FROM FRONTIER

TO SUBURBIA

From Frontier to Suburbia

Loudoun County Virginia

One of America's Fastest Growing Counties

Charles P. Poland, Jr.

Heritage Books
2024

HERITAGE BOOKS
AN IMPRINT OF HERITAGE BOOKS, INC.

Books, CDs, and more—Worldwide

For our listing of thousands of titles see our website at
www.HeritageBooks.com

Published 2024 by
HERITAGE BOOKS, INC.
Publishing Division
5810 Ruatan Street
Berwyn Heights, MD 20740

Copyright © 1976 Charles P. Poland, Jr.

All rights reserved. No part of this book may be reproduced or transmitted in any form or by any means, electronic or mechanical, including photocopying, recording or by any information storage and retrieval system without written permission from the author, except for the inclusion of brief quotations in a review.

International Standard Book Number
Paperbound: 978-0-7884-3187-6

To my Father for his perceptive civic-mindedness and extensive work in community and county activities

TABLE OF CONTENTS

	Page
LIST OF TABLES	ix
LIST OF FIGURES	x

Chapter
1. THE GENESIS OF AN AGRICULTURAL SOCIETY:
   1725 TO 1790   1
   - The Geographical Setting   2
   - The Settlement of Northern Virginia   3
   - Formation of Loudoun County   13
   - Early Agrarian Lifestyle   25
2. DEMOGRAPHIC STABILITY AND AGRICULTURAL
   REFORM: 1790 TO 1828   63
   - Demographic Stability   64
   - Bicorporal Communities   66
   - Agricultural Reform   74
3. POLITICS, NATIONALISM, BANKS, AND THE
   TRANSPORTATION REVOLUTION: 1828 TO 1848   95
   - Politics   96
   - Banks   113
   - Revolution in Transportation   114
4. SLAVERY; STIMULUS FOR DIVISION: 1848 TO 1861   129
   - The Peculiar Institution in Antebellum Loudoun   131
   - The Crusade for a Better World   141
   - The Movement Toward Belligerency   167
5. A COUNTY DIVIDED: 1861 TO 1865   183
   - Mobilization   184
   - Carnage at Ball's Bluff   193
   - Thoroughfare for Blue and Gray Warriors   202

Mosby's Confederacy	209
Supersedure of Civil Rights and Civil Government by Military Might	214
6. A DISHARMONIOUS REUNION: 1865 TO 1877	221
Economic Rehabilitation	222
Social Adjustments	238
Political Resignation, Disillusionment, and Reaction	255
7. THE AUREATE YEARS OF AGRARIANISM: 1887 TO 1917	279
Farm Organizations	280
Dogs, Sheep, and Fences	288
Emergence of Dairying	294
Temperance and Revivalism	295
8. THE LAST DAYS OF UNCHALLENGED AGRARIANISM: 1917 TO 1945	307
The Intrusion of the First World War and Affirmation of Nationalism	308
The Restoration of Civilian and Local Priorities	317
The Trauma of the Great Depression and the Impact of Big Government	326
The Second World War and the Reaffirmation of Nationalism	335
9. THE CRISIS OF CHANGE: 1945 TO 1972	341
The Car as a Vehicle of Change	342
The "Steel Horse" and Scientific Innovations in Husbandry	354
The Suburban Revolution	362
10. THE URBAN FRONTIER AND THE FUTURE OF LOUDOUN COUNTY	381
Current Trends and Futurity	381
Loudoun's Past as a Microcosm of American History	394
EPILOGUE: THE CRISIS OF CHANGE CONTINUES	397
Demographic Revolution	397
Impact of the Demographic Revolution: Revolutionary Changes	398
A Rise in Crime	401
Financing the Demographic Revolution	402
Growth and Political Conflict	404
The End of Traditional Farming: Agriculture's Transition	406
The New Community: The End of the Farm and the Rise of the Subdivision	408

APPENDIX
BIBLIOGRAPHY
INDEX

LIST OF TABLES

Table	Page
1. Yearly Ketocton Association Meetings That Were Held in Loudoun County Baptist Churches from 1776 to 1810	46
2. Data Concerning Loudoun Baptist Churches from 1766 to 1810	47
3. Population of Loudoun County by Decades from 1790 to 1920	65
4. Population of Loudoun's Incorporated Towns from 1900 to 1920	66
5. Towns and Villages That Were Centers of Loudoun's Bicorporal Communities in 1835	72
6. Loudoun's Agricultural Wealth in 1850	77
7. Number and Distribution of Votes Cast by Citizens of Loudoun County in Presidential Elections from 1824 to 1852	106
8. Distribution of Slaveownership in Loudoun County in 1860	133
9. Private Schools Known to Have Existed in Loudoun County during the Nineteenth Century and Early Twentieth Century	154
10. Loudoun's Election of State Legislative Representatives and Ratification of Secession Ordinance	181
11. Military Action in Loudoun during the Civil War	191
12. Report of Funds Raised for America's War Effort in World War I Under the Aegis of the Loudoun County Committee for the United War Work Campaign	313
13. The 1925 Farm Census for Loudoun County by the Department of Commerce	320
14. Statistical Survey of Industries in Loudoun from 1860 to 1920	324
15. Classification of Farms in Loudoun County According to Size	325
16. Agrarian Land Use in Loudoun from 1910 to 1965	360
17. Volume of Milk, Poultry, and Wool Sold by Loudoun Farmers from 1909 to 1964	361
18. Acreage and Yield of Corn and Wheat in Loudoun from 1909 to 1966	363
19. Number of Residents that Lived on Farms in Loudoun from from 1910 to 1960	364

LIST OF FIGURES

Figure	Page
1. Key Topographical Features of Loudoun County	XV
2. Map of Loudoun County Showing Its Propinquity to Washington, D. C., Maryland, West Virginia, and Pennsylvania	5
3. Loudoun's First Subdivision	9
4. Nicholas Minor's 1759 Plan of Leesburg	11
5. A Map of Fairfax County in 1748 Showing Cameron Parish as the Nucleus of Loudoun County	14
6. Rough Map Showing Shelburne and Cameron Parishes that Accompanied the Petition to the Colonial Legislature for the Creation of Cameron Parish as a County	17
7. Plat Showing the Location of the First County Jail (Gaol) Located Two Miles North of the County Courthouse.	21
8. Map of Colonial Loudoun	31
9. Eighteenth-Century Ferries that Crossed the Potomac River from Loudoun to Maryland	35
10. Wheel Configuration with Leesburg as the Hub of Eighteenth-Century Loudoun Life	67
11. Leesburg in 1853 from Yardley Taylor's Map of Loudoun County	70
12. Plan of Middleburg Made by Leven Powell in 1815	73
13. Approximate Location of Three Dozen of the Villages and Towns in Nineteenth-Century Loudoun	75
14. Advertisement of a Woolen Mill in the June 19, 1821, Issue of *The Genius of Liberty*	78
15. The "Y" Configuration of the Two Primary Turnpike Systems in Loudoun	119
16. Survey Made in the 1830's of the Tributaries in Loudoun to be Improved by the Goose Creek and Little River Navigation Company	125
17. Ads in *The Genius of Liberty* from 1818 to 1820 for the Return of Runaways and Hiring Out of Slaves	136
18. Map of Ball's Bluff Battlefield and Vicinity	197
19. Sketch in *Harper's Weekly* of the Execution of Three Deserters from the Army of the Potomac	208
20. A Patriotic Ad that Ran in *The Loudoun Times* from October 11, 1916, to December 4, 1918	314
21. Loudoun County Roads in 1972	343
22. Distribution of Loudoun's Population in 1970	367

23. A 1972 Map of Leesburg, Virginia 371
24. Loudoun County School Sites in 1972 374
25. Premium Farmland in Loudoun County in 1976 393

PREFACE

Most modern historical research has been primarily in the direction of specialization that has benevolently revised and expanded our historical knowledge. Such monographs and similar works are detailed studies often involving a comparatively brief number of years and a broad geographical area. This study is an attempt to reverse this approach by selecting a broad time span, but a small geographical region for examination.

The intent is not to write a traditional local history usually associated with antiquarians, but to use the content of local history of a county in a manner that will provide a microcosm of much of America's national history. The basic organization and analysis of data is presented within a general chronological framework. The central theme is the history of rural and agrarian lifestyles and the transition to an urban society. The study of the shift of Loudoun County in Virginia from a rural to an urban county is especially relevant as an attempt to obtain a degree of perspicuity about one of the central themes in American history. The significance of the demographic growth and planning ordinances of Loudoun's recent history that has attracted national attention is not due to uniqueness as much as it is to the fact that Loudoun's history and problems are representative of numerous areas throughout the nation.

It is hoped this study, originally a doctoral dissertation for Western Colorado University, will provide a microcosm of other historic threads and developments and provide additional insight into the history of the nation as well as into that of a county. Among these threads and developments are the nature and impact of nineteenth-century revolutions in transportation and humanitarian reforms (abolitionism, public education, temperance et al.) and the salient twentieth-century developments, such as the emergence of big government and its attempt to cope with the increasingly complex problems of American domestic life, and the impact of the intervention of the United States in international affairs, such as World War I and World War II, upon the life and attitude of Loudouners.

Other significant aspects of the national experience are reflected in the history of Loudoun during the antebellum and Civil War periods. The internal tension, reprisals, and fighting between residents in the eastern and southern regions of the county who supported the Confederacy and inhabitants in the northwestern section of Loudoun who remained loyal to the Union, the passage of the Army of the Potomac and the Army of Northern Virginia through Loudoun to and from the Antietam and Gettysburg campaigns, the partisan warfare of John S. Mosby and more than forty-six separate military engagements in the county, and Sheridan's use of the torch in Loudoun Valley were indicative of the travail of Southern-border states and the military activity of the Civil War. In addition to the above aspects, an emphasis is also placed upon farming techniques, husbandry, equipment, and the organizations that have been salient elements in Loudoun's agrarian heritage.

Currently Loudoun is facing a problem common throughout much of the nation: suburban sprawl characterized by escalating demographic growth and financial burdens in traditionally rural and agricultural regions. Since 1960 exurban and suburban development in Loudoun has nearly doubled the county's population, eliminated farming in the eastern region and reduced farming in the western portion of the county, dichotomized western agrarians and eastern suburbanites into political factions and induced a contest between the county government in its attempt to control growth and developers who proclaim unfettered growth is synonymous with progress. The contest over development is especially interesting since Loudoun is presently one of the most attractive regions in the nation for investments by developers and land speculators. This attraction is verified by the vast acreage purchased and major communities planned or constructed by corporate giants like United States Steel, Levitt and Sons, I.T.&T., and I.B.M. The legal battles between the county and developers over growth have led to innovations in zoning requirements that have attracted national attention. The outcome of this contest not only is determining the future of this county and the fate of farming in Loudoun Valley, but also is setting legal precedent of national significance in the struggle between the individual's "vested property rights" and the rights of the community to regulate and restrict in the public interest the use of privately and corporately owned realty.

As is usual in historical research, the challenge of objectivity is encountered. Although objectivity is a desirable goal, total objectivity is not claimed or believed possible in interpretative history. For example, the critique pertaining to urban trends in Loudoun is not intended to provide a "nostalgia" tract, but to question the rationale and methods vociferated by proponents of urbanization.

I would like to express my gratitude to all who provided valuable assistance in the preparation of this volume. Among the above were the librarians of the Purcellville and Thomas Balch libraries, Dr. Terry Alford, Jim Birchfield, Dr. Regis Boyle, Edward R. Brown, Esther Brown, Frederick F. Hafner, Dr. G. Melvin Herndon, Asa Moore

Janney, C. Preston Poland, Elisa Poland, Ina Poland, Lynette Poland, Rev. W. W. Hayzlett, Betty Kenyon, Pauline Tooker, Ruth Brown Traynham, and Nancy Uram. Informative primary sources were made available to the author due to the kindness of George Atwell, Arlene G. Janney, W. Emory Plaster, Jr., Leslie W. King, and Frances H. Reid. Finally, I am eternally grateful to my wife, Betty B. Poland, for her dauntless interest and ceaseless diligence and skill in editing and typing that contributed so illimitably to the realization of this book.

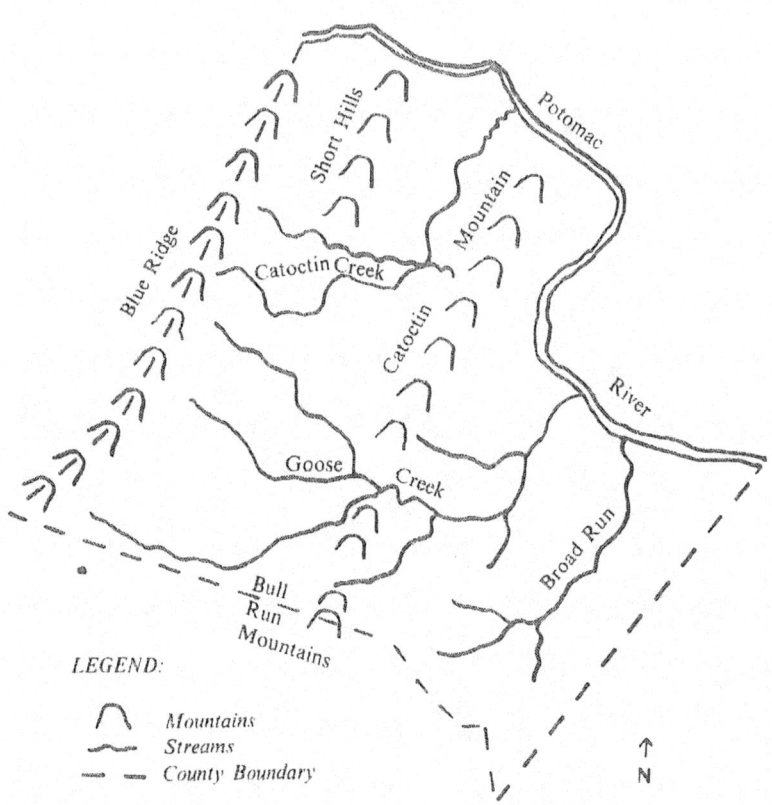

Figure 1. Key Topographical Features of Loudoun County.

Chapter 1

THE GENESIS OF AN AGRICULTURAL SOCIETY: 1725 TO 1790

Man's historical record is in part a significant testimony to the impact of geography as a major determinant of lifestyles of the inhabitants of any given region. Yet, the profound and often adverse impact of man's activities upon topography and ecology have only recently been extensively noticed by members of affluent societies. With the exception of individualists and transcendentalists like Thoreau and Emerson, the limits of nature's resources in the United States were not perceived until Americans were shocked by the impending exhaustion of needed resources.[1] Stunned by the closing of the last frontier, some Americans became aware in the 1890's that their resources were not boundless. They subsequently supported Progressive legislative panaceas for the conservation of land, timber, and petroleum. But as the Progressive era waned, Americans continued to be predominantly motivated by a credo of economic expansion, national security, and progress. All of these were rooted in a tradition of environmental exploitation enhanced by successive technological revolutions that have accelerated Americans' ability to alter their landscape and sap domestic and international resources. Until recently these forces have caused most Americans to relegate conservation as a national priority subordinate to exploitation and act as if nature's resources were inexhaustible. Now as Americans enter the last quarter of the twentieth century they are again shocked by

---

[1] Arthur A. Ekirch, Jr., *Man and Nature in America* (New York: Columbia University Press, 1963), pp. 47, 57. Prior to the nineteenth century enlightened farmers were aware that repetitive cultivation of the same crop depleted the soil of its fertility. However, the abundance of land prevented American farmers from developing an intense concern for conservation.

the realization that they are facing an ominous situation in which shortages of natural resources and ecological damage challenge traditional attitudes and threaten current modes of living. The history of Loudoun County is acutely related to the aforementioned saga.

THE GEOGRAPHICAL SETTING

Located at the northern extremity of the piedmont region of Virginia, Loudoun County has diverse topographical features, many of which are well-suited for agrarian life. Hills and mountain ranges in the county run more or less in a northern - southern direction and parallel to each other while being separated by undulating valleys watered by numerous springs and streams. The most conspicuous features are four ranges of mountains of moderate altitude. The Blue Ridge, the southeasternmost range of the Appalachian system, forms the western boundary of Loudoun and has depressions or gaps every eight to ten miles that have proved necessary and convenient for western travel. Closely paralleling the Blue Ridge and four miles to the east are the Short Hills, a range starting at the Potomac River and extending southward in the county for approximately twelve miles. The topographical backbone of the county is comprised of the Catoctin range which traverses the center of the county from the Potomac River to Aldie. Immediately to the south of Aldie, near where the Catoctin Mountain ends, another range, the Bull Run Mountain, commences and extends into Fauquier County. Of the valleys in Loudoun, the most productive and picturesque is Loudoun Valley, located between the Blue Ridge and Catoctin ranges. The numerous creeks and streams of this valley, as elsewhere in the county, generally flow northerly and northeasterly and are directly or indirectly tributaries of the Potomac River, which forms the boundary between Loudoun and the state of Maryland. By far the largest body of water in the county is Goose Creek. Like another primary stream in Loudoun, Broad Run, Goose Creek's fountainhead is located in a county to the south of Loudoun. Goose Creek meanders through the center of Loudoun for approximately thirty miles, while Broad Run drains the eastern region of the county. The other primary stream, Catoctin Creek traverses the northwestern portion of the county. Goose Creek, Broad Run, and Catoctin Creek empty directly into the Potomac River.[2]

---

[2]James W. Head, *History and Comprehensive Description of Loudoun County, Virginia* ([Leesburg, Va.]: Parkview Press, 1908) pp. 18-20,22-25; (hereafter referred to as the *History of Loudoun County*) Yardley Taylor, *Memoir of Loudo[u]n County* (Leesburg, Va.: Thomas Reynolds, Publisher, 1853), pp. 3-7. Some of the numerous other streams along with abundant springs which made Loudoun one of the "best watered" counties in the state

THE GENESIS OF AN AGRICULTURAL SOCIETY

Vegetation and animal life in Loudoun prior to the advent of the European settler was not unlike most regions east of the Appalachian Mountains. Virgin forest and streams teemed with wildlife that comprised a hunter's paradise. The area not only had animals like fox, raccoon, beaver, otter, squirrel, and rabbit but also abounded with larger species like buffalo, deer, wolf, bear, and elk.[3] Subsequently Indians considered Loudoun a significant part of their hunting grounds. Aborigines were also impressed by the abundance of waterfowl on Goose Creek and the Potomac.[4] They referred to Goose Creek as *Gohongarestaw*, meaning "River of Swans,"[5] and *Cokongoloto*, when translated into English is "Goose Creek."[6] Early explorers found that the prodigious number of swan, geese, and duck in the vicinity of Goose Creek attracted Indians who engaged in trading feathers. The region became a trading center for "Indian millinery."[7]

THE SETTLEMENT OF NORTHERN VIRGINIA

During the colonial era the European settler brought about the first extensive man-made alterations in the vegetation and to a lesser extent in animal life and the topography east of the Appalachian Mountains. These were accomplished by colonists settling upon and clearing the land and tilling the soil. This displacement of the Indians caused successive Indian wars and resulted in treaties that expelled the aborigines from lands their ancestors had lived upon for countless centuries.

Indian warfare did not originate with the coming of the European. Prior to the advent of the white man, Indians in the Northern Neck of Virginia fought with each other over hunting lands and with tribes that inhabited the tidewater region. Algonquin tribes that lived around the Potomac River were far from depraved savages. By the 1600's they had reached the highest stages of neolithic culture, which included a stationary place of residence, fishing, and the cultivation of corn. Piedmont Indians were less advanced and lived exclusively from hunting.

---

are Little River, North Fork of the Catoctin Creek, South Fork of the Catoctin Creek, North Fork of Goose Creek, Beaver-dam Creek, Piney Run, Jeffries Branch, Cromwells Run, Hungry Run, Bull Run, Sycoline Creek, Tuscarora Creek, Horse Pen Run, Sugarland Run, Elk Lick, and Limestone Branch.

[3]Head, op. cit., pp. 68-69.

[4]Fairfax Harrison, *Landmarks of Old Prince William: A Study of Origins in Northern Virginia* (Reprint; Berryville, Va.: Chesapeake Book Co., 1964), p. 100. (This title is hereafter referred to as *Landmarks*.)

[5]Head, op. cit., p. 23.

[6]Harrison, loc. cit.

[7]Ibid.

Their nomadic ways included "firing the forest" to facilitate hunting. This practice thereby created plains which became favorite grazing areas for the buffalo. During the seventeenth century tribes who traditionally inhabited the piedmont of the Northern Neck were driven out by relentless warfare upon them by the tribes of the "Long House," better known as Iroquois, who were intent on establishing their hegemony over eastern America.[8]

Loudoun thus became a part of the Virginia piedmont region that the Iroquois considered their hunting preserve. By the 1720's the Iroquois' claim to this area was so severely curtailed that the way was paved for white settlement. The opening up of the piedmont of northern Virginia was accomplished by Governor Spotswood of Virginia. At Albany in 1722, Spotswood negotiated a treaty with the Iroquois chiefs in which they pledged not to cross the Potomac River or the Blue Ridge Mountains into Virginia without prior permission from the governor of New York.[9] The Albany treaty also removed the Piscataway Indians from a large island in the Potomac River near Loudoun at Point of Rocks, Maryland. The Piscataway had migrated to Conoy Island in 1699 and constructed a fort for their ninety bowmen. Because the Piscataway, also called the Conoy and Moyaones, were subjects of the Iroquois, the governments of Maryland and Virginia feared trouble. The Iroquois were later persuaded to move the Piscataway into Pennsylvania.[10]

The details of Loudoun's topography were not mapped until the early 1700's. Before that time Indian occupation of the area and white preoccupation with more eastern areas were factors that retarded exploration of its topographical features. This veil of mystery was partially lifted in 1692 by the Potomac Rangers, who recorded their impressions of northeastern Loudoun. Later, knowledge of the region was greatly expanded by colonial envoys to the Piscataway of Conoy Island, explorations by topographers, and the movement of colonials interested in establishing settlements in the piedmont and areas farther west.[11] Whites

---

[8]*The Blue Ridge Herald* (Purcellville, Va.), July 21, 1955. A Frederick, Maryland archeologist, Nicholas Yinger, in the mid-1950's supervised an extensive search for graves of aborigines who peopled Loudoun from 800 to 2,000 years ago. One of his finds included the site of a Seneca Indian village near the Potomac River. At that site he found several graves including the remains of a middle-aged male estimated to have died around 1155 A.D. The most unusual find during Yinger's three-year search was the skelton of a large Seneca male with two heads. Other finds included the remains of an infant only fourteen inches in length, numerous artifacts, and the bones of bear and deer. The Senecas later were one of five tribes that formed a powerful confederacy in the fifteenth century known as the "Five Nations."

[9]Harrison, *Landmarks*. pp. 19-21, 24-25, 87. In a later treaty, the Treaty of Lancaster in 1744, the Iroquois relinquished all their land in Virginia.

[10]Ibid., pp. 93-99. The island near Point of Rocks inhabited by the Piscataway bore the name Conoy until it later became known as Heater's Island.

[11]Ibid., pp, 98-101.

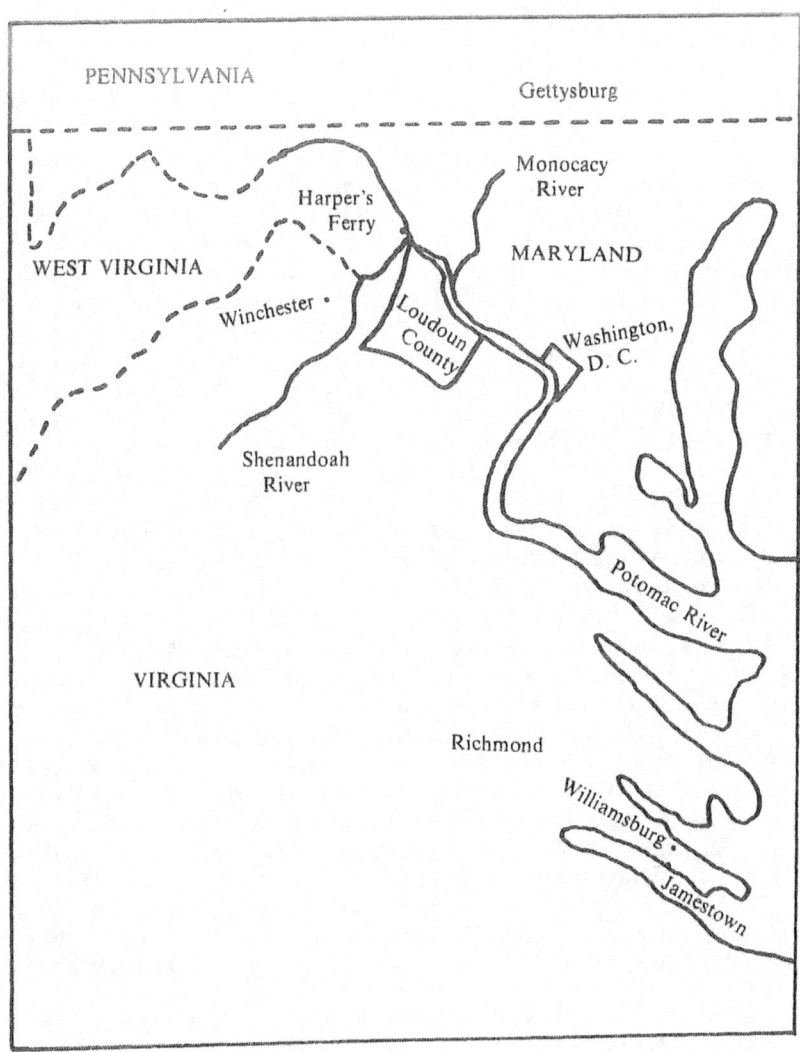

Figure 2. Map of Loudoun County Showing Its Propinquity to Washington, D. C., Maryland, West Virginia and Pennsylvania.

who traversed Loudoun and other regions of the Northern Neck found that the aborigines, except for clearings created by their use of fire, essentially had not diminished wildlife or vegetation. Instead, the most lasting legacy left by the Indian to the colonial was numerous names to identify specific local topographical features and an awareness of new foods, especially Indian corn which became the major food crop of the European settler.

Shortly after Spotswood negotiated the Treaty of Albany with the Iroquois, the settlement of colonial Loudoun began. At that time Loudoun was a small area of what the eminent American historian, Frederick Jackson Turner, later labeled the second American frontier.[12] The first significant settlement of Loudoun took place between 1725 and 1735. During this decade three successive waves of colonists settled in the county. The first thrust of immigrants was of English stock, who located in the eastern and southern Loudoun. The region included the land south of the Potomac River to Middleburg and east of the Catoctin and Bull Run Mountains. Some of the early patents in this region were granted to Philip Noland in 1724 and John Lewis in 1723 near Broad Run. Soon others either leased or purchased land on Goose Creek and the small streams known as Sycoline and Tuscarora.[13] About the same time or shortly thereafter German immigrants from Pennsylvania and New York settled in the northwestern region of the county west of the Catoctin Mountain to the Short Hills and south from the Potomac to Wheatland. This area consisted of 125 square miles that became known locally as the "German Settlement." It is believed that by 1731 sixty German families were living in that region. Also from the north were Quaker pioneers, who entered Loudoun shortly after the Germans. From New Jersey, Bucks and Chester counties in Pennsylvania, Calvert County, Maryland, and directly from England and Wales came Quakers who settled at Waterford and farther south into Loudoun Valley. This core formed a Quaker settlement in the center of the county that separated the English and German settlements. Other important early settlers in the county included the Scotch-Irish, who also settled in the western part.[14]

Two distinct types of communities that had far-reaching consequences developed in Loudoun between 1725 and 1750. English settlers introduced slavery, which became an important part of the labor force of

[12]Frederick Jackson Turner, "The Significance of the Frontier in American History," *The Turner Thesis*, ed. George Rogers Taylor (Boston: D. C. Heath and Co., 1956), p. 4.

[13]Virginia, Northern Neck Land Grant Book D, pp. 86-87. For example on March 20, 1731, Richard Coleman and Peter Rust leased 1,000 acres of land on the northern branch of Tuscarora Creek.

[14]R. Bennett Bean, *The Peopling of Virginia* (Boston: Crescendo Publishing Co., 1938), pp. 147-49; Briscoe Goodhart, *History of the Independent Loudoun Virginia Rangers* (Washington, D.C.: Press of McGill and Wallace, 1896), pp. 3-5; Harrison, *Landmarks*, pp. 265-68; Head, *History of Loudoun County*, pp. 110-13; William Wade Hinshaw, "Fairfax Monthly Meeting," *Encyclopedia of American Quaker Genealogy* (1950), VI, 463-66; Asa Moore Janney, "A Short History of the Society of Friends in Loudoun County," *The*

the eastern and southern regions of Loudoun. The more prosperous of the English colonials developed the larger farms and plantations in the county. In contrast, the German, Quaker and Scotch-Irish, whose acreage was usually that of smaller or yeoman farmers, either spurned slavery or had meager slave holdings. This dichotomy later traumatically divided the county over the issues of slavery and allegiance to the Union and Confederate governments. Other distinctive characteristics and contributions include the moral indignation of Loudoun Friends, who were not only severe critics of the institution of slavery, but who served as the conscience of the county in educational reform and prohibition and provided leadership in progressive farming and related businesses. German settlers were the first to bring sheep and to introduce black cherry trees into Loudoun.[15]

The legal title to land Europeans settled in Loudoun originated from a grant issued by Charles II of England in 1649. This document conveyed all of the 5,282,000 acres of land between the Potomac and Rappahannock rivers to John and Thomas Culpeper and five other men who had befriended the British monarch.[16] The grant was significant because it made the Northern Neck unique from the rest of colonial Virginia. North of the Rappahannock River, land was leased or purchased from the proprietors of the Northern Neck and not the government of Virginia. Neither did settlers in the Northern Neck pay quitrent to the Crown as did colonials in other parts of Virginia. Instead, those in the Northern Neck paid an annual quitrent of two shillings per hundred acres to the proprietors of northern Virginia.[17] Distribution of land under these proprietors led to a system of extensive land speculation and promotional schemes not unlike those of modern America.[18] A pattern

Bulletin of the Loudoun County Historical Society, IV (1965), 29-34; Klaus Wust, *The Virginia Germans* (Charlottesville: University Press of Virginia, 1970), pp. 37-38. Bean in *The Peopling of Virginia* has attempted to determine the ancestry of Loudoun's population by studying surnames found in county records. On this basis he concluded that 43.4 percent of Loudoun's early residents were English, 27.5 percent Scots, 12.2 percent German, 10.2 percent Welsh, 3.9 percent Irish, and 2.8 percent French.

[15]Goodhart, *History of the Independent Loudoun Virginia Rangers,* p. 6; Harrison *Landmarks,* p. 275.

[16]The western boundary of this grant was disputed from 1649 to 1688. By 1719, the proprietorship of the Northern Neck had been consolidated in the hands of one person. This was achieved by the Culpeper family as the result of the marriage of Catherine Culpeper to Thomas Culpeper, the fifth Lord of Fairfax. Their son, the sixth Lord Fairfax, became the sole proprietor of the Northern Neck.

[17]Stuart E. Brown, Jr., "Manors on the Frontier," *Virginia Cavalcade,* XVI (Winter, 1967), 42-47.

[18]The first man to be granted a patent above the Great Falls of the Potomac River was a land speculator by the name of Daniel McCarty. This took place in 1709 and involved 2,993 acres of land in Stafford County that would later be known as the Sugarland tract located in northeastern Loudoun. See page 7 of *Mount Air, Fairfax County, Virginia* (n.p.: Fairfax County Division of Planning, 1970) by Edith Moore Sprouse. The actual settlement of Loudoun was during the latter part of the colonial era.

of land distribution evolved whereby agents of proprietors sold patents to large land speculators, who in turn sold or leased tracts of 100 to 400 acres to settlers. Agents like Robert "King" Carter and Thomas Lee not only provided the services of a modern realtor but used their position to establish themselves among the largest land speculators in the Northern Neck. "King" Carter also granted patents to the numerous members of his family. In Loudoun Carter kept land in the family which included the 5,300-acre Goose Creek tract, the site upon which "Oak Hill" and "Oatlands" were later established, and additional thousands of acres in the Piney Ridge, Broad Run, and Sugarland Run tracts.[19] Agent Thomas Lee patented approximately 16,000 acres in Loudoun, much of which was located on or near the Potomac River, Goose Creek, and Broad Run.[20] It is not surprising that surveyors for proprietors also became land speculators. These included George Washington, John Warner, Amos Janney, and John Hough. The latter two were Quakers.[21]

Other land speculators significant in the early development of Loudoun were Catesby Cocke, John Mercer, Francis Awbrey and John Tayloe. Awbrey has been called "the first citizen of Loudoun" because of his efforts which played a key role in the settlement of the county. Besides being an enormous land owner, he made his place of residence at "Big Spring," a short distance to the north of where Leesburg was later located, ran a ferry across the Potomac, and constructed the first church in Loudoun. In 1748 he sold a tract of about 4,000 acres to Colonel John Tayloe of Richmond County. Tayloe in turn developed the county's first subdivision. He divided his "Kittockton Land" into lots ranging from 150 to 300 acres. He filed a plat with the Fairfax clerk's office and, when Loudoun became a county, had it recorded in that county clerk's office in 1757.[22] By 1757, Tayloe had leased nine tracts of his 1,590 acres yearly rate of forty shillings per 150 acres.[23]

[19]Louis Morton, *Robert Carter of Nomini Hall: A Virginia Tobacco Planter of the Eighteenth Century* (Charlottesville: University Press of Virginia, 1964), p. 70. Robert Carter of Nomini Hall, a grandson of "King" Carter, had land holdings in Loudoun in 1775 that totaled 39,509 acres.

[20]*The Blue Ridge Herald*, July 19, 1956; August 30, 1956; September 13, 1956.

[21]Janney, "A Short History of the Society of Friends in Loudoun," p. 31; *The Blue Ridge Herald*, September 13, 1956. The thousands of acres acquired by Amos Janney, John Hough, plus the 1,289 and 3,000 acres granted to John Mead and Gidney Clark respectively indicate not all land holdings by Loudoun Quakers were limited to several hundred acres.

[22]Harrison, *Landmarks*, pp. 148, 150, 153-55, 287, 395, 427, 434, Loudoun County, Virginia, Deed Book B, pp. 282-83; C, pp. 15, 272, 277, 282; D, pt. 2, pp. 638-39, 641-44, 709-11; E. p. 138; G, pp. 81, 215, 217; H, pp. 119, 144, 151; I, pp. 217, 219, 221, 223, 246, 267; *The Loudoun Times-Mirror* (Leesburg, Va.), July 7, 1960.

[23]Loudoun Deed Book A, pp. 229-32. A shilling in colonial America varied in value from twelve to sixteen cents.

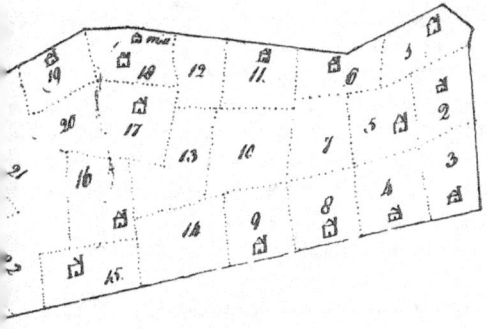

Subdivision (Recorded in 1757). Source: Loudoun County Deed

Another interesting early land developer who had even more in common with twentieth century developers than John Tayloe was one of the county's founding fathers, Nicholas Minor. As soon as Minor realized the colonial Assembly of Virginia had selected a portion of his land as the location of the county courthouse, he hired John Hough to survey sixty acres for a town. Hough surveyed and submitted to Minor a plat that set forth a plan for Leesburg consisting of seventy lots separated by three streets running north and south and four going in an east-west direction.[24] The colonial legislature gave legal sanction to Minor's plans by approving, during September 1758, the erection of a town on Minor's property.[25]

Minor was a shrewd and tightfisted businessman who carefully calculated the naming of his town and conditions for purchasing lots. All stipulations were conceived to enhance the financial remuneration of the developer. During the genesis of the town around Minor's ordinary and the intersection of the Alexandria and Carolina roads on his property, the nascent hamlet was called "George Town" in honor of George II, then the sovereign of England.[26] However, by the time Minor asked the colonial legislature for permission to establish a town, according to one theory, he had decided it would be more financially expedient to forego an appellation based upon his royal proclivity and name the town after someone with more appeal to backwoodsmen of the area than the current British monarch. Subsequently, Minor selected the name of

[24] Penelope Osburn (*The Loudoun-Times Mirror*, October 2, 1958) and Harrison Williams (*Legends of Loudoun*, p. 107) have written that the plat Hough drew was never officially placed in the county records. Nevertheless the plat was a part of a book of records because it has page number "27" on it. It later became legal evidence used in an old Chancery suit, Cavan v. Murray. The plat was rediscovered in 1928 in the papers of that suit.

[25] Hening, *Statutes*, VII, 235-236. The legislature of the colony of Virginia appointed Philip Ludwell Lee, Thomas Mason, Francis Lightfoot Lee, James Hamilton, Nicholas Minor, Josias Clapham, Aeneas Campbell, John Hough, Francis Hague, and William West trustees of Leesburg.

[26] Patrick A. Deck and Henry Heaton, *An Economic and Social Survey of Loudoun* (Charlottesville: University of Virginia, 1926), p. 13. Deck and Heaton contend a "little fort" was built on the present site of Leesburg as "an . . . outpost for the British and Colonial forces during the French and Indian War." The fort was named Georgetown in honor of the British monarch at that time. It is entirely possible a small fort was built there, but it is not mentioned in the available primary sources. The only colonial fort in Loudoun mentioned in such material is "Bacon's Fort" in Plate 33 of *The George Washington Atlas*. Fort Bacon was located on the Colchester Road in southwestern Loudoun on the way to Snickers' Gap between what is currently known as Philomont and Airmont. This fort was probably constructed during the French and Indian War.

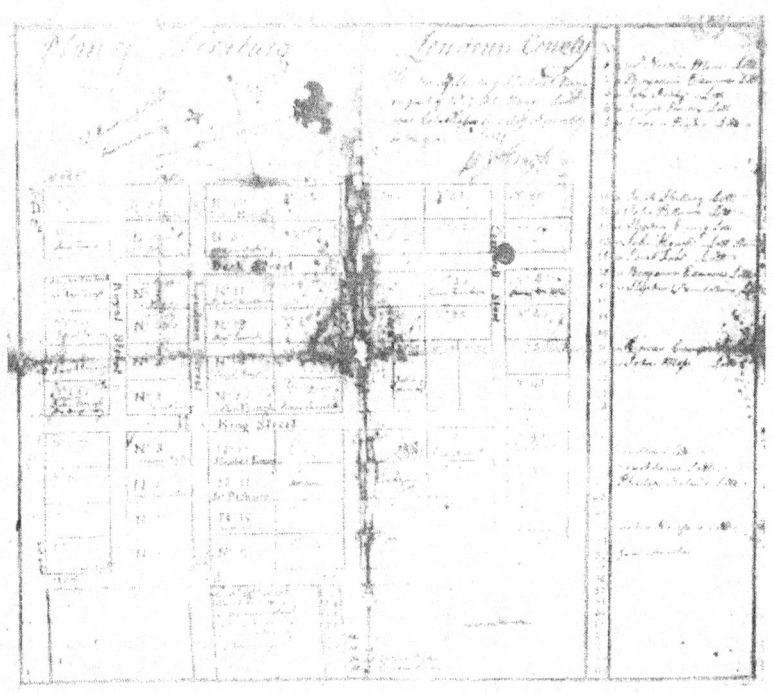

Figure 4. Nicholas Minor's 1759 Plan of Leesburg.

Leesburg after the celebrated aristocratic Lee family of Virginia, of which Francis Lightfoot Lee, the first County Lieutenant of Loudoun, was a member.[27]

Minor apparently did not want others to speculate in land in his town. He therefore required each purchaser to build on the lot for the transaction to be consummated. Most purchasers were given three years to erect a house of brick, stone, or wood twenty feet long and sixteen feet wide.[28] John Poultney, a farmer, purchased lot number two on March 14, 1758, for £ 3. He apparently failed to build on the lot because Minor sold the same lot to Benjamin Edwards for £ 5 on March 10, 1761.[29] Even churches were not exempted from this condition. On September 16, 1767, a plot was sold by Minor for £ 3 to John Miller with the provision that a "Calvinist Church" be constructed within six years. The church not being constructed, ownership of the property reverted to Minor.[30]

Early land speculators, consisting of proprietary agents, surveyors, and investors, helped stimulate and accelerate the settlement of Loudoun and other areas in the Northern Neck.[31] The exact number of settlers in Loudoun prior to 1790 is not known. The closest approach to a census during the colonial period was the tithable list, which did not include women or anyone under sixteen years of age. When the county was

[27]Loudoun County Court Order Book A, Part I, p. 56; *The Loudoun Times-Mirror* (Leesburg, Va.), October 2, 1958. Claims have been made that the town was named exclusively in honor of Francis Lightfoot Lee while others have maintained it was primarily to capitalize on the name of a great family. The name "George Town" was used in early county records and even by Minor until March 1759, six months after the official name was Leesburg. The streets of the town were named King, Back (later changed to Wirt), Royal, Loudoun, Cornwall, and Market. After the Revolutionary experience and the growth of the town, a new street was added called Liberty Street, which became a curious contrast to the earlier pro-monarch appellations.

[28]*The Loudoun Times-Mirror*, October 9, 1958. Minor even spelled out the details of construction of the houses on these lots.

[29]At first Minor received from £2 to £6 per lot. Prices varied because some locations of lots were more desirable than others. After several years Minor was getting as much as £10 per lot.

[30]*The Loudoun Times-Mirror*, October 9, 1958. Some of the early travelers who went through Leesburg were not impressed. A Captain John Davis of the Pennsylvania Line went through Leesburg on June 3, 1781, and recorded in his diary he "was much disappointed in" the appearance of the town. Previously another visitor wrote the town consisted of "insignificant wooden houses."

[31]Lands were often first leased and a few years later purchased. While the land was leased or rented, numerous restrictions were often placed upon cutting wood and the cultivation of crops. Not all settlers had legal title or permission to live upon Loudoun lands when they arrived in the county.

formed in 1757, there were 1,066 tithables compared to 3,126 in 1773 and 3,668 in 1774.[32]

FORMATION OF LOUDOUN COUNTY

As the settlement and population density of the Northern Neck increased, the size of original counties was reduced by the formation of new counties. For example, the region known as Loudoun County was a part of Stafford County from 1664 to 1730, Prince William from 1730 to 1742, and Fairfax from 1742 to 1757.[33] By 1730 the parish was used as the nucleus for the formation of new counties.[34] The geographical boundaries and select governmental functions of what became Loudoun County were provided by Cameron parish, which was formed in 1748 from the upper end of what had formerly been Truro parish. In this period the Anglican Church in Virginia was closely allied with the colonial government. Since the Episcopal Church was often the only officially recognized institution in regions remote from the county seat, it had extensive civil as well as ecclesiastical duties. As a primitive form of local government its civil functions included law enforcement, care of the poor, discipline of vagrants, and the education and "apprenticing of bastards."[35]

In 1754, six years after the establishment of Cameron parish, the inhabitants unsuccessfully petitioned the Virginia Assembly for the creation of another county. In April 1757, the measure to create Loudoun County was reintroduced and passed despite determined opposition

---

[32]"List of Tithables in Virginia, Taken 1773, " *Virginia Magazine of History and Biography*, XXVIII (June, 1920), 81; *The Loudoun Times-Mirror*, July 4, 1957. There were 18,962 people in Loudoun when the first federal census was taken in 1790.

[33]Harrison, *Landmarks*, pp. 365, 312, 320, 327-29.

[34]Ibid., p. 281. The colonial government of Virginia up to 1730 created counties as they were needed. Once a county was created the county court was required to establish a parish or parishes within the county. After 1730 the colonial legislature assumed the function of creating parishes. The significance of this was that parishes were created prior to counties thereby being precursors of them.

[35]Ibid., pp. 282-83, 288-89. The Cameron vestry book is lost; however, Harrison states it is probable that the new parish immediately established a church between the two chapels which were formerly under the jurisdiction of Truro parish, one at Big Spring and the other at Rocky Run. Another old wooden church was located at Sugarland Run but was superseded by a church at Gum Spring near Broad Run which was in turn replaced by the "Frying Pan" church on a branch of Horsepen Run. Of these Cameron churches only Big Spring and Rocky Run continued into the 1800's.

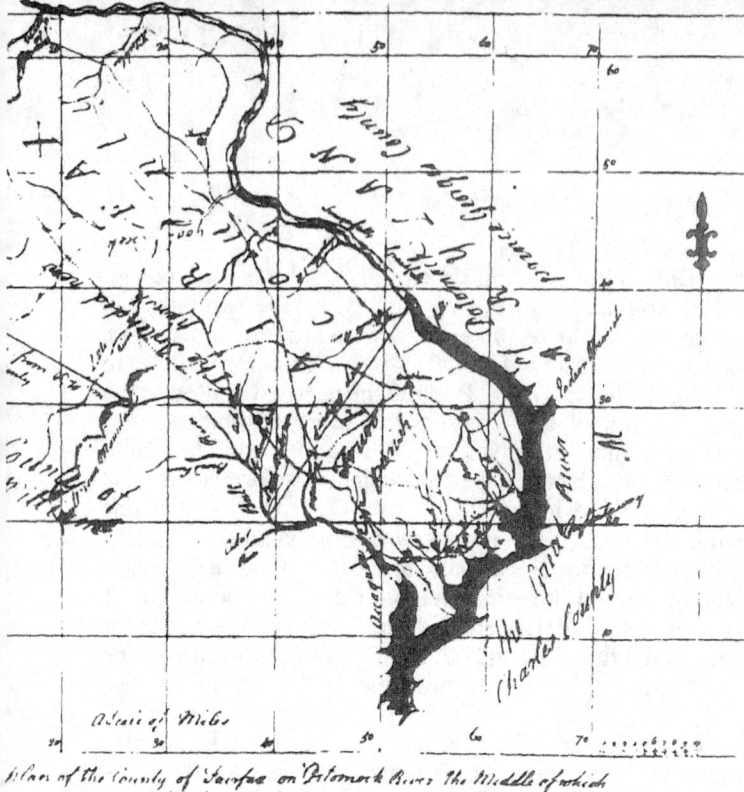

ty in 1748 Showing Cameron Parish as the Nucleus of Loudoun County. (Cameron Parish is ish." Note the early roads, Goose Creek Chapel in the northwest portion, and Ashby's Gap. Old Carolina Road is not shown on this map.)

from representatives of the tidewater section.³⁶ The county was named after John Campbell, fourth earl of Loudoun, who was governor of Virginia and commander-in-chief of British forces in America at the time Loudoun County was established. Campbell's main claim to fame was his ineptitude and indecision, which doomed him to failure and removal from his position as commander-in-chief. The Virginia Assembly named the new county for him in hope he would reverse the disaster of Braddock's defeat in the French and Indian War. Instead the Assembly discovered Campbell lacked administrative and military acumen.³⁷

The boundaries of the new county of Loudoun were essentially those of Cameron parish: the Potomac River on the north, Prince William County, and later Fauquier County, on the south, the Blue Ridge Mountains on the west, and Difficult Run, then called Difficult Waters, on the east. However, the size of Loudoun was reduced by the relocation of the Fairfax-Loudoun boundary from Difficult Run to Sugarland Run in 1798. This reduction culminated from nearly three decades of demand by large planters south of Goose Creek for the creation of a new county in southern Loudoun. These "cavaliers" resented that they could not dominate the local county government of Loudoun and had to compete for local political power with people from western Loudoun, whom they deemed their inferiors. Coinciding with this protest was the creation of Shelburne parish in 1770 in what was formerly the western region of Cameron parish.³⁸ The formation of Shelburne parish served as a stimulant for motivating eastern Loudoun residents into demanding the creation of a new county out of the remaining portion of Cameron parish. This proposal would have left the area of Shelburne parish as Loudoun County.³⁹ Settlers in western Loudoun, op-

---

³⁶Harrison, *Landmarks*, pp. 326-37; Virginia, *The Statutes at Large, Being a Collection of All the Laws of Virginia*, ed. William H. Hening, VII (Richmond: n.p., 1808), 148-49 (hereafter referred to as Hening, *Statutes*). The law creating Loudoun was passed on June 8, 1757.

³⁷Harrison, *Landmarks*, pp. 655-56; Head, *History of Loudoun County*, pp. 109-10. Benjamin Franklin stated Campbell was "like St. George on the signs, always on horseback and never rides on."

³⁸Harrison Williams, *Legends of Loudoun: An account of the History and Homes of a Border County of Virginia's Northern Neck* (Richmond, Va.: Garrett and Massie, 1938), pp. 116-17. Shelburne parish was named after William Perry Fitz-Maurice, Lord Shelburne, a British statesman.

Inhabitants of Cameron parish in Loudoun petitioned the colonial Assembly in May 1769 for the creation of an additional parish. They argued that the size of the parish made it extremely inconvenient to the people who resided north of Goose Creek. Actually the Anglican Church in western Loudoun was of little interest to many settlers such as the Quakers and Germans, who had their own churches.

³⁹Undated Petition from Citizens of Loudoun County to the Honorable Speaker of the Virginia House of Delegates, Archives, Virginia State Library, Richmond, Va. It is not altogether surprising that the petitioners omitted any reference to their rivalry with western Loudouners. The reason stated in the petition for the need for the formation of a

posing such a division of the county, created an impasse until a compromise was worked out in 1798. At that time the land between Difficult Run and Sugarland Run was given back to Fairfax County.[40]

County government in colonial Loudoun, like that of twentieth century Loudoun, derived its power from the Virginia legislature.[41] Major positions in the county government were those of the county court, clerk of the county, and sheriff. Other positions were those of the county lieutenant, who was head of the county militia, constables, surveyors, and coroners.[42] At that time no county official was elected. However, residents within the county prior to 1769 who owned one hundred acres

---

new county was the same that had previously been used in the petition for the formation of Shelburne parish. In both cases petitioners argued the jurisdiction was too large and therefore inconvenienced the inhabitants of the region. The proposed boundary line between Loudoun and the new county was to be the eastern boundary of Shelburne parish, Goose Creek, and Wamkipin Run.

[40]Harrison, *Landmarks*, pp. 291-92, 239-30. The boundaries of the county were later slightly altered, especially the 1798 Loudoun-Fairfax line. Neither were all the citizens during the nineteenth century satisfied with the county. Pro-slave people in Loudoun and Fauquier counties unsuccessfully petitioned the state legislature in 1850 for the formation of a new county out of portions of southern Loudoun and northern Fauquier with Middleburg as the proposed county seat. In 1954 the boundary between Loudoun and Fairfax was resurveyed and moved slightly to the east. Loudoun gained some land that had traditionally been considered a part of Fairfax.

[41]Virginia's status during colonial Loudoun's existence was that of a royal colony with the governor appointed by the crown. Thereby the governor, as the king's representative, exercised considerable power in determining the nature of county government. County officials were usually aristocrats and planters. The county lieutenant, sheriff, clerk of court, and coroner were appointed by the governor. Constables and county surveyors were appointed by the county court. All except justices of the court, who were not paid, received fees in pounds of tobacco for services rendered in accordance to the amount specified by the colonial legislature of Virginia. Many of the positions in local government were patterned after those in England.

[42]Albert O. Porter, *County Government in Virginia* (New York: Columbia University Press, 1947), pp. 32, 34-35, 78-83. The sheriff served in many capacities, both as a county administrator and law official. One of his key functions was to collect taxes. From 1700 to the 1750's in Virginia, there were four kinds of taxes: quitrent (yearly tax of one shilling per fifty acres of land), export tax (two shillings a hogshead on exported tobacco), export tax on tobacco sent to another American colony (one penny per pound), tithe (a tax on free males over sixteen that included a levy on their slave holdings; the rate of the tithe varied according to the desires of the colonial Assembly). By the middle 1700's the job of listing the tithables was taken from the sheriff and given to the county justices (members of the county court). Each county was divided into precincts with one justice assigned for preparing a tax list for each region. Each planter had to report his tithables to the justice. Sheriffs were assisted in their work by deputies and constables. The latter were appointed by the county court to serve in a precinct. Porter states that the first "instance of property taxation" in Virginia emerged during the French and Indian War when the Virginia Assembly levied a tax of one shilling three pence for each hundred acres of land recorded on the quitrent rolls.

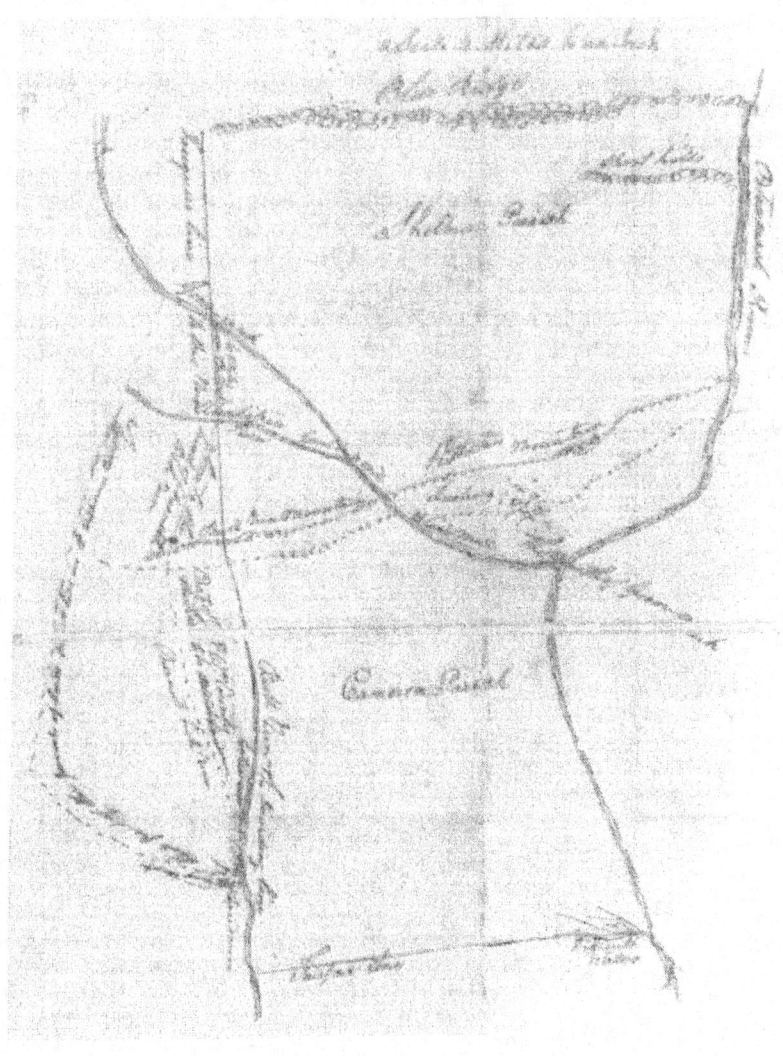

Figure 6. Rough Map Showing Shelburne and Cameron Parishes that Accompanied the Petition to the Colonial Legislature for the Creation of Cameron Parish as a County. (The dotted line just south of the Bull Run and "Kittocton" Mountain represents the old Carolina Road.)

of "wild land" or twenty-five acres of improved or cultivated land could vote for two representatives in the lower house of the Virginia Assembly, known as the House of Burgesses.⁴³ To vote after 1769, a male had to own at least fifty acres of land "if no settlement be made upon it or twenty-five acres with a plantation house thereon at least twelve feet square."⁴⁴

The county court performed both executive and legislative as well as judicial duties. Court was held quarterly, and the men who served as justices were usually the more affluent inhabitants of the county because they received no recompense. The lack of pay was offset by their being the center of local power and attention. On court days not only people who had court business came to Leesburg but many others who desired to witness trials, meet friends, talk and hear news and gossip, and conduct business. Therefore, court days during the eighteenth and nineteenth centuries in Loudoun were of considerable political, social, and economic significance. Among the court's multifarious functions, which were derived from laws enacted by the colonial legislature, were the creation and maintenance of roads,⁴⁵ appointment of county surveyors,⁴⁶ the issuance of licenses and the regulation of ordinaries, ⁴⁷ and the control of the prices of liquor in the county.⁴⁸

---

⁴³Ibid., p. 55. According to Virginia colonial law Loudoun had to pay each "burgess" ten shillings a day when he attended the General Assembly plus "five days for coming and five days for returning" from this body. The county was also to pay transportation costs (Hening, *Statutes*, IIX, 314-15). Loudoun representatives to the colonial General Assemblies from 1758 to 1768 were Francis Lightfoot Lee and James Hamilton; for 1769-1791, Francis Peyton and James Hamilton (Hamilton vacated his seat during May 1770 to accept the office of coroner and was succeed by Josiah Clapham); for 1772-1774, Thomas Mason and Francis Peyton; for 1775-1776, Josiah Clapham and Francis Peyton. The constable remained a minor law enforcement position in Loudoun into the twentieth century but with the advent of cars was superseded by the deputy sheriff (see the *Report of the Secretary of the Commonwealth to the Governor and General Assembly* for 1905, pp. 167-69).

⁴⁴Hening, *Statutes*, IIX, 306.

⁴⁵Loudoun Court Order Book A, Part I, pp. 169,180,182,202.

⁴⁶Ibid., pp. 84-301; Albert O. Porter, *County Government in Virginia*, p. 163. Justices of the court were individually the local magistrates and individually tried petty crimes. The decision could be appealed to the county court. Assisting the county court in its judicial function was the grand jury of Loudouners summoned to serve in that capacity. If the trial concerned a charge that was a felony or treason, it was not tried by the county justices but by a jury of six men from the county. The county court did have control of the legal profession as persons wishing to practice law in the county had to have the approval of the county court and be bonded for good behavior (see Porter, *County Government in Virginia*, pp. 16,50-53,67). By today's standards justice during colonial Loudoun depended upon the effort and attitude of amateurs. However, this system did not deter Loudouners from using the judicial system. If anything they were "sue happy." A British traveler in Loudoun during the 1770's commented: "People seem fond of the law. Nothing uncommon for them to bring a suit against a person for a Book debt and trade with him on an open account at the same time." This is verified by the more than sixty-seven references in

The county government for Loudoun was organized on July 12, 1757.[49] A year passed before a site for a courthouse was selected. Construction of a structure upon this site, which was at the crossroads formed by the junction of the "mountain road" from Alexandria to Key's Gap in the Blue Ridge Mountain with the "Old Carolina road" that traversed the county in a southern direction from the Potomac River, did not take place until 1761.[50] Much of the time and efforts of the justices of the county court during the first decade after the creation of Loudoun County were concerned with the construction of public buildings: the courthouse and the jail. On September 15, 1758, the court hired Aeneas Campbell, also the county's first sheriff, to build a brick courthouse forty by twenty-eight feet for the sum of "Three Hundred and sixty-five pounds current money."[51] At the same time Daniel French

---

the Loudoun County Court Order Books from 1761 to 1800, in which Richard Coleman and his sons and grandsons were either involved in litigation or appointed to positions of public trust such as sheriff, justice, or tax commissioner. (In 1777 a position known as commissioner of taxes was created to collect county taxes; during the 1780's the title was changed to commissioner of revenue.)

[47]Loudoun Court Order Book A, Part I, pp. 11,17,16,75,99,106,113,158,208,219,229-30,233,291,329,344,345; Court Order Book Z, p. 259.

[48]Ibid., p. 7

[49]Harrison, *Landmarks*, pp. 326-27; Loudoun County, Virginia, Court Order Book A, Part I, pp. 1-3. Aeneas Campbell was Loudoun's first sheriff, and Charles Binns was the county's first clerk. Binns served in that capacity from 1758 to 1796, at which time his son, Charles Binns, Jr., took over the position until 1837. From 1837 to 1851, Charles G. Eskridge was Loudoun's clerk. In anticipation of the impending creation of Loudoun, the Council of Virginia's colonial legislature on May 24, 1757, appointed thirteen men to serve as justices of the county court: Anthony Russell, Fielding Turner, James Hamilton, Aeneas Campbell, Nicholas Minor, William West, Charles Tyler, John Moss, Francis Peyton, John Mucklehany, Richard Coleman, Josias Clapham, and George West. Any six of these gentlemen comprised a quorum. At the first meeting on July 12, 1757, all but two justices were present. Court in Loudoun was nevertheless held prior to the American Revolution with as few as four justices present. Often justices of the court helped each other to obtain additional county positions. For example, the court recommended to the governor that William West and Richard Coleman, county justices, be appointed county coroners along with two other gentlemen who were not members of the court.

[50]Ibid., pp. 327-28,344-45; Loudoun Court Order Book A, Part I, pp. 103,166. The site for the county seat was as convenient a location as could have been selected at that time for the inhabitants of the county.

[51]Loudoun Court Order Book A, Part I, pp. 2,84,131,142-43,162,291,166-67. Inside the original courthouse was a court room and a jury room. White oak was used to frame in the structure; the window sashes were made of "well Seasoned Pine of at least 1½ Inches after they were wrought." There were five windows, each with twenty windowpanes, eight by ten inches. Each window was to have "shutters with Hooks & Bolts." The front door was eight feet high and four and one-half feet wide. Inside the courtroom were two galleries for juries with open staircases with banisters leading to the jury boxes. The seats for the county justices were "circular" and "raised with banistered steps leading to them." The

was hired by the court to build the "Gaol and Stocks" for the sum of eighty-three pounds on the sheriff's land at Raspberry Plain, located two miles north of the proposed site of the courthouse.[52] Apparently the sheriff was more successful in supervising the construction of the courthouse than French was in building the jail. The reason was the court issued fairly detailed instructions for the construction of the courthouse, but did not for the jail.[53] Therefore, the court decreed on November 14, 1759, that the jail was inadequate, as it had been constructed, and ruled that the following remedial work was mandatory:

> . . . each Hearth to be laid with brick or stone, two foot deep; the plank butting the Fire place to be taken off nine inches more than it now is, and the chimney [is] to be raised three foot higher than it now is, and outside locks [added] to both doors [and] a trough and passage to carry off the Excrements of Prisoners.[54]

One of the important legislative functions of the court was to levy taxes to obtain funds for the salaries of county officials and other administrative expenses. The first county budget, issued by the court on November 14, 1758, itemized expenditures that amounted to 53,067 pounds of tobacco. At the same time the court issued this budget, it levied a tax of forty-eight pounds current money on 1,156 male inhabitants of the county to cover the costs.[55]

A distinct separation of judicial, executive, and legislative powers did not exist in Loudoun's early county government. Although many of the laws for the county were enacted by the Virginia legislature, the county justices did pass ordinances that they enforced. For example, in 1781

courthouse was constructed on lots number twenty-seven and twenty-eight of what was formerly the property of Nicholas Minor. Successors to the original courthouse were also constructed on the same site: a larger courthouse was built in 1811 and the current courthouse in 1894.

[52]Gaol is the British spelling for jail. It has the same pronunciation as jail.

[53]Loudoun Court Order Book A, Part I, pp. 142-43. On November 14, 1758, 950 pounds of tobacco were appropriated by the court to John Trammell for "building a Prison at Aeneas Campbell's; 9,960 pounds were appropriated to Daniel French for building a prison and Stocks," and 21,900 pounds of tobacco to Aeneas Campbell "in part for building a courthouse for this county."

[54]Loudoun Court Order Book A, Part I, p. 305. By 1767 this jail had been destroyed by fire. On August 12, 1767, the county court composed of James Hamilton, Nicholas Minor, and Philip Noland entered into an agreement with a citizen "for a House to serve as a Prison for this county till such time as one can be built, the old one being burnt down" (see Loudoun County Order Book C, p. 233). At this time the jail was probably moved to Leesburg from Raspberry Plain.

[55]Ibid., pp. 176-77; Wesley F. Craven, *The Southern Colonies in the Seventeenth Century, 1607-1689* (Baton Rouge: Louisiana State University Press, 1949), p. 165. The list of taxable males was called tithables.

Figure 7. Plat Showing the Location of the First County Jail (Gaol) Located Two Miles North of the County Courthouse. Source: Loudoun County Court Order Book A, Part I, p. 103.

the county court decreed: "All persons keeping tippling houses without a license shall be fined 2,000 lbs of tobacco and imprisoned and whipped until their backs are bloody."[56]

Judicial functions of the county court involved attempts not only to provide redress for physical harm and economic damages, but also to punish those involved in illegitimate births and utterances of a vulgar and obscene nature. On September 1, 1757, the court examined Robert Colclough for the rape of Charity Colclough. The case was later terminated due to the "death of the defendant."[57] Justice was often harsh. A slave of George Chilton named Will found that the "mercy of the court" could be uncharitable. Will was charged with "committing a Rape on the body of Sarah Hamrick Windon." He confessed his guilt to the court and threw himself upon its mercy. On Friday, October 27, 1769, he was hung, and his head severed from his body "and set up near the gallows."[58] A less severe sentence was given to another slave named James, who was found guilty of theft. James "broke and entered the House of a certain Mary English in Loudoun" on June 10, 1760. He then "Feloniously took one large Snuff Box of the price of three shillings, three pair of Silver Sleeve Buttons of the price of five shillings." Other items taken included:

> . . .*three Handkerchiefs of the price of ten shillings, one silver Thimble of the price of two shillings, one pair of Silver Studs of the price of two shillings, one Lace of the price of three pence, one Pin Cushion of the price of five pence and ten Needles of the price of ten pence.* . . .[59]

For taking items whose total value amounted to one pound, fourteen shillings, and six pence, the court sentenced James to receive "at the Public Whiping Post thirty-nine Lashes on his bare back well laid on."[60]

The county court also attempted to cope with all social problems, including extreme cases of mental illness. But its solutions, emanating from the necessities of a frontier environment, were often crude and based upon ignorance. Francis Heronimous was ordered by the court on August 11, 1761, to construct a "House ten feet square to secure Paldos

---

[56] Loudoun Court Order Book G, Part II, pp. 364-66. Retailing "spirituous liquor" was a common practice. On May 15, 1871, over thirty county residents were cited by the court for illegally engaging in the retailing of liquor.

[57] Ibid., Book A, Part I, pp. 12,47,94.

[58] Ibid., Book C, p. 275. The court valued "the said slave at 50 pounds of current money." Crimes by slaves against whites were punished even more severely than those committed by whites.

[59] Loudoun Court Order Book A, Part II, pp. 322-23. James was the property of Thomas Gant of Maryland

[60] Ibid.

Heronimous a Lunitik Person until he [recovered] his reason." Two men, Thomas and William Owsley, were ordered to visit the demented male weekly to make sure Francis Heronimous was providing "all necessaries."[61]

After the formation of Loudoun as a county, the church continued to serve in a political capacity. Vestrymen and church officials served the county court in an adjunct capacity that assisted the court in the formation of the list of the tithables, care of orphans and indigent residents, and enforcement of moral codes. In this capacity the church served the communities within the county on the grass roots level and illustrated the union of church and state that continued until destroyed by revolutionary liberalism resulting from America's independence. Use of the church as an instrument of local government is reflected in the following decision of the county court on August 14, 1759, and recorded in the standard writing style of that era which was long on capitalization but short on punctuation:

> *In Pursuance to an Act of Assembly for setting the Tith and bounds of Lands and preventing unlawful shooting and ranging thereupon this Court doth Order and direct that the Vestry of Cameron Parish do divide the said Parish into so many Presints [sic] as to them shall seem most convinient for the Processioning every particular Person's Land within the same that they do appoint the particular Times between the last Day of December and the last Day of March next insuing when such Processioning shall be made in every such Precint [sic] and that they do appoint two intelligent Honest Freeholders in every respective Presint [sic] to see such Processioning preformed and to take and Procession and of the Person's Land they shall Procession and of the Persons present at the same and what Lands in their respective Precints [sic] they shall fail to Procession and the particular reason for such failure.*[62]

Another example of the church being used in a secular capacity was the instructions by the county court on August 9, 1763, to the "Churchmen" of Cameron parish to "bind out according to Law, James Watts of two years of age" and "Elizabeth Watts" five years old to Jacob Schacher, who was to teach the male child "the Trade of a weaver." This action was necessitated by the desertion of the parent or parents who ran off and left the children "in a distressed manner."[63]

Attempts to regulate the sex habits and language of Loudoun colonials proved to be a continuous and time-consuming task as county

[61]Ibid., p. 483.
[62]Loudoun Court Order Book A, Part I, p. 266.
[63]Ibid., Book B, Part I, p. 196.

Court Order Books are full of cases dealing with sexual improprieties and of "swearing oaths." The latter included no less than the county's first sheriff, Aeneas Campbell.[64] Charges of using profanity included the person's name, number of oaths, and month of the alleged utterances. Punishment for "prophane Oaths" was often fines such as the twenty shillings Dennis Dallis had to pay for "swearing four Oaths." Payment, as in other morals cases, was paid to the parish.[65] Residents must have been embarrassed to find they were accused of moral crimes and the charge recorded regardless of the outcome of the trial. Such an example was that of James Coleman and his wife who were ordered to appear at the next court "to answer information exhibited against them for Incestuous Copulation,"[66] or Christian Skinner "for living in a state of fornication with Sally McGinnis," or "Charles Chinn for Cohabiting with Sith Davis," or "Ann Hays for having a base Born Child," or "James Whaley, Jr. absenting from his Wife and taking up with another woman, . . . his Wife's Sister and having a Base born Child by her."[67] Women were fined for having illegitimate children and the father had to pay child support.[68] Sarah Owsley was fined 500 pounds of tobacco or fifty shillings for having a base child.[69] Unwed mothers who could not pay the fine often had to hire themselves out as indentured servants to a man who would pay the fine. William Smith was ordered to pay 800 pounds of tobacco yearly for five years to Cameron parish for the maintenance of a "Bastard Child" of Elizabeth Chilton.[70] Despite zealous reporting by church wardens, sexual conduct and the use of profanity continued to be far below the standards set by the parish.

Other duties of the county court included adopting "some safe mode for preventing the Introduction of" the pestilence into Loudoun. Few words connoted greater fear for eighteenth-century Americans than those of epidemic diseases like smallpox.[71] Such fear was evoked by the news

---

[64] Ibid., Book A, Part I, pp. 98-99; Book E, p. 313.
[65] Ibid., Book A, Part I, p. 177.
[66] Ibid., Book A, Part II, p. 517.
[67] Ibid., Book A, Part I, p. 98; Book G, Part II, p. 365.
[68] Hening, *Statutes*, IIX, 374-75.
[69] Loudoun Court Order Book B, Part I, p. 178.

[70] Ibid., Book G, Part II, p. 285. Not all men who appeared before the court were restrained in their demeanor. For example, Jonathan Monkhouse was put in the stocks for ten minutes for being rude to one of the "judges."

[71] Loudoun County Court Order Book P, p. 272. A law was enacted in Virginia in 1769 that made it illegal to bring smallpox into the colony. After independence the law continued to be in effect with a fine of $3,000 for those that violated it. (See the article by Penelope M. Osburn in *The Loudoun Times-Mirror*, September 19, 1957, entitled "How Loudoun Fought an Epidemic in 1793.")

that smallpox epidemics had erupted in Philadelphia and elsewhere. On the urging of the Virginia governor, the county court of Loudoun on October 2, 1793, placed a quarantine of six days on all travelers to Loudoun from the north. A "Sergeant or Corporal and four men" were to be stationed at each of the ferries that crossed the Potomac River.[72] Their duty was:

> . . .to examine all persons who shall attempt to cross into the county and unless satisfactory proof shall be otherwise made, to Examine such persons on oath or affirmation as to the place from whence they came and if it shall appear that such persons came from Philadelphia or its neighborhood or any other place suspected of being infected with such disease not to suffer them to cross said river in less than six days during which time of their detention the goods or baggage brought with such persons shall during the whole of each day, be exposed to the open air on the other side of the river, after which such persons, if in health, shall suffer to Continue their Journey but if any symptoms of the disease appear, notice thereof shall be given to Doctor Charles Douglas, hereby appointed health Officer for the purpose, who is required to visit such diseased persons [to] determine whether such symptoms are Indicative of the said Malligant fever and according to such determination the Travellor shall be suffered to proceed or be compelled to return to his place of origin.[73]

Apparently the quarantine was not totally successful, because on November 30, 1793, the county court granted the inhabitants of Loudoun the "liberty" for the next three months to receive smallpox inoculations "whenever they conceive themselves to be in danger of taking the infection."[74]

EARLY AGRARIAN LIFESTYLE

Armed with the ax and musket, settlers in Loudoun cleared the land and hunted wildlife. Despite the benefits found in an environment teeming with wildlife and abounding with timber which provided materials for such necessities of life as shelter, fuel, clothing, and sustenance, there

---

[72]Ibid. Each squad served one week in this capacity before being relieved.
[73]Ibid., pp. 272-73.
[74]Loudoun County Court Order Book P, p. 315. The above order was sent to "the Baltimore, Frederick Town and George Town Gazettes" for publication in those papers.

also existed encumbrances.[75] Progress in terms of an eighteenth century frontiersman meant the cultivation of the land. For this to be done successfully, trees had to be removed and animals that menaced the harvest either eliminated or driven away.[76] The abundance of trees, of beasts, and the scarcity of labor to perform the back-breaking tasks of clearing and tilling the land presented the settler with a formidable barrier. Success therefore depended upon the conquest of nature. The extensiveness of forest and wildlife were seemingly so inexhaustible and challenging that it was incomprehensible to the colonial that his way of life was exploitive or wasteful. By modern standards it was not. But in creating an agrarian society and in meeting his needs, the pioneer set in motion a basic tenet of American thought: neither nature nor man can stand in the way of progress.

Central to the colonial lifestyle of Loudouners was the ownership of land. Most of the landholdings in colonial Loudoun by the time of the French and Indian War were those of modest farms. Historian Robert E. Brown in examining 287 landholdings in Loudoun in 1769 found that over seventy-five percent of the landholders owned modest acreage of between 100 and 500 acres. Only eleven out of the 287 landholders owned more than 100 acres. Numerous others in the county leased tracts of several hundred acres or less for an annual rent of two to four pounds.[77] Despite the existence of only a limited number of landholding over 1,000 acres, sizeable ownership of land continued to be significant in the

---

[75]Based on correspondence between Yardley Taylor and N. F. Cabell, January 11, 1854; N. F. Cabell Papers, Virginia State Library, box 2, folder 90. A contemporary list of needed implements for life in colonial Virginia included broad and narrow hoes, a variety of axes (broadax and felling ax), handsaw, shovel, spade, and carpentering tools. Taylor wrote to Cabell in 1854 that "Tradition says that the persons who resided here [western Loudoun] previous to . . . [1730] probably as hunters and squatters, were in the practice of burning the forest the better to secure the game. This practice being stopped, when the settlements commenced, a thrifty growth of timber sprang up, and hence the first settlers could scarcely find timber enough to fence their lands when first cleared. This gave this county a poor appearance, and that was its character through most of the last century. Many old persons have been heard to say, that the timber here now is very much larger than when they first knew it."

[76]Loudoun County Order Book A, Part I, pp. 176-77. The county on November 14, 1758, paid a total of 700 pounds of tobacco for seven wolves killed in the county. For each head of a young wolf that was brought in a bounty of fifty pounds was paid, but for a mature wolf the bounty was 100 pounds. Virginia colonials also had a sense of conservation as indicated by an act passed by the colonial legislature in 1772 to preserve "the breed of Deer," and prevent unlawful hunting. Also in 1772 Loudoun and several other counties got the colonial legislature to repeal the act calling for the destruction of crows and squirrels in their counties.

[77]Robert E. Brown and B. Katherine Brown, *Virginia 1705-1786: Democracy or Aristocracy* (East Lansing: Michigan State University Press, 1964), pp. 14,23. By the 1770's the best land in Loudoun was being sold for three to five pounds per acre.

economic and social status of the owner and in the lives of more humble folk. For example, in Loudoun in 1775 Robert Carter owned tracts of land that totaled 39,509 acres. Much of this land was rented to 177 tenants, who in 1793 paid rents in excess of 950 pounds in currency and 11,124 pounds of tobacco.[78]

The outstanding economic development in Virginia during the eighteenth century was the shift from tobacco to wheat as the main staple of the piedmont region. However, the economy of Loudoun was spared much of this transition. Loudoun's settlement coincided with the period wheat was being cultivated to meet the increased demands of the British market, thus challenging "King" tobacco as Virginia's major staple. Settlement of the western regions of the county was primarily by Germans, Scots-Irish, and Quakers from Pennsylvania, one of the "bread colonies" whose staple was the production of cereals.[79] For these reasons, wheat was an important money crop in Loudoun from the time her soil was first tilled. In 1759, the colonial Virginia Assembly recognized the primacy of the cultivation of cereals in Loudoun and the necessity of authorizing the inhabitants of the county to pay their taxes and fees in money instead of tobacco.[80] Yet tobacco was raised in Loudoun from the beginning of white settlement, especially by English settlers that came from tidewater regions of the colony. Not only were they accustomed to the cultivation of the "golden weed," but also to the institution of slavery which had emerged as the main labor force of a plantation economy. Consequently, slaves accompanied some of the first and more wealthy settlers in Loudoun.[81] Despite the uncertainty of

---

[78]Louis Morton, *Robert Carter of Nomini Hall*, pp. 70,84,280. Robert Carter owned tracts of land in Loudoun at Goose Creek, Broad Run, Sugarland Run, Bull Run, and Piney Ridge.

[79]Lewis C. Gray, *History of Agriculture in the Southern United States to 1860*, I (Reprint; Gloucester, Mass.: Peter Smith, 1958), 166-69 (hereafter referred to as *History of Agriculture*); Harrison, *Landmarks*, pp. 397-401; Morton, *Robert Carter of Nomini Hall*, p. 143. Morton sees the 1760's as the most noticeable period of the shift in Virginia from the cultivation of tobacco to wheat.

[80]Based on correspondence between Yardley Taylor and N. F. Cabell, January 11, 1854; Hening, *Statutes*, VII, 292; Harrison, *Landmarks*, p. 412. The statute passed by the colonial legislature stated that "the inhabitants of the county of Loudoun make but little tobacco and many of them none . . ." Taylor wrote in 1854, "The first settlers here were almost entirely from Pen[n]sylvania, and the adjoining colonies, particularly in the northern and middle parts of the county. The easternpart was more settled by native Virginians. The northern emigrants not being acquainted with the cultivation of tobacco; they cultivated but little of it but turned their attention principally to the raising of grains. This practice, tho it did not reduce the soil as rapidly as raising tobacco, yet after the revolutionary war much of the soil was considered poor and nearly worn out. No grasses had been cultivated and but little attention had been paid to manures."

[81]For a thorough account of the significance and nature of tobacco cultivation in seventeenth-century and eighteenth-century Virginia, consult *Tobacco in Colonial Virginia: "The Sovereign Remedy"* (Williamsburg, Va.: Virginia 350th Anniversary Celebration Corporation, 1957), by Melvin Herndon.

the foreign market for tobacco, soil exhaustion, erosion, and shortage of labor, Robert Carter of Nomini Hall continued to raise tobacco as the main crop of his Leo plantation in Loudoun until 1788. But the records of that plantation were indicative that the history of tobacco production during the late eighteenth century was becoming increasingly more difficult.[82] By 1744, Robert Carter, deciding tobacco cultivation was on the way out, ordered that his plantations cultivate hemp, flax, grain, and cotton.[83] In 1781 he decided that Leo plantation in Loudoun would be devoted exclusively to the cultivation of flax and hemp.[84] As the result of the cultivation of cereals in Loudoun like wheat, corn, rye, oats, and barley during the colonial era, numerous mills were constructed throughout the county.[85] Powered by water from numerous county streams, the grist mills became an integral part of the county's economic life.[86] There were three stages in the cereal economy of Loudoun. The first stage was the raising and harvesting of the grain crop. The second was the transportation of the grain to the mills in Conestoga wagons drawn by six-horse teams where the grain was ground into flour. The

[82] Avery O. Craven, *Soil Exhaustion as a Factor in the Agricultural History of Virginia and Maryland, 1606-1860* (Reprint; Gloucester, Mass.: Peter Smith, 1965), pp. 28-29; Morton, *Robert Carter of Nomini Hall*, pp. 113,137,285. Carter wrote his overseers in 1773 that due to the depression and bad market price, he prohibited "the prizing into hogsheads" even one pound of tobacco in his Loudoun and Prince William plantations. Carter's major tobacco-producing plantations were not in Loudoun but Westmoreland and Richmond counties. For example, his lands in Westmoreland produced 5,455 hogsheads of tobacco in 1784 compared to only twenty-nine in Loudoun for 1783 and 1784.

[83] Morton, *Robert Carter of Nomini Hall*, pp. 155-56,159. Tobacco was held in such disrepute in Loudoun at the end of the eighteenth century persons renting land were forbidden by the terms of their lease from raising tobacco upon the rented land.

[84] Hening, *Statutes*, VII, 384-85; IIX, 38-41,314-15; X, 326-27. Each tithable person in Virginia in 1764 was to pay forty-six pounds of tobacco to defray Virginia's expenses in fighting the French and Indian War. Only the inhabitants of five counties, of which Loudoun was one, were given the option of paying the equivalent in money.

[85] Morton, *Robert Carter of Nomini Hall*, p. 159.

[86] Helen Hirst Marsh, "Early Loudoun Water Mills," *The Bulletin of the Loudoun County Historical Society*, I, (1958),21-26; Loudoun County Order Book A, Part II, p. 533. Marsh's article is a good summary of the early history of mills in Loudoun. One of the first mills in the county was a log mill constructed at Waterford in 1740. The early Minute Books of the county court have numerous references of the court granting permission for the construction of water mills. In 1745 the colonial law of Virginia required permission of county courts for the construction of mills. Loudoun's first sheriff, Aeneas Campbell, was also the first citizen of the county to petition the Loudoun court (1758) for permission to construct a grist mill at his "Raspberry Plain" plantation on Limestone Run. Thomson Mason acquired this property in 1760 and in 1783 built another mill on this property near the mouth of Big Spring Run. Probably the greatest "mill magnate" in Loudoun was John Hough. Hough, a Quaker from Pennsylvania who settled in Loudoun in 1744, was a surveyor for Lord Fairfax for many years. Hough not only acquired thousands of acres of land but had three mills constructed. The first was built in 1761 south of where the present Goose Creek Country Club is located.

third was the transporting of flour, also by Conestoga wagons, to Alexandria, where it was shipped to market in the West Indies and Europe.[87]

Crucial to both the tobacco and flour trade of Loudoun were roads. The genesis of Loudoun's colonial roads were paths traveled by Indians and buffaloes, which included natural northern gateways later known as Noland's Ferry, Snickers' Gap, and Ashby's Gap. One of the early routes for travel between the north and the south was due to the topography of northern Virginia. Aboriginal travelers learned that they could travel from the north to tribes in Carolina and avoid contact with English settlers in the tidewater by going through a trail that traversed the Virginia piedmont. A portion of this trail went through the center of Loudoun just east of the foothills of the Catoctin and Bull Run Mountains.[88] White travelers going to the north or south traveled what they called the Carolina Road after the Indians had been removed from the region. By 1742, the Carolina Road had become such a haven for horse and cattle thieves that it gave rise to another name for the trail, "Rogues Road."[89] Even as late as 1780, the title "Rogues Road" remained appropriate. A traveler from Pennsylvania on his way to North Carolina recorded in his diary that he was robbed at a camp by some of Mr. Noland's Negroes just prior to crossing the Potomac River at Noland's

---

[87]Gray, *History of Agriculture*, I, 165-66; Harrison, *Landmarks*, pp. 405-407. Virginia's colonial legislature enacted legislation that required the inspection of pork, beef, flour, tar, pitch, and turpentine for defects. Every "white man" producing "wheat flower intended for exportation" had to take an oath before a justice of the peace "that the flour he was selling was" fine, clean, and pure, "and not mixed with meal of Indian corn, pease, or any other grain or pulse, and that his casks are justly tared." The justice then granted the producer of flour a certificate he later showed the inspector who "bore the said casks through and diligently views and examine the flower therein contained, and if by him found fine, clean, pure, unmixed, and merchantable, shall stamp or brand on the head of every such cask or barrel the first letter of his county, the letter V for Virginia, the first letter of his own christian name, his whole surname at length, the word fine, the gross, tare and neat weight thereof." (See Hening, *Statutes*, IIX, 143-44). The colonial legislature also attempted to protect cattle in Virginia from "contagious distemper" brought into the colony by cattle from other colonies. During November 1766, a new colonial law required all persons driving cattle from another colony to take an oath before a justice of the peace that he had "known all the cattle" for twenty days and they were free of "contagious distemper." The justice would then have two local men inspect the herd. If the herd was healthy, the justice of peace issued a certificate or bill of health for the herd. Drovers failing to obtain such a certificate could be fined five shillings for each head of cattle (read pp. 245-50 in Hening, *Statutes*, IIX).

[88]Harrison, *Landmarks*, pp. 441,453-55. This trail was extensively used by the Iroquios.

[89]Ibid., pp. 456-57. In an attempt to reduce the theft of livestock, the Virginia Assembly enacted a law in 1742 that required all travelers on the Carolina Road engaged in driving livestock to show a bill of sale on demand of any justice of the peace.

Ferry, and the following night, while encamped two miles from Leesburg, he was again robbed by Negroes who "had a free evening" and roamed everywhere.[90]

Two other important roads ran through colonial Loudoun. Unlike the Carolina Road, these roads went primarily in an east-west direction and connected the Shenandoah Valley with tidewater Virginia. The Colchester Road connected the town of Colchester on the tidewater to the Valley of Virginia via Williams' Gap in southern Loudoun, later known as Snickers' Gap. The other main thoroughfare was known by many names: Sugarland Path, Eastern Ridge Road, New Church Road, Vestal Gap Road, Alexandria Road, and the Old Leesburg Road. In Loudoun this road, running through northeastern Loudoun to Vestal's Gap, connected Alexandria with the Valley of Virginia. Both the Colchester and Alexandria roads were used to some extent as "rolling roads" to transport tobacco to market as well as routes to take flour to market.[91] Tobacco was also rolled to Noland's Ferry over the Carolina Road. Added to these roads were numerous lesser roads in the county. But even the major roadways were often far from satisfactory. Commenting on this, a British traveler in Loundoun recorded in his diary on Nobember 27, 1774, that the:

> Soil produces good wheat but roads very bad, cut [to] pieces with wagons. Their method of mending roads is with poles about 10 ft. long laid across road; stick fast in mud and make an excellent causeway.[92]

[90]Harrison, *Landmarks*, pp. 461-62. The diarist recorded that Noland, his father, and father-in-law had about 200 Negroes on both sides of the Potomac River and that this "neighborhood is farfamed for robbery and theft." Some writers reject the concept of a high rate of crime on this road. Harrison reports (*Landmarks*, p. 501) that an extensive study of the county records of northern Virginia failed to reveal the kind of robbery on Virginia colonial roads as was then common in England.

[91]Charles E. Gage, *Tobacco, Tobacco Hogsheads and Rolling Roads in Northern Virginia* (Falls Church, Va.: Falls Church Historical Commission, 1959), p. 5; Harrison, *Landmarks*, pp. 476,481-82; Herndon, *Tobacco in Colonial Virginia*, pp. 22-26; Virginia, Northern Neck Land Grant Book B. p. 56. Hogsheads of tobacco could be rolled more easily over colonial roads than transported in wagons which would frequently get stuck. Some of Loudoun's tobacco and flour products were not taken to ports primarily by roads but were taken by boat down the Potomac River. Warehouses were located on the Loudoun bank of the Potomac River (see Hening, *Statutes*, XIII, 155). Georgetown became a great market for tobacco grown in Loudoun and other counties bordering the upper Potomac. After the shift to wheat cultivation, Georgetown lost its tobacco trade and was unable to capture the shipment of grain which went to Alexandria and Baltimore for exportation to foreign nations (Avery Craven, *Soil Exhaustion as a Factor in the Agricultural History of Virginia and Maryland, 1606-1860*, pp. 76-77).

[92]Nicholas Cresswell, *The Journal of Nicholas Cresswell, 1774-1777* (New York: The Dial Press, 1924), p. 48. (Hereafter referred to as *The Journal*.)

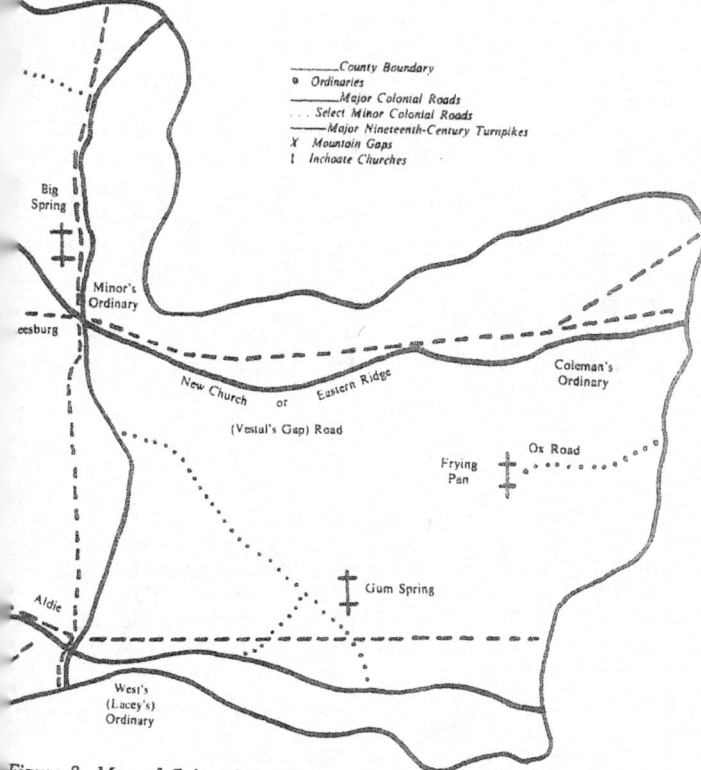

Figure 8. *Map of Colonial Loudoun.*

Also supplementing the colonial roads in Loudoun were ferries that provided more convenient travel across the Potomac River and Goose Creek. At least seven ferries served Loudoun during the 1700's; six crossed the Potomac River and one Goose Creek.[93] The most significant ferry service was provided by the Noland family. In November 1748, Philip Noland petitioned the Virginia Assembly for a license to run a ferry over the Potomac ten miles north of the site of Leesburg, not far from the mouth of the Monocacy River.[94] Despite being denied a permit from the Assembly until 1778, Noland's Ferry was not only an important link in the Carolina Road, but also a shipping point in the Potomac Company line of flatboats on the Potomac River from Cumberland, Maryland, to Alexandria, Virginia.[95]

Ferries were also operated across the widest and deepest portions of Goose Creek near its mouth. In 1747 Fairfax County paid Thomas

---

[93]Loudoun Court Order Book P. pp. 273-74; *The Loudoun Times-Mirror*, September 26, 1957. The Virginia colonial Assembly granted permits to operate ferries in the colony. When a person received such a permit, he showed it to the local justices of the county court who gave the person a license to run the ferry. Records of the county court in 1793 name five ferries that crossed the Potomac River to Loudoun's shores: Edwards', Heater's, Smith's, Belt's, and Conn's. These were probably the names of the men who at that time operated the ferries.

[94]Harrison, *Landmarks*, pp. 503-504. Josias Clapham had petitioned the Assembly for a permit even earlier than Noland, the early 1740's, to run a ferry several miles to the south of where Noland would run his ferry. Clapham later received government permission to run his ferry. Nevertheless, Noland and Clapham were rivals during the early years of Loudoun history. They were later colleagues on the Loudoun Court. In 1778 Philip Noland conveyed his ferry and its landing to his son, Thomas. At that time the Assembly formally repealed the authority for Clapham's Ferry and granted it to Thomas Noland. Interestingly, Clapham was at that time a member of the Assembly.

[95]Ibid., pp. 543,546-47,557. The Potomac Company was in operation during the late 1700's and early 1800's. The company built a series of canals around the falls in the Potomac. Noland's Ferry, according to an old newspaper clipping written by Briscoe Goodhart (see pp. 1-2 of vol. IV of the scrapbooks in the Thomas Balch Library entitled "Loudoun County"), was the site where a number of Hessian prisoners captured at the famous Revolutionary War battle at Saratoga, New York, in 1777 were confined. Goodhart claimed to have found a report while examining old government documents that stated the above developments. Goodhart also wrote that the Hessian prisoners were not confined to any one place but were distributed throughout the county wherever rations could be found and the prisoners put to work on farms. Few of the soldiers were to have returned to Europe after the war. Instead, it has been maintained that they settled in Virginia and Maryland. In the same article the author maintains that a hamlet developed at Noland's Ferry consisting of stores, blacksmith shop, wagon shop, tailor and shoemaking establishments, and a post office that continued until 1822. Canals, railroads, and bridges put the ferry out of business and the hamlet declined. The only remaining ferry currently in operation is White's Ferry, formerly known as Conrad's Ferry. Its origins are also found in the history of colonial Loudoun.

Evans 1,000 pounds of tobacco for running a ferry across Goose Creek.⁹⁶ The Loudoun court on February 9, 1762, granted a license to John Carlyle, an Alexandria businessman and investor, and John Hough to "keep a ferry in this county to the usual place of the said Creek on the Road leading from Leesburg to Alexandria."⁹⁷ The rates for the services of this ferry were set by the same county court:

> ... charge of 7 pence and half penny for a man and horse and two shilling and 6 pence for a wagon team and driver, and one shilling and 3 pence for a hogshead of tobacco with horse and driver.⁹⁸

Land travel was slow and exhaustive in colonial America. It was not uncommon for a traveler, depending on his mode of transportation (wagon, horseback, or foot) and the condition of the road, to go only a distance of ten to twenty miles per day.⁹⁹ Thus along heavily traveled thoroughfares the establishment of places to provide food and lodging at intervals of a few miles was necessary. To this need men of vast and limited means responded, seeing profit in providing for travelers the services of a simple tavern known as an ordinary. Wealthy businessmen constructed special structures for ordinaries and hired others to run them. More humble folk frequently opened up their homes to travelers. The ordinary was an institution that continued until the advent of the automobile, but its golden age in Loudoun was from the 1750's until the 1830's.¹⁰⁰ Stage travel became fashionable around the early 1800's and

---

⁹⁶*The Loudoun Times-Mirror*, September 26, 1957. Roads intercepted by Goose Creek and other streams had to be forded.

⁹⁷Loudoun County Order Book A, Part II, pp. 533-34. Carlyle and Hough were also granted a license by the same session of the county court to "keep an Ordinary [on] the lower side of Goose Creek at the Ferry for one year."

⁹⁸Ibid., Book C, p. 230.

⁹⁹Fairfax Harrison (ed.), "With Braddock's Army: Mrs. Browne's Diary in Virginia and Maryland," *Virginia Magazine of History and Biography*, XXXII (October, 1924), 305-13; George Washington, *The Diaries of George Washington*, ed. by John C. Fitzpatrick, II (Boston: Houghton, Mifflin Co., 1925), 1,064-65. From the 1740's until the American Revolution, Washington traveled extensively over the Alexandria and Colchester roads to western destinations. Consequently he spent innumerable nights at Loudoun's many ordinaries, including those of Coleman, Minor, and West.

¹⁰⁰Loudon County Court Order Book A, Part II, pp. 362, 409, 413, 415, 427, 431, 460, 480, 481, 531, 554, 564, 579, 594, 626, 627; Order Book B, Part I, pp. 25, 29, 35, 59, 60, 72, 77, 105, 108, 110, 161, 192, 193, 232, 235, 240, 250, 260, 278, 315, 319, 324, 335, 338, 358, 391, 491, 494, 506, 535, 673; Order Book B, Part II, pp. 358, 494, 506, 535, 673, 674; Order Book C, pp. 2, 6, 183, 190, 213, 234, 240, 259, 261, 335; Loudoun County Minute Book I, pp. 179, 189, 194, 204, 215, 227, 320, 307; Minute Book XII, pp. 7, 95, 169, 175, 180, 270, 291, 340, 356-59.

tended to limit the need for ordinaries because of the greater distances that could be traveled in a day. But drivers of wagons carrying flour to Alexandria still needed numerous places to spend the night. By the 1830's the Baltimore and Ohio Railroad had diverted most of the flour traffic from Loudoun turnpikes, leaving the pikes for local traffic and drovers who drove hogs, turkeys, sheep, and cattle to Georgetown or Alexandria. Most of the people on long sojourns after 1830 spent the night at hotels in Alexandria, Winchester, or Leesburg instead of the numerous small ordinaries that were decreasing in number. Those remaining often had facilities such as pens and feed for the overnight care of livestock.

Often the more important early Loudoun ordinaries were located at intersections of major roads, mountain gaps, and crossings (ferries and fords) of river and streams. The two most celebrated ordinaries in the county were owned by Nicholas Minor and William West, both located at important intersections of the Carolina Road. Minor's property was located on the Alexandria Road, near where it intersected the Carolina Road; West's ordinary was located at the intersection of the Carolina and Colchester roadways. Both Minor and West were respected citizens of the county. The town of Leesburg was founded on Minor's property, upon which his ordinary was located. William West was also one of the trustees who helped establish the town of Leesburg.[101] Both Minor and West were "gentlemen justices" that made up the first county court of Loudoun and thereby helped launch the county government.[102]

These taverns were referred to as ordinaries because they served "ordinary" or "regular" meals, often consisting of eggs, bacon, hoe cakes, and peach brandy. Though rarely did such establishments have a shield or sign, they were nevertheless easily distinguishable by the numerous papers and advertisements which adorned their walls and doors. These identified such structures not only as a tavern, but a center of the colonial community life where local citizens gathered to drink, gossip, and talk politics. Proprietors of ordinaries that became the center of local social activities often had the exposure and renown that gained them the respect of area citizens and aristocrats of the colony who traveled extensively. This respect often led to ordinary owners being appointed to salient positions in the county government.[103]

---

[101]Hening, *Statutes*, VII, 236.

[102]Loudoun County Court Order Book A, Part I, p. 1. William West was given a license to keep an ordinary at his house by the Fairfax Court in 1754. The license was renewed by the Loudoun Court in 1758 and 1762, which referred to the location of the ordinary at the "Fruit Hill Farm." Charles West, son of William, ran the ordinary until the 1780's. At that time Joseph Lacey seems to have taken over managing the establishment. The building that housed West's ordinary, later known as Lacey's ordinary, was torn down in 1927.

[103]Harrison, *Landmarks*, pp. 484-88. Some of the travelers were important in the colonial legislature and recommended to the governor the appointment of the more respected ordinary keepers to positions in the county government.

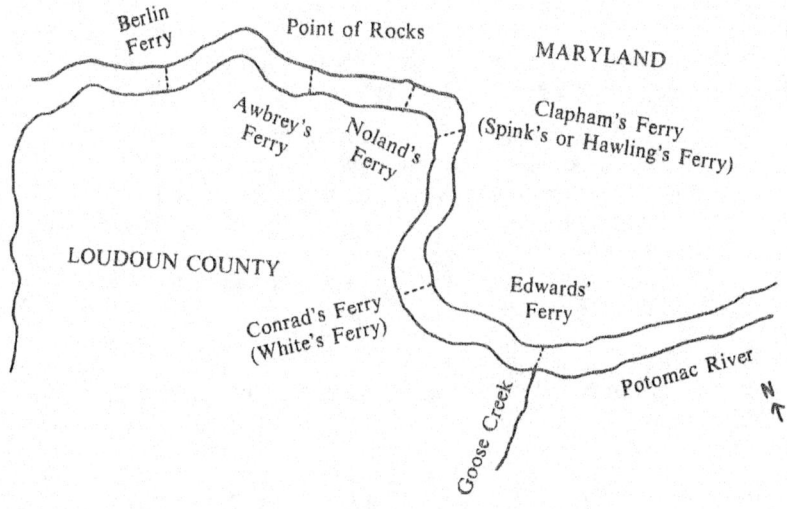

Figure 9. *Eighteenth-Century Ferries that Crossed the Potomac River from Loudoun to Maryland.*

Sleeping quarters at ordinaries were often crowded as all male travelers were usually placed in one room and the females in another. Strangers were required to sleep in the same bed with persons they had never seen before, thereby literally making strange bedfellows. Women frequently slept in their clothes.[104]

More specific examples of the nature of ordinaries and colonial ways can be found in accounts of travelers who passed through the county. Such is the story of an English lady, Mrs. Browne, who followed her brother, a commissary officer attached to Braddock's expedition, to Fort Cumberland during the French and Indian War. This portion of Braddock's force went to Fort Cumberland by way of the Alexandria Road through Loudoun. En route to Leesburg the road was so bad that Mrs. Browne recorded in her dairy that she was so:

> . . . *stiff that I was at a loss to tell whether I had any Limbs. I breakfasted in my waggon and then set of [f] in front [of the marching men]; at which all the rest were very much enrag'd, but to no Purpose for my Coachman told them that he had but one Officer to Obey and she was in his waggon, and it was not right that she should be blinded with dust.*[105]

Upon arriving at Leesburg on June 3, 1775, Mrs. Browne spent the night at Minor's ordinary. While there, she and her companions, which included a preacher who had joined them on the way to the county seat, ordered:

> . . . *some Fowls for Dinner but not one to be had, so was obliged to set down to our old Dish Gammon & Greens. The Officer and the Parson replenish'd their Bowl so often that they began to be very joyous, untill their Servant told them that their Horses were lost; at which the Parson was much inrag'd and pop'd out an Oath, but Mr. Falkner said 'Never mind your Horse, Doctor, but have you a Sermon ready for next Sunday?*[106]

The following day they traveled northwest to the future site of Hillsboro:

> *At break of Day my Coachman came and tap'd at my Chamber Door and said Madam all is ready and it is right*

---

[104]Ibid., p. 486.

[105]Harrison, "With Braddock's Army," p. 312. Shortly after the British disaster at the Monongahela, Mrs. Browne's brother died of the "bloody flux" then in epidemic proportions in the British army. Mrs. Browne almost lost her life to the same disease.

[106]Ibid. The parson was recorded by Browne in her diary as Adams, but Harrison believes this was probably a misnomer for John Andrews, who was at that time the parson of Cameron parish. Gammon was a cured hog ham or side of bacon.

> *early. I went to my wagon and we moved on. Left Mr. Falkner behind in Pursuit of his Horse. March'd 14 miles and halted at an old sage Quaker's with silver Locks [Edward Thompson]. His wife on my comming accosted me in the following manner: 'Welcome Friend sit down, thou seems full Bulky to travel, but thou art young and that will enable thee. We were once so ourselves but we have been married 44 years & may say we have lived to see the Days that we have no Pleasure therein.' We had recourse to our old Dish Gammon, nothing else to be had: but they said they had some Liquor they call'd Whisky which was made of Peaches. My Friend Thompson being a Preacher, when the soldiers came in as the Spirit mov'd him, held forth to them and told them the great Virtue of Temperance. They all stared at him like Pigs but had not a word to say in their justification.*[107]

The travelers spent two nights and one day at Quaker Thompson's preparing to continue on their journey. Mrs. Browne found her quarters lacking:

> *My Lodgings not being very clean, I had so many close Companions call'd Ticks that deprived me of my Nights Rest, but I indulg'd till 7. We halted this Day, all the nurses Baking Bread and Boiling Beef for the march to morrow. A fine Regale 2 Chicken with milk and water to Drink, which my friend Thompson said was fine temperate Liquor. Several things lost out of my waggon, amongst the rest they took 2 of my Hams, which my Coachman said was an abomination to him, and if he could find out who took them he would make them remember taking the next.*[108]

The fact that Mrs. Browne found her lodging unclean was not the result of the government's lack of interest. Both the colonial, and later, state legislatures of Virginia enacted legislation requiring the county courts to rigorously regulate ordinaries. County courts were to grant a yearly license to those establishments that were considered satisfactory. Courts were also to regulate all the fees by putting a ceiling on prices of all services.[109] An example was the rates the county court established for Loudoun ordinaries from June 1806 to July 1807:[110]

---

[107]Ibid., pp. 312-13.

[108]Ibid. After leaving Thompson's on June 6, Browne recorded the roads were extremely bad, due in part to "a great Gust of Thunder and Lightning and Rain, so that" they were "almost drown'd."

[109]Hening, *Statutes*, VI, 72-75.

[110]Loudoun County Court Order Book Z, p. 259.

Breakfast	$.19
Hot dinner with cyder [sic] or Beer	.26
Supper	.19
Ail [sic] and other low wines [per] bottle	.36
Port [per] Bottle	.40
Good Madeira Wine [per] Bottle	.60
Stablage and hay for 24 hrs.	.20
Corn or Oats per Gallon	.09
Lodging in clean sheets	.09
Pasturage 24 hrs	.10

Often the gap was considerable between the theory of the law and common practice followed in running ordinaries. It was not uncommon for proprietors to operate an ordinary without a license or apply for renewal of a permit several years after the expiration of the original license. Like the county officials, proprietors of ordinaries had to be bonded. This procedure was a factor that caused some owners of inns to be reticent in applying for a license. Some lacked the money to post bond, while others, short of capital, solved the problem by taking a partner or entering into an arrangement in which a friend would provide "his security."[111] Occasionally a proprietor was fined for a violation of the law. John Heryford was "convicted of permitting unlawful gaming in his ordinary in Leesburg" and fined "5 pounds of current money," which was given to the church wardens of Cameron parish.[112]

The transformation of a frontier into an agrarian society permeated all aspects of colonial lifestyles in the piedmont of northern Virginia. Even towns had their origins as agrarian trading centers or as providers of services needed in the agrarian society of that age. Colonial urban areas were often a microcosm of the animal husbandry practiced in the more rural areas. All dwellers in small hamlets kept a cow and hogs which, as elsewhere in the county, roamed at large. Hogs, despite serving as useful scavengers and garbage collectors were especially a nuisance as they impeded traffic and did other mischief common to swine.[113] Citizens of the town of Leesburg petitioned the colonial assembly for remedial legislation. In February 1772, the following law was enacted that made it unlawful for hogs "to go at large in the town of Leesburg." If any swine belonging to the inhabitants of Leesburg were found "running or going at large within" the town limits, then it was lawful for:

---

[111] Loudoun County Court Order Book A, Part II, pp. 481, 531, 554, 564, 626, 627. The Loudoun Court granted six licenses to run ordinaries in 1762. Of these six licenses, four depended upon someone else to provide funds for the bond. Under a 1748 law, the bond was 50 "pounds current money."

[112] Ibid., p. 627.

[113] Carl Bridenbaugh, *Cities in the Wilderness* (New York: Capricorn Books, 1964), p. 19.

... *any person whatsoever to kill and destroy every such swine so running at large. PROVIDED ALWAYS, That such person shall not convert such swine, so killed or destroyed, to his or her own use, but shall leave the same where it shall be so killed, and give immediate notice to the owner thereof (if known) and if not, then to the next justice of peace for the said county, who shall order the same to be sold, and shall also cause a description of the said hog to be affixed at the door of the courthouse. . . . And if after notice, published as aforesaid, the owner shall not within ten days appear, and may be lawful for such justice to order the money, arising from such sale to the churchwardens, for the use of the parish.*[114]

Religion was a salient determinant of the lifestyle of colonial Loudoun. The Anglican Church not only played a significant role in the formation of the county, but also acted as a grass-roots regulatory body serving as an extension of the county government. However, religious situations were strongly influenced by the pastoral environment and frontier conditions. The latter made travel to churches scattered throughout the county difficult and qualified ministers hard to obtain and keep. These conditions were reflected in the first church constructed in what is now Loudoun County, the "Chappel of Ease Above Goose Creek."[115] The Anglican parish church was too far for many of the settlers in the area to attend. So a chapel of ease was erected as a place where religious services, including funerals and christenings, were conducted, usually by a lay reader and only occasionally by the minister. When Shelburne parish was created out of the western portion of the parish of Cameron in 1770, the Goose Creek Chapel was the only Anglican, or established church, in the new parish. In accordance with the law, the vestry set about to establish a glebe and church.[116] The glebe

[114] Hening, *Statutes*, IIX, 621-22. This act also stated that it did not in any way prohibit anyone from driving hogs through town to market or to another farm.

[115] Harrison, *Landmarks*, p. 287; *The Loudoun Times-Mirror*, January 17, 1960. Truro parish appropriated 2,500 pounds of tobacco in 1733 to Capt. Francis Awbrey toward building a chapel. The next year the same amount was raised and in 1735 an additional 4,000 pounds for completing the chapel at Big Spring, two miles north of the future site of Leesburg.

[116] *The Loudoun Times-Mirror*, January 17, 1960. The colonial legislature of Virginia enacted legislation that regulated the salary of Anglican ministers: 16,000 pounds of tobacco annual salary, 200 pounds for a funeral, and 150 for a wedding. In addition, the minister must be supplied with a glebe. During November 1773, the vestry of Shelburne parish purchased 465 acres from Joseph Combs and his wife for £465. The glebe house was constructed by Appolis Cooper, who was later killed in the Revolutionary War at the Battle of Brandywine Creek. Minutes of Shelburne parish for November 12, 1772, gave the specifications of the glebe house as a structure of either brick or stone, forty-eight feet long and twenty-nine feet wide. Other details were also spelled out in the minutes.

was a church farm and upon it was the house which was the minister's official place of residence. The Shelburne glebe was located just to the south of the central part of Loudoun Valley near what was later known as Hugesville.[117] No Anglican or Episcopal Church was located in the county seat at Leesburg until 1812. Until that time the Episcopal congregation had to worship in the county courthouse and in the Presbyterian Church.[118] The first Anglican resident minister in Shelburne parish was the Rev. David Griffith, who had been a physician prior to entering the ministry. He served in Loudoun from 1771 until the American Revolution, at which time the parish appears to have been without an Episcopal minister until after the war.[119]

Despite the fact that the Anglican or Episcopal Church was the established religion of colonial Virginia, it was not the most successful denomination in Loudoun, especially in the western half of the county. Factors contributing to the rise of competitive religions in Loudoun were the passage of the English Toleration Act of 1689 and that of Virginia in 1699 which opened the way for the growth of dissenting sects;[120] the at-

---

[117] Nan Lin Kincaid, "The First Churches in Loudoun," *The Bulletin of the Loudoun County Historical Society*, I (1958), 10-11. Not far from the glebe a "Mountain Chapel" was constructed prior to 1773 near what is known today as Philomont. Stephen Roszel and his wife Sarah deeded to the vestry of Shelburne the land upon which the chapel was located. Methodists later used the chapel. During the eighteenth and nineteenth centuries it was not uncommon for the same church building to be shared by several different denominations.

[118] Ibid., pp. 11-12. A small brick church called St. James was built not far from the present Loudoun County jail. A second church was built on the same location in 1836. Pews in the latter building were sold at an auction to churchmembers. The prices ranged from $290 for those near the front of the church to $20 for those in the rear. Some members were extremely disgruntled in the manner the pews had been distributed. One gentleman who vowed never to enter the church again kept his promise. When later a pallbearer, he helped carry the casket only to the church door, where he waited until the service was over and then rejoined the procession as the casket left the church.

[119] Lizzie Worsley (comp.), *Old St. James Episcopal Church, Leesburg, Virginia, 1710-1877* (Leesburg, Va.: n.p., n.d.), pp. 2-5. It is not known if Griffith, the first rector, lived on the glebe or not because the following year after the construction of the glebe house more than £183 was collected from the person or persons who rented the glebe. Prior to the establishment of the glebe, 5,000 pounds of tobacco was added to Rev. Griffith's salary because of the absence of a glebe.

[120] Marcus W. Jernegan, *The American Colonies, 1492-1750* (New York: Frederick Ungar Publishing Co., 1963), pp. 100-101,404-405; Garnett Ryland, *The Baptist of Virginia, 1699-1926* (Richmond, Va.: The Virginia Baptist Board of Missions and Education, 1955), pp. 60-63. Church attendance and support of the Anglican Church was compulsory for all until modified by the acts of 1689 and 1699. Up to that time a marriage was legal only if performed by a clergyman of the established church. But frontier conditions and the lack of American Anglican bishops meant the parishes were not centrally con-

titude of colonial government officials of Virginia and land speculators who were more interested in settling the frontier than in religious conformity;[121] and the settlement of Loudoun, which coincided with a great religious revival that swept America, known as the Great Awakening.[122]

Examples of heterogeneous settlers as a major reason for religious diversity in Loudoun are numerous.[123] Quaker settlers from Pennsylvania during the 1730's and 1840's soon established the Fairfax Meeting (Waterford), Goose Creek Meeting (Lincoln), and Potts' or Gap Meeting (Hillsboro).[124] German settlers established a Lutheran church in the northwestern part of the county near what is currently known as Lovettsville.[125] The zeal of revivalism associated with the Great Awakening was responsible for the establishment and growth of the

---

trolled. Virginia did not have religious freedom after 1699, but it did have a degree of toleration of denominations other than that of the established church. County courts as late as the 1760's sometimes brought charges against what they considered to be vagrant and itinerant persons for illegally assembling themselves on Sunday as Anabaptists. Such lawbreakers were ordered to give bonds and security for future "good behavior" or else go to jail.

[121]Carl Bridenbaugh, *Cities in the Wilderness* (New York: Capricorn Books, 1964), p. 131; Jerenegan, op. cit., p. 406.

[122]Wesley M. Gewehr, *The Great Awakening in Virginia, 1740-1790* (Durham, N.C.: Duke of University Press, 1930), p. 33.

[123]According to Kincaid in her article, "The First Churches in Loudoun," there were a number of "papists," or Catholics, included in the list of tithables in 1749.

[124]Bliss Forbush, *A History of Baltimore Yearly Meeting of Friends* (Sandy Spring, Md.: Baltimore Yearly Meeting of Friends, 1972), p. 33; Hinshaw, "Fairfax Monthly Meeting," *Encyclopedia of American Quaker Genealogy* (1950), VI, 464-65; Asa Moore Janney, "A Short History of the Society of Friends in Loudoun County," *The Bulletin of the Loudoun County Historical Society*, IV (1965), 30-33. A preparative meeting was organized at Waterford in 1735 which became the Fairfax Monthly Meeting in 1744. During the early 1750's a regular meeting was established at Goose Creek. The first Goose Creek Meeting house was a log structure believed to have been built on the site where Hannah Janney, who with her husband, Jacob had emigrated with her from Bucks County, Pennsylvania, held their first devotions. The Potts' or Gap Meeting during the 1760's was weakened by constant bickering between the Potts and Janney families, causing delegations of Friends from other meetings to attempt to mollify disputes. Early Quaker settlers in Loudoun often met in their homes until a meeting house could be erected. These pious and hard-working settlers had not only the most democratic organization of all colonial religions, but they were also the least ostentatious in the architecture of their churches. They intentionally built their meeting houses so externally they looked like private dwelling houses instead of churches.

[125]William E. Eisenberg, *The Lutheran Church in Virginia, 1717-1962* (Roanoke, Va.: The Trustees of the Virginia Synod, Lutheran Church in America, 1967), pp. 54,90,192. The first Lutheran Church in Loudoun was built in 1765 at the above site. Two churches have since been constructed there. The last "New Jerusalem" has a seating capacity of 500. During the nineteenth century, Lutheran churches were organized at Neersville (1835), Tankerville (1866), and Mt. Zion (1895) in Loudoun.

other major religious denominations established in colonial Loudoun: Presbyterian, Methodist, and Baptist. Rev. Amos Thompson's efforts as a missionary in Loudoun during the 1760's were responsible for the establishment of two Presbyterian churches, the Catocton Presbyterian Church near Waterford and a church at Gum Spring (Arcola).[126]

From the 1760's to the 1790's, Methodist and Baptist churches established their primacy as dominant religions to such an extent they have retained this status in the county into the 1970's.[127] The establishment of these two religions in the county was testimonials to one important aspect of the Great Awakening: the appeal to the backwoodsman and small farmer, limited in education and often illiterate, of a fundamentalist faith that stressed emotionalism instead of complex doctrines and rituals as embraced by the aristocracy in the Anglican Church.[128] Nicholas Cresswell, an English visitor who held Loudouners and their culture in disdain, talked about the prevalence of Methodist and Baptist in the county. On December 17, 1775, he recorded in his diary that he "Went to hear Bombast, Noise and Nonsense uttered by a Methodist and an Anabaptist preacher" in Loudoun.[129] Two years later, February 24, 1777, he wrote:

---

[126]James L. Graham, *The Planting of the Presbyterian Church in Northern Virginia* (Winchester, Va.: George F. Norton Publishing Co., 1904), pp. 78,84-90,102-103; Kincaid, "The First Churches in Loudoun," pp. 16-17. Thompson was a graduate of the College of New Jersey (Princeton). On April 7, 1769, John Caven gave one acre of land for the erection of a Presbyterian church. This church remained a place of worship until 1814. It was also the precursor of the current Presbyterian Church in the town of Waterford. The Gum Spring church established by Thompson was apparently not used by the Presbyterians after 1782. In all likelihood the building was used as a free meeting house for different denominations prior to being taken over by the Methodists. A Presbyterian church was not built in Leesburg until 1804 despite references to a Presbyterian Society in that town as early as the American Revolution. Both the establishment of the society and church were due to the work of Rev. Thompson, who died three months after the church was dedicated. He was buried a few feet west of this structure. The plans and dimensions of the Leesburg Presbyterian Church were used in the construction of Presbyterian churches at Bluemont and on Harper's Ferry Road.

[127]Kincaid, "The First Churches in Loudoun," p. 19. For example, there were fifteen Methodist churches in Loudoun in 1851, forty-four in 1906, and nineteen in 1958. The last figure was not due so much to a decline in Methodism as consolidation of churches made possible by the automobile. In 1972 there were fifty-three churches in Loudoun, twenty of which were United Methodist and thirteen were Baptist.

[128]Bernard A. Weisberger, *They Gathered at the River* (Chicago: Quadrangle Books, 1966), p. 53; Louis B. Wright, *The Atlantic Frontier* (Ithaca, N.Y.: Great Seal Books, 1963), p. 330. The Great Awakening also stimulated a missionary movement for Indians and Negroes. Yet, it was also a turbulent era for Congregational and Presbyterian denominations as they bifurcated into liberal and conservative factions.

[129]Cresswell, *The Journal*, pp. 133-34. On December 27, Cresswell wrote of a Methodist meeting in Leesburg which attracted many people who came in sleighs.

> Expected to have a Methodist meeting here to-day. The Company, or congregation of Canting, Whining Hypocrites met, but the Parson disappointed them. I am sorry Captn. Douglas [s] should be such a dupe to these religious quacks. He keeps a good table, is a good-natured man, easily led, and rather unsteady in his religious principles, always glad to see or converse with these Fag-end-of-the-Scripture mongers, and as long as his house is open to them they will haunt him as bad as they tell us the Devil haunts their meetings. They are a set of the noisiest fellows I ever heard. Instead of enforcing their arguments, they only exalt their voices.[130]

Methodist missionaries came to Loudoun during the 1760's, preached in "Free Meeting Houses," and participated in holding revivals.[131] It is believed that one of them was Robert Strawbridge. The spread of Methodism was so infectious that land was purchased in Leesburg in 1766 for the construction of a Methodist meeting house and cemetery. The Old Stone Church constructed on this site has been proved by a Methodist historian to be the first Methodist Church in Virginia, and the deed of May 11, 1766, in which Nicholas Minor sold lot number fifty in the town of Leesburg to Robert Hamilton[132] for £4 "current money of Virginia" for the establishment of the above church, to be the "first Methodist deed in America."[133]

---

[130]Ibid., p. 185. Cresswell was a worldly chap who was not only opinionated but liked to drink. On numerous occasions, while in Loudoun he would write in his diary, he stayed drunk for several days at a time. It is not surprising he held the professed piety of Methodists more than he could stand. For example, Cresswell wrote of meeting a Methodist parson in Leesburg whom he considered as "one of the most affected bigoted little people" he had ever met. Captain William Douglas was a local justice and planter who befriended Cresswell as well as others.

[131]Kincaid, "The First Churches in Loudoun," pp. 17-19; William W. Sweet, *Virginia Methodism: A History* (Richmond, Va.: Whittlet and Shepperson, 1955), pp. 46,48,79. Early Methodist churches still standing in Loudoun are those at Arnold Grove, near Hillsboro; Salem, on the Harper's Ferry Road; Bluemont; and Roszell Chapel. The first organized Methodist Society in America was established in 1763 near Windson, Maryland. Preachers from there came to northern Virginia as missionaries. Later a Methodist Society was formed in Leesburg. It was a common practice for most religious denominations in the county prior to the Revolution to refer to their church buildings as "Meeting Houses." The Quakers are the only sect in the county that currently continues to use this appellation.

[132]Robert Hamilton was a "cordwainer," later called a shoemaker, who acquired considerable property in Leesburg.

[133]Melvin Lee Steadman, Jr., *Leesburg's Old Stone Church* (Manassas, Va.: Virginia-Craft Printing Co., 1964), pp. 2-3,7-9,11-13. The first Leesburg Old Stone Church was completed in 1770 as a temporary structure made of "soft stone." During May 1778, the Sixth Conference of American Methodism was held in this structure. Noted Methodist

Like Methodism, Baptist churches were established throughout the county due to emotional appeal, efforts by evangelists, and settlers converted to the denomination prior to their settlement in the county. By 1840 seven Baptist churches were in Loudoun: Ketoctin, Little River, New Valley (Lucketts), Goose Creek, Leesburg, Ebenezer, and North Fork. Baptist settlers purchased land in 1763 and built their first church in Loudoun, the Ketoctin Baptist Church. The first Baptist Association, formed in 1776, was called the Ketocton Association.[134] From that year on into the nineteenth century this association held yearly conferences of four days duration during August at the various churches that belonged to the association. Thursday and Friday of the yearly meetings consisted of business discussions of matters dealing with the association; Saturday and Sunday were devoted to preaching.[135] The success of the latter was

evangelists, including Francis Asbury, also preached there. In 1785 to 1790 a new structure was built on the same site as the first church. This old stone structure, which was apparently enlarged in 1802, stood until 1901. Its interior was unadorned. The pulpit towered above the plain benches upon which the congregation sat (later pews were purchased). Galleries were built on three sides of the interior to accommodate Negro members of the congregation. Negroes, slave or free, attended early white churches as a common practice. Kincaid writes that all records of denominations in Loudoun prior to 1850 that she has read included Negroes on their rolls (see Kincaid, "The First Churches in Loudoun," p. 16). The Old Stone Church became the subject of two lawsuits. In 1850 a suit was filed, Head v. Hough, that developed out of the formation of the "Methodist Episcopal Church South" when Methodists in the North and South reached an impasse on the issue of slavery. The renamed Methodist church at Leesburg had to prove it had legal title to the land upon which the Old Stone Church was located. This title was proved to the satisfaction of the court and former members of the Old Stone Church, who had after the split erected another church on the site where the current United Methodist Church of Leesburg is located. The second suit, Norwood v. Gaver, involved a dispute in 1900 between white and black members over the possession of the Old Stone Church. The court decreed the church was to be sold. It was sold to Benjamin V. White for $416.65. After the sale the church was soon torn down. The parsonage was sold, and many of the old gravestones were removed to pave the way for a tennis court. Buried in this cemetery are early leaders like Richard Owings, Christopher Frye, and Stephen A. Roszel. Steadman contends Owings, who died in 1786, was the "first born Local Preacher in America." Owings was born in Baltimore County, Maryland, November 13, 1738. Currently the site of the Old Stone Church and cemetery is owned by the Northern Virginia United Methodist Board of Missions.

[134]Kincaid, "The First Churches in Loudoun," p. 15; Garnett Ryland, *The Baptist of Virginia, 1699-1926* (Richmond, Va.: The Virginia Baptist Board of Missions and Education, 1955), p. 17; Robert B. Semple, *A History of the Rise and Progress of the Baptist in Virginia* (Richmond, Va.: By the Author, 1810), pp. 299-300. The Philadelphia Association of Baptists at its meeting in October 1765 agreed that Virginia should form her own association. Four churches met at the Ketoctin Meeting House on August 19, 1766, after which the association was named. The name of the church and association was an Indian word that is spelled in numerous ways: For example, the Association is "Ketocton," the Baptist Church is "Ketoctin," the Presbyterian Church is "Catocton," the Valley is usually "Catoctin." In early records, the creek and mountain are spelled "Kittoctin."

[135]Semple, *A History of the Rise and Progress of the Baptist in Virginia*, pp. 302-03.

determined by the number of persons converted and baptized. On this basis the greatest success was in 1771 at the New Valley Church, where 275 of 912 persons attending that annual meeting were baptized.[116] Despite the comparative rapid establishment of Baptist churches in Loudoun, not all were maintained with ease. In spite of the colonial need for supernatural reassurance of protection from malevolent forces, such as disease and weather detrimental to humans, livestock, and crops, it still took, in order to maintain a steady church attendance, a predicant who knew the scriptures, had a crude eloquence and excitative sermon, and intrepid tenacity to stir up the emotional conscience of the yeoman. Men with such an aptitude were frequently not available. An example was the ministry of John Marks, the second minister of the Ketoctin Baptist

Business transacted during the first two days of the annual meetings of the Ketocton Association occasionally dealt with issues that divided and agitated those in attendance. Three of the most divisive issues involved (1) a Methodist preacher, James Hutchinson, who later became a Baptist preacher, (2) the desirability of requiring each of the members of the Baptist churches to "contribute to the expenses of their church according to their property," and (3) the morality of church members owning slaves. In 1787, the Ketocton Association declared "hereditary slavery was a breach of the divine law" and drew up a plan of gradual emancipation which created "considerable tumult in the churches." During the 1790's the same association ruled it was lawful to exclude anyone from the "privileges of the church" who did not contribute to defraying church expenses in accordance to the church member's wealth. Those churches in the association that tried to enforce this levy met great opposition and were forced to discontinue the practice. James Hutchinson was born in New Jersey and raised in Loudoun County. He later went to Georgia, where he first became a Methodist minister and later a Baptist preacher. In 1791 he came to Loudoun to visit his relatives. While here, he converted and baptized many persons. The Ketocton Association thus became upset because they doubted that the baptisms performed by Hutchinson were valid since he had been previously baptized as a Methodist. The association created "considerable agitation" when it ruled in 1791 that all persons baptized by Hutchinson would have to be rebaptized and the ordinance readministered. The association ruled this procedure was imperative because to make an exception for those baptized by Hutchinson could eventually be applied in other matters and thereby "produce confusion." Prior to 1791 the association had considered the question of those being baptized by someone who had not been originally baptized a Baptist, and in every case it had ruled that being rebaptized was unnecessary or had left it to the conscience of the party involved.

[136]Ibid., pp. 301-02. The number of persons baptized decreased appreciably from the end of the American Revolution in 1783 until 1802. In 1789 the Ketocton Association was divided into two associations, Ketocton and "Chapawanfech," but in 1792 the two associations were reunited. This separation, which reduced in half the number of churches sending members to the yearly meetings, does not completely explain the drastic decline in the number baptized. Even after the reunion of the Chapawanfech district with the Ketocton the number baptized was low while attendance of the yearly meetings was high. For example in 1794 the association met at Little River where 2,017 people attended from thirty-one churches; only thirty-two persons were baptized. After 1800 the number baptized increased to between 153 and 216. Factors influencing the number baptized were the evangelical acumen of those preaching at the yearly meeting plus the emergence of a new unbaptized generation.

Association Meetings that Were Held in Loudoun County Baptist Churches from

	Number Baptized	Number of Total Attendance	Number of Corresponding Churches
	—	—	4
	275	912	10
	270	1,050	17
	38	1,007	21
ek	21	624	14
ek	12	486	10
	32	2,017	31
ek	39	1,898	31
	216	1,901	30
	185	2,004	28
	153	2,036	31

A History of the Rise and Progress of the Baptist in Virginia, p. 302.

cerning Loudoun Baptist Churches from 1766 to 1810.

umber of Original embership	Number of Membership in 1810	By Whom "Planted"	Former Pastors	Pastor in 1810
—	29	J. Garrard	Garrard J. Marks R. Major	W. Gilmore
81	75	D. Thomas	J. Hickerson J. Thomas	
30	30	J. Thomas	W. Thrift	W. Gilmore
37	76	---	---	---
30	57	---	A. Weeks	W. Gilmore
27	40	W. Thrift	Thrift	---
19	49	W. Fristoe	Fristoe	Fristoe

the Rise and Progress of the Baptist in Virginia, p. 398.

Church. Although a man who maintained "a spotless reputation of piety and steadiness," as a preacher he was "sensible, yet cold and phlegmatic." His "dry and cold method," responsible for his lack of success as a preacher, in turn led to small congregations that could pay little and thereby constantly kept him in a state of poverty.[137] It was not an uncommon occurrence for churches in Loudoun to be without a minister for years. The most remarkable example was Goose Creek Baptist Church. During the first thirty-five years of its existence it was without a regular pastor, and yet few churches in the Ketocton Association were more prosperous. This situation was extremely unusual. Most churches without an effective regular ministry struggled to stay in existence. The early history of Leesburg and Ebenezer Baptist churches until 1810 had not been "distinguished by anything remarkable," nor at that time did they have resident pastors.[138] The Little River Church was the most successful of all the early Baptist churches in Loudoun. This church originated from the revival efforts of a Rev. Thomas and the subsequent work of its first pastor, Richard Major. After being in existence for only two years, it had the largest membership, 272 members, of any church in the Ketocton Association.[139]

Although the churches in Loudoun, except the Anglican Church prior to the American Revolution, did not enjoy the privilege of an established church that could use the county government to punish those guilty of improper or immoral behavior, all denominations, nevertheless, attempted to discipline their members both prior to and after the American Revolution. Erring members were called before church of-

---

[137]Ibid., pp. 304-05. Other Baptist churches in the county also struggled to keep from closing. For example in 1793 New Valley had only thirteen members. Few of the early Loudoun ministers had extensive formal education.

[138]Ibid., pp. 305-07.

[139]Ibid., pp. 305-06. Even the membership of this church declined as the result of new churches being formed in communities that formerly supported Little River. Another factor in the decrease in the size of Little River was the death of Major and the inability of the congregation to get a new minister for several years. Finally Robert Latham was hired. The first Little River Church was constructed on one acre of land located at the forks of the road to Williams' Gap and Leesburg. William West sold this tract of land to Benjamin Hutchinson, John Smarr, John Shippy, and William Berkeley, trustees for the public good, for one shilling, to be used for a school and a meeting house. This deed stated that a meeting house had previously been constructed on that site prior to the transfer of the title. There have been four additional Little River churches built on a site a mile or so to the east of the original log structure. The shift in location probably resulted from the Baptist of the area asking Robert Carter for several acres of land upon which to build a church. He apparently readily assented to their wishes on February 25, 1783 (see Louis Morton, *Robert Carter of Nomini Hall*, p. 237). On December 16, 1971, the fourth Little River Baptist Church, the third in that location, was destroyed by fire. Since that time a new structure has been constructed on the same land.

ficers of such denominations as the Presbyterian, Baptist, and the Society of Friends. Usual punishment was denial of participation in church services and suspension of church membership. Moral crimes included everything from poor church attendance, to "foul mouth," and fornication. For example a member of the New Valley Baptist Church had his membership suspended for frequenting a place "where there was mirth and dancing."[140] Likewise the Society of Friends in Loudoun, in addition to devoting time to the normal mechanics of running their meeting, also spent considerable time attempting to right the behavior of straying individuals.[141] If the Friends Meeting heard of wrongdoing, several men were appointed to talk to males indicted by rumor, and a small delegation of women would talk to suspect females. They would then recommend whether the Meeting should draw up a testimony against the accused. Essentially, what was demanded by the Meeting was a confession of wrongdoing and a promise to do better. Members who pleaded they were innocent frequently had their membership suspended until they confessed their sins.[142] Quaker leaders rarely wanted membership permanently denied to any wayward person. For example, Rebecca Gibson lost her membership in the Goose Creek Society of Friends until "she becomes truly sensible of the crime committed and condemns the same to the satisfaction of Friends, which is desired for her."[143] Another illustration was testimony produced against Sarah Newton that was approved and signed and handed to the Women's Meeting of Goose Creek. They ruled Miss Newton should lose her membership due to her:

> . . . inattention to the dictates of *Truth in her own Breast* hath so deviated as to be guilty of fornication, for which reproachful conduct we deny her any longer a right of membership until she be enabled and make suitable satisfaction for her offence, which is our desire for her.[144]

---

[140]Kincaid, "The First Church in Loudoun," p. 16.

[141]All religious denominations in the eighteenth and nineteenth century Loudoun felt that their church alone was the true or correct church of God. Therefore, marrying outside the church was a major source of consternation. For example, when it was reported to the Goose Creek Meeting that a member had married outside the church, a committee was appointed to investigate the situation and to recommend disciplinary action.

[142]Minutes of the Goose Creek Monthly Meeting, February 25, 1819; July 29, 1819. Members of one monthly Meeting who wished to transfer their membership to another had to wait until their old Meeting sent an answer to an inquiry by the new Meeting that it had no objection. Meetings that expelled members rarely blocked attempts by the wayward to join other Meetings.

[143]Ibid., October 30, 1819.

[144]Ibid., January 38, 1819.

Another aspect of eighteenth-century Loudoun life was military service, especially in the local militia. The county supplied a limited number of soldiers and supplies in the French and Indian War and extensive supplies and a number of men in the American Revolution.[145] The legacy of the French and Indian War included not only the eviction of France from North America but impedimental administrative burdens and financial woes for England. These problems were not only salient determinants of British policy from 1763 to 1776, but also the source of growing distrust of the "mother country" by the more recalcitrant colonials who envisaged a British conspiracy that would destroy liberty in British colonial America and the last hope of mankind against abusage and degradation.[146] Apparently a majority of Loudouners were believers in this nascent ideology that evolved into a credo stressing the unique position and mission of the American people. From 1763 to 1776, reaction to British colonial policy in Loudoun was often a microcosm of the revolutionary movement in America. Emotional protest of Loudouners first took the form of a denunciation of Parliament while professing loyalty to the British monarch. Aroused and angered by the British response to the Boston Tea Party that resulted in the enactment of punitive "Intolerable" or "Coercive" Acts, Loudouners met at a public meeting at the county courthouse in Leesburg on June 14, 1774, over which Francis Peyton presided. In addition to condemning the Intolerable Acts, this meeting also denounced the Tea Act and the Admiralty Courts. The resolutions formed at this meeting referred to the British Parliament as "utterly repugnant to fundamental laws of justice" and its recent behavior as "a despotic exertion of unconstitutional power designedly calculated to enslave a free and loyal people." The Loudouners at this meeting also resolved to "have no commercial inter-

---

[145]William Fletcher Boogher (ed.), *Gleanings of Virginia History* (Baltimore: Genealogical Publishing Co., 1965), pp. 111, 216-22; Head, *History of Loudoun County*, pp. 123-24. The French and Indian War (1754-1763) started four years prior to the formation of Loudoun as a county, but a few Loudouners no doubt fought in this war and provided supplies. In 1757 Thomas Gore and James Clemons were each paid "four pounds, ten shilling for a rifle gun impressed," thirteen shillings were paid to Stephen Emorie "for dressing guns for militia"; in 1763 Captain Moss was paid six shillings a day for sixty days' service and Lieutenant Gore three shillings, six pence a day for sixty days' service. In 1764, the colonial legislature of Virginia offered a bounty of forty shillings for every person who voluntarily served in the militia. If enough men did not volunteer then the number needed could be drafted (Hening, *Statutes*, IIX, 11-12). Every tithable person in Virginia was taxed forty-six pounds of tobacco to help defray the expense of Virginia in fighting the French and Indian War (Hening, *Statutes*, IIX, 38-41).

[146]Bernard Bailyn, "A Fear of Conspiracy Against Liberty," *The America Revolution: The Critical Issues*, ed. Robert F. Berkhofer, Jr. (Boston: Little, Brown, and Co., 1971), pp. 78, 101-104; *The Blue Ridge Herald*, September 22, 1955.

course with Great Britain" until the above grievances were resolved.[147] Following the suggestion of the First Continental Congress, Loudoun formed and maintained a committee of Safety from 1774 to 1776. This committee of fifteen Loudouners served as a local extension of the Continental Association to make sure county residents neither purchased nor sold items to England.[148] At the meeting in Loudoun in 1774, residents expressed their allegiance to the King. But in a series of resolutions that emanated from a meeting of the committee of Safety of Loudoun County on Friday, May 26, 1775, after the battles of Lexington and Concord, statements were made not only that George III had "forfeited the confidence of the good people of this Colony, but that he may be justly esteemed an enemy to America."[149] At that time, Loudouners considered themselves in a state of war with England. Troops from the county marched as far as Fredericksburg, Virginia, during the spring of 1775 on their way to Williamsburg for the purpose of assisting other Virginians into taking reprisals against the crown for an order that had led to the confiscation of powder from a magazine belonging to Virginia. The Loudoun militia returned to the county upon the request of Peyton Randolph, who pointed out that the people of Williamsburg were under "no apprehensions of danger."[150] Loudouners were intolerant to the expression of any Tory views even months prior to the Declaration of Independence. The revolutionary Committee for Loudoun's Public Safety demanded absolute conformity and support of the "patriot's cause." Anyone who dared to criticize this movement had to answer to the Loudoun Committee for Public Safety:

> *Richard Morlan being summoned to appear before this Committee, for speaking words inimical to the liberties of America, and tending to discourage, a Minute-man from returning to his duty; and also publickly [sic] declaring he would not muster, and if fined would oppose the collection of the fine with his gun: The charge being proved against him, and he heard in his defense, the Committee think*

---

[147]Head, *History of Loudoun County*, pp. 128-29. Loudoun's protest committees were active in seeing the county was represented in Virginia's meetings. For example, there were Loudoun delegates to the Virginia convention of 1774 (August 1-6, 1774). In the series of Virginia conventions held during March 1775, July 1775, December 1775, and May 1776, Loudoun was represented by Francis Peyton and Josias Clapham.

[148]Charles W. Coleman, "The County Committees of 1774'75 in Virginia," *William and Mary Quarterly*, 1st ser., V (October, 1896), 94-106. This committee consisted of Francis Peyton, Josias Clapham, Thomas Lewis, Anthony Russell, John Thomas, George Johnston, Thomas Shore, Jacob Reed, Leven Powell, William Smith, Robert Jamison, Hardage Lane, John Lewis, and James Lane.

[149]Head, *History of Loudoun County*, p. 130. Officials of the county court on August 12, 1776, issued instructions for the Declaration of Independence to be read aloud in front of the courthouse.

[150]Ibid.

proper to hold the said Morlan up to the publick [sic] as an enemy to their rights and liberties; and have ordered that this resolution be published in the Virginia Gazette.[151]

The dissatisfaction in Loudoun with British colonial administration was amply testified to by Nicholas Cresswell, who traveled extensively in Loudoun and the rest of the colonies from 1774 to 1777. Prior to 1776 he wrote in his diary that the people of Loudoun were revolutionaries and that he was "very uneasy, Dam the rascals."[152] On January 16, 1776, Cresswell recorded that he left Leesburg to go to Alexandria to obtain passage home to England and that he planned to keep his "intentions of going home a secret or I am certain to be imprisoned. D--m the Rascals." Unable to leave America, he returned to Leesburg and found "nothing but Independence will go down. The Devil is in the people."[153] On May 24, 1776, he recorded "A great riot in Town [Leesburg] about Torys. Mr. Cavan obliged to hide himself."[154]

Intolerance to Tories and unabashed support of the Whig or the Patriot cause continued in Loudoun during the American Revolution. The most severely hit were the Quakers in the county whose religion prohibited them from performing any military service. As attempts to compel them to bear arms in the militia were unavailing, a law was enacted that levied a tax upon their property. This legislation being unacceptable to them, they refused to pay all taxes for several years during and after the war on the grounds that the money either supported the war effort or went toward discharging the war debt. Consequently, some of the properties of Loudoun Quakers were confiscated and sold.[155]

The war had a profound impact upon most people within the county. Every freeman that was able-bodied and between the ages of sixteen

---

[151]Ibid., p. 131. Another outspoken loyalist was John Osburn, who lived near Hillsboro. He desired to debate with a local preacher the subject of the American Revolution, but the debate was said to have been cancelled due to "heated tempers." Osburn had two sons. The father made up for the younger son's being born on July 4 by naming him Tarleton in honor of the British General. (See *The Loudoun Times-Mirror*, November 2, 1972.

[152]Cresswell, *The Journal*, 1. 132.

[153]Ibid., p. 136.

[154]Ibid., p. 144. While in Loudoun, Cresswell was sick during most of March 1776. March 3, he wrote, "Violent pains all over my body. Some symptoms of a nervous fever." The next day he "applied for the Doctor, who assures me it is a complication of the Nervous Fever and Rheumatism. Gave me a physic." He went outside on March 22, the first time since March 3, and became sick again for five days. His impatience made Cresswell call the doctor a "Blockhead." Cresswell had another relapse on April 3, 1776.

[155]Head, *History of Loudoun County*, pp. 132-33; Hening, *Statutes*, IIX, 242-44. In 1776, the General Assembly legislated that all Quakers between the ages of eighteen and sixty were to be included on the militia rolls, but they could furnish a substitute if the militia had to fight. Any Quaker refusing to fight or hire a substitute was to be fined "ten pounds . . . to be levied by distress and sale of the estate of the Quaker so refusing . . ."

and fifty was enrolled in the county militia. In 1780 and 1781 Loudoun had the largest militia of any county in the state, with 1,746 men.[156] Many Loudouners who served in the war left families that could not support themselves in the absence of the head of the household. For these dozens of needy families, the county court appointed men of some means to supply the needy with the "necessaries of life":

> *1788, November 9th: John Alexander to furnish Elizabeth Welch, her husband being in the army. 1778, Nov. 15th: George Embrey to furnish the child of Jacob Rhodes, said Jacob being in the Continental army. William Douglas to furnish Mary Rhodes, her husband being in the army. George Summers to furnish William Gilmore, his son being in the army.*
>
> . . . .
>
> *1779, April:. . . Josias Clapham appointed to apply to the Treasurer for 500 pounds to be placed in the hands of John Lewis, Gent, to supply the necessaries of life for those who have husbands or children in the Continental army.*
>
> . . . .
>
> *1780, July: Simon Triplett to furnish Jermima Coleman, wife of Joel, not exceeding two barrels of flour and 200 pounds of Pork.*
>
> . . . .
>
> *1781, April: William Owsley to supply Hannah Rice & two children, the family of James Rice, who died in the Continental army.*
>
> . . . .
>
> *1782, March: William Douglas to furnish Eleanor Wilcox, agreeable, to an order of the last court directed to John Lewis, Gent, the said Lewis declining.*[157]

The county treasurer usually reimbursed men like Jacob Tracey, who provided for the needy families of soldiers. Tracey received twenty pounds "for nursing and burying Sophia Harris, the wife of a continental

---

[156]Thomas Jefferson, *Notes on the State of Virginia*, ed. William Peden (Chapel Hill: University of North Carolina Press, 1955), pp. 88-95, 118; "The Number of Men of Military Age in Virginia in 1776," *Virginia Magazine of History and Biography*, XVIII (December, 1910), 34-35. In 1776 Loudoun's militiamen numbered 1,600. The militia of the counties of Virginia were formed into companies and the companies into one or more battalions according to the number in the county militia. In every county the county lieutenant was the head commander of the whole militia. From March 1778 to December 1782 the court of Loudoun recommended to the governor of the state over 100 Loudoun men as officers in the Continental army (see the Loudoun County Court Order Book G, pp. 517-22).

[157]Loudoun Court Order Book G, Part II, pp. 519-22.

soldier." Those who furnished supplies were also compensated.[158] The state government made specific demands upon the counties of Virginia for supplies for the army, such as clothing, food, and wagons. On October 5, 1780, the Virginia General Assembly enacted legislation that required Loudoun to furnish fifty-three suits, each suit to consist of two "shirts of linen or cotton, one pair of overalls, two pairs of stockings, one pair of shoes, one wool, furr or felt hat, or leather cap." The county was divided into districts by the county court and the commander of the county militia. Select people within each district contacted other citizens with the intent that their quota would be furnished within fifty days. Each of these districts was also required to furnish "one good beef, weighing at least three hundred nett." For six months from the time the act was passed, Loudoun like other Virginia counties had to "furnish . . . one good and serviceable wagon with a good cover and a team of four horses and complete harness with a driver, who shall serve as a driver" for one month at the expense of Loudoun. The county court was to enact a levy on the tithable persons for the sum necessary to supply the above wagon, team, and driver.[159]

If persons within a district or the district failed to provide their quota of the clothing or beef, they were subject to additional taxes to make up the difference. All of the above was to be set in motion by the governor's asking the "eldest acting justice in the county" to call the other justices of the court together to make the necessary arrangements for supplying the clothes, beef, and wagon. If the justice or "field officer" failed to comply, he was to be fined 5,000 pounds of tobacco.[160] Also in 1780 the state drew upon Loudoun's human resources in asking a quota of 117 men to serve in the Continental army.[161]

Cresswell gave a fascinating glimpse into a few aspects of Loudoun life and how it was affected by the war:

> *October 10, 1776 — The 6th Regt. of Virginians are camped in Leesburg on their way to the northward. A set*

---

[158]Ibid., p. 137. "Virginia State Troops in the Revolution," *Virginia Magazine of History and Biography*, XXX (December, 1922), 56-59. Harrison Williams, *Legends of Loudoun* (Richmond, Va.: Garrett and Massie, 1938), p. 140. Apparently by 1781 as the fighting of the war neared an end, Loudoun had a fair accumulation of the accoutrements of war. Lafayette wrote Washington on July 1 of that year that "100 Saddles, 100 Swords, 100 pairs of pistols may be soon expected at Leesburg. . . ." On the 26th of the same month William Davis, a colonel, wrote there "are 920 muskets and 486 bayonets" at "Noland's." The transporting of these supplies from Noland's Ferry presented a difficult task for Captain A. Bohannan. There were few wagons in the area of Leesburg that could be impressed because most needed repairing. To get transportation, Bohannan had to pay Loudouners for the use of their wagons.

[159]Hening, *Statutes*, X, 348-41. A sheriff, receiver, or constable failing to carry out his duty in the above were to be fined 10,000 pounds of tobacco.

[160]Ibid., pp. 326-27.

[161]Cresswell, *The Journal*, p. 163.

of dirty ragged people badly clothed, badly disciplined and badly armed.

Oct. 11, 1776 — Salt sells here at 40 shillings, Currency, per bushel. This article is usually sold for four. If no salt comes in, there will be an insurrection in the Colony.

. . . .

December 4, 1776 — A Ducth mob [Loudouners] of about 40 horsemen went through the town to-day on their way to Alexandria to search for Salt. If they find any they will take it by force. All of them armed with swords or large clubs. This article is exceedingly scarce, if none comes in the people will revolt.[162]

. . . .

Jan. 7, 1777 — News of Washington taking 760 Hessian prisoners at Trenton confirmed causing the people of Loudoun to change their mind of the war a few days ago being a lost cause. Their recruiting parties could not get a man (except he bought him from his master) no longer since then last week, and now the men are coming in by companies. D—them all.[163]

. . . .

Jan. 17, 1777—. . . Washington's name is extolled to the clouds. Alexander, Pompey, and Hannibal were but pigmy Generals, in compairson with the magnanimous Washington.[164]

. . . .

Jan. 26, 1777 — Eleven English prisoners arrived and are to be stationed here, all of them soldiers. Have been summoned to mount guard over them but absolutely refused . . . determined to go to jail myself rather than guard an English prisoner.[165]

---

[162] Ibid., p. 173.

[163] Ibid., p. 179. By March of the same year the glamor had worn off and Cresswell wrote, "Great tumults and mumuring among the people caused by pressing the young men into the Army."

[164] Ibid., p. 181.

[165] Ibid., Other aspects of Loudoun life during the Revolution are also revealed in Cresswell's diary. On March 25, 1777, he recorded he "Dined at Mr. Elyey's. The Miss Elyeys very sensible but not killing beauties." The next day at Leesburg, Cresswell "Got into a terrible fray. Six waggoners attacked Mr. Dean in his store, all of them armed with whips. He called to me for assistance. I got a good stick and knocked 2 of them down when Mr. Cavan came to our assistance. Cavan broke one man's arm, I bared another's scull for about 6" long and hurt anothervery much. Mr.Dean fainted several times with loss of blood. [Two] men gave security for future good behavior and paid doctor." Three days later while still at Leesburg Cresswell was "Employed in directing workmen about the pump, find them to be profoundly ignorant. (Mem. never to employ a negro if white man is to be got.) The people here are much bigoted by their own ways" (see pp. 190-91 of Cresswell's *Journal*).

Unlike the Tory views of Cresswell and a few Loudouners, and the neutral posture the Quakers had hoped to take, the rest of the county's population was for the most part composed of vociferous supporters of the Revolution. Representative of the broad base support in Loudoun for the Revolution were the lives of John Champe, a yeoman; Rev. David Griffith, M.D., minister of the established church for the Shelburne parish in Loudoun; and Leven Powell, Loudoun planter and member of the Virginia aristocracy. Their lives are indicative of those of pro-revolutionary supporters, whose traditional lifestyles were interrupted by their military service.

John Champe has been traditionally embraced as the Revolutionary War hero from Loudoun.[166] The saga of Champe's military career has all the needed components for adulation. A large muscular youth of humble origin, he distinguished himself in military service and was subsequently recommended by his commanding officer, Light Horse Harry Lee, to carry out a plan Washington had contrived to capture Benedict Arnold (who had deserted the American army and joined the British).[167] According to the plan, Champe was to feign desertion from the American forces and enlist in Arnold's command. At the first opportunity, Champe was to capture Arnold and bring him to Washington.[168] The plan failed because shortly prior to the night Champe was to abduct Arnold and deliver him to Lee at Hoboken, New Jersey, Arnold and his force were sent by ship to Virginia. Champe accompanied the British to Virginia and North Carolina, where he rejoined the American forces under General Greene.[169]

---

[166] Head, *History of Loudoun County*, pp. 133-34; Williams, *Legends of Loudoun*, p. 142.

[167] Briscoe Goodhart, who authored an article found in newspaper clippings collected in scrapbook ("Loudoun County," III, 10-33, Thomas Balch Library, Leesburg, Virginia), stated nothing is known of Champe's boyhood, which was probably lived near Waterford. Goodhart states that the old War Department records reveal that John Champe enlisted in 1776 at the age of nineteen as a private in Captain Harry (Light Horse Harry) Lee's Company of 1st Light Dragoons of the Continental army. He was first "mustered for pay" on November 1777 and transferred to Lee's Legions. On April 7; 1778, he was given the rank of corporal and on January 1, 1779, promoted to Sergeant-Major. The records also reveal at the end of the war Champe was appointed to the position of doorkeeper or sergeant-at-arms of the Continental Congress at Philadelphia. Soon afterwards Champe returned to Loudoun, married and lived on a small farm at Dover. He later moved to Kentucky, where he is believed to have died around the year 1797. Briscoe Goodhart contends that the report that Champe went to what is now West Virginia and died there in 1808 is false.

[168] L. Carroll Judson, *The Sages and Heroes of the American Revolution* (Philadelphia: By the Author, 1852), pp. 423-24. Washington had originally hoped that Champe could determine if any other American generals were being disloyal.

[169] Williams, *Legends of Loudoun*, pp. 143-55. The details of Champe's mission are described in Light Horse Harry Lee's *Memoirs of the War in the Southern Department of the United States*. Williams quotes extensively the material relating to Champe. For the details

David Griffith's role in the war was not as dramatic but perhaps more significant than that of Champe's. Unlike the meagerly educated youth of nineteen seeking adventure, Griffith was an extremely erudite man. Born in New York City, he was later granted the degree of M.D. in London in approximately 1762. In 1763, he commenced practicing medicine in New York but later decided to enter the ministry. So he went back to London in 1770 and was ordained as an Anglican minister. Soon thereafter he went to New Jersey as a missionary, after which he came to serve Shelburne parish in Loudoun. In 1776, he left his position in Loudoun and became a chaplain of the Third Virginia Regiment. The army, however, soon used his medical skills, and by December 1776, he was serving in the capacity of a surgeon in the Continental army in Philadelphia. From 1780 until his death in 1789, he served as the rector of Christ Church in Alexandria, Virginia.[170]

Griffith was a close friend of Leven Powell and communicated extensively with him during the war; both were staunch supporters of the American cause. Powell was born in Prince William County, Virginia, in 1737.[171] During the 1760's he moved to Loudoun, where he purchased five hundred acres of land upon a portion of which he later established the town of Middleburg. During the 1770's he became actively "engaged in stirring up his fellow citizens to protest against British policy." In 1775 he was made a major of a battalion of Loudoun minutemen that was "employed in harrassing Lord Dunmore's troops" in the vicinity of Norfolk, Portsmouth, and Hampton, Virginia. During January 1777, General Washington appointed Powell a lieutenant-colonel of the Six-

---

of Champe's adventures see pp. 142-58 of Harrison's *Legends of Loudoun*. Champe may not have officially joined the British army, but he apparently served in a company commanded by a Captain Cameron, who after the war recorded in a diary that while caught in a violent thunderstorm one evening in northern Virginia, he went to the nearest house for shelter and much to his surprise it was the home of Champe. According to Cameron, both men greeted each other like long lost friends. Briscoe Goodhart in "The Story of John Champe" maintained that during the Undeclared Naval War with France, Washington wrote Lee to have Sergeant Champe called into service and "placed at the head of a cavalry command." Lee allegedly sent a courier to Loudoun in search of Champe, who had moved to Kentucky and died. However, Ida M. Judy in a romantic biography of Champe, *John Champe: The Soldier and the Man*, states that county court records reveal that Champe moved three times after the Revolution: from Loudoun to West Virginia, back to Loudoun (to Dover), and finally to Botetout County, Virginia, (not Kentucky), where Champe died (after 1807).

[170]"Letters of Rev. David Griffith, To Leven Powell, 1776-1778," *The John P. Branch Historical Papers of Randolph Macon College*, I (June, 1901), 39-53. At the second annual convention of the Diocese of Virginia, May 1786, Dr. Griffith was selected as the bishop of that religious jurisdiction. Unfortunately the financial condition of the Episcopal Church in Virginia was such the money could not be raised to send Griffith to England for the consecration ceremony.

[171]In 1763, he married Sally Harrison, a daughter of Burr Harrison of Chapawamsic.

teenth Regiment of the Virginia Continentals. He joined the American forces at White Marsh Plains near Philadelphia and spent the winter of 1777-1778 at Valley Forge, where illness impeded his military function.[172] Powell, on January 21, 1778, wrote his wife from Valley Forge of his condition:

> My dear,—Since I wrote you by Capt. Grant I have had the misfortune to have a severe spell of sickness, the effects of which I have not got quite clear of. A few days after he left I was taken with a flux, which, however, left me in 8 or 9 days, and in its place came on the Yellow Jaundice. This was more lasting, but at length got the better of. During the time of the Jaundice I was seized with a small pain in the upper part of the forehead, just over my left eye. This after several days became very troublesome, and at length began to swell, particularly about the eye, and to break out in little sores. The swelling increased until I lost the sight of that eye, and which was very near being the case with the other. Dr. Griffith, who was at the same house with me, prepared an ointment, which was applied to the place as a plaster; this with two blisters which I have had drawn and the blessing of God, has so far restored me as to see pretty well again out of that eye; the other is perfectly well. The breaking out in my head and forehead seems now to be my only complaint, except the redness and weakness in my eye; these seem to be healing, and I trust will be nearly cured in 8 or 10 days. The Doctor calls it St. Anthony's fire; be it what it will, it has given me great pain and confined me a great while to my room. I walked out to-day for the first time for these many days past. I have as comfortable quarters as any one could wish at the house of John Rowlands, who is an able farmer, and the people are remarkably kind and cleanly.[173]

This illness compelled Powell to return to Virginia and later resign his position in the army in 1778. After the war he took an active part in politics and was the county's most significant political figure from the 1780's to the early 1800's, when his Federalist mantle was passed on to Charles F. Mercer.[174]

[172]"Leven Powell," *The John P. Branch Historical Papers of Randolph-Macon College,* I (June, 1901), 22-24.

[173]Ibid., pp. 36-37.

[174]Ibid., pp. 22. After Powell returned to Virginia from Valley Forge, Washington sent Powell a furlough with the request to use it as long as necessary, and not to resign his commission unless his health made it impossible for him to again serve in the war. The Virginia Assembly later voted Powell a full share of public land as if he had served throughout the war.

The American Revolution was undeniably a monumental and pivotal episode in America's history, especially her political life. Yet for a small locality like Loudoun County the consequences can be overstated. To be sure, the immediate impact was an intensified Whig intolerance to Tory views and Quaker pacifism. Family life was disrupted by Loudouners going to war where some of the latter were killed or their health impaired while families of the less affluent became indigent and dependent upon relief provided by those assigned by the county court. Neither did Loudouners like sending their sons off to war after the first few years of belligerency had paled the romanticism associated with the early stages of the revolutionary movement. Loudouners were also less than willing to suffer in silence the scarcity of salt, so indispensable at that time as a preservative and condiment, or to charitably provide supplies and wagons for the American cause. Economic sanctions the colonials applied against England in retaliation for the Intolerable Acts and the impact of the war upon Loudoun's export of flour were certainly disruptive of Loudoun's economy.[175] Loudoun was also spared the devastation of enemy invasion as the area remained free of military fighting. Regardless of the immediate impact of the war and its immediate aftermath, the long-term effect of the war and independence had a negligible long-range impact upon the county's economy, social structure, and political institutions.[176] The major alteration in institutions within the county was that of the Anglican Church, defrocked of its established status by revolutionary liberalism.[177] The Anglican Church lost the revenue from parish levies, glebe lands, and residences, as properties of the former established church were seized by the state of Virginia and

---

[175]Gray, *History of Agriculture in the Southern United States to 1860*, II, 572-81. Although specific evidence concerning Loudoun's economy during this period is unavailable, the revolutionary movement prior to the Declaration of Independence, according to Gray, had not notably impaired the agricultural prosperity of the Southern colonies. While the British maintained a blockade during the war against the colonies, she was unable to stop all trade involving the Southern colonies. It was not until 1782 that most trade was severely hampered. Another fact that meant the war was of limited impact upon Loudoun's economy was the numerous small and subsistent farmers who had a meager quantity of agricultural produce to sell. During the war some of Loudoun's agricultural produce was used to support the American cause and thus less was left to export. Yet exportation was not determined solely by the war need and the British blockade. In 1778-79 there existed a shortage in the supply of commercial grain, due to the wheat crops of Maryland, Virginia, and North Carolina being seriously damaged by the Hessian fly.

[176]Porter, *County Government in Virginia*, p. 100.

[177]Ibid., pp. 128-31; Hamilton J. Eckenrode, *The Revolution in Virginia* (Hamden, Conn.: Archer Books, 1964), pp. 295-96. In 1777, commissioners of taxes were established as a part of the county government of Virginia to collect taxes. During the 1780's those positions were replaced by the commissioner of revenue which still exists.

sold.[178] In accordance with state law, the care of the poor in the parish after the Revolution was no longer the responsibility of the vestry but that of a new county official known as the overseer of the poor. The law also required that glebes be sold and the money given to the overseers of the poor to be used in the care of the indigent.[179] Unlike most vestries which complied with the law, the vestrymen of Shelburne parish refused to sell the glebe, whereupon the overseer of the poor took the case to court to force compliance with the law. Litigation continued until the Superior Court of Virginia in Seldon v. the Overseers of Loudoun (1827) ordered the glebe to be sold.[180]

[178]Worsley (comp.), *Old St. James Episcopal Church, Leesburg, Virginia, 1710-1877*, p. 5. Apparently the vestry in Shelburne parish did not meet between May 22, 1776, and April 27, 1779. The condition of the Anglican Church in Shelburne was critical; no levy had been collected since prior to 1775. The parish was without a minister from May 1776, when Griffith joined the army, until 1794. At that time Rev. Alexander Jones served Shelburne parish for one year for the modest sum of fifty pounds of tobacco. From 1796 to 1810 Alexander McFarlan was the Episcopal minister of the parish. He preached two Sundays a month at Leesburg, one at the Pot House, and one at Middleburg. Upon McFarlan's recommendation when he resigned, John Dunn was chosen as his successor. Dunn served in that capacity from 1801 until his death in 1827. He was buried under the floor of Old St. James Church in Leesburg and a monument erected "over the spot" by his congregation.

The Anglican Church was disestablished in 1784, and Thomas Jefferson's religious freedom legislation was enacted by Virginia in 1786, thus officially establishing the separation of church and state in the Old Dominion. Dissenting churches felt a sense of gratitude to the sage of Monticello for the statute of religious freedom. The Ketocton Baptist Association, which was formed in Loudoun, later wrote to President Thomas Jefferson in 1808, thanking him for their "deliverance from the galing chains of ecclesiastical Establishment." This letter, plus Jefferson's response, can be found in the Jefferson Papers in the Manuscript Division of the Library of Congress. They are also reproduced in "Jefferson and the Ketocton Baptist Association," *The Bulletin of the Loudoun County Historical Society*, I (1958), 57-60. Charles F. James in his *Documentary History of the Struggle for Religious Liberty in Virginia* (Lynchburg, Va.: J. P. Bell Co., 1900) on p. 197 asserts that the "Baptist were the only denomination that maintained a consistent record" in working for the end of the established church in Virginia.

[179]By the first decade of the nineteenth century a poorhouse was established in a square-shaped stone building in Leesburg (*The Loudoun Times-Mirror*, May 22, 1962).

[180]*The Loudoun Times-Mirror*, January 17, 1960. During the litigation several members of the vestry either died or retired, but Dr. Wilson Cary Seldon continued his fight until 1827. The property was purchased by John Aldridge and remained in his family for several generations. For the opinion of Chancellor Henry St. George Tucker in Seldon v. the Overseer of the Poor of Loudoun, consult pages 1-16 in the Appendix of volume two of his book, *Commentaries of the Laws of Virginia* (Winchester, Va.: By the Author, 1837). Tucker maintained the crux of the case was the constitutionality of the laws authorizing the sale of glebe lands in Virginia. In his opinion the Virginia acts of 1798 and 1802 that sanctioned the sale of glebe lands were constitutional (p. 15). Seldon v. the Overseers of the Poor caused much discussion in Loudoun, although most of the citizens appeared to have favored the sale of the glebe. The court's decision in 1827 even became an issue in the elec-

The basic social structure of Loudoun after the Revolution remained essentially the same. There had been few Tories within the county, and the perseverance of the Quakers enabled most of the Friends to weather the storm. Neither had the Revolution significantly changed the political base in Loudoun. Men like Leven Powell remained influential in the county because their service and support of the Revolution increased their popularity and consequently their political influence. For example, Powell was elected to the Virginia convention of 1788 that ratified the Constitution of the United States.[181] A man of strong convictions, he is credited with being the founder of the Federalist party in Loudoun. In 1798 and 1800 he was elected to Congress, where he participated in the struggle for political supremacy between America's nascent two political parties.[182]

---

tion of 1832 for the House of Delegates, when it was rumored falsely by an opponent of candidate C. Douglas that he was against the sale of the Loudoun glebe. Despite the publication of a disclaimer in the April 14, 1832, issue of the *Genius of Liberty*, Douglas lost the election.

[181]"Leven Powell," *The John P. Branch Historical Papers of Randolph-Macon College*, I (June, 1901), 22-23. Four candidates ran to represent Loudoun in the Virginia ratification convention: Powell, Colonel Clapham, who favored the Constitution, and General Stephen Thomas Mason and William Ellzey, who were opposed to ratification. In a bitter campaign Powell and Mason were elected and represented the county. Stephen Mason, like his uncle George Mason, was opposed to ratification because of the absence of a Bill of Rights.

[182]Ibid., pp. 22-23. In 1796, Powell was the only Presidential elector in Virginia who voted for John Adams in opposition to Thomas Jefferson. Prior to the Twelfth Amendment to the Constitution that went in effect in 1804, separate balloting for the President and Vice-President did not exist. Each elector could vote for two candidates for the Presidency. This led Burr, the Republican Vice-Presidential candidate, to receive the same number of electoral votes as the Republican Presidential candidate, Jefferson. The Federalist-dominated House of Representatives, of which Powell was a member, had to decide which of the Republican candidates would ascend to the Presidency. Powell considered both Jefferson and Burr "far short of what they ought to be for that important office." Powell considered abstaining from voting, but wrote his friends to "be governed by their opinions." Some favored Burr, like Thomas Sims of Leesburg.

Chapter 2

DEMOGRAPHIC STABILITY AND AGRICULTURAL REFORM: 1790 TO 1828

The three-quarters of a century prior to 1790 witnessed the first significant ecological change induced by man within the political frontiers of Loudoun. The advent of white settlers in this region led to the displacement of the aborigines, bison, and wolves; the clearing of thousands of acres of forests; and the establishment of basic demographic and economic patterns and social and political institutions that were later moderately modified, but nevertheless remained the nucleus of an agrarian lifestyle throughout the nineteenth century into the twentieth century.[1] Although the years from 1790 to 1917 represent the golden age of an agrarian lifestyle for Loundouners, it was far from being a halcyon era. Politically, the second and third quarters of the nineteenth century were dominated by the tenebrous clouds of sectionalism that broke into

---

[1] For example, many of the old colonial county offices like those of sheriff, clerk of court, and coroner still remain. Most of these are now elected instead of appointed positions. The county commissioner of revenue and the attorney for the commonwealth emerged during or at the end of the Revolutionary period and are still salient positions in Loudoun's government. Extensive changes in county government did take place as the result of the Virginia Constitution of 1867, which created townships in each county. Each township elected a representative to the Board of Supervisors which replaced the county justice forming the traditional county court which had served as the key administrative agency in Loudoun. The township was abolished and replaced by districts by constitutional amendent in 1874, but the elected Board of Supervisors still remains as the key governing body of Loudoun's county government (consult Porter, *County Government in Virginia*, pp. 243-45, 270, 348).

the destructive storm of 1861 to 1865, disrupting economic prosperity and civil government, and left psychological scars lingering into the twentieth-century.[2] Besides these developments the dominant characteristics of the lifestyle in Loudoun County from the Revolutionary period to the First World War were (1) the relative numerical stability of the county's population, (2) the prevalence of agrarian community life consisting of farms and a nearby hamlet, and (3) agricultural reform and specialization.

DEMOGRAPHIC STABILITY

The demography of Loudoun appeared to have been amazingly constant when the statistics of 20,523 people in 1800 are compared to the 20,577 residents in the county in 1920. This situation is true especially when it is realized that only fifty-four more people lived in Loudoun in 1920 than in 1800. Despite the relative stability of Loudoun's population, it would be incorrect to conclude that significant fluctuations within the period from 1790 to 1920 did not occur. For example, during this span of years the highest number of people recorded by the federal census as residing in the county was 23,634 in 1880. The lowest was 18,962 in 1890, a difference of 4,672.[3] Two major trends also occurred during this period. Loudoun's population increased from 1790 to 1820 and then decreased from 1830 until 1920, except for increases during the decades from 1840 to 1850 and 1870 to 1880.[4] A great deal of the decrease in Loudoun's population was due to blacks leaving the county, especially from 1880 to 1920, during which time the county's Negro population decreased 2,433 or 33 percent.[5] Whites in Loudoun decreased only 624 or 3.8 percent during the same period. Yet a greater percentage of whites probably left the county in the early 1900's than the above figure would indicate because the average death rate from 1913 to 1924 for whites in Loudoun was 12.1

---

[2]These developments will be discussed in later chapters.

[3]Deck and Heaton, *An Economic and Social Survey of Loudoun*, p. 62.

[4]Ibid.; H. R. Sanders, Eliza D. Lunceford, and Virginia Fenton, *Loudoun County Geography Supplement* (Charlottesville, Va.: Loudoun County School Board, 1925), p. 26. The increase from 18,962 in Loudoun in 1790 to 20,523 in 1800 was greater than the statistics indicate because counted in the 1790 census were residents between Difficult Run and Sugarland Run. By 1800 they were residents of Fairfax County as the result of the boundary realignment between Fairfax and Loudoun in 1798.

[5]Prior to the Civil War, free blacks and slaves fled to Pennsylvania. Slaves were also sold to the deep South. The decrease in Loudoun's Negro population after 1880 into the early twentieth-century coincided with a mass exodus of blacks from the south to the west and especially to industrial centers of the North. See pp. 298-99 of *From Slavery to Freedom* (3rd ed.; New York: Alfred A. Knopf, 1967) by John H. Franklin.

per 1,000 as compared to the average birth rate for the same period, which was 22.8 per 1,000.[6] The same point can also be made for Loudoun's black population. From 1913 to 1924 the death rate of the county's black residents was 16.4 per 1,000 and their birth rate 27.9 per 1,000.[7]

Table 3. Population of Loudoun County by Decades from 1790 to 1920.

Year	White	Negro	Total Population	Percentage Increase	Percentage Decrease
1790	14,749	4,213	18,962	—	—
1800	15,200	5,323	20,523	8.2	—
1810	15,577	5,761	21,338	3.9	—
1820	16,144	6,558	22,702	6.3	—
1830	15,497	5,442	21,939	—	3.4
1840	13,840	6,591	20,431	—	6.9
1850	15,081	6,998	22,079	8.0	—
1860	15,021	6,753	21,774	—	1.4
1870	15,238	5,691	20,929	—	4.0
1880	16,391	7,243	23,634	12.9	—
1890	16,696	6,578	23,274	—	1.5
1900	16,080	5,868	21,948	—	6.0
1910	15,946	5,221	21,167	—	3.6
1920	15,767	4,810	20,577	—	2.8

Source: United States Census Statistics printed in *An Economic and Social Survey of Loudoun* by Deck and Heaton, pp. 62-64.

By 1920, 3,587 of Loudoun's population of 20,577 lived in incorporated towns. These towns were still small and remained a vital part of Loudoun's rural life. For a population to be classified as urban, the census of 1920 maintained that the people must reside "in incorporated places of 2,500 inhabitants or more." By this criterion Loudoun was still completely rural.[8] Not only did these hamlets not qualify to be classified

---

[6] Deck and Heaton, *An Economic and Social Survey of Loudoun*, pp. 62-67. There are no birth and death rate statistics for the years prior to 1913.
[7] Ibid. The number of people in Loudoun in 1920 born in a foreign country was practically negligible: 111.
[8] Deck and Heaton, *An Economic and Social Survey of Loudoun*, p. 63.

as urban, but, like the county as a whole during the late 1800's and early 1900's, most Loudoun towns had a decrease in population. Leesburg in 1830 had 1,700 and in 1850, 1,688 inhabitants. By 1900 population in the county seat had declined to 1,513.[9] Other old towns also decreased in numbers. During the 1830's Waterford had approximately 400 residents, but by 1910 only 266 resided there. Middleburg's population declined from 430 in the 1830's to 263 in 1910. During the same period Hillsboro's population witnessed a less dramatic decrease from 172 to 138. The most noticeable exception to the trend of diminution was the town of Purcellville, a comparatively new town in the county, where the number of residents jumped from 388 in 1910 to 549 in 1920.[10]

Table 4. Population of Loudoun's Incorporated Towns from 1900 to 1920.

Town	1920	1910	1900
Leesburg	1,545	1,597	1,513
Purcellville	549	388	—
Round Hill	359	379	318
Hamilton	287	315	364
Middleburg	283	263	296
Waterford	266	331	383
Lovettsville	167	192	97
Hillsboro	131	138	131

Source: United States Census Statistics in *Loudoun County Geography Supplement* by Sanders, Lunceford, and Fenton. p. 26.

BICORPORAL COMMUNITIES

Nineteenth-century agrarian life in Loudoun evolved around the farm and nearby village. The needs and services of the grange belt and town complemented each other and gave rise to a bicorporal community

[9]Joseph Martin (ed.), *A New Comprehensive Gazetteer of Virginia* (Charlottesville, Va.: Moseby and Tompkins, Printers, 1835), pp. 211-12; Sanders, Lunceford, and Fenton, *Loudoun County Geography Supplement*, p. 26; National Archives of the United States, Population Schedules of the Census of Loudoun County, Virginia, for 1850, microcopy no. 252, roll no. 69.

[10]Martin, *A New Comprehensive Gazetteer of Virginia*, pp. 211-16; Sanders, Lunceford and Fenton, *Loudoun County Geography Supplement*, p. 26.

STABILITY AND AGRICULTURAL REFORM: 1790 TO 1828

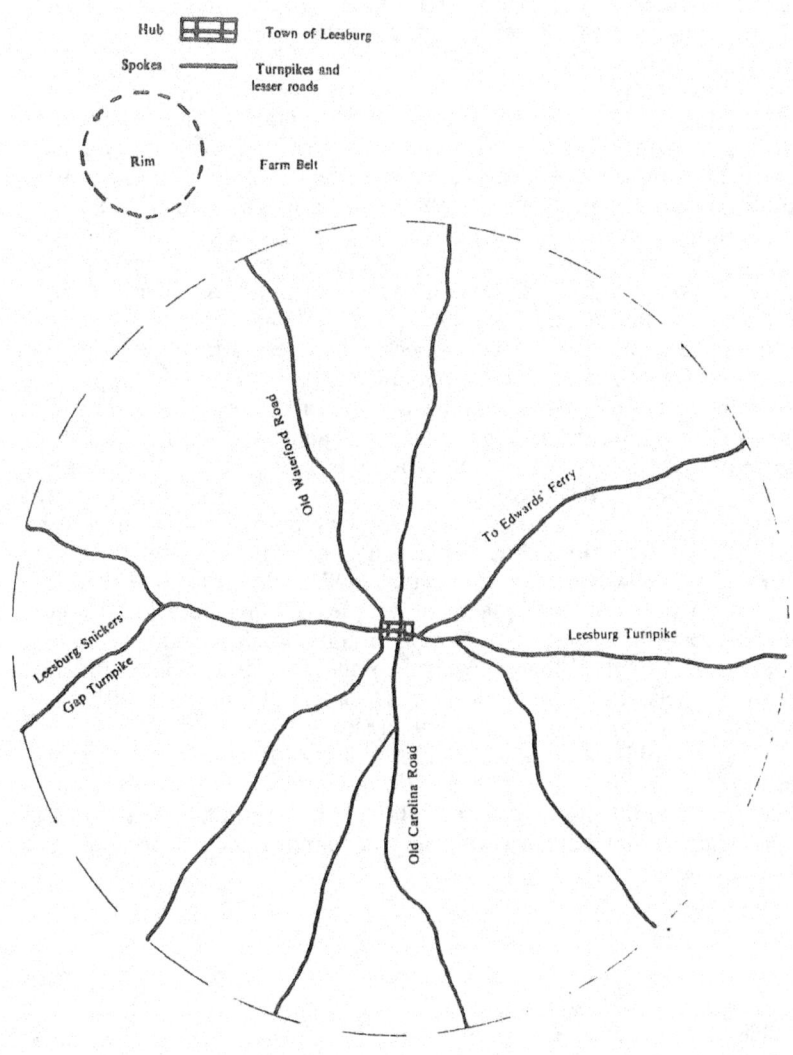

Figure 10. Wheel Configuration with Leesburg as the Hub of Eighteenth-Century Loudoun Life.

with a configuration analogous to the wheel: the axle or hub being the town: farms surrounding the town forming the outer rim; and the numerous roads, turnpikes and lesser roads, forming the spokes that connected these two salient parts of the community. The complementary relationship between farm and town took place in innumerable ways. Towns provided for the farmer institutional and economic services by being the site of stores, churches, schools, taverns, and places of business for physicians, cobblers, blacksmiths, wagon makers, tanners, tailors, and lawyers. Although Loudoun staples were usually sent to market outside the county, the cultivation of wheat by the farmer and the transportation of the grain to a mill, usually located in a town or village, is a good example of the dependent relationship of the two dominant segments of Loudoun's nineteenth-century community, the farm and the hamlet.[11]

Although towns and farms varied greatly in size throughout the county, all were a part of the more than three dozen communities scattered over Loudoun. Each of these communities became to varying degrees an economic and political microcosm of the county as a whole. Each of the communities had respected families or persons who were looked to by others in the immediate vicinity for civic and political leadership. Institutions like churches and the country store provided centers for religious, intellectual, and social activities. The country store, referred to as a mercantile store in the nineteenth century, had a special drawing power in the bicorporal community. It served not only the economic needs of the community as a combined grocery, hardware, clothing, and feed store, but also often housed the post office for the community and was used as a precinct polling place during elections.[12] The store was a common place for people to congregate for frequent lively discussions about politics, community affairs, and gossip. Expressions of the will of the bicorporal community, other than at precinct balloting, were often by resolutions passed at citizen meetings in response to a crisis, like events that preceded the Civil War.[13]

Only the older and usually larger villages—Leesburg, Middleburg, Waterford, Hillsborough (Hillsboro), Aldie, Union, and Snickersville—that had been established by legislative acts of the Virginia legislature had anything approaching municipal government.

---

[11] Bicorporal communities were not unique to Loudoun County, but existed throughout much of nineteenth-century America.

[12] Martin, *A New Comprehensive Gazetteer of Virginia*, pp. 210-14.

[13] *The Democratic Mirror* (Leesburg, Va.), November 24, 1858; June 20, 1860; June 27, 1860; July 17, 1860; July 25, 1860. The existence of militia units in many bicorporal communities prior to the Civil War was also an expression of community consciousness and identity.

The state legislature appointed from four to ten men to serve as the trustees of from ten to sixty acres expropriated to be the site of a new town.[14] The trustees were empowered to "lay off ... lots ... with convenient streets." A majority of the trustees were also "authorized to make such rules and orders for the regular building therein ... and from time to time ... settle and determine all disputes concerning the bounds of the lots."[15] Rule by appointed trustees was certainly anything but democratic. Trustees were generally aristocrats or leading businessmen within the county; frequently they did not reside within the town they supervised; and some lived at great distances from the given hamlet.[16]

Boundaries between one bicorporal community and another were determined by what the nineteenth-century mind considered a convenient distance for travel by horseback, horse and buggy, oxen and wagon, or by foot to stores, churches, and mills.[17] This judgement stimulated the rise of towns and villages on roads that would serve farm families in a radius of generally two to five miles.[18] Stores and other accouterments of town life often evolved where a mill or church had been established during the colonial era.[19] After the Civil War, rail travel in Loudoun created new villages or expanded the size and significance of

---

[14]Harrison, *Landmarks*, pp. 661-69; Hening, *Statutes*, VII, 235; XII, 605-06. Also established in what was considered Loudoun in the early 1700's were Matildaville and Centreville. But due to Fairfax's reannexation of lands in eastern Loudoun in 1798, the above hamlets became a part of Fairfax County. If a trustee died or resigned, the remaining trustees could select a replacement. With the exception of Leesburg, none of Loudoun's towns had a genuine form of town government until after 1870.

[15]Hening, *Statutes*, XII, 605.

[16]Harrison, *Landmarks*, pp. 661-69. William West, an ordinary keeper near what later became Aldie, became one of the original trustees of Leesburg despite living a considerable distance from the town. Ludwell Lee and Francis Lightfoot Lee, like West, were original trustees of Leesburg who did not live in that town. The primary function of the trustees was to establish the town. By the 1820's supervision of Leesburg had ceased to be by trustees as it was then governed by a mayor and "common council." Incorporation of a few towns in Loudoun took place after the Civil War: Middleburg was incorporated in 1872, Hamilton in 1875, and Purcellville in 1908.

[17]Boundaries between one community and another were rarely precisely drawn. This was true especially if farm families lived approximately an equal distance from two hamlets. They no doubt frequented both villages depending upon the services offered and the site of their church and residences of friends.

[18]Consult the map by Yardley Taylor, *Loudoun County Virginia from Actual Surveys* (Philadelphia: Thomas Reynolds and Pearsall Smith, publishers, 1853).

[19]For example, towns emerged around the establishment of mills at Aldie and Waterford, Goose Creek (Lincoln) emerged from the site of a Quaker Meeting House.

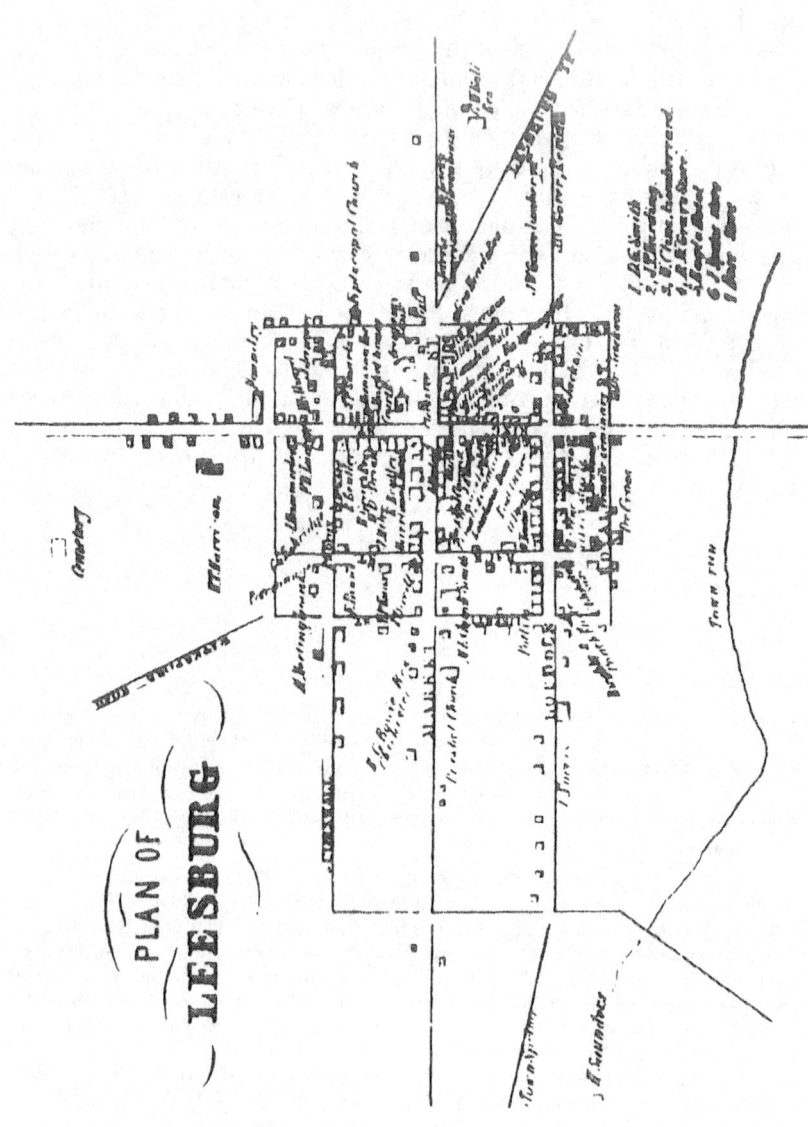

Figure 11. *Leesburg in 1853 from Yardley Taylor's Map of Loudoun County.*

old ones.[20] Families left in an area more than three or four miles from a town were often serviced by church, store, or mill that stood alone. Such an example was Griggsville, located nine miles west of Leesburg. This meager pretense of a hamlet consisted of one family, a store and post office that served a "densely settled" farming area during antebellum Loudoun.[21] Similar hubs of communities were Evergreen Mills, located ten miles from the mouth of Goose Creek, consisting of a store and flour mill; and the small but legitimate hamlet of Oatland Mills. The latter was several miles farther west on Goose Creek and included several stores, a post office, and several much used mills.[22]

The opposite to these small isolated villages of limited significance was Leesburg. Its influence as the result of being the county seat and its proximity to the center of the county gave it a political and legal radius that included the complete county. Its economic appeal was almost as great. This economic factor was testified to by the fact that Leesburg was by far the largest town in area and in the number of stores, mechanics, houses of worship, hotels, physicians, dentists, and attorneys.[23]

---

[20]Towns or hamlets that emerged or grew due to being railroad stops were Guilford Station, Farmwell (Ashburn), Belmont, Leesburg, Hamilton, Purcellville, Round Hill, and Snickersville (Bluemont).

[21]Martin, *A New Comprehensive Gazetteer of Virginia*, p. 211. Other small villages in Loudoun were Taylorstown, Paeonian Springs, Ryan, Sterling, Trappe, Silcott Springs, Waxpool, Neersville, North Fork, Leithton, and Wheatland.

[22]Ibid., p. 214. Transcending the bicorporal communities were magisterial districts created in each of the counties of Virginia in 1851. During the 1850's, Loudoun had ten districts (consult map of Loudoun in 1853 by Yardley Taylor). Due to the disruption of county government because of the Civil War, in 1869 the county government was reorganized and decentralized with the establishment of townships. Officers elected for each township in the county were clerk, assessor, tax collector, commissioner of the roads, township supervisors, three constables, overseer of the poor, and justices of the peace. After five years the township in Virginia was abolished and replaced by the magisterial district. At this time, 1874, Loudoun was reorganized into six magisterial districts: Broad Run, Mercer, Mt. Gilead, Jefferson, Lovettsville, and Leesburg. Each of these districts elected a supervisor, one constable, one overseer of the poor, and three justices of the peace. Tax collection was taken over by the county treasurer, and the duties of the assessor, by the county commissioner of revenue. The duties of the commissioner of roads and overseers of the roads were transferred to the new position of road surveyors. However, from 1874 well into the 1900's the magisterial districts remained more than an election district. They remained a unique and peculiar political institution. By popular vote the people of each district could borrow money for the construction of roads and schools in their district, yet the actual administration of the spending of the funds was usually conducted by county officials such as the board of supervisors. As the result of this system each district spent varying sums of money, which in turn led to each district often having different tax rates. (Porter, *County Government in Virginia*, pp. 270-72.)

[23]Ibid., pp. 211-12.

Villages that were Centers of Loudoun's Bicorporal Communities in 1835.[a]

Population	Dwelling Houses	Mercantile Stores	Mills	Churches	Schools	Post Off.	Taverns or Hotels	Physicians	Dentists	Lawyers	Mechanics & Artisans
1810	ca.100			1		1					
	20	8	2		1	1					ca. 5
	40	12	2		1	1					ca. 4
	(1 fam)	1	1			1					
1802	172	30	3	2	1	1	1	1	1		10
				2			1				ca. 6
1758	1,700	500	22		3	11	1	4	5	2	7	ca.28
		14	4		2	1	1	1				6
1787	430	70	7	ca.2	2	4	1		4		2	20
	62	10	1		1	1	1		1			5
	71		1	1		1	1	2				ca. 5
					1							
		6	1			1	1					2
1824	98	16	2		1	1	1	2	2		1	8
1813	135	25	2		3	1	1	1	3		1	ca. 6
1801	400	70	6	1	2	2	1	4	3			12

villages in Loudoun, nor does this chart list all the places with post offices. Most of the above *Comprehensive Gazetteer of Virginia* (1835), edited by Joseph Martin, pp. 210-16. See also Hening, *Statutes*, XII, 605-06.

ans are tanners, saddlers, tailors, house carpenters, cabinetmakers, tin plate workers, rs, milliners, and coach makers.

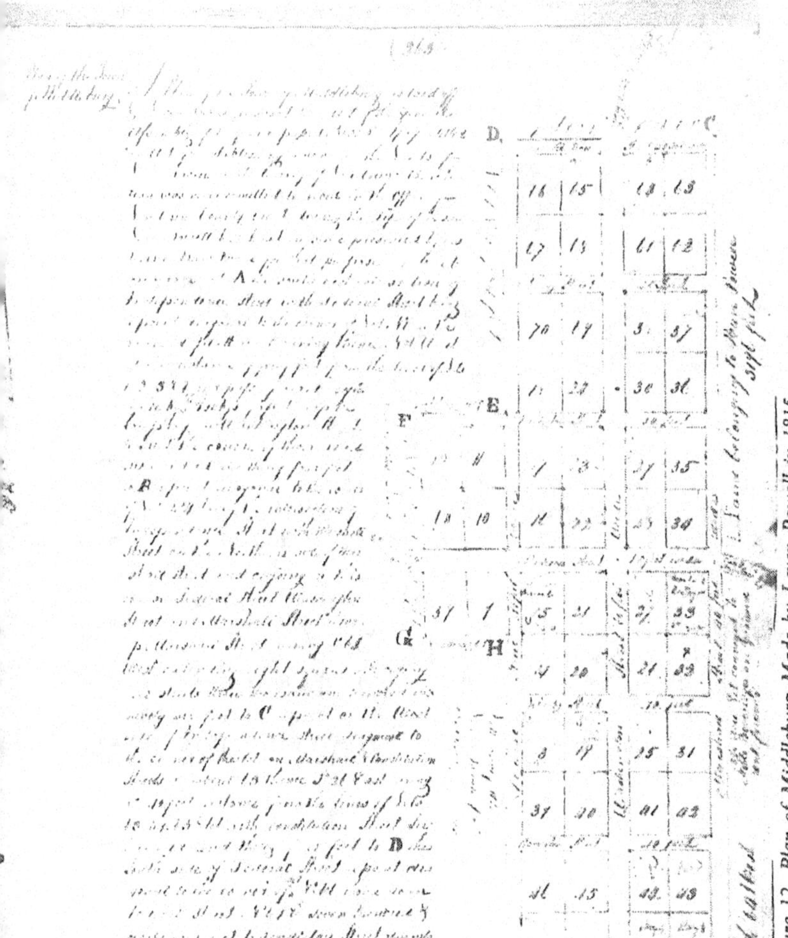

Figure 12. Plan of Middleburg Made by Leven Powell in 1815. Powell, a staunch Federalist, named most of the streets after prominent Federalists: Marshall, Washington, Hamilton, Pinckney, Pendleton, Pickering, Jay, and Madison. During much of the nineteenth century Middleburg was Loudoun's second largest town.

AGRICULTURAL REFORM

While farm life has always demanded long hours of work, life in colonial Loudoun to the Civil War was based essentially upon hand labor from sunrise to sunset, with some assistance from crude implements drawn by horse or ox. During this era the ceiling placed upon production by hand cultivation was gradually raised by technology and improved methods of husbandry.

Wheat continued as Loudoun's key staple while corn, the major food crop since the colonial period for man and livestock, also found its way into foreign markets.[24] The abundance of water power and cultivation of cereals led to the establishment by 1850 of "Seventy-seven water powers... principally merchant, Grist and Saw mills."[25] One spring near Leesburg was large enough to turn a "merchant mill capable of manufacturing 75,000 bushels of wheat a year."[26] Before 1850 most of the county's wheat was made into flour and sent to Alexandria. Prior to the existence of turnpikes, transporting a barrel of flour to Alexandria often cost a dollar. When the Little River turnpike was completed and the Leesburg turnpike started, the price was reduced to seventy-five cents, and after the construction of the C. & O. Canal it was further reduced to forty-five cents per barrel. By 1850 farmers in the county started sending large quantities of their wheat to markets outside Loudoun instead of having it converted into flour.[27] Rye, corn, oats, and buckwheat, which were also raised, were "mostly consumed at home."[28] Other staple articles were pork and beef. "Many hundred head of cattle" were "annually grazed"

---

[24]Gray, *History of Agriculture*, I, 169-72. The native maize the white settler found in Virginia consisted of a number of varieties. These varied in color from white, red, and yellow to blue.

[25]Taylor, *Memoir*, p. 27.

[26]Martin, *A New and Comprehensive Gazetteer of Virginia*, p. 209. During the 1830's one of the most significant, if not the largest producer of wheat, was the ten-mile circumference around Middleburg. In that region alone there were eighteen flour mills, "all plentifully filled by the annual harvest" that "produced in the average acre, about 25 bushels of superior wheat."

[27]Taylor, *Memoir*, pp. 25,27; *The Loudoun Times-Mirror*, July 4, 1958; July 17, 1958; May 22, 1962. A good Quaker and foe of hard drink, Taylor lamented the "distillation of grain and the production of Spirituous Liquors... [as] the cause of so much vice and misery to the human family."

[28]Martin, op. cit., p. 210. Grasses cultivated for pasture and hay for livestock included red and white clover, timothy, "herds grass," and orchard grass.

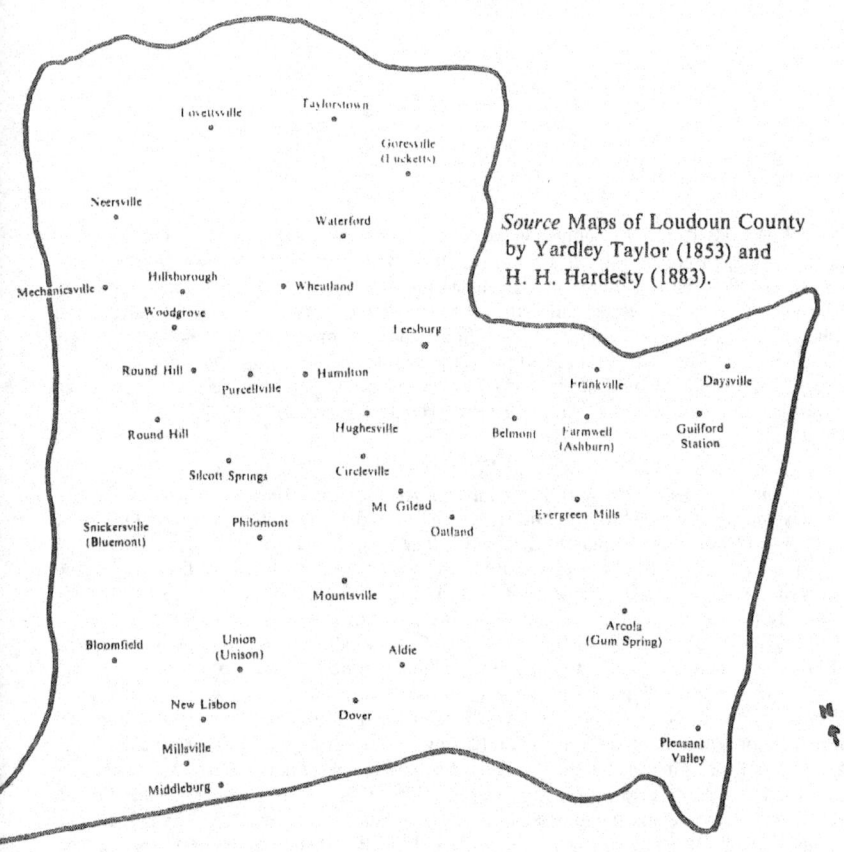

Figure 13. *Approximate Location of Three Dozen of the Villages and Towns in Nineteenth-Century Loudoun.*

and, like hogs raised in the county, driven to markets in Baltimore, Maryland, and Georgetown in the District of Columbia.[29]

Next to hogs, sheep were the most numerous animals raised in nineteenth-century Loudoun.[30] Woolen "factories" were established along streams in the county for carding and fulling of wool.[31] The Phoenix Factory near Aldie also offered to barter with anyone lacking cash to pay for having his wool processed.[32] In addition to livestock a great variety of vegetables was raised, and apple, peach, and cherry orchards provided fruit for Loudouners.[33]

---

[29] Ibid.; based on correspondence between Yardley Taylor and N. F. Cabell, January 11, 1854. Hogs were also driven from the county to these markets. During the late 1700's and early 1800's, Israel Janney "made it his business to go up into the mountainous parts of Virginia and purchase cattle and drive them into this county for the use of himself and others; and, as he kept a team to convey flour from his mill to Alexandria, he frequently slaughtered his fat cattle at home and sent the beef to market by wagon when the season was favorable. This would now [1853] be considered a small business, yet it serves to show the commencement of what is a very large and important trade."

[30] Taylor, *Memoir*, p. 23.

[31] *The Genius of Liberty* (Leesburg, Va.), May 30, 1829; Fenton M. Henderson, *Loudoun County, Virginia: Its Social, Agricultural and Manufacturing Advantages* (Leesburg, Va.: By the Author, 1868), p. 5. Numerous ads were printed in *The Genius of Liberty* of wool carding business throughout the county. The majority of the carding machines were advertised as being either new or repaired. These machines combed and disentangled the fibers of the wool, thereby preparing it for spinning. After carding, the wool was returned in rolls to the owner. Wool carding machines were usually run by water power, but William H. Hough's establishment on Beaver Creek, two and a half miles north of Waterford, had to "erect an inclined wheel" to work his machines by horses "due to a lack of water." Proprietors of the carding business usually required that wool be "well washed and cleared of sticks" prior to being brought to them. Hough also required "one pound of soft grease be put on, or sent with, every 8 to 10 pounds of wool." For fine wool he urged the use of oil "as the wool will spin much better." The most extensive service in the 1820's was offered by the Crooked Valley Factory near Middleburg. This establishment provided the carding of wool and fulling (cleaning) and dyeing of cotton, silk, linen, and woolen cloth in the most popular colors of the period, which were blue and black. Other colors were also available.

[32] *The Genius of Liberty*, June 19, 1821. A superior breed of wool-yielding sheep, merino sheep, was introduced into Loudoun prior to 1812. According to Yardley Taylor, "the late Pheneas Janney of Alexandria being in Europe on a mercantile voyage, previous to the last war with Great Britian; sent to his father," Israel Janney, a Loudoun farmer, miller, and merchant, "a lott of *merino sheep*, and thus they were introduced" in the county.

[33] Taylor, *Memoir*, pp. 18-22. Due to the slow growth of pear trees and their "liability to blight," they were not a common fruit tree in the county. In the early 1850's, a disease affecting the morello cherry tree hit the county and threatened to destroy this type of tree as it had previously done to such trees in Pennsylvania.

Table 6. Loudoun Agricultural Wealth in 1850.

Area of County in Square Miles	525
Assessed Value of Real Estate	$9,100,221.00
Tax on Real Estate	$16,380.40
Tax on Personal Estate, Salaries, etc.	8,030.57
Tax on Merchants' Licenses	3,942.79
Total	$28,353.76
Acres of Land in Farms, Improved	208,454
Acres of Land in Farms, Unimproved	86,222
Acres of Land in Towns, other lots, and waste lands thrown out of cultivation	41,325
Total	336,001
Cash Value of Farms	$8,349,371.00
Value of Farming Implements and Machines	$145,744.00
Number of Horses	6,727
Number of Asses and Mules	52
Total	6,779
Number of Milk Cows	5,958
Number of Work Oxen	425
Number of Other Cattle	16,005
Total	22,388
Number of Sheep	20,727
Number of Hogs	25,967
Value of Livestock	$9,375.92
Bushels of Wheat	563,930
Bushels of Rye	8,633
Bushels of Corn	749,428
Bushels of Oats	117,055
Bushels of Buckwheat	3,751
Bushels of Barley	75
Bushels of Irish Potatoes	21,735
Bushels of Sweet Potatoes	115
Bushels of Peas and Beans	920
Bushels of Seed	338
Bushels of Other Grass Seed	182
Pounds of Butter	422,021
Pounds of Cheese	12,120
Pounds of Wool	60,228
Tons of Hay	11,990
Value of Household Manufacturing	$4,171.00
Value of Slaughtered Animals	$165,259.00
Value of Orchards	$11,458.00

Source: Yardley Taylor, Memoir, p. 23.

Phœnix Factory,
NEAR ALDIE.

AMERICAN MANUFACTURES

The Subscriber,

RESPECTFULLY informs the public that his factory for Carding, Fulling, Dying, &c. &c. is now in complete operation, and will continue as a

Permanent Establishment,

Ready at all times and seasons to do any of the above work that may be offered, with the utmost despatch, and at as low a rate as any of his rivals may think proper to dictate. None but the first rate workmen will be employed.

☞ The prices will be as reasonable as any reasonable man could wish. In order to accommodate business to the *hard times*, all kinds of grain will be received in payment; or, if it will suit better, I will card for one seventh part of the wool.

⁂ Wool and cloth will be received at the house of Mr. William Dewer, at the toll-gate near Aldie; also at Mr. Hugh Rogers's, near Middleburg, and returned to the above places when finished.

CASH will be given for wool.

F. BROOKS.

Phœnix Factory, June 19, 1821.—23 3t.

Figure 14. Advertisement of a Wooden Mill in the June 19, 1821, Issue of The Genius of Liberty.

Generally farmers are paradoxically individualists and at the same time traditionalists. Each having his own methods of husbandry, he is usually very reluctant to abandon either his agrarian philosophy or the farm techniques he empirically acquired from his father and from common practice. Different philosophies and procedures for farming have traditionally existed in the same community from the colonial to modern eras. The rate of change in attitude and farm methods occurred slowly from the colonial period to the Civil War. During most of the colonial period it was not uncommon for farmers in Virginia to plant and cultivate small grain in hills or drills with only a hoe. During this same time span, wheat and other grains were harvested with a sickle. It took a motivated and sinewy man to reap, bind, and stack three-quarters of an acre of wheat per day.[34] The cutting, gathering up by hand, and tying small grain into bundles and placing the bundles into shocks or stacks, and subsequently threshing the grain by the use of the flail or a long pole or club were time-consuming and exhaustive. To beat out the product of twenty acres required three men three weeks.[35] Corn also took considerable physical effort to cultivate and harvest, but, compared to wheat, it was less expensive and relatively easier to harvest. Also, its being less vulnerable at harvest time explained in part the popularity throughout the county of corn as the most entensively grown food crop for man and beast. Corn in colonial Virginia was planted in hills from three to five feet apart. Five to six kernels were planted in each hill and later thinned to two or three stalks. Corn was usually thinned once or twice. It was also customary to pull leaves from the plant while still green and wrap them in a bundle to feed the livestock during the winter. Another common colonial practice was to cut off the top of the stalk just above the top ear and cure the top for fodder. Cutting the whole stalk and shocking it were not introduced in Virginia until after 1780.[36]

During the colonial period the hoe was more valuable than the plow. This preference was due in large part to the heavy and clumsy nature of plows with wooden moldboards which did little more than scratch the surface of the topsoil, plus the fact that for newly cleared land

---

[34]Gray, *History of Agriculture*, I, 169-74. It was not uncommon in the 1770's for farmers in northern Virginia to plant additional crops between the hills of corn, wheat, or other small grain. Landon Carter planted barley in hills every three feet and planted spelt (a hard-grained variety of wheat) between the hills of barley. It was also common to plant wheat and barley between the hills of corn. The volume of seed sowed per acre seemed to vary greatly. Anywhere from a half to two bushels of wheat were sowed per acre.

[35]Ibid., pp. 170-71. To thresh their small grain more imaginative farmers constructed devices in which their livestock would repeatedly run over the stalks placed upon a circular floor or platform.

[36]Ibid., p. 174. Shelling corn was done either by hand or by putting the ears in a pile and beating them with flails. By hand a man could shell only six bushels a day as compared to twenty bushels an hour by using the flail.

with stumps the plow was totally impracticable. At the advent of the nineteenth century, other farm implements were also crude: harrows, sickles, scythes, and threshing machines. During the next sixty years, 1800 to 1860, major technological breakthroughs occurred that would dominate the nature of American farming into the twentieth century. The cradle was substituted for the scythe and sickle; the occasional adoption of mechanical reapers, tremendous improvement in the composition and design of plows; the hoe was superseded by horse-drawn tillage implements, such as the cultivator; mechanical seeders, threshing machines and horserakes also made their appearance. A summary of the emergence of improved farm equipment was written by Yardley Taylor in 1854:

> *The constant intercourse of the citizens of this county who emigrated from the north, with the places of their nativity, soon made them acquainted with improvements there. The iron mould [sic] board plough was introduced here soon after it was first used in Pen[n]sylvania. BENJAMIN BRADFIELD, then of this neighborhood [Purcellville], brought a mould board from Pen[n]sylvania ABOUT 1808, and had a plough made to it. An ingenious ploughmaker here, named GIDEON DAVIS, seeing the mould board and believing it to be too small for our purposes, soon made a PATTERN FOR A LARGER ONE, and had some cast and tried and they soon came into general use. This pattern is substantially the same now used here for barshare ploughs. The NORTHERN PLOUGHS, particularly those with cast shares, DO NOT SEEM TO TAKE generally with our farmers. Our soil contains considerable amount of flint gravel with sharp angles, and this with the sand of the soil, will soon bevel . . . even of the best temper, and unless it can be sharpened it will not plough well. Hence wrought iron shares are prefered, and they often in dry weather have to be sharpened every day, to enable them to do good work.*
>
> . . . .
>
> *I might have mentioned that other labor saving implements were introduced here soon after their value became known. HORSE POWER THRESHING MACHINES were first used ABOUT 1822 and soon generally adopted. WHEAT DRILLS ARE COMING INTO USE, and they will no doubt soon become general. The farmers of this county have been sometimes charged with being indifferent to the improvement in farming implements, but the truth of the matter is they are a calculating people, and as they are generally laboring men themselves, they are not willing to spend their money,*

without having some evidence of the value of the proposed improvement.[37]

Except for improved plows, the universal use of the above equipment that amounted to the first significant revolution in American farming, did not occur until after the Civil War. Habit, inertia, plus the dependence upon the local blacksmith for construction of the above items, were strong retardative factors. Crude plows were still used by many farmers until the Civil War. During the same period harvesting small grains in Virginia was probably done more by cradling than with the reaper. The human body still remained a vital source of power.[38]

Farm laborers have always been an indispensable part of American agriculture. Mechanization of farming has gradually transformed the need for a large unskilled labor force, such as was originally provided by indentured servants and slave labor, to a smaller number of laborers on each farm who were more skilled and could appropriately operate the increasing number of complex and sophisticated machinery. However, Loudoun's agrarian civilization prior to 1860, if it did not need a sophisticated labor force on the farm, did need goods and services provided by artisans such as blacksmiths and cobblers. The training of these artisans was done by an apprentice system that evolved from Europe.[39] Loudoun County records record minors between the ages of ten and eighteen years being apprenticed by parents or guardians. One way to handle adolescent orphans was to "bind them out" as apprentices.[40] In exchange for room and board and being taught a skill or trade, the youths were legally bound to work until they were twenty-one for their new guardians. It was a common practice for apprentices in Loudoun to run off prior to becoming twenty-one. In 1818, Adam Grubb advertised a six-cent reward for the return to him of John Wallman, a nineteen-year-old apprentice in stone masonry who had "absconded" from Grubb six months earlier.[41] A reward of the same amount was offered for Balaain Smith, an apprentice "to the blacksmith business."[42] One of the highest rewards offered during this period was $5.00 for the

---

[37]Based on correspondence between Yardley Taylor and N. F. Cabell, January 11, 1854. Cast iron plowshares were brittle and easily broken by rocky soils, whereas wrought iron plowshares were less likely to break.

The cradle was a frame fastened to a scythe with fingerlike rods so grain could be laid evenly as it was cut. The device was also often referred to as the cradle-scythe. By laying the stalks of grain evenly, the device made them easier to pick up and tie into small bundles called sheaves. On the average a cradler could cut two and one-half acres a day. Specific procedures used after the small grain was cut varied; however, a common practice was to stand eight to ten sheaves into stooks (shocks), later to be removed to larger shocks prior to threshing. Many farmers in eastern Virginia did not bind at all, but put the loose wheat in small stacks and later either put it into larger stacks or threshed it.

[38]Gray, *History of Agriculture*, II, 792-97, 799-800.
[39]Ibid., I, 342.
[40]Loudoun County Order Book H, p. 196.
[41]*The Genius of Liberty*, March 17, 1818.
[42]Ibid., May 12, 1818.

return of nineteen-year-old John Duncan, who was an "indentured apprentice to the wagon making business" under John James.[43] The lowest reward was one cent offered for the return of Charles Gordon, "an apprentice to the boot and shoe making business" operated by William King in Leesburg.[44]

Far more significant for the Loudoun farmer after the Civil War was the economic and psychological adjustments necessitated by the manumission of American slaves prior to the end of 1865 and the migration of Loudoun's male youths to the cities, especially Washington, D.C., during the late nineteenth and early twentieth centuries. Readjustments due to the termination of slavery resulted in most of Loudoun's black citizens becoming tenants. However, during this transition many Loudouners doubted that blacks would provide a dependable labor force as freedmen. It was at this time, the late 1860's and 1870's, that Virginia and other ex-Confederate states unsuccessfully attempted to attract European immigrants.[45] This search was not to attract poor European immigrants for tenantry, because Loudouners, like other Americans, had a strong nativistic bias against poor European immigrants that was second only to racism.[46] John A. Carter, a Loudoun delegate in the Virginia legislature and chairman of the Standing Committee on Immigration in the House of Delegates, in letters to the voters of Loudoun published in *The Democratic Mirror* stated there existed no "just cause for fear of pauper labor coming to this State; for the simple reason that we already have an abundance of labor, in proportion to our capital and means of paying for it."[47] In short, Virginians hoped to sell their surplus land to European immigrants and persons from Northern states with a degree of wealth as the way to stimulate the economic growth of the state. Delegate Carter strongly urged that:

> . . .every man, not only in this county [Loudoun], but in the State, to warmly espouse the cause of Immigration to the State, of "Land purchasers and actual settlers," with

---

[43]Ibid., June 27, 1820.

[44]Ibid., February 3, 1818.

[45]E. Merton Coulter, *The South During Reconstruction 1865-1877* (Baton Rouge: Louisiana State University Press, 1947), pp. 102-104; Jack P. Maddex, Jr., *The Virginia Conservatives, 1867-1879: A Study in Reconstruction Politics* (Chapel Hill: University of North Carolina Press, 1970), pp. 178-83. Of the 213,000 immigrants who arrived in the United States in 1868, only 713 went to Virginia.

[46]William D. Sheldon, *Populism in the Old Dominion: Virginia Farm Politics, 1885-1900* (Reprint; Gloucester, Mass,: Peter Smith, 1967), p. 9. During the last decades of the 1800's, 29 to 35 percent of Loudoun adult males were tenant farmers.

[47]*The Democratic Mirror* (Leesburg, Va.), August 12, 1875; August 19, 1875. The purpose of this committee was to advertise the advantages for people from Northern states and European countries in buying land in Virginia.

capital, to aid in the development of our dormant resources, and to give active employment to our laboring and mechanical fellow-citizens; and thus keep them from having to leave their present homes for want of work at inadequate pay.[48]

To benefit financially from this movement, companies in the United States were formed to entice colonists to America "from all parts of Europe" and help them "select and occupy Cheap Lands, where good soil and a general climate will insure health and prosperity." Such a company was the United States Land and Immigration Company, which hired J. William Foster and Fenton M. Henderson of Leesburg as land agents for their company in Loudoun County. To attract immigrants to the county, Henderson wrote a pamphlet entitled *Loudoun County, Virginia: Its Social, Agricultural, and Manufacturing Advantages.*[49] Despite the overly optimistic tone of this tract in regard to life in Loudoun in 1868, it apparently enticed few, if any, immigrants to the county. By 1884, the Catoctin Farmers' Club had given up attempting to attract affluent foreign settlers to Loudoun. A committee was established at that time by this organization "to open correspondence with emigrant agents" in an attempt to obtain "less affluent but nevertheless good foreign labor" for the county.[50] Failing in this search, a plan was presented to the club in 1904 to get "colored brethren to emigrate from the crowded parts of the south" to Loudoun. After "a long and spirited discussion of the subject" most members of the Catoctin Club stated that the proposal was "not acceptable" and "would not work."[51] Like the rest of Loudoun farmers at the advent of the twentieth century, farmers in the Catoctin Club of Waterford continued to face a shortage of "farm hands." On April 6, 1907, R. B. Abel, a member of the above organization, lamented that he was paying a seventeen-year-old boy $15.00 a month, and "it was hard to find a hand at any price." He also suggested that farmers in farm organizations should attempt to control wages of farm employees by setting a uniform wage. Other members rejected this suggestion as impractical due to the great number of farmers scattered over such a vast area. One member felt the farmers' only salvation was in

---

[48]Ibid., August 12, 1875. This eagerness for outside money no doubt was a pivotal force in the turning away from the bitterness of war and reconstruction and the evolution of Henry Grady's call for "a new South," in which the North and South could exist and complement the needs of each other free of sectional tensions for the first time in well over half a century.

[49]Fenton M. Henderson, *Loudoun County, Virginia: Its Social, Agricultural and Manufacturing Advantages* (Leesburg, Va.: By the Author, 1868), pp. 1-8.

[50]"Minutes of the Catoctin Farmers' Club," III, 219.

[51]Ibid., VII, 125.

the use of modern machinery.⁵² The shortage of labor was exacerbated by the migration of farmers' sons to urban areas. On April 18, 1914, the Lovettsville Farmers' Club attempted to formulate solutions to counteract this trend. H. M. Nisewarner stated the best practice was to give their sons "inducements where they" were "personally interested by attending to poultry on the share, or to have some of their own, or to have a patch of ground that they can claim for their own."⁵³ The other members agreed this was the most that could be done to offset the deceptive but nevertheless seductive lure of the city as a glamorous place of action, thrills, and economic advancement.⁵⁴

Salient changes in farming techniques in northern Virginia and elsewhere from the end of the colonial period to the Civil War were (1) the plow superseded the hoe, (2) corn was seeded in drills instead of hills,⁵⁵ (3) the cradle became the major implement for harvesting small grains instead of the scythe or sickle, and (4) improved management of fields through the rotation of crops and experimentation with fertilizers and soil conditioners like lime and gypsum.⁵⁶

Loudouners, especially John A. Binns, made contributions to the growing agricultural reform of the late eighteenth and early nineteenth centuries. Binns advocated deep plowing, the extensive use of gypsum,⁵⁷

---

⁵²Ibid., VII, 199-200.

⁵³"Minutes of the Lovettsville Farmers' Club," I, 70.

⁵⁴The strain of late nineteenth-century farm life can be found in *The Democratic-Mirror* which recorded the occasional deaths in July and August of field hands, usually Negroes, who succumbed to heat prostration.

⁵⁵Gray, *History of Agriculture*, II, 813-14. At the start of the post-colonial era, plows had for the most part replaced the hoe and hill methods of planting corn. Many farmers at that time did not plow the entire field but prepared a "list" or row by running a narrow plow several times up and down the row and once across if the corn was to be cross-checked. Although plowing the complete field soon became in vogue, the issue of cross-checking versus drill husbandry along with debates as to the proper distances between rows and proper distance of planting the seed in the row continued into the twentieth century. After the first tilling of the soil, plows were used less in cultivation as farmers relied more on harrows and cultivators. When seed failed to germinate, farmers replanted by hand. Removal of suckers or extra stalks was also done by hand throughout the 1800's and like the practice of replanting continued into the 1900's.

⁵⁶Ibid., pp. 793,797,809; based on correspondence between Yardley Taylor and N. F. Cabell, January 11, 1854. Although drills were invented prior to the Civil War, they were not used extensively until later. Most small grain was generally sown by hand up to the 1860's. A practice that did develop prior to the war in an attempt to reduce the problem of soil erosion in the piedmont region was to plow horizontally on the sides of hills instead of the traditional vertical direction.

⁵⁷Gypsum is a hydrated sulfate of calcium that can be found naturally in sedimentary rocks and is used for making plaster of Paris and in treating soil. Binns referred to gypsum

and raising clover as among the essentials of good farming practices that became known throughout Virginia and Maryland as the "Loudoun system." These procedures gained a degree of currency for restoring exhausted and depleted soil to fertility and for significantly increasing crop yields.[58]

John Alexandria Binns was the oldest son of Charles Binns, a founding father of Loudoun County, local aristocrat, and the county's first clerk of the court. John was probably born in the year 1761 and died in 1813.[59] The gentleman justices of the county recommended to the governor of Virginia that Binns, despite being a young man, be appointed a first lieutenant in the county militia.[60] In 1782, his father gave him a farm near Leesburg of 220 acres. Within two years after acquiring this farm, young Binns set about experimenting with gypsum and other farm techniques.[61] By 1803 he had developed a formula that he deemed to be indispensable for successful farming. He had these views published during 1803 in a tract entitled *A Treatise on Practical Farming*.[62] This work was known for its simplicity in literary style and phraseology as well as for its being the only official published pronouncement on the Loudoun system. In it Binns set forth an agrarian philosophy predicated upon the optimistic premise there existed no disorder to befall "the human race, or

---

as plaster; others wrote of using plaster of Paris on their land. The gypsum stone was ground into powder by Loudoun mills (see *The Genius of Liberty*, August 29, 1820).

[58]Avery O. Craven, *Soil Exhaustion as a Factor in the Agricultural History of Virginia and Maryland, 1606-1860*, pp. 87-90, 111-112; Gray, *Agricultural History*, II, 803-09.

[59]The exact dates of John A. Binns' birth and death are not known. It is known he died during 1813 and apparently had no children because he left his estate ultimately to his nieces. His widow, Dewanner, later married a Methodist minister who died long before her demise at Cumberland, Maryland. In his will Binns gave the place of his last earthly residence, a plantation called Clover Hill, to his "loving wife." It was Binns' will that she hold all his young slaves until they reached the age of twenty-five. At that time his brother, Thomas Neilson Binns, to whom John had bequeathed $500 for the purpose of seeing that his slaves were liberated, was to take the slaves from all the farms the late John Binns had owned to Maryland to be freed. If Thomas refused "to assist" Binns' blacks in obtaining their freedom, then the $500 was to go to any relative who would carry out this provision of the will. If no relative stepped forward, then "any other person stepping forward to bring about the emancipation" was entitled to the "aforesaid sum of five hundred dollars."

[60]Rodney H. True, "John Binns of Loudoun," *William and Mary Quarterly*, 2d ser., II (January, 1922), 28-31. Charles Binns' will was written in December 1800 and probated in July of the following year. His will disposed of 2,109 acres of land among his five sons. Two hundred and forty acres of this land was in Loudoun; the rest was located in Kentucky.

[61]Ibid., p. 31. He apparently lived on the land his father gave him until 1793. At that time he "exchanged it" for another place. In 1792 Binns started purchasing a number of large and small tracts of land in Loudoun. He continued this buying until 1797, after which he actively sold land as well as purchased it.

[62]Ibid., pp. 25-26. In 1804 a second edition of this work was published. It differed from the first in that a few short essays on various aspects of farming were added as well as a long list of certificates from persons testifying to the authenticity of Binns' findings.

disorder to the vegetable creation, but what the all-wise author of our being had provided a remedy."[63]

Binns recorded the genesis of his gospel of gypsum in the following manner:

> In the year 1784, I procured from the captain of a ship at Alexandria two small stones, weighing about 15 lbs. which I beat with a sledge hammer, pounded it fine in a mortar, and sifted it through a hair sifter. I then gave it to a tenant, who agreeably to my directions, put it on four or five hundred corn hills. In about two or three weeks the color of the corn was much altered, exhibiting a deeper green than the other; but on gathering there appeared little or no difference as to the quantity, which discouraged me from making any further attempt the year following. When harvest came on, the wheat was nearly double; this circumstance was remarked by several persons in the neighborhood who would not agree with my opinion, that the use of the plaister was the cause.[64]

Stimulated by this success, Binns experimented with gypsum on both grass and grain. He ran innumerable experiments by applying gypsum to the soil prior to planting, to the seed before the planting, and sometimes to the plants in the field.[65] He also experimented with different types of gypsum from Nova Scotia and France, and their effects upon various types of soils. The results were amazing. He doubled the yield of his hay and corn per acre and greatly increased his yield in oats and wheat.[66] In 1975, he planted fifty-four acres of corn in a field so

---

[63]Ibid., p. 62. His booklet was sold for fifty cents and probably printed in a limited edition. If Jefferson had not read and saved a copy of this tract, posterity may have heard little about John Binns. Neighbors W. H. Washington, Samuel Tillett, Israel Lacey, and William H. Harding testified that Binns told the truth. Conrad Verts, who helped cradle Binns' grain, told others of his difficulties in cutting Binns' bountiful crops. Samuel Ward, for years Binns' right-hand man, also spoke of the accuracy of Binns' statements.

[64]John A. Binns, *A Treatise on Practical Farming* (Frederick-Town, Md.: Printed by John B. Colvin, 1803), p. 1. Wheat was planted in the field gypsum had been applied to after the corn crop had been cut.

[65]Ibid., pp. 3-13. Binns also experimented with growing corn in hills and rows. In 1798 he planted only ten acres of corn. It was planted in rows four feet apart and the corn seed from ten to fifteen inches apart. The corn had been rolled in "plaister." He also sowed one bushel of plaster on each acre. The field produced 155 barrels of corn. During 1810 he planted fourteen acres of corn in hills four feet apart. A top yield for Binns in corn was forty bushels to the acre.

[66]Ibid., pp. 30-41. One way Binns urged farmers who used plaster to know if they had good "plaister was to break open a small stone of it." If it looked moist and dissolved "quickly in the mouth, then it is good; but if upon breaking the stone it appeared dry, and upon biting it you find a grit on the teeth, and dissolving slowly in the mouth, the plaister is but indifferent."

barren and devoid of fertility that his neighbors declared it "to be entirely worn out; and if" Binns "raised corn there it might" as well "be raised in the main roads." Binns rolled each bushel of seed corn in a bushel of plaster before planting the seed. He was unable to apply later more plaster as he exhausted his supply and was unable to get more in time. Nevertheless, those who traversed the road by this field proclaimed it "to be the best upland corn in the county, and equal if not superior to the river Bottoms."[67]

Binns' faith in gypsum came close to knowing no bounds. He had reason to have faith in it; after using it for nineteen years, he had prospered to the point that Thomas Jefferson referred to Binns as "tolerably rich."[68] By the time of his writing his treatise dealing with the pragmatic life of farming, Binns confidence had reached the point that he believed gypsum to be the panacea for many agrarian woes. He incorrectly asserted gypsum was a complete fertilizer and considered "one bushel to be equal to one hundred loads of straw-manure, on old poor land."[69] In his opinion plaster was the "best and richest ... manure ... in the world."[70] He used animal manure extensively and planned to cover more than "one sixth of [his] plantation" with it in 1803. But it was no match in his view for plaster. He wrote that:

> ...if it was not for the health of my family, and its tendency in correcting, loosening, and meliorating the soil made stiff by plaster, I should never think it worth the expense or trouble of carrying it [manure] out. ...[71]

He blamed the effluvium from manure in warm weather for causing

---

[67]Ibid., pp. 10-11.

[68]True, "John Binns of Loudoun," p. 36.

[69]Ibid., p. 25. At best gypsum added three essential elements, calcium and sulphur and, by promoting the growth of legumes, nitrogen (Craven, *Soil Exhaustion as a Factor in the Agricultural History of Virginia and Maryland, 1606-1860*, pp. 111-12).

[70]Ibid., p. 28. Other benevolent contributions of gypsum, according to Binns, were (1) when applied to "a light soil it would stiffen and close the ground and thereby prevent it from washing in gullies," (2) it possessed "a cooling nature to the earth and vegetation in the summer," (3) when applied "about the roots and the bark of" fruit trees "white-washed with lime, and gypsum stones thrown over the roots, it will prevent the worms, sheep and cattle from destroying them; and farther, will prevent hares from destroying a young nursery of fruit trees, and still not injure their growth;" and (4) it would greatly increase tobacco and hemp production.

[71]Ibid., p. 28. Binns carried out many experiments with various kinds of manure and fertilizer. He considered horse-manure and, surprisingly, salt "excellent manures;" lime, soot, ashes, sheep-manure were rated good while cattle-manure was "tolerably good;" and straw the most inferior manure of all.

fevers and in "cold moist weather . . . quinsies and pleurisies." From his travels he concluded that where he discovered fevers he has "always observed either dirty, filthy stables, hog-pens or water standing in . . . cellars, or ponds of water not far off." He also warned these "places were most liable to dysenteries." If people would "cleanse their stables, stockyards, cow-pens, hog-pens, wood-yards and ash heaps by the first of June," Binns contended, they "would have little need of having recourse to the apothecary shop, too commonly resorted to in" his neighborhood.[72]

Some of Binns' neighbors copied his methods especially his agronomical triad consisting of the gypsum, deep plowing, and the cultivation of red clover.[73] Binns modified the traditional three-field crop rotation system of corn, wheat, and pasture. Traditionally, after corn had been raised in a field, it was followed the next year by wheat, and the third year left unplowed and uncultivated as cattle and hogs grazed on such vegetation that grew spontaneously. Binns modified the procedure by using gypsum and planting clover during the third year.[74] He also greatly preferred raising red clover for hay instead of timothy.[75] Additional conclusions reached by Binns from his comprehensive empirical experimentations were the "advantages of thick over thin sowing" of small grains, the undesirableness of rye, appropriate methods of raising sheep, and theories about why the Hessian fly and other insects attacked crops.[76]

---

[72]Ibid., pp. 43-45. "Quinsies" was an inflammation of the throat. Binns proudly asserted that his family, which consisted of "about sixteen or seventeen, little and big for eighteen or nineteen years past," since he practiced his manure removal program had been, except for a couple of exceptions and spells of being "layed up" for a few days, "clear of those epidemical complaints" that affected his neighbors. During the almost two decades Binns referred to, he had only one death in his family, "an infant which was suffocated by mother's milk, it was supposed, in the night." One member of his family "was attacked by the rheumatism," and another "by the Small Pox during the same time span."

[73]Ibid., p. 44.

[74]*Gray, History of Agriculture*, II, 808-09.

[75]Binns, *A Treatise on Practical Farming*, pp. 54-56. In making clover hay, Binns used the following procedure, the first day he cut the clover; the next day he turned the hay over to aid drying and that afternoon he hauled the hay to the "mow, barrack, or stack." He then "put down a layer of . . . straw six inches thick; then . . . layer of clover twelve inches thick, and so on with straw and clover, alternately, until" all the hay was stored. "This system he claimed prevented hay from becoming mouldy or "mow burnt."

[76]Ibid., pp. 51-52,57,58-59,61-71. He investigated the advantages of sowing wheat thinly and thickly by sowing some acres with only half a bushel of seed and another patch with one and a half bushels. He found the wheat sown thinly not only did not grow as well as that sown thickly, but also was more prone to damage from freezing. Binns advised "every person in the farming line to quit sowing" rye because it impoverished the soil, failed to yield as much as wheat, and mysteriously caused fruit trees to decay when planted near an orchard. On raising sheep, he advised farmers not to allow their rams "to run" with the flock "until late in the fall" so "ewes will not drop their lambs until the snowy season is

An indication that many Loudouners in 1818 were practitioners of deep plowing, as advocated by Binns, can be found in a letter authored by another county resident, Robert Russell. In an epistle to a friend, Russell stated that the practice of shallow plowing had been abandoned by most farmers in his community. He further maintained this subsequently necessitated improvements in the construction of plows by making them larger and stronger with moldboards consisting of cast iron.[77] Loudouners, as well as people elsewhere, developed plows to improve tilling the land during the second and third decades of the nineteenth century. During this era the best known plow in Virginia, except for Jefferson's, was the one developed by Stephen McCormick of Loudoun. John Balthrop of the same county invented a "double shovel" plow which was used to cultivate corn.[78]

Other examples of Binns' impact upon his agrarian neighbors included his claim that they had increased their wheat production by three to fourfold since using gypsum. Some complained that the use of gypsum created too "luxuriant [a] growth" and the yield thus taxed a labor force that became insufficient "to get the wheat threshed and manufactured in the season, so as to get their flour to market before the next season."[79] Commenting upon the expanded production Binns wrote:

> *I do not think that the millers in the compass of ten miles square, in the settlement where I live. . .will be able to manufacture much above one half; there are some in the*

over." This procedure, Binns proclaimed, reduced the morality rate of lambs due to exposure to the point of being minuscule. Prior to using this method, Binns stated he "generally lost one third of the lambs, and a good many of the old sheep, with rot [footrot] , by housing them.

[77]Craven, *Soil Exhaustion as a Factor in the Agricultural History of Virginia and Maryland, 1606-1860*, p. 90. To provide greater power in order to use the improved plows more efficiently, farmers in Loudoun seldom used less than three horses to a plow.

[78]Richard B. Davis, *Intellectual Life in Jefferson's Virginia, 1790-1830* (Chapel Hill: University of North Carolina Press, 1964), pp. 167-68. Stephen McCormick's plow was not registered until 1828. Other Loudoun inventors of this period included Andrew Glendening, who during one year, 1824, put on the market an apple cutter, fly killer, washing machine, and a sausage machine. He obtained patents for all of these. Glendening was not the only or first Loudoun resident to invent washing machines. In 1809 Robert Robinson of Leesburg developed such a machine as did David Dungan of the county in 1811 (see A. J. Morrison, "Virginia Patents," *William and Mary College Quarterly*, 2d ser., II (July, 1922), 149-50).

[79]Binns, *A Treatise on Practical Farming*, p. 17,18,39. The increased growth was disliked by the laborers. Reapers were paid on the average of four shillings per day; but they turned down six from Binns to harvest a wheat field in which the crop had fallen over due to heavy wind and rain. Others quit after starting the harvest, declaring they would rather reap for half the wages in wheat that stood regularly up; some complained of their wrists and thumbs being strained. Binns wrote it took nearly five weeks before "he got the . . . grain cut and secured."

settlement that will be obliged to desist from threshing, being unable to find room in the mills, or yet deposit any more in their granaries.[80]

Binns' experiments were noticed outside of Loudoun. While President of the United States, Jefferson was so pleased with Binns' findings he sent copies of the Loudouner's treatise to his English friends, including the head of the English Board of Agriculture, with endorsements praising the little book for restoring Loudoun's prosperity and stopping emigration to the South.[81]

Not all of his neighbors applauded Binns' extensive work. Many were indifferent; others no doubt ridiculed him and impugned his veracity.[82] Unfortunately, the long-range impact of Binns' general agrarian reform program became adynamic as the result of his excessive claims for gypsum. His followers often neglected other aspects of improvements. Thus some advocates of gypsum came to denounce it as an impoverisher of their soils or a stimulant that rapidly depleted the land of its fertility. They soon declared their lands to be "clover" and "plaster sick," and many came to abandon the use of both.[83] Loudoun Quakers refused to accord Binns the honor of introducing gypsum and red clover into the county. They maintained that this honor should go to one of their own, Israel Janney. Apparently, they felt that Binns' publication of his treatise was an ostentatious act in an attempt to intumesce his reputation at Janney's expense.[84] A manifestation of this rivalry appeared in an insidious manner long after the deaths of Loudoun's two precursors of agrarian reform. N. F. Cabell, a Virginian gathering material for a book he later wrote entitled *Early History of Agriculture in Virginia*, corresponded with Loudoun Quakers, Daniel Janney and Yardley Taylor, during the 1840's and 1850's concerning the causality of Loudoun's

---

[80]Ibid.

[81]Gray, *History of Agriculture*, II, 803; True, op. cit., pp. 20-21.

[82]Binns, *A Treatise on Practical Farming*, pp. 4; 49,61-62. Some of Binns' neighbors felt his bold statements, which included the claim that his method of raising wheat "defied the ravages of the [Hessian] fly," were "presumptuous" and would anger the Lord, and thus bring "some heavy judgement" upon Binns or his wheat.

[83]Craven, *Soil Exhaustion as a Factor in the Agricultural History of Virginia and Maryland, 1606-1860*, pp. 111-12.

[84]True, "John Binns of Loudoun," pp. 36-38. Actually neither Janney or Binns was the first to introduce clover and plaster husbandry. Both had developed previously in Pennsylvania. However, they were significant for introducing them into northern Virginia (Gray, *History of Agriculture*, II, 779).

prominence as a prosperous agricultural area."⁵ Both responded that much of the credit should be attributed to the county's pioneer agrarian reformer, Israel Janney, who not only was the first to use "plaster and red clover" in the county, but also improved "grazing and the county roads." No reference to Binns' contributions was made.

Not all of Loudoun agrarians turned their back on the use of gypsum and the other aspects of the Loudoun system advocated by Binns and Janney. Those who used a manure in addition to gypsum, as Binns did, continued to believe in plaster's curative power for the soil. Much evidence indicates the use of gypsum and other aspects of the Loudoun system continued throughout the remaining nineteenth century. In 1875 Shroff and Company at Leesburg advertised plaster for sale.[86] The Loudoun Manufacturing Company of Purcellville during the 1870's advertised it kept "Fine GROUND PLASTER . . . on hand at" its mill.[87] Plaster seemed to have withstood fairly well the emergence of new competition from commercial fertilizers that started during the 1840's, such as Poudrette, one of the first patented commercial fertilizers to be sold, which was believed to have been made from the refuse from sewers and garbage heaps of large cities mixed with other substances. But the most significant craze after plaster was the eagerness for guano, the manure of sea birds found especially on islands off the coast of Peru, which was extremely high in nitrogen. Guano mania struck especially in the cotton belt of the antebellum South, but was not limited to it.[88] Yardley Taylor

---

[85]Ibid., pp. 36-37; based on correspondence between Yardley Taylor and N. F. Cabell, January 11, 1854; October 11, 1954; N. F. Cabell Papers, box 2, folder 91; Gray, *History of Agriculture*, II, 959; N. F. Cabell, "Some Fragments of an Intended Report on the Post-Revolutionary History of Agriculture in Virginia," ed. E. G. Swen, *William and Mary Quarterly*, 1st ser., VXVI (January, 1918), 164-65. Daniel Janney, the only survivor of Israel's seven sons, in the 1840's was a physician who lived near Purcellville. He wrote Cabell in 1845 that he remembered well hearing his father tell friends that he first tried gypsum on oats as he had brought a small quantity in his saddle bags given to him by a friend in Chester County, Pennsylvania. Dr. Janney also wrote that his father ran a store and from his father's store records he discovered that during June 1792, Israel Janney purchased ten tons of plaster "and used it much more extensively than before, being convinced of its power by the small experiment made heretofore." In April 1794, Daniel Janney curiously mentioned, with no further explanation, that John Binns was charged with purchasing one ton of plaster from his father. Israel Janney's records also reveal that during March 1794 he sold all of his clover seed to neighbors. These purchases were small, rarely more than a quart, as farmers first wanted it proven by their own experiments that clover was a good crop. While all this evidence does indicate that Israel Janney was a pioneer in Loudoun agricultural reform, it does not disprove the precursory work of John Binns. Binns' extensive usage of gypsum started in 1784; Israel Janney may have experimented earlier with gypsum, but he apparently did not use it extensively until 1792.

[86]*The Democratic Mirror*, August 12, 1875.

[87]Ibid., May 11, 1876; July 12, 1877.

[88]Gray, *History of Agriculture*, II, 805-06.

in his *Memoir of Loudo[u]n County, Virginia*, wrote that since 1849, "the use of Guano" and "other amendments in agriculture" were largely responsible for the increased production of wheat in Loudoun.[89] The demand for guano continued into the latter part of the nineteenth century as companies produced guano attachments for more efficient application of that material upon fields.[90]

Agricultural reform in Loudoun prior to the Civil War, in addition to the invention and application of some of the new farm equipment and use of commercial or imported fertilizers, manifested itself in the demand for a county agricultural society. The decade immediately following the War of 1812 witnessed a great interest in the formation of agricultural societies throughout the South.[91] Loudoun was no exception. The editor of *The Genius of Liberty* decried the absence of such a county organization. This sentiment was elaborated in a lengthy article printed in *The Genius of Liberty* that had been penned by a Loudoun farmer. He lamented the lack of a Loudoun agricultural society to diffuse general agricultural information to county farmers.[92] The cry for such an organization was partially met in 1825 and 1826 with the founding of the Agricultural Society of Loudoun, Fauquier, Prince William, and Fairfax.[93] A separate Loudoun society does not appear to have been formed until March 1842.[94] This organization, the Agricultural Society of Loudoun, subsequently sponsored an annual county fair during the 1850's,

---

[89]Taylor, *Memoir*, p. 25. Taylor wrote in a letter written in 1854 to N. F. Cabell that from "an examination of the census tables it will be perceived, that every field of 32 acres on an average yields 220 bushels of the different varieties of grain cultivated here, besides furnishing pasture and fodder for 1 horse 1 cow 2½ other cattle 3 sheep and 4 hogs annually. Since the census was taken, by the introduction of Guano, the amount of grain has been greatly increased, particularly in the eastern part of the county where the soil had been the most reduced."

[90]*The Democratic Mirror*, August 12, 1875. Sheroff and Company advertised during the 1870's Crowell's guano attachments along with Pitt's threshing machines, Montgomery wheat fans, Willoughby grain drills, Bickford and Huffman drills, plows, cutting boxes, pumps, and churns. The Loudoun Manufacturing Company served as an agent of Aultman and Taylor threshers, Buckeye reapers and mowers. It also claimed to have the best threshing engine on the market as well as having "a commodious Foundry and machine Shops" for "special attention to REPAIRING AND RE-BUILDING OLD Implements—at a great saving to farmers." A fertilizer ad in *The Democratic Mirror* on June 20, 1860, stated the availability at "reasonable cash prices, Peruvian Guano, and all other Fertilizers, Ground and Lump Plaster of best quality."

[91]Gray, *History of Agriculture*, II, 784-85.

[92]*The Genius of Liberty*, July 25, 1820.

[93]Davis, *Intellectual Life in Jefferson's Virginia, 1790-1830*, p. 168.

[94]*The Loudoun Times-Mirror*, November 26, 1959. An ad in a county newspaper called for those interested in forming an agricultural society in the county to meet in the courthouse on Monday, March 14, 1842.

which stimulated competition for cash awards varying from $1 to $10. After the Civil War the Loudoun society renewed the annual fair.[95] Under the supervision of marshals appointed for the occasion, county residents could compete for prizes not only in livestock and culinary classes but also in "Domestic Manufactures, Household Fabrics, and Home Manufactures" made in Loudoun.[96] The Agricultural Society of Loudoun was apparently assisted after the Civil War by the formation of the Loudoun County Livestock Exhibition Association during the latter part of the nineteenth century.[97] To further promote and improve agricultural knowledge and farming techniques, The Loudoun County Agricultural Academy and Chemical Institute was formed in 1854 by Benjamin Hyde Benton.[98] Commonly called "The Institute" and located three miles north of Aldie, it offered "instruction in all branches of mathematics and science useful to the farmer and man of Science."[99] This represented the first attempt to offer vocational training in Loudoun. Students not only were taught just the theories of agriculture but also were "instructed in the practical application of their studies to every-day affairs of life." The Institute advertised in 1854 courses of study pertaining to aspects of agronomy which touched almost every need of an agrarian community:

---

[95]*The Democratic Mirror*, August 9, 1871; August 30, 1871. The annual county fair was discontinued during the Civil War, but renewed during the reconstruction period. A Loudoun county fair has continued to the present, long after the demise of the Agricultural Society of Loudoun. Most of the twentieth-century fairs in the county have been sponsored by Loudoun 4-H clubs.

[96]Ibid., August 30, 1871. For example, for the three-day fair of September 13,14,15, 1871, all members of the Agricultural Society of Loudoun were given badges which admitted them free. The families of members were also admitted without charge. All others had to purchase a ticket which amounted to fifty cents for an adult and twenty-five cents for a child. Fees for membership in the society were $3. All male exhibitors at the fair, then held at the new fair grounds west of Leesburg, had to become members of the society and have their "animals and articles entered at the Business Office before taking them into the enclosure." Ladies were exempted from the prerequisite of membership to exhibit items. Domestic manufactures classes had eighteen categories, such as the best ten yards of fulled cloth, carpeting, factory flannel, and linsey.

[97]Virginia, *Acts of the General Assembly of the State of Virginia*, 1884, p. 155 (hereafter referred to as *Acts of the General Assembly*). The properties of the Loudoun County Livestock Exhibition Association and several other agricultural societies in the state were exempted from taxation by state law in 1884.

[98]Philip V. diZerega, "History of Secondary Education in Loudoun County, Virginia" (unpublished Master's thesis, University of Virginia, 1948), p. 22. Benton had previously operated a boarding and day school at New Lisbon.

[99]*The Washingtonian* (Leesburg, Va.), June 2, 1854. In this issue is an advertisement for "The Institute" written by its founder and principal Benjamin H. Benton.

> ...the phenomena of nature...the properties of soils, the requirements of plants, the composition of minerals, the utility of different kinds of rocks, laws of mechanical forces, calculation of cost, quantity and strength of materials used for building and other purposes, surveying farms, levelling water courses, laying out roads, making maps, mechanical drawing calculations required in the construction of machinery....[100]

Agricultural "chemistry," which included "how to prepare pure chemicals, analyze soils, minerals, marls," was taught to advanced students. Farmers were urged to have their soil analyzed by The Institute. The school also had a furnace, turning lathe, "and a great variety of tools for working in wood and metal." The regular sessions went from the first of October to the first of the following August. For this ten-month session the cost was $200. This fee included tuition, board, lodging, washing, fuel, and lights.[101] Unfortunately this school closed in 1861 due to the Civil War and never reopened.[102]

---

[100] Ibid., The ad also stated that sons of preachers and editors would be charged only $150 to attend a session at The Institute.
[101] Ibid.
[102] diZerega, "History of Secondary Education in Loudoun County, Virginia," p.22. The original building that housed The Institute has been restored by the Beagle Club of America. This organization currently continues to use this structure as a clubhouse.

Chapter 3

POLITICS, NATIONALISM, BANKS, AND THE TRANSPORTATION REVOLUTION: 1828 TO 1848

The years from 1828 to 1848, referred to by Glyndon Van Deusen as "the Jacksonian era," were dominated by nationalism and sectionalism competing for centrality.[1] Nationalism during this period of America's adolescence was nourished by extensive demographic, territorial, economic, and technological growth that included multifarious developments, such as: the continued westward migration of American settlers, increased immigration, annexation of Texas, settlement of the Oregon issue, acquisition of the Mexican Cession, revolution in transportation, rise of corporations, accelerated industrial and agricultural growth, and the extension of suffrage and application of political procedures that promoted egalitarianism benefiting the white male and subsequently helping to elevate Jackson to the Presidency. Intellectually the response to such national vitality was the belief in a credo that reflected the confidence and arrogance of a youthful country. Americans believed that their nation was the land of God's chosen people, due in part to their agrarianism and self-reliance. The nation's blessings were believed to have been ordained by divine providence and to include the inevitability of American progress and unencumbered geographical predestination best symbolized by the popular slogan of the

---

[1]Glyndon G. Van Deusen, *The Jacksonian Era, 1828-1848* (New York: Harper and Row, 1959), p. xi.

1840's "manifest destiny."[2] A triad of God, nature, and individualism not only was believed to be the reason for American greatness, but also was associated with Jackson in such a manner that he became the symbol for that age.[3]

During the "age of Jackson" nationalism appeared to be rampant and unfettered. Yet during this period of dynamic growth there emerged sectional tensions over the federal government's policies pertaining to internal improvements, land, banking and currency, tariffs, and the numerous issues associated with slavery. American society was indicted by religious evangelicalism for its sin, by millennialists and perfectionists for its crass materialism, and by humanitarian reformers because of America's inhumanity to the disadvantaged, which included the mentally ill, criminal, tippler, woman, and the slave.[4] As the Jacksonian era waned, the dialectic conflict between nationalism and sectionalism intensified so sectionalism not only challenged nationalism but also came close subsequently to superseding it through the use of such instruments as secession and war.

Since the democratization of politics and the revolutionary breakthroughs in transportation, along with other forms of economic growth, were determinants of the American idea of progress and salient aspects of the more positive developments in America during the Jacksonian and antebellum eras, they will be examined as they relate to the history of Loudoun County, Virginia.

POLITICS

Residents in Loudoun County during the Jacksonian era were not imbued with sympathy for either the Democratic party or the majority of the Presidential policies of "Old Hickory." Instead the bulk of Loudouners supported the National-Republican party and subsequently the Whig party. Allegiance to these parties was consistent with the support given by Loudoun to the Federalist party prior to its demise and the

---

[2]Albert K. Weinberg, *Manifest Destiny* (Chicago: Quadrangle Books, 1963), pp. 89,100-01.

[3]Marvin Meyers, *The Jacksonian Persuasion: Politics and Belief* (Stanford, Calif.: Stanford University Press, 1966), pp. 31-32,274-75; John W. Ward, *Andrew Jackson: Symbol for an Age* (New York: Oxford University Press, 1962), pp. 207-13.

[4]Hans Kohn, *American Nationalism* (New York: Collier Books, 1961), pp. 106,110-15; Charles S. Sydnor, *The Development of Southern Sectionalism, 1819-1848* (Baton Rouge, La.: Louisiana State University Press, 1962), pp. 116,121,126-27,132,231,321; Alice F. Tyler, *Freedom's Ferment* (2d ed.; New York: Harper and Row, 1962), pp. 113,140,166,196,225,265,338-39,454,548.

interest within the county in internal improvement programs that would expedite the exportation of Loudoun's staple, flour, to markets outside the county.[5]

Exemplification of the politics of Loudoun during the 1820's and 1830's can be found in the career of Charles F. Mercer, the most significant political spokesman of the county during that span of the Jacksonian era.[6] As a politico, Mercer was a significant force in the Virginia legislature from 1810 to 1817, the House of Representatives from 1817 to 1830, and the Virginia constitutional convention of 1829-1830. He was an effective leader of movements and policies concerning most of the dominant issues of the Jacksonian period. His energy was amply spent in attempting to create in his native state a sound banking system, the colonization of the free Negroes from America to Africa, and the establishment of a comprehensive educational system that included public schools. While in Congress, Mercer was a critic of many of President Jackson's policies and championed the cause of internal improvements for the nation as a whole. He also became the first president of the Chesapeake and Ohio Canal Company. His political career spanned the period from the demise of the Federalist party to the advent of the Whig party. He was a Federalist during most of his political life until the rise of

---

[5]Charles H. Ambler, *Sectionalism in Virginia from 1776 to 1861* (Chicago: University of Chicago Press, 1910), pp. 77,87-90; Harrison, *Landmarks*, p. 401. James W. Head in his zeal for stating Loudoun's historical significance asserts in the *History of Loudoun County* (p. 139) that Leesburg, Virginia, ". . . for a little more than two weeks . . . was the Capital of the United States during the War of 1812." This claim is based upon the storage of federal records either in or near Leesburg when the British burned Washington, D. C., in 1814. Writers are still debating if federal records were actually stored in Leesburg or several miles to the south of the county seat at the country estate known as "Rokeby."

[6]Charles Mercer was born on June 16, 1778, at Fredericksburg, Virginia. He was the youngest son of Eleanor and James Mercer. Young Mercer was the grandson of John Mercer, an Irish immigrant, who was also an author and a lawyer. In 1795 Charles Mercer entered the College of New Jersey (Princeton) and graduated in 1797 first in his class. During his last year in college he started reading law. During 1802 he was licensed to practice law in Virginia. On December 26, 1839, his resignation from his seat in the House of Representatives brought to an end a career in the Virginia state legislature and Congress that spanned nearly thirty years. He then became a cashier of a bank in Tallahassee, Florida, and was a key member of the Texas Association. The latter was a company to settle colonists in Texas. From 1847 to 1853 he lived near Carrollton, Kentucky. After selling his property there, he traveled for three years in Europe and worked for the abolition of the slave trade. Suffering from cancer of the lip, he returned to the United States and settled in Fairfax County, Virginia, where he died on May 4, 1858. Mercer's body was interred at the Union Cemetery in Leesburg. See the biographical sketch of Charles Fenton Mercer in the *Dictionary of American Biography* (VII, 539), as well as James M. Garnett, *Biographical Sketches of Hon. Charles Fenton Mercer* and the master's thesis by Olliver O. Trumbo entitled "Charles Fenton Mercer, 1778-1858."

the Whig party in 1830's, at which time he became a Whig.[7] It was appropriate that one of the political subdivisions of Loudoun, Mercer District, was named in honor of this active politician.[8]

Charles Mercer inherited a tract of land in southern Loudoun from his father, who had earlier inherited it from Charles' grandfather, John Mercer. Upon this tract of land Charles Mercer established his Loudoun home and founded a village he named "Aldie" in tribute to Aldie Castle in Scotland, believed to have been the home of his ancestors. He also constructed a mill in Aldie which became the economic hub of that community and remained in operation until 1971.[9]

Although the political preference of the county was first the Federalists and later the Whig party, the two-party system existed in Loudoun throughout most of the antebellum era.[10] This two-party allegiance was illustrated by the stormy elevation of Mercer from the Virginia legislature to the United States Congress. Mercer's Republican opponent for the seat in the House that represented Loudoun, Fairfax, and Fauquier counties, was Armistead T. Mason. Both men were Loudouners and landed gentry, with progenitors from influential Virginia families.[11] Mason, a graduate of William and Mary College and

---

[7]Olliver O. Trumbo, "Charles Fenton Mercer, 1778-1858" (unpublished master's thesis, Madison College, 1966), pp. 13-14,20-30,46-50,52-56. So solid was the support in Loudoun for Mercer, his constituents re-elected him on three occasions to the General Assembly while he was absent from the county. The first was during his military service in the War of 1812, the second absence resulted from an illness he contracted during that war, and the third absence was due to a trip to Canada for his health.

[8]Harrison, *Landmarks of Old Prince William*, p. 263.

[9]Ibid., pp. 260,236,668; Trumbo, "Charles Fenton Mercer, 1778-1858," pp. 6-7; telephone interview with James E. Douglas, Aldie, Virginia, August 18, 1973; *The Loudoun Times-Mirror* (Leesburg, Va.), February 22, 1962. The mill is believed to have been completed between 1807 and 1809. Construction was time-consuming since the several-story structure has brick walls one and a half feet thick. The bricks were made by Mercer's slaves. Shortly after the completion of the mill, Mercer sold it to Captain John Moore, whose progeny ran the mill until it was closed. Moore's great-grandson James E. "Ned" Douglas ran the mill until 1971. Among the people the mill serviced was a former President of the United States, James Monroe, whose estate, Oak Hill, was located a few miles north of Aldie.

[10]Ambler, *Sectionalism in Virginia*, pp. 134-35,222-23,330-31; Charles Sellers, "Who Were the Southern Whigs?" *Essays on Jacksonian America*, ed. Frank O. Gatell (New York: Holt, Rinehart and Winston), pp. 230-35; Henry H. Simms, *The Rise of the Whigs in Virginia* (Richmond, Va.: The William Byrd Press, 1929), pp. 62,87,116,138,159. The two-party system in Loudoun supports the thesis set forth by Charles Sellers in his article "Who Were the Southern Whigs?" Sellers rejects the concept of a monolithic antebellum South politically devoted to States' rights and slavery and hostile to the nationalist and antislavery capitalistic North.

[11]Ambler, op. cit., pp. 100-101. Mason was a relative of the family of George Mason, and Mercer was related to a general of Revolutionary War fame, General Hugh Mercer.

former commander of a cavalry regiment in the War of 1812, resigned his seat in the Senate in 1817 to campaign for the House of Representatives.[12] Federalists Mercer won the election by a narrow margin, which gave rise to six months of acrimonious debate between the two former candidates. Their feud was aired in *The Genius of Liberty* and *The Washingtonian* and culminated in Mason's demanding satisfaction in a duel.[13] The feud started with Mason writing Mercer on April 5, 1817, accusing Mercer of making disrespectful comments during the campaign. When Mercer denied having made any such remarks, the dispute seemed to have come to an end. But Mason demanded a recount of the ballots. The former general and "Chief of Selma"[14] objected to alleged irregularities, such as persons voting who lacked the proper length of residence, insufficient property, or improper registration. Mercer countered with an article to the "Federalist of Loudoun" that stated Mason was attempting to deprive many citizens of their right to vote.[15] Invective correspondence was authored by both men until November 19, 1817, at which time Mason attempted unsuccessfully to force Mercer into a duel.[16] Mercer declined the duel on the grounds that it would

---

[12]Trumbo, "Charles Fenton Mercer, 1778-1858," p. 31. Mason served in the U.S. Senate from January 3, 1816, until March 3, 1817. Mason had been appointed by the state legislature to the Senate to fill the vacancy created by the resignation of William B. Giles.

[13]*The Genius of Liberty* (Leesburg, Va.), October 7, 1817, and October 14, 1817.

[14]Head, *History of Loudoun County* p. 140. Mason was referred to as "The Chief of Selma" because of his residence four miles north of Leesburg called "Selma Plantation."

[15]Trumbo, "Charles Fenton Mercer, 1778-1858," pp. 31-32. Mason also demanded that the votes be examined for incorrect spelling.

[16]Ibid., pp. 32-33; *The Genius of Liberty*, October 14, 1817. Mason petitioned Congress to reverse the election in his favor. In an attempt to gather evidence of election irregularities, Mason went to various taverns in northern Virginia during November, including Austin's tavern in Leesburg. Congress, nevertheless, upheld Mercer's election. Ironically, Mason met his death at the hands of his cousin, John M. McCarty, on February 6, 1819. Both were residents of Loudoun and met upon the famous dueling field in Bladensburg, Maryland. The political differences of the two cousins started over McCarty's calling Mason a coward after the latter had introduced a bill while in the Senate that would have allowed Quakers of Loudoun to pay a fee of $500 in lieu of military service. A succession of bitter political quarrels followed that led to the fatal duel. Mason's reluctance to participate in a duel with McCarty led the latter to refer to Mason in *The Genius of Liberty* as a "disgraceful coward." The two antagonists fought with muskets loaded with only a single ball and fired at each other at a distance of only ten feet. Mason was killed at the age of thirty-two. His body was taken to Leesburg and buried in the Episcopal churchyard with an imposing masonic ritual. (See Head, *History of Loudoun County,* p. 140, and pp. 74-76 of the January 1927 issue of the *Virginia Magazine of History and Biography*, Vol. XXXV.)

Insight into the character of McCarty was given by an elderly voter in a letter "To the Freeholders of the County of Loudoun," published in the March 24, 1818, issue of *The*

violate the tenets of his religion. To this reply, Mason blurted that Mercer was a "consummate hypocrite and a most contemptible coward."[17]

Bipartisan politics failed to disappear in Loudoun during the latter half of the "Era of Good Feelings." Despite the demise of the Federalist party as a national party and statements by politicians like Colonel Mercer that no party spirit existed in Loudoun, political partisanship did appear in the county during the spring of 1821 in the campaign to determine Loudoun's congressional and state legislative representatives. There were five candidates for these positions of whom only one was a Democratic-Republican. *The Washingtonian* openly urged the election of Federalists. In a letter to the editor of *The Genius of Liberty* an annoyed Loudoun Democratic-Republican, Algernon Sidney, protested bitterly about deceitful campaign practices of Loudoun Federalists. Sidney felt county Federalists leaders, by maintaining that political partisanship was dead, deceitfully flattered Democratic-Republicans in an attempt to eliminate their candidates and to flood the campaign with candidates of Federalists persuasion. Loudoun Federalists, he contended, were:

> ...*hot-headed politicians who wish to affect moderation, and bury party distinctions, for the plausible purpose of gaining their point in the congressional election....In one hand they hold the olive branch, and in the other the scalping knife. In one ear they whisper in soothing accents, let us AMALGAMATE, there are no party distinctions, we are all federalists, we are all republicans; while in the other they proclaim away with your democracy; we'll have none of it.*
>
> *Now my fellow citizens, does this look like candour—does it appear like the era of good feelings?... Will the enlightened freeholders of Loudoun suffer themselves to be gulled and duped by a few designing, ambitious, and I may add factious individuals? Will they be led by some half-dozen crazy partisans, and hair-brained politicians, who cannot keep consistency in view?*[18]

Genius of Liberty. In the article the author commented upon McCarty's qualifications as a political candidate seeking to represent Loudoun in the General Assembly of Virginia. The elderly gentleman tactfully commented that McCarty's qualifications were weak due to his youth, temper, and lack of long-term residence in the county. The author of the letter advised McCarty before running for political office to "first make the county . . . his permanent residence, settle upon his estate, marry a wife, mix with his fellow citizens, learn family duties, moral habits, experience in social affairs," and "acquire a firm disposition and a steadfast mind" free of a "heart boiling with violent passions" and revenge.

[17] Trumbo, op. cit., p. 33.

[18] *The Genius of Liberty,* April 3, 1821.

Sidney's support for the lone Loudoun Democratic-Republican candidate, Captain Rust, was shared by many county freeholders. Rust received 638 votes as compared to his Federalist opponents, Braden and Grayson, who received 478 and 397, respectively. Both Rust and Braden were elected to represent Loudoun in the Virginia House of Delegates. In the congressional election, Mercer nosed out another Federalist by sixteen votes. Mercer received 394 votes to 378 for Bailey.[19]

Others in Loudoun during the decade after the War of 1812 interpreted the "Era of Good Feelings" as a transitional period in America's two-party system. Such was the view of the publisher of *The Genius of Liberty*, B. W. Sower, who in 1820 advocated that "former party distinctions shall be done away, and the very terms by which we were politically distinguished shall be forgotten." In the place of the traditional Federalists and Republican parties, according to the publisher, two new parties would emerge, dedicated, respectively, to one of the "two leading questions of national policy . . . commerce and manufactures."[20] Sower was on the side of "manufactures." During November 1819, he blamed the shortage of specie in Loudoun and the United States on American imports:

> . . .*we have ruined ourselves by continuing our importation of foreign merchandise, with the balance of trade against us; instead of fostering our own manufactories at home, and this at a time when our own staple commodities could scarcely find a market abroad. It is this state of things, and this alone, which has almost reduced us to poverty and bankruptcy; and, must ultimately tend to national ruin.*[21]

Concern for national economic development and subsequently internal improvements did not immediately soften Sower's belief in States' rights. During the 1820's he and his paper continued as an organ of the opposition party, attempting to counter remnant Federalism in Loudoun, which politically dominated the county by speaking out against the growing power of the central government.[22] Thus Sower looked upon the expansion of slavery and Missouri's statehood as the most significant issue since the "adoption of the federal constitution." To him the central issue was not the expansion of slavery, but political centralization:

> . . .*for the general government to restrict Missouri in the formation of her constitution and state government in relation to slavery, or in any other manner, not authorized*

[19] Ibid., April 10, 1821.
[20] Ibid., June 20, 1820.
[21] Ibid., November 23, 1819.
[22] Ibid., November 9, 1819.

> by the constitution of the United States . . . would be not only subversive of HER rights and liberties, but would tend to form such a relation between the general government and the confederated states, as was never contemplated by the federal compact. Such an assumption of power, on the part of congress, would at once, we conceive, prostrate our noble political fabric in the dust, a sad spectacle of ruined greatness.[23]

None of the elections in Loudoun during the Jacksonian period of the 1820's to the 1840's had the degree of bitterness and acrimonious exchanges as the Mason-Mercer feud that emanated from the congressional election of 1817. Lethargic Loudoun voters in the Presidential election of 1824 expressed limited interest in that election. The several hundred voters that participated in that election was an abnormally small number, even when one considers that universal white male suffrage did not exist at that time in Virginia. Throughout the Jacksonian era Loudoun voters supported political candidates for state and congressional positions and the Presidency who strongly supported economic nationalism in the form of internal improvements. This was a significant factor in John Quincy Adams' receiving 102 votes in 1824 to 68 votes for William H. Crawford, and 62 for Andrew Jackson.[24] The fourth candidate, Henry Clay, failed to receive a single Loudoun vote despite his comprehensive plan for internal improvements and protective tariff known as his "American System." Loudouners found Clay unacceptable at that time because they did not consider him a serious candidate with a chance of winning nor were they overjoyed with the prospects of a high protective tariff. Adams' strong endorsement of internal improvements, evasive stand on the tariff issue, his reputation as Secretary of State, and his being the son of a former Federalist President made him the most acceptable of the four Democratic-Republican Presidential candidates.[25] In 1828 more than three times the voters in the county went to the polls in this Presidential election than in the previous one. Adams received 525 votes to 229 for Jackson, who won the election.[26] After four years as President, Loudouners still found Jackson un-

---

[23]Ibid., February 8, 1820.

[24]Presidential Election Returns of Loudoun County, Virginia for 1824 (MSS in the Archives of the Virginia State Library, Richmond, Va.), Election Records No. 265. The vote was light throughout Virginia as less than half of the eligible voters voted. Crawford received the highest number of votes in the state.

[25]Ambler, *Sectionalism in Virginia*, pp. 127-32; George Dangerfield, *The Awakening of American Nationalism, 1815-1828* (New York: Harper and Row, 1965), p. 218. The Federalist party ceasing to exist as a national party after the War of 1812, made, for a time, the Democratic-Republican party the only major party in existence.

[26]Presidential Election Returns of Loudoun County, Virginia, for 1828, Elections Records No. 266.

acceptable.[27] The candidacy of Clay and his zealous championing of internal improvements, in comparison to Jackson's veto of the Maysville Road Bill,[28] resulted in Loudouners casting 837 votes for Clay and 319 for Jackson in the 1832 election.[29]

The Whig party emerged in Virginia in 1834 to oppose what critics contended was excessive executive power wielded by "King Andrew the First," especially in his removal of the remaining deposits from the Bank of the United States prior to the expiration of its charter.[30] Loudoun's anti-Jackson position continued in the 1836 Presidential election. Consequently, Martin Van Buren, the political heir of Jackson, received only 254 votes as compared to the 935 for the Whig candidate.[31] The Whig party dominated Loudoun's political life from the early 1830's until the early 1850's in local, state, and national elections. For example, in Presidential elections during this period William H. Harrison in 1840 received 1,269 votes to 381 for the Democratic candidate, Van Buren; Clay in 1844 got 1,505 votes to 474 for James K. Polk; Zachary Taylor obtained 1,453 votes in 1848 to 420 for Lewis Cass; and Whig Winfield Scott in 1852 received 1,813 of Loudoun's ballots compared to 788 for his handsome Democratic opponent, Franklin Pierce.[32] All of Loudoun's

---

[27]Henry H. Simms, *The Rise of the Whigs in Virginia, 1824-1840*)Richmond, Va.: The William Byrd Press, 1921), p. 28. John Janney was a leader of the state National Republican Convention that met at Staunton during July 1832.

[28]Van Deusen, *The Jacksonian Era*, pp. 51-52. Jackson was far from hostile to internal improvements. He approved projects and expenditures during his first term that were twice those approved by Adams' administration.

[29]Presidential Election Returns of Loudoun County, Virginia, for 1832, Election Records No. 267. Seven votes were cast for other candidates. There were six precincts or polling places in Loudoun at this time: Leesburg, Union, Lovettsville, Hillsboro, Gum Spring, and Mount Gilead.

[30]Simms, *The Rise of the Whigs in Virginia*, pp. 84-86,183.

[31]W. Dean Burham, *Presidential Ballots, 1836-1892* (Baltimore: The Johns Hopkins Press, 1955), p. 828.

[32]Ibid., From the late 1840's and early 1850's Loudoun had at best only a few supporters of the third party movement, known as the Free Soil party. During 1848, Samuel M. Janney, according to the September 28, 1848, issue of *The National Era*, rejected nomination as an elector on the Free Soil ticket on the grounds that, although he was in "sympathy with the Free Soil movement," he did not believe it was "expendient for ministers of the Gospel to take any office by which they may become involved in the turmoil of a political contest." In a letter stating the above, the Loudoun Quaker also stated his objections to the Mexican War of 1846-48 on the grounds that American participation was unjustifiable. He not only condemned the attempts to expand slavery into newly acquired territory but feared for "the large proportion of the existing inhabitants of New Mexico and California" that were "of mixed blood." Janney reasoned that because of "the

representatives in the state House of Delegates from the early 1830's to 1840 were Whigs.³³ The Loudoun press was also dominated by the Whig point of view. *The Washingtonian*, established in 1818, originally espoused the Federalist line, but during the 1830's into the 1850's it was a Whig organ. Although *The Genius of Liberty* originally was pro-Democratic-Republican, it became a spokesman for Whig views until its demise in the early 1840's. Another paper, *The Loudoun Chronicle*, established in the 1840's, also exposed the Whig viewpoint.³⁴ To counteract the lack of a newspaper in the county to champion the positions of the Democratic party, *The Spirit of Democracy* was printed in 1840.³⁵ This sheet failed to make a significant impact upon the political climate of Loudoun as it probably ceased publication during 1842. Not until the Whig party disintegrated as a national party during the 1850's did a Democratic newspaper become a successful and influential paper in Loudoun.³⁶

A substantial increase in the number of Loudouners who voted occurred long before the realization of universal white male suffrage in Virginia. This did not exist in the state until the constitution of 1851 went into effect and eliminated as a voting prerequisite the ownership of at least twenty-five acres of improved land.³⁷ The greatest increase in the

Indian, the Spaniard, and the African" were mingled in every variety of hue, should the laws of the slave states be introduced" in lands known as the Mexican Cession then "everyone... who has *negro blood* in his veins will be liable to be reduced to slavery, unless he takes measures to prove his freedom."

In the state political conventions held in 1851 John Janney, Charles B. Tebbs, and James Kilgour represented Loudoun Whigs at Charlottesville on September 25, and Colonel Joel L. Nixon, John Norris, and Captain Charles Douglas attended the Democratic convention at Staunton, held on September 21 of the same year.

³³Simms, *The Rise of Whigs in Virginia, 1824-1840*, pp. 167-91. For example, Loudouners elected the following Whigs to the House of Delegates of the Virginia state legislature that met in: 1843, John Janney, Lewis Beard, and John M. McCarty; 1835, Lewis Beard, George C. Powell, Timothy Taylor, Jr.; 1836, Robert T. Luckett, N. S. Braden, Lewis Beard; 1837, Robert T. Luckett, Lewis Beard, Timothy Taylor, Jr.; 1838, Lewis Beard, Sanford J. Raney, Timothy Taylor, Jr.; 1839, Lewis Beard, Sanford J. Raney, H. T. Harrison; 1840, Lewis Beard, Sanford J. Raney, and H. T. Harrison.

³⁴Lester J. Cappon, *Virginia Newspapers, 1821-1935* (New York: Appleton-Century-Crofts, 1936), pp. 111-13. The original founder of *The Loudoun Chronicle* sold the paper during the late 1840's, and the new owner took a position more favorable to the Democratic party.

³⁵Ibid., pp. 5,113.

³⁶Ibid., pp. 111-13.

³⁷Ambler, *Sectionalism in Virginia from 1776 to 1861*, pp. 137-38. For a time after 1776, to vote in an election in Virginia one had to own fifty acres of land. Until 1831, merchants, mechanics, and others unattached to the soil were ineligible to vote. The constitution of 1831 did extend the right to vote to select non-landowners: housekeepers or heads of

percentage of Loudoun voter participation in Presidential elections occurred between 1824 and 1844. During that span the number of ballots cast by Loudoun voters increased from 232 to 1,971. Demographic increase was not the reason for the increase in the number of voters because the population of the county decreased from 22,702 in 1820 to 20,431 in 1840. Since realty qualifications were not altered during this period and demographic increases were not a factor in explaining the increment in voter qualification prior to 1851, the only plausible explanation is that property qualification was not a salient encumbrance upon males in Loudoun's agrarian antebellum society. Voter participation, instead, depended primarily upon voter interest in elections.[38]

Opposition in Loudoun to the politics of the Democratic party during the age of Jackson was not due to a rejection of nationalism and a supreme allegiance to the philosophy of States' rights. Instead, it resulted from a belief in nationalism that differed from that of the Jacksonians which many Loudoun citizens assumed to be incorrect.[39] Loudouners wanted Jackson to take a more positive stand on some aspects of economic nationalism, namely internal improvements and the Bank of the United States (B.U.S.) They viewed his limited support of internal improvements and his vigorous opposition to the national bank as negative forms of political nationalism that were bringing about an excessive concentration of political power in the Presidency. Mercer expressed this view openly, thereby making him an anti-administration spokesman who incurred the displeasure of Jackson. In retaliation, Jackson had Mercer

---

families who were residents for one year and leaseholders who could produce legal verification of their status. However, this provision only modestly increased the number of voters in Loudoun as the ownership of realty remained the major prerequisite for voting in Virginia until 1851.

[38]Ibid., p. 137; Virginius Dabney, *Virginia: The New Dominion* (4th ed.; Garden City, New York: Doubleday and Co., 1971) pp. 213,214,222; Robert E. Brown and B. Katherine Brown; *Virginia 1705-1786. Democracy or Aristocracy* (East Lansing: Michigan State University Press, 1964), pp. 14,212. Ambler and Dabney contend that only about half of the freedmen in Virginia prior to 1831 could vote. The Browns, who made a comprehensive study of voting in eighteenth-century Virginia, refute the traditional view set forth by Ambler and Dabney and maintain eligible male voters were so numerous prior to the American Revolution that Virginia could be called a "representative democracy." To be sure, the 728-vote increase in the Presidential election the year after the constitution of 1851 went into effect was the largest numerical increase in voter participation in Loudoun during the period from 1824 to 1852. But the significance of this figure is greatly reduced when compared to the dramatic increase in percentage of ballots cast in the county in Presidential elections from 1824 to 1848. The latter tends to support the thesis set forth by Robert Brown and his wife.

[39]Margaret (Peggy) O'Neal's marriage to Jackson's Secretary of War, John H. Eaton, created a rift in Jackson's cabinet. This vivacious daughter of a Washington tavern keeper was born in a log house in Loudoun County, located five miles north of Round Hill.

removed as the president of the Chesapeake and Ohio Canal Company in 1833, a position Mercer had held since 1828.[40]

The one aspect of economic nationalism to which Loudoun citizens did not give their unflinching support was high protective tariffs. Their representative in Congress, Charles Mercer, voted against the Tariff of Abominations of 1828. However, he voted for the Tariff of 1832 due to the meek compromise feature, despite the fact that the 1832 act retained protectionism, with duties only slightly lower than those of the act of 1828.[41] Not all Loudouners found protective tariffs offensive. S. B. T. Caldwell in a broadside stating his views on the issues of his day supported the concept of protectionism and was proud to announce:

> ... I have ever been a warm advocate of the "American system," and of internal improvements--and as decidedly opposed to the doctrine of NULLIFICATION, in all its

Table 7. Number and Distribution of Votes Cast by Citizens of Loudoun County in Presidential Elections from 1824 to 1852.

Year	Political Party			Total
	Democrat (or precursor)	Whig (or precursor)	Other	
1824	62	102	68	232
1828	229	525	0	754
1832	317	838	7	1,162
1836	254	935	2	1,191
1840	381	1,269	0	1,650
1844	474	1,505	0	1,979
1848	420	1,453	0	1,873
1852	788	1,813	0	2,601

[a]All Presidential candidates in the 1824 election were technically Democratic-Republicans.

---

[40]Ambler, *Sectionalism in Virginia*, pp. 184-85; Trumbo, "Charles Fenton Mercer, 1778-1858," pp. 62-65. Mercer had earlier denounced Jackson in 1819 in a speech in Congress, in which he condemned the general's execution of two British citizens, Alexander Arbuthnot and Robert Ambrister, in Florida. In 1832, Mercer proposed that Congress consider ways of reducing the powers of the executive branch. All of these were factors in Jackson's dislike of Mercer.

[41]Ambler, *Sectionalism in Virginia*, pp. 122-23, 204-05; Trumbo, "Charles Fenton Mercer, 1778-1858," p. 45.

modes and tenses. And permit me to add, that at no period of my life have I been more thoroughly convinced, that the stability of our government, and the prosperity of our common country, essentially depends upon the steady pursuit of, and adherence to these doctrines.[42]

In the constitutional crisis that resulted from South Carolina's nullification of the Tariffs of 1828 and 1832 and Jackson's insistence upon state compliance to federal law, Loudoun's representatives in the state legislature reflected the county's dedication to nationalism. They voted against a resolution that mildly approved South Carolina's course of action in the nullification controversy.[43] The continuing impact of nationalism in Loudoun throughout the 1830's and 1840's was also significant in altering the political stance of one Loudoun paper, *The Genius of Libery*, from a States' rights position held prior to 1820 to one by 1840 dedicated to "ONE CONSTITUTION — ONE COUNTRY — ONE DESTINY."[44]

The nationalistic posture of the majority of Loudoun voters on internal improvements, their views on slavery, and the need for political reform within the state were echoed by their representatives in the state and federal legislatures, and often allied the cismontane area of Loudoun with the transmontane counties of the Old Dominion.[45] Since the colonial period, a regional or sectional strife had existed between the older society of the east and the areas later settled farther west.[46] During the Jacksonian era northern and western regions of the state, peopled primarily by small farmers, were at odds with the piedmont and tidewater areas controlled by slave-holding planters. They argued over representation, suffrage, and abuses in state and local governments. Loudoun voted in 1828 with the western counties for the calling of a state constitutional convention to remedy these problems.[47]

---

[42]S. B. T. Caldwell, *To the Voters of Loudoun*, August 5, 1831.
[43]Ambler, *Sectionalism in Virginia*, pp. 216-17.
[44]*The Genius of Liberty*, November 14, 1840. (This paper by 1840 was officially called *The Leesburg Genius of Liberty*.) Also a factor in the paper's shift in political ideology was the change in publishers. By 1840 the paper was being published no longer by the Sower's family, but by George Richards.
[45]Ambler, op. cit., pp. 1-5, 70-71, 130-31, 134-35, 144-45, 198-99, 216-17.
[46]Ibid., pp. 1-5.
[47]Ibid., pp. 137-44; Dabney, *Virginia*, pp. 214-15; Simms, *The Rise of the Whigs in Virginia*, pp. 36-37. By 1828 on the basis of population, representation in the state legislature heavily favored the eastern section of the state. Voting was limited to owners of property. A free-holder could vote several times during the same election if he owned property worth at least twenty-five dollars in several nearby counties. By riding furiously a man could cast a ballot in one precinct in three or four counties. County courts also were often dominated by a few or limited number of gentry within the county. Members

The Virginia constitutional convention of 1829-30 was "the last gathering of giants" of Virginia political figures of the late 1700's and early 1800's.[48] In attendance were such venerable men of national prominence as Madison, Marshall, and Monroe. Monroe one of three delegates from Loudoun that included Charles F. Mercer and Richard H. Henderson, was unanimously elected president of the convention. Ill health soon forced the former President of the United States to resign as chairman of the convention. Mercer took an active role in the convention, which included speaking out for reforms, such as supporting fairer representation for the western counties in the state legislature.[49] The results of the convention and the changes set forth in the new constitution it drafted were meager and fell far short of the goals of western delegates and reformers. Only discontent in the counties of the northern piedmont and Shenandoah Valley was appreciably decreased as the result of constitutional reform. As a northern piedmont county, Loudoun was a beneficiary of the increased representation granted to that region and the Shenandoah Valley. The number of Loudoun's delegates in the lower house of the General Assembly was increased from two to three. Subsequently Loudouners voted for ratification of the constitution of 1830, which went into effect due to the heavy pro-constitution vote of the eastern counties of the state.[50]

A common political practice in Loudoun during the Jacksonian period was the political rally.[51] Such an occasion was a "Whig Festival" held at Leesburg on Tuesday and Wednesday, October 15 and 16, during the Presidential campaign of 1844. A "string of carriages" brought people from all regions of the county. Rain and muddy roads forced the first day celebration to be held at the courthouse. On the second day a multitude gathered in Leesburg to march to a grounds in "a beautiful woods" set aside for the occasion, located three-quarters of a mile from town. The parade to the speakers' stand consisted of carriages of those

---

of the county court were appointed by the governor, but on only the recommendation of the sheriff. The court's role combined executive, legislative, and judicial functions of county government. Its duties ranged from that of a court of law to appointing civil officers and all military officials below the rank of brigadier-general to setting the rate of county taxes. The sheriff was often too close to the court to suit many people because this office was often rotated among members of the county court who accepted the position as a means of compensating for their "gratuitous services as judges."

[48]Dabney, *Virginia*, p. 216; Richard B. David, *Intellectual Life in Jefferson's Virginia* (Chapel Hill: University of North Carolina Press, 1964), pp. 22-23.

[49]Virginia, *Proceeding and Debates of the Virginia State Convention of 1829-30*, pp. 1,4,21; Trumbo, "Charles Fenton Mercer, 1778-1858," pp. 55-57.

[50]Ambler, *Sectionalism in Virginia*, pp. 165-66, 170-73.

[51]Simms, *The Rise of the Whigs in Virginia*, p. 90. Loudoun Whigs turned out in large numbers at Leesburg on June 26, 1834. At this political rally letters were read from Clay, Calhoun, and others praising Virginia on "her stand against executive encroachment and arbitrary power." Such political rallies were frequently held at Leesburg.

who had not already assembled at the grounds and instrumental and vocal musical groups comprised of bands from many places, including "Glee Clubs" from Alexandria, Georgetown, Harper's Ferry, and Charlestown. Once at the festival grounds Charles F. Mercer, the main speaker who had formerly been elected upon numerous occasions to represent Loudoun, gave a lengthy address that included his views on tariffs, annexation of Texas, United States Bank, and the distribution of the proceeds from the sale of public land among the states. John Janney, the man who would succeed Mercer as Loudoun's most respected politician and at that time Whig elector in the forthcoming election, made a few succinct remarks predicting that Loudoun would vote overwhelmingly for Clay for President.[52]

While attendance at the county Whig festival at Leesburg in 1844 was truly extensive, its magnitude was considerably less than that associated with Lafayette's visit to Loudoun in 1825. For the latter event an estimated crowd of 10,000, almost half of Loudoun's population, turned out for what has been called "the greatest social event in the history of Leesburg." The Leesburg celebration grew out of General Lafayette's and President John Q. Adams' three-day visit with ex-President Monroe at the latter's home, Oak Hill.[53] Lafayette and Adams accepted an invitation by the citizens of Leesburg to visit their town located approximately nine miles north of Oak Hill.[54] A troop of cavalry commanded by Captains Chichester and Bradfield escorted the illustrious guests to Leesburg.[55] As the procession drew near to Leesburg

---

[52] *The Loudoun Times-Mirror*, August 7, 1959. Reprint of excerpts from the diary of Samuel S. Birkley, a carriage-maker who lived in Leesburg during the Jacksonian age. His diary also records Major Fairfax of Fairfax County making a short speech at the Leesburg courthouse during 1846 in an attempt to get Loudouners to join him in forming a company to go to Mexico and fight in the Mexican War. Birkley's diary also mentions a meeting held at the courthouse which adopted resolutions to raise money and provisions for the relief of the Irish, who were suffering a famine due to the "failure of the potato crop."

[53] Head, *History of Loudoun County*, pp. 142,144. Monroe's palatial three-story home with a Grecian facade and a portico with hugh Doric columns was not constructed until after he became President. Tradition maintains Monroe lived for a time prior to his ascendancy to the Presidency in a humble wooden structure near where he constructed his new home. Later burdened by the lack of money, failing health, and the death of his wife in 1830, the former President reluctantly sold Oak Hill in 1831 and went to live his remaining years in New York.

[54] Robert D. Ward, comp., *An Account of General Lafayette's Visit to Virginia* (Richmond, Va.: West, Johnson, and Co., 1881), pp. 103-04. Mr. Ball, a member of the committee of arrangements, and Mr. Henderson, of the town council, went to Oak Hill and invited the famous men to Leesburg for a public celebration in their honor.

[55] Ibid., p.104. The General, the President of the United States, the ex-President, and Mr. Henderson were in the first carriage, "drawn by four elegant bay horses, provided for the occasion."

on August 9, the artillery of Captain Shreve's company was fired and according to one observer:

> Multitudes of people lined the road, and crowded forward to behold the veteran apostle of Liberty, attended by the Chief Magistrate of a great and free people, and by one of his brave companions-in-arms, himself recently retired from the first honors of the republic.[56]

Upon arrival at Leesburg they alighted in the field of William M. McCarty, and under the shade of an oak tree Lafayette was introduced to the town's committee members and officials who planned the celebration. He then reviewed Loudoun's current militia and was introduced to a few Loudoun veterans of the Revolutionary War.[57] The procession then moved to Colonel Osborne's hotel, where the mayor, Dr. John H. McCabe, and the "common council of Leesburg" were introduced to their guests and a welcome address was delivered by McCabe. After the guest had partaken of "slight refreshments" in "a large room of the hotel," they toured all of the main streets of the town: Loudoun, Market, Back, Cornwall, and King streets. Next the procession proceeded to the courthouse, where a tribute to Lafayette was made by a Loudoun youth that reflected the pervasive influence of the classics and was reminiscent of a tribute to a Roman warrior or emperor. From the gate of the courthouse square to the portico of the courthouse an avenue was formed by two lines of area school children. One line was comprised of the young ladies of the Leesburg Female Academy dressed in white with blue sashes and their "heads adorned with evergreens." As the General passed them, they put sprigs of laurel they held in their hands in his path as the left line formed by lads of the Leesburg Institute dressed in "sashes and white and black cockades" watched attentively.[58] Just prior to Lafayette's reaching the portico of the courthouse, a boy gave "a very neat address" followed by a little girl holding a "wreath of laurel" who gave the following tribute:

---

[56]Ibid. This description was provided by a Mr. Le Vasseur, who accompanied Lafayette to Oak Hill and Leesburg.

[57]Cuthbert Powell, the chairman of the committee on arrangements, and General Rust, marshal of the day, were among those introduced to the famed Frenchman. The military force consisted of two volunteer troops of cavalry, commanded by Captains Chichester and Bradfield; Captains Moore and Cockerill, and two rifle companies commanded by Captains Henry and Humphries.

[58]Head, *History of Loudoun County*, p. 143; Ward, *An Account of General Lafayette's Visit to Virginia*, p. 105.

> *Hail! patriot, statesman, hero, sage;*
> *Hail! freedom's friend! Hail, Gallias's son!*
> *Whose laurels greener grow in age,*
> *Plucked by the side of Washington.*
>
> *Hail! champion, in a holy cause!*
> *When hostile bands our shores beset,*
> *Whose valor blade the oppressor pause,*
> *Hail! holy warrior, LaFayette!*[59]

Lafayette responded by taking the hand of the young speaker and saluting her. On behalf of the adult citizens of the county, Ludwell Lee "addressed the General in a patriotic speech," to which Lafayette "replied in a handsome manner."[60] The concluding ceremonies started at four o'clock in the afternoon when the honored guests:

> . . . were escorted to the courthouse square, in which, under an extensive awning, a splendid and elegant dinner, prepared by Mr. Henry Peers, was set out and tastefully ornamented by arches of evergreens with appropriate devices and mottoes.[61]

Innumerable toasts were made by President Adams, Lafayette, Monroe, and more than thirty-five county figures who honored the triumvirate of international fame, the town of Leesburg, and the people of Loudoun, and the uniqueness and nobility of the American mission for mankind in securing the "republican blessings of independence, freedom, and equal rights" that emanated from the American Revolution, in which the venerated Lafayette played a benevolent role. Lafayette and his party spent the night at the mansion of Ludwell Lee east of Leesburg and the following day set out for Washington, D. C.[62]

Leesburg was the center of Loudoun's political, and to a lesser extent, economic life during the Jacksonian era. One of Loudoun's leading Quakers, Yardley Taylor, described the town of 1,700 people in 1835 as "a neat village located near a small ridge of mountains." This post village and seat of justice was located thirty-one miles northwest

---

[59] Ward, op. cit., p. 105.
[60] Ibid., p. 106.
[61] Ibid. Head maintained two hundred people "participated in this banquet."
[62] Ibid., pp. 107-08. Before spending the night at the Lee mansion, the guests went to the residence of W. T. T. Mason in Loudoun, where Mason's two young daughters were baptized, "for one of whom General Lafayette stood god-father, and for the other the late and present President."

of Washington and 153 miles north of the state capital, and one and one-half miles south of the Potomac River. The hamlet contained about 500 houses, twenty-two general stores, three churches, one bank, two apothecary shops, three schools, and four taverns.[63] In an attempt to offer greater security for these structures, the town formed a fire company in 1827. The official name for this "bucket brigade" was "The Leesburg Star Fire Company." Their equipment consisted primarily of buckets made entirely of heavy hide, shaped similar to a stovepipe hat. Every member of the fire company was equipped with two buckets, one for each hand.[64]

Numerous skilled mechanics and related establishments were located in the town in 1835. These consisted of tanners, three saddlers, four house carpenters, four shoe factories, three tailor establishments, one cabinet maker, three tin plate workers, one coppersmith, one locksmith, three blacksmiths, one coachmaker, one wagon maker, one turner and chair maker, two hat factories, and two printing offices, each issuing a weekly paper. Professional medical and legal services were provided by the town's five practicing physicians, two dentists, and seven "resident attorneys."[65] A "barbering business" was also located in the town. During 1820, Thomas Williams advertised that "he flatters himself that he cannot be surpassed by any in the county for good shaving, and neatness of cutting and dressing hair." Barber Williams offered gentlemen of the area the option of paying for his services by the year, half year, or every three months.[66]

The streets of Leesburg were "well paved" and the "town supplied with fine water, in pipes of wood from a spring issuing at the base of the Kottoctin mountains." Taylor also claimed that Leesburg was "not excelled for morality by any town in Virginia."[67] Officials of the county court who handed out justice hoped that the fear of trial and possible incarceration inspired acceptable social behavior for not only the town

---

[63] During May 8, 1820, a bad hail storm hit the Leesburg area. Exceptionally large stones broke 3,000 to 4,000 panes of glass from windows of buildings in town and "completely covered" the streets with hail. In 1836, another vagary of the weather hit Loudoun. Rain commenced on June 1 and continued until the eleventh day of that month. From June 11 showers came daily until June 21, when unabated rain set in for several days.

[64] *The Loudoun Times-Mirror*, August 9, 1934. Each hide bucket held about two gallons of water. At the meetings of the Leesburg Star Fire Company, any member refusing to comply with the rules or who used "disorderly" expressions was fined fifty cents. Every violation of the company's by-laws was punishable by a one dollar fine.

[65] Joseph Martin, ed., *A New Comprehensive Gazetteer of Virginia* (Charlottesville: Mosely and Tompkins, Printers, 1835), pp. 211-12.

[66] *The Genius of Liberty*, July 25, 1820. The daily services of Williams for one year cost $12, three times a week for one year $8, twice a week for a year $6, and once a week for a year $4.

[67] Martin, op. cit., pp. 211-12. The town was governed by a mayor and twelve councillors.

but also the county as well.⁶⁸ Records of the county jailor reveal that during much of the Jacksonian era, the latter years of the 1820's and the early 1830's, about seven people were committed to the county jail a month. For example, during the above period 182 were jailed. Among them, six were charged with felonies, including two persons for murder, twenty-two with "breaches of the peace," one with petty larceny, and four with counterfeiting. In addition to horse thieves, slaves believed to have run away from their owners, and lunatics were also housed in the county jail.⁶⁹

BANKS

The first bank in Loudoun County was located in Waterford. It was established by The Loudoun Company, which was organized on March 28, 1815, by local investors who met in Waterford at Joseph Talbott's tavern.⁷⁰ Facilities were certainly unpretentious as the directors rented Isaac Steer's "store room" in his Waterford home for $75 a year. The inability of The Loudoun Company to obtain a charter for its bank doomed that financial institution to bankruptcy. In an attempt to unite efforts in petitioning the state legislature for charters, the directors met several times at Winchester, Virginia, with the directors of other unchartered banks of northern and western Virginia. But the legislature was dominated by easterners who opposed the creation of additional state banks. The General Assembly during 1816 passed an act suppressing all unchartered banks in the state, including that of The Loudoun Company.⁷¹

In 1817 the state did incorporate the Bank of the Valley, located in Winchester.⁷² During the same year the state legislature approved

---

⁶⁸County court was held on the second Monday in March, June, August, and November. The Circuit Court of Law and Chancery was held during April and in September.

⁶⁹*The Loudoun Times-Mirror,* May 14, 1964. This period extended from August 5, 1828, to January 1, 1831. During this period three lunatics were put into the county jail.

⁷⁰Helen Hirst Marsh, "The Loudoun Company," *The Bulletin of the Loudoun County Historical Society,* III (1962), 43-44. Twelve directors of The Loudoun Company were elected at this meeting: James Moore, Robert Braden, Asa Moore, John Williams, Abiel Jenners, George Janney, Samuel Clapham, John Hamilton, Joshua Osburn, Cornelius Shawen, John Morgan, and Jacob Mendenhall. On April 12, 1815, Daniel Eaches was appointed a director to fill the vacancy created by the appointment of Jacob Mendenhall to cashier.

⁷¹Ibid., 44-48; Ambler, *Sectionalism in Virginia,* pp. 237-38. The last board meeting of the directors was held on January 10, 1824. The western counties of Virginia wanted the incorporation of "additional independent state banks." They argued this move was necessary to provide financial aid for internal improvements.

⁷²Ambler, *Sectionalism in Virginia,* p. 238.

establishing a branch of this bank at Leesburg. *The Genius of Liberty* notified the public that:

> ... the commissioners appointed by the last legislature of Virginia, to receive subscriptions, for stock of the bank of the Valley, at Leesburg, will open books for this purpose on the 1st day of Nov. next at Mr. Austin's tavern in the town of Leesburg. The books will be kept open ten days.[73]

The branch of the Valley Bank opened its doors in Leesburg in 1818 at the corner of Market and Church streets.[74] During March 1818, two men, Grub and Master, traveled two days to reach Leesburg from Alexandria with a wagon carrying $60,000 in specie for the branch bank. The importance of the arrival of specie was interpreted by the editor of *The Genius of Liberty* as "laying" the "foundation for the emission of a paper currency predicated upon specie capital," which the editor correctly pointed out was at that time "the chief corner stone in all monied institutions; without it they must eventually fall."[75]

During the age of Jackson the bank at Leesburg helped finance important segments of the county's economic life. By 1838 the most significant clients of this bank were those involved in thirty-nine accounts, each owing the bank in excess of $5,000. Leesburg merchants alone had borrowed more than $45,697, although most of the borrowers were Loudoun farmers. A Loudoun slave trader got $5,900 from the bank to enable him to purchase slaves to sell to the lower South.[76]

REVOLUTION IN TRANSPORTATION

The catalyst for much of America's economic growth prior to 1860 can be attributed to the revolution in transportation. Technological innovations, coupled with the public demand for cheaper and faster modes of transportation, led enterprising men to maintain that turnpikes, then canals, and finally railroads and steamboats were transportation panaceas.[77]

---

[73] *The Genius of Liberty*, October 14, 1817. The capital stock was divided into shares of $100 to be paid in five installments of $20 each. The first "at the time of subscribing and the remaining four on the first day of January, March, May, and July" 1818.

[75] *The Genius of Liberty*, March 31, 1818.

[76] Virginia, House of Delegates, *Journal*, 1838, Doc. No. 53, pp. 1-4. The thirty-nine accounts consisted of both single and joint accounts.

[76] Virginia, House of Delegates, *Journal*, 1838, Doc. No. 53, pp. 1-4.

[77] George R. Taylor, *The Transportation Revolution, 1815-1860* (New York: Harper and Row, 1951), pp. 22-23, 32-33, 74-75.

Aspects of the transportation revolution that touched Loudoun involved the turnpike, canal, and railroad. Not only did these not turn out to be a cure-all for mobility, but in many instances they were a resounding failure.

Turnpikes in northern Virginia resulted from the establishment of trade during the latter part of the colonial period between towns on the Potomac River and the Shenandoah Valley. As the traffic increased between the two regions, the primitive road systems between the Potomac River and the gaps in the Blue Ridge Mountain steadily deteriorated not only from use but also the lack of proper maintenance. The latter resulted from a statute of 1748 under which all roads were considered to be the responsiblity of the local communities. Maintenance was directed by the county courts with conscripted labor of the "tithables," all residents who lived two or three miles from a road being called to work upon the pike. Local residents who resented having to work a local road for their own use were not about to repair damages to byways inflicted by foreign wagoners who traversed their community from the transmontane region to the tidewater. Merchants at Alexandria were keenly aware of this barrier to their economic prosperity and lobbied during the Revolutionary period for remedial legislation. In response to this situation, the legislature enacted legislation from which would emerge the turnpike system, private road companies chartered by the state to build and maintain roads for profit by charging toll at select intervals.[78]

One of the first and few successful private turnpike companies in Virginia, the Little River Turnpike Company owned and operated thirty-four miles of "paved" road from Alexandria to the ford of Little River, the location of a village later known as Aldie. This company, organized in 1802, opened its road for traffic in 1806. This was one of the few turnpike companies in Virginia which paid regular dividends to its stockholders. Credit for this achievement was due to the able and pragmatic management by the president of the company, who was also an energetic Quaker and Alexandria businessman, Phineas Janney. Other turnpike companies soon built roads that connected the Little River Turnpike with roads leading to Warrenton and the Valley of Virginia. Two such companies, the Snickers' Gap Turnpike Company and the Ashby's Gap Turnpike Company, chartered at the end of the first decade of the nineteenth century, constructed new roadbeds or improved existing

---

[78]Harrison, *Landmarks of Old Prince William*, pp. 561-62. A state law of 1785 authorized the trustees appointed by the county courts of Fairfax and Loudoun to collect tolls and erect toll gates across roads from "Snigger's and Vestal's gaps to Alexandria." The original tolls under this act were 1s, 3d. for a coach or other four-wheeled riding carriage; two-wheel riding vehicle the charge was 8d; loaded or unloaded wagon, 1s.; cart, 6d. These fees were modified shortly because the above rates were collected without regard for the distance traveled.

ones in southwestern Loudoun from the Little River Turnpike at Aldie to the two mountain gaps in the Blue Ridge after which the two companies were named. This network of roads emerged as the most vital and significant link between Alexandria and the Valley of Virginia prior to the advent of railroads.[79]

Aid for turnpike construction was obtained in part by the efforts of a Loudoun delegate to the General Assembly, Charles Mercer. Mercer labored from 1812 to 1817 for the construction of turnpikes and waterways in Virginia. He introduced bills that were instrumental in the establishment in 1816 of a state fund for internal improvements under the supervision of a Board of Public Works.[80]

The act of 1801 that granted legal permission for the formation of the Little River Turnpike Company aptly described the mode and nature of travel in Loudoun and elsewhere in Virginia during the age of Jefferson and Jackson. For instance, for every ten-mile segment on this road the following sums were to be paid by travelers or drovers driving livestock to market:

> *For every score of sheep. . . hogs . . . twelve cents, for every score of cattle twenty-five cents, and so in proportion for any greater or lesser number; for every horse six cents, for every two wheeled riding carriage twelve and a half cents, for every four wheeled riding carriage twenty-five cents, for every cart or wagon the wheels whereof do not exceed four inches in breadth, six cents, for each horse drawing the same; if the wheels exceed four inches, and are less than seven inches in breadth, three cents for each horse drawing the same, and where the breadth of the wheels exceed seven inches, two cents for each horse drawing the same, and every mule or ox drawing a wagon or cart shall be estimated in paying the said tolls as equal to a horse . . . .[81]*

---

[79]Ibid., pp. 564-65, 577-78; Virginia, Board of Public Works, *Annual Reports*, 1816-1818, pt. 2, pp. 13-14. (Hereafter referred to as *Annual Reports*.) The earliest private turnpike company chartered in Virginia, the Fairfax and Loudoun Turnpike Company, was chartered by the state in 1796 to build and manage a road from Alexandria to the ford of the Little River. The company was not successfully organized, so in 1801 a law was enacted by the state legislature that stated the Little River Turnpike Company was to supersede the Fairfax and Loudoun Turnpike Company, Commissioners appointed from Loudoun for the unsuccessful Fairfax and Loudoun Turnpike were Levin Powell of Middleburg, Thomas Lewis of Leesburg, Richard B. Lee, and Samuel Love.

[80]Jean Gottmann, *Virginia in Our Century* (rev. ed.; Charlottesville: The University of Virginia Press, 1969), p. 106; Trumbo, "Charles Fenton Mercer, 1778-1858," pp. 22-24. The Board of Public Works was the predecessor of Virginia's Department of Highways.

[81]Virginia, *The Statutes at Large, Being a Collection of All the Laws of Virginia*, edited by Samuel Shephard (Richmond, 1823-36), II, 385-86. (Hereafter referred to as Shephard, *Statutes*.

This act and subsequent legislation strongly encouraged the use of wide wheels on wagons in an attempt to reduce the problem of ruts being cut in the turnpike during wet weather by loads conveyed in wagons with narrow-width wheels.[82] Weight limitations in accordance with width of wheels were to be rigorously enforced from December to May, and at no season of the year were any wagons to carry more than five tons.[83] Rules regulating the use of these early turnpikes and fines for failing to observe them were precursors of modern traffic laws and fines. For example, on the Little River Turnpike "all drivers of every kind of carriage. . .except in the passing of a carriage of slower draft, shall keep their horses and carriages to the right hand side of said road." Violations of this rule could result in a two-dollar fine. Persons evading the payment of tolls were subject to penalty of "not less than three nor more than ten dollars."[84]

Motivated by the thought of emulating the success of the Little River Turnpike, businessmen in northern Virginia and Georgetown formed another major turnpike system that later traversed the northeast and northwest portions of Loudoun County. Farmers and businessmen in the area of Leesburg were anxious to become a part of the Little River road complex, which would greatly improve travel between the county seat and Alexandria. In an attempt to realize this goal, the people of Leesburg formed a corporation, awkwardly named the "President, Directors and Company of the Leesburg Turnpike Road." As this company slowly constructed a new road east from Leesburg in the direction of Sugarland Run, the businessmen of Georgetown, envious of their competitors in Alexandria, were able to divert the course of the Leesburg Turnpike and prevent its connection with the Little River Turnpike. Under the enticement provided by the directors of the Georgetown Turnpike Company, who promised to construct a road from Georgetown to Loudoun's eastern boundary, the Leesburg company had its original charter amended.

During late 1822 the Leesburg Turnpike merged with the Georgetown Turnpike near Loudoun's eastern boundary and Sugarland Run at Drane's tavern, the site of a hamlet later known as Dranesville.[85] After achieving a better connection with the nation's capital and

---

[82]Ibid., pp. 386, 452-53. Returning wagons and carts carrying less than 500 pounds were exempt from paying toll.

[83]Ibid., II, 452-53. Legislation of 1803 authorized the Little River Turnpike Company to erect scales at tollgates to ascertain the weight contained in wagons. Those guilty of carrying weight more than the law allowed were subject to a fine imposed by the justice of the peace of "five dollars with costs."

[84]Ibid., pp. 453-54.

[85]*The Genius of Liberty*, January 7, 1823; Harrison, *Landmarks of Old Prince William*, pp. 566-67, 570, 577-80. In 1813, two companies were chartered in the District of Columbia to construct turnpikes connecting Leesburg with Georgetown and Alexandria. It appears

Georgetown, enterprising dreamers at Leesburg planned to extend their modern road to the northwest to join the Cumberland Road and thereby place Leesburg on a major route for western traffic. In 1828, Richard H. Henderson and others obtained a charter for the Northern Turnpike Company in a futile attempt to achieve this lofty goal. More successful was the Leesburg and Snickers' Gap Turnpike Company, chartered in the early 1830's, which soon opened an improved road from Leesburg west to Snickers' Gap in anticipation of diverting traffic from the older Snickers' Gap and the Little River turnpikes.[86] Later a branching off from the Leesburg Turnpike at Clark's Gap in a northwestern direction became an improved road, constructed by the Hillsborough (Hillsboro) and Harper's Ferry Turnpike Company chartered in the late 1840's. This road was constructed to join northern Loudoun with the B. & O. Railroad. Also chartered during the 1840's was the Waterford and Point of Rocks Turnpike Company. Prior to the Civil War, travel north and south through Loudoun was improved as the results of the work of the Leesburg and Point of Rocks Turnpike Company and the Leesburg and Aldie Turnpike Company. These two companies constructed roads that connected Leesburg with Point of Rocks, Maryland, and the Little River Turnpike near Aldie.[87] However, of all the turnpikes constructed in Loudoun the most important were those systems related to the Little River Turnpike and the Leesburg Turnpike. These turnpikes curiously formed parallel "Y" configurations.

Turnpikes in Loudoun and other areas of northern Virginia were constructed from funds obtained from individual stockholders, with a small percentage of money obtained from shares purchased by the State Board of Public Works. This method is illustrated by the Ashby's Gap Turnpike Company, which sold, as did other companies, shares for $100

---

that Leesburg offered to trade at either of the two places, depending on which would offer the best deal. Alexandria merchants, who already had a successful link with the Valley of Virginia, were less anxious to make as appealing an offer as the businessmen of Georgetown. The road from Dranesville to Alexandria remained too defective to charge tolls until the end of the 1830's, at which time the Middle Turnpike connecting Alexandria and Dranesville was completed.

[86] Virginia, *Acts of the General Assembly of the State of Virginia, 1827-28*. An ad was placed in the April 14, 1832, issue of *The Genius of Liberty* by the president of the Leesburg and Snickers' Gap Turnpike Company, Presley Cordell of Leesburg, for road contractors to make "sealed proposals for M'adamizing four miles of the Leesburg and Snickers' Gap Road.". Conditions to be met by the contractor getting the job were the division of the road into sections of a half mile each, "with paving to be eighteen feet wide and ten inches thick, on the average" with "stones to be broken to the weight of six ounces."

[87] Harrison, *Landmarks of Old Prince William*, pp. 568, 579. Another turnpike company formed during the late antebellum era concerned with Loudoun was the Alexandria, Loudoun, and Hampshire Turnpike Company. It filed reports with the Board of Public Works in 1853 and 1854. Note that Hillsboro was spelled Hillsborough until the town of Hillsboro was incorporated in 1880.

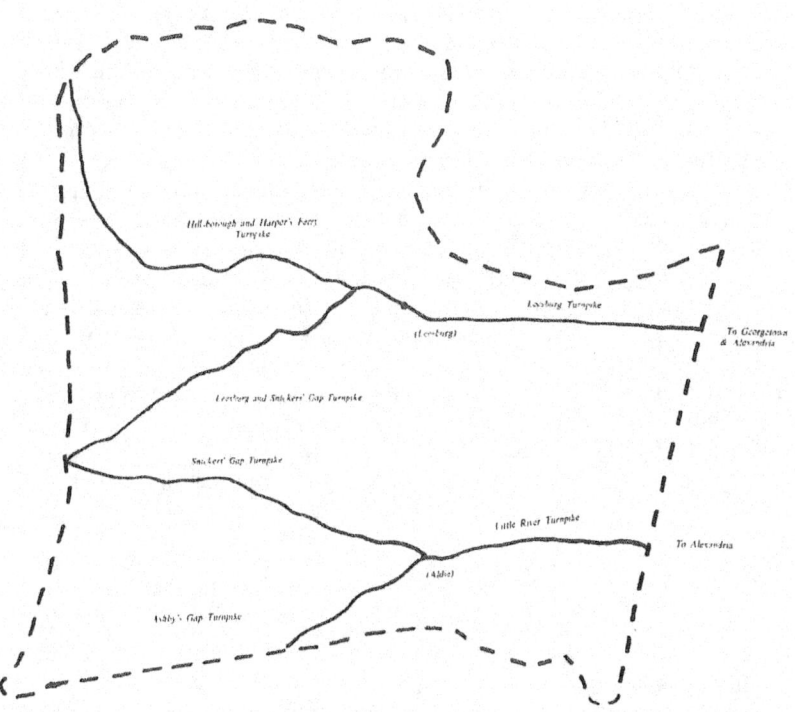

Figure 15. The "Y" Configuration of the Two Primary Turnpike Systems in Loudoun.

each, 1,246½ shares to individuals and 140 to the Board of Public Works.[88] With the exception of the successful Little River Turnpike Company, the other turnpike companies in Loudoun were shaky investments.[89] Anent this situation, a letter was printed in *The Genius of Liberty* in 1820 in an attempt to bolster the sagging confidence of stockholders who had invested in one of the major turnpike companies in Loudoun. The author pleaded to "the Stockholders in the Leesburg Road" to keep their stock as he optimistically wrote, "it is obvious this stock will yield at least 3 to 4 percent."[90] His appeal was not heeded, and even after the completion of the fifteen miles of turnpike from Leesburg to Drane's tavern many of the stockholders in the Leesburg Turnpike Company remained delinquent in their final payments due on their stocks. A notice in the January 7, 1823, issue of *The Genius of Liberty* admonished "all delinquent stockholders that if the balances due" were not paid by February 12, "then such shares will be" considered as forfeited and "will be offered at public sale, for CASH, before the Court House door, in the town of Leesburg."[91]

Despite a modicum of financial success, the turnpike systems that traversed Loudoun lingered throughout most of the nineteenth century, the last tollgates disappearing in the county after the advent of the twentieth century. However, the impetus for forming new turnpike companies had been curtailed long before the 1900's by railroads and the Civil War. This curtailment was reflected in legislation enacted in 1866, which became the obituary of turnpikes in Virginia. Under this act roads deemed abandoned by turnpike companies became the property of the counties.[92] Loudoun's two major turnpikes, Little River and Leesburg turnpikes, ceased in 1896 to be toll roads. In 1910, the state chartered a new corporation, the Washington and Leesburg Turnpike Company, to take possession and improve roads from Leesburg to

---

[88]*Annual Reports*, pp. 186-87; *The Genius of Liberty*, April 14, 1832. For example, in 1832, 1838 to 1842 dividends of four per cent were paid to stockholders in the Little River Company. Unlike this company, other turnpike companies rarely paid dividends to investors.

[89]Ibid., p. 354.

[90]*The Genius of Liberty*, February 8, 1820. Investors purchased stock on an installment plan.

[91]The town of Leesburg in 1818 had a lottery to raise $8,000 "for the purpose of paving the streets of the town." Six thousand tickets were offered for sale at five dollars each. Out of the 6,000 tickets 2,012 won prizes. First prize was $4,000. Conjecture about roads in Leesburg during the nineteenth century is stimulated by a newspaper clipping in "Loudoun County," vol. III of scrapbooks in the Thomas Balch Library, Leesburg, Va., written during the early 1900's. This clipping records that while excavating to install piping of a new water system in Leesburg in the early twentieth century, workmen dug up a piece of white oak wood. W. D. Hempstone concluded this was a part of the old corduroy road that he believed was established through the town in 1858.

[92]Harrison, *Landmarks of Old Prince William*, p. 575; *The Globe* (Fairfax, Va.), March 23, 1972.

Georgetown and Alexandria, as it was ruled that former turnpike companies of these roads had abandoned them. During the 1920's the state took over the construction and maintenance of many of Loudoun's major roads, including by the end of 1928 the stretch between Leesburg and Dranesville, formally managed by the Leesburg Turnpike Company and its successor.[93] The positive contributions of turnpikes in Loudoun have had a long-range impact upon the county. By improving old colonial roads and cutting new roadbeds, turnpike companies provided not only more reliable facilities for land travel during the nineteenth century but also roadbeds upon which the modern network of roads was constructed. The derivations of many of the roads currently traveled in Loudoun are still distinguishable from the lingering appellations derived from their turnpike origins. For example, portions of the state highway system, such as Route 50, are still known as the Little River Turnpike and Route 7 as the Leesburg Pike.

The immediate impact of the turnpike system upon Loudoun, in addition to providing more accessible roads for travel by man and livestock and the transporting of produce, was the extensive increase in stage travel and improved postal service. By 1820, mail arrived three times a week to the Leesburg post office from "Washington City" and twice a week from Winchester, other regions of western Virginia, Ohio, Kentucky, Tennessee, Alabama, Mississippi, Missouri, Indiana, and Illinois.[94] Mail from Waterford and Hillsboro, Charlestown, and Martinsburg was received only once a week.[95] By 1841 mail service to and from Leesburg to other hamlets within the county had appreciably increased. Mail delivery to Neersville, Hillsboro, and Waterford was increased to three times a week, and new weekly mail routes were established to carry mail to and from Upperville, Hughesville, Circleville, Philomont, Union, Bloomfield, Middleburg, and Noland's Ferry.[96] Areas in the county without postal service were aided by *The Genius of Liberty*, which listed from 1818 to the 1840's the names of all who had mail in the Leesburg post office. Residents were given four months to pick up their mail before it was "sent to the general post-office as dead letters."[97]

[93]Ibid., p. 580; "Minutes of the Catoctin Farmers' Club of Waterford, Virginia," X (First and Merchants National Bank, Leesburg, Va.), newspaper clipping dated August 30, 1928, p. 271.

[94]For example, mail arrived every Sunday, Tuesday, and Thursday at "4 o'clock P.M. from Washington, eastern and southern points and left Leesburg for the same at 7 o'clock P.M." on the same days.

[95]*The Genius of Liberty*, March 14, 1820. In the December 21, 1819, issue of this paper the postmaster of Leesburg, William Woodly, advertised for a post rider "to carry the mail on sundry routes" and pledged "liberal wages will be given." He further stated "a lad from 14 to 18 years of age would be preferred—None need apply but such as can come well recommended."

[96]Ibid., April 10, 1841.

[97]Ibid., April 7, 1818; April 10, 1841.

Passenger service was also provided by the mail stages. For example, Thomas J. Noland and Company ran a mail stage from Washington to Winchester via Leesburg on Tuesdays, Thursdays, and Saturdays. On these days a coach left Washington at 4:00 A.M. and completed the grueling journey to Winchester around 6:00 P.M. the same day. The return trip to the nation's capital occurred on Sundays, Wednesdays, and Fridays. Stops by Noland's stages were made in Loudoun at Leesburg, Hamilton's Store, and Purcell's Store. One-way fare to or from Washington and Winchester was $4.00, whereas the fee to travel from Leesburg to Washington was $2.50.[98]

Like the rest of the nation, a canal craze hit Loudoun during the 1820's and 1830's. But unlike the turnpike craze, which was at least a qualified success, the canal ventures in Loudoun resulted in total failure.

Inland waterways served as major highways in many areas during the colonial era. As such, the Potomac River in 1762 was looked upon by Loudouners and others as a valuable commercial asset with an even greater potential.[99] Enterprising men in Loudoun from 1785 to 1812 eagerly supported the "Patowmack Company's" attempts to enhance the navigability of the Potomac and connect it with Ohio and the rest of the area known as the Northwest Territory. Disillusioned by the failure of the "Patowmack Company" to realize its grandiose promises, Loudouners partitioned the General Assembly in 1812 and 1816 for a charter that would allow them to cut a canal parallel to the southern bank of the Potomac River from eastern Loudoun to Alexandria. Their requests were blocked by the "Patowmack Company" until 1817. During that year the Alexandria Canal Company was chartered to cut a canal from Goose Creek in Loudoun to Hunting Creek in Alexandria. Although this route was surveyed in 1818, the canal was never constructed. The construction in the 1820's of the Chesapeake and Ohio Canal not only eliminated the proposed canal from Goose Creek, but also altered appreciably the ambitions of Loudoun supporters of water transportation. During the early 1830's the C. & O. Canal was operating opposite the mouth of Goose Creek. At that location officials of the canal had a lock constructed to lift boats from the Potomac to their canal.[100] Loudoun owners of mills along Goose Creek and its tributaries, Little River and Beaver Dam, envisioned not only transporting Loudoun flour and other

---

[98]Ibid., April 10, 1841.

[99]Harrison, *Landmarks of Old Prince William*, pp. 540, 551, 555. James Hamilton, a burgess for Loudoun, and John Hough, a justice of Loudoun, attended a meeting at Frederick, Maryland, in 1762 for the purpose of planning the union of western rivers with the Potomac.

[100]The installation of a lock at that location was no doubt due to the influence of Loudouner Charles F. Mercer, who was not only the first president of the C. & O. Canal Company, but was also vitally interested in the Loudoun navigation project.

farm produce more cheaply to market, but also intercepting the wagon trade from the Valley of Virginia at the ford of Little River at Aldie. It was believed the latter would bring additional financial remuneration for investments in the project to improve the navigability of Loudoun's principal streams.[101] A memorial (memorandum), dated December 20, 1831, was sent by Loudoun citizens to the Virginia General Assembly, asking for permission to improve Goose Creek and its tributaries in order to make a navigable waterway for canal boats, which would allow Loudouners to take advantage of the C. & O. Canal.[102] The legislature responded favorably, granting a charter on March 15, 1832, to the Goose Creek and Little River Navigation Company.

Prior to state approval the "sundry proprietors of the banks of Goose Creek and Little River" had met at Leesburg on November 14, 1831, and agreed upon "A Plan of Inland Navigation for the County of Loudoun." This plan optimistically projected that twenty-six miles of navigation could be obtained by constructing a series of short canals around each mill and mill dam on Loudoun's major streams. This project was to be accomplished by cutting canals that totaled seven miles and constructing two dams across Goose Creek and one at or near the mouth of Beaver Dam, plus installing twelve locks and excavating seventeen miles of tow paths. The total cost for construction was estimated at $50,000. Annual expenses for the maintenance and operation of the facility were calculated not to exceed $3,000. The report concluded that the anticipated volume of exports to and from Loudoun, Fauquier, and "the upper end of Prince William" would rapidly defray constructional costs and operational expenses. It further suggested that a toll of four cents per mile for each ton of produce conveyed over the Loudoun waterway would yield a handsome profit.[103]

Unfortunately this early plan, like later projects, turned out to be more speculative than prophetic. Construction of the system was not

---

[101] Harrison, *Landmarks of Old Prince William*, p. 551; W. E. Trout, III, "The Goose Creek and Little River Navigaion," *Virginia Cavalcade* (Winter, 1967), 31.

[102] Virginia, Memorial of the Citizens of Loudoun County on December 20, 1831, to the Virginia General Assembly, Archives, Virginia State Library, Richmond, Va.; Legislative Petitions, Loudoun Co., 1822-1831, Box F, No. 9868.

[103] Goose Creek and Little River Navigation Company, *A Plan of Inland Navigation for the County of Loudoun* (n.p.: November 14, 1831), pp. 1-8; *The Loudoun Times-Mirror*, September 8, 1960; Trout, "The Goose Creek and Little River Navigation," pp. 31-34. Construction specifications for the canals, locks, and boats indicate planners were aware from the start of keeping construction costs to a minimum. Locks were constructed of stone with lock chambers 52 by 11 1/2 feet, only half the length of the locks on the C.&O. Canal. The boats to be used on Loudoun canals were to be 90 feet long and 7 feet four or five inches wide. Further costs were to be reduced by using millers and proprietors as attendants, since the locks were in the vicinity of mills. It was believed only eleven lock-tenders would be needed and each should receive an annual salary of $100.

started until 1849, three years after the death of the first president of the company, George Carter of Oatlands. After taking office as the new president in 1849, Colonel Humphrey B. Powell of Middleburg initiated action that culminated in the construction of only part of the company's project. After Powell had a final survey made, James Roach of Alexandria was hired to build the first twelve miles of "slackwater navigation," from the mouth of Goose Creek on the Potomac River to the mouth of Little River.[104] Finally by 1854, this span was opened after $100,750 had been expended. The construction of nine locks, four canals, and four dams had cost more than twice the original projected cost for the completion of the whole project.[105] With only approximately half of the project completed, the Goose Creek and Little River Navigation Company was bankrupt. Though the company had been weakened by financial duress inflicted by rising construction costs, the lethal blow was administered by obsolescence. Construction upon the project had not started until after the canal age had been replaced by the "iron horse" age. In 1857, Colonel Powell wrote the obituary of the project in his last report to the Board of Public Works. He confessed the system was of little or no value either to the state or investors as the result of the attraction to "speedy railroad facilities" being constructed at that time in Loudoun by the Alexandria, Loudoun, and Hampshire Railroad.[106] Although the Goose Creek improvement project died stillborn, at least one canal boat travelled the improved navigation.[107] But its voyage confirmed the failure of the Goose Creek facility. It is alleged that the contractor would not be paid until a boat arrived at Evergreen Mills. To obtain his wages, the contractor had a boat taken up the system as far as the appointed mill. The accumulation of mud in the channel impeded progress so badly that the contractor had the boat dragged by several yoke of oxen and pushed from the rear by a "crowd of colored" laborers,[108] an accomplishment technically fulfilling the contractor's contractual obligations, but hardly verification of the creation of a practicable and usable facility.

[104]In 1849, Powell hired General Gibbs McNeil as head engineer and J. H. Alexander as assistant engineer to make the final survey of the project.

[105]Harrison, *Landmarks of Old Prince William*, pp. 552, 560; Trout, "The Goose Creek and Little River Navigation," p. 32. Sixty thousand of the more than $100,000 had been subscribed by the Commonwealth of Virginia. Many vestiges of what were constructed still remain as landmarks. All were indicated on Yardley Taylor's map of Loudoun, made in 1853.

[106]Harrison, *Landmarks of Old Prince William*, p. 552; Trout, "The Goose Creek and Little River Navigation," p. 34.

[107]A "test boat" was ordered by the company in 1854 from a boat builder who lived in Cumberland, Maryland. It was to have a capacity to carry 250 barrels or thirty-one tons.

[108]*The Loudoun Times-Mirror*, September 8, 1960. Penelope M. Osburn stated the above details were quoted by J. R. Lintner, who obtained the information from Joshua Ritocor, who claimed to have witnessed this event as a boy. Although boats with the capacity

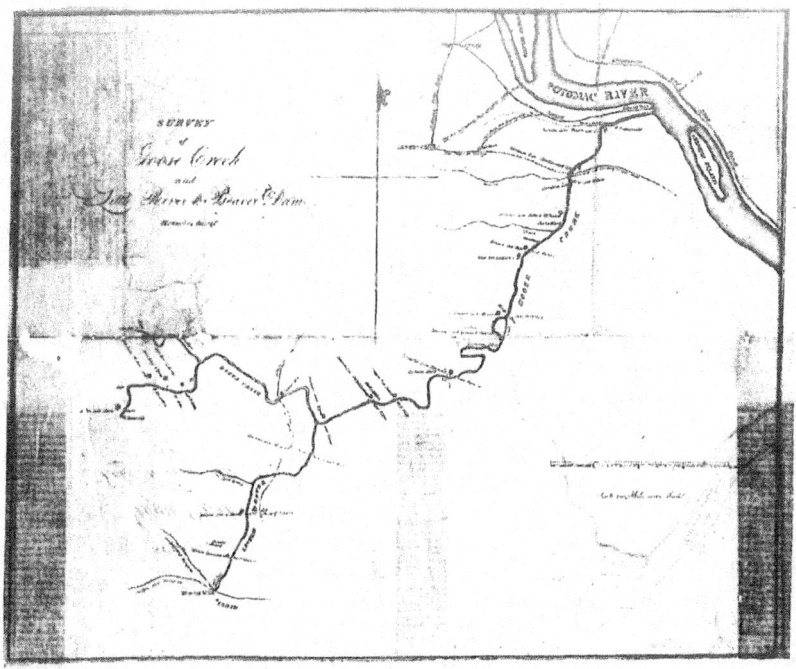

Figure 16. Survey Made in the 1830's of the Tributaries in Loudoun to be Improved by the Goose Creek and Little River Navigation Company.

Not all of Loudoun's visionaries during the Jacksonian era thought exclusively in terms of one transportational system as the panacea. During the 1830's some local planners dreamed of integrating land and water conveyances to obtain greater transportation efficiency. Thomas Philips and others received a franchise in 1831 from the state to attempt to implement this concept. They planned to construct a railroad from the mouth of Catoctin Creek to Upperville, where the proposed railroad would connect with the Ashby's Gap Turnpike. In 1832, Richard Henderson and eight others received a charter for "The Leesburg Rail-Road Company,"[109] giving enterprising gentlemen of Leesburg permission to construct a railroad from Leesburg to the closest point on

of carrying considerable tonnage could not be used, it is probable that in light of the fact that the C. & O Canal was in operation until 1924, light boats may have been sparingly used for the conveyance of items to and from the Potomac and the lower regions of Goose Creek.

[109]Richard Henderson may have been the most active county resident during the antebellum era in attempting to establish new transportational facilities within and through Loudoun.

the Potomac. The terms of the charter were never implemented.[110]

Despite other extensive plans of the late 1840's and early 1850's rail transportation in Loudoun was not a reality until shortly before the Civil War. Rail transportation in the county resulted from an attempt by Alexandria merchants to regain the trade of wheat and flour from the Valley of Virginia that had been formerly conveyed by turnpike from this valley to Alexandria. By 1836 the wagon trade to Alexandria had been diverted to Baltimore, Maryland, as the result of the construction of the Baltimore and Ohio Railroad. Much of this trade had heretofore been carried over the Little River Turnpike and other roads in Loudoun. Wagon trade over these routes was reduced to a trickle "by the mid-1830's thereby gravely affecting" the economic life of Loudoun hamlets like Middleburg, Dover, and Aldie that once thrived as important stations or stops for wagoners.[111]

One of the railroads calculated to restore the economic primacy of Alexandria was the Manassas Gap Railroad. This reversal was to be achieved by providing rail travel from Harrisonburg in the Valley of Virginia to Alexandria. Planners of this road also planned to open a Loudoun branch off the main line near Loudoun's southeastern boundary. This line was to proceed north through Aldie and Carter's Gap to Purcellville. The Loudoun Branch Railroad was designed not only to carry Loudoun Valley's staples of wheat and flour, but to be extended eventually to Harper's Ferry and thereby additionally increase Alexandria's contact with western trade. By 1858 most of the grading of the Loudoun Branch of the Manassas Gap Railroad had been completed as far as Purcellville.[112] But financial problems, the priority of construction of the main line, and the intervention of the Civil War led to the permanent abandonment of the Loudoun Branch. The railroad bed from southern Loudoun to Purcellville still remains as a monument to an unrealized dream and the tenacity of engineers and Irish laborers, who with oxen, horses, carts, wagons, and shovels excavated the proper grade for the railroad by making cuts thirty to forty-five feet deep in elevated terrain and raising the bed thirty feet above the natural

---

[110]Harrison, *Landmarks of Old Prince William*, pp. 583,596; Virginia, *Acts of the General Assembly of the State Virginia, 1831-32*, pp. 153-61. The state legislature placed the following conditions upon the Leesburg company. At least 180 shares of stock had to be sold, and work upon the railroad had to be started within two years from the date of the issuance of the charter. If these conditions plus the completion of the railroad within a decade after 1832 were not met, then the Leesburg Railroad Company would forfeit its charter and have to disband.

[111]Harrison, *Landmarks of Old Prince William*, pp. 576, 582-85.

[112]Ibid., pp. 588, 592; Statement by Ed Brown, personal interview, March 19, 1972. Near Purcellville, a field currently owned by Sam Brown is called the "Irish Lot" because it was formerly a camp site of Irish laborers who worked on the nearby railroad. The northern end of the cut near Purcellville was used by that town for approximately forty years, ca. 1930 to 1970, as the town dump. Other portions of the cut farther south have also been used as a dump and occasionally as a burial ground by farmers for their dead livestock.

topography in depressed areas. Stone culverts were erected where the roadbed crossed small streams. One-ton rectangular stones eight feet long were quarried from the Short Hill Mountain in Loudoun. After being transported by wagon to the appropriate construction sites, they were placed on top of each other without the use of mortar until a culvert approximately nine feet high and eighteen feet wide with a rectangular opening less than four feet wide and five feet high was completed.[113]

Only one of all the companies chartered during the antebellum period made rail transportation a reality for Loudoun. But this company like it unsuccessful contemporaries left a legacy of financial problems that continued to plague the companies operating the line in Loudoun until service was discontinued in 1968.

In 1847 a charter was issued to the Alexandria and Harper's Ferry Railroad to connect the two places after which the Company was named. When the Alexandria and Harper's Ferry Company was unable to launch construction, a new charter was granted to the Alexandria, Loudoun, and Hampshire Railroad Company to build a railroad from Alexandria to the coalfields of what is now West Virginia. This company had two prospective routes surveyed. One was to follow an old colonial road through Dranesville, Leesburg, Clark's Gap, and Hillsboro while the other proposed route was to extend west from Horsepen Branch through Carter's Gap in the Catoctin Mountain (where the Loudoun branch of the Manassas railroad was to cross) and under the Blue Ridge by a tunnel at Snickers' Gap. Neither of these routes was used; instead, a compromise route located between the two above routes became the site of the railway. Track was laid from Alexandria to Leesburg, where the first train arrived on May 17, 1860. Service was later expanded by extending the track through Clark's Gap to Hamilton in 1871, to Round Hill in 1874, and finally to the base of the Blue Ridge at Snickers' Gap (Bluemont) in 1900.[114]

Not all developments in Loudoun County during the age of Jackson are typical of the salient phenomena that are associated with the national history of that era. For example, being an eastern region of the country, Loudoun did not enjoy substantial demographic growth between the 1820's and the 1840's. During this period the political tenor of the majority of Loudoun voters was strongly anti-Jackson and anti-Democratic. This political persuasion was not the result of an adherence to a States' rights philosophy, but resulted from the belief that the

[113]Statement by Ed Brown, personal interview, March 19, 1972. It took one day for a wagon to carry one stone from the Short Hill Mountain to the Purcellville area. The dimension of the various culverts are not identical. These structures in the 1970's remain essentially as they were originally constructed.

[114]Harrison, *Landmarks of Old Prince William*, pp. 592-94; Herbert H. Harwood, Jr. *Rails to the Blue Ridge* (Falls Church, Va.: Pioneer America Society, 1969), pp. 1-2, 9, 11, 13, 35, 43, 51, 55, 90-91, 106, 107; Ames W. Williams, *The Washington and Old Dominion Railroad* (Springfield, Va.: Capital Traction Quarterly, 1970), pp. 1-3, 42-43, 95, 110, 146. The Alexandria, Loudoun, and Hampshire Railroad Company was

centralization of political power in the Presidency due to Jackson's measures was an incorrect form of nationalism endangering the political system. Loudouners, as led by their most significant politician of the early nineteenth century, Charles F. Mercer, espoused that true nationalism stressed federal economic aid and development of the country through the promotion of internal improvements. These were looked upon as vital to Loudoun's economic well-being. Businessmen, like Richard H. Henderson of Leesburg, dreamed of establishing turnpikes, canals, and railroads through Loudoun that would lead to lucrative dividends resulting from increased trade and travel from the Shenandoah Valley and points farther west to eastern termini like Georgetown and Alexandria. County agrarians likewise looked upon improved transportation as the key to their prosperity in the belief that more of their produce could be transported more economically and efficiently to market. Economic interest thereby resulted in strong support within the county for the Whig party and its strong endorsement of economic nationalism. Although transportation systems in Loudoun frequently failed or fell far short of anticipated goals, the rationale set forth by local businessmen and farmers in memorials and plans were indicative of one aspect of the mind of Jacksonian America: the belief in the inevitability of progress that would manifest itself in economic expansion and financial aggrandizement.

extensively subsidized by the state of Virginia, which was willing to invest $853,000. This subsidy was given on the condition that the state be given extensive representation on the company's board of directors.

Rail transportation did play a role in the mining and processing of iron ore in Loudoun from 1830 into the 1850's. As early as 1814, land speculator Ferdinando Fairfax advertised his land for sale in Loudoun along the Potomac River as excellent for the development of an "Iron Company." Apparently no one at that time was interested. During the 1830's, Thomas Johnson started mining iron ore from the eastern side of the Catoctin Mountain near the Potomac River and Point of Rocks, Maryland. The ore was shipped elsewhere to a furnace until 1839. At that time a furnace was installed near the mine. The ore was melted with charcoal burned on the property. As production rapidly increased, the melting capacity of the Catoctin furnace became inadequate. Ore was once again sent elsewhere to be processed until the owners belatedly agreed to allow the construction of a new furnace approximately a half-mile east of the old plant. The new plant, completed in 1857, had twice the capacity of its predecessor. In an attempt to take advantage of this increase, a track was laid from the B.&O. Railroad across the Point of Rocks Bridge to the mine and new furnace. Nevertheless, business was still hampered by the lack of adequate transportation. The bridge was erected only for wagons and only one railroad car was allowed to cross the bridge at a time. The success of this mine from 1830 to 1860 did stimulate the development of a community in Loudoun in the vicinity of the furnace. About twenty-five dwellings were constructed plus a large boarding house called the "Shanty." A new flour mill was constructed and was run by water from the Catoctin Creek that was conveyed to the mill by a tunnel under a spur of the Catoctin Mountain. The mining operation was also instrumental in the erection of a bridge across the Potomac at Point of Rocks in 1850 and the opening of a new road from the Potomac to Taylorstown, Virginia. However, the Civil War permanently terminated the activities of mining and the Catoctin furnace.

Chapter 4

SLAVERY; STIMULUS FOR DIVISION: 1848 To 1861

No aspect of American life has been as conspicuously contradictory to American theories of democracy, egalitarianism, and individualism as the institution of slavery.[1] The incongruity of slavery with American ideals become especially apparent during the Jacksonian era. At the advent of the Jacksonian period, slavery had erupted from a local to a national issue as a result of the Tallmadge Amendment of 1819 and the situation in territories seeking statehood. Despite the temporary solution provided by the Missouri Compromise of 1820, the issues associated with the anachronistic institution of slavery, such as the expansion and abolition of slavery and fugitive slaves, not only would continue as major political issues but also would emerge as the dominant and paramount problem demanding resolution during the antebellum era. Superficially it would appear that the issue of slavery from the Compromise of 1820 to the start of the Mexican War in 1846 was not an insurmontable problem for the federal government. The tariff crisis, the status of the

---

[1]Arthur A. Ekirch, Jr. *The American Democratic Tradition: A History* (New York: Macmillian Co., 1963), p. 128. Interesting extracts of letters from former Loudoun slaves, Jesse and Mars Lucas, can be found on pages 72 and 73 of *Legends of Loudoun Valley* by Joseph V. Nichols. In letters written between March 10, 1830, to April 24, 1836, to their former owner, Dr. Albert Heaton of Leesburg, Virginia, (who was addressed in the letters as "Dear Master"), Jesse and Mars wrote of their disillusionment with "freedom" in Africa. Accustomed to life in America, they considered the African natives lazy and cruel "heathen" and life in Caldwell, Liberia, as harsh. They complained of the aloofness

Bank of the United States, and the issue of internal improvements were the dominant problems of Jackson's Presidency. Although closely connected to sectional politics, these did not on the surface appear to be directly related to slavery. Congress worked out a modus operandi for handling the innumerable abolitionists' petitions by discarding such petitions through procedures specified in "gag rules."[2] While Congress attempted to ignore abolitionists' demands, a growing sectional awareness developed in the Northern, Western, and Southern regions of the United States that the uniqueness of their respective economies based upon industry, wheat, and cotton meant that federal policy that promoted the economic welfare of one section could adversely affect the economic well-being of another. Superimposed upon this geographical economic difference was the institution of slavery that made the South unique over the other.two major geograhical sections. Southern sectional consciouness of her uniqueness became acute when slavery emerged as a national issue. This awareness burgeoned into a paranoia that included the belief that the continued existence of Southern civilization was imperiled by (1) the implementation of economic policies by the federal government that promoted the economic well-being of non-slave states at the expense of the South and (2) the attacks upon the institution of slavery by the North to block the expansion of slavery into the territories. Southerners were also exasperated by Northerners' refusal to comply with federal fugitive slave legislation and by what they believed to be the activities of supercilious abolitionists which enhanced the likelihood of slave insurrections.[3] These fears promoted States' rights as the political theory in which the South placed her ultimate hope for counteracting federal policies that were believed to menace the South's well-being. During the Jacksonian period political leaders in South Carolina had the greatest awareness of the South's uniqueness and the greatest dedication to States' rights. During the 1830's they stressed that the issues of tariffs and internal improvements were indirectly connected to the defense of slavery. If the federal government was allowed to enact extensive legislation on those issues, then the sovereignty of states would recede and be replaced by centralization so it would be likely that the "general welfare" clause of the federal Constitution would be used to advance the cause of the

and theft by natives, of numerous leopards and other wild beasts, of killing a snake thirteen and a half feet long, and of rarely having meat to eat due to the great difficulty in catching the very elusive monkey. Jesse and Mars Lucas also pleaded with their former master for permission to return to America. They considered their life in Liberia far inferior to that they had known as American slaves.

[2]Van Deusen, *The Jacksonian Era*, pp. 133-35.

[3]The North also developed a persecution complex during the antebellum era. Northerners felt the South was threatening their economic life by blocking legislation the North needed or wanted and aggressively attempting to extend slavery throughout the nation via the Kansas-Nebraska Act and the Dred Scott Decision.

abolitionists as well as that of the road builders.⁴ This fear was indicative of the rapidly accelerating trend of the antebellum era that, as sectional tensions increased, slavery somehow became involved in all the major issues so by the latter part of the pre-Civil War period slavery was the symbol of all sectional differences.

THE PECULIAR INSTITUTION IN ANTEBELLUM LOUDOUN

Slavery in Loudoun County became an alienating force for certain Loudouners' disenchantment with the North and emerged as the major force for division among citizens within the county. Slavery had been established by English settlers in eastern and southern regions of Loudoun during the eighteenth century. It became the feature most distinguishing those regions from the northern and western portions of the county settled during the same century by German, Scotch-Irish, and Quaker settlers from Pennsylvania.⁵ These areas had smaller farms and little or no slave labor. During the early settlement of Loudoun both slaves and free laborers cultivated tobacco and grain. But as the eighteenth century waned, both forms of labor were concentrated upon the production of cereals as the staple of the Virginia piedmont shifted from tobacco to wheat.⁶ From the end of the 1700's until the extinction of slavery, Loudoun slaves were used to raise wheat and corn, and tend livestock, and perform multifarious other jobs associated with nineteenth century northern Virginia agrarian life.

From 1800 to 1860, Loudoun's population fluctuated between 20,000 and 22,000.⁷ Approximately one-fourth of the county's population during this period was slaves.⁸ By 1810 the population of both free and slave in Loudoun totaled 21,180. Of this number, 878 people owned 5,001 slaves. Due to incomplete statistics the size of slaveholdings in 1810 can be determined for only 830 owners. Of this total the most numerous group consisted of 287 who owned only one slave. Equal in number were the 275 owners of two to four slaves. One hundred and sixty Loudouners were masters of five to nine slaves. The number of owners of more than

---

⁴William W. Freehling, *Prelude to Civil War: The Nullification Controversy in South Carolina, 1816-1836* (New York: Harper and Row, 1968), pp. 87, 127-28.

⁵Goodhart, *History of the Independent Loudoun Virginia Rangers*, pp. 3-4; Head, *History of Loudoun County*, p. 112; Joseph V. Nichols, *Legends of Loudoun Valley*, (Leesburg, Va.: Potomac Press, 1961), pp. 11-12.

⁶Harrison, *Landmarks of Old Prince William*, p. 397.

⁷For example in 1830, the county had 21,939 inhabitants; in 1840, 20,431; in 1850, 22,079; and in 1860, 21,774.

⁸Head, *History of Loudoun County*, p. 85.

ten slaves was small. Eighty had between ten and nineteen slaves, twenty-eight owned twenty to forty-nine slaves, and only one man, W. C. Seldon, had more than fifty. Seldon was the proprietor of fifty-two slaves. The most prominent features of Loudoun slave demography during the early nineteenth century were the relatively limited number of slave-owners and limited number of persons with substantial human chattel.[9] This trend continued until the Civil War.

The number of slaveowners in the county declined from 878 in 1810 to 670 in 1860,[10] while the number of slaves in the county during the fifty years preceding the Civil War varied from 5,001 in 1810 to a high of 5,729 in 1820.[11] From 1820 to the Civil War the number of slaves in the county declined slightly,[12] whereas free Negroes in Loudoun increased from 604 in 1810, to 831 in 1820, and 1,373 in 1850, but had declined to 1,252 in 1860.[13]

There is no indication that the condition and treatment of slaves in antebellum Loudoun was noticeably different from that of human chattel in other areas of northern Virginia.[14] Apparently some Loudouners attempted to teach Loudoun slaves to read and write. This instruction prompted a letter to the editor of *The Genius of Liberty* signed "Judex," in which well-meaning persons were admonished that they were violating the state's slave code, which made it illegal for slaves to congregate and be taught to read and write. "Judex" further stated that the law declared that "a slave attending such" a meeting "shall receive twenty lashes on his bare back," and any white person present at such an unlawful meeting "shall pay three dollars for every offence" or "receive twenty lashes on his bare back, well laid on." In conclusion "Judex" stated, "Negroes, teachers, and justices look to it: the order of society must prevail over the notions of individuals." Otherwise the

---

[9]National Archives of the United States, Population Schedules of the Census of Loudoun County, Virginia for 1810; microcopy no. 252; roll no. 69.

[10]Population Schedules of the Census of Loudoun County, Virginia for 1810; Head, *History of Loudoun County*, p. 85.

[11]Population Schedules of the Census of Loudoun County, Virginia for 1820; microcopy no. 33; roll no. 69.

[12]Head, *History of Loudoun County*, p. 85; Taylor, *Memoir of Loudoun County, Virginia*, p. 23. In 1850 there were 5,641 slaves in the county compared to 5,501 in 1860.

[13]Head, op. cit., p. 85; Population Schedules of the Census of Loudoun County, Virginia for 1810 and 1820; Taylor, op. cit., p. 23.

[14]United States, National Archives, Slave Schedules of the Census of Loudoun county, Virginia for 1850; microcopy no. 432; roll no. 989. Census records give only a cursory glimpse of the health of slaves. The only indication of physical and mental defects of Loudoun slaves in the slave schedule of 1850 were two slaves recorded as being blind, one deaf and dumb, another an idiot, and one insane. This was far from being a complete and accurate analysis. Thirty-five per cent of the slaves recorded in the Loudoun schedule of 1850 were mulattoes.

Number of Owners	Size of Slaveholding
124	1
84	2
61	3
83	4
46	5
39	6
35	7
27	8
22	9
80	10-14
36	15-19
23	20-29
4	30-39
4	40-49
1	50-69
1	100-199

Table 8. *Distribution of slaveownership in Loudoun in 1860.*
Source: Head, *History of Loudoun County*, p. 85.

problem of fugitive slaves and the practice of selling slaves to local farmers and slave traders were as common in Loudoun as in other regions of the upper South.

Advertisements in Loudoun newspapers during the antebellum era for runaway slaves are indicative of a sense of dysphoria within the minds of at least a small minority of the slaves in Loudoun.[15] Ads for fugitive slaves included items to aid in the identification of a runaway: slave's name, age, physical appearance, clothing, and reward. Reward varied from $5 as offered for a Negro named Jim, who was described as being about thirty years of age, approximately "five feet eight or nine inches high, of a black complexion . . . flat nose, part of his upper teeth gone," and scars "on his nose between his eyes, a large one on his breast and several others about his body," to $200 for another male slave named Joe. Joe was about the same age and height as Jim, but stooped "in the shoulders, was of thin visage and habit of body," and had a downcast look, "and stammered in his speech." It was not apparent from the ads why the

---

[15] *The Genius of Liberty*, February 3, 1818; March 10, 1818; May 4, 1818; April 16, 1819; October 26, 1819; May 23, 1820; June 13, 1820; August 8, 1820; *The Democratic Mirror* (Leesburg), April 6, 1859; April 13, 1859; April 20, 1859.

reward for Joe was substantially greater than that offered for the return of Jim. Armistead T. Mason, the owner of Joe, was a member of the local aristocracy and was a person of far greater wealth than Edward Hammat, the owner of Jim.[16] Other variables that may have influenced the size of the reward for the return of fugitive slaves, in addition to the wealth of the owner, were the skill of the slave and the size of slave holding. The larger the number of slaves owned, the more incumbent it was for the owner to obtain the return of the fugitive in hopes of discouraging others from attempting to escape from bondage. To increase the chance of having fugitives returned, many slaveowners raise the reward the farther the fugitive was found away from the owner's residence. This course was also true for the reward Armistead T. Mason offered for the mulatto Joe, who had absconded during Mason's absence from home. If found in Virginia, Mason would pay only $50 reward; in Maryland or the District of Columbia, $100; and "if apprehended in Pennsylvania or in any other state or territoy;" $200. In addition to the reward Mason advertised he would "pay all reasonable charges" for returning Joe to him.[17] Stephen C. Roszel offered a reward for Dick, a slave "six feet high, coarse, and strong built, of quite dark complexion," also dependent of the distance away from Roszel's home that the fugitive was captured; twenty miles from home, a $10 reward would be paid; if fifty miles away, $30; and for all greater distances $50 plus "reasonable charges" encountered by the person in the return of the fugitive.[18]

Frequently the fugitive slaves had scars, sores, and some deformity that resulted from an injury. For example, a $40 reward was offered for a young female slave named Charlotte, who had a "scar above her left arm, occasioned by a burn."[19] Armistead Mason's slave, Joe, had severely bruised fingers on his left hand; Hammat's slave, Jim, was extensively scarred. Another slave, Ned Biays, had a bruised right eye when he ran away.[20] Another young male fugitive named Dick had a scar on his face believed to have resulted from a burn sustained as a young child.[21] A thirty-year-old, "sprightly well set" fellow "about five feet tall, named Hanson, who took with him" on his freedom trip "a fur hat, nearly new; a fine yellow striped searsucker coat; a pair of new shoes, and sundry other clothing," had a crooked little finger resulting from "an original bruise." Hanson was also "very talkative," but had

---

[16] *The Genius of Liberty,* May 4, 1818. The following was published in the August 19, 1829 issue of *The Richmond Whig:* "Died at his residence in Loudoun County, Virginia, a few days since, Tommy Tomson, a black man, aged 130 years. He was born and lived in Virginia, and retained his mental and physical faculties, to a few days previous to his decease."
[17] Ibid.
[18] Ibid., May 31, 1818.
[19] Ibid., February 3, 1818.
[20] Ibid., November 2, 1819.
[21] Ibid., March 31, 1818.

"an impediment in his speech."²² Escaping with Hanson was "a likely black negro woman named Ann" about five feet in height and twenty-six years of age. According to her owner, Ann had "no particular marks . . . only that her middle finger, on her right hand, stood nearly or perfectly straight, while the others closed tableside."²³ Conclusive evidence can not be found to substantiate the number of the above injuries that were sustained from abusive treatment as opposed to those resulting from accidents and carelessness. A slaveowner, Joel Osburn, was tried in the county court for "alleged maltreatment of his Negro slave servant" that resulted in the slave's death. The court in a not altogether surprising verdict ruled Osburn was innocent.²⁴

Fugitive slave ads often revealed that some of the runaways were clever, cunning, and in a few cases literate. Such a man was John Owens, a fugitive whose "cunning and artful" ways enabled him to escape from the Loudoun jail.²⁵ Another fugitive, twenty-seven-year-old Major Buoy, was described as having a "very black complexion and being well made and handsome; with considerable cunning."²⁶ A dark young mulatto male, named Bill Johnson, who ran away wearing a yellow vest was depicted as "very active, and communicative; reads and writes tolerably well."²⁷ Other slaves had more pragmatic skills that were valued by their owners. George Gulick, who lived near Aldie, lamented the loss of Ned Biays, who ran away. Biays was "a handy fellow about a farm," a "rough carpenter," and could make "coarse shoes."²⁸

Pennsylvania seemed to have been the favorite refuge for fugitive slaves as well as free blacks from Loudoun because that was the nearest free state to Loudoun County.²⁹ An additional factor was the cooperation between Loudoun Friends and Quakers in Pennsylvania, who befriended fugitive slaves via the underground railroad from Loudoun to the Quaker State. The migration of Loudoun blacks was attested by Samuel Janney. In his *Memoirs*, he recorded that in a visit to Pennsylania in 1845 he saw a "considerable number" of blacks from his native county, including one elderly Negro man who said "he had nursed" Janney when the latter was a child.³⁰ The number of fugitive slaves that fled from Loudoun would

---

²²Ibid., June 13, 1820.
²³Ibid.
²⁴*The Democratic Mirror*, January 19, 1959.
²⁵*The Genius of Liberty*, October 26, 1819.
²⁶Ibid., June 13, 1820. A notice in the August 29, 1820, issue of *The Genius of Liberty* advertised for the owner of James Hall, John Hoe, to "come forward, prove property, pay charges, and take" the slave away.
²⁷Ibid., October 26, 1819.
²⁸Ibid., November 2, 1819.
²⁹Ibid., May 4, 1818; March 31, 1818.
³⁰Samuel M. Janney, *Memoirs of Samuel M. Janney* (Philadelphia: Friend's Book Association, 1881), pp. 92-93.

Notice.

WAS COMMITTED to the jail of Loudoun county, on the 14th inst. a Negro man, who calls himself

James Hall,

About five feet ten or eleven inches high, stout and well made, has the appearance of having lost an upper fore tooth, appears to be about 22 or 23 years of age. Says he belongs to John Hue Washington, King George county, Va. from whom he ran away about eighteen months since. Had on when taken up, a domestic striped roundabout, and pantaloons of the same.

The owner is requested to come forward, prove property, pay charges, and take him away, or said negro will be dealt with as the law directs.

Giles Hammat,
Jailor.

Aug. 22, 1820.—32 tf

☞ The editors of the Richmond Enquirer are requested to insert the above three times, and forward their bill to the editor of the Genius of Liberty.

$50 Reward.

RAN away from the subscriber on the 25th August last, a black man who calls himself

NED BIAYS.

About 30 years of age, 5 feet 8 or 9 inches high, stout and well made. His right eye was bruised when he went off and had the appearance of continuing so. Had on a blue surtout coat of fine cloth, blue cloth pantaloons, twilled linsey short coat, and had with him other clothing. He is a handy fellow about a farm, can make coarse shoes, and is a rough carpenter. The above reward will be given on bringing him home to the subscriber, living in Loudoun county, Va. near Aldie, or lodging him in jail so that I get him again.

GEORGE GULICK.

November 2—31.

☞ The editors of the 'Palladium of Liberty,' the 'Virginia Reformer,' and the 'Political Examiner,' are requested to insert the above three times in their respective papers, and to forward their bills to this office.

I wish to hire out,

FOR the ensuing year, 12 or 19 negroes, consisting of men, women, boys, and girls.— Among which are a good blacksmith with his tools, and two or three excellent ploughmen and cradlers, an excellent female house servant, that is capable of any kind of house work.

Any application should be made between this and the first day of January next, as at that time they will certainly be hired.

Mary Mason.

Nov. 21, 1820.—45 6t.

Figure 17. Ads in THE GENIUS OF LIBERTY *from 1818 to 1820 for the Return of Runaways and Hiring Out of Slaves.*

be impossible to determine. Entries in the private notebook of Edward Hammett, jailer of Loudoun County during the age of Jackson, seem to indicate that runaways from, or passing through, Loudoun were a common occurrence. For example, during a span of two years and five months, from 1828 until 1831, Hammett recorded "fourteen runaway Negroes" and keeping forty-three Negroes for return to their owners.[31] During the last decade of the antebellum period, Loudoun's population decreased from 22,079 in 1850 to 21,744 in 1860. Most of this decrease was in the county's Negro population. Slaves in Loudoun decreased from 5,641 in 1850 to 5,501 in 1860. The county's number of free Negroes declined during the same period from 1,373 to 1,252.[32] The preponderant number of free blacks and fugitive slaves that left Loudoun during that period went to Pennsylvania. However, the decline in Loudoun's slave population was also due to blacks' being sold to other areas of the South, especially to the cotton kingdom.

Slaves were sold in Loudoun due to (1) a surplus of slave labor, (2) punishment for slave crimes, and (3) financial remuneration. Central to an analysis of the reasons why slaves were sold are the issues of the efficiency and profitableness of slavery in antebellum Loudoun.[33] A native Loudouner and critic of slavery, Samuel Janney, charged that slavery was an inefficient and wasteful labor force which was also responsible for retarding manufacturing in Virginia.[34] This view was not accepted universally by Janney's contemporaries or by all modern historians.[35] The hiring out and sale of slaves in Loudoun due to a moderate surplus of slaves,[36] settling up estates of deceased slaveowners, and the need for cash can be documented.[37] The extent that inefficiency and

[31] *The Loudoun Times-Mirror*, May 14, 1964. "Keeping Negroes" probably referred to blacks put in jail on suspicion of being runaway slaves.

[32] Head, *History of Loudoun County*, p. 85; Taylor, *Memoir of Loudoun County, Virginia*, p. 23. There were 305 fewer people in Loudoun in 1860 than in 1850. However, there were only forty-five fewer whites in the county in 1860 that in 1850 as compared to a decrease of 260 Negroes (free and slave) during the same decade.

[33] Stanley L. Engerman, "The Effect of Slavery upon the Southern Economy: A Review of the Recent Debate," in *Did Slavery Pay?*, ed. by Hugh G. F. Aitken (Boston: Houghton Mifflin Co., 1971), pp. 301-07.

[34] Samuel M. Janney, *The Yankee in Fairfax County* (Baltimore: Snodgrass and Wehrly, 1849), p. 10.

[35] The issues of the profitableness, efficiency, and future of slavery in antebellum America, and the treatment of slaves are still being spiritedly debated by American historians.

[36] *The Genius of Liberty*, November 21, 1820; January 7, 1823; December 30, 1823. Slaves were usually hired out for a year. On January 1, 1824, Mary Mason took a dozen slaves to the tavern of John Drish in Leesburg for interested parties to negotiate for the service of her slaves. By 1860, the annual hiring rates in Virginia were $105 for men and $46 for women.

[37] Ibid., January 21, 1820; November 21, 1820; January 30, 1821; January 7, 1823; December 30, 1823; *The Democratic Mirror*, September 29, 1858; October 20, 1858; December 7, 1859; January 11, 1860.

unprofitableness of slavery led to the disposal of Loudoun slaves is more difficult to substantiate. Evidence exists that shows slaves were far from lacking in skills. Many females were "well acquainted with the duties" of being a house servant as well as with the techniques of sewing and spinning.[38] Male slaves possessed skills that included being "excellent ploughmen," cradlers, and blacksmiths.[39]

Slaveholders in antebellum Loudoun usually inherited their slaves.[40] This method of acquiring slaves substantially reduced the cost of slave labor in Loudoun to essentially that of providing sustenance, clothing, and shelter for those in bondage. If the majority of male slaves in the county possessed any competence in agrarian work, especially in the cultivation of cereals, and the females a modicum of skill and motivation for household work, then it was very probable that slavery in Loudoun was not only efficient but financially profitable.[41] The relatively high prices Loudoun slaveowners received for slaves sold to slave traders also offer a degree of credence for the thesis of Conrad and Meyer that slavery was profitable in the upper South due to the continuous demand for slave labor in the cotton belt.[42]

Often the time and place for the sale of slaves in Loudoun occurred on court days on the front steps of the courthouse. Administrators of wills frequently took advantage of these occasions and site to hold public sales of real estate and personal property, which often included slaves.[43] Aware of such an event, agents in the domestic slave trade made a point to be present. Charles P. McCabe, a Loudoun agent, often advertised in *The Democratic Mirror* for 100 slaves.[44] During the fall of 1859 the following ad was placed in the above paper by W. B. Noland: "Wanted; Any number of likely Young Negroes for which the highest Cash price

---

[38] *The Genius of Liberty*, November 21, 1820; January 7, 1823.

[39] Ibid., November 21, 1820.

[40] Population Schedules of the Census of Loudoun County, Virginia for 1810 and 1820.

[41] Alfred H. Conrad and John R. Meyer, "The Economics of Slavery in the Antebellum South," in *Did Slavery Pay?*, ed. by Hugh G. J. Aitken (Boston: Houghton Mifflin Co., 1971), pp. 172-73. Conrad and Meyer argue that the cultivation of cotton made slavery profitable in the lower South, which in turn led to the purchase of surplus slaves from the upper South.

[42] Ibid., p. 174. Interpretations contrary to those of Conrad and Meyers, and K. M. Stampp are those of U. B. Phillips and Eugene D. Genovese. Genovese, in *The Political Economy of Slavery* (New York: Random House, 1965), pp. 141-44, 275-79, challenges the profitability thesis of Stampp, Conrad, and Meyer. Like Phillips, Genovese maintained slavery was inefficient and unprofitable but was dearly embraced by Southerners in order to maintain white supremacy.

[43] *The Democratic Mirror*, September 29, 1858; January 5, 1858; December 7, 1859.

[44] Ibid., September 24, 1858; October 6, 1858; October 13, 1858; October 20, 1858.

will be paid."⁴⁵ Slave traders, B. M. Campbell and W. L. Campbell, had their agent at Winchester, John Avis, also to compete for Loudoun slaves by advertising:

> *I wish to purchase a large number of Negroes for the Southern market—Men, Women, Boys, Girl, and Families, for which I will pay the highest price in CASH. Persons having Slaves to dispose of will find it to their interest to give me a call before selling. Any letters addressed to me at Winchester, Va. will receive prompt attention. I may be seen in Leesburg on court or other public days.*⁴⁶

The January 5, 1858, issue of the *Mirror* stated that "a good many negroes" had "changed owners in Loudoun last week." The premium price was $1,500 for a blacksmith and $1,590 for a woman and her children. During December of the same year "an ordinary looking negro sold for $1,350."⁴⁷ These prices were above the average prices paid in Virginia at that time for prime field hands.⁴⁸

Although money was the main reason for slaves being sold in Loudoun, the problem of obstreperous slaves was also a factor. Erring Negroes were often sold to slave traders or deported by them to other areas in the South. A number of slaves were tried for crimes, and those found guilty were deported to the lower South. The cases of Marietta and Tom are examples of Loudoun slaves convicted for crimes and deported. Marietta was found guilty of infanticide, and Tom of second degree murder.⁴⁹ Tom killed a free Negro, Rueban Hurley, near Aldie late one Friday night in an argument that ensued from Hurley's refusal to pay the money he owed Tom. During the altercation Hurley attacked Tom with a mowing scythe. Tom responded by throwing a rock that struck and killed his assaulter. The court ruled that Tom's failure to

---

⁴⁵Ibid., September 21, 1859; September 28, 1859; October 5,1859; October 19, 1859. Noland was an agent for a slave trading company owned by Joseph Bruin.

⁴⁶Ibid., August 15, 1860.

⁴⁷Ibid., December 15, 1858.

⁴⁸Ulrich B. Phillips, *American Negro Slavery* (Baton Rouge: Louisiana State Press, 1966), pp. 370-71. The price paid in Virginia for able-bodied young male slaves fluctuated considerably during the antebellum era: $1,000 in 1819, $400 in 1825, $1,000 in 1839, $500 in 1844, $1,000 in 1858. Usually slaves in Loudoun were sold for cash, but near Upperville during October 1858, John T. Ross, administrator of the estate of Mahlon Baldwin, sold "Twelve likely young Negroes . . . on a credit of Three months; bond and security" were given in addition to interest from the date of the sale.

⁴⁹*The Democratic Mirror*, November 10, 1858. Tom was owned by Mrs. Leah Hutchinson.

report the incident immediately and the fact he covered the body up with leaves necessitated Tom's removal from Loudoun to the lower South.⁵⁰

Despite the lack of any collective slave uprising in Loudoun, malcontent did exist, as indicated by slaves running away and by problems in slave management. Rebellious slaves occasionally struck out violently at those in authority. A slave belonging to A. H. Rogers attacked an overseer with a butcher knife. Armed, the overseer shot the Negro.⁵¹ A similar incident occurred when a slave of Colonel Sanford I. Ramey assaulted an overseer known as "Mr. Hope." Hope repulsed his assailant by shooting the slave in the leg.⁵² A far better comprehension of these incidents would be possible if the circumstances surrounding these outbursts were known. However, the fact that overseers in Loudoun were armed is proof that the relationship between slaves and those in authority was far from being wholly amicable.

The threat of being sold or having relatives or friends "sold down the river" in the domestic slave trade was disconcerting to slaves. *The Genius of Liberty* reported with some disapproval in 1821 the act of "a drove of negroes consisting of about one hundred . . . unhappy wretches" that included men, women, and children passing through Leesburg one Saturday on their way to "a southern destination."⁵³ According to one Loudouner who wrote a letter dated March 10, 1828, to the *Genius of Universal Emancipation*, at least one Loudoun slave committed suicide after being sold to a slave trader and two others ran off. The latter two sought and found Loudouners to purchase them so they could remain in the county. The author of this letter stated the details of these developments and decried the slave trade in an interesting and emotional, though not altogether lucid and grammatically correct, manner:

> A most tragical occurrence had lately taken place in this vicinity, occasioned by those monsters who traffic in HUMAN FLESH. A man by the name of Crooks, living near Hillsborough in this county, lately sold his FAMILY OF BLACKS to some of those inhuman traders. I have been informed that the men were sent to a smith's shop on an errant [sic] where the traders were in readiness to secure them—but being warned of their danger by the way, absconded until the rest of the family were driven off. The number was about eight or

⁵⁰Ibid., November 17, 1858. Tom did tell others about the fight the morning after the incident.
⁵¹Ibid., December 16, 1861.
⁵²Ibid., April 20, 1859. The paper reported the wound was not serious.
⁵³*The Genius of Libery*, September 4, 1821.

ten. They accordingly started, with the women and children, and put up about 14 miles from where they started. They were secured in a room that night, and in the morning when they went to awaken them, Lo! a middle aged woman had laid down to rise no more!! — IT WAS SUPPOSED SHE HAD TAKEN SOMETHING BY WHICH SHE PUT A PERIOD TO HER EXISTENCE: *choosing death rather than be dragged off by these tyrants. — Can it be possible that such a state of things will be suffered long to continue in this land of boa[s]ted Liberty. How unequal those laws, which give one man the power to deal thus with his brother man. Numerous instances occur to show that the Blacks, (however destitute they are supposed to be of feeling) who thus choose death in preference to transportation to a distant market.*[54]

THE CRUSADE FOR A BETTER WORLD

Inspired by the contradiction of an expanding democracy for the white male during the Jacksonian era while disadvantaged minorities continued to be treated in a manner that perpetuated subservience and servility, liberals and reformers decried the existence of such practices that were contrary to the concepts of democracy, Christianity, and humanitarianism. Most of the people who demanded humanitarian reforms did so not because they rejected the idea of American progress but because they considered reformism imperative for the continued and accelerated progress of the nation and the perfection of the American people.[55] As the most blatant contradiction of individualism and egalitarianism, slavery became the salient and most controversial target of humanitarian reform movements.

Antebellum reforms in Loudoun were limited to the protest against slavery and the demand for public education. Leadership for both crusades was provided by members of the Society of Friends. Quakers had been the outstanding spokesman for humanitarianism since colonial America. During the colonial period, under the leadership of John

---

[54]*Genius of Universal Emancipation* (Baltimore, Md.), March 29, 1829. This letter also stated that the "notorious Legg" was the slave trader "engaged in the above diabolical transaction."

[55]John L. Thomas, "Romantic Reform in America, 1815-1865," *Ante-Bellum Reform*, ed. by David B. Davis (New York: Harper and Row, 1967), pp. 153-61; Alice F. Tyler, *Freedom's Ferment*, pp. 23, 46.

Woolman, Friends were working for the termination of slavery.[56] This activity also influenced Loudoun Friends. John Hough, instructed by the Fairfax Meeting in Loudoun, wrote James Pemberton on May 29, 1762, to send him six dozen copies of John Woolman's *Some Considerations on the Keeping of Negroes.*[57]

A complement to the Quakers' efforts to fight slavery through colonization was made by the Methodists. During the latter part of the eighteenth century the Methodist Church in Virginia was a dedicated opponent of slavery. Like the Quakers, Methodists worked for colonization and decreed all members of the church must liberate their slaves. By 1801 the Methodist Church had waned as a vibrant crusader against slavery. The church then took a neutral position in regard to the good and evil of human chattel.[58] As sectional tensions by the 1840's made neutrality untenable, American Methodism was split into Northern and Southern organizations.[59] However, prior to 1830, while Methodist officialdom maintained a neutral posture, Loudoun Methodists worked for the termination of slavery through colonization. This trend was illustrated by the holding of an annual meeting of the Loudoun Auxiliary of the American Colonization Society on May 2, 1820, at the Leesburg Methodist Church.[60] Quakers, Methodists, and others who attended included slaveowners like Burr Powell and William Noland. Both gentlemen were elected to positions as vice-presidents of the Loudoun Colonization Society.[61] During the 1840's the same church that housed the colonization conference in the early 1820's had become a Southern Methodist Church and took the position that slavery was a "positive good," morally right, and sanctioned by the Holy Bible.[62]

---

[56] Merle Curti, *The Growth of American Thought* (2d ed.; New York: Harper and Row, 1951), pp. 72-73; Robert McColley, *Slavery and Jeffersonian Virginia* (Urbana: University of Illinois Press, 1964), pp. 145-54. Friends in the yearly meeting of 1784 ruled that Quakers in Virginia could no longer own slaves.

[57] James Hough to James Pemberton, Pemberton Papers, Historical Society of Pennsylvania, Philadelphia, Pa., XV, 153.

[58] McColley, *Slavery and Jeffersonian Virginia*, pp. 152-53.

[59] Sydnor, *The Development of Southern Sectionalism, 1819-1848*, pp. 297-99; *Loudoun Times Mirror*, August 7, 1958.

[60] *The Genius of Liberty*, April 25, 1820; May 1, 1820. Officers were again elected for the next term that had served in the same capacity the previous year: president, Rev. John Mines; vice-presidents, Samuel Murray, Ludwell Lee, Israel Janney, James Moore, Mahlon Taylor, Samuel Nichols, Isaac Brown, Sydner Bayley, Johnson Cleveland, Burr Powell, James Heaton, William Ellzey, William Noland; managers, Asa Moore, John Rose, George Carter, Jacob Mendenhall, Prestley Cordell, Charles B. Ball, S. C. Roszel, L. P. W. Balch; treasurer, R. H. Henderson; recording secretary, R. H. Lee. The society also met in the Leesburg Methodist Church in 1821

[61] Ibid., May 16, 1820; Census of Loudoun County, Virginia for 1810. In 1810, Burr Powell owned twenty-one slaves and William Noland thirteen.

[62] The Baptists and Presbyterians in America were also divided into separate denominations due to sectional bitterness over slavery.

From 1810 to 1839, Charles Mercer, despite being a slaveowner, championed colonization. In 1816 Mercer introduced a resolution in the Virginia legislature that passed the General Assembly. The measure requested that the Governor urge the President of the United States to promote the purchase of land either in the United States or Africa for the voluntary colonization of free Negroes. Continuing this approach, he was one of the founders and long-time enthusiast of the American Colonization Society, founded in 1817, and the Virginia Colonization Society founded in 1828.[63]

The high point of the antislavery movement in Loudoun occurred during the 1820's and early 1830's due to (1) the existence of at least two colonization societies in the county, the Loudoun Auxiliary of the American Colonization Society and the Loudoun Manumission and Emigration Society, and (2) the requests by Loudouners of their state representatives that the latter bring an end to slavery within Virginia. The Manumission and Emigration Society was formed at a meeting held at the Goose Creek schoolhouse on August 21, 1824. Composed primarily of Friends in the county,[64] the society dedicated itself:

> . . . to expose the evils which result from the existence of African slavery, invite the co-operation of our fellow citizens generally, in order to effect its gradual abolition, consistent with the laws and constitution of our country; and to aid and encourage, by voluntary contribution the emigration of our colored population to Hayti [sic], Africa or elsewhere.[65]

Although the above position embraced the identical basic approach of gradualism and colonization espoused by the American Colonization Society and its Loudoun auxiliary, the Goose Creek organization, which included few, if any, slaveowners, took a stronger moral stand against slavery in general and the evil of the domestic slave trade in particular.[66]

---

[63]Trumbo, "Charles Fenton Mercer, 1778-1858," pp. 21-22, 46-50, 69, 71. Pro-colonization resolutions were passed by the Virginia legislature in 1800, 1802, and 1816. Charles Mercer later served as vice-president of the Virginia organization. He gave substantial amounts of his time and money to both the Virginia and American Colonization societies. While in Congress, he obtained the passage of a bill that made engaging in illicit foreign slave trade an act of piracy. Not only did Mercer consider slavery an intolerable evil, but the condition of free blacks in America more disgraceful than that endured by slaves.

[64]The president of the society was a Quaker, Yardley Taylor. At the meeting on August 21, 1824, a constitution for the organization was adopted.

[65]*Genius of Universal Emancipation*, July 4, 1825; October 29, 1825.

[66]*The Genius of Liberty*, July 3, 1821; September 4, 1821; September 25, 1821; October 2, 1821; October 9, 1821. During 1821 *The Genius of Liberty* printed that about one hundred slaves had passed through Leesburg on their way to the lower South. It was also

The Loudoun Manumission and Emigration Society hoped to realize their goals by appealing to the magnanimity, self-interest, and patriotism of slaveowners through newspapers such as *The Genius of Liberty* and *Genius of Universal Emancipation*. In an eloquent address to the public printed in these newspapers during 1825, the society identified slavery as "such an atrocious debasement of human nature" as to demand immediate extinction." References were made to the fact that the institution of slavery violated the national rights stated in the Declaration of Independence, such as "life, liberty, and pursuit of happiness," of which "no human authority can justly deprive" anyone. Slavery was "entirely inconsistent with the principles of a republican government." The welfare of society did "not require that any portion of its members should be enslaved." Instead, slavery was an inferior form of labor that had "a tendency to nourish indolence, to discourage industry," and injure materially "those areas where it existed." It was argued that the increase in the number of slaves and the spreading of the institution into Western territories compelled the immediate termination of the institution by colonization to Africa or Haiti of those in the state of thraldom.[67] Failure to take such a course of action immediately would inevitably result in bloody slave insurrection that would "be attended with the most awful consequences."[68] The Loudoun antislavery organization implored Loudouners and citizens elsewhere to recognize:

> . . . that slavery cannot be justified; that it is a pernicious and dangerous evil. . . .
>
> We ask you in the name of justice, of which our country ought to be the palladium; we conjure you by your love for that country; by all those ties which connect you with posterity; by your interest in its future welfare, to save it, by a timely effort from destruction, and your character to future ages from reproach.[69]

reported that a little more than half of that number of "unhappy wretches had been sold by Judge Washington, of Mount Vernon, President of the Mother American Colonization Society." This evoked a number of letters to the Loudoun paper, including those authored by Judge Washington and Loudoun members of the American Colonization Society. All rebuked the paper for insinuating that Bushrod Washington was guilty of impropriety and that selling slaves was inconsistent with the principles of the colonization society. Finally the editors of the paper issued an apology which included the statement: "it does not appear that Judge Washington, in the sale of his slaves, did violate any *prescribed* rule of the Society."

[67]The position of the Loudoun Manumission and Emigration Society was that the distance and expense of sending blacks back to Africa made Haiti a superior site for colonization.

[68]*Genius of Universal Emancipation*, November 5, 1825.

[69]Ibid. Jonathan Taylor, Jr., a Loudoun Quaker, was the authorized agent from 1826 through 1828 in the county for Benjamin Lundy's *Genius of Universal Emancipation*.

On August 21, 22, and 23, 1827,[70] the Loudoun Manumission and Emigration Society was host to the first annual convention in Virginia for the abolition of slavery.[71] Twenty-one delegates from seven local societies met in the Goose Creek schoolhouse.[72] After the election of officers, a "Constitution of the Virginia Convention for the Abolition of Slavery" was adopted.[73] The convention then addressed itself to issues concerning the practicableness of colonization of American slaves in Africa and desirability of the separation of blacks and white peoples. Support was proclaimed for colonization, gradual emancipation, and the boycott "as far as practicable" of products made by slave labor. The internal slave trade was denounced as an intolerable and "tyrannical" proceeding that the convention must attack.[74] Further transactions consisted of the appointment of five delegates from the Goose Creek meeting to the American Colonization convention to be held in Philadelphia on October 2, 1827,[75] and the selection of a standing committee of five to transact business during the recess of the local convention.[76]

Antislavery feeling in Loudoun was not limited solely to Quakers and other non-slaveholders. A public meeting held at the Leesburg courthouse on December 17, 1831, resulted in the appointment of a committee that drafted a petition to Loudoun delegates, James M'Ilhaney, Presley Cordell, and Samuel B. T. Caldwell, in the Virginia legislature to strongly urge the General Assembly to abolish slavery in the Old Dominion.[77] Five of the nine men on the committee that drew up the petition owned approximately 120 slaves.[78] The stimulus for the

[70]Ibid., April 26, 1828.

[71]Patricia C. Hickin, "Antislavery in Virginia, 1821-1861" (unpublished Doctor's dissertation, University of Virginia, 1968), p. 434.

[72]At the convention from Loudoun were Daniel Janney, David Smith, William Holmes, Sr., William Holmes, Jr., Henry S. Taylor, Yardley Taylor, Benjamin F. Taylor; from Alexandria: Elisha Talbot; from Waterford: Isaac E. Steer, Noble S. Braden, Jesse Gover; from Union: Edward Beeson, Elisha Fawcett.

[73]Daniel Janney of Loudoun was elected vice-president of the convention.

[74]The convention was to investigate the slave trade and gather "such facts that may be of use when the abolition of that traffic shall become the object of legislative consideration."

[75]Delegates included Noble S. Braden of Waterford and Benjamin F. Taylor of Loudoun local societies.

[76]*Genius of Universal Emancipation*, May 3, 1828. The committee of five consisted of Daniel Janney, Yardley Taylor, Isaac E. Steer, George Sharp, and Thomas Wright.

[77]Theodore M. Whitfield, *Slavery Agitation in Virginia, 1829-1832* (rpt; New York: Negro University Press, 1969), pp. 68-69, 147.

[78]Members of the committee that were slaveholders were Richard Henderson, chairman of the committee; Wilson C. Seldon, Jr., Henry Clagett, George M. Chichister, and J. A. Carter. Other members of the committee were John Janney, William B. Tyler, Langette Ball, and Joshua Osburn.

petition from Leesburg calling for an end to the slavery in the state and the reason it was supported by some of Loudoun's most prominent slaveowners was the chilling impact of Nat Turner's insurrection that had occurred in Southhampton County, Virginia, during August 1831. Loudoun's petition made several references to that carnage and insisted the only method to prevent similar slave revolts was the "gradual emancipation of slaves of the Commonwealth, and . . . removal of the entire colored population."[79] Supplementing the fear of slave insurrections were arguments that the "labor of slaves, in a community" like Loudoun, was "the most expensive that can be used" and that slavery tended to "lay waste" to the regions in which it was supported. In short, the basic tenor of the petition was not only negative but also reflective of fear:

> It is most clear, then, that the public interest and safety of individuals call aloud for energetic, but prudent measures having for their object the ultimate extinction of involuntary servitude, and the removal of a race irreconcilably antagonistic to ours.[80]

M'Ilhaney, Cordell, and Caldwell, members of the House of Delegates representing Loudoun, in accordance with the wishes of the framers and supporters of the Loudoun petition, voted for the Preston Amendment which maintained it was "expedient to adopt some legislative enactments" that would abolish slavery in Virginia. The repudiation of this concept by the Virginia legislature proved to be a significant turning point in the momentum of antislavery movements in the state.[81]

Efforts and support by many slaveowners for abolitionist schemes after 1830 waned. This decline was due in large part to the lessening

---

[79]Petition from Loudoun County on December 23, 1831, to the Virginia General Assembly, Archives. Virginia State Library, Richmond, Va.

[80]Ibid.

[81]Charles S. Sydnor, *The Development of Southern Sectionalism, 1819-1848* (Baton Rouge: Louisiana State University Press, 1962), p. 225; Theodore M. Whitfield, *Slavery Agitation in Virginia, 1829-1832*, pp. 83, 93-94. For interpretations rejecting the year 1831 as a time of significant shift in attitude of Virginians away from emancipation, consult pp. 768-69 of the unpublished dissertation by Patricia C. Hickin entitled "Antislavery in Virginia, 1821-1861" and pp. 182-83 in *Slavery and Jeffersonian Virginia* (Urbana: University of Illinois Press, 1964) by Robert McColley. Hickin sees the paramount shift occurring in 1835 while McColley believes the 1780's witnessed a decisive shift in the state away from emancipation and to the defense of slavery. Whitfield, in *Slavery Agitation in Virginia, 1829-1832*, feels the early 1830's was a turning point. Whitfield argues that Virginia was close to bringing about the abolition of slavery in the state at that time. He further maintains that Virginia as the state with the largest slave population, one-fifth of the total slave population in the United States, failure to abolish slavery during the early 1830's was a significant and far-reaching missed opportunity.

in gradual emancipation and colonization as the dominant approach and the rise of immediatism supported by Northern reformers like William Lloyd Garrison, whose vociferation and condemnation of the Southern slaveowner evoked resentment after 1830 even in abolitionists in the South like Samuel M. Janney.[82]

Samuel Janney, a member of the Goose Creek Meeting of the Society of Friends in Loudoun County, was the outstanding reform leader of antislavery and free schools movements not only in antebellum Loudoun but also in the state. His progenitors were English Quakers who originally settled in Pennsylvania and later in Loudoun.[83] Raised in an environment concerned with education and piety, young Janney thrived upon the challenge of educational lessons even from the early age at which he was sent to school. Along with his intellectual awakening emerged an acute and sensitive awareness of religious and moral precepts of the Bible and his faith. He later wrote in his *Memoirs* that at a "very early age I experienced the operation of divine grace condemning me for evil, and inciting me to goodness."[84] From this milieu emerged a man of considerable literary abilities dedicated to the improvement of America's disadvantaged. The application of an adroitness for writing and proclivity to befriend the mistreated resulted in Janney's authoring numerous books and articles, traveling extensively throughout the Eastern part of the United States on behalf of his religion, and championing the cause of public education, antislavery, and the American Indian.[85]

Janney's labor against slavery started in the 1820's, when he was in the mercantile business at Alexandria.[86] There he, along with other Friends and Methodists, formed the Benevolent Society of Alexandria dedicated to the rescue "from the possession of slave traders, persons illegally held in bondage and to enlighten the public mind in regard to the evils of slavery."[87] To aid the work of this oganization, Janney wrote a series of essays dealing with slavery and the domestic slave trade.[88] Published in the *Alexandria Gazette*, these set the tone of his future antislavery writing. Although he identified the degrading impact slavery had upon both blacks and whites, Janney acknowledged the Benevolent Society had no intention of interfering with the legal rights of the slaveholder. In a shrewd attempt to appeal to the slaveowner, Janney

---

[82] Hickin, "Antislavery in Virginia," pp. 760-63.
[83] Janney, *Memoirs*, pp. 1-6. Janney was born in 1801 and died in 1880.
[84] Ibid., p. 6.
[85] Ibid., pp. 52-80, 86-96, 106-10, 254-84.
[86] Janney's father had moved to Alexandria while Samuel was still a child.
[87] Janney, *Memoirs*, p. 28.
[88] Ibid., p. 29. The Alexandria Benevolent Society with the help of Janney and others like him gathered about 1,000 signatures on a petition that was sent to Congress demanding the abolition of slavery in the nation's capital. Janney also supported during the 1820's a colonization society to aid in the removal of free blacks and liberated slaves from the United States to Africa.

discarded what he felt was the excessive devotion by most antislavery writers to the argument that slavery oppressed the black. Instead, the main thrust of his indictment of slavery was on more pragmatic grounds which he hoped would be more persuasive for the Southern white. He compared Virginia with free states of the Northeast in an attempt to prove that a free economy was far superior in prosperity to one encumbered by the existence of slave labor, which also demeaned the republican form of government.[89]

Janney's crusade against slavery was interrupted from 1830 to 1839 as he moved south of Alexandria to Occoquan to live and participate in a partnership with his brother-in-law as a proprietor of a cotton factory.[90] Finding that business venture financially unrewarding, Janney moved to Loudoun County in 1839, where he opened up a boarding school for girls called Springdale. For a while it provided him with a degree of solvency and time so that with financial aid from Friends in Philadelphia he could renew his crusade against slavery.[91] He believed that public sentiment in Virginia during the 1840's was advancing in favor of emancipation. The Loudoun Quaker planned to vigorously carry out his attack upon slavery through the press in such a tactful and judicious manner that would compel slaveholders, he hoped, to liberate their slaves. Cognizant that the danger of offending Southern whites was increasing as the South became more aware and sensitive to her sectional uniqueness, Janney repudiated during 1844 the approach of both the Liberty party and the American Antislavery Society. Spokesman for the latter organization who stated during that year that "dissolution of the Federal Union is one of the principal objects to be aimed at as a means of abolishing slavery" greatly irritated Samuel Janney. He denounced and countered such nonsense by stating:

> This measure I cannot sanction. The Constitution of the United States, so far as it upholds slavery, ought to be amended, but not destroyed; for if we let go our hold upon this anchor, we know not where the vessel of state may be carried by the tumultuous waves of party spirit. Anarchy and confusion may ensue, and then, when it is too late, we may have to weep over the wreck what our hands have made.[92]

Practicing restraint but not deception, Janney stated, but did not belabor the fact, that since the late 1820's he favored "immediate and

---

[89]Hickin, "Antislavery in Virginia, 1821-1861," pp. 527-28.
[90]Janney, *Memoirs*, p. 3.
[91]Ibid., pp. 50-51.
[92]Ibid., p. 75.

unconditional emancipation . . . ; but knowing the prejudice against it in the minds of people," he would settle "for gradual emancipation."[93] He advised fellow Quakers to always take a stand against slavery "under the influence of the meek, lamb-like spirit of Christ" and avoid "the excitement of passion, which too often hurries the unwary into rash and improper measures."[94] The approach he had developed during the 1820's was used far more extensively and ardently during the 1840's. This approach stressed the publication of articles in Southern newspapers illustrating how slavery was responsible for the economic decline of Virginia.[95]

Concerned with reaching as many slaveowners as possible, Janney, nevertheless, devoted considerable energy to addressing himself to the problem of the institution of slavery in the county where he resided as well as throughout the South. During 1849, he persuaded the editor of *The Loudoun Chronicle*, Thomas C. Connolly, to attempt to establish a newspaper dedicated to the promotion of public education and emancipation.[96] Janney was to be the corresponding editor, while Connolly was to own and edit the news sheet. The two Loudouners hoped their paper would be read extensively throughout Virginia.[97] From the outset Janney and Connolly lacked the money needed for their publishing venture.[98] If the paper was ever published, which was unlikely, it was

---

[93]Ibid., p. 33.
[94]Ibid., p. 114.
[95]Janney, *The Yankee in Fairfax County*, pp. 10-23. This influential essay is a reprint of an article originally published in the *Richmond Whig*. It is an excellent example of Janney's sophisticated attack upon slavery. In this essay he does not mention slavery but lauds the impact of free labor and improved farm techniques employed by Northern farmers who had recently settled in Fairfax. Janney also made a plea for Virginia to "become a manufacturing state," contending that she had an abundance of natural resources, such as coal and iron. The *Alexandria Gazette, Richmond Whig, Baltimore Saturday Visitor*, and *Loudoun Chronicle* printed most of his pieces during the 1840's. Janney apparently converted both editors of the *Visitor* and *Chronicle* to the crusade against slavery.
[96]The paper was to be patterned after antislavery tracts of *The National Era* and *Louisville Examiner*. Both were admired by Janney and Connolly.
[97]Hickin, "Antislavery in Virginia, 1821-1861," pp. 503-04. Janney and Connolly needed to raise five hundred dollars since neither had adequate resources of his own to launch the publishing venture. Janney believed one hundred dollars could be raised in Loudoun. He wrote Henry Ruffner in July 1849, asking for names of people sympathetic to emancipation in other counties to whom he could write for financial assistance.
[98]*The Loudoun Chronicle* (Leesburg, Va.) August 10, 1849. It would seem that a man with substantial business acumen would be chary about establishing another newspaper in Loudoun County during the 1840's. During that decade the county was served by the following papers published at Leesburg: *The Washingtonian, The Loudoun Chronicle (Loudoun Whig), The Spirit of Democracy*, and *The Genius of Liberty*. *The Genius of Liberty* started publication in 1817 by S. T. B. Caldwell and apparently stopped around

for an extremely brief period. It is possible that Connolly sold *The Loudoun Chronicle*, then called the *Loudoun Whig*, to W. S. Hough of Fairfax in August 1849, with the intent of launching a new tract.⁹⁹ But it can also be surmised that Connolly had planned originally to make the *Chronicle* a reform tract since circumscribed evidence indicates the paper was greatly concerned with antislavery. Nevertheless, it is also possible that the sale of the paper may have been based solely upon financial motivation.¹⁰⁰

Related to Janney's antislavery crusade was his quest for the establishment of public education in Virginia. He took an active part during 1845 and 1846 in the movement for educational reform. He believed the establishment of free schools was a necessity: (1) to educate "the white children in order to elevate and enlighten the governing class." and (2) serve as "the means of promoting the antislavery sentiment which was obstructed by ignorance and prejudice."¹⁰¹ Janney during this time was appointed a delegate from Loudoun to an educational convention at Richmond. To his surprise he found himself highly regarded by the other delegates and was able to take an active part in the proceedings

---

1841. After finding it difficult to establish a newspaper, Caldwell soon sold the paper to B. W. Sower for $1,200 but kept the book and stationary business. Little is known about *The Spirit of Democracy*. It was edited and published by Richard W. Claxton. The only existing copy of this paper is the March 8, 1842, issue in the possession of the Loudoun County Historical Society. It is also unfortunate that only scattered issues exist of the county's longest published newspaper, *The Washingtonian*. This paper was published for more than ninety years and spanned most of Loudoun's nineteenth-century history. Incomplete issues are still in existence for the years 1851 to 1903 in the Thomas Balch Library in Leesburg, Virginia. *The Washingtonian* was established in 1808 by Patrick McIntire. Upon Patrick McIntire's death, his son, C. C. McIntire continued publication until 1851. At that time the paper was purchased by William B. Lynch. Publication of *The Washingtonian* was suspended during the Civil War but resumed during 1865. In 1903, *The Washingtonian* merged with *The Mirror* of Leesburg which had been established in 1855. The paper formed as the result of the combination of these two papers in 1903 was known as *The Washingtonian-Mirror*.

⁹⁹Janney, *Memoirs*, p. 105; *Loudoun Whig* (Leesburg, Va.), April 28, 1849; *The National Era* (Washington, D. C.), September 28, 1848. It is interesting to note that Janney failed to mention in his *Memoirs* the attempt to establish a crusading newspaper. His only reference to the *Loudoun Whig* in his *Memoirs* was in regard to an editorial on W. A. Smith's speech on slavery. The only copy of the *Loudoun Whig* that has been located is an April 28, 1849, issue currently located in the office of *The Loudoun Times-Mirror* in Leesburg, Virginia. An article from the *Loudoun Whig* was quoted in the September 28, 1848, issue of *The National Era*.

¹⁰⁰Unexplained is the reason Connally changed the name of the *Chronicle* to *Loudoun Whig* around 1848. Hough, the new owner and editor, changed the name back to the *Chronicle* because he did not plan to continue the publication as "an out and out Whig paper."

¹⁰¹Janney, *Memoirs*, p. 93.

of the convention.¹⁰² Although Janney's views were too liberal for a majority of the delegates, the convention did persuade the state legislature to enact legislation for the establishment of a free school system in counties where two-thirds of the citizens voted to initiate public education. When Janney came back to Loudoun after the convention, he "found the cause of popular education had gained ground." Janney's efforts on behalf of public education were supported by *The Loudoun Chronicle*. In one of the latter's editorials, a plea was made for the establishment of "common schools" on the grounds that public education was a "political necessity" for the existence and perpetuation of a "free government." According to the editor of the *Chronicle*, public education would promote a "free government" by providing control and refinement of the masses in such a way as to "repress the ignoble" and restrict the "scrutiments of the proud."¹⁰³ Public education would also make the ballot in the hands of the average less threatening as they would be less likely to fall victims to "misplaced esteem" and "bold presumptuous, and unblushing ignorance."¹⁰⁴

Contrary to Janney's optimism, only six counties in the state accepted the challenge and attempted to establish public schools. Much to Janney's surprise, Loudoun was not one of them. Slaveholders in the county generally opposed free schools on the grounds that it was an "entering wedge for" the abolition of slavery.¹⁰⁵ This view aborted the efforts of educational reform not only in Virginia but also in the Southern states, where it was held by a majority of Southern slaveholders during the waning years of the Jacksonian era. The South was thus increasingly hostile to crusades for humanitarian and benevolent changes on behalf of the disadvantaged.

---

¹⁰²Ibid., pp. 93-94. During the convention, Janney spoke in opposition "to the *pauper system* then existing" in the state. He condemned it for its "inefficiency and its degrading effect in making a distinction between the rich and the poor." He instead advocated "a system of free schools such as were in successful operation in New York and New England." While attending the convention, Janney had an interview with Governor James McDowell, at which time Janney pressed his antislavery views.

Loudoun County expended $1,230.18 and $1,073.60 for the education of poor children in 1832 and 1833.

¹⁰³*The Loudoun Chronicle*, September 7, 1849.

¹⁰⁴*The Genius of Liberty*, December 30, 1825.

¹⁰⁵Janney, *Memoirs*, pp. 94-95; Virginia, House of Delegates, *Journal*, 1846-47, Bill No. 82. This bill was passed on February 25, 1846, and gave Loudouners the option, which they rejected, to establish free schools in the county. Bill No. 82, in addition to dealing with the mechanics of selecting local school commissioners (to be elected annually, two from each school district within the county), also dealt with the selection of teachers and textbooks. This law also covered methods of financing free schools. The financial sources for free schools were to include the state Literary Fund, glebe income, local school tax, plus a "tuition to be charged for each scholar" of not "less than fifty cents nor more than one dollar per quarter, or term of three months." No tuition fee was to be demanded of those who in the opinion of the commissioners were unable to pay.

Education in antebellum Loudoun was above the level of the majority of other counties in Virginia.[106] This achievement was true especially in the number of private schools which arose in towns and included boarding and day schools like the Leesburg Academy (1799-1879) and other Leesburg schools;[107] Middleburg Academy (ca. 1803-1861); William Williamson's Middleburg School (1805-1830) and other Middleburg schools; Hillsborough Academy (1845-1855) and other Hillsboro schools; Rev. Ben Bridges' School in Broad Run District (1845-1870); Upperville Academy (established in 1833), Rehoboth Academy (established in 1834), and schools established by Friends, such as Franklin Taylor's school near Hughesville (1825-1860), the Waterford School (1761?-1861), and Samuel Janney's Springdale Boarding School Association (established in 1839)[108] Predecessors of these institutions were family schools. Governesses or tutors were hired by the wealthy and social elite to instruct the children of their families. A variation of this was the cooperation of two or more families in securing an instructor and setting

---

[106] A. J. Morrison, *The Beginning of Public Education in Virginia, 1776-1860* (Richmond, Va.: Davis Bottom, Superintendent of Public Printing, 1917), pp. 127-83.

[107] *The Genius of Liberty*, April 10, 1841; Philip V. diZerega, "History of Education in Loudoun County, Virginia" (unpublished Master's thesis, University of Virginia, 1948), pp. 26-32. (Hereafter referred to as "History of Education in Loudoun.") A number of private schools existed in Leesburg by the 1820's. Many stressed literature and English grammar like Edward Hazen's school, Bashaw's English School, John Woods English School, and Samuel A. Jackson's English School. Hazen was especially proud of a "new and improved" teaching technique. He claimed by the use of lectures and charts more English literature could be taught in five or six weeks than could normally be learned by "usual methods in one year." Other Leesburg schools were P. Saunder's School, which taught subjects on the high school level, and the Leesburg Female Academy, which replaced Mr. and Mrs. Gibson's Female School.

[108] diZerega, op. cit., pp. 130, 137, 177, 182. In 1834, Middleburg had one classical school, one English school for males, and two female academies while Leesburg had one classical school for males, two English schools for males, and three schools for females. The Middleburg Academy was in operation from 1803 to 1861. During all or a portion of that time it was a military academy. The Virginia legislature in 1827 enacted a law authorizing the principals of the Middleburg Academy, Enos W. Newton and Ozro P. Jenison, to have "seventy-five stand of muskets, of cartouch boxes and belts for the use of the pupils in the said seminary." An extensive ad for the Middleburg Academy was placed in the December 30, 1829, issue of *The Genius of Liberty* by E. W. Newton. Tuition for the elementary branches was $3 per quarter, more advanced work in English grammar, geography, bookkeeping, arithmetic, elocution was $4; rhetoric, history, chemistry, philosophy, astronomy, logic, ethics, mensuration, surveying, $5; and the higher branches of mathematics, Latin and Greek languages $8. Good board could be obtained in respectable families, including the home of Principal Newton. Boarding with the Newton family was $100 per annum. This included "washing." If students did not furnish their own beds, they had to pay $10 extra.

up on one of their estates a school for the children of the neighborhood.[109]

Of all Loudoun's private schools the institution probably the most esteemed was the Leesburg Academy, which was in existence throughout most of the nineteenth century.[110] The school year of the academy consisted of forty-four to forty-six weeks, divided into two semesters that extended from early September to the end of July.[111] Principals of the academy prior to the Civil War rarely stayed on the job more than a few years because of the financial problems and the inadequacies of the school building.[112] The latter are illustrated by a plea of one headmaster to the trustees that they had to do something to improve the "warming" of the academy during the winter.[113] Principals were first business managers and secondly educators. They could elect, as the "Rev." Dr. Neil did, to accept an annual fixed salary,[114] or they could agree to a more flexible arrangement by which their salary would depend upon the enrollment.[115] Ultimate authority for the academy rested with a board of trustees, who held monthly meetings to resolve problems and issues relating to the institution. This board appointed all principals and teachers.[116] Discipline was of paramount importance to the trustees. During August 1845, they fired a Mr. Hunter because in their judgment he did not command the discipline "indispensably necessary, although in many other respects" he was an "eminently qualified" instructor.[117]

[109]Ibid., pp. 20-21. Family schools were held on the plantations and country estates known as Springwood, Raspberry Plain, Belmont, Coton, Oatlands, Rokeby, Benton, Llangollan, Morrisworth, Chestnut Hill, Rockland, Exeter, Selma, Aldie Manor, Morven Park, and Oak Hill.

[110]The Leesburg Academy was not the first school in Leesburg. There was a Latin school there in the 1780's. In 1783, Dr. Schoepf, while traveling south, noticed that a proposal had been made to establish a Latin School in Leesburg. The first building for the Leesburg Academy was a house the trustees rented. Students boarded with "respectable families of the town." The trustees also hired Rev. Allen "to preside over the Seminary."

[111]Leesburg Academy, Minutes of the Board of Trustees, August 12, 1845, Thomas Balch Library, Leesburg, Virginia.

[112]The following were principals of the Leesburg Academy during the antebellum era: Rev. John A. Getly (1833-34), John F. Keenan (1834-37), "Rev." Dr. Neil (1837-184?), W. B. Benedict (1846-1852), J. J. Sanborn (1853), Rev. Charles H. Nourse (1854-59), and J. B. Wilson (early 1860's).

[113]Leesburg Academy, Minutes of the Board of Trustees, December 4, 1840.

[114]Ibid., December 2, 1837. Dr. Neil's annual salary was $800.

[115]Ibid., September 13, 1833. Such an arrangement was accepted by Rev. John A. Getly, who was guaranteed for one year "a number of scholars whose tuition fees would amount to $1000.00." Enrollment in the academy averaged between twenty-five and fifty students.

[116]During August 1845 the board of trustees appointed a Mr. Converse to teach English for a yearly salary of $350.

[117]Leesburg Academy, Minutes of the Board of Trustees, August 12, 1845.

ation	Type		For			Opened	Closed	Enroll.
	E	HS	B	G	Coed			
urg		x	x			1799	1879	25
urg	x	x	x			—	—	—
urg	x	x			x	—	—	—
urg	x	x		x		—	—	—
urg		x	x			—	—	—
urg		x		x		—	1874	35
urg	x	x	x			—	1897	60
urg	x	x	x			—	—	—
leburg	x	x			x	1803	1861	—
n	x	x	x			—	—	—
rford	x	x			x	1761?	1861	—
lleburg	x	x	x			1805	1830	—
esville	x	x	x			1825	1861	—
ln	x	x		x		1839	1854	—
boro	x	x			x	1845	1855	—
boro	x	x		x		1855	1861	—
boro	x	x	x			1815	—	—
urg	x	x		x		1836	1861	—
ing	x	x			x	1845	1870	—
e	x	x	x			1854	1861	—

on	x	x		x	1850	1853	—
		x		x	1869	1888	70
g	x	x	x		1865	1873	32
	x	x	x		1870	—	—
		x		x	1909	1915	60
g	x	x		x	—	—	—
e					ca. 1870	—	—
	x	x		x	1866	—	—
	x	x		x	1855	1888	35
	x	x		x	1894	1903	30
	x	x		x	1894	1896	32
rg	x	x		x	1897	1899	20
ill	x	x		x	1901	1903	16
	x	x		x	1902	1903	20
ill	x	x		x	1903	1904	15
ill	x	x		x	1904	1906	12
rg		x		x	1914	—	100

ted in Loudoun County during the Nineteenth Century and Early Twentieth Century.

Secondary Education in Loudoun County, Virginia," p. 63; *The Democratic
e for Young Ladies Near Leesburg, Virginia: Session 1866-7*. With the exception
above chart is the same as that prepared by diZerega for his study of Loudoun

Although motivated by frugality, the trustees nevertheless felt a sense of humanitarian duty to consider the possibility of admitting free to the academy a few students who could not afford the tuition and boarding.[118] Often the trustees asked the town council for financial assistance. While town leaders did provide some financial assistance, such as the $250 they appropriated during 1837 for the repair of the school building,[119] they were not amicable toward all requests. During July 1837, the town council refused to allow a lottery to take place, out of which at least $150 would have gone to the academy.[120] By 1843 both the trustees and the town planners concluded that a new building was to be constructed at a cost not to exceed $5,000.[121] The construction costs of the new structure were financed by a local lottery. The success of the lottery was due in part to the inspirational eloquence of a speech given at Leesburg by a prominent educator then teaching at the University of Virginia and author of the "McGuffey Reader," William H. McGuffey.[122]

Despite the relatively high number of private boarding and day schools operating in Loudoun during the first half of the nineteenth century, a large percentage of Loudoun's population remained uninitiated into rudimentary education and the experiences that beset students erring in behavior or academic performance, such as having the teacher strike their knuckles with a ruler or stinging their "backside" with a switch. Poor schools initiated by state legislation enacted during the second decade of the 1800's nominally existed in antebellum Loudoun. Fifteen school commissioners in the county reported in 1832 that Loudoun had seventy-five schools for the poor that were attended by 900 indigent pupils on the average of only seventy days during the year.[123] Yardley Taylor, a Loudoun Quaker and surveyor who succinctly and accurately assessed the state of antebellum education in Loudoun, wrote:

---

[118]Ibid., January 6, 1846. A special committee was created by the trustees to consider if the tuition from other students would make it economically feasible to admit select, promising students free.

[119]Ibid., February 7, 1837.

[120]Ibid., July 22, 1837.

[121]Ibid., July 21, 1843.

[122]Penelope M. Osburn, "The True American," *The Bulletin of the Loudoun County Historical Society*, 1 (1958), 33-34; Ralph Walker, "American Schoolmaster: McGuffy and His Reader," *American History Illustrated*, VIII (May 1973), 22-23. The new structure was completed in 1846 and used as a school until 1879. It was then purchased by the county for $7,500 and used as a Clerk's Office building for the county government. The proceeds from this sale were partially used to purchase a lot and move the academy to a site south of the town's cemetery, where Leesburg's high school was later constructed and remained in operation until the 1950's.

[123]Joseph Martin, ed., *Gazetteer of Virginia* (Charlottesville: Moseley and Tompkins, Printers, 1835), p. 77.

> The citizens of this county have not been unmindful of the advantages of education. . . . Good boarding schools, in different parts of the county have been supported, and in many neighborhoods, good day schools are kept up throughout the year, yet it must be confessed that, in too many places, an indifference is manifested, not very creditable to those concerned. The importance of good schools is not sufficiently appreciated by all. It is to them that we must look, to furnish the elements of education to the masses. The rich can obtain education for their children, but the poor should have it provided for them. Our State is providing funds for educating the children of the indigent, but, from the imperfection of the school system, now in use, this fund cannot be properly applied. In many parts of the county, school houses are not within the reach of all, and as those interested with the distribution of this fund, have no control in the selection of teachers, or the management of the schools, its advantages are but partially felt.[124]

Taylor went on to propose that the existing funds be increased by the addition of a modest property tax to provide "a good system of public schools" in Loudoun.[125]

Taylor's conclusions about education in Loudoun were reached as early as 1817 by a representative of the county in the General Assembly, Charles Mercer. To remedy the inadequacies in Virginia's education, Mercer introduced a comprehensive bill that would have created a system of education for both sexes through the establishment of primary schools, academies, colleges, and an university.[126] Unfortunately this measure was not passed. Samuel Janney's efforts during the 1840's on behalf of public

---

[124]Taylor, *Memoir*, p. 29.
[125]Ibid.
[126]Morrison, *The Beginnings of Public Education in Virginia, 1776-1860*, pp. 10-11, 15. Although Mercer's bill failed to pass the General Assembly in 1817, it was the forerunner of provisions later enacted into law. Thomas Jefferson in 1779 proposed the first bill for public education in Virginia. In 1810, the state established the Literary Fund which appropriated certain escheats, penalties, and forfeitures for the education within the state. However, it was not until the 1818 Act that even the pretense of public education existed within Virginia. Under the 1818 legislation, the county courts had to appoint school commissioners whose major function was to establish schools for indigent children. The next significant education legislation that attempted to establish free schools throughout the state was enacted in 1846. Like previous legislation successful implementation of the law depended upon the initiative of the county and community. Consequently few counties within the state had an adequate system of public education prior to the Civil War.

education, like those of Mercer, were, nevertheless, a positive contribution to education throughout the state. Janney lamented the failure of public education to be extensively realized in Virginia not only because it was a setback for humanitarianism, but also because it was a blow against future pride one could take in the intellectual and scientific achievements of the state. He wanted Virginia to stop being dependent:

> . . . upon the North not only for many of our best teachers, but for nearly all our literature. How seldom do we hear of a book being written by a Virginian! How few scientific discoveries have we made? Nearly all the best developed intellect in this State has been devoted to law and politics, because these have been considered the roads to distinction. If the great mass of our people were educated, a part of their intellectual energies would be directed into different channels, and we might have our distinguished authors and savants as well as other states.[127]

Loudoun's repudiation of public education at a time when Janney had realized prominence within Virginia was a severe rebuff to him and his belief that the state was on the verge of an enlightened social reformation. However, a few years later Loudoun dealt him an even greater blow. Unlike the earlier rebuff, the latter was an indictment of Janney personally by the county court in an attempt to censor and silence him from making future antislavery pronouncements.

In September 1849, William A. Smith, president of Randolph Macon College in Virginia and a Southern Methodist minister, delivered in the courthouse at Leesburg a verbose address ostensibly on education, which in reality was predominately a defense of slavery.[128] Since Smith's views, which included the denunciation of the Declaration of Independence and the assertion that slavery was "right in itself, and sanctioned by the Bible," were heard by a large audience, many of whom applauded, and the opposing view was not represented, Janney was greatly concerned and annoyed. To refute Smith's arguments, Janney wrote three critical essays pertaining to Smith's speech.[129] Two of these were published in the Leesburg *Washingtonian*. The third article was not published because of threats made against Janney which caused the editor of the *Washingtonian*, C. C. McIntire, to withhold publication.[130]

---

[127]Janney, *Memoirs*, p. 95.
[128]Hickin, "Antislavery in Virginia," p. 504; Janney, *Memoirs*, p. 97.
[129]The first essay appeared in the August 10, 1849, issue of the *Washingtonian*.
[130]Hickin, op. cit., p. 505.

Soon after the publication of the first essay, the grand jury of Loudoun "presented" Janney for publishing an article which they contended "was calculated to incite persons of color to make insurrection or rebellion."[131] Although the accusation was false, it was the charge's being expressed in an illegal manner that prevented the county court from bringing him to trial on this presentment.

Loudoun slaveowners were not satisfied. They wanted Janney punished for his antislavery statements to prevent him and others from making such outbursts in the future. This action reflected the growing paranoia about slavery and slave insurrections in the South that manifested themselves in a demand for conformity to an illiberal conservatism of protecting and defending the "peculiar institution" of slavery.[132] Conformity was demanded of individuals as well as intellectual, political, religious, and legal institutions of the South.

At the next quarterly court in November 1849, the grand jury again indicted Janney for the same essay, in which they now maintained he contended "owners 'had no right of property in their slaves.' "[133] The trial was set for March 1850, but due to a motion by the attorney for the commonwealth it was postponed until June 11.[134] While awaiting trial, Janney concluded that it was unlikely that he would be found guilty and subsequently receive a heavy fine and imprisonment. He, nevertheless, worried about "the opprobrium intended by the attempt to persecute" him and "cast out his name as evil." Therefore, during his usual numerous prayers he "endeavored to draw nigh to Him who is mighty to save."[135]

Janney pleaded his "own cause" without the aid of legal counsel. By basing his case upon legal technicalities and broad principles of constitutional liberties in a highly effective manner, he was considered to have presented a "brilliant" defense.[136] The core of his defense was set forth in four points he stressed in a written argument to the court. First, the charge that his article published in the *Washingtonian* stated " 'that masters have no right of property in their slaves' " was not valid. An examination of his article, he argued, would reveal the reverse was

---

[131]Janney, *Memoirs*, pp. 97-98.

[132]Clement Eaton, *The Freedom-of-Thought Struggle in Old South* (New York: Harper and Row, 1964), pp. 298,352.

[133] Janney, *Memoirs*, p. 98.

[134]Ibid., 98; Loudoun County Minute Book of 1850, pp. 10-11. See Commonwealth v. Samuel M. Janney.

[135]Janney, *Memoirs*, p. 98. While charges were pending against Janney, he authored a lengthy article for *The National Era* (see January 31, 1850, issue) that was a caveat about the decline of Virginia. Janney's stand on slavery in this article was very moderate. In reference to the existence of slavery in the South and its expansion into the territory, Janney wrote: "If the South is content with Slavery where it now exists, we are. All we ask is that it shall remain where it is."

[136]Eaton, *The Freedom-of-Thought Struggle in the Old South*, p. 136.

true. In the article Janney had correctly defined that under the law a slave was property and a creature void of any legal rights as a person.[137] This was his basic objection to "the whole system of American slavery . . . it degrades men by regarding them as property."[138] Second, he declared that the statute he was accused of violating, when compared with the constitution of Virginia, did not apply to his case because the latter document stated " 'the Legislature shall not pass any law abridging the freedom of speech or of the press.' " He further maintained that as a member of " 'a religious society' " that found slavery a violation of its creed, it was his religious duty to speak out against slavery, not to " 'incite slaves to make insurrection or rebellion' " or " 'meddle with the slave, but to appeal to the master.' "[139] Third, if the court deemed that the statute of 1848, under which he was charged, did apply in his case, then the law should be voided since it was in violation of the Virginia state constitution. Janney cited legal precedent for such action in Judge Roan's decision in the case of Peter Kemper versus Mary Hawkins.[140] Fourth, he argued that it was grossly unfair to accord freedom of speech and press to a person from another county, a learned predicant, who traversed the county to speak on education but instead defended slavery and ridiculed the Declaration of Independence,[141] while the same rights were denied to a Loudouner. He concluded:

> . . . can it be possible that freedom of speech and of the press are so completely prostrated in Virginia, that a native citizen of the county may not be permitted to answer an address thus publicly delivered, in which were maintained doctrines at variance with the sentiments of Washington, Jefferson, Madison, Patrick Henry, and all the great statesmen of Virginia.[142]

After the commonwealth attorney responded to Janney's written argument, the defendant concluded his defense by stating orally to the

---

[137] Janney, *Memoirs*, p. 100. Janney's article elaborated that " 'A slave is to all intents and purposes a *chattel personal*, and may be taken and sold for his master's debts; he cannot acquire nor hold property; he can make no contract that his master may not annul; he cannot even contract matrimony, for there is no legal marriage for slaves.' "

[138] Ibid.

[139] Ibid., pp. 100-03.

[140] Ibid., pp. 103-04; Eaton, *The Freedom-of-Thought Struggle in the Old South*, p. 136.

[141] Janney, *Memoirs*, p. 105. Janney mentioned that the nature of W. A. Smith's address was discussed in detail in an editorial in the *Loudoun Whig*.

[142] Ibid.

magistrates of the county, most of whom were slaveholders,[143] that "the longer you keep this subject before the people the more there will be to my way."[144] The justices were fearful of making the Janney case a local "cause celebre" so they stopped the trial.[145] Before dismissing Janney, the chairman of the court, Hamilton Rogers, admonished the Friend about "the necessity of great care and caution in meddling with the delicate question of slavery." Janney "cared little" for "the lecture and proceeded without delay in obtaining the publication in a local newspaper his written defense, which he entitled "The Freedom of the Press Vindicated."[146] But the trial may have had the ultimate impact upon Janney that the magistrates and slaveowners in the county wanted.[147] While Janney did not forsake or recant his antislavery views after 1850, he was far less active in the antislavery cause. Instead, he concentrated on writing religious histories concerning the Society of Friends, thus making the decade of the 1850's his most productive period as an author.[148]

As illustrated by the trial of Samuel M. Janney, attitudes in Loudoun since the late 1840's had been bifurcated into vociferous critics of slavery led by Loudoun Quakers and proponents of slavery who were intolerant of even moderate criticism. Slaveowners in the county had shifted from their open demand for the end of slavery by gradual colonization. The awareness that colonization of blacks would not be realized, the fear of slave insurrection, which had earlier made slave-owners in the county work for colonization, and the intemperate attacks upon the institution of slavery and Southern slaveowners by Northern abolitionists were among the salient reasons that Loudoun slaveowners became intolerant of any indictment of slavery. Accompanying this sharp division in Loudoun over slavery not only intolerance but also bitterness.

---

[143]Loudoun County Minute Book of 1850, pp. 10-11; Slave schedules of the Census of Loudoun county, Virginia for 1850. The county magistrates were Hamilton Rogers, Asa Rogers,Thomas S. Ellzey, and John A. Carter. All were slaveowners except Ellzey. Hamilton Rogers in 1850 owned twenty-five slaves, Asa Rogers seventeen, and John A. Carter thirty-two.

[144]Janney, *Memoirs*, p. 98.

[145]Ibid.; Loudoun County Minute Book of 1850, pp. 10-11. The clerk was ordered to enter in the Minute Book a "nolle prosequi" for Janney's trial, which technically meant the prosecutor would proceed no further on the indictment.

[146]Janney, *Memoirs*, pp. 99-106; *The National Era*, June 27, 1850.

[147]Hickin, "Antislavery in Virginia," pp. 511-13. Hickin states that Janney may have backed away from his crusade against slavery due to his increasing dismay at the extremism of Northern abolitionists, the increasing zeal of the South to protect slavery, and the failure of the emancipation movement in Kentucky.

[148]Janney, *Memoirs*, pp. 106-11. The following works were written or started by Janney during the 1850's: *The Life of William Penn* (Philadelphia: Hogan, Perkins, & Co., 1852); *The Life of George Fox* (Philadelphia: Lippincott, Grambo & Co., 1853); *History of the Religious Society of Friends* (4 vols., Philadelphia: T. Elwood Zell, 1859-1867).

The activities of Quakers at Goose Creek during the 1820's, such as the formation of the Manumission and Emigration Society and acting as host to the Virginia abolition convention did not greatly concern or excite Loudoun slaveowners. But an antislavery meeting held by the Friends at Goose Creek in 1856 was the source of great consternation in the county, especially throughout the eastern and southern regions of Loudoun.

Indicative of the increasing acrimony and hostility in the slave-owning community in the county toward the Goose Creek Quakers is a lengthy single page publication dated July 28, 1857, written by a Loudoun slaveowner to Yardley Taylor.[149] The author described Taylor as a "heavy set, hugely footed" aging Quaker leader. The latter was known locally as the county's topographer and antislave advocate, whose activities included being the first president of the Loudoun Manumission and Emigration Society. The author of this article made the following reference to the fame of Taylor's antislavery activities:

> There are but few persons in the county, I presume, who have not heard of you as the Chief of the abolition clan in Loudoun. I am free to award to you this position, for the boldness and daring which you have uniformly exhibited in promulgating the odious doctrines of your sect, fully entitles you in my opinion, to [this] distinction.[150]

This publication was in response to Taylor's attempt to obtain another interview with the author of the article in order to presumably try to convince him that owning slaves was sinful. This printed outburst was not only to reject the idea of an interview, but also to chastise Taylor and the Goose Creek Quakers for their antislavery activities, during which they allegedly maliciously maligned the slaveowner's good name in a discussion of the gentlemen at this antislavery meeting and by circulating throughout the community, according to the slaveowner, an anonymous "slanderous, blackguard, scurrilous, dirty, vile, miserable doggerel letter."[151] In regard to Taylor's role and comments pertaining

---

[149] *To Yardley Taylor, Esq.*, July 28, 1857. This broadside was probably originally published in one of the county newspapers. The author signed the article, but that portion of the broadside is missing.

[150] Ibid.

[151] Ibid. Taylor reputedly referred to the slaveowner in the 1856 Goose Creek antislavery meeting as: "He is poor—unsustained by family influence, or wealthy connexions, and it will be an easy matter to shift the burden of our sins on his shoulders; for we are powerful: - it will crush him and save us." This statement was also published in the *Alexandria Sentinel*. Rumor also had a critical letter about the gentleman in question being read to the pupils at the Goose Creek school.

to the underground railroad, the slaveowner commented: "Monstrous! Monstrous!" and "Yardley, Yardley! who would have dreamed that your own confession could make your guilt so clear."[152] But the greatest shock to the slaveowner was Taylor's utterance that it was difficult to find "any more valid objections against" whites "marrying a negro wench, than in wedding an Indian beauty."[153] The slaveowner also accused Taylor and his antislavery allies of being the stimuli for fear that plagued the minds and hearts of many Loudouners. Not only Loudoun antislavery crusaders were believed to be responsible for producing conditions that debilitated the efficiency of the county government, but also they unleashed upon the "community evils which the laws were powerless to remedy."[154]

Goose Creek, a Quaker settlement, was referred to as the center of the underground railroad in Loudoun. The number of slaves assisted to freedom by the Friends of that community is not known. Yardley Taylor was arrested and tried for participation in the escape of a fugitive. A runaway came to Taylor's menage, where the fugitive was fed and given a letter by the Quaker to a friend in Pennsylvania.[155] Rumors circulated in Loudoun that years earlier Taylor had assisted a slave named Phil to escape to freedom and was behind an unsuccessful foray of Loudoun Quakers into a neighboring county to liberate those in bondage.[156]

The outstanding female antebellum reformer in Loudoun and participant in the underground railroad was Miss Margaret Mercer. Although she was not a Quaker, this remarkable woman fought against slavery, ran a private girls' school at Belmont, and was an advocate and leader in the women's rights movement.[157] She greatly reduced her affluence by emancipating her slaves and sending them to Liberia.

The escalating debate and emotional accusations between detractors and proponents of slavery in Loudoun and the occasional trial of an

---

[152] *To Yardley Taylor, Esq.*
[153] Ibid.
[154] Ibid.
[155] Ibid. Taylor is reported to have commented that Quaker friends in Pennsylvania criticized him for not doing more to aid runaway slaves.
[156] Ibid.
[157] *The Loudoun Times-Mirror*, May 14, 1964; diZerega, "History of Education in Loudoun," p. 40. Miss Mercer was born in 1791, the daughter of John Francis Mercer of Cedar Park, Maryland. Mr. Mercer served as Governor of that state. Miss Mercer purchased Belmont, the former home of Ludwell Lee, after Lee's death. At Belmont she conducted a school for young ladies from 1836 until her death in 1846. Miss Virginia Kephart succeeded Miss Mercer and conducted the school for approximately a decade after which the school was moved to Leesburg and held in a house later the residence in the 1940's and 1950's of General George C. Marshall. Miss Mercer offered a comprehensive curriculum, which included English grammar and literature, music, French, chemistry, botany, morals, philosophy, theology, graphics, geography, mathematics, and Latin.

abolitionist produced heated discussions and espousal of political theories in an attempt to rationalize the sanctity of one position and incorrectness of the opposing view. Yardley Taylor defended his position in aiding a fugitive slave and thereby violating the Fugitive Slave Act of 1850, because the act was in contradiction to the "higher law" of his religion. Furthermore, Taylor contended that man's obligation to government extended no farther than the submission to legal penalties. Slaveowners maintained that allegiance to a "higher law" was a dangerous doctrine that justified resistance to any man-made legislation and could culminate in anarchy. On the issue of the Fugitive Slave Act of 1850, Loudoun slaveowners did not take a States' rights posture, but one of fervent nationalism. They argued man's moral and legal duty were the same: to support the government and laws of that government that granted him protection. This position was stated very forcefully by one of Taylor's most vociferous critics:

> The principle of moral and positive laws is the same, and the same obligation rests upon us to obey the one as the other. The good man makes no distinction. The object of penalties is to enforce obedience to the laws, by detering men from their violation. They are not designed as an equivalent for the commission of an offence. A man is, therefore, very far from performing his whole duty to society by simply submitting to the penalty of a violated law. He is under a high moral obligation to do more than this—he must obey that law. The Bible, morality, and patriotism, all alike unite in enjoining it as a solemn duty which every man owes to the government which affords him protection.[158]

Loudoun slaveowners were also disenchanted with the enforcement of the Fugitive Slave Act in Northern states. This sentiment was true especially in the settlement of the case involving Loudoun's most celebrated fugitive, Daniel Dangerfield, alias Daniel Webster. Dangerfield escaped in 1853 from Loudoun, where he had been a slave of French Simpson. Six years later, on April 4, 1859, Dangerfield, then approximately twenty-five, was arrested at Harrisburg, Pennsylvania, by a deputy United States marshal, who handcuffed and took the fugitive to Philadelphia for the United States Commissioner Lonstreth to determine, in accordance with the Fugitive Slave Act of 1850, whether Dangerfield was a runaway slave or a free man.[159]

---

[158] *To Yardley Taylor, Esq.*
[159] *The Democratic Mirror*, April 6, 1859. (Hereafter referred to as the *Mirror*.) Dangerfield's arrest emanated from a warrant issued at the behest of the widow of French

SLAVERY/ STIMULUS FOR DIVISION: 1848 TO 1861

The arrest of Dangerfield and the hearing that followed caused a lot of excitement in Philadelphia and throughout Pennsylvania. Speeches denouncing the arrest of Dangerfield as an outrage were made in the Pennsylvania state legislature. Sympathetic and emotional accounts of the trial were published in Pennsylvania newspapers.[160] Pennsylvanians found the young Negro, who had endured recent personal tragedy with the death of his last child, plus his impending re-enslavement an easy subject for great sympathy. Hundreds of Negroes gathered around the courthouse during the first day of Dangerfield's trial, causing the chief of police to send 400 policemen to disperse the crowd.[161] Lucretia Mott, the venerable Philadelphia Quakeress and abolitionist orator, attended the trial and sat next to Dangerfield, giving him encouragement. During the trial in the heated debate among the lawyers, she threw her arms around Dangerfield and verbally interrupted the hearing. An official removed her arms and persuaded her to return to her seat. Even Marshal Yost, who was determined to keep order at the trial, offered to give from $50 to $200 toward the $1,300 purchase price of Daniel if the decision rendered declared Dangerfield was a fugitive slave.[162]

The hearing was a turbulent event. Legal counsels for the plaintiff and defendant debated legal technicalities, the intent and application of the Fugitive Slave Act of 1850, and examined witnesses all day and night. The night session continued without a recess from four o'clock in the afternoon until six o'clock the next morning. The crux of the case was the number of years Dangerfield had lived in Pennsylvania. Had he lived in Harrisburg since 1850, as he claimed, or had he been a slave in Loudoun until 1854, as five witnesses for the plaintiff testified? Those

---

Simpson, Elizabeth Simpson. His capture resulted from action by J. H. Gulick, a Loundouner. On a trip North Gulick stopped off for a few days at Harrisburg in February 1859 because he had heard in Loudoun that Dangerfield was in Harrisburg. After he discovered Dangerfield, Gulick wrote Sandford P. Rogers, an attorney, friend, and relative of Mrs. Simpson. At the trial, Gulick testified that he identified Dangerfield for the marshal and assisted in the arrest by grabbing the fugitive and informing the crowd that Dangerfield was a burglar. This apprehending he stated, was to discourage others at the scene of the arrest from befriending Dangerfield.

[160] For example, *The Philadelphia Bulletin*, *The Philadelphia Journal*, and *The Harrisburg Telegraph* were among the newspapers of that state that carried detailed accounts of the Dangerfield case. *The Philadelphia Bulletin* described Dangerfield as a "good-looking stalwart man" with "an inoffensive countenance," who had lived in Harrisburg during the past nine years where he made fences. The paper stated that Daniel was arrested at six-thirty on a Saturday morning at a market place on the pretense he had committed a crime. When interviewed, according to the *Bulletin*, Daniel stated with "tears in his eyes . . . he had a wife and two children." Both of the children were dead. The last child was buried just a week prior to Dangerfield's arrest.

[161] Fifty special deputy marshals were assigned to keep order at the Dangerfield trial.

[162] *Mirror*, April 6, 1859.

testifying on the behalf of Mrs. Simpson were Dr. Francis Lucketts, formerly of Loudoun, who had treated Daniel for typhoid while he was a slave on Simpson's farm; John W. Patton, a Loudoun constable who had formerly worked as a farm hand for French Simpson, where he claimed he saw Dangerfield as a slave until July 1854; William L. Bogue, who currently ran the Eagle Hotel in Leesburg but earlier was in the "boot and shoe business at Aldie," where he knew Daniel when the latter worked as a mill boy. J. H. Gulick, who refused to swear to tell the truth because he had joined the Baptist Church and had not sworn for two or three years, testified he had known Daniel for twenty years and last saw him in 1853;[163] Sandford P. Rogers, an attorney and relative of Mrs. Simpson, who was instrumental in procuring the warrant that led to the subsequent arrest of Dangerfield, testified he had known the defendant since he was a boy. Rogers claimed he last saw Dangerfield in 1853. Although several Negroes testified they had seen Daniel Dangerfield in Harrisburg, Pennsylvania, and in Maryland prior to 1853, all but the testimony of one of these witnesses was disproved as contradicting Dangerfield's own testimony. The sole remaining testimony on behalf of Dangerfield was that of an elderly illiterate Negro named Smith, who admittedly had a bad memory. Evidence supporting the return of Dangerfield to Loudoun seemed irrefutable. However, the inexperience of Lonstreth as a commissioner and the overwhelming opposition in Pennsylvania to the return of Dangerfield to thraldom made Lonstreth, on the basis of Smith's testimony, rule Dangerfield was not a fugitive slave and was free to remain in Pennsylvania. The verdict was received in the City of Brotherly Love with great exultation and excitement. In a carriage Dangerfield was driven through the streets where he was cheered by approximately 1,000 Negroes.[164]

To the decision that Pennsylvanians received with euphoric jubilation, many Loudouners reacted with disdain and contempt. The *Mirror*, which had given the Dangerfield case extensive coverage, stated:

> The decision in this case, is one of the most unblushing, infamous prostitutions of the dignity, honesty and independence which should ever envelope the judiciary. [It] . . . blackens the record of fallen Pennsylvania, and if there is any power lodged in the Executive of Virginia, that will enable help to demand separation, we trust that he will not be slow in its exercise.[165]

---

[163]Ibid., April 13, 1859. Gulick took an affirmation to tell the truth instead of the traditional oath.
[164]Ibid.
[165]Ibid.

Not all white residents in Loudoun, especially in the northern and western regions of the county, were dismayed by the outcome of the Dangerfield case. The other county newspaper, *The Washingtonian,* accused the *Mirror* of attempting to exploit the case in a manner that would benefit the candidacy of a county Democrat in an impending election. This accusation touched off a feud between the two Loudoun papers, resulting in the publication of numerous excoriative editorials.[166]

The lack of unanimity within the county over the significance of the Dangerfield case does not deny that this case and others where the North circumvented or refused to comply with federal fugitive slave legislation were salient contributions to the erosion of nationalism in the mind of Loudouners and other Southern slaveholders and exacerbated their apprehension about Northern creditability and reliability to abide by, and comply with, federal legislation that the North deemed was malevolent. In short, Northern rejection of the fugitive slave legislation that was an indispensible component of the Compromise of 1850 helped nourish Southern sectional fears into a paranoia that included grave reservations about the workability of federalism and the continuation of the Union.

THE MOVEMENT TOWARD BELLIGERENCY

From 1848 to 1861, the nation moved through one of its most discordant periods. The paranoia of sectionalism after 1848 continued to weaken the bonds of union until distrust and fear resulted in secession and civil war. Sectional rivalry, which threatened nationalism, originated from the divergent economic interests of the North, South, and West. This divergence caused conflicting and competing stands as to what should be the policy of the federal government on issues involving Western territories, internal improvements, a national banking system, tariffs, and slavery. Of all these issues, slavery dominated American political life during the thirteen years prior to the Civil War. It became the symbol of all sectional differences and was directly related to the growing lacuna between the people of states where slavery was prohibited and those who not only tolerated human bondage, but proclaimed it a "positive good."

Sectional tensions, acrimony, and virulent rhetoric had a profound and unsettling impact upon the residents of Loudoun. They responded with a hyperactivity in the form of holding countless local and county

[166]Ibid., April 20, 1859.

political meetings from 1847 to 1861 to express concern about the state of the nation. The stimulus for the first wave of gatherings after 1848 was the political aftermath resulting from an American victory in the Mexican War. The acquisition of land west of Texas to the Pacific Ocean, known as the Mexican Cession, by the United States revived the divisive issue of the expansion of slavery. Prompt resolution of this issue became vital as the discovery of gold in California dramatically peopled that territory and led to its application for statehood.[167] The consequence was a sense of immediacy that stimulated partisan and discordant utterances by sectional spokesmen. This conflict frightened Loudoun County residents. Consequently, Loudouners expressed their devotion to the Union and disdain for extremist positions that threatened the continuation of the existing national political system.

Such was the tone of a political gathering of county Whigs and Democrats on February 22, 1850, at the Loudoun courthouse. Ostensibly this occasion was to pay tribute to George Washington. In reality the preamble and eight resolutions introduced by John Janney, and ultimately endorsed by the leading civic-minded citizens of the county, focused upon the state of the nation and the issue of slavery.[168] Land recently acquired from Mexico was blamed as the cause of the "new difficulties" within the nation. Generally the resolutions combined a pro-Southern position and support for the Union that included a fervent opposition to the Wilmot Proviso, a demand that fugitive slaves be returned to their owners and the contention that the South had been "wronged" by the North, but not to the point of warranting radical action and secession.[169] However, a Southern rights convention convened in Nashville, Tennessee, in June 1850 to consider whether the South should secede from the Union was denounced in the Loudoun resolutions as illegal and unrepresentative of the true will of the people of the South.[170] The conciliatory tone of the resolutions and the concern of the Loudoun people for the continuance of the Union are illustrated by the following excerpt from the lengthy preamble that introduced the resolutions:

---

[167]A letter written in 1849 and published in the December 31, 1953, issue of *The Blue Ridge Herald* reveals that Loudouners were attracted by the lure of gold strikes in California: "The winter has been remarkably dull [in Loudoun]. . . . The young men are all leaving and going to California. There is a company fitted out in Union, which will leave in a few days."

[168]Only one dissenting vote was cast as all the remaining men at the meeting voted for the adoption of the resolutions.

[169]The sixth resolution was copied verbatim from a speech that the venerable spokesman of the antebellum South, John C. Calhoun, had recently made before a subcommittee in the U. S. Senate. It stated that the prohibition of slavery in a territory as a prerequisite for statehood was inconsistent with the Constitution since the latter required only a republican form of government.

[170]*The Loudoun Chronicle,* March 1, 1850.

> That the unity of government which constitutes us as one people, is justly dear to us, for it is a main pillar in the edifice of our real independence; the support of our tranquility at home; our peace abroad, of our safety, of our prosperity, and of that very liberty which we so highly prize.
>
> We pause at this period and ask dispassionate men if any act has been passed by the National Legislature which will justify us as Southern men, in resorting to the extreme measures which have been suggested in certain quarters, as a remedy for our grievances.[171]

A similar posture was exhorted by W. S. Hough, the editor of the Whig organ in the county known as *The Loudoun Chronicle*. His editorials included statements such as, "Our country is our larger home. . . . The fountain of our plentous prosperity is our union from which all of us drink."[172] For those who castigated the Union, he denounced by writing:

> There has been nothing so exquisitely painful as the light and reckless tone of menace detraction in which certain men have spoken of the sacred and priceless jewel - the Union of the States.[173]

During January 1850, when the exigent issues of slavery demanded resolution, Hough stated it would be best if Southern fire-eaters and secessionists were to leave the country. He maintained the vast majority of the people were strongly for the Union, and this exodus would bring about a compromise that would solve the nation's problems.[174] During the Great Debate in the Thirty-first Congress, his paper called for the admission of California as a state in the Union and for Congress to adopt a policy of non-intervention on the issue of slavery in the remaining territories. If the latter was done, Hough argued, the South would withdraw all her opposition to the admission of California as a free state.[175] He emphasized that the new Fugitive Slave Act must be

---

[171] Ibid.
[172] Ibid., August 31, 1849.
[173] Ibid., December 21, 1849.
[174] Ibid., January 11, 1850.
[175] Ibid., March 29, 1850. Hough praised the work of Henry Clay for introducing the bills that eventually emerged as the Compromise of 1850. In a September 27, 1850, editorial, Hough did not view with alarm the Georgia Convention which stated Georgia would acquiesce in the Compromise, but only as long as the North complied with the compromise and did not attack the institution of slavery. He confidently stated there were too many moderate men in the South who strongly supported the Union to allow its dissolution.

enforced. In reference to a mob at Boston that attempted to block the return of a fugitive slave, Hough vehemently condemned such participants as "Boston outlaws."[176] Hough also strongly endorsed the idea of free blacks leaving the United States, especially the South, where they were considered "wily agitators of the servile population."[177] Hough's concern for the welfare of the South was also expressed in editorials that lamented the economic dependence of the South upon the North. Like more eminent Southern spokesmen, such as Edmund Ruffin, William Gregg, and James D. B. DeBow in his influential *DeBow's Review*, Hough called for the economic diversification and independence of the South.[178] Economic independence for the South, according to Hough, could best be achieved by Southerners not using Northern industrial products. The Loudoun editor cheered the formation of several Southern associations formed to boycott Northern products. If Southerners complied with such an economic policy of non-intercourse with the North, then Hough believed the South would be forced to erect her own manufacturing establishments which would bring about the economic independence of the South and force the North to have the proper respect for the region south of the Mason-Dixon line.[179]

Although sectional tensions were temporarily lessened by the enactment of the Compromise of 1850, sectional issues, especially those related to slavery, had not been laid to rest. Not only sectional bitterness and fears were exacerbated by the Kansas-Nebraska Act of 1854, but also the lacuna between the North and South continued to widen during the second half of the decade.[180] During this period the fear of Loudouners reached its highest peak after John Brown's raid October 16-18, 1859, on the federal arsenal at Harper's Ferry, Virginia. The threat of a slave insurrection had always haunted Southerners. What made Brown's raid especially ominous to residents of Loudoun was the fact that it had taken place literally only several hundred yards from the northwestern boundary of the county. *The Democratic Mirror* reflected the local hysteria and in its eyes the despicable role that abolitionists played in the violence at Harper's Ferry:

---

[176]Ibid., November 8, 1850.

[177]Ibid. Hough was encouraged by the rumor that a British West India Committee was attempting to obtain additional labor for the plantations of the British West Indies and British Guiana. Furthermore, it was rumored that free blacks would be given free passage, small grants of land, and citizenship if they emigrated to the above British territories. As a part of this canard was the belief that the West India Committee would pay owners of emancipated slaves a bonus if their ex-slaves settled in the British West Indies.

[178]Avery Craven, *The Coming of the Civil War* (Chicago: University of Chicago Press, 1957), pp. 278-82.

[179]*The Loudoun Chronicle*, October 18, 1850.

[180]Due to the non-existence of copies of Loudoun newspapers from 1852 to 1858, a detailed political study of the county during that period cannot be made.

> It will be seen upon calm consideration of this affair that it was one of the most complete and fearful plans for revolution which this or any other country had ever witnessed.... We think we see in it the direction and control of more intelligence than old Brown had yet shown.
>
> We continue to occupy our Columns with details of the insane and atrocious attempt of the Abolitionists to excite a servile insurrection in Virginia and the South, by their desperate adventure at Harper's Ferry.[181]

Residents of Hillsboro and Lovettsville, Loudoun hamlets nearest to Harper's Ferry, naturally displayed the greatest anxiety. Ironically, the first reaction of the people of Hillsboro was one of only slight concern since they were originally told only a minor affray had occurred among laborers. Shortly thereafter the news came of a slave uprising under the leadership of John Brown, whose fanaticism had earned him notoriety for his role in the Pottawatomie Creek massacre in the "Bleeding Kansas" crisis of the mid-1850's. Rumors then reached Hillsboro that inaccurately claimed Brown had 500 men.

In spite of the rapid subjugation of less than two dozen insurgents by the United States Marines under the command of Robert E. Lee and the execution of John Brown on December 2, 1859, by the state of Virginia, the hysteria of Loudouners remained at a fever pitch into 1860. Fear prompted public meetings on October 29, 1859, at Hillsboro and Lovettsville to find ways to protect the county from additional fanatics like John Brown that the Northern abolitionists might send to lead slave rebellions in the South. Both meetings sent a delegation to the governor of Virginia to ask for arms for the county militia units, established special patrols to protect Loudoun boundaries, and denounced and attempted to prohibit peddlers, book agents, travelers, and vendors of goods from traveling through the county since their real intention might be to incite slave insurrections.[182]

The response to John Brown's raid not only brought about the establishment of border guards to vigilantly protect the county from outside agitators, but also pointed out the woeful inadequacies of the Virginia militia system in Loudoun. Prior to the raid at Harper's Ferry, unenthusiastic attempts were made from time to time to muster county

---

[181] *The Democratic Mirror*, October 26, 1859.

[182] Ibid., November 9, 1859. In addition to resolutions denouncing peddlers, book agents, travelers, and vendors of good, the Hillsboro meeting enacted resolutions that also condemned teachers for stirring up the slave population in the county.

residents for militia drill and parades.[183] So sloppy were the periodic parades in which these militia units participated, an editorial in *The Democratic Mirror* called for the abolishment of the entire militia.[184] Discipline was so languid and leadership so ineffectual that it was not uncommon for feuds to develop between members of the militia. Such was the case in which a militiaman was tried by his commanding officer, a colonel, in a court of inquiry, composed of militia officers in which the colonel was the presiding officer. For misconduct during a parade, the militiaman was charged with mutiny. The trial was marred by even less order than the parade; the proceedings were characterized by shouting, yelling, throwing of chairs, exploding of "torpedoes" as bedlam reigned supreme. Finally the trial was terminated as the accused was found guilty of disobedience and fined five dollars.[185]

Under more somber circumstances the inadequacies of militia units in the county were further revealed. A week after John Brown had been captured, fifty men from Hillsboro, who were part of the 56th militia regiment, marched to the northwestern frontier of the county, believing they were protecting their community from abolitionist incursions. Fifteen members of this force were so young their mothers begged them not to go, while some of the others in the militia were in their seventies. Armed ineptly with outdated and inferior weapons like flint pistols, bludgeons, and blunderbusses, this band of Loudouners made at best a feeble gesture to protect their homes from an imagined imminent danger.[186]

Alarm and fear did bring about an improved militia in the county as many residents prepared to fight throughout the fall and winter of 1859-60. In addition to the Hillsborough Border Guard, the Loudoun Guard and Leesburg Civil Guard were formed and drilled daily.[187] Bridges and landings along the Potomac River were guarded. The Hillsborough Border Guard was ordered into the service of the state militia and scouted the Short Hills and Blue Ridge Mountans. Incidents were reported of exchanges of gunfire between Loudoun forces and unknown assailants. Arms and munitions were procured.[188] When uniforms were ordered, to the dismay of the editor of *The Democratic Mirror* they were purchased from a company located in Philadelphia

---

[183]Ibid., May 4, 1859. The 56th Regiment was composed of eight companies of residents from the northwestern region of the county, ten companies that formed the 57th Regiment were made up of men from northeastern and eastern sections of Loudoun, and six companies in the 132nd Regiment drew from residents in southwestern Loudoun. There were other state militia units in Loudoun.
[184]Ibid., April 6, 1859.
[185]Ibid., November 24, 1858.
[186]Ibid., October 26, 1859.
[187]Ibid., November 30, 1859;December 7, 1859.
[188]Ibid., November 30, 1859. Eighty carbines with ammunition, sabres for the cavalry, and one hundred precision muskets for the infantry were purchased and brought to the county.

instead of a Southern company. To finance the outfitting of county militiamen, a military fair was held in Leesburg, and numerous oyster suppers were organized in several of the major hamlets throughout the county.[189] Such fund raisings were also occasions for militant speeches. None reflected the combative spirit within the county better than the speech of Captain A. L. Rogers in early January 1860.[190] Rogers stated that three months previously, at the time of John Brown's raid, not an armed company and scarcely a musket were in Loudoun, but as of the first of 1860 there were eight organized and equipped companies of volunteers. He stated that he believed the true feelings of most county residents to be for "the Union, Constitution, and peace," but in view of John Brown's raid:

> ... [Loudouners] are armed to the teeth and ready for war! Being determined to defend our institution from all assaults of abolitionists, if need be, at the point of bayonets and cannon's mouth.[191]

By 1860 the attack upon slavery, real or imagined, dominated the thinking of Southerners. This was a form of conservatism and conformity that demanded the defense of slavery by citizens and institutions of the South. In Loudoun, total conformity in the defense of slavery did not take place. Nevertheless, support of slavery in the county was considerable, and the Methodist churches in Loudoun during 1860 were affected by the sectional conflict that resulted in the separation of American Methodists into Northern and Southern denominations. Because of the issue of slavery most Methodist and Baptist churches in the South had terminated their affiliation with their Northern counterparts during the 1840's.[192] Loudoun Methodists remained a part of the Northern General Conference until after John Brown's raid. The latter made Loudoun slaveowners, many of whom were members of Methodist churches within the county, intolerant to attacks upon slavery. Subsequently, when the General Conference of the Methodist Churches of the North met at Buffalo, New York, in 1860 and took a strong stand

---

[189]Ibid., December 7, 1859; December 28, 1859.

[190]This was also an occasion for one of the county's military units to display its newly acquired uniforms.

[191]*The Democratic Mirror*, January 11, 1860. During March 1860, Captain D. T. Shreve arrived from Richmond with approximately $6,000, the amount the state paid the Loudoun Cavalry and Loudoun Guard "for service in the John Brown War."

[192]E. Merton Coulter, *The Confederate States of America* (Baton Rouge: Louisiana State University Press, 1950) p. 521.

against slavery, Loudoun responded with church meetings that denounced the action of the Buffalo Conference, which demanded non-slaveholding as a qualification for church membership.[193] In March 1861, this dissatisfaction culminated in the churches of the Baltimore Conference, of which Loudoun Methodist churches were a part, in breaking with the General Conference of the Methodist Church and organizing a Central Conference dedicated to the idea of non-intervention with the institution of slavery.[194]

Slavery and related sectional issues were responsible for extensive political activity during the late 1850's and early 1860's. Numerous local precinct meetings were held by Whig and Democrats for the selection of delegates to county, regional, and state nominating conventions, which in turn would determine the choice of party candidates for positions in the state and national government.[195] Despite the demise of the Whig party as a viable national political organization during the second half of the 1850's, it remained the dominate political force within Loudoun until the Civil War. The strength of county Whigs was due in part to the Whig heritage in Loudoun and in part to the espousal of unpopular positions of States' rights and secession by Democratic candidates. Even the vigor and enthusiastic support of *The Democratic Mirror* for all Democratic candidates and platforms did not weaken support for Whig candidates with Loudoun.[196] For example, Whig candidates in the state and congressional election of 1859 received three times the votes in Loudoun as their Democratic opponents. This plurality in turn prompted the county Whigs to be jubilant. Their celebration at Leesburg included bonfires, balloons, and the shooting of "loud-mouth blunderbusses."[197] As a result of the Whig victory and the acrimony between local Whigs and Democrats, *The Democratic Mirror* advised Democrats to stay out

---

[193] *The Democratic Mirror*, June 20, 1860; June 27, 1860; July 17, 1860; July 25, 1860.

[194] Ibid., March 27, 1861. John A. Carter of Loudoun was the temporary chairman of the Baltimore meeting until the election of a president. Carter was later appointed chairman of a committee that recommended breaking with Northern Methodist churches over their opposition to slavery.

[195] Ibid., November 3, 1858; November 10, 1858; December 8, 1858; December 22, 1858; January 19, 1859. The Odd Fellows Hall and the county courthouse were popular meeting places for county political conventions.

[196] Ibid., November 24, 1858; December 27, 1858. The partisan tone of the *Mirror* was such that it claimed the progress of the United States was due to the Democratic party while "Abolitionists, Black Republicans, Free Negroes, Spiritualists, and Know Nothings" have been malevolent forces. *The Washingtonian* defended the Whig candidates and criticized the Democrats. This defense evoked the wrath of the *Mirror* and continued editorial feuds between the two papers.

[197] Ibid., June 1, 1859.

of Leesburg for a few days and be "a little shy of certain [other] localities" inhabited by county "Know-nothing-Whigs."[198]

Even the excitement and argumentation displayed in the county during the election of 1859 were surpassed the following year during the Presidential election. Whig and Democratic rivalry increased and was fanned by editorial feuds between *The Washingtonian* and *The Democratic Mirror*.[199] Perceptive county residents, Whigs and Democrats, were well aware that the nation was facing a major political crisis. Many wondered about the future of the Union.[200] Such disquietude was expressed on February 13, 1860, at Odd Fellows Hall in Leesburg at the county Democratic convention to select delegates for the state Presidential nominating convention.[201] Six enacted resolutions expressed concern for the welfare of the nation and the need for delegates at the forthcoming national Democratic convention in Charleston, South Carolina, to allay the anxiety of Loudoun Democrats and people throughout the county by a display of wisdom and moderation that would continue the "preservation" of the Union.[202]

The aspirations of Loudoun Democrats as well as of others throughout the nation, except those of Southern radicals, were unfulfilled as the ten-day Charleston convention not only adjourned without nominating a Presidential candidate after fifty-seven ballots, but also evoked an irreparable schism within the national Democratic party. This split was an ominous development for the future of the Union. Sectional tensions over slavery had finally severed the major unifying political force of Northerners and Southerners, the Democratic party.[203] Sensing this break, the *Mirror*, which a few months earlier had claimed that the possibility of a split occurring at the Charleston convention was absurd, stated:

[198]Ibid., June 8, 1859.

[199]Ibid., August 8, 1860; August 23, 1860. John Janney, Loudoun's most prominent political figure of this period was one of the county delegates to the Whig state nominating convention held in Richmond, Virginia. Janney was elected president of the gathering, which enacted resolutions that supported popular sovereignty, expressed opposition against reopening the African slave trade, and denied that the federal government had the right to "interfere" with slavery in the United States.

[200]The June 22, 1859, issue of the *Mirror* took a more confident stand than that expressed eight months later at the county convention. It refuted as absurd the forecasts that the candidacy of Stephen A. Douglas would "disturb the harmony of the National Democracy by thrusting new and hazardous issues upon the Charleston Convention." The *Mirror* went on to say that, although it did not like Douglas' views on slavery in the territories, it did not believe Douglas' candidacy would cause discord in the Democratic National Convention.

[201]*The Democratic Mirror*, February 22, 1860.

[202]Ibid., February 15, 1860.

[203]Roy F. Nichols, *The Disruption of American Democracy* (New York: Macmillan Co., 1948), pp. 305, 516-17.

> *A party disruption has now taken place, and the danger of its speedy dissolution on purely sectional basis is imminent. The question is suggested to every thoughtful mind. If the Union between the Democracy of the North and of the South is dissolved in the year 1860, how long will this Union of the States be likely to continue?*[204]

The divisiveness within the nation was reflected in the candidacy of the four men who vied for the Presidency in the election of 1860. Of these the *Mirror* vigorously supported the Southern Democratic party candidate, John C. Breckinridge, finding the candidacy of Stephen A. Douglas of the Northern Democratic party and John Bell of the Constitutional Union party far less acceptable, and the Republican candidate, Abraham Lincoln, abominable. While most Loudouners agreed with their paper's assessment of the candidacy of Lincoln, they did not share its enthusiasm for Breckinridge. Loudouners cast 2,037 votes for Bell as compared to 778 for Breckinridge, 120 for Douglas, and 11 for Lincoln. Loudoun Whigs were responsible for the tremendous support Bell received from Loudoun voters.[205] It was not, however, surprising that a border region like Loudoun with strong devotion to the Union as well as to the institution of slavery would overwhelmingly support the party and Presidential candidate who intentionally evaded the issues concerning slavery and instead stressed solely the Constitution, the Union, and the enforcement of laws.[206]

The election of Lincoln did not diminish the devotion of county residents for the Union. Loudouners considered the secession by some Southern states in response to Lincoln's election as unwarranted. Even *The Democratic Mirror*, which often espoused a more radical sentiment than that supported by most people in the county, condemned secession as a response to the election of Lincoln as hasty and unwise since the

---

[204] *The Democratic Mirror*, May 9, 1860.

[205] Ibid., May 23, 1860; July 11, 1860; July 18, 1860; July 25, 1860; August 8, 1860. The *Mirror* referred to Lincoln as the common enemy of the country and the first great issue of the campaign. County conventions were held in Loudoun during the summer of 1860 for the support of all the candidates but Lincoln. For example, at Mt. Gilead, Southern Democrats held a meeting to promote support for Breckinridge while a Bell and Everett Club was established in Leesburg for the support of the Constitutional Union party. Local campaigning became more heated as the result of resolutions introduced by John Janney which blamed Southern Democrats for renewing the sectional conflict in 1854 by repealing the Missouri Compromise with the passage of the Kansas-Nebraska Act. This stand in turn prompted a less than temperate denouncement by *The Democratic Mirror*.

[206] Ibid., November 7, 1860; November 14, 1860.

South still maintained decisive power in Congress that could be used to check undesirable Presidential action.[207] Nevertheless, Loudouners were worried about the future of the Union, as were most people throughout the nation, as hope for its preservation dwindled with each waking day. On December 10, 1860, ten days prior to South Carolina's secession from the Union, a public meeting was held at the courthouse in Leesburg to consider the alarming condition of the federal Union.[208] A committee of nine prominent county residents, headed by John Janney, drafted a preamble and series of resolutions.[209] The preamble stated that the imminent danger in which the Constitution and the Union were should not exist because no law had been enacted by Congress that justified disunion. It furthermore declared that disunion would not resolve but only acerbate sectional problems. Specific solutions for the nation's political malaise were spelled out in the twelve resolutions.[210] Generally conciliatory and conservative in nature, they opposed secession. The paramount concern of the vast majority of Loudoun males who attended the convention for the preservation of the Union is indicated by the vote of 92 to 65, surprisingly rejecting the resolution that stated the federal government must not use force against states to prevent their secession from the Union.[211]

Loudoun's support for the Union was carried into the special state convention that assembled in Richmond on February 13, 1861, to consider the fate of the Old Dominion. Yet of the seven candidates who sought to represent Loudoun in that convention, all denounced the use of force to prevent secession. The two elected, John Janney and John A. Carter, not only were the most prominent county politicians but also were strong supporters of the Union who worked for an amelioration

---

[207]Ibid., November 14, 1860. The *Mirror*, however, had nothing complimentary to say about Lincoln. Although the *Mirror* rejected Lincoln's election as legitimate justification for secession, it did claim it was just reason for indignation and gloom, since, according to the *Mirror*, it was the first time a President was elected who was concerned solely with promoting Northern interests.

[208]Local apprehension about the fate of the nation also resulted in meetings being held at two precincts.

[209]This committee was appointed by Thomas W. Edwards, who was elected chairman of the meeting.

[210]The salient positions expressed in these resolutions were (1) all Northern states should repeal personal liberty laws and other legislation that interfered with fugitive slave laws; (2) Virginia must not secede under any circumstance until conferring with all Southern and border states; (3) if the border states were willing to stay in the Union, South Carolina should be willing to do the same since she had far less to suffer than the border region; (4) opposition to the reopening of the African slave trade was expressed; (5) federal coercion of states to prevent secession was denounced; (this was the only resolution which was rejected by the convention); (6) the necessity of settling the slavery question was stressed; (7) it was urged that the state and federal officials use patience and forbearance in an effort to prevent war. Each resolution was voted upon separately by the men who attended the Leesburg convention.

of the discord within the nation. The most radical candidate, John R. Carter of Philomont, espoused secession.[212] Because of this stand he was overwhelmingly repudiated by county voters by receiving only 269 votes compared to 1,945 for Janney and 1,411 for John A. Carter.[213] Janney's concern for the preservation of the Union was a key factor in his election as chairman of the Richmond convention.[214] Upon becoming the presiding officer, while he recognized the gravity of the situation which had necessitated the state convention, he fervidly spoke for the preservation of the Union:

> It cannot be that a Government thus founded and administered can fail, without the hazard of bringing reproach, either upon the wisdom of our fathers, or upon the intelligence, patriotism, and virtue of their descendants.[215]

At first the convention followed Janney's sentiment. Instead of promptly passing an ordinance of secession, as the lower South had done,

---

[211] *The Democratic Mirror* December 12, 1860. The editor of this paper maintained that the defeat of this resolution was not representative of county sentiment as he claimed nine-tenths of the residents of Loudoun were opposed to the use of federal coercion against seceding or seceded states. However, this statement is not consistent with an account in the January 25, 1861, issue of the *Mirror*, which stated during December 1860 the county was not yet opposed to the use of coercion to preserve the Union.

[212] Ibid., January 30, 1861, February 13, 1861. John Janney and John A. Carter during the early 1850's had represented Loudoun in the Virginia constitutional convention. Carter was a senator in the state legislature at the time of the secession crisis. While campaigning for the special state convention to deal with status of Virginia, he stated, "I do not believe that a State has the Constitutional right to secede." To emphasize his opposition to secession, John Janney in the campaign reiterated a part of the preamble he had written during the county convention held the previous December: "So long as Virginia can remain in the Union, without sacrificing her honor or imperiling her safety, she will never desert her sisters. . . ." During the end of January, Janney set forth a position that Lincoln later took regarding Fort Sumter. Janney stated that the President of the United States did not have the constitutional right to surrender voluntarily possessions of United States property and territory. He further reasoned if South Carolina claimed to be wholly independent of the United States and foreign to it and tried to capture Fort Sumter, it was an act of war and the President of the United States would be bound by his constitutional duties to defend the fort.

[213] John Janney's popularity was such that he was considered a winner prior to the election. The real contest was between John A. Carter and Asa Rogers. The latter polled 1,103 votes and lost the election. In the February 6, 1861, election, Loudouners also voted 2,108 to 472 for a referendum that stated if the special state convention proposed that Virginia secede from the Union, the matter would have to be ratified by the voters of the state.

[214] Beverley, B. Munford, *Virginia's Attitude Toward Slavery and Secession* (New York: Negro University Press, 1969), pp. 258-59.

[215] *The Democratic Mirror*, February 20, 1861.

it proceeded to study the situation and seek a resolution to sectional differences through reconciliation and compromise.[216] On April 4, 1861, the convention rejected a motion for Virginia's secession from the Union. But the fall of Fort Sumter and Lincoln's proclamation calling for troops to fight for the Union led to a sudden reversal of the convention's position regarding secession. In a secret session on April 17, 1861, it passed an ordinance of secession for Virginia, despite the vote of Loudoun's two delegates, Janney and Carter, who as in the previous vote cast their ballots against secession.[217]

During the six months following the December 1860 convention in Leesburg, which indirectly embraced, although reluctantly, the coercion of seceding states to prevent them from leaving the Union, the mood of many Loudoun residents had been dramatically altered by national events. Torn between a concern for seceded sister Southern state and an allegiance to the national union of states, most Loudouners, as well as other Virginians, during the first part of 1861 attempted to reconcile and accommodate their divided loyalties by espousing a position of support for the Union while repudiating both secession and the use of force to coerce seceded states back into the Union.[218] However, Lincoln's call for volunteers after the fall of Sumter to restore the Union by force put the people of Southern border regions like Loudoun County in an unenviable quandary. No longer could they accommodate their contradictory national, sectional, and regional allegiances. They had to decide whether to fight for the continuance of a federal Union against Southern neighbors or to secede and resist Federal troops. This choice made a majority of Loudouners and other Virginians cast their plight with seceded states, because to fight against fellow Southerners was even more repugnant than the demise of the Union.

Political gatherings within Loudoun during April and May reflected the accelerating recalcitrancy and shift in paramount allegiance from national to sectional goals.[219] Even during early April, prior to the fall

---

[216]This attempt for compromise was true especially regarding the Peace Convention held during February 1861 in Washington, D.C., sponsored by Virginia to solve the crisis created by the secession of the lower South.

[217]Head, *History of Loudoun County*, p. 148; James G. Randall and David Donald, *The Civil War and Reconstruction* (2d ed.; Boston: D. C. Heath and Co., 1961), pp. 156-57. The ordinance of secession was submitted as a referendum to the people of the state for rejection or ratification on May 23, 1861.

[218]Henry T. Shanks, *The Secession Movement in Virginia, 1847-1861* (New York: AMS Press, 1971), pp. 154-57, 205; Randall and Donald, op. cit., pp. 156-57.

[219]*The Democratic Mirror*, April 3, 1861. Head in the *History of Loudoun County* (p. 148) and Nichols in *Legends of Loudoun Valley* (p. 92) maintained a meeting was held in Leesburg prior to the passage of an ordinance of secession by the state convention. The county convention, according to the above authors, due to the eloquence of J. Mort Kilgour, a Maryland resident with large landholdings in Loudoun, passed a resolution demanding the Richmond Convention vote that Virginia secede from the Union.

of Fort Sumter, county slaveowners held a "Southern Rights Meeting" and proclaimed that if the South was to remain in the Union then the federal government must legalize, renew, and foster the African slave trade with America.[220] But such theoretical utterances as this and the debates over the legality of secession expressed in county newspapers since South Carolina withdrew from the Union were replaced by the reality of voting the "Old Dominion" out of the Union on May 23.[221] Not surprisingly, talk of this somber choice dominated county political activity prior to the referendum on the above date. The personalities of the candidates for the state legislature were overshadowed by this issue as their support and chances of winning were determined solely by their stand on secession. Subsequently, the county elected two secessionists, B. P. Noland and Nathaniel Harrison, to the state legislature and endorsed the ordinance for Virginia's secession by a vote of 1,628 to 726. Only three out of fifteen precincts voted against secession: the non-slave-holding areas of Lovettsville, Waterford, and Waters.[222] An accompaniment to this election was an intolerance unknown even in the most heated of previous elections. A number of disturbances occurred at the polls, and reprisals were taken against Unionist supporters. A number of them left the county and sought refuge in Maryland prior to the election. Those staying, who composed a sizable minority of the county's population and insisted on voting against secession, did so at the risk of personal injury. A gentleman living near Leesburg who voted against secession was treated to a "bath in a mud hole." Several others were thrown into the Potomac River for the same reason.[223] Such acts of retaliation sprang from a conviction that Loudouners who condoned fighting against other Southerners by voting against secession were not rational and conscionable persons and therefore should be punished. Such inflexibility and intolerance to deviation from what was conceived as the only correct position, the hallmark of all belligerents, set the stage for a most uncivil war.[224]

---

[220] *The Democratic Mirror*, April 3, 1861. Shanks in *The Secession Movement in Virginia, 1847-1861* (p. 10) ranks Loudoun County as one of the counties in the state where twenty to thirty-nine per cent of the white families owned slaves in 1860.

[221] *The Democratic Mirror*, January 25, 1861; March 6, 1861; March 13, 1861. The Mirror reported that T. C. L. Hatcher of Loudoun, a student at Columbia College in Washington, D.C., at the time of Lincoln's inauguration attended the reception at the White House, where upon being seen by Mr. Lincoln, the new President allegedly called to Hatcher, "Stranger! I never allow anyone taller than myself to pass me unchallenged, I acknowledge myself beaten."

[222] Ibid., May 29, 1861.

[223] Goodhart, *History of the Independent Loudoun Virginia Rangers*, pp. 12-13.

[224] B. J. Sheetz, the editor of *The Democratic Mirror*, chided Lincoln in editorials for the President's inability to perceive the reality of disunion and for his bungling of the Fort Sumter crisis, which subsequently caused war.

Table 10. Loudoun's Election of State Legislative Representatives and Ratification of the Secession Ordinance.

Nathaniel Harrison	John W. Minor	John George	J. J. Henshaw	W. F. Mercer	For Secession	Against Secession
385	155	11	1	8	400	22
92	18	4	11	18	102	19
24	92	16	9	8	117	19
80	3	0	0	0	108	0
83	3	2	0	0	135	5
53	24	0	17	23	82	31
16	16	4	201	209	31	220
17	34	37	0	0	115	0
29	9	51	279	279	46	325
75	17	5	0	0	114	3
63	29	7	26	28	84	38
23	0	5	40	44	26	39
27	10	4	1	0	150	0
26	7	2	0	0	54	5
21	36	3	0	0	62	0
914	543	151	585	617	1,628	726

May 29, 1861.

BALLS BLUFF, HARRISON'S ISLAND IN THE FOREGROUND

Chapter 5

A COUNTY DIVIDED: 1861 TO 1865

The border states proved to be the primary battleground for the American Civil War. Loudoun, as a minute part of this region, proved to be a classic example of the fate of the border area. Like other border areas, a sharp and hostile cleavage existed between citizens who gave avid adherence either to the Confederacy or to the Union. In Loudoun the genesis of this division of loyalty stemmed from colonial settlement. The English who settled in eastern and southern parts of the county developed large farms dependent upon slave labor. This lifestyle was continued by their descendants, who consequently became supporters of the Confederacy, whereas in northern and western Loudoun, Quakers and Germans had established smaller farms without slavery and with contempt for human chattel. During the Civil War their heirs remained loyal to the Union. This microcosm of sectional differences manifested itself in bitterness and animosities that frequently led to skirmishes between citizens of the county and the confiscation of each other's property.

In addition to the divarication in loyalties, two other factors were salient determinants of military activities within Loudoun during the Civil War. One was Loudoun's strategic location. As a border area located between two belligerents, Loudoun was frequently beleaguered as numerous Confederate and Union scouting and reconnaissance parties traversed, fought, and established temporary hegemony over the county. Much of this activity was due to Loudoun's being located approximately twenty-five miles west of the Union capital, Washington, D.C. The protection of this city, and of Union territory in Virginia east of Loudoun County, prompted extensive Union reconnaissance into Loudoun and was a prime factor in attracting Mosby and his partisans, who desired to raid and harass the Federal forces who defended Washington. As if this situation were not enough, specific topographical features encouraged the movement of major Confederate and Union armies through Loudoun. For example, the numerous fords along the county's northern boundary on the Potomac River were important factors in the traversal of Loudoun by the Army of Northern Virginia and the Army of the Potomac. Lee also used the Blue Ridge Mountains, which formed the western boundary of Loudoun, as a screen to protect his army from the Union forces during the Gettysburg campaign.

The third significant determinant of military activity within Loudoun was the county's agricultural wealth. Not only the small military commands formed within Loudoun took county produce, but also the Army of Northern Virginia and the Army of the Potomac lived off the county when they passed through. While local Confederate units like that of Mosby tried to preserve Loudoun as an exclusive Confederate "bread basket," Union forces attempted to divest the county of Confederate partisan warriors not only with bullets, but also by carrying off supplies that could be used by any Confederate soldier. But the Union failure to destroy the "Gray Ghost" and the knowledge that he supplied much of his command from Loudoun agriculture caused the Federals to burn the western half of the county and drive off its livestock. Consequently, agricultural productivity, along with divided loyalties and the geographical location and topography of the county, were paramount factors during the four years of blood-letting known as the Civil War in producing extensive movement of Blue and Grey warriors through the county and more than forty-six episodes of fighting, that varied in size from a battle to lesser contests, nebulously referred to in the massive volumes of the *War of the Rebellion* as skirmishes, engagements, actions, and affairs.[1]

MOBILIZATION

Accompanying the movement toward secession during April and May 1861 was the mobilization of the county for war. Neither the county nor the state government waited for the people to ratify the ordinance of secession before mobilizing. When the convention at Richmond voted to secede on April 17, the governor immediately sent messages to county militia units to prepare for war. On Friday, April 19, members of the

---

[1] N. E. Warinner (comp.), *A Register of Military Events in Virginia 1861-1865* (Richmond, Va.: Virginia Civil War Commission, 1959), pp. 1-12, 20-22, 24, 28, 31-35, 39-43.

Loudoun militia were mustered into the service of Virginia in anticipation of being needed for the seizure of the federal arsenal at Harper's Ferry.² Stirred by the imminent possibility of fighting and a macabre fascination for war common to that of most nineteenth-century Americans, Loudouners gathered in large numbers on April 24 and enthusiastically cheered the Loudoun Guard to what proved to be an uneventful trip by rail to Alexandria.³

An atmosphere of crisis and excitement was created due to daily recruiting, the sale of one hundred dollar county bonds,⁴ increased county taxes, and the appropriation of $50,000 by the county government to arm Loudoun militiamen and assist families whose heads departing for war left their farms unattended or shorthanded or their families without an income or breadwinner.⁵ Concern for their families was especially acute among county militiamen. They met in a convention in Wheatland on May 11 to consider ways "to provide" for dependent members of their families. A few weeks later the mayor of Leesburg held a similar meeting, at which time a committee was established to collect money, wood, bacon, flour, candles, and butter for soldiers' families. Assistance for families of Loudoun soldiers was necessary from the start of the war. Even prior to the advent of combat, during the spring and early summer of 1861, militiamen were required to be away from their homes and live in a camp outside of Leesburg. By the fall of 1861, all residents felt the acute shortage of coffee, sugar, and salt as village groceries were unable to procure these items to replace their diminished stock.⁶

In addition to raising and arming Loudoun militia units, the county pursued an ambitious program of building three forts on elevated ground

---

²*The Democratic Mirror*, April 24, 1861. By May 1, Loudoun had 400 volunteers in the Loudoun Guard, Loudoun Artillery, Loudoun Cavalry, and the Hillsborough Border Guard. On April 9, Governor Letcher appointed Asa Rogers as Major General of the 2nd Division of the Virginia Militia and Robert L. Wright as Brigadier General of the Second Division, 6th Brigade of the Virginia Militia.

³Ibid., May 1, 1861. The Loudoun Guard returned to the county a few days later.

⁴Ibid.

⁵Ibid., May 15, 1861. The arrival of two brass cannons in Leesburg during the last of April created quite a stir among local citizens as the two weapons were looked upon as an example of the growing military might within the county.

⁶Ibid., May 1, 1861; June 5, 1861. Loudoun contributed men to a number of Confederate organizations during the Civil War. Men from the county predominantly formed the 8th Virginia Regiment, a company (Loudoun Guard) of the 17th Virginia Regiment, and 35th Virginia (White's) Battalion, while many of Loudoun's men later served in the 43rd Virginia Battalion (Mosby's Rangers). Other organizations served by Loudoun's men included the 1st, 2nd, 4th, 6th, and 7th Virginia Cavalry, the 1st Maryland Cavalry, the 1st Richmond Howitzers, Stuart's Horse Artillery, Chew's Battery, Stribbling's Artillery, Letcher's Artillery, Gillmore's Battalion, the 34th Virginia Artillery, Loudoun Artillery, and 40th Virginia Infantry, and the 1st and 7th Georgia Infantry.

outside of Leesburg.⁷ Work on these fortifications proceeded from the summer of 1861 into 1862. The local paper reported in July 1861 that the 57th Regiment of Virginia Militia marched through the streets of Leesburg "armed with pomp and circumstance of glorious digging spades, hoes, mattacks" to construct forts around the town.⁸ During the winter of 1861-62, D. H. Hill, the Confederate officer who at that time was in charge of fortifying Leesburg, sent Lige White of Loudoun to the southern part of the county and to Fauquier County with the unpopular task of taking from residents of that area wagons, teams of draft animals, and blacks that could be "spared."⁹ The Loudoun County government in the meantime ruled that all able-bodied free blacks in Loudoun between the ages of eighteen and fifty were to labor in building batteries and entrenchments as directed by General Hill.¹⁰ Despite this effort and the expense of constructing Forts Evans, Johnson, and Beauregard, such fortification proved to be of insignificant military value as the town of Leesburg, like the rest of the county, frequently came under the control of Union forces during the war.

Of even less effectiveness was the work of the Goresville militia, which had been ordered to guard one of the fords on the Potomac River and to prevent Union soldiers from crossing. Due to the absence of the captain of this Loudoun militia unit, the quartermaster, Campbell Belt, was in charge. Belt had harrows placed in the fording area of the river. He claimed this maneuver would "tangle up the Yankee army" if they attempted to cross. However, when Union soldiers on the Maryland side of the Potomac learned of the submerged harrows, two companies were sent and removed the tillage implements, which were later sent north and sold.¹¹

Although the first year after the fall of Fort Sumter was truly an improvised war, the strain of war was intense. Life in Loudoun was abruptly changed. Businesses had to be abandoned, farms were left improperly attended, and local governmental services were disrupted. By

---

⁷There were Fort Evans, located east of Leesburg; Fort Johnson, on the crown of a hill, one and a half miles west of Leesburg; and Fort Beauregard, built to the south of the town near Tuscarora Creek. According to the Account Book of John Norris, a Leesburg merchant, his business was the supplier of hundreds of pounds of nails, large amounts of oak, apparently used for the construction of these forts. From May until August, these items were charged to the state of Virginia; after August they were charged to the Confederate States of America. Norris also rented a team of horses, a wagon, and driver to the Confederates for $4 a day.

⁸*The Democratic Mirror*, July 10, 1861.

⁹Frank M. Myers, *The Comanches* (Baltimore: Kelly, Piet, & Co., 1871), pp. 19-21.

¹⁰Loudoun County Minute Book, 1862, pp. 62-63. The county justices met and selected workers from a list of able-bodied free Negro males. The county sheriff then notified the selected men to meet at a time agreed upon by the justices and General Hill.

¹¹Goodhart, *History of the Independent Loudoun Virginia Rangers*, pp. 19-29.

May 1, the editor of *The Democratic Mirror* was compelled to greatly reduce the size of that newspaper as employees were on duty in the Loudoun Guard. The county government during June 1861 suspended the road tax in Loudoun and left the care of roads to civic-minded local residents. This step was to compensate for the increased taxation of Loudouners necessitated by the mobilization of the county for war. As the war progressed, civilian life in Loudoun was disrupted more and more.[12]

Disruption of civilian life was accelerated by the dichotomy in the loyalties of county residents. Supporters of the Union, in the minority, often became the object of ostracism, intimidation, arrest, and even confiscation of their property.[13] Such was the case of Samuel C. Means, as excellent example of the fate and treatment of non-Confederate supporters. Means was a prosperous Waterford businessman who owned and operated the county's largest flour mill.[14] When Confederates failed in their attempts to talk Means into joining their ranks through friendly persuasion, they issued him an ultimatum. Either he join the Confederate army or leave the state and have his property confiscated. Finally, on July 1, 1861, Means left his family in Waterford and fled to Point of Rocks, Maryland. In response to his departure, Confederates confiscated Means' twenty-eight horses, forty-two hogs, large quantities of flour, and many other items. Finally, during the last month of 1861, Means was blamed, probably falsely, for leading raids into Loudoun. Subsequently, Confederate authorities in Richmond branded him a renegade and offered a $5,000 reward for his capture.[15]

This treatment was no doubt an influential factor in Means' acceptance of a commission from the Union Secretary of War, Edwin M. Stanton, to go into Loudoun and recruit a company of cavalry to be mounted on horses that belonged to men who had joined Confederate

---

[12]*The Democratic Mirror*, June 12, 1861; November 20, 1861. One of Loudoun's citizens, B. P. Noland, was appointed Quartermaster General of the Confederate Army. By July 23, 1861, he had held this position without pay and had given 3,000 bushels of his own wheat and 150 head of cattle from his herd to the Confederate Army.

[13]Goodhart, *History of the Independent Loudoun Virginia Rangers*, pp. 20-21. Union support was especially strong in the German community of Lovettsville and Quaker settlements of Waterford and Lincoln. Unionists were threatened with arrest if they did not support the Confederacy. This move prompted some to leave the county and go to Maryland. However, upon doing this, they sacrificed their property as the Confederate Army usually confiscated everything but the land. If Unionists returned to the county, they were usually arrested and sent to a Confederate prison. Unionists who never left the county were forced to grant goods or perform services for the Confederate Army. For example, Confederates took teams and wagons from German and Quaker residents. If these Union farmers had neither of these items, then they were forced to serve as drivers of Confederate supply wagons.

[14]Means also had business interests which he shared with a brother at Point of Rocks, Maryland. Ironically, one of Samuel Means' brothers served in the Confederate army.

[15]Goodhart, *History of the Independent Loudoun Rangers*, pp. 23-26.

forces. Means joined the Union army on June 20, 1862, and immediately established his headquarters at his home in Waterford, where he recruited Unionists, mainly German, Quaker, and Scotch-Irish from the communities of Lovettsville and Waterford.[16] This force, known as Loudoun Rangers, was the only organized military unit from the state of Virginia that fought in the Union Army.[17]

The counterpart of the Loudoun Rangers was the 35th Virginia Battalion, sometimes referred to as "White's Battalion," better known as the "Comanches." Like the Rangers they were originally organized as an independent command and recruited from county residents.[18] Also like the Loudoun Rangers, the Comanches were organized and commanded by a Loudouner, Elijah (Lige) Viers White. After the Penisular campaign Lige White wanted an opportunity to destroy the Loudoun Rangers, whom he considered to be a "pestilence upon Loudoun."[19] This goal resulted in a skirmish at Waterford on August 27, 1862, which was truly that of a "Brother's War" as this engagement gave vent to indignation, wrath, and acrimony possible only in the border areas where neighbors and, in some cases, members of the same family became bitter enemies as the result of an adherence to conflicting political ideologies.

The inexperienced Rangers were camped in the Waterford Baptist Church, their main base from the genesis of the organization. Shortly before dawn, on August 27 they were attacked at that location.[20] This

---

[16]Ibid., pp. 1,9,27-28,225-34.

[17]John Divine, "The Passage of the Armies Through Loudoun: 1861-1865," *The Bulletin of the Loudoun County Historical Society*, II (1960), 37.

[18]Williams, *Legends of Loudoun*, pp. 207-09. Lige White during the Civil War fought in thirty-one battles, fifty-nine recorded engagements, and was wounded seven times. Prior to organizing the Comanches, White had won distinction for his heroism as a scout during the Battle of Ball's Bluff. White had great difficulty in obtaining recruits during the winter of 1861-62 because of General Hill's use of Loudoun's men in constructing fortifications. For example, during this time the Comanches had only twenty-five men as compared to nearly 700 at the end of the war. After seeing action in the Peninsular Campaign and later achieving a victory over the Loudoun Rangers at Waterford, White was able to get the Comanches officially recognized as an independent unit of the Confederate army on October 28, 1862. During 1863 White's force became a part of General W. E. Jones' Brigade and continued as a part of the regular Confederate militia organization until the war was terminated.

[19]Myers, *The Comanches*, pp. 95-95. After the Peninsular campaign, White was given permission by General Ewell to return to Loudoun.

[20]Goodhart, *History of the Independent Loudoun Virginia Rangers*, pp. 38-39. Prior to the Waterford skirmish, the Rangers' only combat experience was infrequent encounters in Loudoun with a few "Rebels." Until the early summer of 1862, no Loudoun Ranger understood even the basic drilling procedures. By fall of the same year their most experienced and capable member was the unscrupulous Charles A. Webster. He was knowledgeable in cavalry tactics, skillful in shooting and wielding a sabre, a "lady's man,"

attack occurred in spite of Ranger pickets who had earlier been stationed on each of the six roads that led into the hamlet. These entrances had been circumvented by White and approximately fifty men whom several local citizens had guided through a cornfield to near the Union camp. There White divided his force in an attempt to trap and capture his opponents. He stationed about twenty men on foot in the cornfield in front of the church, with orders to withhold their fire until they reached the church. At that time the remainder of the Comanches on horseback would "dash down" from a nearby hill and hopefully capture the fleeing enemy. This order was improperly executed. Instead of holding their fire until reaching the two dozen Federals, who were gathered in front of the church listening to the noise made by the advancing Confederates, the dismounted Comanches fired prior to leaving the cornfield. The Rangers fled inside the church. Nevertheless, White's force wounded several, including a Lieutenant Slater, who relinquished leadership of the small beleaguered force to the intrepid drill master, Charles A. Webster. After thirty minutes of rapid exchange of fire, White sent Mrs. Virts, whose home was across the street from the church, under a flag of truce demanding the Rangers' surrender. Webster refused in emphatic and graphic language very rarely, if ever, heard in a church. Fighting was renewed for another hour. Then Mrs. Virts was sent under a second flag of truce to talk to Webster, who again refused to surrender and informed her if she came again, he would shoot her. Fighting was renewed and continued until six-thirty or seven o'clock in the morning.[21] At this time the Rangers, nearly out of ammunition, responded favorably to the message brought for the third time by Mrs. Virts. They agreed to surrender on the condition that they be immediately paroled and released. Unaware of the Rangers' scarcity of ammunition, White, who was about to kill the Union horses and leave, since his men had also almost depleted their supply of ammunition, agreed to parole his arch rivals.[22]

The aftermath of this fighting between county residents was anything but pleasant. The Baptist church looked more like a slaughter house than a house of worship. Remarkably only one Ranger had been killed, but of the approximately two dozen Union soldiers, eleven were wounded. Many of the wounded were lying on the church pews in pools of their own blood and in excruciating pain.[23] The surrender scene was an unique

and braggart. Prior to the Waterford skirmish, while attacking a squad of Confederates recruiting Loudouners at Mount Gilead, Webster killed a Southern captain in a manner that prompted criticism from his fellow Rangers as too hasty and unwarranted.

[21] Myers, *The Comanches,*, pp. 97-98.

[22] Goodhart, *History of the Independent Loudoun Virginia Rangers*, pp. 33-35; Myers, *The Comanches*, pp. 95-96. Charles A. Webster later during the war was recaptured and hanged by Confederates at Richmond, Virginia, on April 10, 1863.

[23] Twenty-one Rangers were captured, but only nineteen were paroled. Four other Rangers escaped because they hid in the basement of the church and were not found by the Confederates. The Rangers' historian, Briscoe Goodhart, was in the church during the

one because many of the men of the Rangers and Comanches had been former schoolmates and friends. But the war and divergent loyalties had replaced friendship and brotherhood with bitterness and revenge. This fact was poignantly illustrated by the animosity displayed after the surrender of the Rangers when William Snoot, a member of the Comanches, wanted to kill his unarmed brother, Charles, because the latter was a member of the Union force. Only the intervention of Confederate officers prevented William from murdering his brother.[24]

The Waterford skirmish severely weakened and almost terminated the existence of the Rangers.[25] Much of the responsibility for the debacle was due not only to the inexperience of the Rangers, but also to the questionable leadership of their commander, Sam Means, who had anticipated an attack but spent part of the night of skirmish in his Waterford house. When the fighting commenced, instead of attempting to assist his men, he fled from the area.[26]

battle as a member of the Rangers. He had just joined and was still in civilian clothes. White, mistaking Goodhart for a civilian, did not bother to parole him with the other Rangers. Ranger Henry Dixon died five days after the engagement due to a mortal wound sustained from a "ball passing through his bowels." Two Comanches were killed; the number wounded is not known.

[24]Myers, *The Comanches*, pp. 100-02.

[25]Ibid., pp. 100-04. The Comanches seized fifty-six horses, saddles, bridles, 100 fine revolvers, many carbines, and other items that formerly belonged to the Rangers. Upon learning of the capture of Means' horses, pro-Confederate citizens of Loudoun went to Manassas to claim their livestock, since they had been taken from them by the Rangers. Captain Lige White was obliging and returned their animals. The Rangers, however, were not the only military unit that depended on Loudoun residents to furnish mounts. After the Waterford skirmish, White had both men and horses recruited from the county.

[26]In 1864, Means resigned from the Rangers in protest to the consolidation of the Loudoun unit with the 3rd West Virginia Cavalry. But prior to leaving, he got embroiled in a more humorous controversy. He had agreed to send Stanton "a good fresh milk cow" from Loudoun. To fulfill his promise to the Union Secretary of War, Means sent William Bull, one of his Rangers, to Washington, D.C., with the cow and sent by telegraph a message to Stanton that stated, "I send you today Sgt. Bull with cow and calf." However, in transmitting the telegram the word "Sgt." was omitted, which made the message read, "I send you today bull with cow and calf." Upon receiving this news, the bellicose Stanton went into a tirade, in which he denounced Means and refused to accept the livestock when Sgt. Bull arrived at his office. After Stanton's staff was able to convince the Secretary of the error, he accepted the cow and calf.

Table 11. Military Action in Loudoun During the Civil War.

1861

August 8	Skirmish at Lovettsville
October 4	Skirmish near Edwards' Ferry
October 21	Battle of Ball's Bluff

1862

March 8	Occupation of Leesburg by Union Forces
May 27	Skirmish at Loudoun Heights
August 27	Skirmish at Waterford
September 2	Skirmish near Leesburg
September 14,17	Skirmishes at Leesburg
September 20-22	Skirmishes at Ashby's Gap
October 21	Reconnaissances to and skirmishes near Lovettsville
October 22	Skirmish near Snickersville
October 31	Skirmish at Aldie
October 31	Skirmish at Mountville
November 1	Skirmish at Philomont
November 2-3	Skirmishes at Union
November 9	Skirmish at Philomont
December 12,13	Skirmish between Harper's Ferry and Leesburg

1863

January 26-27	Skirmish at Middleburg
February 14-16	Affair on the Hillsboro Road
March 2	Skirmish near Aldie
April 1	Skirmish near the mouth of Broad Run
June 17-18	Engagement at Middleburg
June 17	Action at Aldie

June 19   Skirmish at Middleburg
June 21   Skirmish at Ashby's Gap
June 22   Skirmish near Dover
July 12   Skirmish at Ashby's Gap
July 30   Skirmish near Aldie
August 8   Skirmish at Waterford
September 1   Skirmish at Leesburg
September 14   Skirmish at Leesburg
September 30   Skirmish at Neersville

1864

January 10   Skirmish at Loudoun Heights
February 5   Skirmish near Aldie
February 21   Skirmish near Circleville
March 6   Skirmish at Snickersville
April 19   Affair at Leesburg
July 6   Action at Mount Zion Church near Aldie
July 15-16   Skirmishes near Hillsboro
July 16   Skirmish and capture of Confederate
                   wagon train at Purcellville
July 16   Skirmish at Woodgrove
July 19   Skirmish at Ashby's Gap
November 28   Skirmish at Goresville

1865

January 18   Affair near Lovettsville
February 19   Skirmish at Ashby's Gap
March 21   Skirmish near Hamilton

CARNAGE AT BALL'S BLUFF

Unlike Samuel Means, Lige White had had battle experience prior to the Waterford skirmish. In White's military background was participation in the largest single engagement to take place in Loudoun County during the Civil War, the Battle of Ball's Bluff. Fought on October 21, 1861, this was a diminutive battle when compared to the massive numbers of soldiers that participated in such titanic conflicts as Antietam, Gettysburg, and Cold Harbor; yet, because of the time and aftermath of the Battle of Ball's Bluff, also known as the Battle of Leesburg, it was of national military and political significance.[27]

After the first Battle of Bull Run, Confederate and Union forces stationed pickets on each side of the Potomac River to closely monitor and prevent each other from making a surprise attack. Crucial in the Confederate vigil of the fording areas across the Potomac into Loudoun was a brigade located near Leesburg at Fort Evans under the command of Colonel Nathan George ("Shanks") Evans.[28] His antagonists across the Potomac, General Charles P. Stone, had a division of Blue warriors to help protect Washington, D. C., from a Confederate attack.[29] In an attempt to determine Confederate strength in Loudoun and discourage any movement of Rebel forces into Maryland, Union scouting and raiding parties were sent into Loudoun, which resulted in skirmishes at Lovettsville on August 8 and Edwards' Ferry on October 4. As the aftermath of this activity a sense of hysteria gripped the county because it anticipated a major invasion by Union forces.[30] Such anxiety was reflected in the bold headlines of the *Mirror*, in referring to the Union raid upon Lovettsville as "Federal Troops in Loudoun" and "Burning of Private Property, Arrest of Unoffending Citizens, Three Federal and One Confederate Soldier Killed, Six Men and Twenty Horses Captured by Enemy."[31]

---

[27] *The War of the Rebellion: A compilation of the Official Records of the Union and Confederate Armies* (Washington, D. C.: Government Printing Office,1881), Ser.I, V, 237-38,567,582 (hereafter referred to as *Official Records*).

[28] For an excellent and precise summary of the Battle of Ball's Bluff, the movement of major Union and Confederate forces through the county, and the burning of Loudoun Valley, consult *Loudoun Civil War: A History and Guide* by John Divine et al. (Leesburg, Va.: Potomac Press, 1961).

[29] Stone's division was only one among several stationed by General George B. McClellan along the Potomac to Harper's Ferry.

[30] *The Democratic Mirror*, October 2, 1861.

[31] Ibid.,August 8, 1861. Although shots were exchanged between pickets on opposite sides of the Potomac after Bull Run, it was common for Confederate and Union soldiers stationed on the banks in Loudoun and Maryland to talk to each other "across the river," often in "a most friendly nature, guying (kidding) one another." They also often agreed not to fire upon each other "and were of the opinion that the shooting of pickets (was) all foolishness."

Ironically it was the attempt to probe the strength and intimidate the Confederate force to leave the vicinity of Leesburg that led to the Union debacle at Ball's Bluff. General George McClellan had instructed General Stone to keep a vigilant lookout on Evans' activities around Leesburg and to determine whether the movement of a Union division under General McCall, which had been sent to Dranesville, would intimidate the Confederates into leaving the vicinity of Leesburg. If not, "Little Mac" added in his message to Stone, "A slight demonstration on your part would have the effect to move them away."[32]

Stone, believing he had been instructed to assist McCall in a southern movement, positioned his men at Conrad's Ferry, Harrison's Island, and Edwards' Ferry.[33] Early during the night of October 20, Captain Philbrick with a scouting party of twenty men left Harrison's Island and surveyed the Virginia shore. He reported that a Confederate camp was located near Leesburg, which consisted of approximately thirty tents but no pickets posted in any direction of the Potomac. Not willing to pass up such a seemingly lucrative opportunity to hit the enemy, Stone ordered Colonel Devens to move silently during the night to the enemy camp and at daybreak destroy it. After this action, if no additional Confederate forces of sufficient strength were in the immediate vicinity to endanger the Union force, Devens was to stay on the Virginia side of the Potomac and to make further reconnaissance of the whereabouts of other Confederate forces.

This maneuver set in motion what would result in the Battle of Ball's Bluff.[34] Topography would play a key role in the fighting on that October 21. It posed a problem for Union movement, which demanded sagacity and perfection in the execution of troop movement and battle tactics. Salient among the topographical features of the battle area were (1) the Potomac River, which separated the belligerents and necessitated the Union's use of boats to reach the Virginia shore; (2) Harrison's Island, a sizeable land mass used as a stepping stone, the halfway point for Union forces crossing the river; (3) Ball's Bluff, seventy to ninety feet high and facing the river, compelling Union troops to take a path to the left of the bluff prior to and during the battle; and (4) the battlefield, which consisted of a clearing of eight to ten acres trapezoid in shape surrounded by a wooded area, hills to the left of the bluff, and a ravine which formed a semi-circle of the battlefield.[35]

[32]Robert V. Johnson and Clarence C. Buel (eds.), *Battles and Leaders of the Civil War*, II, 123-24.

[33]Stone was unaware that on the morning of October 21, the day of the Battle of Ball's Bluff, McCall had been withdrawn from the vicinity of Dranesville.

[34]Although the Battle of Ball's Bluff was fought on one day, preliminary action took place preceding and after the battle. Two days prior to the battle the Federals across from Edwards' Ferry commenced a heavy cannonading of Fort Evans, Leesburg Pike, and Edwards' Ferry. An anti-climactic skirmish occurred on the afternoon of the day after the Battle of Ball's Bluff as the result of another Union crossing at Edwards' Ferry.

[35]*Official Records*, Ser. I, V, 320-21.

The Battle of Ball's Bluff took place in three phases, each phase more intensely fought than the preceding one. The first phase was a skirmish at seven in the morning; the second, several encounters that occurred around noon; and the third, a series of Confederate attacks from 3:00 to 6:00 P.M. that drove the Union forces back to and over the bluff.

The genesis of the first stage of fighting was the movement across the Potomac River at midnight on October 20 of Colonel Devens' reconnaissance force. Their objective was to destroy what was believed to be an ill-guarded Confederate camp a mile from the river. This Union force of 300 experienced considerable difficulty in crossing the swollen Potomac due to an inadequate number and the type of boats.[36] Finding no camp but only a grove of trees, which Philbrick and his men during the previous night had mistaken in the filtering moonlight as tents, Devens continued his reconnaissance toward Leesburg. By seven o'clock in the morning a brief skirmish between Devens' men and an outpost of Confederates under the command of Captain W. L. Duff was fought in an area north of Leesburg and west of Ball's Bluff. This fighting was terminated by Colonel Devens, who, after hearing that a body of Confederate cavalry were approaching, withdrew his men into a wooded area.[37]

In the meantime to divert attention from Devens' movement on the Virginia side of the Potomac, Stone sent Union troops under General Willis A. Gorman across the river to Loudoun three miles south of Harrison's Island at Edwards' Ferry. However, the commander of the Confederate forces in the vicinity of Leesburg, Colonel "Shanks" Evans was not deceived by this feint. Earlier in the day he had shifted his forces from Burnt Bridge, located on Goose Creek, to the area of Fort Evans.[38] Upon hearing of Duff's skirmish with Federals, Evans sent four companies of infantry under Colonel W. H. Jenifer and at noon an additional regiment under Colonel Eppa Hunton to assist what was previously a small Confederate outpost to the west of Ball's Bluff. At noon the combined forces of Jenifer and Hunton struck at Devens' right flank. To prevent being outflanked, Devens was soon forced to retreat sixty yards, which put his men approximately a half-mile west to the bluff. At about 2:00 P.M. he was again forced to fall back nearer the bluff, where reinforcements were slowly arriving.

Throughout most of the day the Union soldiers under Devens were in a precarious position. Their backs were near a bluff that dropped nearly

---

[36] Johnson and Buel (eds.), *Battles and Leaders of the Civil War*, II, 124-25. It took Devens' force from midnight to four in the morning to cross the Potomac in three boats, which had a total carrying capacity of approximately thirty men.

[37] *Official Records*, Ser. I, V, 295, 309, 349, 363.

[38] A few days earlier Evans had sent his men to Burnt Bridge to counter any possible movement to Leesburg of the Union forces under McCall.

100 feet to a swollen river, where an inadequate number of boats negated any opportunity for a hasty retreat, while in front of the Federals was a Rebel force that constantly increased in number. Devens had been informed at ten o'clock in the morning that soon Colonel Edward D. Baker would arrive with sizeable reinforcements. Reinforcements slowly arrived, and Colonel Baker, a friend of Lincoln and Senator from Oregon, did not arrive on the battlefield and take charge of the Union force until after 2:00 P.M. He had wasted valuable time of more than an hour by personally supervising the lifting of a boat from the C.&O. Canal instead of delegating this task to a person of lesser rank.[39] Upon arriving at the battlefield, Baker immediately displayed a lack of military acumen and judgment that greatly imperiled the Union soldiers. The plight of the Union forces at mid-afternoon was aptly described by Colonel Milton Cogswell of the "Tammany" or 42nd New York Regiment:

> Arrived at the landing opposite Harrison's Island, I found the greatest confusion existing. No one seemed in charge, nor was anyone superintending the passage of the troops, and no order was maintained in their crossing. I immediately crossed the island to make the passage of the second branch of the river, and there found still greater confusion existing than at the first landing. I ascended the bluff (about 70 feet high) and reported myself to Colonel Baker. Colonel Baker welcomed me on the field, seemed in good spirits, and very confident of a successful day. He asked my opinion of his disposition of troops, and I told him frankly that I deemed them very defective. I advised an immediate advance of the whole force to occupy the hills.[40]

However, Baker, ignoring the advice of Cogswell, made the position of the Union force untenable. This result is verified by the fact that from three to six in the afternoon the Federals were being driven back to the bluff.[41]

---

[39] *Official Records*, Ser. 1, V, 296-97, 307, 309-10, 349, 369. Despite difficulties in transportation, the Union force was able to get three pieces of artillery, two howitzers and one six-pounder in the center of the line by two o'clock in the afternoon. Confederates later nullified this maneuver by rapidly killing the Union artillerymen.

[40] Ibid., 320-21.

[41] The following was the disposition of men during the final struggle of the day. Between Leesburg and the Federal forces, Evans had from left to right three companies of Virginia cavalry under the command of Colonel W. H. Jenifer, and three infantry regiments. On his left flank he had Company K of the 17th Mississippi, two companies of the 18th Mississippi, and Company D of the 13th Mississippi, all under the command of Colonel Jenifer. To the right of those companies were three infantry regiments: the 8th Virginia, which was commanded by Colonel Hunton, and the 17th Mississippi, which was commanded

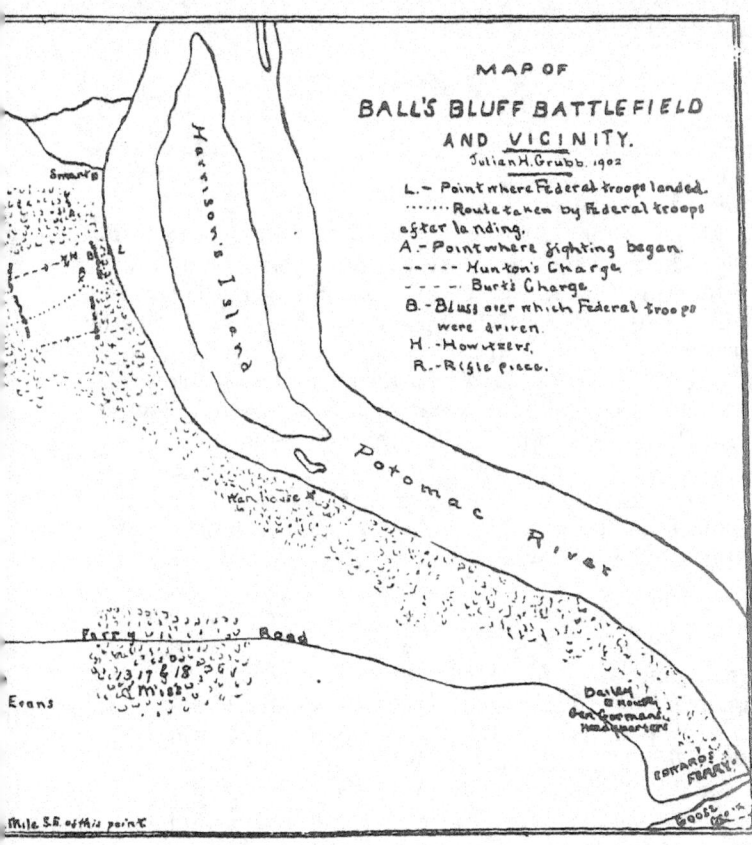

Figure 18. Map of Ball's Bluff Battlefield.

At 3:00 P.M., General "Shanks" Evans launched the heaviest Confederate attack of the day; Colonel E. R. Burt led the 18th Mississippi Regiment in a savage charge on the Union left flank. Burt was soon reinforced by the 17th Mississippi Regiment under the command of Colonel Winfield S. Featherson. While Burt and Featherson were driving back the Union left flank, Colonels Hunton and Jenifer were leading their troops in a hammering drive upon the center of the Union line.[42] At the same time the Confederate cavalry was hitting the Union right flank. Confederates soon occupied the high ground that Baker had earlier foolishly spurned. Confederates then formed a semi-circle around the beleaguered Federals. The few pieces of artillery the Union soldiers had been able to transport across the Potomac soon became virtually useless as Confederate skirmishers killed off Union artillerymen.[43]

During the late afternoon Colonel Baker was killed by Confederate skirmishers. A dramatic and somewhat imaginative account of this event has been provided by Captain Francis A. Young of Baker's staff.[44] According to Young, Baker was

> . . .at all times in the open field, walking in front of the men lying on the ground, exhibiting the greatest coolness and courage. The fire of the enemy was constant, and the bullets fell like hailstones, but it was evident that the enemy was firing into the open field without direct aim. Colonel Baker fell about 5 o'clock. He was standing near the left of the woods, and it is believed he was shot with a cavalry revolver by a private of the enemy, who after Colonel Baker fell, crawled on his hands and knees to the body and was attempting to take his sword, when Captain Bieral with 10 of his men rushed up and shot him through the head and rescued the body.[45]

by Colonel Burt; the 13th Mississippi was held opposite Edwards' Ferry to check General Stone, who was supervising Gorman's action. Facing the Confederates in front of the bluff was a Union force, which during the day was gradually being formed from men that arrived from across the river. This force was composed of the 15th Massachusetts, 20th Massachusetts, the 71st Pennsylvania or 1st California, and 42nd New York, also called the Tammany Regiment.

[42] At approximately 4:00 P.M. while leading this charge, Colonel Burt was mortally wounded.

[43] *Official Records*, Ser. I, V, 297, 310, 322, 328, 359.

[44] Young was near Baker at the time of the latter's death.

[45] *Official Records*, Ser. I, V, 328. Young also reported that "at the time Colonel Baker was shot he was looking at a mounted Confederate officer, who rode down a few rods into the field from the woods, who, being shot by one of our men, returned to the woods and appeared to be falling from his horse. Colonel Baker, turning about, said, 'See he falls,' and immediately fell, receiving four balls, each of which would be fatal."

Colonel Cogswell assumed command after some confusion among the remaining Union colonels as to who would be Baker's successor. Shortly after taking command, Cogswell rejected the wishes of Devens and Lee to retreat across the Potomac. Such a venture Cogswell deemed too hazardous. Instead, he hoped to have the Union soldiers fight their way through the left of the Confederate line and attempt to move to safety through Edwards' Ferry. However, this plan soon became impossible to implement as the Tammany Regiment apparently mistakenly followed a Confederate officer, Lieutenant Charles B. Wildman, who in a state of confusion had ridden rapidly toward and in front of the Tammany line; mistaking it for Confederate soldiers, he beckoned the Union regiment to charge what was in reality the Confederate line. Unfortunately for the Union, the Confederate line poured a murderous fire into the approaching Yanks. The Federals, unable to move forward, were forced to choose between surrender or retreating off a bluff. What occurred at the wooded bluff was a carnage. Confederates forced many of the Union soldiers over the cliff, not giving them a chance to retreat to the path at the side of the precipice which they had formerly climbed. Union soldiers fell, jumped, were bayoneted, shot and clubbed over the steep hillside to a narrow beach near the Potomac River. Some sprang down from the bluff upon the heads and bayonets of fellow soldiers. Such was the case of a ponderous "Tammany" soldier who broke his neck in the fall and mashed the head of a gray-haired private between two rocks.[46] Survivors on the beach searched in vain for the few boats available to escape across the river. The men who found such vessels overloaded and swamped them. For most, the only means of escape was to jump into the swollen river and attempt to swim to Harrison's Island. As chaos and panic reigned, Colonel Devens attempted to get soldiers to throw their muskets into the river and swim across. Many stripped themselves of swords and muskets and hurled them into the river, then jumped in themselves. A few kept their weapons and miraculously managed to swim across with them. Some soldiers who could not swim floated on logs while other comrades hugged the bank and searched hopelessly for an escape route while Confederates fired down from the top of the bluff. The scene was pathetic as the whole surface of the river seemed filled with heads or struggling bodies screaming and dying.[47]

---

[46]Henry Steele Commager (ed.), *The Blue and Gray* (New York: The Bobbs-Merrill Co., 1950), I, 115-19. Lige White, a young local farmer and hero of Ball's Bluff who rendered valuable service as a courier and guide for the Confederates, led a small force at the end of the battle to capture stranded enemy who were keeping a watchful vigil for boats to carry them to safety. He attested to the pandemonium on the beach as he frequently stumbled across Union corpses and wounded, the latter frequently screaming in agony.

[47]*Official Records*, Ser.I, V, 247-48, 311, 319-20, 325, 361.

By 7:00 P.M. the rout of the Union force was complete; by 8:00 P.M. most of the remaining soldiers on the Virginia side had been captured and taken to Leesburg. Later, they were marched twenty-five miles to Manassas on their way to Confederate prisons. The Confederates had achieved victory only by strain and a maximum effort. Near the climax of the fighting at 5:00 P.M. Colonel Hunton and his famed 8th Virginians were nearly out of ammunition. Hunton, after distributing the few remaining cartridges, was forced to rely almost completely on the use of the bayonet as his men charged the center of the Federal line, driving it back and capturing two howitzers. After this gallant charge, this Virginia regiment was exhausted and out of ammunition.[48]

Activities on October 22, the day after the Battle of Ball's Bluff, consisted of caring for the wounded, burying the dead, another Union crossing at Edwards' Ferry, and a skirmish there in the afternoon. All of this action was anticlimactic compared to the action of the previous day. Nevertheless, Harrison's Island, Leesburg, and Ball's Bluff presented a somber aftermath of the occurrences of the previous day.

Confederate hospitals were set up in the churches in Leesburg, and the Union established a temporary hospital on Harrison's Island to care for their wounded until they could be taken to the Maryland shore. A few of the wounded, including a future Supreme Court Justice, who went to Maryland via Harrison's Island were:

> Captain Dreher, shot through the head from cheek to cheek, possible recovery; Captain J. C. Putman, right arm taken off at the socket, doing well; First Lieutenant O. W. Holmes, shot through leg and small of the back from side to side, doing well; First Lieutenant J. J. Lowell, shot in the leg, not serious; and Second Lieutenant Putnam was shot in the bowels, died in this camp yesterday. His body was sent to Boston this morning.[49]

On October 22, the Confederates refused to allow Federals to send a surgeon to the battlefield or to remove their wounded from Virginia. However, a Union burial detail under a flag of truce was allowed to cross to Virginia and bury forty-seven Union bodies, which were reported to be about two-thirds of the number left dead on the field.[50] Confederate dead were interred in the Union Cemetery at Leesburg.

---

[48]Ibid., pp. 361, 367, 370.
[49]Ibid., p. 317. Harrison's Island was also a place where some of the bodies of Union dead were temporarily taken. Among the dead was the corpse of Colonel Baker, which had been carried along with the wounded in a leaky boat that sank on its next trip.
[50]Today this burial site is Ball's Bluff Cemetery.

The casualty statistics of the battle attest to its tragedy. Although both sides were similar in strength, approximately 1,700 each, estimates of the other's strength, numbers engaged, and casualties were grossly exaggerated in official reports and newspaper accounts. Union losses numbered 921, about half of their total force engaged, of whom 49 were killed, 158 wounded, and 714 captured or missing. Confederate losses were much lighter: out of about 1,700 men, 33 were killed, 115 wounded, and 1 missing, for a total of 149 casualties.[51]

Most Loudouners rejoiced over the Confederate victory. They read with jubilation the headlines printed in *The Democratic Mirror*, calling the victory at Ball's Bluff "The Grand Fight Near Leesburg."[52] Numerous county residents visited the battlefield immediately after the fighting and carried off much of the Confederate spoils of war. This foray caused Shanks Evans to issue a proclamation that required the local citizens to return to him the large number of Springfield Minie muskets and other enemy arms they had carried from the battlefield as souvenirs.[53]

The defeat of Federal forces at Ball's Bluff had national repercussions far greater than other Civil War battles of similar size. The Federal loss had not denied the Union control of strategic territory; the battle neither influenced the overall military course of the war nor altered its outcome. It is extremely doubtful that the Union would have continually occupied and defended the land in Loudoun bordering the Potomac if they had won the battle. The most significant result of the Battle of Ball's Bluff was the impact it had on Union and Confederate morale. This factor was true especially for the Union. Perplexing the government in Washington was the problem of gaining and keeping the support and confidence of Union citizens in a war six months old where the military forces of their government had failed to win a significant battle in the eastern theater. An additional reason the Battle of Ball's Bluff became a determinant in morale was the extensive attention given it by the 3,000 newspapers in the United States. However, reporting in papers, whether in the North or South, presented jaundiced accounts of both the military action and significance. Confederate newspapers exaggerated the event and claimed that its resulting in disaster for Union soldiers was inevitable. While Northern newspapers also stressed the battle as a Union disaster, they unfairly and fiercely blamed the Union defeat on General Stone. He became the unfortunate scapegoat for the wrath and vindictiveness of radical Congressmen who were to challenge Lincoln's leadership during the remainder of the war. The inevitable comparison of Ball's Bluff with the first Battle of Bull Run and the realization of two consecutive Union defeats in the Eastern theater, and

---

[51] *Official Records*, Ser. I, V, 308, 353.
[52] *The Democratic Mirror*, November 27, 1861.
[53] Ibid., October 30, 1861.

the death of Colonel Baker were factors in the formation of a Congressional Joint Committee on the Conduct of the War. Although this committee was active throughout the war, its immediate purpose was to investigate the cause of the disaster at Ball's Bluff. Convinced that Stone was not in sympathy with radical war aims and finding him loyal to McClellan, whom radical members of Congress also disliked, the committee, with Stanton's support, engineered Stone's arrest and imprisonment. Stone was never formally charged or given a trial, but rumors of his alleged treason and disloyalty swept through the North. Later released from prison, Stone had been, nevertheless, sacrificed for political vengeance.[54] His military career never recovered. Relegated to relatively minor military assignments and viewed constantly with suspicion, he resigned from the Union Army in 1864.

Ironically, the press and Joint Committee on the Conduct of the War extolled the name of Colonel Baker and depicted him as a martyr whose death resulted from the mismanagement and treachery of Stone. The defeat of the Union at the hands of a Confederate force of approximately equal strength was not the fault of Stone. In spite of the fact Federal soldiers had fought well, as Confederate reports attest, the incompetent leadership of Baker made them victims of defeat. His blunders, resulting from naivete and inexperience, were costly. His improper management of the crossing of the Potomac and his failure to take command of the hills which commanded much of the battlefield were the salient reasons for the Union defeat.[55]

THOROUGHFARE FOR BLUE AND GRAY WARRIORS

Shortly after the Battle of Ball's Bluff, General D. H. Hill replaced Shanks Evans as the ranking Confederate officer in Loudoun. Hill concentrated his efforts upon the fortification of Leesburg in anticipation of a significant Union advance to Centreville via Loudoun's county seat.[56]

---

[54] *Official Records*, Ser. I, V, 34-35, 341-46. The Battle of Ball's Bluff also was news because it came at a time when the war was young and few battles had occurred. Ball's Bluff would have received less interest and attention if it had occurred during the later years of the war.

[55] Ibid., pp. 34-35, 341-46.

[56] Prior to Stone's arrest in February 1862, a few Union soldiers stole horses from Loudoun and fired across the Potomac upon private carriages carrying ladies. Hill sent a letter to Stone threatening to hang Northern soldiers caught while committing such acts. After consulting McClellan, Stone replied he would not sanction robbery, and, if such persons were turned over to him, they would be tried and punished.

During the first part of March 1862, General Hill and his Southern soldiers left the county as General Joseph E. Johnston pulled the Confederate force back toward Richmond. As Hill left Loudoun, he complied with Johnston's orders to put the torch to hay and grain stacks and other items that would be of benefit to the Union army. Consequently as Hill left Leesburg on a cloudy March morning, the flames that flared up from the stockyards and mills created an atmosphere of gloom and desolation that would become all too common during the remaining war years.[57]

Shortly prior to Hill's evacuation of Leesburg, a Union force of 700 to 800 men under the command of Colonel John W. Geary entered the northwestern region of the county. There he found a "majority of the inhabitants . . . hailed" his presence "with gladness, and willingly took the oath of allegiance" to the Union government.[58] However, during Geary's one-month stay in Loudoun, the first time the county was occupied and controlled by Union troops, he found the people in the rest of the county anything but enthusiastic about his presence. For example, his occupation of the forts around Leesburg, the courthouse, bank and all other public buildings hardly endeared him to local residents. Finding a strong secessionist sentiment in the county seat, Geary established a rigid provost marshalship in an attempt to maintain order. His announcement of a general impressment of Leesburg residents into the Union army was considered by many Loudouners to be Geary's most abominable act. To avoid having to comply with this order, many Confederate suppporters, including John Janney, took a oath of allegiance to the Union Government.[59]

Geary roamed through the county during his transient stay in Loudoun, believing he solely was responsible for "liberating" the county from "Rebel" rule and soldiers.[60] In fact, this was only the initial step in a process that would be repeated for the remainder of the war: contending forces alternating in the control of the county. At times a large segment of the county was controlled by Union or Confederate forces. At other times small reconaissance forces or raiding parties controlled only one or two communities. The oscillation of Union and Confederate control over the county was due to the location of Loudoun as a border area. However, only during times of large troop movement through the county was it necessary to exert control over the entire region and its accessible roads and mountain gaps. This was the case in the Antietam and Gettysburg campaigns, during which the Army of Northern Virginia and Army of the Potomac traversed Loudoun.

[57]Myers, *The Comanches*, pp. 31-33; *Official Records*, Ser. I, V, 513, 1091, 1095-96. The Union soldier that pursued Hill's retreat from Leesburg found a path "blackened with devastation hurriedly committed."
[58]*Official Records*, Ser. I, V, 512.
[59]Ibid.
[60]Ibid., 514-15.

After the second Battle of Bull Run, Robert E. Lee and the Army of Northern Virginia moved through Loudoun to invade Maryland. By moving his army east of the Blue Ridge Mountains through northern Virginia, Lee hoped the Federals would fear for the safety of the cities of Washington and Baltimore and would subsequently withdraw their troops north of the Potomac River. If the latter occurred, Lee's supply lines would be in less danger.[61] Lee, who had entered Leesburg in an ambulance due to injuries, [62] made his headquarters for two days at Henry Harrison's home as the Army of Northern Virginia traversed Loudoun County.[63] While in Leesburg, the community made many social demands on Lee, who faced pressing problems. Among these was straggling, caused by bruised feet due to the lack of shoes and a diet of green corn, which induced serious and debilitating diarrhea and evoked an extensive number of absences without leave.[64] While at Leesburg, Lee reorganized much of his artillery, cut excess baggage, removed unfit horses as draft animals, and attempted to rid himself of bruised and slow-footed stragglers by sending them to Winchester.[65] A total force of 64,000 Confederate soldiers of the Army of Northern Virginia entered Loudoun between September 4 and 7 and used many of the county's products. Yet due to straggling, probably not more than 55,000 of this number crossed into Maryland.[66] Even the Army of Northern Virginia

---

[61]Douglas Southall Freeman, *R. E. Lee* (New York:Charles Scribner's Sons, 1934), II, 353. Additional reasons for selecting routes through Loudoun were the numerous fording areas on the Potomac.

[62]John Divine, "The Antietam Campaign," *Loudoun County and the Civil War*, p. 41. Lee's favorite horse, Traveller, had shied, probably due to a sudden noise, while the general was dismounted but holding the reins. Lee was suddenly jerked to the ground, spraining one hand and breaking several bones in the other.

[63]A brief skirmish occurred near Leesburg on September 2, 1862, as Colonel Tom Mumford's 2nd Virginia Cavalry entered Leesburg in advance of Lee's main army, found the town occupied by Loudoun Rangers and Cole's Maryland Cavalry. After defeating the Union force and a six-mile chase, Mumford and his men moved into Maryland. D. H. Hill's command on September 4, was the first division of the Army of Northern Virginia to arrive in Leesburg. It was followed by the divisions of Longstreet and Jackson. The latter two divisions entered the county from Dranesville via what is today Route 7.

[64]Douglas Southall Freeman, *Lee's Lieutenants* (New York: Charles Scribner's Sons, 1943), II, 149-52. The movement through Loudoun by Lee's army has been referred to as the "Green Corn Campaign."

[65]Divine, "The Antietam Campaign," *Loudoun County and the Civil War*, pp. 40-44; Official Records,Ser. I, XIV, Pt. 2, 592-93. While moving through Loudoun, Jackson placed his only experienced division commander, A. P. Hill, under house arrest as the result of an argument over straggling.

[66]G. F. R. Henderson, *Stonewall Jackson and the American Civil War* (New York: Longmans,Green and Co., 1911), II, 207-03. Shortly after Lee crossed into Maryland, an additional Confederate force under General John G. Walker crossed back into Loudoun from Maryland at Point of Rocks and traversed the northern end of the county on his way to help Jackson take Harper's Ferry.

that crossed White's Ford into Maryland after Lee's reorganization was anything but an awe-inspiring sight. Eyewitnesses reported that they had never seen such a ragged, dusty, filthy, and ill-provided for group of men.[67]

Lee left behind in Loudoun a disgruntled Lige White, who had unsuccessfully pleaded with J. E. B. Stuart to accompany the Army of Northern Virginia across the Potomac. After spending several days in Waterford, White went to intercept a Union force under General Hugh J. Kilpatrick that was seizing control of Leesburg. After bombarding the town with artillery, during which "Shrieking shells came crashing through walls and roofs in the center of . . . town," Kilpatrick's cavalry rode through the hamlet. Upon reaching the western outskirts of Leesburg, he was attacked by White's small command. Fighting was abruptly terminating when the "Chief of the Comanches" was seriously wounded. Although Federals searched vigilantly, they were unable to capture the wounded White. His men frequently moved him to various homes throughout the county to prevent his seizure by the Federals.[68]

Loudouners witnessed some of the horrors of the aftermath of the bloody Battle of Antietam. A Confederate hospital was established at Middleburg, and the area from Leesburg to Warrenton was filled with sick and convalescent soldiers of the Confederacy.[69] This situation was complicated by the crossing of the Union's Army of the Potomac into Loudoun from Harper's Ferry and Berlin from October 26 to November 2.[70] At the head of this movement was General Alford Pleasonton's cavalry, assigned the task of clearing Loudoun Valley of "Rebels" so the Union Army could move southward to Warrenton. In carrying out this assignment, Pleasonton led his men in skirmishes with outposts of the enemy at Philomont and Bloomfield. He also thwarted attempts by Loudoun "secessionists" to send horses to the Confederate cavalry and prevented a Confederate doctor, who was anxiously impressing wagons, from sending sick and wounded Southern soldiers from Aldie and Middleburg to Winchester. The presence of Pleasonton's command at Aldie was violently protested by women of the hamlet. The ladies threw

---

[67]Freeman, *R. E. Lee*, II, 354-55.

[68]Myers, *The Comanches*, pp. 111-12; *Official Records*, Ser. I, XIX, Pt. 1, 1091-92.

[69]*Official Records*, Ser. I, XIX, Pt. 1, 1091-92. After the Battle of Antietam, Stuart completed a hasty and exhausting second ride around McClellan by crossing White's Ford in Loudoun. September and October were not only the time of the passage of mighty armies to and from combat through Loudoun but also a period of extensive secondary movements, such as Union and Confederate reconnaissance and scouting trips, which at times culminated in skirmishes in Loudoun by contending forces.

[70]Ibid., 86-88. Pontoon bridges were constructed, which enabled McClellan's forces to cross the Potomac River at Berlin, Maryland, and the Shenandoah River at Harper's Ferry.

stones at the Union soldiers and waved a Confederate flag. The Union command withstood the feeble stoning but confiscated the Confederate flag from the hands of hostile females.

While these events were occurring, Lee's army was moving southward near the western slopes of the Blue Ridge as McClellan's forces entered Loudoun east of the same range of mountains. A contingent of Confederates guarded the gaps of the Blue Ridge to prevent a sudden Union attack on Lee's long-faded and ragtag lines while Confederate partisans like Lige White looked upon the long Federal columns of thousands of men, horses, mules, and wagons as inviting targets for raids.[71] J. E. B. Stuart was assigned the special task of monitoring and impeding Union movement. After learning of Federal movement in Loudoun and attacks by the enemy upon his pickets, Stuart fought hotly contested skirmishes with Union soldiers at Philomont and Union (today called Unison) during the first two days of November. Due in part to the efforts of the "Stuart Horse Artillery" under the leadership of the gallant Captain John Pelham, supported by dismounted cavalry sharpshooters behind numerous stone fences, Stuart was able to contest the rolling farm land of Philomont and Union. He slowly retreated as he gave up each hill only after a fight, which thereby obtained time for Lee's army to move farther south.[72]

The year 1863, like in 1862, saw Loudoun a thoroughfare for Union and Confederate armies as Lee invaded the North for the second time. After his victory over "Fighting Joe" Hooker at Chancellorsville, Lee again moved northward, again using the Blue Ridge Mountain as a screen. J. E. B. Stuart was given the difficult job of screening the Confederate army by keeping the enemy east of the Blue Ridge. Pleasonton's Union cavalry proved to be a strong opponent for Stuart's command as Pleasonton tried to dislodge the Confederates from the mountain gap at Aldie and the two in the Blue Ridge, Snickers' Gap and Ashby's Gap. From June 17 through June 21 the roads from Aldie to Snickers' and Ashby's gaps were the scene of frequent cavalry battles,

---

[71]Ibid., Pt. 2, 86-88, 96-97. White raided the enemy's rear columns moving throughout the county. According to Myers, the Comanches' historian, White captured approximately 1,000 prisoners and 200 wagons, but at a cost of having a considerable number of men of his own command captured. In December 1862, Major-General Henry W. Slocum moved his corps through Loudoun on its way to aid General Burnside, who was then fighting the Battle of Fredericksburg. White tried unsuccessfully to capture Slocum's wagon train, but managed to capture about 100 Union stragglers, some of whom were found asleep in a mill. Finally giving up his efforts to capture the Union wagon train, White concentrated on again attacking and scattering his arch enemy, Sam Means, and the Loudoun Rangers at Waterford.

[72]Ibid., Pt. 2, 141-43, 145, 147. On the night of November 2, 1862, Stuart's command bivouacked east of Upperville, leaving the disabled and wounded at Union with surgeons and nurses. The next day, Stuart gradually withdrew his men to Ashby's Gap.

the most severe being fought at Aldie, Middleburg, and Upperville.[73] Pleasonton's cavalry slowly pressed Stuart's cavalry to Ashby's Gap as the result of cavalry charges, counter charges, and hand-to-hand sabre fighting. At the end of four days of fighting the Confederates had lost a total of 505 men compared to the Union's 827 casualties.[74]

As Lee moved northward toward the Potomac River, the Union Army of the Potomac was set in motion to check the enemy's northern advance. Hooker's entire army, all seven infantry corps and his cavalry under Pleasonton, converged upon Loudoun from Fairfax, Herndon, Germantown, and Dranesville. This mammoth force, the largest to move through Loudoun under one command, descended upon the county with its long columns forming the shape of a giant fan. From June 17-27 all accessible roads in Loudoun were used to reach and cross the pontoon bridges at Edwards' Ferry.[75]

After the immortal three-day struggle at Gettysburg, Loudoun was once again traversed as Confederate and Union armies moved southward. The swollen Shenandoah River thwarted Lee's plans to retreat by moving through Loudoun. When Lee's army crossed into Virginia, it moved southwest of the Blue Ridge, while Meade's forces moved in the same direction but crossed the Potomac east of the same mountain range and moved through Loudoun Valley from July 17-27. Although Union cavalry went in advance of the long Union lines to scout the mountain passes and protect Federal infantry from attacks from Southern soldiers moving through the passes, Confederate partisans Mosby and White were active in the county, capturing Union supplies and stragglers.[76]

---

[73]The fighting at Aldie on June 17, 1863, has been called the bloodiest small cavalry battle of the Civil War.

[74]Freeman, *Lee's Lieutenants*, II, 52-54; Divine, "The Passage of the Armies Through Loudoun: 1861-65," II, 33-35; H. B. McClellan, *Life and Campaigns of Major General J. E. B. Stuart* (Bloomington: Indiana University Press, 1958), p. 307-14; *Official Records*, Ser. I, XXVII, Pt. 2, 688-89. More casualties occurred in Loudoun between June 17 and 21 than at any other time of the war.

[75]Freeman, *Lee's Lieutenants*, III, 51-56, 62-65; *Official Records*, Ser.I, XXVII, Pt. 2, 142-43.Three Union soldiers of the 12th Corps of the Army of the Potomac were executed near Leesburg on June 19, 1863, for desertion. Details of the grim event were set forth in the August 8, 1863 issue of *Harper's Weekly*: " . . . a little after noon, the Corps was formed in three sides of a square, with the fourth side occupied by three open graves and three empty coffins, seated upon which, bound hand and foot and blindfolded, were the three unfortunate men (William M'Kee, William Groover, and Christopher Krumbar). A squad of eight men were placed at a distance of about three rods from each of the condemned, and a reserve in readiness, should the first fire not prove fatal; but at the single volley the whole three dropped at once lifeless upon their coffins, into which the bodies were then placed, and after the Corps had been marched in columns past them, buried on the spot."

[76]Freeman, *R. E. Lee* III, 144-45; *Official Records*, Ser. I, XXVII, Pt. 2, 988-92; Myers, *The Comanches*, p. 206; James J. Williamson, *Mosby's Rangers* (New York: Ralph B. Kenyon, Publisher, 1896), pp. 85-86.

THE ARMY OF THE POTOMAC—EXECUTION OF THREE DESERTERS

in HARPER'S WEEKLY of the Execution Outside of Leesburg
ne 19, 1863, of Three Deserters from the Army of the Potomac.

During the summer of 1864, the third consecutive year of major troop movement through Loudoun, General Jubal A. Early, after winning the Battle of the Monocacy and frightening Union leaders by fighting the Federals on the outskirts of Washington, retreated into Virginia by crossing the Potomac on July 14 at White's Ford.[77] Early brought with him prisoners taken at the Battle of the Monocacy, captured livestock, and $220,000 in Union currency filched from citizens of Hagerstown and Frederick, Maryland. After resting at Leesburg for two days and writing a report about his "successful" raid upon the Union capital, he retreated westward through the county into the Shenandoah Valley via Snickers' Gap. The Federal pursuit of Early through Loudoun resulted in a number of skirmishes between July 15-19, including clashes at Leesburg, Hillsboro, Purcellville, and Woodgrove. Approximately 15,000 men of Major General H. G. Wright's 6th Corps and Major General W. H. Emory's 19th Corps of the Union Army chased Early westward through the county, while a smaller Union force of 700 infantrymen and 2,000 cavalry crossed the Potomac near Harper's Ferry and into northern Loudoun and proceeded southward in pursuit of Early. Union forces were unsuccessful in stopping Early's retreat into the great Valley of Virginia. However, Early's retreat to safety was short-lived as the inexorable Sheridan not only defeated Early in the Shenandoah Valley but also destroyed "Old Jube's" command.[78]

MOSBY'S CONFEDERACY

Much of the military activity in Loudoun from 1863 into 1865 was due directly or indirectly to the "Gray Ghost" or "Scarlet Cloak," John Singleton Mosby. Slight of build, but wiry and dauntless, Mosby had a definite proclivity for guerrilla warfare or partisan service. Like his mentor and hero, J. E. B. Stuart, Mosby liked the spectacular and viewed himself as a chivalrous knight or Robin Hood of the Confederacy. His

---

[77]Frank E. Vandiver, *Jubal's Raid* (New York: McGraw-Hill Book Co., 1960), p. 172. Unlike the previous major troop movements through the county in 1862 and 1863, which proceeded in northern and southern directions, Early and his Federal pursuers moved primarily westward through the county.

[78]Divine, "Early's Attack on Washington," *Loudoun County and the Civil War*, pp. 51-53; *Official Records*, Ser. I, XXXVII, pt. 1, 270-75, 283-85, 295, 320, 322, 349. In pursuit of Early, the 6th Corps crossed the Potomac at White's Ford (the route of Early's retreat) and shelled the rear guard of the fleeing Confederates at Leesburg. The Union's 19th Corps pursued Early through Loudoun via Edwards' Ferry. This corps turned back at Snickers' Gap and returned to Washington, D.C.

daring nature and individualism found ample opportunity for expression in a border region like Loudoun and elsewhere in northern Virginia that formed what was referred to as "Mosby's Confederacy."[79] Mosby's battle tactics and fighting methods were not complex. When discovering Union soldiers in his "Confederacy," Mosby relied on the element of surprise. He considered the saber useless in cavalry skirmishes and instead had his men use revolvers, shotguns, and rifles. His attacks were also, devoid of complex deployment of his Rangers. Instead, once the order to attack was given, it was every man for himself. Each partisan was to ride as rapidly as his mount would carry him into the midst of the enemy where he discharged his weapons as many times as possible. If the attack was successful, a confused opponent would flee or surrender.[80] The drama and excitement emanating from this style of combat, the booty and seizure of goods from the enemy, and only periodic fighting while frequently living at home and having the comforts of civilian farm life made it easy for Mosby to attract followers, some of whom were not leading citizens of the community, but deserters from the regular Confederate Army or ruffians and hoodlums looking for adventure.[81]

Often Mosby's success was not only the result of intrepid behavior, but also luck. The latter was true especially during early 1863, when Mosby was attempting not only to enhance his reputation but also to insure the permanency of the Rangers as an independent partisan organization. For example, on March 2, 1863, Mosby's runaway mount caused the "Gray Ghost," against his better judgment, to lead a charge at Aldie against fifty dismounted Vermont cavalrymen. Luckily for Mosby, the surprised Federals believed they were greatly outnumbered and fled. Many were captured as some had hidden in the wheat bins

---

[79]V. C. Jones, *Ranger Mosby* (Chapel Hill: University of North Carolina Press, 1944), pp. 130-33; John S. Mosby, *Mosby's War Reminiscences and Stuart's Cavalry Campaign* (New York: Pageant Book Co., 1958), pp. 27-32. Although Mosby had operated as a partisan since December 1862, the official organization of his 43rd Batallion, or Mosby's Rangers, did not take place until June 10, 1863, at Rector's Cross Roads in Loudoun, four miles north of Middleburg. He insured his permanency as a partisan by daring and bold raids, capped by his capture of a Union general, Brigadier General Edwin H. Stoughton, near the Fairfax County Court House during early March 1863. Most of Mosby's activities during the last half of the war years were in an area from the Blue Ridge Mountains east to Fairfax County, known as Mosby's Confederacy. Loudoun County was the geographical heart of his confederacy.

[80]*Official Records*, Ser. I, XXV, Pt. 1, 19; pt. 2, 5-6. These procedures were used whether raiding Union supply lines when the Army of the Potomac traversed Loudoun prior to and after the Battle of Gettysburg or the numerous Federal cavalry reconnaissance parties sent into Loudoun from Washington to capture the "Gray Ghost."

[81]Mosby, *Mosby's War Reminiscences and Stuart's Cavalry Campaigns*, pp. 98-106. A few former infantrymen, disabled for infantry duties due to wounds received in former combat service, also joined Mosby's Rangers. Many of these men tied their crutches to their saddles and eagerly waited a chance to try their hand at partisan warfare.

of the town's mill.⁸² Ironically, Mosby's victory resulted more from the boldness of his horse than from the dauntless behavior of the partisan leader.

One month later, on April 1, good fortune again intervened in a situation that could have terminated the military career and life of not only Mosby but also that of his command. The genesis of the episode was Mosby's pursuit of a Federal force he believed to be at Dranesville. Failing to find the "Blue Coats" at Dranesville, he returned to eastern Loudoun and camped at midnight at Miskel's farm, located near where Broad Run empties into the Potomac River. Although not an ideal place to be if attacked, Mosby selected the site because of the scarcity of forage elsewhere. Mosby incorrectly assumed that because he was a mile from Leesburg Turnpike, he and his men were safe; he therefore failed to post pickets. That night tired and cold Confederates slept in the hayloft of the barn and on the floor of the Miskel house while their horses were tied to a high fence surrounding the barnyard. In the meantime, a citizen notified the Federals of Mosby's location. A force of 150 men of the 1st Vermont Cavalry under the command of a Captain Flint was sent to destroy Mosby's smaller force.

Early the next morning, Mosby was looking across the Potomac at a Union force when Dick Moran, one of the Rangers who had spent the night two miles away and had learned of the pursuing Federal force, rode as rapidly as possible across open fields to warn Mosby. Upon arriving at the Miskel farm, Moran waved his hat and screamed that the Yankees were coming. Almost simultaneously with this caveat, Flint's force arrived on Miskel's farm, catching the Rangers totally unprepared. Mosby and his men, many running from the farmhouse, raced for the barnyard where only one-third of their mounts were saddled and bridled. As the approaching Federals were only 200 yards from the barnyard, Mosby ordered his men not to fire but to "saddle up." Despite this seeming lack of hysteria in a precarious situation in which the Rangers had no avenue of escape while being attacked by a force of more than twice their numbers, Mosby later admitted he had felt that his final hour had come. Meanwhile, Union soldiers gathered along the Maryland bank of the Potomac to cheer their comrades on to what seemed the inevitable rout of the Confederates. Mosby's men were caught in a barnyard and only partially mounted when the Federals fired upon them. This attack was followed by a saber charge by the Union cavalry, which was very ineffective due to the barnyard fence separating the two contingents. Waiting until the fence had checked his opponents' charge, Mosby then had his men fire into the Federals. This volley surprised the Union cavalrymen, who panicked and fled. The Rangers relentlessly pursued

⁸²Ibid., pp. 50-61. At the time of the attack the Federals were preparing to feed their horses.

the fleeing 1st Vermont Cavalry for several miles. Miraculously, Mosby's calm judgment, the barnyard fence, and desperate fighting had not only overcome certain disaster but also led to the killing and wounding of twenty-five and the capture of eighty-two of the Union force, while Mosby's sixty-nine Rangers sustained only one death and three slightly wounded partisans.[83]

During the remainder of the war, Mosby's Rangers and Federal cavalry units scouted Loudoun in search of each other. When they clashed in combat, Mosby almost always emerged as the victor. Such was the case in his most successful and bloodiest engagement in Loudoun, the action on July 6, 1864, fought near the Mount Zion Church. Both forces were approximately of equal strength, about 150 men. However, the Rangers routed their opponents so badly, that only thirty-four of the Union force returned to their Falls Church camp the day after the skirmish.[84]

The battlefield at Mount Zion immediately after the skirmish presented an all-too-common sight of the seamy side of war that people want to forget. The ground was strewn with pistols, guns, blankets, and other equipment. Dead and injured soldiers covered the ground while wounded horses, maddened with pain and fear, ran wildly over the area or feebly attempted to rise but continued to fall to the ground, where they trembled until death consumed them. That night Mosby's pickets could hear the sickening groans and noises of wounded men and horses.[85]

Mosby's growing reputation, due to coverage by Northern newspapers of his numerous defeats of Union forces sent into Loudoun to destroy him, presented the Union command with a vexing and embarrassing problem. During August 1864, General U.S. Grant, general-in-chief of the Union forces, wrote Sheridan and asked whether he could spare a division of

---

[83] James J. Williamson, *Mosby's Rangers* (New York: Ralph B. Kenyon, Publisher, 1896). pp. 51-53; *Official Records,* Ser. I, XXV, Pt. 1, 78-79. On June 10, 1863, Mosby's Rangers were mustered into the Confederate Army as the 43d Battalion of the Virginia Cavalry.

[84] *Official Records,* Ser. I, XXXVII, Pt. 1, 359-61. Some members of the Union cavalry returned to their camp at a later date. Nevertheless, Union casualties were heavy: 13 killed outright, 37 wounded, 12 of whom were said to have been mortally wounded. Mosby claimed to have captured 51 prisoners out of the Union force of 150. Mosby's Rangers had only one man killed and six wounded. While attacking at Mount Zion, Mosby and his men were described by a Union soldier as "yelling like Indians."

[85] J. H. Alexander, *Mosby's Men* (New York: Neale Publishing Co., 1907), pp. 91-96; Wiliamson, *Mosby's Rangers,* pp. 187-89. Near the battlefield was a red brick house that was used as a hospital after the battle. It was in this structure that two doctors labored into the night, attending the wounded and mangled bodies of fighters. A Union cavalry force, consisting of 250 men, went the day after the fighting to Mount Zion, where they buried their dead and carried off their wounded. They failed to discover four bodies of Union soldiers that were later buried by local citizens.

cavalry to be sent through Loudoun to destroy farm produce, and carry off animals, Negroes, and men under fifty capable of bearing arms. Sheridan, unable to send a division of men, dispatched a much smaller force into the county, which failed to get rid of the elusive Mosby. Finally, after Sheridan had destroyed Early's command and burned the Shenandoah Valley, he ordered Major General Wesley Merritt and his 1st Cavalry Division into Loudoun Valley to consume and eliminate all forage, burn all barns, destroy milk or other contents in barns, and drive off all livestock in the region. Sheridan stressed dwellings were not to be burned nor personal violence to be inflicted upon the citizens. However, he justified the destruction of property as necessary to rid the area of "lawless bands" of "guerrillas." For five days the heart of Mosby's Confederacy, Loudoun Valley, was put to the torch, and thousands of head of livestock were driven from the area in an attempt to rid the region of Mosby and White. Loudoun was experiencing one of the major transitions the Civil War marked in warfare: total war. Despite the destruction inflicted on Loudoun Valley from Monday afternoon, November 28, until Friday morning, December 2, 1864, Mosby and his elusive men not only avoided being captured, but continued to operate in the area until the end of the war.[86]

A revealing and penetrating account of the burning of Loudoun Valley was recorded by a Union soldier who participated in the incendiary action:

> *The necessity of destruction is one of the many dark phases of war. As we descended the eastern slope of the Blue Ridge, nothing could be more beautiful than that garden of Virginia flanked on the farther side by the Bull Run Mountains. It is one of the richest counties in cattle and pasturage, with splendid stock in horses and sheep. It fell to the lot of our brigade to go through the beautiful Valley between Loudoun Heights and the Short Hills, and flankers were sent out so as to sweep the whole Valley. Some idea of the general destruction may be formed when I relate that in one day two regiments of our brigade burned more than one hundred and fifty barns, a thousand stacks of hay, and six flour mills, besides driving off fifty horses and three hundred head of cattle. This was the most unpleasant task we were ever compelled to undertake. It was heart-piercing to hear the shrieks of women and children, and to see even men crying and beating their breasts, supplicating for mercy on bended knees, begging that at*

---

[86] *Official Records,* Ser. I, XLIII, Pt. 1, 672; Pt. 2, 730. The last skirmish in Loudoun was fought near Hamilton on March 21, 1865, between Mosby and a Union force sent into the county to stop the Rangers from impressing supplies and conscripting citizens into Confederate service. This skirmish was Mosby's last victory. On April 20, 1865, he disbanded his Partisan force of approximately 200 men.

least one cow - an only support - might be left. But no mercy was allowed. Orders must be obeyed. All that could subsist guerrillas must be destroyed. If citizens would not themselves cease harboring guerrillas, then we must compel them to desist in the only way open to us. It was a terrible retribution on the county that had for three years supported and lodged the guerrilla bands and sent them out to plunder and murder.[87]

SUPERSEDURE OF CIVIL RIGHTS AND CIVIL GOVERNMENT BY MILITARY MIGHT

During the war years local civil government, civil rights, and peacetime conveniences were subordinated and frequently forfeited to the will and needs of the military. Like most other areas of the nation contested by Union and Confederate armies, Loudoun County ceased to have either a republican or democratic system of local government during this period. County court was not held from February 1862 until July 1865,[88] properties of civilians were confiscated by both the forces of the Union and Confederacy, county residents were frequently arrested as spies or suspicious citizens, travel by civilians was greatly encumbered, postal service was impaired,[89] religious services were often hindered by

---

[87]Charles A. Humphreys, *Field, Camp and Prison in the Civil War, 1863-1865* (Boston: Press of George H. Ellis Co., 1918), pp. 191-92.

[88]At the start of the Civil War all Loudoun County Court records were removed to Campbell County, Virginia. Also at the beginning of the war, an unsuccessful attempt was made by the Virginians to provide for future gaps in judicial facilities caused by war. An ordinance was passed which stated that any business that was required by law to be performed by a county court that could not be held due to the conditions of war could be transacted in any of the neighboring county courts in the state.

[89]Janney, *Memoirs*, pp. 218-24; *The Democratic Mirror*, July 10, 1861. Mail service in particular was severely hampered. In an attempt to alleviate this problem, people in Loudoun went to the federal post office at Point of Rocks, Maryland, where letters from north of the Potomac River were picked up. Jacob Lemon, an elderly man who had carried mail between Point of Rocks and Waterford, during the early part of the war frequently carried letters between the two areas. He was soon arrested by Confederates and charged with "being the bearer of treasonable correspondence." He was acquitted on the grounds that he was not responsible for the content of the letters. By 1864, the Federals maintained a strict blockade along the Potomac. No mail was allowed to pass north or south across the Potomac, and no one could cross without a pass from the Union government except refugees to the North and people bringing grain from Virginia into Maryland. Confederate forces also hampered travel to Maryland as early as 1861. After the Battle of Ball's Bluff, Samuel Janney crossed the Potomac into Maryland without permission from General Evans. Janney was rebuked by Evans for violation of a military order and detained in Leesburg for four days as a face-saving device for Evans, who did not know what to do

the use of churches as hospitals or barracks,[90] and county newspapers were forced to cease publication due to labor and paper shortages. As bad as these conditions were, the fact that Loudoun suffered less than many other areas in the South was of little comfort to county residents.

The Civil War soon destroyed civilian government and any pretense of impartial rule in Loudoun as martial law replaced civil law. Both Union and Confederate established provostships over the county while soldiers of the Blue and Gray swept through Loudoun. Although both administered oaths of allegiance and granted paroles throughout the war, these failed to establish or maintain civicism as reprisals and agitation between Union and Confederate supporters in Loudoun compounded disorder and instability caused by skirmishes and troop movement. It was also common for residents of the county to keep the military informed on the loyalties and attitudes of neighbors in their respective communities.[91]

However, the military became the greatest decimator of basic civil rights and freedoms. Whenever the county was occupied by Confederate troops and under their transitory control, Union supporters like the Quakers were under surveillance. The reverse was true when Union troops controlled the county. It was common for forces of both sides to arrest county citizens and charge them with espionage, supporting the enemy, or failure to back the contingent doing the arresting.[92] Often, unlike the judicial prosecution during peacetime, civilians were charged not so much for what they had done, but for what they might do. Such "preventive action" was based on martial law and the doctrine of military necessity.[93]

The military not only arrested civilians who supported the opposing side, but also seized local residents as hostages. An excellent example was an incident during the fall of 1863 in which the Confederates

---

with the resolute Quaker. By 1862 no one could go through the Confederate military lines in Loudoun without a pass. The same year travel in the county was restricted even further when General J. E. Johnson ordered General Hill not to issue any passes in Loudoun to "market people" or others who lacked military business in the county.

[90] No religious services were held in the Loudoun Ketoctin Baptist Church during the war because its minister enlisted in the Confederate Army as a chaplain and was later captured by the Yankees.

[91] Janney, *Memoirs*, p. 189

[92] *Official Records*, Ser. I, XXXIII, 113.

[93] James G. Randall, *Constitutional Problems Under Lincoln* (Urbana: University of Illinois Press, 1951), pp. 120-27, 140. At the start of the war, Union supporters were threatened with arrest and punishment for not supporting the Confederacy. This threat caused a number of them to leave the county. However, in December 1861 when four Unionists tried to return to Loudoun to visit their families, they were arrested and sent to Libby Prison in Richmond. While there, they suffered from malnutrition and starvation.

retaliated against the arrest and imprisonment of two Loudouners, Henry Ball and Campbell Belt, who had refused to take the oath of allegiance to the United States. After appeals to Union authorities to obtain their release were unsuccessful, an order was supposedly procured from the Confederate Secretary of War for the retaliatory arrest of several Loudoun Unionists.[94] A small detachment from Colonel Lige White's Comanches was sent to Waterford to arrest three of that community's prominent Quaker citizens and Unionists supporters: Asa Bond, William Williams, and Robert Hollingsworth. Mr. Bond, the father-in-law of Captain Samuel Means of the Loudoun Rangers, escaped arrest because Mrs. Bond and her sister assailed the several Confederate soldiers with such domestic weapons as broomsticks and rolling pins. They also rang the dinner bell and fired a few shots from a revolver, which forced the squad of Confederates to settle for the arrest of William Williams and Robert Hollingsworth.[95]

In an attempt to obtain the release of Williams and Hollingsworth, Samuel M. Janney, accompanied by the wife and brother of Williams, went to see President Lincoln in hopes that the "Great Emancipator" would release the two Loudoun secessionists held by the Federals. Lincoln, who spent most of his weekdays receiving just such citizens, treated them kindly and sent them to see Edwin M. Stanton. The Secretary of War, lacking Lincoln's tact and being unafraid to disappoint, refused to consent to their request. However, all was not lost. The Loudouners petitioned the authorities in Richmond, who released the Loudoun Quakers. In return Stanton promptly released the Confederate supporters from the county. Not all county residents arrested as political prisoners or hostages were as fortunate because a few of the less hardy died or had their health impaired due to the strain of prison conditions.[96]

The arrest of the two Quaker Unionists from Waterford was not an isolated incident. During 1864 dozens of county civilians were carried from their homes by the military and placed in prisons. Many of these arrests stemmed from an order from General Grant that stated Loudoun was to be cleared of all citizens liable to Rebel conscription. However, in compliance with the order, a detachment of Federal cavalry arrested a number of Loudoun residents, including some Quakers returning home from a religious service. Samuel Janney, who continued to the end of

---

[94]Myers, *The Comanches*, pp. 219-20; *Official Records*, Ser. I, XXIX, Pt. 109. Upon hearing of this plan, Major Cole of the Maryland Cavalry notified two prominent Confederate sympathizers in the vicinity of Waterford that he would hold them as hostages if Union citizens from Waterford were seized.

[95]Goodhard, *History of the Independent Loudoun Virginia Rangers*, pp. 130-31; Myers, *The Comanches*, p. 220. Williams and Hollingsworth were taken to Richmond and imprisoned at Libby. Later, due to the intervention of Quaker citizens of Richmond, they were transferred to a privately operated prison.

[96]Janney, *Memoirs*, pp. 202, 218-24.

the war to work for the release of Loudoun civilians he felt were arbitrarily arrested and imprisoned, appealed to the major who had supervised the arrests. Those whom Janney could testify were loyal Union supporters were released. However, not knowing many, he could not testify on their behalf, although he argued for their release. The latter were, nevertheless, taken and imprisoned in Washington. In particular, Janney attempted to obtain the release of a doctor, not because he was loyal to the Union, but because his professional services were needed in Loudoun. When the major refused to release the physician, Janney once again traveled to Washington, where he visited army officials, including the Assistant Secretary of War, C. A. Dana. Dana sent Janney to see General Sheridan. The dauntless Quaker traveled to Harper's Ferry to see Sheridan, where he received a lecture from the general that Loudoun, as other areas, must bear her burden of the war. After the lecture the general agreed to release not only the doctor, but also all old men of Loudoun who were over the age for conscription. Sheridan assured Janney that he would telegraph the appropriate authorities in Washington.

But upon arriving in Washington, Janney discovered that Sheridan had not informed authorities of his decision. An exasperated Janney went again to see Assistant Secretary Dana. Janney adamantly expressed to Dana his apprehension about the policy of the Federal government frequently leading to the arrest of citizens of Loudoun who had committed no overt act against the Union, but who were arrested because of their political opinions. Janney emphasized that such measures did the Union little good and could have disastrous consequences because Confederate authorities would retaliate by arresting an equal number of Union supporters in the county. Further admonishing the Assistant Secretary of War, Janney warned that Federal troops continuing to destroy Loudoun's crops and carrying off her livestock would inflict suffering upon the residents and not appreciably increase the Union war effort. Impressed by Janney's oratorical effort and logic, Dana agreed to parole twenty-eight Loudouners.[97]

---

[97]Ibid., pp. 218-24. Janney furnished Dana with information about the character and peaceful nature of the twenty-eight men prior to their parole. (Janney does not state in his *Memoirs* whether the doctor was among the twenty-eight men released.) Shortly after the release of the aforementioned, Janney learned that thirty-two more Loudoun residents had been arrested and imprisoned in Washington. Among this group was a former state senator and county judge, Asa Rogers, who with twenty-five others of Confederate sympathies were held as hostages in hope Confederate authorities would agree to exchange them for twenty-six residents of Pennsylvania that Southern forces had carried off during the Gettysburg campaign. Janney worked for the release of Rogers, who refused to take the oath necessary to be paroled because he had a son and nephews in the Confederate army. He stated if they came to his house he would not only admit them, but attempt to prevent their capture by Union forces.

Of similar severity and annoyance as arbitrary arrests of civilians were the conscription of reluctant residents into military service and the pressing (seizing) of supplies from farmers. Conscription of county residents was primarily done by Confederates, particularly Mosby and White.[98] To counteract these pressures, as previously shown, Union patrols carried off citizens likely to be conscripts of Confederate forces. For the Quakers, who opposed war and most of whom refused to fight, the Confederate government was required to adopt an alternate policy. The Confederacy subsequently required Friends to pay fines to exempt them from military service.[99]

Other than the burning of Loudoun Valley, the systematic pressing of crops and livestock by Union and Confederates caused the most significant reduction in the wealth and economic well-being of county residents. Examples of Union and Confederate soldiers helping themselves to the county's agricultural wealth are numerous. Stonewall Jackson, while at Harper's Ferry, sent a small force during April 1861 to buy or press horses from the Quakers of Loudoun to obtain good draft horses for his artillery.[100] Later on, Means mounted his company of Rangers as much as possible on horses taken from the farms owned by county residents who had joined the Confederate army.[101] Throughout the war, combatants of both sides seized horses, the Confederates for mounts and the Union to prevent them from being used by Southern forces. Demands on Loudoun's forage and grain were especially great during major troop movements through the county, such as before and after bloody battles of Antietam and Gettysburg. During Early's retreat through the county after his raid on Washington, Confederates so extensively consumed Loudoun's produce that Union pursuers could not subsist to any extent off of the county.[102]

Partisan forces such as Mosby's Rangers and the Loudoun Rangers considered Loudoun their exclusive bread basket and attempted to guard

---

[98] Janney, *Memoirs*, pp. 232-33; *Official Records*, Ser. I, XXIX, Pt. 1, 95. The notable exception to Union conscription in Loudoun was an order of dubious legality issued by Samuel Means of the Loudoun Rangers. On July 15, 1863, Captain Means issued an order which was of the nature of a general conscript law for Loudoun. A detachment of Rangers was sent into the county to notify a large number of citizens of suitable age for military service that the time was right for them to enlist in the Rangers. However, few men responded as this statement was taken more as a request than as an order.

[99] Myers, *The Comanches*, pp. 18-19.

[100] Buel and Johnson, *Battles and Leaders of the Civil War*, I, 122. The Quakers were noted for their agricultural prosperity and fine horses.

[101] Goodhart, *History of the Independent Loudoun Rangers*, pp. 27-28.

[102] *Official Records*, Ser. I, XXXVII, Pt. 1, 268, Pt. 2, 297. Mosby and his men attempted to restrict Unionist troops in pursuit of Early from taking forage and grain from the county.

it from the enemy.[103] Tolerance by area Confederate and Federal partisans to each other's pressing activities was especially low. Mosby and Means not only attempted to impede each other from taking Loudoun's produce but also condemned the other's pressing as the activity of lawless gangs, ruffians, and guerrillas. Mosby was also an exceptional irritant to Union forces, who in turn carried off extensive amounts of Loudoun produce in an attempt to rid the area of the Gray Ghost.[104] Whereas Federal reconnaissance parties preferred to seize properties of Confederate supporters, Mosby and the Confederates often selected the farms of Union sympathizers, especially those of the industrious and prosperous Quakers for "hay soldiering" or "pie rooting."[105] The practice of pressing farm products in Loudoun, extensive throughout the war, was increased as the war stretched into the third and fourth year. By 1863, pressing was so common one eyewitness wrote:

> *What had been considered an impossibility the year before was not demonstrated to be perfectly feasible, and to the great discomfort of the border land both uniforms were daily seen by the citizens, and very frequently followed each other so rapidly that when not in actual chase, one party would scarcely be out of sight before the other would be demanding rations and horse-feed, and making awful threats against Rebels or Yankees as the case might be.*[106]

[103]The Loudoun Rangers often camped across the Potomac from Loudoun at Point of Rocks, Maryland. From there they frequently visited Loudoun and collected hay and corn, for which they gave the citizens vouchers of the United States Government, promising to pay at a future date for the supplies taken.

[104]*Official Records*, Ser. I,XXIX, Pt. 1,110; Pt. 2,94-96; Ser. I,ILVI, Pt. 1,552,1303-8. Typical of the Union attitude as the report filed during September 1863 by a Federal cavalry officer who had just completed a scouting trip into Loudoun: "I noticed a great many fat cattle in Loudoun which indirectly find their way to the rebel army. Allow me to suggest the propriety of seizing the same for the benefit of the Government."

[105]Alexander, *Mosby's Men*, p. 30. "Hay soldiering" applied to taking forage from farmers to feed horses of a military force. "Pie-rooting" referred to securing food for soldiers from residents along any given route the force traveled. Mosby usually placed William Hibbs, a Loudoun blacksmith and father of two sons in the Confederate army, in charge of such activities. Although Hibbs was not an officer, he was affectionately referred to by Mosby's men as "Major."

[106]Myers, *The Comanches*, pp. 226-27. Raiding provided opportunities for daring adventure that became a fervency for some. One example was that of a Loudouner, young John Mobberly, a detached scout of White's Comanches, who made numerous nightly attacks upon Federal pickets stationed in Loudoun. He also seized livestock in the county. Prior to 1860, Mobberly was considered by many of his neighbors to be a dimwitted youth. Yet during the war he developed a lust for raiding that was abnormal and a reputation as an indomitable "guerrilla." His activities were so exasperating to Union officers stationed at Harper's Ferry and northwestern Loudoun during 1864 and 1865 that numerous Federal expeditions were sent with instructions to bring back the corpse of the "desperate" Mobberly

Even the burning of Loudoun Valley and the attempt by the Union during the fall of 1864 to remove all livestock from Loudoun Valley did not terminate either Mosby's command or their pressing of farm produce.[107] Although Loudoun graineries were at their lowest ebb, only four months after the burning of the western half of the county, Mosby was active not only in conscripting men into service for the Confederacy, but also in pressing corn, wheat, and bacon. Also, his seizing of the few remaining head of livestock left many farmers with the perplexing problems of few provisions and no horses for spring plowing.

As the war came to an end, weary county residents, even Confederate supporters, eagerly greeted the termination of what they considered unfair harassment by Union and Confederate troops. Samuel Janney ably summarized the treatment and feeling of county Unionists during the war:

> During four years we have been exposed here to the deprivation of the soldiers, our young men liable to rebel conscription, our loyal citizens sometimes arrested and imprisoned by the rebels, the crops on some farms taken or destroyed, and the people kept in a state of feverish anxiety.[108]

and exterminate his "gang of murderers infesting Loudoun." Extensive raids were made in western Loudoun, where numerous homes were searched, and in one instance the pursuit of Mobberly was attempted in a blinding snow storm with "snowdrifts that were leg deep." Mobberly's small force of about fifteen was gradually killed or captured. Finally, during the first part of April 1865, Mobberly was killed by Union soldiers who had set a trap for him by using horses as bait for a raid that drew the partisan into the deadly range of Federal rifle fire.

[107]Janney, *Memoirs*, pp. 232-35. To aid distressed Friends in Loudoun, Northern Quakers gave financial assistance. Residents of Loudoun were promised compensation or payment for the seizure of their property at various times during the war by both belligerents. These were rarely fulfilled.

[108]Ibid., p. 234.

Chapter 6

A DISHARMONIOUS REUNION: 1865 TO 1877

The most dramatic and traumatic series of events in American history were those associated with the disruption and reconstruction of the Union. Citizens of Loudoun County, Virginia, regardless of their views concerning union and secession, welcomed the termination of carnage and strain inflicted upon them by the existence of four years of civil war. The county had been traversed and trampled by innumerable warriors of the Blue and Gray.[1] Civil government in the county had been superseded early in the war by military rule that oscillated back and forth between Union and Confederate officers. Mail service had been suspended, travel by civilians restricted and their civil liberties negated by arbitrary arrests and incarceration.[2] The war effort had demanded sacrifice not only in human life, but also in materials, especially agricultural resources. Her agricultural products had not been always voluntarily granted to military forces. Loudoun paid dearly for being a part of Mosby's Confederacy. Mosby's harassment of Union forces brought from Washington, D. C., and Alexandria, Virginia, numerous cavalry incursions into Loudoun in an attempt to destroy the "Gray Ghost." Union incompetence doomed such ventures to failure. Subsequently, General Sheridan had the western half of the county burned and livestock seized in an attempt to destroy Loudoun's capacity to sustain Confederate partisans.[3]

---

[1] *Official Records*, Ser. I, XXVII, pt. 2, 297.

[2] Goodhart, *History of the Independent Loudoun Virginia Rangers*, p. 131; *The Democratic Mirror*, July 10 and August 21, 1861 (hereafter in Chp. 6 referred to as the *Mirror*); Janney, *Memoirs*, pp. 218-24.

[3] *Official Records*, Ser. I, XXIX, Pt. 2, 94-95; and Ser. I, XLVI, Pt. 1, 552, 1307-08.

All of this devastation made Loudouners yearn for normalcy despite a reluctance by many to resign themselves during the waning days of the war to the imminent demise of the Confederacy and the death of slavery. Soon new hope and optimism emerged from the belief that rapid restoration of the Union was forthcoming due to the Lincoln-Johnson reconstruction plans. These plans were based upon the President's power to pardon and the promise by ex-Confederates of future fidelity to the Union. But as Congressional hegemony emerged in 1866 and reconstruction became more protracted, a far greater political and social retribution was being demanded of the South. Before Radicals would acknowledge proper atonement had been made by ex-Confederates for their sins of secession, hope and optimism turned to dismay and bitterness. Loudouners found little solace in the fact that Virginia was spared the degree of subjugation endured by other ex-Confederate states.[4]

ECONOMIC REHABILITATION

Rapid economic recovery for regions ravaged by war is theoretically more likely for an agrarian society rather than an industrial one. This premise is true in the sense that a crop can usually be planted and harvested sooner and more easily than factories and cities can be rebuilt. But for the Southern farmer during the summer of 1865, economic reconstruction involved more than the successful harvesting of a crop. Barns and, in many cases, houses had to be rebuilt. The war had destroyed livestock that would take years to replenish. Basic concepts of property rights, upon which the antebellum South had emerged, were shaken or destroyed. In addition to losing investments in the black man as chattel, ex-Confederates faced possible confiscation of their lands and its redistribution to the freedmen. The abolishment of slavery and the shortage of cash necessitated readjustments in labor relationships. The results were the modification of the plantation system and the rise of sharecropping and the crop-lien system, which replaced the wage system, increased tenantry, augmented the indebtedness of tenants to the country store, subsequently elevating it to the position of the dominant financial institution in the South during the reconstruction era.[5]

The general economic condition in the South at the end of the war was desolate indeed when compared to that of the North. The latter was an area which fortunately had been spared from being part of the major

[4]Randall and Donald, *The Civil War and Reconstruction*, pp. 560, 620-21; Kenneth M. Stampp, *The Era Of Reconstruction, 1865-1877* (New York: Alfred A. Knopf, 1965), p. 62.

[5]E. Merton Coulter, *The South During Reconstruction* (Baton Rouge: Louisiana State University Press, 1947), pp. 1-22; Randall and Donald, *The Civil War and Reconstruction*, pp. 531-38, 550-51.

arena for battles and whose agricultural and industrial development had been stimulated rather than destroyed by America's civil blood-bath.[6] The War Between the States resulted in not only a victory of nationalism over sectionalism, but also in supremacy of the factory over the farm, of such irreversible magnitude that the "Lost Cause" can be viewed as "The Second American Revolution" or watershed of modern American industrialism.[7]

The precise degree of Loudoun's economic deterioration induced by the rigors of war is difficult to determine. There is enough evidence to sustain the view that, while the country endured extensive damage, it had not been reduced to economic prostration.[8] During the war years the absence of civil government and political stability due to the almost continuous movement of hostile forces across the county and occasional fighting and the enlistment of Loudouners in the armies of the Blue and Gray reduced the county's labor force, impeded Loudoun's normal agrarian lifestyle, and reduced its wealth. Both "Johnny Reb" and "Billy Yank" demanded sustenance from Loudoun's wheat, corn, cattle, sheep, and hogs and appropriated mounts and draft animals. A comparison of the number of livestock in Loudoun five years after the war with the number at the advent of hostilities is indicative of part of the Civil War's economic impact upon the county. In 1860 there were 7,503 horses, 105 mules, 571 oxen, and 23,153 hogs as compared to 5,572 horses, 82 mules, 620 oxen, and 14,594 hogs in the county in 1870. At the end of the war there was a shortage of horses in Loudoun. Many of the remaining animals had been saved from being seized by soldiers because of their age and unfitness for use. Adding to the farmer's woes was the difficulty in replacing farm equipment that had been destroyed or seized during the war. Despite the above problems the farmer's plight after the war was not saturnine. Wheat production in 1870 was 537,026 bushels compared to the 396,297 bushel yield in 1860.[9]

As early as June 14, 1865, a county newspaper optimistically reported:

> We are glad to hear from all parts of the coun-
> ty—growing crops are looking remarkably well and

---

[6]For a rebuttal of the thesis that the Civil War greatly accelerated Northern industrial development see Thomas C. Cochran, "Did the Civil War Retard Industrialization?" *Views of American Economic Growth: The Agricultural Era*, eds. Thomas C. Cochran and Thomas B. Brewer, I (New York: McGraw-Hill, 1966), 252-61.

[7]Charles A. Beard and Mary R. Beard, *The Rise of American Civilization*, II (Rev. ed.; New York: Macmillan Co., 1962), 99. For an evaluation of Beard's "Second American Revolution" thesis consult Staughton Lynd, ed., *Reconstruction* (New York: Harper and Row, 1967), pp. 82-88, 114-29.

[8]Penelope M. Osburn, "The Road Back," *Loudoun County and the Civil War* (Leesburg, Va.: Potomac Press, 1961), p. 6.

[9]Ibid., pp. 68-69.

promise a good yield. The wheat crop is not as large as in former years, but there is a fair proportion of corn. Loudoun is a great county—her agricultural resources are immense.[10]

Ironically one of the factors that kept the prices of farm products from Loudoun and nearby areas after the Civil War higher than they may have normally been was the shortage of livestock and cereals caused by the spoilation and devastation sustained during the war. Loudoun farmers sent their produce to Georgetown in the District of Columbia and Baltimore, Maryland, where prices after the war were generally higher than those received at the same markets prior to 1861. Prices, which were very high immediately at the end of the war, decreased as farm products became more plentiful:

	1850 (November)	1865 (July)	1872 (August)
Wheat (per bu.)	$1.20-1.40	$ 2.05- 2.15	$1.40-1.75
Corn (per bu.)	$ .65- .83	$ .94- .97	$ .71- .74
Cattle (per 100 lbs.)	$4.50	$ 7.75- 8.25	$6.00-6.75
Hogs (per 100 lbs.)	$5.75-7.00[11]	$14.75-15.00[12]	$6.75-7.00[13]

It has been stated that the small, or yeoman, farmer fared better in Loudoun during and after the war than the planter.[14] For the most part this situation is true. However, in the mind of the small granger his sacrifice was proportionately as great as that of his more wealthy counterpart. Both had livestock and crops seized by military forces of the North and South. Eastern and western regions of the county were affected in different ways by the war. Slavery had existed primarily in

---

[10] *Mirror*, June 14, 1865.
[11] Ibid., November 24, 1858.
[12] Ibid., July 26, 1865.
[13] Ibid., August 28, 1872. The economic impact of the Civil War upon Loudoun is reflected in the decline from 296,142 acres of land farmed in 1860 to 276,291 acres in 1870.
[14] Osburn, "The Road Back," pp. 69-70.

the eastern and southern regions of Loudoun,[15] where 670 slaveowners owned 5,501 slaves in 1860.[16] The termination of slavery, therefore, had the greatest economic impact upon the eastern and southern portions of the county. Although the northwestern region was spared this loss, it, along with the southwestern part of the county, suffered in 1864 from Union incendiarism that inflicted by far the greatest destruction and confiscation of property during the Civil War in Loudoun County. The specific number of livestock seized and the value of property destroyed are not known. The Union officer who supervised the operation estimated that 5,000 to 6,000 cattle, 4,000 sheep, and 6,000 hogs were driven off or destroyed.[17] The same officer stated that, although he did not know the number of mills, barns, or quanity of forage destroyed, he estimated the damage was in the millions of dollars.[18] Union citizens petitioned Congress for redress. Under the leadership of Samuel Janney, who authored the original petition to the government and visited Secretary of War Stanton as well as numerous members of Congress, the loyalists won part of their demands. On January 23, 1873, a law was enacted that paid loyal citizens of Loudoun $61,821.13 for livestock losses.[19] Another bill, which was introduced periodically from 1865 to 1894, would have made payments to them totaling $199,220.24 for property losses.[20] This bill never became law, despite having passed both Houses of Congress at different sessions.[21] The sum of money requested in both bills was based upon claims made by loyal citizens during the latter part of the war.[22] At that time, officers of the Union army attempted to authenticate the claim and loyalty of each petitioner by requiring him to take an oath of loyalty to the United States. Later affidavits from appraisers and loyal citizens that verified the claimant's damages and his loyalty to the Union were also demanded and obtained. The following petition shows how they were authenticated:

[15]Williams, *Legends of Loudoun*, p.59.
[16]*Mirror*, December 12, 1860; Osburn, op. cit., p. 61.
[17]*Official Records*, Ser. I. XLIII, Pt. 2, 730.
[18]Ibid., Pt. 2, P. 673. One of the three brigades that participated in crippling Loudoun Valley alone destroyed 230 barns, 8 mills, 1 still, 10,000 tons of hay, and 25,000 bushels of grain.
[19]Janney, *Memoirs*, pp. 229-32. Some members of Congress were afraid that this law would set a precedent for numerous and immense claims against the government.
[20]Ibid., pp. 229-30. Janney estimated that, if supporters of the Confederacy had sought financial redress, their claims for damages would have been close to $196,000. This is a conservative appraisal.
[21]U.S. Congress, House, *Certain Loyal Citizens of Loudoun County, Virginia*, H.R. Rept. 806 to accompany H.R. 2451, 53rd Cong., 2nd sess., 1894. Congress refused to make any compensation for property destroyed on the premise that the federal government was not liable or responsible for property destroyed in states that seceded from the Union.
[22]Four Negroes petitioned the government for $1,775 for loss of property at the hands of Union soldiers. They received $1,300.

UNITED STATES TO THOMAS YOUNG

1864 - To property burned by United States troops, by order of General Sheridan —
  November 30 - To straw of three hundred bushels of wheat-$15.00

To ten bushels of white wheat, at $2.50 - 25.00

$40.00

·*I hereby certify on honor that the above accounts, amounting to forty dollars, are correct and just.*

THOMAS YOUNG

We, the undersigned, do solemnly affirm that Thomas Young is loyal to the government of the United States, and that he has never voluntarily given aid to the rebellion; and further, that the within account is just, as appraised by us, to the best of our knowledge and belief.

JOSEPH NICHOLS
GEORGE GREGG
WILLIAM HOLMES

Sworn to and subscribed before me this 28th of January, 1865, at Lovettsville, Virginia.

A. W. Chamberlain
Lieutenant First New York Dragoons
Acting Assistant Adjutant General, Second Brigade
First Cavalry Division, Middle Military Div.

Oath prescribed by act of Congress Approved July 2, 1862. COUNTY of Loudoun, State of Virginia, ss:
  I, the undersigned, of the county of Loudoun and state of Virginia, do solemnly affirm that I have never voluntarily borne arms against the United States since I have been a citizen thereof; that I have voluntarily given no aid, countenance, counsel, or encouragement to per-

sons in armed hostility thereto; that I have neither sought nor accepted nor attempted to exercise the functions of any office whatever under any authority of pretended authority in hostility to the United States; that I have not yielded a voluntary support to any pretended government, authority, power, or constitution within the United States hostile or inimical thereto. And I do further affirm that, to the best of my knowledge and ability, I will support and defend the Constitution of the United States against all enemies, foreign and domestic; that I will bear true faith and allegiance to the same; that I take this obligation freely, without any mental reservation or purpose of evasion.

THOMAS YOUNG

Sworn and subscribed to before us this 16th day of February, 1866 -

MAHLON THOMAS, J.P.
ENOCH FENTON, J.P.
LOT TAVENNER, J.P.
ELI I. HOGE, J.P.

STATE OF VIRGINIA, to wit:

    I, Charles P. Janney, clerk of the county court of Loudoun County, in the state aforesaid, do certify that Mahlon Thomas, Enoch Fenton, Lot Tavenner, and Eli Hoge, whose genuine signature appear to the above certificate, are justices of the peace for the county and state aforesaid, duly commissioned and qualified.

    Given under my hand and the seal of said court, at Leesburg, this 26th day of February, 1866.[23]

    Unionists, especially Quakers, economically recovered more rapidly than Confederate supporters, due not only to the partial financial compensation for damages by the federal government but also to the fact they were primarily small farmers who did not believe in or have slaves. Loudoun Friends were especially fortunate in that they sought and

---

[23] U. S. Congress, Senate, *A Bill for the Relief of Loudoun County, Virginia*, S. Rept. 99 to accompany S. 48, 43rd Cong., 1st sess., 1874.

received immediate aid from Quakers in Philadelphia and New York.[24] The hardest hit were the larger farmers and planters in the southwestern portion of the county. They not only lost their slave labor force as the result of the war, but also endured heavy property losses from the Union raids in 1864 that burned and confiscated property throughout the western half of the county.[25] An indication of the decrease in Loudoun's wealth brought on by the Civil War can be obtained from an examination of the census records pertaining to the county in 1860 and 1870. For example, C. F. Hempston, a farmer near Leesburg, was recorded in 1860 as having realty amounting to $30,000 and personalty to $7,500.[26] In 1870 the value of his real estate had declined to $2,000 and his personal property to $1,321.[27] Although Hempston was not among the wealthiest citizens of Loudoun, his assets were far above the county average.[28] The degree of reduction in his wealth from 1860 to 1870 is fairly representative of what had happened to other Loudouners. However, conditions were not as dismal as the general 1870 county census would indicate. In that survey only a small percentage of Loudoun's residents were listed as having any realty or personalty.[29]

During the post-war period it was not uncommon for several farms or tracts of land consisting of 100 to 200 acres to be sold each month in Loudoun. A few estates were sold by the county court due to the owners' inability to remain solvent.[30] But on the whole, there does not appear to have been a drastic shift in proprietorships. There is some evidence the shortage of cash in the years immediately after the war was responsible for land prices being lower than they were prior to 1861. For example, two tracts of land were sold during June 1866 for $38.75 and $39.75 per acre. During the 1850's the same land would have probably brought around $50 per acre.[31] However, land prices in Loudoun were not severely depressed. Good farm land with dwellings and other

[24]Janney, *Memoirs*, p. 231.

[25]Penelope Osburn contends that the county deed books for the twenty-five years after the war reveal that many of the larger farms were sold. She assumed it was because of the lack of capital to operate the farms and pay taxes. See page 70 in *Loudoun County and the Civil War*.

[26]U.S. National Archives, Population Schedules of the Censuses of Loudoun County, Virginia For 1860, Microfilm, roll no. 297, micro-copy no. T.7, Fairfax County Library, Fairfax, Virginia. (Hereafter referred to as Censuses of Loudoun.)

[27]Ibid., 1870, roll no. 1659, micro-copy no. 593.

[28]Elizabeth A. Carter was appraised in 1860 as having $150,000 in realty and $250,000 in personalty.

[29]Censuses of Loudoun, 1870.

[30]*Mirror*, December 7, 1865; May 30, 1866. On December 4, 1865, the county court ruled that unless Syddah Williams appeared within one month to face his creditors and a debt amounting to $1,553.99 plus interest his estate would be attached.

[31]Ibid., June 6, 1866.

structures in the spring of 1866 sold from $50 to $65 per acre.³² By the 1870's land prices in the county had risen to an average of between $58 and $80 per acre.³³

Approximately ten months after the burning of Loudoun Valley and six months after Lee's surrender, Loudoun residents were stunned when they read in the August 31, 1865, issue of *The Democratic Mirror* that more than 15,000 acres of land, plus homes and stores belonging to ex-Confederates in Loudoun, were being confiscated by the Freedmen's Bureau to be redistributed later among blacks.³⁴ Loudoun's 81 pieces of confiscated land varied in size from 1 to 1,000 acres. Ownership was being denied to small farmers as well as aristocrats like Francis Mason, who was to lose several tracts totaling 2,800 acres.³⁵ The editor of *The Democratic Mirror* denounced confiscation in a statement that lacked total factual correctness but was nevertheless eloquent:

> Since the cessation of hostilities the people of the South have evinced a spirit of hope, charity and forebearance at which their enemies doubtless marvelled. Broken in fortune, crushed in spirit, a magnanimous conqueror might at least afford to spare her the bitter humiliation of being trampled in the dust, and seeing thousands of her helpless women and innocent children turned homeless and penniless upon the world for the benefit of "loyal refugees" and "freedom." Was it for this that seven long years the men of the Revolution struggled to throw off the yoke of British tyranny? Aye, men of the Federal army was it for THIS that you perilled your health and your lives on the bloody fields of the South?³⁶

Confiscation of property in Loudoun was done under the authority of the Confiscation Act of 1862 and legislation in 1865 that established

---

³²Ibid., March 14 and April 11, 1866.

³³Ibid., August 2, 1871; March 13, 1872; February 3 and April 6, 1876. Poor, uncleared, or hilly land was sold as low as $8 per acre. Occasionally a special tract would be sold for $100 or slightly more. The *Mirror* on September 21, 1865, reports that a 200-acre tract of land near Arcola owned by Dr. Wicks was sold to a gentleman from Washington for $35 per acre. The same land a few years earlier was sold for $7.50 an acre.

³⁴*Mirror*, December 31, 1865. The *Mirror* got its information from an article in a Richmond newspaper.

³⁵The town of Leesburg had several lots and houses confiscated. Although all of the people whose property was being confiscated in all likelihood had supported the Confederacy, not all had voted for secession.

³⁶*Mirror*, August 31, 1865.

the Freedmen's Bureau. As in the application in other areas of the South the purpose of confiscation was to (1) punish those who defiled the sanctity of the Union by supporting the "Rebellion" and (2) provide "forty acres and a mule" for "freedmen" and "loyal refugees."[37] The more than 15,000 acres of confiscated land in Loudoun would have provided more than forty acres for each adult Negro in the county. Unfortunately for the blacks, the land was not transferred to them.[38] Shortly after the land in Loudoun had been theoretically confiscated, the Freedmen's Bureau restored ownership to Loudoun's former white owners.[39] At the very time that Loudouners learned of the confiscation of property in their county and state, forces were at work to counteract such sequestration. President Johnson, despite having endorsed the order by General O. O. Howard to seize the lands of select ex-Confederates in Virginia, believed in lenient treatment of most Southerners. In late September the President ordered that confiscation in Virginia stop. By that time General O. O. Howard had already suspended activities relating to confiscating property in Loudoun.[40] Most white citizens of Loudoun and elsewhere in the South were relieved that the plans of radical proponents of comprehensive confiscation, like Thaddeus Stevens and George W. Julian, had been rejected by the majority of Republicans and Democrats. The latter failed to see the necessity of extensive confiscation and deemed it a dangerous assault upon property rights.[41] Loudoun ended 1865 with the realization that, in spite of the fright of confiscation, land would not be redistributed in the county.

Like agriculture, business in Loudoun rapidly responded to the cessation of hostilities. War had disrupted commercial life so badly during 1861 and 1862 that many businesses remained closed until the spring of 1865. The commercial as well as the political center of the county was the county seat, Leesburg. Modest in size, with approximately 1,500 residents, it was, nevertheless, the largest hamlet in Loudoun County.

---

[37]John W. Burgess, *Reconstruction of the Constitution* (New York: Charles Scribner's Sons, 1902), p. 44; Randall, *Constitutional Problems Under Lincoln*, pp. 276, 331. Some of the properties seized throughout the South by the federal government was abandoned land. Apparently only a portion or little of the land in Loudoun confiscated had been abandoned. *The Democratic Mirror* also recorded that the news of the loss of properties discouraged many Loudoun proprietors from making repairs or improvements.

[38]*Mirror*, November 2, 1865. Few if any of the whites had moved. Some Loudoun citizens received confiscation notices that instructed them to go to Alexandria on September 4: B. P. Noland, R. S. Chinn, William Beanton, Jr., W. B. Cockran, Robert C. Bounan, Howard Reith, Gibson Gregg, Dr. Philo Crane, J. R. Carter, and Richard Dulaney.

[39]Ibid., September 28, 1865. By October 19, the Freedmen's Bureau had returned to eleven people in Loudoun property valued at over $200,000. This property, like other Loudoun property, was "held by the" government under the pretext that it was abandoned. Few Loudoun properties marked for confiscation were actually abandoned.

[40]Ibid., September 14, 1865.

[41]Stampp, *The Era of Reconstruction, 1865-1877*, pp. 124-27, 129-31.

The type of inhabitants and business establishments of Leesburg is indicative of the economic and intellectual tenor and lifestyles of the reconstruction era. Most of the businesses and many of the former proprietors resumed activities during the spring and summer of 1865. Among them were lawyers, barbers, blacksmiths, booksellers, butchers, bakers, coopers, carriage and coach makers, carpenters and builders, cabinet makers, druggists, proprietors of clothing stores, hardware stores and dry goods stores, grocers, hatters, painters, tailors, silversmiths and jewelers, shoemakers, saddlers, harness makers, tinners, brickmakers, brick masons, plasterers, saw mill and foundry operators, bankers, hotel managers and owners, marble workers, and wheelwrights.[42] Both newspapers, *The Washingtonian* and *The Democratic Mirror*, published in Leesburg, had suspended publication during the last several years of the war due to the shortage of paper and labor. On June 14, 1865, *The Democratic Mirror* resumed publication and set the philosophical tone for peace: "We are aware of the ravages of the last four years." Many of "our former patrons have passed away, but as our present business is with the living, we shall send our paper to such of our former subscribers as we know" where to find them.[43] For several months after the war papers were sent via anyone who would see or be near the residence of a subscriber. This practice continued until the mail service was re-established.[44] The *Mirror*, as other businesses in town, was compelled to pay cash for all its purchases. They urged customers and patrons "to do unto" them, as they had "to do unto others": pay cash at the time of purchase.[45] John H. Lewis, a blacksmith, stated his business terms most succinctly and directly: "terms being invariably CASH"![46] John Grimes' advertisement of fresh meats for sale, issued on July 5, 1865, indicated a similar plight of "stock is high and finances low . . . will be compelled to sell for Cash only."[47]

[42] *Business Directory of Leesburg* (Leesburg, Va.: William L. Stork, publisher, 1860), pp. 1-6. In 1860 there were in Leesburg: six lawyers, one banker, six blacksmiths, one bookseller, four butchers, one baker, four coopers, two carriage and coach makers, four clothing stores, two druggists, four dry goods stores, three carpenters and builders, two cabinet makers, eleven grocery stores or grocers, plus five grocery and variety stores, one hatter, two hardware stores, three painters, two tailors, two milliners, two silversmiths and jewellers, six shoemakers, two saddlers and harness makers, four tinners, two brickmakers, two brick layers, two plasterers, one steam saw mill, one iron foundry, one potter, one "fancy" store, one marble worker, two wheelwrights, one livery stable, one gardener, one bank, post office, county offices, two hotels, and two newspapers, and one fair grounds.
[43] *Mirror*, June 14, 1865. Annual subscription rate was $2 in advance and $3 as one received the paper.
[44] Papers were continually sent to pre-war subscribers until the newspapers were sent back with the word "no" written on them.
[45] *Mirror*, June 14, 1865.
[46] Ibid.
[47] Ibid., July 26, 1865.

Holders of worthless Southern paper currency and bank notes also suffered financial losses. During 1861, $30,000 worth of "Corporation of Leesburg" notes were placed in circulation, mainly in Loudoun, notes redeemable in current Southern bank money.[48] The mayor of Leesburg assured the holders of notes that "in case the town was destroyed by the enemy" securities were in the Leesburg bank, which would make possible the redemption of the notes. These notes were not redeemed after the war despite the demands of owners of such notes.[49]

The Civil War forced some businessmen to make significant adjustments. For example, prior to the war Charles P. McCabe was one of the largest agents in the slave trade in the county.[50] After June 14, 1865, he made a comfortable living by manufacturing and selling boots, shoes, harness, bridles, collars, whips, and other leather items.[51] War also disrupted the income of those who worked in the capacity of civic officers. The county sheriff and deputies were not paid for services rendered prior to the war until several years after 1865. Their salaries were dependent upon their collection of taxes and county levies, bills and militia fines. The war prevented many of these from being collected. A relief bill was passed by the Virginia General Assembly in 1867 that belatedly resolved the issue of uncompensated service.[52]

The war had even disrupted the business of running a cemetery. To the north of the town of Leesburg, several acres of land had been incorporated by local businessmen in 1852 as the Union Cemetery. Large oak trees with the background of the Catoctin Mountain provided a scenic and tranquil setting for a burial ground.[53] Despite accelerated usage between 1861 and 1865, no annual meeting of the lot-holders was held from 1860 until June 1865. The cemetery grounds, unkept during the war years, resulted in grounds and fencing being in disrepair.[54] After the war Thomas Littleton and John W. Hammerly provided mortuary services for Union Cemetery and the Leesburg vicinity. They were competitors in making cabinets and furniture as well as in providing

---

[48] These notes were presumedly issued to finance the building of three forts on the outskirts of Leesburg and mobilization efforts in preparation for war.

[49] *Mirror*, February 7, 1866.

[50] Ibid., September 15, 1858.

[51] Ibid., August 9, 1865; April 17, 1872.

[52] Virginia, *Acts of the General Assembly of the State of Virginia*, 1866-1867, p. 529.

[53] *Mirror*, September 15, 1858. By the late 1850's burial lots of eighteen by twenty feet in Union Cemetery were $20. Other lots five by five feet were nine cents per square foot. The fee for digging and sodding a grave for a person under five years of age was $2, for a person between five and twelve $3, and for anyone over twelve years of age $4. Disinterment was $2 and reinterment was the same. The gates to the cemetery were kept locked, but keys could be borrowed from five of the business proprietors in town.

[54] Ibid., June 28 and July 26, 1865.

undertaking services.⁵⁵ This was a combination that was not as odd as would first appear because business for morticians in the town of Leesburg during the reconstruction period was uncertain. Citizens of the area found the work of doctors and dentists more constructive but still intimidating. Soon after Dr. W. P. Witherow renewed his dental practice following the war, he issued a caveat that people had better immediately use his services because after July 4, 1865, he would not make house calls.⁵⁶

The medical career of Dr. Alexander R. Mott, like that of other doctors who practiced in Loudoun, was disrupted by the war. Mott's training included studying medicine under the aegis of another physician prior to entering, and subsequently graduating from, Jefferson Medical College in Philadelphia in 1845. From that time, except for the years from 1861 to 1865, he practiced medicine in Leesburg for the next half century. A man of medium stature, he traveled throughout the county during all seasons in a light buggy. He had considerable confidence in the use of tincture of veratrum viride, using it to check incipient pneumonia. He was also confident that bleeding, when properly used, would control puerperal convulsions. Mott was one of a group of physicians who helped bring venesection back into favor. As a preceptor he launched the medical career of at least seven men who became successful physicians.⁵⁷ By June 28, 1865, Mott had opened with an associate a drug store in Leesburg.⁵⁸ With the help of his associate he developed "Mott and Metzger's Anodyne Cream Liniment." It was advertised in the county papers as an "invaluable liniment for rheumatism, sprains, bruises, frost bites, chillblain, chapped hands, ringworm, tetter, scratches," and "galls of all kinds." One of several published testimonials by local citizens about this medical panacea stated:

> *I have been using your Cream Liniment on a badly sprained arm and find it by far the best Anodyne I have found, both to relieve stiffness of the joints and to ease pain. I have also cured one case of inveterate Scratches with the same. I will not be without it in my family, and among my horses, in the future.*⁵⁹

⁵⁵Ibid., August 22, 1866. Undertakers were not limited to Leesburg. April 24, 1872. A. C. Wyckoff of Gum Spring, later called Arcola, advertised he had "fitted up a neat and substantial HEARSE" and was prepared to "furnish COFFINS and attend funerals, at the shortest notice" and moderate charge.

⁵⁶*Mirror*, June 14, 1865. Dentists, like Witherow, usually made periodic trips to several offices they kept throughout one or more counties.

⁵⁷*The Loudoun Times* (Leesburg, Va.), December 25, 1919. Venesection is a medical procedure of opening a vein to let blood (bleeding).

⁵⁸*Mirror*, June 28, 1865.

⁵⁹Ibid., August 9, 1871.

A contemporary of Dr. Mott also returned to Loudoun after the Civil War, Dr. George Emory Plaster. Dr. Plaster served the ailing in the western regions of the county around Snickersville. Unlike Dr. Mott, his specialty was extracting teeth with a pocket knife in the absence of proper instruments. This feat earned him the lengthy title of "the doctor who took out teeth with a pocket knife."[60] Still another doctor, Dr. J. F. Zacharias, came back to Leesburg in 1865 not only to help the sick, but also to collect back fees. He ran ads in county newspapers requesting patients indebted to him for the year 1862 to call at his office as soon as possible. Those who did so prior to August 15, 1865, would receive a ten percent reduction in their bills.[61]

Suffering was a way of life for some of the county's residents who were unfortunately afflicted with disorders that doctors were powerless to remedy. Such a person was Charles T. Chamblin. As a lieutenant in the 8th Virginia regiment he had been wounded at the Battle of Seven Pines on June 1, 1862. A one-ounce minnie ball struck him in the head, entering the side of the nose just below the left eye and narrowly missing the brain. Surgeons probed the wound and determined that the bullet which had penetrated four inches into Chamblin's head was inoperable. Discharged from service, Chamblin returned to Loudoun, where he continued to live in pain and experience great difficulty in swallowing. During June 1866, four years after being wounded, Chamblin coughed from his throat the minnie ball. The only after-effect was a "soreness in the throat and giddiness in the head for a day or two."[62]

Members of another profession also rehung their shingles in the spring and summer of 1865. Lawyers were aware that the legal questions in Loudoun were less than settled. William B. Downey, John M. Orr, Charles B. Tebbs, George A. Thacher, and others who had law offices in Leesburg found this situation financially rewarding. Claims against the federal government pertaining to property losses in the burning of Loudoun Valley in 1864 and the confusion over Gen. O. O. Howard's order confiscating land in the county during the late summer of 1865 provided extensive legal work for attorneys in Leesburg and other towns of Loudoun, like Middleburg and Hamilton.[63] Downey advertised that persons having had their barns, forage, and other property burned by order of United States officers, would do well "to call at his office" and "have their claims adjusted."[64] Attorney Orr likewise urged people to

---

[60] *The Loudoun Times*, January 1, 1920.
[61] *Mirror* August 9, 1865.
[62] Ibid., June 20, 1866.
[63] Ibid., September 21, 1865.
[64] Ibid., July 26, 1865. Members of the bar practicing in Loudoun County met in Leesburg on November 13, 1866, and drew up a "Tariff of Minimum Fees." These minimum fees, which included $5 for advice, writing a bill of sale, deed of trust, taking depositions and $10 for a will, examining title to land, for service, if employed all day,

see him for "the prosecution and collection of all description of claims on the government."⁶⁵

Many of Loudoun's residents found it far more entertaining to seek out Leesburg's "drinking saloon's" that reopened in 1865. *The Democratic Mirror* boastfully commented in 1866:

> *If well ordered saloons can be taken as evidence of the virtue and prosperity of a people, Leesburg is the most virtuous and prosperous county-town in the State. She enjoys the presence of four Saloons, Roberts', Timms', Lloyd's, and Pickett's, . . . Each are fixed up in the highest style known to the profession, while the latter two have recently undergone a thorough refitting, ala New York. Handsome rooms, good attention, delicious oysters, foaming ale, and sparkling elceteras [sic], exhibit themselves with marvellous promptness at the sight of a greenback.*⁶⁶

Numerous stores were available in the town for those who desired to do some serious shopping. Among them was a general store whose owner sought bargain-hunters by advertising his establishment as "The Cheap Store."⁶⁷ It is not known how effective this appellation was in attracting customers.⁶⁸

One of the results of renewed economic growth and business activity in Leesburg in 1865 was the increasing shortage of houses. People lamented not only the lack of housing but soaring rent prices. A one and a half story brick house "heretofore rented for $69.00, brought $120.00" a year in 1866. An old "log shell that in antebellum time was considered a hard bargain at $5.00 rented after the war for $42.00."⁶⁹ *The Democratic Mirror* commented that "houses were never in greater demand than at present—every shanty in town is under rent at almost fabulous rates."⁷⁰ This situation no doubt was a salient factor in the

---

were to be adhered to by all lawyers practicing within the county. Among the more expensive services of an attorney were "instituting a suit for slander, false imprisonment, assault and battery . . . seduction, or defending under the bastardy act,"$20; "defending a prosecution for a Felony," $25; instituting chancery suit in circuit court or an action of ejectment, $30.

⁶⁵Ibid., July 26, 1865.
⁶⁶Ibid., October 10, 1866.
⁶⁷Ibid., August 16, 1865.
⁶⁸Ibid., July 5, 1871. During late June of 1871 a wild horse ran through King Street in Leesburg and into Russell's Cheap Store. The horse "mounted the counter" before being caught and led from the store.
⁶⁹Ibid., October 10, 1866.
⁷⁰Ibid., September 28, 1865. The *Mirror* by fall of 1865 also urged that ten to fifteen new homes be constructed at a cost of $600 to $1,000 each and rented from $60 to $100 a year.

formation of the Leesburg Building Association, which made by 1871 periodic loans up to $400. Another oganization, the Loudoun County Building Association, also provided competition for the town banks by offering loans from $700 to $1,000 to its members who would show up the first Tuesday night of every month at the courthouse in Leesburg.[71]

At least one discerning resident was concerned about the state of the town of Leesburg in November 1865. As a method of displaying his displeasure, he wrote a letter to the *Mirror* that indicted the townspeople for increasing the chance of a cholera epidemic and allowing slovenliness and decadence to manifest itself over the town in the form of unsightly leaves that clogged the gutters, malodorous and shabby hog pens, saloons plus twenty merchants, many of whom sold "ardent spirits" without a license. The latter was unfair to tax-paying citizens of the town, and the sale of intoxicants with or without a license was deemed detrimental by creating a milieu that encouraged and incited the area children to "run the downward road" toward damnation.[72]

Vital to the economic reconstruction of Loudoun was the return to unfettered transportation and renewed communication. By the middle of June 1865, the daily mail between Leesburg and Point of Rocks, Maryland, was reopened, which according to *The Democratic Mirror* put the county "once more in communication with the world at large."[73] Postal service returned more slowly to outlying regions of the county. It was not until December 1865 that anything approaching normal postal service returned to the county.[74] The Post Office Department did not close bidding for the transportation of the mails in the state of Virginia until the November after Appomattox.[75] The granting of mail contracts was an important stimulus for the resumption of extensive stage travel in Loudoun. By December, two stage lines were operating in the county, one carrying the mail and passengers from Leesburg, Alexandria, and Washington, D.C.,[76] and the other providing passenger service three days

---

[71] *Mirror*, August 2, 1871. On December 19, the Virginia General Assembly passed an act incorporating the Loudoun Savings Bank.

[72] Ibid., November 30, 1865.

[73] Ibid., June 14, 1865. The August 2, 1871 issue of *The Democratic Mirror* noted that the Virginia Telegraph Company would immediately construct a line from Alexandria to Leesburg so the telegraph service to the town would be available in sixty days.

[74] *Mirror*, December 20, 1865. For example, the postmasters for Snickersville and Arcola were not appointed until December 1865.

[75] Ibid., November 23, 1865. The bids for yearly transporting mail involving Loudoun routes were from Middleburg to Alexandria $750; Leesburg to Washington (twice a week) $900; Hillsboro to Harper's Ferry $200; Lincoln to Barry, Md. (three times a week) $274. Many of the bids and others throughout the state were so high the government found them unacceptable.

[76] Ibid., December 7, 1865. From May 31, 1860, until the Civil War the mail was carried daily between Leesburg and Alexandria by train.

a week between Washington, Leesburg, and Winchester, Virginia.[77] One-way fare between Leesburg and Washington or Leesburg and Winchester was $3.50.[78] It took approximately eight hours to travel the less than forty-mile route between Leesburg and Washington.[79]

Railroad companies provided menacing competition for proprietors of stagecoaches. By 1866 the Alexandria, Loudoun, and Hampshire Railroad Company had taken mail carriage between Alexandria and Hamilton, in Loudoun County, away from stage lines. Stagecoaches were no match for the speed of the train or its capability to provide daily service to and from the county at reasonable rates.[80] The failure of railroad entrepreneurs to extend the railroad from Loudoun to Winchester extended the life of the stagecoach companies in the county.[81] By 1866 the railroad from Alexandria to Hamilton served as the trunk of Loudoun's transportation facilities. Stagecoaches bridged the approximately thirty-mile gap between Hamilton and Winchester. During 1871 Kemp's stagecoaches went daily to and from Snickersville, Berryville, and Winchester to the terminus at Hamilton. Reamer's stagecoaches accommodated travelers to and from Aldie and Middleburg to the railroad station in Leesburg. Stages, therefore, formed the limbs or arteries that complemented the incomplete train system. However, residents in the western portion of the county were anxious to extend rail service into that region of the county. Numerous meetings

---

[77]Ibid., March 7, 1866. A trip from Washington to Winchester was $6.50 in December 1865. At that time stages left Washington for Winchester, and Winchester for Washington, on Tuesday, Thursday, and Saturday.

[78]By March 1866, one-way fare for stage travel between Leesburg and Washington was $2.50. At that time passengers could leave Pickett's House in Leesburg for Washington in a four-horse coach at 7:00 A.M. every Monday, Wednesday, and Friday.

[79]*Mirror*, March 7, 1866. The route between Leesburg and Winchester was approximately thirty-three miles.

[80]Ibid., April 11, 1866; June 20, 1866. Railroad service from Alexandria to Leesburg was not renewed after the war until late spring or early summer of 1866. The reason for the delay was the rebuilding of bridges and the reconstruction of track between Herndon and Guilford (Sterling) that had been "completely destroyed" during the War between the States. By 1871 the Washington and Ohio Railroad, which earlier bought out the Alexandria, Loudoun, and Hampshire Railroad, ran two trains, except Sunday, daily between Alexandria and Hamilton. At 8:45 A.M. the mail train left Alexandria. It passed through Leesburg at 10:35 A.M. and arrived at 11:00 A.M. at Hamilton. It left Hamilton for Alexandria at 12:50 P.M. At 4:00 P.M. an accommodation train left Alexandria for a trip to and from Hamilton. Fare was four cents a mile on the mail train; commutation tickets were three cents per mile, and annual tickets sixty dollars. In 1866, a trip by rail from Alexandria to Leesburg was $3, from Alexandria to Winchester $5.50.

[81]A factor retarding the connection with Winchester via Loudoun was the Blue Ridge Mountain in the western frontier of the county. Although it did not pose insurmountable engineering problems, the cost made it economically prudent not to extend the line. An additional factor was that Winchester and the Valley of Virginia had been previously connected to Baltimore, Maryland, and Washington, D. C., by other railroads.

were held to extend the railroad to Snickersville.[82] Aroused citizens around the milling town of Aldie also held civic meetings to promote the construction of the Piedmont and Potomac Railroad, chartered on June 28, 1870. Although rail service was eventually extended to Snickersville, the Piedmont company failed to construct a railroad connecting Washington and the Shenandoah Valley by way of Aldie.[83]

Rehabilitation of the county's transportation facilities after the war was completed by the activities of numerous turnpike companies that rebuilt bridges and improved existing dirt roads and constructed additional ones throughout Loudoun. The need for improvement was indicated by the comment of travelers and the practice of stagecoach drivers to "roam at large" over open fields that were not fenced to avoid the unpleasant holes and "bed stones" of the turnpike.[84]

SOCIAL ADJUSTMENTS

The most difficult readjustment demanded of the South in social and political reconstruction was the relinquishment of attitudes about blacks and centralized government. By spring 1865, States' rights and slavery were terminated. The acceptance and compliance with this revolutionary change in America was an arduous task for the people of an area who had previously given allegiance to the indispensability of decentralized political sovereignty and the maintenance of human chattel. This was an allegiance that became recalcitrant from the experiences of sectional bitterness and the tragedies of war. The Southerner's inability to totally reverse his adherence had long-range manifestations upon race relations and politics in the South until the present.

Traditional statements regarding race relations in Loudoun County during the years immediately after the abolition of slavery contend that there was little if any racial animosity and that blacks were more content and responsible than in many other Virginia counties and Southern states.[85] Cursorily this appraisal may appear to be accurate. Whereas the Ku Klux Klan was short-lived in Virginia, unlike most ex-Confederate states, it never existed as an organized force in Loudoun.[86] The Klan's failure to make its malicious presence felt in the county was because of (1) the

---

[82]*Mirror*, August 28, 1872.

[83]Ibid., December 13, 1871.

[84]Virginia, *Acts of the General Assembly of the State of Virginia*, 1869-1870, pp. 477-78; *Mirror*, September 21, 1865; June 6, 1866. Travel by turnpike to Washington was not a pleasant journey during the winter. One Loudouner remarked in 1866 that one of the advantages of traveling to D. C. in private conveyance was the more one was "enabled to bless the inventor of bad roads."

[85]Harrison Williams, *Legends of Loudoun*, p. 225.

[86]Allen W. Trelease, *White Terror: The Ku Klux Klan Conspiracy and Southern Reconstruction* (New York: Harper Torchbooks, 1972), p. 65.

absence of a threat by blacks to the continuance of white political supremacy within the county and (2) the existence of a significant number of residents who had been non-slaveowners during the antebellum era, many of whom had vociferously opposed slavery.

Despite the lack of extensive and outrageous mistreatment of Negroes in Loudoun like that which occurred in many areas of the South, it is not surprising that blacks in Loudoun were not instantly accepted or treated as equals by the white community. Neither were all blacks content with their status. Like many areas in the United States, while Loudoun's attitude and adjustment to Negro freedom and civil rights did not erupt into sensational racial strife, the civil rights issue still remained in need of amelioration.[87]

During reconstruction the freedmen's greatest native ally within the county was no doubt the Society of Friends, an organization that had a tradition of crusading for the betterment of Negroes. However, the freedmen gained few white friends from the threat of confiscation of properties by the Freedmen's Bureau on the behalf of ex-slaves.[88] A majority of Loudoun whites not only were resentful of such action, but also considered the freedmen inferior. Local politicians during October 1865 attempted to hurt each other's chances of winning the election by accusing each other of being in favor of Negro suffrage.[89] Editorials and letters to the editors for the first few years after the war maintained the unsuitability of blacks to participate intelligently in the political process.[90] They were also depicted as being promiscuous and disrespectful of laws.[91] On July 12, 1865 *The Democratic Mirror* stated:

> Now that civil law is once more established, we hope this community may not be soon again disgraced by such a pugilistic exhibition as was witnessed on Sunday afternoon last, between a party of FREEDMEN of both sexes. . . . Nobody was severly hurt, but the sooner these disorders are remedied by the infliction of severe punishment, the better for the peace and good name of the town [of Leesburg].[92]

---

[87]Alrutheus A. Taylor, *The Negro in the Reconstruction of Virginia* (New York: Russell and Russell, 1961), pp. 68-69, 77.

[88]Loudoun County, along with all of the state of Maryland, Washington, D. C., Alexandria, and Fairfax counties of Virginia formed the first district of the "Bureau of Refugees, Freedmen, and Abandoned Lands," better known as the Freedmen Bureau.

[89]*Mirror*, October 12, 1865.

[90]Ibid., November 28, 1866.

[91]Ibid., August 22, 1865.

[92]Ibid., July 12, 1865. Blacks by no means had a monopoly upon violence and lawlessness. The November 30, 1865, issue of *The Democratic Mirror* was very critical of an item in the *Washington Chronicle* entitled "Outrage in Leesburg, Va.," which exaggerated the nature of disorderly conduct by some men who formerly served under

The white population felt there was a need to control and force Negroes to behave more responsibly. To help control blacks during large gatherings like their camp religious revival, a "special colored police" force was formed.[93] Though blacks comprised one-fourth of the county population, the preponderance of persons arrested in the decades following the Civil War were Negroes. For example, during 1875 thirty-two persons were incarcerated in the county jail in Leesburg on charges varying from misdemeanors to felonies, twenty-six of whom were blacks.[94]

Original jurisdiction for trying and passing judgment in cases involving lesser crimes, like assault and battery and petty larceny, rested in the hands of the local county justices. Defendants had the right to appeal to the county court.[95] Court justices handled numerous cases

Mosby. During the spring of 1872, a "shooting affray between whites occurred on King Street between two young men, George Wright and James H. Cross." The incident stemmed from an earlier incident in town, when Cross hit Wright's father in the head with a brick.

The most celebrated criminal case in Loudoun County during the reconstruction period involved a white mother, Mrs. Lloyd, charged with killing her four children with arsenic. The reports of the disinterment at Union Cemetery in Leesburg and examination of the bodies during April 1872 provided macabre and grisly reading: "In the presence of a group of curious spectators, who gathered around the . . . graves, over and about which there hovered a solemn stillness, the work of disinterment proceeded. At length the coffins were reached. And that of HENRY who died on the 24th day of July, 1870, was gently raised and in the presence of Drs. Mott, Cross, and Fauntleroy, the lid was removed only to reveal a body so far decomposed and covered with the mosses of death, that nothing remained save the skeleton frame, which was fast crumbling to pieces. . . . Then came the opening of the grave of ANNIE, the child that died on the 16th of February, 1872. The coffin was raised and opened, and there lay the childish form, beautiful even yet, though for two months locked in the silent grave. Every portion of her grave clothes was bright and perfect, from the white ribbon that held back the golden curls from the brow of death, to the tiny slippers that first encased her icy feet, while the bracelets upon her arms, and the golden chain that girdled her neck, placed there by a mother's hand, sparkled in the calm sunlight of that April evening. . . . The body was in an almost perfect state of preservation,—and the stomach and liver were dissected, placed in a glass jar, securely sealed, and turned over to Mr. Barrett, who next morning carried them to Prof. Tonery, of Baltimore to be analyzed . . . ." Mrs. Emily E. Lloyd was acquitted of murder during the first week of November, 1872.

[93] *Mirror*, August 19, 1875; April 6, 1876. The population in Loudoun in 1876 was 20,929, of whom 5,218 were Negroes. During the mid-1870's fifty-five paupers were kept in a poorhouse at a cost of $1,670. The salary for the superintendent of the poorhouse was $500, and the physician fees amounted to $525.

[94] Ibid., February 10, 1876. Five of the Negroes committed to jail were females. Of the thirty-two prisoners only one was sent to the state penitentiary. Six of the thirty-two were in jail due to improperly selling whiskey.

[95] Ibid., June 28, 1871. Every year approximately ten of these cases were appealed to the county court at a cost to the taxpayer of about $20 per case. One Loudoun citizen complained in the *Mirror* that this was a heavy financial burden upon the taxpayer. He was especially critical of justices allowing the county court to originally try cases that should be handled by them.

involving blacks. Justice E. B. Powell, within several days during August, 1875, handled two cases involving Negroes. Special "colored police" brought before Powell a Negro whom they had arrested for selling whiskey on a campground during a religious revival. Powell imposed a fine equal to the amount of money the man had on him and then sent the offender to jail for ten days. A day or two later another black man was brought before the same justice for stealing a pair of boots. Justice Powell "found him guilty, and ordered him to be given ten lashes, which was duly administered in the jail yard."[96] Powell was apparently less severe in the sentences in cases in which both the offender and the victim were black. Of these cases, one of the more unusual involved dissension between the pastor and congregation of the Providence Baptist Church. One of the church trustees had the minister arrested for "levelling a loaded pistol" at the trustee's "pious head and threatening him with the contents." Powell dismissed the case against the "parson and made the complainant pay" court costs of $1.80.[97]

The county court handled what were considered to be the more serious crimes. During December 1871, William Carter, a black youth about twenty-one years of age was found guilty of stealing a horse and sentenced to twelve years in the state penitentiary. This sentence was comparable to the fourteen-year sentence given a white man, Landon T. Lovett, in the fall of 1866 for stealing a horse. By this comparison it would appear that a degree of equal justice regardless of color existed. This was not the case; Lovett in addition to horse-stealing shot a Negro male. For this offense he received only one year for a total sentence of fifteen years for both offenses.[98] Sex crimes of Negro males against white females were especially odious to the white community. Though such offenses were rare in Loudoun during the late 1860's and 1870's, even attempted rape of a white female by a black carried a heavy sentence. Burr Pollard, a Negro, was sentenced to eighteen years in the state penitentiary for attempting to rape a white woman. During the same session of the county court, a man by the name of Beamer who was found guilty of assault with intent to kill, was given only one year in the state penitentiary.[99] Nevertheless, after the war, racial tensions in Loudoun were far less intense than in other areas of the South. No event in Loudoun came close to approaching the Negro militia companies' use of the torch against whites in York County, South Carolina, in 1871.

[96]Ibid., August 19, 1875.
[97]Ibid., August 24, 1876.
[98]Ibid., December 13, 1871. In June 1876 Loudoun County started using the technique of a chain gang to punish persons confined to the county jail. The sheriff was directed to "procure six balls and chains." Prisoners required to work on the chain gang were hired out for fifty cents a day. Convicts worked ten hours a day and had to be returned to the jailor at the end of the day.
[99]Ibid., July 20, 1876; December 21, 1876.

Arson was a popular form of Negro retaliation against whites in racial conflicts.[100] Indicative of the comparatively limited instances of racial antagonism erupting into violent acts in Loudoun during the era of reconstruction was the existence of but a few cases of arson in the county.[101] Negroes served as special policemen, and on at least one occasion a black citizen who lacked deputy status caught, and testified against, a black who had attempted to rape a white woman.[102]

Racial slurs were fairly common in issues of *The Democratic Mirror* published from 1865 to 1876. While only infrequently was the term "nigger" used in the paper, use of the term "darkey" was more prevalent.[103] Blacks emulated white lifestyles in Loudoun not only in religious camp meetings, but in having their own fairs and tournaments.[104] In reference to a Negro tournament at Leesburg, the *Mirror* reported that the "dusky population from the surrounding country gathered in

---

[100]Trelease, *White Terror*, pp. 364-65.

[101]*Mirror*, March 4, 1866. A black girl was committed to jail during March 1866 on the charge of attempting to burn the house of Rufus Smith.

[102]Ibid., July 12, 1871. During July 1871, Benjamin Hibbs of Aldie offered a $50 reward for the capture of a young Negro male named Euroch Corum, who allegedly attempted to rape a white woman. Corum had been shot at several times, one bullet going "through his face near his mouth, going in one side and coming out of the other." He was caught, due to the assistance of another Negro male, and sent to jail. However, there was widespread fear that blacks represented a significant threat to the well-being of white women in the county. In the September 6, 1877, issue of the *Mirror* a story entitled "Another Brutal Outrage" told of the experience of a Miss Newton, who was "outraged" (raped) on a Saturday morning near Round Hill, by "one or both of two colored men, who were concealed in a corn field . . . to which place she had gone for the purpose of gathering some beans. Her screams were heard by her brother, but he supposing she had been frightened by the sight of a snake or something of that sort, did not go to her assistance until the fiends had made their escape." The report also states that one of the blacks was caught and identified by the young lady. Several men continued to look for the other man. In the next issue of the *Mirror*, September 13, the father of the attacked girl, Charles A. Newton, corrected the earlier report. Miss Newton was severely frightened but not raped. There had been only one attacker, who shortly fled because the girl's family came immediately to her rescue.

[103]Ibid., September 7, 1865; November 7, 1866; August 19, 1875. The memory of the institution of slavery tainted the attitude of whites during and after the era of reconstruction. This attitude included a condescending view of blacks, the continued use of slave names like "Gilmore's Alford" or "Uncle Alford," and the insistence that freedmen accept a subservience to whites in the "new order" of society. A decade after the Civil War the *Mirror* praised the life of a late black minister. His life was apparently exemplary and deserving of praise. Yet, while bestowing tribute upon the dead devine, the editor of the *Mirror* made subtle references to the inferiority of blacks and the desirableness for them to be simplistic and docile.

The practice of referring to elderly, cooperative, and likable blacks as "Uncle" and "Aunt" was continued well into the twentieth century as was the custom of black domestics showing respect for the children of their employers by placing "Miss" or "Master" in front of the child's Christian name.

[104]Ibid., June 12, 1867; September 5, 1866; September 18, 1872.

great" numbers. That it was a "dark affair, truly so dark indeed, as to have been invisible to people of the region."[105] These references were typical. County newspapers always indicated if a person mentioned in the paper was black. Mention was usually made by reference to them as "negro" or "colored". At times, references were complimentary. Blacks frequently came from Washington, D. C., to Loudoun by train to attend black fairs, tournaments, or revivals. On September 25, 1872, the *Mirror* noted a "good band of colored musicians" of the "Sons and Daughters of Moses—a benevolent Association (colored)—from D. C. and Alexandria" arrived in Leesburg by special train.

Among the more recalcitrant in attitude and reluctant to accommodate the new status of blacks were former slaveowners in Loudoun. Many had severe doubts during the summer and fall of 1865 about the probability of the Negro making the transition from slave to free laborer in such a manner that would provide an adequate and desirable labor force for farming. One such former slaveowner wrote the following lament to the *Mirror* and signed it "Agricola":

> The prospect of this state of affairs to improve in this county, where the fates are against us is hope against hope. You may make a contract with a negro to serve you in a specified condition for a twelve months, and knowing the disposition and nature of the african as well as you do, have you any confidence that he will fulfill the stipulations of the contract? None in the least. You are almost sure that the very time you want him most, your neighbor has offered him six pence more than you, and off he has gone, leaving you and crop in the lurch. They are ignorant of the obligation a contract imposes, and were they to forfeit a sum of money as a penalty for such violation, some officious ass would easily persuade them that you had acted in bad faith and taken advantage of their condition to agrandize yourself. . . .
>
> The negro will never constitute much of a bugbear in this county. Destined to share the same fate of the 'poor Indian,' falling back at the gradual approach of the white man, will in the course of a few short years, if the proper inducements are extended, have a hardy, laboring industrious and honest class of white people here, and produce a change in the laboring interests of the county for good, beyond the expectations of those most sanguine. Farmers whose slaves have left them should without delay

[105] Ibid., September 7, 1865.

> move their cabins to convenient locations on their premises
> and I will guarantee that the best class of white laborers
> can readily be found to occupy them with whom contracts
> can be made, and faith plighted, and every interest of
> society subserved.[106]

To be sure, freedmen in Loudoun, as throughout the South, were ill-prepared and often had little comprehension of the responsibilities of liberation. However, the dismal prophecy of the fate of the Negro in Loudoun by "Agricola" was not realized. By the 1870's many landowners in Virginia shifted from a view they formerly shared with "Agricola" in 1865. While considering the Negro intellectually, politically, and socially inferior to the white, they recognized that many blacks were good free laborers.[107] A majority of Loudoun's Negro population became tenant farmers, some remaining on the farms where they formerly worked as slaves.[108]

To assist the Negro in adjusting to freedom, relief, educational, and economic services were provided by Freedmen's Bureau.[109] How much assistance was rendered to freedmen in Loudoun during the latter half of the 1860's is not known. *The Democratic Mirror*, with the exception of the Bureau's aborted attempt to confiscate lands for freedmen, made only occasional reference to the Freedmen's Bureau. Historians have generally lauded the relief work of the Bureau in caring for the needy, but how effective it was in Loudoun in that regard is unclear. During February 1866, Negroes of Leesburg and the vicinity formed a "Colored Man's Aid Society" to assist indigent and ill blacks. This move was applauded by the *Mirror* as a necessary one by county blacks toward self-reliance. The *Mirror* further warned that, unless Loudoun blacks took care of the wants of their destitute, many helpless Negroes would frequently "go supperless to miserable beds, Freedmen's Bureau to the contrary notwithstanding."[110] Doubt was vindicated in the eyes of the critics of the Bureau when the superintendent of the Bureau for Loudoun County, James J. Ferree, resigned on February 26, 1866, while being accused of "malfeasance in office." Ferree, also a minister, had been ordered to restore the property of Thomas W. Edwards that had been earlier confiscated by the Bureau. He withheld the papers that restored ownership to Edwards until the latter did the parson a favor. Ferree was

---

[106]Ibid., September 21, 1865. The second line of the last paragraph is incoherent.

[107]Taylor, *The Negro in the Reconstruction of Virginia*, pp. 121-22.

[108]Ibid., p. 281. Another example of the comparative compatibility of some blacks and whites in Loudoun after 1865 is that, unlike most Negroes who voted the Republican ticket, a small number of blacks in Loudoun voted the Democratic ticket in the state election of 1881.

[109]Randall and Donald, *The Civil War and Reconstruction*, p. 576.

[110]*Mirror*, February 7, 1866.

unable to force Edwards to bring him a load of wood or pay the Bureau agent's livery bill of $5.50. Edwards did pay Ferree a fee of $5.50, which he was told was the standard practice in such cases. Ferree signed a receipt for the bogus fee that was sent by Edwards to General O. O. Howard, head of the Freedmen's Bureau, with an explanatory letter. Howard's response was that Ferree was guilty of malfeasance in office and that Ferree had been earlier relieved as superintendent of the Bureau for Loudoun.[111]

There is evidence of positive contributions of agents of the Bureau in Loudoun, such as supervision of labor contracts entered into by freedmen, the establishment of schools for use by Negroes, and the census of the county's black population.[112] Extension in 1866 of the Freedmen's Bureau for six years, in spite of President Johnson's veto, empowered the Bureau with almost complete control over the Negro. This authority left the local and state government of Virginia with only a minimum control of blacks until 1870.[113] For this and other reasons, many white residents in Loudoun were chary and contemptuous of the purpose and activities of the Bureau.[114] The practice of the county's providing assistance for the indigent was reviewed after the war and in select cases provided limited relief for the destitute freedmen. An example was an order in 1866 by an overseer of the poor for district eight in Loudoun that the county was to support Margaret Nergin and her two children, ages five and two. Once this black woman recovered from her illness, she and her children were to be removed to "the county of Fairfax, whence, they had migrated . . . to Loudoun during the past year."[115]

During the four years of the Civil War most of Loudoun's schools were not in operation. A few schools reopened during the fall of 1865 for an academic year that continued until the latter part of June of the following year.[116]

[111]Ibid., February 14, 1866; March 4, 1866. Ferree resigned prior to Howard's reply to Edwards on March 5, 1866, on the pretext of ill health. In all likelihood once Edwards informed Ferree that a complaint was sent to Gen. Howard, Ferree decided to resign.

[112]Ibid., August 31, 1865; September 7 and 21, 1865; October 5, 1865; Taylor, *The Negro in the Reconstruction of Virginia*, pp. 15,23,70. A squad of fifteen to twenty soldiers during August 1865 aided the Freedmen's Bureau in taking a census of the Negroes in Leesburg.

[113]Taylor, op. cit., p. 23.

[114]*Mirror*, September 21, 1865.

[115]Loudoun County, Virginia, *Minute Book of the County Court*, No. 17, p. 374.

[116]Philip V. diZerega, "History of Secondary Education in Loudoun County, Virginia" (unpublished Master's thesis, University of Virginia, 1948), pp. 65-66. (Hereafter referred to as "History of Education in Loudoun.") Philip diZerega in the above master's thesis concluded that only four private schools that had been in operation prior to the war were reopened after the cessation of hostilities, whereas seventeen schools in operation prior to the Civil War did not reopen after 1865. The latter is somewhat of an overstatement since

During August 1865 the following schools advertised extensively in *The Democratic Mirror* the impending resumption of classes: the Leesburg Academy, Leesburg Female Seminary, Leesburg Male School, Belmont School, Dover School, and the Middleburg Seminary. Tuition depended not only upon the school, but also the level of study within each school. The average tuition for the 1865-66 school year ranged from $15 to $20 a month.[117] By 1875 the Leesburg Female Institute, the Loudoun Valley Academy in Hamilton, the Mountsville Academy and the Springwood Select Home School for Young Ladies, the Loudoun School and the Blue Ridge Academy had joined the older private schools in providing educational facilities for children from select middle and upper class families.[118]

Academic life in Loudoun's private schools during the postwar period is illustrated by the educational milieu associated with the Loudoun Valley Academy, the first institution in the county established to prepare students for the profession of teaching. Founded in 1869 by Jonathan

---

some of the schools diZerega lists were closed several years prior to the war and not because of it. For example, Janney's Springdale boarding school closed in 1854 because of financial reasons. Nevertheless, the overall conclusion of diZerega that most private schools in operation in 1861 did not reopen after 1865 is correct. The private schools diZerega lists as reopening after 1865 were the Leesburg Female Academy, which provided elementary and secondary instruction for girls,; the Rev. Ben Bridges in Sterling, which offered elementary and secondary instruction for both sexes; the Leesburg Academy, located in Leesburg; and McCormick's English and Classical School in Dover. The latter two institutions provided elementary and secondary "schooling" for boys. Elementary and secondary institutions not reopening after the war, according to diZerega, were schools for girls, Margaret Mercer's School and Gibson's School in Leesburg, and Rev. Dr. Wicks' School in Hillsboro; coeducational schools that were not reopened included the Middleburg Academy and the Waterford School. Schools for males not reopened included P. Saunder's School in Leesburg, Gilbert and Tenny's School in Leesburg, the Union Academy in Unison, the Flint Hill Academy in Hughesville, and the Loudoun Institute near Aldie.

[117]*Mirror*, August 9, 1865; September 21, 1865.

[118]*Springwood Select Home for Young Ladies near Leesburg, Virginia: Secession 1866-7* (n.p.; n.d.); diZerega, "History of Education in Loudoun," pp. 46, 63. Springwood Select Home for Young Ladies, near Leesburg, was established to provide an education for the children of G. Washington Ball. In order to provide what was considered to be quality education and instruction in English, mathematics, and the classics, a limited number of young ladies from ages ten to sixteen of other families were taken into Ball's home. Monthly report cards for the forty-week school year were sent to the student's home by mail. Final examinations were given on work covered over the whole year, not just the semester. Restrictions were rigid by modern standards. For example, girls were barred from receiving letters except from their families. Letters from the parents were not to be sent to the child but directly to the principal.

The Loudoun School was located at "Buzzard's Roost," Middleburg. It was opened after the Civil War under the direction of "Professor" Virginius Dabney. Tuition and board was $300 per session. Dabney closed the school in 1873 and went to Princeton, New Jersey, where he opened another preparatory school.

The Blue Ridge Academy, a college preparatory school, was established in 1870 at Snickersville, but closed after a few years of operation.

K. Taylor, who also served as the principal, the school served mainly Quakers and a few other Loudouners interested in quality education.[119] The school, located in an old mill, was a success from the start, as its enrollment increased from fifty-three students in 1869-1870 to ninety-six in 1872-1873.[120] Classes usually started during the first week in September and terminated in the middle of June the following year, comprising an academic year of forty weeks divided into two twenty-week sessions.[121] Tuition depended upon the age of students and their area of study, with the minimum each session for each subject $5 and the maximum $25.[122] Textbooks were usually purchased by the students, although English books could be rented for twenty cents a session.

Most of the students at the academy were day students. A few were boarders and lived with local families approved by the principal so students would "enjoy all the comforts of home, and not be exposed to . . . injurious influences."[123] Oral and written examinations were given once a week, at the end of each month, and the last week of each term or session. Parents received a monthly grade report, consisting of six pages and including the numerical averages of their children's grade on each subject and their general average minus demerit marks.[124] The use of

---

[119]*Catalogue of Loudoun Valley Academy for Young Ladies and Gentlemen: Session 1869-1870* (Alexandria, Va.: Printed at the Commercial Advertiser, 1870), pp. 3-5. (Hereafter referred to as the *Catalogue of Loudoun Valley Academy*.) In 1861, Taylor had established the Chester Valley Academy in Coatesville, Pennsylvania. In 1867 he sold that academy and moved to Loudoun.

[120]Ibid., pp. 3-4; *Circular for 1872-73 of the Loudoun Valley Academy* (n.p.; n.d.), p. 3; diZerega, "History of Education in Loudoun," p. 45. There were six females in the school in 1869-1870 as compared to thirty-six in 1872-1873. Taylor changed the name of Loudoun Valley Academy in 1873 to the Virginia Normal Institute.

[121]The first session ended and the second started in late January.

[122]*Catalogue of Loudoun Valley Academy*, p. 9. The academy was divided into branches or departments: (1) English, for students under twelve, tuition per session was $12.50, for those over twelve tuition was between $20 and $25 per session; (2) Languages each were $10 per session; (3) Latin and Greek, together amounted to $15 each twenty weeks of study; (4)Bookkeeping was $10 per session. One half of all fees were to be paid in advance, and the remainder in the middle of the term or session. The price of fuel was divided among the students. The academy also had a normal department to prepare students to become teachers. It consisted of emphasizing subjects taught in "common schools" and instruction in the art of teaching. Those who completed the full course and deemed competent to teach by the principal J. K. Taylor were assisted by him in obtaining teaching positions. Since public schools were just starting in Loudoun, the job market for teachers was good.

[123]*Catalogue of Loudoun Valley Academy*, p. 9. Most of the students were from Hamilton and other communities in Loudoun near the academy; a few students were from other Virginia counties, Fauquier and Frederick, and Maryland. One student was from Omaha, Nebraska.

[124]Ibid., pp. 7-8, 11. A perfect score in each lesson was ten. If one question was missed, then the student received a score of eight. More than five demerits in one month was considered by Taylor as "decidedly censurable" and would cause "a change in" the "mode of correction."

"tobacco in any form, rum, profane language, irregular attendance or ungentlemanly conduct" by a student whether at the school or boarding house were grounds for expulsion from the academy.[125] Despite a rigid academic and behavior code, Jonathan K. Taylor was liberal on the controversial educational procedure of having boys and girls in the same classroom. From past teaching experience in schools that separated and mixed the sexes, Taylor decidedly preferred heterogeneous grouping. He maintained that it improved both the academic performance and behavior of both sexes as each sex inspired "the other to greater intellectual efforts" and that the boys were "less rude and more chaste in their language" and the girls "more guarded in their behavior." The headmaster also recommended that "each student should study at least two hours out of School in the preparation of the Lessons for the subsequent day." He strongly urged parents to provide "a quiet room" for homework as it was folly "to expect a child to prepare a lesson within hearing of the family business and conversation: better study in earnest for a short time then play in earnest, than to spoil both."[126]

The most innovative development in private education in Loudoun during reconstruction was the establishment of night schools. They attempted to provide schooling in the three "R's" for Loudoun's more humble folk, members of families of small farmers and mechanics who could not afford to attend private day schools. During each week night, classes were held that included "one hour . . . devoted to exercises on the Black Board, by which means any one of moderate ability may in a short time be well versed . . . in Arithmetic." Tuition was $1.50 per month, paid in advance.[127] Night schools failed to become popular, due in part to the advent of Virginia's public education system. Private day schools, after public schools were established, continued for a short time to function unhampered by the new competition.

The spread of free or public schools throughout Virginia in the 1870's was the culmination of the efforts of educational reformers that started in 1779.[128] Education in Loudoun and elsewhere in the state was revolutionized by this phenomenon. A part of this revolution was the gradual elimination of most private schools and academies in Loudoun.[129]

---

[125]Ibid., p. 9.

[126]*Catalogue of Loudoun Valley Academy*, pp. 7, 12-13. Taylor maintained that as a general rule day pupils were not as prepared in their lessons as boarders.

[127]*Mirror*, October 3, 1866; April 24, 1872.

[128]A. J. Morrison, *The Beginning of Public Education in Virginia, 1776-1860* (Richmond, Va.: Davis Bottom, Superintendent of Public Printing, 1971), pp. 7-8. In 1779 Thomas Jefferson drew up a comprehensive education bill that included the creation of a system of public education in Virginia. This bill was not passed and had no immediate impact upon education in Virginia.

[129]diZerega, "History of Education in Loudoun," p. 89. In 1888, the superintendent of public schools in Loudoun, L. M. Shumate, reported that the popularity of public schools in Loudoun had forced "nearly all efforts to run private schools" to be abandoned.

One of Loudoun's oldest educational institutions, the Leesburg Academy, was compelled to make the transition from a private to public school. In 1875 the academy was moved from a building it had occupied since 1846 to a three-story building constructed on a site donated by one of the trustees of the academy, H. T. Harrison. The old building was sold to the county in 1879 and was therafter used to house court records and county offices.[130] When the academy was forced by declining enrollment to go out of business in 1879, the trustees allowed the public school system to use the building. Although replaced by a public school, the new school was still advertised as the Leesburg Academy even after the academy building constructed in the 1870's was destroyed by fire in 1893.[131] As a public institution the Leesburg Academy was in some aspects not totally unlike traditional modern public education in the division of students according to age, basic subjects taught, and length of school year.[132] McGuffey's famous readers were used in both the primary and intermediate departments.

One of the most distinguishing features of the Leesburg Academy was the degree of difficulty of the senior department or high school, which was equivalent to a four-year college education of the mid-twentieth century. To graduate from the Leesburg Academy, a student had to have earned a certificate of proficiency in at least ten subjects, including mathematics through algebra, "junior" Latin, and all of the English courses. Certificates of Proficiency were awarded to those students who had obtained at least a mark of eighty percent upon the final

---

[130]*Announcement of the Twelfth Session of [the] Leesburg Academy* (Leesburg, Va.: Mirror Office, 1898), p. 1.

[131]diZerega, op. cit., pp. 92-93, 138. The public school established in 1870 with Mr. John W. Wood as the principal and Frank Brawner and Mrs. Wood as assistants was moved from the corner of Cornwall and King Streets, a site upon which the school was located form 1870 to 1879, to the new academy building. Mr. John S. Simpson in 1888 became principal, after three others had succeeded Mr. Wood as headmaster. Simpson served in that capacity until 1901, at which time he resigned to teach in a private school in Fayetteville, North Carolina. After fire destroyed the academy building, school was conducted in area churches and private buildings from 1893 to 1894 while a two-story brick building consisting of sixteen classrooms was being constructed. In 1914, Charles P. Janney, the last surviving trustee of the Leesburg Academy, gave the property to the county, which in turn in 1925 transferred the title of the property to the Loudoun County School Board.

[132]*Announcement of the Twelfth Session of [the] Leesburg Academy*, pp.3-6. The school was divided into four departments: primary, intermediate, junior and senior. Subjects taught were orthography (spelling), reading, writing, geography, history, English grammar, natural philosophy, physiology (health), civil government, English and literature, chemistry, Latin, French, German, Greek, and mathematics. School started in September and closed in June. Report cards were sent home every three months. Mid-term and semester examinations were given. Like other educational institutions "profanity, vulgarity, fighting, and smoking were not tolerated."

examination.¹³³ Graduation from the academy qualified graduates to apply for teaching positions in Loudoun's public schools. The principal of the academy, Professor J. S. Simpson, maintained that a certificate of graduation from the Leesburg Academy as the equivalent "to an examination by the County Superintendent" of those seeking teaching positions in Loudoun's public schools.¹³⁴ Another feature of the Leesburg Academy in the latter 1800's that distinguished it from the Loudoun Valley Academy and most public schools was the segregation of students according to sex after their first few years of instruction.¹³⁵

The Underwood Constitution of 1869 committed Virginia to the establishment of public education. Despite foibles within the nascent system of public education, 1869 is significant for establishing an instrument that would slowly move the Old Dominion in the direction of egalitarianism.¹³⁶ The immediate as well as the long-range implementation of the commitment to public education was a major task. Between 1869 and 1871, land for school sites had to be obtained, buildings constructed, and teachers hired. By August 1871, the state had a total of 3,000 schools, fifty-five of which were in Loudoun County.¹³⁷

As in the rest of the state, the public schools opened in the fall of 1870 with a faculty that lacked the prestige and experience of teachers in private institutions. The following summer, in preparation for another new school year and in an attempt to improve the quality of instruction, the county superintendent of schools organized a teachers' institute that was held in Wood's schoolhouse in Leesburg on July 18 and July 19. Twenty-five to thirty teachers, mostly young men, attended what was

---

¹³³Ibid., pp. 3, 6. A greater emphasis was also placed upon the classical languages, Greek and Latin, than in modern education.

¹³⁴*Announcement of the Twelfth Session of [the] Leesburg Academy*, p. 6. In 1897 the instructional staff of the Leesburg Academy included in addition to the principal, Professor Simpson, Miss A. Deane Johns, S. V. Watkins, S. G. Thompson, Miss C. W. Wise, and Miss E. K. Lewis.

¹³⁵Ibid., p. 1.

¹³⁶J. L. Blair Buck, *The Development of Public Schools in Virginia* (Richmond: State Board of Education, 1952), p. 69; Virginia, *Acts of the General Assembly of the State of Virginia, 1869-1870*, pp. 402-17.

¹³⁷*Mirror*, October 25, 1871, June 28, 1872; diZerega, "History of Education in Loudoun," pp. 84-85, 94. Forty-six of Loudoun's first public schools were for whites and nine were for blacks. The average salaries for male teachers were $33.88 per month; white female instructors were paid only $21.74 per month. Uniform school terms of nine months were not realized for Loudoun white schools until 1928-1929. From 1870 to 1902 the length of the school year varied from five to ten months. The average number of months schools were in session during the first year 1870-1871 was a little more than four and one-half months. In accordance with state law anyone from five to twenty-one was entitled to attend these schools free. There were 6,644 Loudoun youths of school age. Of this number, 5,813 were white and 1,831 were Negroes. However, only about one-third of Loudoun's eligible school-age population attended school during 1870-1871.

to become a common event involving all county public school teachers. As would be expected, pragmatic issues were discussed at the 1872 institute, including topics like proper discipline and organization of a school. An animated discussion developed about the advantages and disadvantages of "mixing the sexes in schools."[138] At this meeting men were also appointed to present lectures at the next institute on instructional techniques for arithmetic, English grammar, geography, and reading.[139]

In Virginia, financing public education has been the dominant problem facing local and state officials, educators, and taxpayers from the inception of the public school system to the present. The 1870's were no exception. At that time a combination of state and local funds provided the money from which the public school system operated.[140] State money was divided among the school districts on the basis of the number of children in each district between the ages of five and twenty-one years of age.[141] Loudoun's property for the early 1870's was valued at approximately $15,000,000. The state property tax of ten cents per $100 took from Loudoun about $15,000, of which the state returned to Loudoun $6,680 in 1871. As total cost of the first year of public education in Loudoun was $8,255.87, Loudoun parents soon discovered that state funds would cover only a portion of the county's educational costs.[142] During the early 1870's, Superintendent Wildman went "begging" for money from patrons in Waterford and Lovettsville. After making a plea "in the strongest possible light," he was able to secure supplementary funds of $550 and $450, respectively, from the two towns.[143] A notice in the *Mirror* on August 28, 1871, apprised the citizens in Hillsboro and vicinity of a special meeting "to make such arrangements as will be necessary to keep" the school operating for the year. The notice also stated that the state Literary Fund was "sufficient to defray the expenses of the school" for not more than five months. Failure of patrons to make proper financial arrangements would have meant that the Hillsboro school would have been closed for the last five months of that academic year.[144] During the 1870's additional money for Loudoun's schools was

---

[138]*Mirror*, July 24, 1872.
[139]Ibid.
[140]State funds were obtained for public education from the interest on the Literary Fund, capitation tax, and state property tax. While local taxation for education was not compulsory, each county could raise additional funds by an additional property tax that originally was not to exceed 'five mills on a dollar in any one year." (One mill is one-tenth of a cent.)
[141]J. L. Blair Buck, *The Development of Public Schools in Virginia*, p. 69; Virginia, *Acts of the General Assembly of the State of Virginia*, 1869-1870, p. 415; diZerega, "History of Education in Loudoun," p. 85.
[142]*Mirror*, October 18, 1971.
[143]diZerega, op. cit., p. 86.
[144]*Mirror*, August 28, 1872.

obtained from county and district school taxes.[145] The necessity of having to levy local school taxes when the county paid far more in state property taxes than the amount the state provided for Loudoun schools annoyed numerous taxpayers within the county. One local citizen protested:

> ... we send to the education of the non-tax paying people of South side Virginia ... more than we get back ... We ... pay out ... about half of our entire State tax for the privilege of education of the hordes of negroes of lower Virginia.
> Education is a good thing but surely people should take care that too much is not done for them by other people.[146]

This attitude was also indicative of a segment of the county who questioned the need for the new "free schools." Loudoun's first Superintendent of Schools, John W. Wildman, wrote in his report to the State Superintendent of Public Instruction in 1872 that the public school system in Loudoun had "encountered the most determined opposition by the educated and refined portion" of the county, who regard public education "as an organization to promote the interests and elevate the condition of the negroes and lower classes [of] whites at the expense of the property holders." Wildman also revealed that Loudoun's aristocrats were contemptuous of the quality of public education because the "very limited amount of funds ... prevented the employment ... of thoroughly competent and experienced teachers." Wildman concluded his report on the more optimistic note that the general will of the majority of the people in Loudoun favored public education and that public education would be successful in the county.[147] Nevertheless, it took many decades before the majority of the citizenry took full advantage and had confidence in the public school system. For example, in 1897 the members of the Catoctin Farmers' Club of Waterford concluded that education was important, but "our county public schools were little

---

[145]Ibid., May 1, 1872. School taxes levied during 1872 in the county districts or townships were the following cents per hundred dollars of assessed property: Mercer, four; Leesburg and Lovettsville, five; Mt. Gilead, Jefferson and Broad Run, six cents.

[146]Ibid., October 18, 1871. Criticism of education costs within the county emerged with the initiation of the public school system. In August 2, 1871, issue of the *Mirror*, the superintendent of Loudoun public schools was challenged by a concerned taxpayer to answer a series of questions in the newspaper to allay fears of a "great and growing dissatisfaction" in the county "as to the management of School Funds."

[147]diZerega, "History of Education in Loudoun," pp. 84-86. Wildman was a graduate of Virginia Military Institute and a former trustee of the Leesburg Academy.

better than no school as now run."[148] Blame for this situation was attributed to the apathy of Loudoun parents, who did not "care whether their children attended school or not." Yet, these same parents were "at all times" able to "find fault with the teacher because their children were not further advanced in their studies."[149]

Experiences of the reconstruction period were frequently anything but enjoyable. Yet people during the postwar period in Loudoun did not forsake merriment. Revelry and divertissement were obtained not only from the "bottle" but also from the infectious jocularity of a crowd on a festive occasion. Extensive references were made in the *Mirror* to such activities that indicate life in the county was far from morose. The favorite form of mass entertainment from the end of the Civil War to the end of the century was associated with an event simply referred to as a tournament.[150] This was a contest symbolic of medieval jousting tournaments and chivalry. Young men, often dressed in costumes and given titles like "Young America," "Knight of Shenandoah," "Unknown Knight," "Guerilla," and "Ivanhoe," matched skills in spearing a ring with a lance while riding a horse at a rapid speed. Marshals and judges supervised the tournament and helped determine the winner and runners-up. The victorious knight crowned his girlfriend "Queen of Love and Beauty." Knights that were runners-up selected "Maids of Honor." Often such tournaments would be an all-day affair, like the one near Bloomfield on Tuesday, October 10, 1865. Twenty-five knights participated from 9:00 A.M. until noon in that contest, which was followed immediately by the crowning of the queen and her court and a picnic. Once dinner was over:

> . . .*music struck up and the beaus and belles whirled the mazes of the giddy dance until the disappearance of the sun behind the Blue Ridge warned them to return to their respective homes.*[151]

An occasional horse race provided excitement for area citizens. Near Leesburg during October 1866 a much-talked-about race occurred between a Loudoun horse and a Fauquier mare for the prize of a $75 suit of clothes. Loudouners were disappointed in the outcome as reflected in the caustic report in the *Mirror*:

---

[148]"Minutes of the Catoctin Farmers' Club of Waterford, Virginia, 1868-1943," VI (First and Merchants' National Bank, Leesburg, Va.), November 6, 1897.
[149]*Mirror*, December 4, 1897.
[150]*Mirror*, August 21, 1865; September 14, 1865; October 19, 1865; October 6, 1872; July 26, 1877.
[151]Ibid., October 19, 1865.

> *The Loudoun nag, like Loudoun nags generally, felt his keeping and cavorted 'round at such a rate before the race, that his more staid and less pampered feminine competitor 'won the breeches,' by about twenty feet.*[152]

During the 1870's baseball clubs were formed in Loudoun. The Potomac Baseball Club of Leesburg had an ad printed in the *Mirror* challenging any club in the county for a game to be played at Leesburg on Friday, September 21, 1877. The winning team was to receive a "bat and ball" and the title of baseball champions of Loudoun.[153] Additional entertainment was provided by the circus, which usually visited the county once a year. For example, W. W. Cole's "New and Greatest Show on Earth" performed at Leesburg on October 1, 1877. Naturally it was advertised as being "10 Times Larger! 100 Times More Grand!"[154]

Numerous social gatherings, like picnics, strawberry festivals, and oyster suppers were held by the Grange and other farmer organizations and temperance and civic organizations. Such festivities were usually accompanied by a band such as the Hamilton cornet band.[155] Even religious retreats, revivals, and camp meetings were far more than pious and sanctimonious occasions. Despite being in violation of the law, peddlers frequently sold intoxicating "spirits." Any gathering offered needed relief from the tedium resulting from the relative isolation of nineteenth-century agrarian living. The annual Loudoun agricultural fair, held at Leesburg since the antebellum era except during the Civil War, was one of the social highlights of the year,[156] sponsored by Loudoun Agricultural Society. During early November in 1873 President U. S.

---

[152]Ibid., October 10, 1866. Horse racing was a favorite pastime of colonial America. Therefore, it was probably enjoyed by Loudoun's eighteenth-century citizens. By 1811, according to the July 23, 1811, issue of *The Washingtonian*, the Jockey Club of Leesburg sponsored races at Tutt's Hill near Leesburg on the 405-acre plantation, Locust Hill, owned by the secretary of the club, Charles P. Tutt. The Jockey Club of Leesburg advertised in the October 14, 1817, issue of *The Genius of Liberty* a purse of $200 "for a three mile race and repeat" race to be run on October 15, 1817, and a two-mile and repeat race on October 16. On Friday, October 17, a purse of $100 for a "one mile and repeat" contest was advertised. The following day, Saturday, a purse of $150 plus "an elegant saddle, bridle, and martingale, worth at least fifty dollars," was to be given to the winner.

[153]*Mirror*, September 6, 1877. The Potomac Baseball Club resented a newspaper's reference to another Loudoun team as the champions of northern Virginia. It was this team the Leesburg team wanted to play. Baseball has been played in the county since 1871, if not earlier. The October 11, 1871, issue of the *Mirror* tells of a youth names J. B. McCabe, who broke his arm playing baseball. The *Mirror* also believed boys would be killed as a result of playing this "silly game."

[154]Ibid., September 20, 1877. Cole's circus came by train from Alexandria.

[155]Ibid., December 30, 1871; October 2, 1872.

[156]Ibid., August 9, 1871.

Grant and his cabinet came to Leesburg by train to visit a Loudoun fair. His arrival, tour of Leesburg, attendance of the fair, and departure at the depot attracted large crowds and produced "huzzahs."[157]

One of the unique methods of entertainment was the rattle-band serenade of newlyweds.[158] This custom was an informal wedding reception whereby friends would attempt to startle honeymooners after they had gone to bed by serenading the couple "by the use of tin horns, bells, and such other instruments as are best calculated to make [the] night hideous." Not all newlyweds appreciated this light-hearted harassment. One such person was Joseph B. Mann, who lived near Lovettsville. Joseph's brother, acting on the advice of Joseph, attempted to stop the organization of a rattle-band club. Paying no attention to this caveat, the group, led by their captain, John Brislan, went to Joseph Mann's house. They had scarcely marched around the house one time when they were fired upon "three times in rapid succession" by Joseph Mann. "No one being hurt by the firing, and the party" believing it was in no danger "continued their demonstration, when two other shots were fired, one of them taking effect in the back of the neck of the Captain, John Brislan." Brislan was not killed instantly. He was carried into Mann's house, where he lingered until about eight o'clock the next morning. Mann then fled, but returned the following day and "surrendered himself to the officers of the law" to be charged with murder.[159]

POLITICAL RESIGNATION, DISILLUSIONMENT, AND REACTION

Political reconstruction demanded the South's acceptance and compliance to rule by a central government that was formerly her enemy. This subservience required a drastic and sudden realignment in allegiance, which was not an easy transition for many adamant Confederate supporters. Readjustment to the preservation of the Union, although not easy, was less difficult than the acceptance of blacks as citizens. The South did not make the complete shift in racial attitudes that would have granted the Negro equality along with freedom; neither was the transformation of white Southerners' political theory absolute. Conservatism evolved as a theory and organization whereby white

---

[157]Osburn, "The Road Back," pp. 72-73. Grant's visit to Leesburg in many ways was very similar to General Lafayette's visit to Loudoun on August 9, 1825.

[158]This custom continued to be used in the western part of the county until the mid-twentieth century. As a general rule, rattle-band visitations were not made on the wedding night but any night thereafter.

[159]*Mirror*, November 15, 1877.

Southerners titularly accepted nationalism and Negro freedom, but counteracted many of the demands of radical reconstruction.

Loudoun County, as the rest of ex-Confederate areas of the South, went through three stages in political reconstruction: the first was a period of hope based upon a rapid return to a degree of political normalcy believed possible due to the Lincoln-Johnson reconstruction policy. This period was followed by a time of frustration and disillusionment resulting from Congressional control of reconstruction, which repudiated Johnson's reconstruction and exacted that the South resubmit to more rigorous and protracted rehabilitation. Reaction to Congressional demands was that of a begrudging compliance by Southern conservatives. The final stage was more agreeable to the majority of Southerners as they cheerfully welcomed the termination of Congressional reconstruction and the return to "home rule" and the subsequent end of reconstruction.

Virginia's political reconstruction was less traumatic than the experiences of other Southern states. This difference was due to the lack of the traditional radical or black reconstruction government plus the moderation of Major General John M. Schofield as commander of Virginia during Congressional reconstruction. Loudoun was fortunate enough to have an easier time than many other Virginia counties. A strong migrating force in the transition in Loudoun's allegiance from the Confederacy to the United States was the Society of Friends and other anti-slavery Unionists. Although they formerly had been a divisive force during the antebellum and Civil War era, they provided the county with a nucleus of political support and sympathy for nationalism during the reconstruction period. The county was still divided between the Unionists, who supported the Republican party, and ex-Confederate supporters, who backed the Conservative party for county, state, and Congressional positions and the Democratic candidates for President. While political dialogue between opposition candidates was often vociferous, it was free of violence and retaliation that had occurred during the late antebellum period and during the Civil War. Indicative of a decline in animosity between people of the county of conflicting political concepts was the general lack of hatred of Northerners who settled in the county after the war. Unless they were associated with, or held, positions of authority under the federal government in some capacity, such as an agent of the Freedmen's Bureau, the *Mirror* surprisingly objected to the characterization of them as "straggling adventurers." The *Mirror* rebuked those who used the term carpetbagger for the decent Northern settlers in Loudoun and elsewhere in the state as the work of "oily tongued demagogues [radicals], who never discovered the great beauty of Virginia — her inexhaustible wealth — her unsurpassed curative powers."[160]

---

[160] *Mirror*, October 25, 1871.

Unionists within the county mourned Lincoln's death. Their feelings regarding the martyred President were eloquently expressed by one of their leaders, a Quaker, Samuel M. Janney:

> The joy of the loyal people at the prospect of deliverance from rebel oppression and anticipated restoration of National authority, is suddenly turned into mourning for the loss of our beloved and venerated President. . . .[161]

News of Lincoln's being shot surprisingly did not reach Loudoun until April 16, two days after that dreadful ordeal at Ford's Theater. This lag was due to the rigid "blockade at the Federal lines on the Potomac." Janney received a newspaper on April 17 that confirmed:

> . . .the sorrowful report, and now we feel the sad bereavement which had brought deep and universal distress upon the people of the loyal states. For myself, I can say that I felt for him an affection and reverence that I never felt for any other statesman, and having had some acquaintance with him, I mourn his death as the loss of a personal friend. Many of the secessionists who four years ago reviled his character, having lately become convinced of his benevolent disposition and remarkable lenity towards his enemies, now regret his removal by the hand of the fiendish assassin, and look forward with dread to the rigid measures anticipated from his successor.[162]

Loudoun Friends provided not only political support for Presidential administrations during the reconstruction periods, but also were participants in President Grant's "Quaker Indian Policy" of appointing Quakers Superintendents and Indian agents.[163] Samuel Janney served as Superintendent of Indian Affairs in Nebraska from 1869-1871. His brother, Asa M. Janney, served for a time as Agent of the Santee Sioux.[164]

Union supporters in Loudoun during the war years, while numerous, nevertheless formed only a minority of the county's total population. The preponderance of Loudouners had ratified Virginia's secession from the Union by a vote of 1,628 for secession to 726 against.[165] The lack of

---

[161] Janney, *Memoirs*, p. 235.
[162] Ibid.
[163] Ibid p. 250.
[164] Ibid., pp. 254, 286.
[165] *Mirror*, May 29, 1861.

unanimity was sufficient so that Loudoun County at various times during the Civil War was in the unique position of being claimed by three state jurisdictions: Virginia of the C.S.A., Pierpoint's "Virginia" of the U.S.A. and West Virginia.[166] Pierpoint's Union administration at Alexandria, Virginia, did receive limited support from Loudoun's Unionist supporters. Delegates from Loudoun helped reorganize the Pierpoint government in Alexandria in 1863 after it had been forced to move from Wheeling as the result of the formation of West Virginia. Loudoun sent as many as three delegates to the constitution convention of Virginia Unionists at Alexandria in 1864: Dr. J. J. Henshaw, J. Madison Downey, and E. R. Giver. Downey, elected speaker of the House of Delegates of the Peirpoint government in 1863, was re-elected to the same position in 1864.[167]

While the Unionists in Loudoun responded to the news of the end of the Civil War with jubilation, the majority of the county population, which had supported the Confederacy, reacted with hopeful resignation. One of the most influential spokesmen for the latter was the editor of *The Democratic Mirror*, Benjamin F. Sheetz. His partisan journalistic support for Conservative and Democratic party candidates until his death during the 1890's made him one of the most influential men within the county. On June 14, 1865, his editorial "To the People of Loudoun and the Adjoining Counties" presented the following summation of the South's antebellum and Civil War history as well as what her attitude should be now that the war was lost:

> . . .*war has swept over the land, like a terrible sirocco, desolation and ruin marking its pathway. . . . For years previously, the mad passions of men, lashed into fury by a wild fanaticism, had convulsed both sections of the nation, until those convulsions, culminated into a strife the most magnificently horror that the world ever witnessed — one section battling for what she believed to be a principle of our common Constitution the doctrine of States Rights.*

---

[166]Hamilton J. Eckenrode, *The Political History of Virginia During the Reconstruction* (Gloucester, Mass.: Peter Smith, 1966), pp. 13-14. During the war years, "Pierpoint" was the spelling used by the governor. After the war, he signed his name "Pierpont."

[167]Eckenrode, *The Political History of Virginia During the Reconstruction*, pp. 15-20. Anyone present at the Alexandria convention of 1863 from northern counties of Virginia was admitted as a delegate regardless whether he represented constituents. In Pierpoint's re-election as governor of Virginia Unionist government in 1863, only two of Loudoun's fifteen polls were open for voting. Henshaw, Downey, and Giver were elected as delegates from Loudoun on a very small vote. The area under Pierpoint's administration by the last year of the war had diminished to that of two counties: Alexandria and Fairfax. However, conditions greatly improved for Pierpoint on May 9, 1865, when President Johnson recognized Pierpoint's Alexandria government as the true state government of Virginia.

> *Blood has flowed like water with grief and woe. . . . The struggle, however, has at length ended and in its close has settled for us the hitherto difficult problem of where our paramount allegiance is due, viz.: to the government of the United States. The South defeated at the ballot-box, resorted to the sword, and as 'peace hath her victories no less renouned than war,' now that that has failed her, it becomes her citizens as good and lawabiding people, to conform at once to the new order of things. . . .*[168]

In regard to the freedmen Sheetz commented:

> *The 'peculiar institution' — the fruitful source of all our trouble—is extinct. If their last end prove better than their first; or in their changed condition they realize a greater degree of happiness, freed from care and suffering than they have done in the past—it will be a consolation, atoning in a great measure for their natural guardians and protectors, and who in thousands of instances regard them with almost paternal affection.*[169]

Sheetz in the same editorial, extolled President Johnson as a man of "justice, firmness, and calm judgement . . . reared in that school of politics which allowed to the states respectively the largest library consistent with the public good." Concluding his appraisal, Sheetz placed the hope and protection of the South in the hands of the new President:

> *. . . we have too much confidence in his wisdom and patriotism to believe that he will suffer himself to be forced into those wild schemes of ambitious men the inevitable tendency of which must be to retard that spirit of union, harmony and good feeling which has so conspicuously set in throughout the 'late Confederacy.'*[170]

Civil government partially returned to Loudoun during June 1865. A flag-raising ceremony took place in Leesburg on May 31 that signaled the symbolic return of Loudoun to the Union. In preparation for the first county-wide election of county officers since the war started, a pole

---

[168] *Mirror*, June 14, 1865.
[169] Ibid.
[170] Ibid. Sheetz befriended the beleaguered President in editorials during the next four years. The main exception was during the late summer of 1865, when the confiscation of land in Loudoun was imminent.

approximately forty feet long was placed on the top of the county court house with "a very pretty flag, emblazoned with the stars and stripes,"[171] after which event candidates for county positions gave speeches before "quite an assemblage of persons."[172] The next day Loudoun citizens elected justices and other county officials; the first post-war county court was held later, July 10, 1865.[173] Several who were in key county positions prior to the war were defeated badly when seeking re-election in 1865.[174] County records that had been stored in another area of Virginia for safe-keeping were returned to the county during the first part of August 1865 by the former clerk of the court, George K. Fox, Jr.[175] Civil law was not re-established, even in a limited sense, until three months after Lee's surrender. From April until August, a degree of lawlessness abounded throughout the county, with serious offenders often being pursued by Federal soldiers.[176]

The *Mirror* reported that civil law "asserted her supremacy" in Loudoun during the latter part of July and that "transgressors had better beware."[177] This statement was premature. Civil authority was not truly supreme in Loudoun until the termination of Congressional reconstruction of Virginia in January 1870.[178] During the first part of August 1865, all paroled prisoners in Loudoun of the late "Rebel" armies were ordered to report immediately to the nearest provost marshal. Such persons were restricted from extensive travel without prior approval of the provost marshal.[179] At the end of the same month, Thomas E. Allen, provost marshal at Leesburg, ordered that "all citizens of Loudoun County . . . having in their possession horses or mules branded U.S. or C.S." register such livestock with his office.[180] On February 7, 1866, the provost marshal of Loudoun County had printed in the *Mirror* a warning

---

[171] Ibid., June 14, 1865.

[172] Ibid. Numerous "gentlemen justices" were elected along with the clerk of the court, Charles P. Janney; sheriff, Samuel Luckett; commonwealth attorney, William B. Downey, and commissioners of revenue. Sheetz commented upon the campaign speeches: "Now that the election is over, anything like an epitome of what they said would be as a last year's almanac." Other county officers elected were overseers of the poor and constables of the ten polling places in Loudoun, one of which was not open on June 1, 1865.

[173] Osburn, "The Road Back," p. 63.

[174] *Mirror*, June 14, 1865. George K. Fox, Jr., was soundly defeated in his attempt to continue as Clerk of the Court. Former sheriff, David Hixon, received only nineteen votes in the 1865 election. This was due in large part, according to the *Mirror*, to "a large majority" of county people being "denied the privilege to vote."

[175] Ibid., August 9, 1865. According to the *Mirror*, Fox returned from Devil's Kitchen with the county records.

[176] Ibid., June 14, 1865.

[177] Ibid., July 26, 1865.

[178] Eckenrode, *The Political History of Virginia During the Reconstruction*, p. 40.

[179] *Mirror*, August 9, 1865.

[180] Ibid., September 7, 1865. Allen in the order stated it was not the intent of the government to take possession of such animals as long as they were registered.

that anyone in Loudoun who appeared in public with the insignia of his rank of the "late rebel army" would be subject to arrest. It was acceptable to wear old uniforms as long as they were devoid of any insignia or military buttons. The order specified that in the event plain buttons were unattainable, the military buttons were to be covered with cloth.[181] Troops were periodically stationed in Loudoun until 1870.[182] Their appearance rarely pleased members of the white community, who looked upon the arrival of soldiers as the response to " 'frequently reported' falsehoods of bad treatment to the darkies."[183] Another example of the military rule in Loudoun during reconstruction is illustrated by an event that occurred during the early part of February 1866. Shortly prior to the beginning of a religious service at Harmony Church in Hamilton by the traditional minister of the church, Rev. Waugh, a Southern Methodist, the military prohibited him from using the church so the facility could be used by a newly appointed preacher, Rev. Ross of the Baltimore conference.[184] On the following Sunday, four disgruntled parishioners retaliated by trying to block Rev. Ross from holding services. They stole from the church the Bible, hymn books, the sabbath school library, and a pine table. For this sacrilegious act they were arrested by soldiers and placed in a guardhouse.[185]

Former Confederate supporters in Loudoun from June to December 1865, with the exception of the confiscation scare, continued to be relatively optimistic about their future. A contributing factor to hopefulness was the belief that by Christmas of that year reconstruction of the state would be complete. This optimism helped reduce some of the bitterness of the war and the sadness of human sacrifice, of which they were continually reminded by the absence of deceased members of their families. In Union Cemetery at Leesburg were the remains of about 200 "defenders of the 'Lost Cause' representing nearly every state in the Confederacy."[186] The return of bodies to the county during the post-war years of Loudoun men killed elsewhere also stimulated emotionalism.[187] Reverence for these dead led to the formation of "The

---

[181]Ibid., February 7, 1866. Capt. John T. Macaulet was the provost marshal of Loudoun County. This order did not originate with him nor was it limited just to Loudoun.

[182]*Mirror*, January 31, 1866.

[183]Ibid., July 18, 1866.

[184]Ibid., February 7, 1866. From 1861 until February 1866 the ministers of the Hamilton church were appointed by the Staunton conference. A similar difficulty as the one in Hamilton occurred during September 1865 in the Methodist Church of Leesburg. The traditional minister, Rev. Wilson, was arrested by an officer of the provost guard when a new minister arrived who had been appointed by the Baltimore conference. The congregation overwhelmingly supported Rev. Wilson.

[185]Ibid., February 21, 1866.

[186]Ibid., June 27, 1866.

[187]Ibid., January 31, 1866.

Ladies' Central Memorial Association of Loudoun County," dedicated to the preservation of the memory of Confederate war dead by caring for their graves.[188] But the possibility of rapid and total restoration of Virginia's political relationships within the Union encouraged Loudouners to look beyond their sorrow and pay the direct tax levied upon them by the federal government. Notwithstanding "hard times and scarcity of money," the vast majority of county residents responded promptly during the early fall of 1865 and paid by November 15 of that year all but $1,630 of the $31,446.90 levied upon them. Even the U.S. tax collector, Spencer A. Coe, who spent sixty days in Loudoun receiving the above money, was impressed with the "prompt payment and courtesy" displayed by county taxpayers.[189]

Compliance with Johnson's "easy" reconstruction policy was the vehicle upon which Loudouners sought to restore political normalcy and prevent the realization of schemes of radical politicians, such as the confiscation of their property. The *Mirror* not only praised Johnson, but pleaded:

> . . . the absolute necessity of every man taking the Oath of Amnesty prescribed by the President in his proclamation of the 29th of May. Thousands have already done so, and those who have not are only deterred therefrom by a spirit of procrastination which whispers of a more convenient reason. Let no such syren song lull you late delay. By taking the oath you place yourself on equal footing in all respects, with your fellow-man; and besides, confiscating agents are abroad in the land, whose interest no less than their instructions impell them to libel the property of every citizen. With the evidence in your possession of having subscribed the oath, you may bid defiance *except in certain cases,* to their proceedings—but when such proceedings have once begun before you have taken the oath, you are at least subjected to cost, delay, doubt, and anxiety of mind, all of which, if you ultimately succeed in having your property released are vexatious annoyances.[190]

Any justice of peace or notary public in Loudoun was authorized to administer the oath.

In courting speedy reconstruction, the South not only embraced Johnson's reconstruction policy, which was essentially based upon taking

---
[188]Ibid., June 27, 1866.
[189]Ibid., November 23, 1865.
[190]Ibid., September 7, 1865.

an oath of future allegiance to the United States, but developed a rationale why she should not be the recipient of chastisement, retribution, and punishment. It included: (1) the South's acceptance of Negro freedom, although not equality with whites, and (2) the need for the South to display allegiance to the government and Constitution of the United States.[191] The Constitution in this rationale was considered to be a conservative document that allowed the states a notable degree of autonomy. Such a rationale attempted to soothe the South's psychological needs by stressing the purity of her past and present actions. This attitude was to become the central theme of innumerable editorials by Sheetz in the *Mirror*. The terms "disloyalty" and "treason" were unacceptable to him as valid assessments of secession as they impugned the South's honor. Furthermore, Sheetz set forth the rationale in his editorials that emphasized the "people of the South entered into secession believing they had a constitutional right to do so." The result to be sure was a war that the South lost, but, this defeat, the Loudoun editor maintained, did not justify radicalism "sucking the life-blood of Andrew Johnson in its endeavors to thrust upon the South negro equality, and military power to force her to accept it." The editor also reasoned the South after the war was "infinitely the most peaceable and law-abiding of the two great sections of the nation." Crime and violence, rationalized Sheetz, had never been less than in August 1865, which he stated was illustrated by the limited cases to be tried by the Loudoun court.[192]

An outstanding example of the attitude and rationale for reconciliation that existed in the county from June to December 1865 was displayed at a special meeting held in the courthouse in Leesburg on September 11, 1865, resulting from the turmoil in the county at the end of August, when citizens learned that Loudoun property would be confiscated. A few hotheads in the county were unrealistically talking about desperate measures. However, the tenor of the Leesburg meeting was set by J. Mortimer Kilgour, who dwelled at some length upon the point that the question of slavery and of permanent dissolution of the Union had been settled and should be accepted as final. Kilgour maintained it was time for the people of Virginia to show "their loyalty . . . to the Government of the United States." His sentiment echoed the attitude of those in the courthouse as resolutions were written that

---

[191]Ibid., September 14, 1865. Rollin G. Osterweis in *The Myth of the Lost Cause, 1865-1900* (Hamden, Conn.: Archon Books, 1973) argues that Southern romanticism continued after the Civil War in an efficacious credo that consisted of white supremacy, the pristine nature of the Southern female, and the valorous and chivalric character of the Confederate soldier (see pp. 60, 65, 93, 101, 117, and 143).

[192]*Mirror*, August 23, 1865. It is doubtful the lack of cases handled by the county court during August was representative of the law-abiding nature of Loudouners. Many offenders were at that time arrested by federal soldiers, who often did not use the civil authorities or their facilities, which included the county court.

pledged support for the Johnson administration and allegiance to the government of the United States.[193]

Notable in what Loudouners believed to be the last phase of Presidential reconstruction of Virginia was the election of representatives to Congress as well as the state legislature on October 12, 1865. Loudoun voters supported a conservative candidate, Robert Y. Conrad, over Louis McKenzie, a key figure in the restored government of Virginia at Alexandria during the war, by a vote of 754 to 423.[194] There seemed to be "less feeling with regard" to this election than Sheetz could ever remember. The total votes cast were less than half of the 2,800 votes that were cast in the 1860 Presidential election.[195] Feelings were displayed in this election by Loudoun Unionists who were not ready to forget and forgive. Two hundred and eighty-seven of them voted against amending the state constitution, formed in 1864 by Unionists, at Alexandria, which disfranchised persons in the state who held civil or military offices above the county level under the "rebel" government of Virginia. However, the majority of Loudouners who voted, 834, like the majority throughout the state, voted to delete the above provision from the constitution of Virginia.[196]

From December 1865 to 1870 the majority of Loudoun's residents became increasingly disillusioned and embittered, as did the rest of the South, with reconstruction. By December 1865, the requirements set by Johnson had been met by all ex-Confederate states except Texas.[197]

---

[193]Eckenrode, *The Political History of Virginia During the Reconstruction*, p. 36; *Mirror*, September 14, 1865.

[194]Conrad was elected Congressman for the 7th Congressional district of which Loudoun was one of nine counties.

[195]*Mirror*, October 19, 1865. Randall and Donald, *The Civil War and Reconstruction*, pp. 560-61. Apathy was, no doubt, a major factor in this reduction. The exact number of Loudouners ineligible to vote is not known because Johnson's May 29, 1865, proclamation pardoned supporters of the Confederacy except those whose taxable property exceeded $20,000. This number was in all likelihood only a minor factor in explaining the small voter turnout. Johnson liberally granted thousands of special pardons for those who did not qualify under his 1865 proclamation. For example, by September 1865, the President had granted special pardons to George W. Ball, Thomas W. Edwards, and Sanderson Thrift of Loudoun. These pardons carried with them the return of property that had been seized by the Freedmen's Bureau. On December 25, 1865, Johnson "unconditionally" granted a "full pardon and amnesty" to all who had supported and participated in the "rebellion."

[196]Eckenrode, *The Political History of Virginia During the Reconstruction*, p.21; Jack P. Maddex, Jr., *The Virginia Conservatives* (Chapel Hill: University of North Carolina Press, 1970), pp. 38-39; *Mirror*, October 19, 1865.

[197]Lawanda Cox and John H. Cox, *Politics, Principle and Prejudice, 1865-1866* (Englewood Cliffs, N. J.: Prentice-Hall, 1963), p. 137. Johnson's policy for reconstruction of the South, in addition to requiring an oath of allegiance, included that ex-Confederate states must (1) enact state laws abolishing slavery and ratify the Thirteenth Amendment, (2) nullify legislation for secession, and repudiate all debts resulting from supporting the "War for Confederate Independence."

Loudouners rejoiced when the President in his first annual message to Congress, on December 6, informed Congress that reconstruction was over and the Union had been restored. Rejoicing ceased when Congress responded by rejecting Johnson's reconstruction of the South by refusing to seat representatives of the ex-Confederate states. This move was the start of an acrimonious contest between Johnson and Congress over reconstruction policy that would emasculate executive power to the point of political impotency, come close to imposing, if not impose, legislative hegemony over the nation, and rekindle and exacerbate Southern resentment.

The year 1866, often referred to as the "critical year" in reconstruction, saw Congressional power and reconstruction policy supersede those of Johnson. Paramount in this transfer of power and change in policy was the Presidential veto of bills to extend indefinitely the life of the Freedmen's Bureau and to enact Civil Rights legislation. These vetoes drove moderate Republicans in Congress into the camp of the radicals.[198] Before the year was over, Republicans, under the leadership of the radicals, had substantially increased their control over both houses in Congress due to the humiliation of Johnson by paid hecklers as the President maladroitly attempted to attain the election of moderate representatives to Congress in a speaking tour known as the "swing around the circle."[199] The year also witnessed Congress' setting in motion what was to be a key phrase of its reconstruction program, the Fourteenth Amendment.[200] From 1867 until the termination of Congressional reconstruction, radicals completed their consolidation of power, which included a further reduction in executive power by (1) enacting the Command of the Army Act, Tenure of Office Act, (2) impeachment of Johnson, and (3) implementation of Congressional reconstruction under the Reconstruction Act and supplementary legislation. The Reconstruction Act divided the South into five military dis-

---

[198]Cox and Cox, *Politics, Principle and Prejudice, 1865-1866*, pp. 231-32; Randall and Donald, *The Civil War and Reconstruction*, pp. 578-80. The most important recent reinterpretation of reconstruction is by Michael Perman in *Reunion Without Compromise: The South and Reconstruction, 1865-1868* (Cambridge: Cambridge University Press, 1973). Perman rejects the views traditionally projected by the pro-Southern and revisionist schools of interpretation. Perman maintains that reconstruction failed during 1865-1868, not because of Johnson's administrative failures, but because reconstruction policy was incorrectly based upon the assumption that the South wanted reconciliation, when in reality conservatives in most Southern states were frantically attempting to "stop reconstruction dead in its tracks." Therefore, no reconstruction policy could have been successful unless it was radical and strong enough to circumvent through cohesion the recalcitrant and non-compromising attitude of the South (see pp. 10-11, 337-42). Although it would be unfair and incorrect to reject Perman's thesis on the basis of an analysis of one county, his interpretation is, nevertheless, not a completely accurate assessment of Loudoun's attitude from 1865 to 1868.

[199]Randall and Donald, *The Civil War and Reconstruction*, p. 589.

[200]Ibid., pp. 580-86.

tricts, subject to martial law in order to protect the freedmen and establish the Republican party in the South.[201] For Virginia, Congressional reconstruction was comparatively mild and lasted only from March 2, 1867 to January 28, 1870.[202] Nevertheless, Loudoun and other sister counties reacted to the chain of events from 1866 to 1877 with a feeling of victimization and disenchantment.

During the first few months of 1866, conservative Loudoun residents continued to believe that Johnson would "restrain the radical wave that" was "threatening to submerge the whole country."[203] But nevertheless, they were concerned. Sheetz, in an editorial to the people of the county, warned that the issue was "fairly and squarely presented": Johnson either maintained "his own well-known policy," or succumbed "to the dictation of Congress."[204] Johnson's veto of the bill to extend the Freedmen's Bureau and Congressional inability to override the veto bolstered the faith of Loudoun conservatives in the President. Sheetz saw the failure to override the veto as the greatest blow that had "been struck at the abolition mongrels."[205] This was the last Johnsonian victory that Loudouners would be able to cheer. Their concerns were renewed even prior to Congressional passage of the Civil Rights bill on March 16, 1866. A few days prior to the passage of the Civil Rights Bill by Congress, the *Mirror* voiced the following opinion in regard to additional reconstruction measures:

> *The Southern States, since the surrender of Gen. Lee's army, and the consequent collapse of the Confederacy, have done, and done speedily and well, all that reason, justice or common sense could required that they should do. They subscribed, in good faith, to all the oaths of loyalty required of them—they repudiated their war debt—adopted the constitutional amendment declaring negro slavery forever at an end—and so changed their code of laws as to allow negroes to sue and be sued—to marry wives and hold property—to testify in Courts of Justice, and perform such other acts of a resident upon the soil, as was guaranteed to the white man . . . . We are even now maliciously taunted with being sworn abolitionists, because we have sworn to the oath of loyalty prepared for us—but let it never be said that by legislative enactment we declared ourselves no better than a nigger.*[206]

[201] Ibid., pp. 592-600, 604-05, 607-08.
[202] Eckenrode, *The Political History of Virginia During the Reconstruction*, p. 40.
[203] *Mirror*, January 24, 1866.
[204] Ibid.
[205] Ibid., February 28, 1866.
[206] Ibid., March 14, 1866.

Upon learning of the passage of the Civil Rights Bill, the tone of the reporting in the *Mirror* became more caustic. While Loudoun conservatives still had faith that Johnson would be able to negate Congressional action by his use of veto power, they did not like the intent of the Civil Rights Bill, which in their eyes would "place power in the hands of the negro at the expense of the white man."[207] This conclusion was supported by the observation that the "poor Indian," the "original owner of the soils" and "a higher type of man than the negro ever can be," was excluded from the privileges and rights" of the Civil Rights Bill.[208] Upon learning that Johnson vetoed the bill, the *Mirror* praised Johnson by stating a President of "less nerve, less statesmanship, less public virtue, less Roman firmness" would allow radicalism to "run riot in the halls of legislation, and this" land "of liberty would degenerate into the vilest despotism" and rule "by mongrel imbecility such as never disgraced the halls of the Montezumas in the darkest days of their fallen glory."[209] Shocked by Congressional enactment of the Civil Rights Bill into law over the President's veto, Sheetz condemned the legislation as "revolutionary" and "distasteful, inexpedient, if not unconstitutional." Furthermore, in the judgment of the editor, it reflected "on the part of Congress a spirit of deadly hostility to the administration, and a determination to 'rule or ruin.' "[210]

Deterioration of hope for immediate reconciliation was accompanied by a disturbance in Leesburg during March 1866. A resident of the town, John W. Head, was unloading at his home a "load of fish"he had purchased. His house was opposite the barracks of federal troops stationed in the town. Several inebriated soldiers started taking the fish. When Head protested, he was beaten and kicked in such a manner as to bloody and break his nose and inflict other injuries. This was only one phase of the incident. During the melee a local butcher, John T. Grimes, had expostulated with Head's assailants. A short time after the disturbance had ceased, three or four soldiers had additional "words" with Grimes, who was standing in front of his store. As the argument became more heated and the number of the soldiers increased, Grimes stepped in his shop and "emerged through an open window, butcher-knife in one hand and cleaver in the other, bidding defiance to his assailants."[211] The soldiers "speedily repaired to" their barracks "to recruit their force and get their guns"; some "appeared in the street with their weapons creating an ominous situation." Fortunately, their rifles were not used,

---

[207]Ibid., March 21, 1866.
[208]Ibid.
[209]Ibid., April 4, 1866.
[210]Ibid., April 11, 1866. Many Congressmen supported the Fourteenth Amendment because they thought the Civil Rights Act was unconstitutional.
[211]Ibid., March 14, 1866.

as an officer arrived on the scene and quelled the disturbance. Although the *Mirror* praised the majority of soldiers for their propriety, the incident was, nevertheless, considered an example of unwarranted abuse made possible by the needless extension of federal authority that garrisoned troops in the county seat.[212]

By July 1866, Loudoun conservatives like Benjamin Sheetz became even more strident in their rhetoric. Congressional submittal to the states for ratification of the Fourteenth Amendment evoked the following response by the *Mirror:*

> We do not for one moment entertain the idea that this bastard amendment, the offspring of the brain of such political harlots as Sumner, Stevens & Co., will ever receive the sanction of a sufficient number of the States of this Union to make it a law.[213]

Despite a growing disdain for Congressional policy, Loudoun conservatives still retained a glimmer of hope for blunting what they believed to be radicalism. In the coming together of Johnson supporters from both the North and South for a convention in Philadelphia during September 1866 prior to the Congressional elections of that fall, they saw a true example of partial reconciliation. It was hoped this meeting would inspire Northern voters to elect to the contested seats representatives that held moderate views regarding the reconstruction of the South.[214] Reasons and observation soon displaced this limited optimism with fear and pessimism. Even prior to the November elections, Sheetz was losing hope for any reconciliation. He warned there was a grave possibility of not only protracted but permanent "disunion." This division would be very likely, he contended, if "the nation" endorsed "the policy of the Radicals at the coming elections, and the Southern States are reduced to the condition of conquered provinces." He contended that, after a few years of a Congressional policy of keeping the South out of the Union, "the people will cease to regard the outrage as they did when it was first projected." Thus "the first step will have been taken towards a permanent change in the structure of our government."[215]

The results of the Congressional election in the fall of 1866 and the impeachment of Johnson, who had been looked upon by ex-Confederates in Loudoun as their savior from radicalism, were

---

[212]Ibid.
[213]Ibid., June 20, 1866.
[214]Coulter, *The South During Reconstruction, 1865-1877,* pp. 45-46; *Mirror,* September 5, 1866. The radicals countered the convention of conservatives by later holding a convention in Philadelphia for the purpose of bringing Southern Unionists in touch with Republicans from the North.
[215]*Mirror,* October 10, 1866.

depressing developments for Loudoun conservatives. Sheetz expressed their attitude regarding the reassembling of Congress in 1867 after the Christmas holidays. According to Sheetz, the spirit of Christmas was "entirely lost" on that "radical body," who "instead of returning to their posts with a spirit of amity and patriotic fellowship," were "full of hatred, malice and all uncharitableness."[216] By 1867, the attitude of Loudoun conservatives had shifted from urging reconciliation and compliance to passive resistance to radical policy.[217] The latter attitude was reflected in Sheetz's response to the passage, in March 1866, of the Reconstruction Act that subsequently made Virginia the First Military District under the rule of General Schofield:

> It may be that a little time and consideration will develop the propriety of the South swallowing this tub of garbage, set before her by Congress—if so, let it be done in honesty and good faith—but let us in the meantime be careful not to voluntarily assist in carrying through the flames of faction, this condemnation of all that we have heretofore held sacred, only to find that our sole reward is a blistered hand.[218]

After the passage of the first Supplementary Reconstruction Act of March 22, 1867, Sheetz shifted to compliance of the existing Reconstruction Acts. He feared that the continuation of passive resistance would allow radicals and blacks to gain complete supremacy in the Old Dominion. Sheetz contended that the application of the disfranchisement provisions of the above legislation would not adversely affect Loudoun voters. At best, he felt less than "a half dozen men," except for those that held significant positions in rebellion governments, would be disfranchised or, at worst, it would affect less than "one man in fifty of all voters of the county." Consequently, Sheetz pleaded with Loudoun's conservative population to register! He charged them:

---

[216] Eckenrode, *The Political History of Virginia during the Reconstruction*, pp. 49-51; *Mirror*, January 9, 1867. A view of Congress during reconstruction that differs greatly from that set forth in this paper is the thesis of Michael Les Benedict in *The Impeachment and Trial of Andrew Johnson* (New York: W. W. Norton and Co., 1973). Benedict rejects the concept of impeachment as an attempt to establish Congressional supremacy. He instead maintains impeachment was a defensive move by Congress against a President who claimed broad powers, appointed provisional governors without the approval of the Senate, and nullified Congressional legislation (see pp. 13 and 180). Although this view represents the current trend in reconstruction historiography, it is difficult to square Benedict's thesis with his characterization of Johnson as a "strict constructionist" (see p. 12).

[217] Eckenrode, op. cit., pp. 49-50.

[218] *Mirror*, March 13, 1867. This fear was no doubt prompted by the removal of Virginia's moderate governor, Francis H. Pierpoint, and General, Schofield, from command of the First Military District.

> *If it is wrong and unjust for congress to disfranchise a portion of our people—how much more criminally improper is it for the remainder to disqualify themselves by a refusal on their part to register.*[219]

Although the specific details of the reaction of Loudoun conservatives to developments from 1868 to 1871 cannot be documented, there is little doubt their sense of frustration continued as they saw a combination of whites and blacks of "radical political persuasion" dominate the state constitutional convention of 1868 and delay until 1870 Virginia's readmission into the Union.[220]

In the eyes of Virginia conservatives, the 1870's was the first decade after the Civil War during which complete "home rule" had returned to Virginia. The distinguishing characteristic of this period was the paramount power of conservative forces. Emblematic of their ascendancy was the emergence of the Conservative party. The genesis of this organization was the attempt by Virginians at the end of the Civil War to shift from the ashes of the ideology that had led to the formation of the Confederacy to a modified version of racism and States' rights. While slavery and secession were recognized as dead, the belief in the inequality of whites and blacks and the limited power of the central government remained the credo of the majority of ex-Confederate supporters. Johnson's reconstruction program was eagerly embraced by many Southern conservatives because it was regarded as the most prudent course to pursue for the realization of these maxims. Also, in the eyes of conservatives, radical or Congressional reconstruction was conceived as an odious and fatal threat to white political supremacy. In Virginia it was not the military regime that was feared, but the prospect of a radical civil government composed of white and black Republicans dedicated to Negro equality and the disfranchisement of former supporters of the Confederacy.[221] The beginning of the organization of what was to become known as the Conservative party in the state was at a state convention held in Richmond on December 11, 1867. The executive committee of the Conservative party of Richmond and members of old Whig and Democratic central executive committees jointly called for this convention to consolidate their efforts to counter the growing

---

[219] Ibid., June 12, 1867.

[220] Eckenrode, *The Political History of Virginia During the Reconstruction*, pp. 87-88. The attitude of Loudoun conservatives from 1868 to 1871 regarding specific developments can not be analyzed due to the lack of preservation of any of the issues of Loudoun County newspapers published during that period. Specific reaction to the ratification of the Fifteenth Amendment to the U. S. Constitution as an additional prerequisite for Virginia's readmission into the Union remains hidden.

[221] Maddex, *The Virginia Conservative, 1867-1879*, pp. 46-47.

power of Virginia radicals.²²² In 1869 conservative members of a bifurcated Republican party in the state transcended traditional party affiliations and formed a coalition with other conservatives within the state. The broad base appeal attempted by the "new movement"of Virginia conservatives was to include whites of Republican and Democratic parties and former Whigs. Shocking to many traditionalists was the eagerness of some conservatives to appeal to Negro voters.²²³ The efforts of a coalition of conservatives was rewarded by obtaining the ratification on July 6, 1869, of the Underwood Constitution and the rejection of disfranchising and test-oath clauses of that document.²²⁴ This victory was a major turning point in Virginia's reconstruction history. It terminated Congressional reconstruction of the state, gained Virginia official readmission into the Union, and elevated conservatives within the state into political superiority.²²⁵ By September 1871 the Conservative party of the state had organized itself in such a manner so as to integrate the efforts of the state organization with that of cities and counties.²²⁶

Loudoun conservatives, Democrats and former Whigs, were participants in the movement of 1869 that terminated reconstruction in the state and vaulted the forces of conservatism to the political forefront.²²⁷ This accomplishment, the extensive grass roots organization of the Conservative party of 1871, and the intensive support of the *Mirror*, which became an organ, under Benjamin Sheetz's editorship, for the Conservative party within Loudoun, ignited extraordinary political activity within the county during the 1870's, resembling the extensiveness of political activity preceding the Civil War.

The origin of the Conservative party in Loudoun can be traced to a series of political meetings in Leesburg during 1865 and 1866. During a meeting in September 1865, resolutions were passed to show Loudoun's "loyalty" to the Union and endorse Johnson's reconstruction policy because it was based "upon conservative principles in accordance with the Constitution of the United States."²²⁸ In April 1866, conservatives

---

²²²Eckenrode, *The Political History of Virginia During the Reconstruction*, p. 85.

²²³Maddex, *The Virginia Conservatives*, pp. 80-81. Local committees of the Conservative party held biracial barbecues; Conservative employers were urged to cajole or threaten black employees into voting the Conservative ticket.

²²⁴Voters were allowed to vote separately upon the disfranchising and test-oath clauses of the Underwood Constitution.

²²⁵Eckenrode, *The Political History of Virginia During the Reconstruction*, pp. 116, 120-21.

²²⁶*Mirror*, September 6, 1871. According to party organizational rules, each county was to "hold" popular meetings, have people of each township to select two representatives to a county committee. The chairman of the county committee was to "act as superintendent . . . for the county" and control all matters of organization and registration.

²²⁷Maddex, *The Virginia Conservatives*, pp. 79-80; *Mirror*, October 25, 1871.

²²⁸*Mirror*, September 14, 1865.

held a county convention that nominated for sheriff Loudoun's top war hero, Colonel Elizah V. White, who had served in the Confederate army. White won the election from the incumbent, Samuel G. Luckett, by 1,855 votes to 1,596.[229] The *Mirror* attributed the colonel's victory over an opponent the paper acknowledged as a good man because of White's "honest conservatism and manly adherence to the President's [reconstruction] policy."[230] But the paramount force for the emergence of a Conservative party in Loudoun, as in the rest of the state, was the disillusionment of the majority of ex-Confederate supporters with Congressional reconstruction policy.[231] The formation of the Conservative party in Loudoun was not a revolutionary act. The term "Conservative" was deemed by many Loudouners to be simply the Democratic party's local name.[232] This fact is illustrated by the diminishing usage of the word "Democratic" in the title of the *Mirror*, which had been a Democratic paper since antebellum days.[233] Without any appreciable shift in basic political theory the *Mirror* during the 1870's became the mouthpiece for the Conservative party. Grateful conservatives soon made the editor, Sheetz, the head of the county organization of the Conservative party, with the title of "Superintendent."[234] Primarily the advantage of using the title "Conservative party" was to attract the support of those who preferred not to think of themselves as Democrats. Interestingly some of the Negro citizens in the county in 1871 either refused to vote or voted the Conservative party ticket, as illustrated by a dozen or more black residents of Leesburg. This trend was due not so much to the appeal of the Conservative party but to the disenchantment of a few blacks, who according to the *Mirror,* were "tired of being led by the nose and used for the advancement of strangers."[235]

During the 1870's members of the Conservative party held meetings on Saturday afternoons on the precinct, township, and county levels to nominate and elect conservative candidates for political offices.[236] The practice of organizing Conservative clubs on the precinct level was started in Loudoun during the summer of 1871.[237] The salient duty of these local organizations was to canvass the community in such a manner as to make

---

[229]Ibid., April 11, 1866.

[230]Ibid., May 30, 1866. Luckett had been elected on June 1, 1865, in an election in which many Loudouners did not, or could not, vote.

[231]Ibid., October 25, 1871.

[232]Maddex, *The Virginia Conservatives*, pp. 130-31.

[233]*Mirror*, August 27, 1876.

[234]Ibid., September 13, 1877. At times Sheetz's editorials used Conservative and Democratic synonymously.

[235]Ibid., November 15, 1871.

[236]The Underwood Constitution changed the name of political divisions within the counties of Virginia from districts to townships.

[237]Ibid., July 26, 1871; August 2, 1871; August 9, 1871; August 16, 1871; August 23, 1871; August 30, 1871; August 26, 1875; September 2, 1875; September 16, 1875.

sure all Conservative voters were properly registered and voted.[238] Clubs were organized not only for conservative local, state, and congressional candidates, but also for Presidential aspirants. Support for Democratic Presidential candidates was manifested in the formation of "Greeley and Brown" clubs in 1872 and "Tilden and Hendricks" clubs in 1876.[239]

Conservative and Democratic candidates usually received the majority of Loudoun ballots cast during the decade of the 1870's.[240] But the concept of the "solid south" was not applicable to the border county of Loudoun during the 1870's as the two-party system existed within the county. Republicans, referred to as radicals by county Conservatives, although not so strong or well-organized as the Conservatives, held county meetings and conventions and were organized in a manner similar to that of the Conservative party within the county. The executive committee of the Republican party of Loudoun had persons assigned to each of the county's five townships to promote the candidacy of Republicans.[241]

An example of Republican strength in Loudoun was the Presidential election in 1872. Grant carried the county by thirty-three votes.[242] However, Conservatives in Loudoun were divided in this election. One faction led by Sheetz found Greeley, who had favored a liberal policy toward the South, an attractive candidate to defeat, politically, Grant, who had militarily thrashed Lee into surrender during the late war.[243] Others voted with Republicans in the county for Grant because, except for Greeley's attitude on reconstruction which was no longer germane for Virginia, they found little to cheer about in the candidacy of a man who was one of the founders of the Republican party and noted for his liberal

---

Conservative clubs of each precinct elected a president, vice-president, secretary, treasurer, and several delegates and alternates to attend township and county nominating conventions or other meetings. For example, township meetings were held during August 1871 to choose delegates to a county convention on September 2, where two candidates for the House of Delegates of the Virginia legislature would be nominated and delegates would be elected to attend another convention to elect a party candidate for the state senate.

[238]Ibid., August 2, 1871. Members of local Conservative clubs were assigned to committees composed of two people to canvass each road district.

[239]Ibid., September 11, 1872; August 24, 1876.

[240]Coulter, *The South During Reconstruction*, p. 377; *Mirror*, September 6, 1871; November 13, 1872; November 1, 1875; November 9, 1876. Simkins, *A History of the South*, pp. 313-14.

[241]*Mirror*, April 24, 1872; August 27, 1876; November 9, 1876.

[242]Ibid., November 13, 1872. Grant received 1,549 votes to 1,516 for Greeley.

[243]Ibid., May 8, 1872. Sheetz commented about the nomination of Horace Greeley at the Cincinnati convention as an event where "Liberal Republicans" working with Democrats "fills us with hope and encourages us to look upon the overthrow of Grantism as a foregone conclusion." Sheetz's optimism may have been inspired by his dislike of Grant, whose speeches Sheetz referred to in the *Mirror* on October 25, 1871, as sounding "more like the chattering of an imbecile than the acknowledged chief of a great nation."

reformism. In this election, 1,471 of Loudoun voters chose, out of apathy or protest against both Presidential candidates, not to vote. Sheetz concluded that nine-tenths of these "stay-at-home" were "Democratic-conservatives."[244]

Far more interest was evident in the county during the Presidential election of 1876. For more than two months, from September to the election on November 7, political activities touched all parts of the county, led by Sheetz and his paper and the Leesburg Tilden-Hendricks Club.[245] The campaign within Loudoun for the Democratic Presidential hopefuls was launched by a pole-raising in Leesburg on Saturday afternoon, September 3.[246] Weekly meetings were held thereafter by the Leesburg Tilden-Hendricks Club until the election. Such meetings were primarily occasions for campaign speeches, usually by ex-Confederate officers like that of Colonel Richard H. Lee of Clarke County, who at Leesburg on Friday night, September 14, spoke on "The Republican Party." For one hour and twenty minutes, according to Sheetz, Lee spoke in "a clear, logical and forcible manner," pointing out that the Republican party of the 1870's was synonymous with "grand larceny ... conceived in corruption, and christened in fraud."[247] At one of the October meetings Captain George R. Head of Loudoun addressed the "colored people" in the crowd and told them to abandon their "suicidal policy" of "banding themselves together as an 'Invincible Club'—and arraying themselves as a class against what nine-tenths of their white fellow-citizens believe to be for the best interest of all the people."[248]

Head's speech was in reference to black Republican meetings at Leesburg in September, during which the history of slavery was discussed and the Democratic party was indicted as the party whose policy has been "detrimental to the welfare of the colored man." Loudoun Negroes at these meetings also maintained they were indebted to the Republican party for their "freedom and rights." As the result of these meetings at Leesburg, blacks in the county formed a club known as "The Invincible Republican Club of Leesburg, Virginia." Their motto was "May God help us to be invincible." The tone of this slogan was considered threatening by ex-Confederates, who considered the Invincible Club a

---

[244]*Mirror*, November 13, 1872. Another example of white Republican interest was shown in 1876 by the nomination of James M. Hoge of Loudoun for the state Senate by a Republican convention in Alexandria. In that election 1,721 Loudoun voters voted for Hoge as compared to 2,614 for his opponent.

[245]Ibid., October 26, 1876; November 2, 1876.

[246]Ibid., September 7, 1876. The pole was about 115 feet long and 18 inches in diameter at the base. An American flag twenty by thirteen feet was flown from the pole.

[247]Ibid., September 21, 1876. This was in reference to the Grant scandals. The core of the campaign against Republicans was the need for reform to purge the government of corruption.

[248]Ibid., October 12, 1876.

"menace to the white people." For example, Sheetz not only considered the black meetings and club strident, but also considered the fact that blacks held their meeting at a chapel constructed "largely by the contributions of the Democrats" of the community a display of ingratitude toward the white community.[249]

Increasing in tempo during the month of October, Conservative efforts generally dwarfed by comparison Republican efforts in the county. Speakers on behalf of Conservative and Democratic party candidates appeared in most of the county's hamlets on Saturdays of the last three weeks prior to the election.[250] The highlight of Conservative efforts in the county was a barbecue and "grand demonstration" for Tilden and Hendricks held on Thursday, October 26, at Leesburg, sponsored by the Leesburg club.[251] Between 1,000 and 1,200 gathered in the courthouse square on a "raw" and cool day for proceedings that went from noon into the night and included "nine stirring speeches," mainly by ex-Confederate officers, a "substantial dinner for all," and a torch-light procession. At about 6:30 P.M. throughout the town "business houses" and "private residents were aglow with brilliant lights and handsome and appropriate devices," which included over 600 Chinese lanterns. A torchlight procession was formed on the east end of Market Street at seven o'clock, headed by the brass band of Leesburg and followed by a "couple of colored men" from the Tilden-Hendricks Club of Lewinsville displaying a large American flag. Several hundred people were in the procession, carrying over one hundred torches and twenty-five to thirty "transparencies," including one each of Tilden, Hendricks, and General Hunton, a candidate for Congress from the eighth district. As the parade marched through the town, "sky-rockets, from time to time went whirling through the air, illuminating the heavens with their lurid glare." A small cannon that had been brought by train from Alexandria, "belched forth its thunderous peals" in anticipation of sending Republicanism to its "grave." After the parade additional speeches were given until after 11 P.M.[252]

Due to the efforts of visitation committees sponsored by county political clubs and the excitement induced by celebrations like that of October 26, people registered and voted in record numbers. The Leesburg precinct alone had ninety newly registered voters, making a total for the county seat of more than 800 registered voters.[253] Of this number 688 voted on November 7, including, according to Sheetz, "Africa," which "was out in full force and polled over 200 votes, only about 21 of which

[249]Ibid., September 14, 1876.
[250]Ibid., October 26, 1876. For example, on October 28 at 2:00 P.M. speakers delivered addresses at Aldie, Snickersville, Union, Hughesville, Hillsboro, Farmwell, and Woodgrove. The following Saturday, campaigning occurred at Woodgrove and Gum Spring.
[251]Ibid., October 12, 1876; October 26,1876.
[252]Ibid., November 2, 1876.
[253]Ibid., November 2, 1876. Thirty-eight were newly registered Negroes.

were deposited for Tilden and the balance of his ticket."²⁵⁴ As a whole, the county voted overwhelmingly for Democratic and Conservative candidates. Tilden received 2,643 to 1,705 votes for Hayes. Hayes' strongest support came from the four precincts he carried: Hughesville, Waterford, Lovettsville, and Luckett's Store, all of which were located either in the northern or western part of the county.²⁵⁵

Elated by the enthusiasm for Tilden's support in Loudoun and his 250,000 popular-vote margin throughout the nation over Hayes, the *Mirror* in its largest headlines up to that time stated:

> USHER IN THE NEW BORN DAY
> THE YEAR OF JUBILEE HAS COME
> Tilden Our Next President
> *'Let us have Peace'*²⁵⁶

The following week in an editorial entitled "The War Is Ended," Sheetz concluded:

> *The election of Tilden is the fulfillment of Grant's 'Let us have peace.' It has broken the backbone of the Republican party, whose real strength was in the passions and prejudices of the North. The 'bloody shirt' has lost its power, and 'the war' no longer exists as the tocsin to array section against section. The Democratic triumph is but the triumph of home rule and the equality of the States. It gives to the South the assurance it sought and failed to receive from the Republicans, that it is a component of the Union, not a vassal of the North. It welds and certifies the Union as the Union of equals. It breaks down the color-line. It makes us one people.*²⁵⁷

Though usually jaundiced and showing partisanship in the tenor of his rhetoric, Sheetz was, nevertheless, an astute student of the political process. From the beginning he was aware of an "agonizing suspense"

---

²⁵⁴Ibid., November 9, 1876. The vote in the Leesburg precinct was 457 votes for Tilden as compared to 228 for Hayes.

²⁵⁵Ibid., November 16, 1876. Votes for Tilden and Hendricks at Gum Spring precinct were "thrown out . . . by reason of a mistake made by the commissioner of election of that precinct, in certifying to the vote of Tilden and Hendricks, instead of certifying to the vote of the electors."

²⁵⁶Ibid., November 9, 1876. Although 1876 was the centennial year of American independence, it evoked little, if any, celebrating in Loudoun. Since the majority of Loudouners had been avid supporters of the Confederacy, they looked upon the federal government as a malevolent force that had subverted the attempt to establish a "new independence" through secession.

²⁵⁷Ibid., November 16, 1876.

as to the results of the election because of twenty disputed electoral votes from South Carolina, Florida, Louisiana, and Oregon. But he maintained that logic and the will of the American people dictated that Tilden was the victor as he needed only one of the contested electoral votes to become President and Hayes needed all twenty.[258] As the fall of 1877 waned, the above view diminished. The factional decision of the special election commission and the subsequent awarding to Hayes all of the contested electoral votes was deemed by Sheetz to be "wholesale robbery" and a "perfidy unparalleled."[259] As in all his editorials, Sheetz liked to discuss current developments in terms of what he felt were their historical context:

> . . . the student of our national history will read, that in the centennial year of our national existence, a man was elevated to the highest position known to our system of government, by a fraud so palpable, so gross, and so enormous, that in any other land than our own, it would have been followed by bloodshed.[260]

The editor of the *Mirror* was also suspicious of "Hayes' much vaunted Southern policy," referred to by historians as the Compromise of 1877, "would turn out a snare and a delusion."[261] Sheetz, however, greatly tempered his view of Hayes when the withdrawal of the last of federal troops from the South finally terminated reconstruction.[262]

Although the Presidential election of 1876 had been a source of considerable disenchantment for Virginia Conservatives, it, nevertheless, represented in Loudoun the high tide of the Conservative party. During the campaign for state offices in the fall of 1877, Conservatives within the county split over the issue of state funding. "Antifunders," or "readjusters," C. P. McCabe and Captain John R. Carter, who previously were active within the Conservative party, ran as Independents and defeated for the House of Delegates of the Virginia General Assembly Cooke D. Luckett and William Matthew, who favored the controversial fiscal program and had been nominated by the Conservative party of Loudoun.[263] This cleavage within the ranks of the Conservative party

---

[258]Ibid., November 16, 1876; November 23, 1876; Randall and Donald, *The Civil War and Reconstruction*, pp. 687-93.

[259]*Mirror*, February 22, 1877.

[260]Ibid., March 8, 1877.

[261]Ibid., March 22, 1877; Randall and Donald, *The Civil War and Reconstruction*, pp. 700-01. The compromise of 1877 was an informal agreement by the Republicans that if Democrats would not filibuster in Congress and allow Hayes to "be elected," then (1) the remaining federal troops would be withdrawn from the South, (2) a Southerner would be appointed to Hayes' cabinet, and (3) federal money would probably be allocated for internal improvements in the South.

[262]*Mirror*, April 26, 1877.

[263]Ibid., November 1, 1877; November 8, 1877; November 15, 1877.

would soon bring about the demise of the party in Loudoun, as a majority of her citizens would in the future refer to themselves as Democrats on issues and in support of candidates for local and state positions as well as in matters concerning Presidential candidates and national political issues.

An examination of Loudoun County's history during the era of reconstruction does not provide profound insight into all aspects of reconstruction or all the salient historiographical issues, such as the extent of corruption within state reconstruction governments or the validity and degree of acumen displayed in Presidential and Congressional reconstruction programs.[264] It does reveal much of the essential nature of what reconstruction meant to ex-Confederate supporters: economic readjustment, the forced recognition and accommodation of the recently emancipated freedmen if a degree of social concinnity was to be obtained, the re-establishment of local government, and compliance with Presidential and Congressional programs to obtain the readmission of ex-Confederate states into the Union. At least as difficult for the ex-Confederate to cope with as material and institutional readjustments was the readjustment of traditional Southern attitudes on race and political theory. A majority of Loudouners responded to this challenge with an attitude that represented a pragmatic synthesis of the conservative antebellum mind, with adaptations necessitated by the loss of the Civil War and compliance with federal reconstruction policies. Motivated by the possibility of an expeditious reconciliation with the North under executive reconstruction policy, the ex-Confederate conceded that slavery was terminated, secession was not a constitutional right of each state, and all owed allegiance to the government of the United States. Prompt consummation of reconstruction was considered obligatory to escape the demands of radical miscreancy that menaced the continued implementation of white supremacy as well as limited federal intervention in state and local life during the postwar era. This threat was accelerated by the refutation of Presidential reconstruction and supersedure by Congressional programs. In response, conservatives throughout the state of Virginia, Democrats and former Whigs, formed the Conservative party. This party became the vehicle by which ex-Confederates blunted and terminated control by the coalition of white and black Republicans within the state and restored white political supremacy. Further, the party ended federal intervention and provided the opportunity for the continuance in modified form of many of the political and social attitudes of the pre-Civil War era.[265]

[264]Staughton Lynn, ed., *Reconstruction* (New York: Harper and Row, 1965), pp. 1-9; Seth M. Scheiner, ed., *Reconstruction: A Tragic Era* (New York: Holt, Rinehart and Winston, 1968), pp. 1-8; Edwin C. Rozwenc, ed., *Reconstruction in the South* (2nd ed.; Lexington, Mass.: D. C. Heath and Co., 1972), pp. vii-xi.

[265]For a view of the Conservative party being more than a reactionary movement and possessing liberal programs, see Maddex, *The Virginia Conservative*, pp. 292-95.

Chapter 7

THE AUREATE YEARS OF AGRARIANISM: 1877 TO 1917

From the era of reconstruction to World War I, basic farm techniques and equipment that had been developed prior to the Civil War shaped the agrarian lifestyle in Loudoun. The horse, which had joined his "homo sapiens" master as a partner and assistant in agrarian toil during the colonial period, became more important after the Civil War. Into the 1900's the horse continued to extensively pull farm implements invented and produced prior to 1861, such as metal plows, cultivators, mowers, and reapers.[1] The horse was also indispensable in pulling wagons used for multifarious tasks from carrying hay to the mow, sheaves of wheat to the horse-powered, and later steam-driven, threshing machines, or grain to the mill or local market. After the Civil War, Loudouners still relied greatly upon their own technological ingenuity, and the mechanical skill of local smiths in the production of tools, farm implements, and smitheries. One example was Richard Henry Taylor's establishment in 1866 of the Loudoun Valley Foundry near Lincoln. Originally this establishment specialized in plows. Taylor advertised he was "prepared to furnish the Loudoun County Iron Beam Double Plow; points for Cummins' No. 10 and 12 Plows, Barshear Mould Boards; Woodcock Points and Shares." He also stated he would gladly "make points for any Plow" if there "existed a proper pattern, or Point furnished to mould from." In an attempt to launch his business after a destructive

---

[1] Horses were also used to pull the binder, which later superseded the reaper.

war in which local residents lacked cash, Taylor accepted "old iron" in exchange for his work at the rate of $1 for each hundred pounds of scrap metal he was given.[2]

The postwar fairs, sponsored by the county's agricultural society, also testified to the dependence and encouragement of locally manufactured and homemade items, such as clothing and farm equipment. In 1871, the Eleventh Annual Fair and Cattle Show of the Loudoun Agricultural Society demanded all exhibits in the classes of "Domestic Manufactures and Home Manufactures" be made within the county by Loudouners. This class included items like carriages, saddles, hats, clothing, brooms, foot-mats, barn shovels, pottery, washing machines, and "hay and dung" forks.[3]

FARM ORGANIZATIONS

Joined to the more traditional elements of Loudoun agrarianism between the Civil War and World War I was a growing concern for husbandry and improved breeds of farm animals, stimulated by the county fair and the emergence of farmer organizations in many of the major bicorporal communities.[4] Numerous local farmer clubs were formed during the era of reconstruction due to (1) the desire to resume the county's pre-Civil War tradition of agricultural reform through continuous promulgation and dissemination of improvements in husbandry,[5] (2) the need and wish to rebuild economically and expand after the weary years of a military holocaust, (3) a nascent awareness that in spite of the existence of considerable local mechanical and technical ingenuity, Loudoun farmers were becoming increasingly dependent on sources outside the county for such items as commercial fertilizers and farm implements, a course giving rise to the economic imperative of cooperative purchasing,[6] and (4) the need for decentralized

[2] *The Democratic Mirror*, October 3, 1866.
[3] Ibid., August 30, 1871.
[4] Gray, *History of Agriculture*, II, 846-48. The first significant movement for an improved breed of farm animal in Virginia and the other Southern states was the merino sheep craze that developed just prior to the War of 1812.
[5] *The Democratic Mirror*, November 1, 1871.. The Aldie Club held its first meeting on October 21, 1871. At that time it had "a nucleus of a library consisting of over fifty volumes on agriculture and its kindred subjects."
[6] Ibid. This issue of *The Democratic Mirror* printed that the benefits of the farmers club were as follows: "The members of the club can join together in the purchase of fertilizers, seeds, labor saving implements, stock, etc., etc., and get them all at a much less cost than they could if each individual made the purchases for himself."

organizations to represent and expound upon local agrarian needs in the community and work for remedial action.⁷

The most succinct and illuminating statement of the multifarious purposes and rewards of such organizations was a letter to the editor of *The Democratic Mirror* written on October 24, 1871, by the secretary of the Aldie Farmers' Club, Alfred L. B. Zerega. Members of farmer clubs had an additional duty, he stated, to carry out agricultural experiments and aid their club in keeping "on record, prices current of the various markets, thereby giving" all members "an oppportunity of judging when and where to sell or buy."⁸ He also maintained that a farmers' club "by a combined action of its members and other clubs in the county" could "to some extent regulate the price of labor."⁹ He concluded the letter by calling upon the farmers of the county to unite by organizing community farmer clubs. Zerega stated:

> *In all cities the Merchants, Lawyers, Tradesmen, etc. have organizations of their own for their mutual protection and advantage. Every little town has its chamber of commerce, its exchange and its trade unions, and why should the largest and most important class of the people alone attempt to make a living, single handed, against the minority who are all bound together in some shape or other.*
>
> *There is one golden maxim which ought to be kept constantly in view by farmers: United we stand, Divided we fall, or in other words, In Union there is strength.*¹⁰

---

⁷Ibid. Zerega in the same letter stated "Farmers' Clubs are organized for the purpose of affording the farming community opportunities of meeting together once or twice a month to consider matters pertaining to the farming interest . . . ." The initiation fee to join the Aldie Club in 1871 was two dollars. Additional monthly dues of twenty-five cents also had to be paid (*The Democratic Mirror*, August 23, 1871).

⁸Ibid. "Minutes of the Catoctin Farmers' Club of Waterford," III, 53-54, 61. The Aldie Club received in 1871 sixteen quart packages of seed from the Agriculture Department for various members of their club to plant and carefully note and report their yields. Other clubs, especially the members of the Catoctin Farmers' Club of Waterford, carried out extensive experimentations during the 1870's, which included the use of fertilizers and other aspects of crop husbandry.

⁹*The Democratic Mirror*, November 1, 1871; October 16, 1872. The Catoctin Farmers' Club at its October 8, 1872, meeting added other dimensions to the role of the farmer club by resolving to exhibit the best possible products of county farming and "do all they could collectively and individually to prevent horse-thieving" and, when horses were stolen in the vicinity of Waterford, "to make exertions to recover the property, and to secure the arrest of the thief."

¹⁰Ibid.

A seminal cognizance by Loudoun farmers of a changing America manifested itself in amalgamation of agrarians in what were called farmers' clubs and by 1875 led to the establishment of local units of the Patrons of Husbandry, better known as the Grange. As members of such organizations, Loudouners attended, in addition to the meeting of local Grange organizations, district meetings of the Grange of Northern Virginia in towns like Alexandria and Culpeper.[11] The Grange clubs of Loudoun also frequently held county picnics.[12] These activities were especially frequent during the summer and fall of 1875 and no doubt helped give rise to a meeting at Leesburg on May 8, 1876, in which delegates from Aldie, Loudoun Valley, Catoctin, Goresville, Tankerville, South Fork, and the Mercer Grange met and organized a county Grange called the Pomona Grange, with headquarters at the Grange hall in Hamilton.[13] The year 1876 represented the zenith of the Grange in Loudoun and Virginia. After that year the Grange rapidly declined, giving way in the latter half of the 1880's to the Farmers Assembly and the Farmers' Alliance of Virginia. The latter in turn went through an organizational metamorphosis and emerged in 1892 as the Populist party in the state.[14] Populism received meager support from Loudoun farmers. The county newspapers that have been preserved from the decade of the 1890's devoted little space to Populism. However, Populist

[11]Ibid., September 2, 1875. Among the local units of the Patrons of Husbandry in Loudoun that were represented in the district meeting at Alexandria in 1875 were the Catoctin Grange, No. 433; Snickersville Grange, No. 237; Loudoun Valley Grange, No. 437; South Fork Grange, No. 376. Oliver H. Kelly founded the Patrons of Husbandry in 1867 to unite the farmers of America to improve their conditions by cooperative buying and opposition to monopolies. It was far more active in politics in the midwest than in northern Virginia.

[12]Ibid., July 15, 1875; August 12, 1875; September 14, 1876. For example, under the auspices of the Patrons of Husbandry of Loudoun County, "Three Grand Grange Basket Pic-nics" were held during September 1876 at Benton's much frequented Camp Ground, at Ewell's Chapel, and in Hamilton. The Philomont brass band attended all three outings, and the general public was invited.

[13]Ibid., May 11, 1876. Pomona in Roman mythology was the goddess of fruit and fruit trees. The preamble to the county Grange stated its purpose was "to establish more intimate relations between" the "subordinate Granges in Loudoun" and "to succeed more effectually in accomplishing the" purposes of "their order; viz: In meeting together, buying together, selling together, and in general acting together, for" their "mutual protection and advancement, as occasion may require. . . ."

[14]Sheldon, *Populism in the Old Dominion*, pp. 22-27. At its height in 1871, there were 16,000 members in the Grange in Virginia. In 1885 the Farmers' Assembly was organized at a meeting in Richmond. This organization was not involved in the Farmers' Alliance but served as a clearing house for the grievances of Virginia farmers and as an agrarian lobby in the state capital to obtain benevolent farm legislation. Each local grange or farmers' club having a dozen active members was entitled to one representative at the annual meeting of the Farmers' Assembly in Richmond. There were several unsuccessful attempts during the first half of the 1900's to reorganize a local organization of the Grange at Lincoln (Statement by Edward R. Brown, personal interview, January 27, 1974).

candidates on the state level did campaign in Loudoun, and Loudoun was represented in a Populist convention held in Alexandria in 1894 to nominate a candidate for the eighth congressional district of Virginia. At this slimly attended meeting, John G. Herndon of Loudoun was elected chairman. Nevertheless, Populism failed even to challenge seriously the political supremacy of the Democratic party in Loudoun.[15]

Of greater significance for the county and possessing greater longevity than the Grange were the Loudoun farmer clubs. They existed prior to the Grange and continued to exist long after the demise of local units of the Patrons of Husbandry. The Catoctin Farmers' Club of Waterford has been in existence since 1868.[16] More recently formed, the Lovettsville Farmers' Club, established in 1911, continues to be the most active and influential local farm lobby organization within Loudoun.[17]

By the end of the 1870's basic organizational procedures of county farmers' clubs emerged that have since been continued as standard practice of such organizations. Among the customary characteristics and procedures were monthly supper or dinner meetings at various members' homes, with business meetings usually held prior to eating. The business meeting included the reading of the minutes of the last meeting, a recording of current prices of farm products, appointment of members to make a presentation at the next meeting, and a guest speaker or presentation and discussion of a topic germane to Loudoun farming by members of the club. Frequently after the meal and the completion of the business meeting, members would be given an informal tour of the

---

[15]Ibid., 91, 104, 151; *The Democratic Mirror,* September 14, 1893; October 12, 1893; November 16, 1893; March 15, 1894; September 6, 1894. In the state election of 1893, Democratic candidates received the preponderance of Loudoun's votes. Prohibition was more significant in Loudoun in this election than the Populist crusade. For example, the Democratic candidate for the House of Delegates, John F. Ryan, received 1,486 votes to 708 for D. J. Hoge, the Prohibitionist candidate. The only Populist candidate for the House of Delegates voted upon by county residents was J.G. Herndon, who ran "for Floater Delegate." He received only 519 votes in Loudoun, compared to 1,874 for his Democratic opponent, the popular Eppa Hunton, Jr. From the limited and scattered copies of Loudoun newspapers that exist from the 1890's, definitive evidence does not exist as to the reason Populism failed to appeal to Loudoun farmers. Unlike the tobacco-producing counties in the southern region of the state, Loudoun had a more diversified economy, was closer to markets, and was more prosperous in the 1890's. Loudoun farmers had grievances, but they apparently were less severe than those of farmers in the southern part of the state. One of the few positive contributions of Populism in Virginia was the state's adoption of the Australian, or secret ballot, in 1894.

[16]"Minutes of the Catoctin Farmers' Club," III, 7.

[17]"Minutes of the Lovettsville Farmers' Club," I, 1. Another farmers' club in Loudoun formed during the twentieth century was the Planters' Club. This organization was established in 1913.

livestock, crops, equipment, or barn of the host.[18] An additional characteristic was the limitation of membership to fifteen. The paramount reason was that the average farmhouse could comfortably seat this number, and the farmer's wife could set a bountiful "spread."[19] The hostess took pride in providing as much food as possible for her guests. She believed this largesse to be the most important element in being hospitable. In turn, the male guests took pride in consuming as much of the feast as possible. Such indulging was deemed to reflect favorably upon the culinary prowess of the hostess. Minutes of the meetings usually recorded that meals were "bountifully prepared, to which all did justice and enjoyed."[20]

The limited membership and a familiarity between members who were almost always neighbors led to a degree of informality in the business meetings. Occasionally members either forgot or refused to prepare themselves for their assigned presentations.[21] Neither was it uncommon for farmers to consider their monthly meeting as a quasi-stag gathering, at which they had male companionship and an opportunity to tell an off-color joke when the ladies were in the kitchen and unable to hear such expressions of jocosity. While "politics" were to be "kept out of the discussions," this stipulation often asked for more restraint than was possible in a meeting that often was an informal seminar with each member expressing his views and practices on numerous agrarian issues.[22] Membership at times slipped below the maximum number of fifteen due to an occasional rift between members in a club. Such an occurrence apparently prompted the first and only president of the Lovettsville Club from 1911 to 1920 to resign "for reasons he would not explain."[23] Nevertheless, the above characteristics and foibles did not prevent farmers' clubs from being dedicated to the identification of agrarian problems and their solutions and the improvement of farming techniques.

---

[18]Howard M. Hoge, Loudoun's first county Agricultural Demonstration Agent, helped organize the Lovettsville club.

[19]"Minutes of the Catoctin Farmers' Club," II, 7-11; "Minutes of the Lovettsville Farmers' Club," I, 1-4. These meetings were usually held on Saturday. Occasionally a small initiation fee was required of new members, but usually expenses for postage, stationery, flowers for ill or deceased members were raised "by a direct assessment of the membership." Currently meetings of the Lovettsville Farmers' Club are frequently not held in homes but in local restaurants.

[20]"Minutes of the Lovettsville Farmers' Club," I, 13, 35, 116, 162, 164, 174.

[21]Not all presentations were entirely satisfactory. For example, the presentation by Charles Carpenter of the Lovettsville Club on the topic of whether it was profitable to breed undersized mares for saddle and driving horses consisted of the succinct and simple reply of "yes."

[22]*The Democratic Mirror*, November 1, 1871.

[23]Loose letter from H. L. Rodeffer to B. O. Compher in Volume I of the "Minutes of the Lovettsville Farmers' Club."

Transportation and communication inadequacies, including road, railroad, and telephone facilties, continued to be among the major grievances of Loudoun farmers from the Civil War to World War I. Loudoun wanted more roads to be macadamized, and telephone service to be expanded and improved.[24] In a monthly meeting held during 1915 by the Lovettsville Club, the topic was discussed "Which would be the most beneficial to this Farming Community, an Electric line running through this [Loudoun] valley or improved public-roads, with [a] free Bridge at Brunswick?" The club considered the road and free bridge to be the most important.[25] The management of rail facilities as also a source of dismay. On April 10, 1872, the Farmers' Association, meeting in Hamilton, concluded that the Washington and Ohio Railroad was:

> . . being prostituted to serve the purposes of certain monoplies, to the detriment of the farmers, who have been continually appealed to for pecuniary aid, in extending the road.
>
> . . . .
>
> Whereas, the material interests of the farmers of Loudoun are unnecessarily depressed from the want of direct communication with Washington—inasmuch as our produce in reaching that city, is handled, transferred and reshipped, thereby imposing a burdensome and useless tax, upon the pockets of the farmers. And whereas a railroad track is already laid connecting the W. & O. R. R. with the aforesaid city and is frequently used for the accommodation of certain speculators, but is inaccessible to other parties.
>
> . . . .
>
> . . . a trip of 50 miles from Washington to Hamilton was attended with more fatigue than a trip from the former place to New York, a distance of 240 miles, and there was no reason for such a state of affairs.[26]

---

[24]"Minutes of the Catoctin Farmers' Club," IV, 8, 55, 183; VII, 176, 181; "Minutes of the Lovettsville Farmers' Club," I, 6, 9, 16, 25, 82-83, 85. People in the Lovettsville area were displeased with having to pay toll to cross the Brunswick Bridge, but they were especially vexed with the inadequate road from Lovettsville to Brunswick, Maryland. The Lovettsville Farmers' Club was instrumental in the acquisition of private as well as public funds that enabled the construction of a macadam road from their community to Maryland. In 1906 the Catoctin Club wanted a long distance telephone facility between Waterford and Washington, D. C. A Mr. Church, the owner of the local line, offered to connect Waterford with the long distance line then in existence at Paeonian Springs at a cost of $125.

[25]"Minutes of the Lovettsville Farmers' Club," I, 85.

[26]*The Democratic Mirror*, April 10, 1872; October 16, 1872. The Catoctin Farmers' Club lamented the discontinuance of the evening train to Hamilton: "Winter is the season

At home the farmer faced problems in animal and crop husbandry. Animals were susceptible to maladies and debilitation by parasites and vermin. From 1879 to 1899, numerous cattle died in the county from tick fever. One farmer in 1899 claimed to have heard "of ticks being so thick on cattle that [they] could be scraped off with a stick."[27] The only remedy for this problem was to wash the cattle with carbolic acid as soon as ticks were discovered.[28] Lice were also a serious problem. J. C. Souder stated in 1914 that he "did not believe" he had "ever raised a colt that did not have lice on it in the spring." Furthermore, he added that stock do "not necessarily have to be thin in flesh to get lousy." His remedy was to "mix coal oil and grease and rub all the way from [the] ears to tail" of the animal. H. L. Rodeffer recommended clipping the hair of colts to get rid of lice. But he added he had "known of cases where even that" failed. Farmers in the Lovettsville Club also correctly identified the common fly in 1914 as the cause of disease. In a discussion of the best way to eradicate the fly, members recommended the destruction of "all breeding places by spraying, burning, and tearing out all such places." In conclusion, the members conceded that "no satisfactory way could be found to really eradicate the fly."[29] In 1879, J. E. Walker spoke "of sore eyes in his cattle" but did not know the reasons they were afflicted. Others claimed that bringing cattle from Alexandria to Loudoun introduced disease into their livestock, such as pneumonia. Members of the Catoctin Club advocated that, if pneumonia struck their livestock, the use of "crude petroleum" was a "good remedy."[30] When Loudouners purchased some sheep from Ohio, they found that area was selling numerous defective sheep to them. An additional difficulty that Loudouners had with their sheep was a disease known as "foot-rot" that attacked the hoofs. The common remedy was the application of "blue stone" on the feet of the animals that suffered from the disease.[31]

Sheep were not the only animals to suffer from this malady. E. B. White purchased a "car load of Buffalo calves" in the fall of 1900 to "raise for meat." He maintained they did well but would have done better if they had not suffered from "an attack of hoof-rot" in the spring of 1901.[32] Other problems, such as cows aborting, also plagued farmers. Some believed this condition resulted from cows' "eating rye-straw" while

---

of leisure with farmers, and many of them like to make visits to Washington and Alexandria, for business or pleasure. . . ."

[27] "Minutes of the Catoctin Farmers' Club," VII, 63.
[28] Ibid., III, 51.
[29] "Minutes of the Lovettsville Farmers' Club," I, 72-73.
[30] "Minutes of the Catoctin Farmers' Club," III, 17. It was not specified the amount of "crude petroleum" an ailing animal was forced to swallow.
[31] Ibid., p. 55.
[32] Ibid., p. 67. Among the uses of blue-stone or copper sulfate, a blue crystalline substance, is that of a germicide.

others blamed it on injuries inflicted by the horns of other cattle.[33] Often farmers not only did not know the cause of what afflicted their livestock, but also did not always know what disease their animals had. In 1888, Henry Virtz reported the prevalence of the "Epizootic" among horses in the county. Virtz stated he did "not doctor" such animals but was careful "not to feed too heavily" and to keep his "horses well sheltered."[34] Occasionally farmers attempted to be humorous regarding an unusual death of an animal. Such was the statement of C. H. Van Devanter, who in 1896 purchased a sow and pigs. The "pigs died of cholera,"[35] while "the sow ate all the lambs, turkeys, and chickens on the farm." Finally the sow, according to Van Devanter, "committed sowicide by jumping into the swill barrel."[36]

Remedies used to combat maladies afflicting animals were often old ones. A discussion at the Catoctin Club on May 1, 1882, centered around the topic of how "to stop horses from slobbering." The only remedy the members knew was an "old one of cabbage leaves."[37] Also commonly used for ailing cows was a procedure that seems very unusual by today's standards. The minutes of the Catoctin Club recorded in 1880 that:

> R. J. T. White. . . found a favorite cow sick. Symptoms were loss of milk, loss of appetite and a great difficulty of breathing accompanied by a loss of blood thro [sic] the nostrils.[38]

One member of the club, Amos Hughes, upon hearing of this cow claimed the animal had suffered from a disease known as "hollow-horn." The members then discussed "the old and infallible remedy for for this disease." A hole was bored in the horn of the ailing animal and its tail split; "salt and pepper" were put in the cut on the tail and "a mixture of turpentine and . . . other ingredients" was poured in the hole in the horn.[39] In 1882 one county farmer strongly recommended a piece of rope

---

[33] Ibid., VI, 8.
[34] Ibid., III, 95.
[35] Cholera has long been the most prevalent disease afflicting hogs. It usually results in death of the ill swine.
[36] "Minutes of the Catoctin Farmers' Club," VI, 46. Swill or garbage was put in a barrel with water and later fed to hogs in a trough.
[37] Ibid., IV, 152. It was not stated how the cabbage leaves were used. Possibly they were fed to the horse.
[38] Ibid., III, 89.
[39] Ibid. This treatment no doubt shocked the sick animal because it causes the animal to suffer a great deal of pain. It is questionable how therapeutical this treatment really was. Did the animal survive due to this shock to its system or did it survive in spite of this treatment and farmers confused the loss of listlessness and renewed activity induced by pain as improvement or recovery?

as an effective means of dislodging matter in the throat of choking cattle.[40] Farmers also had measures to assist in the weaning of a colt from a mare. Upon the recommendation of a veterinarian some farmers burned "camphor and let the fumes go around the mares bag to dry her up." Others had different solutions, which included keeping the mare and foal in separate stables for a few days. Another piquant practice was the method some farmers advocated as the most rapid way to fatten cattle for market. A Major Jones in 1882 claimed he knew of a system used in England called the "stalling or boxing of cattle." This procedure simply consisted of "placing the animal to be fattened in a rectangular box or put" the animal "in the ground to a depth exceeding the height of the steer. . . . In this box stall he is fed [un]til he has made manure enough to fill up the stall sufficiently to enable him to walk out, by which time he is ready for market."[41]

DOGS, SHEEP, AND FENCES

Dogs also menaced livestock in Loudoun after the Civil War until well into the twentieth century. Sheep were especially vulnerable to canine marauding. The degree of damage that was inflicted is illustrated by *The Democratic Mirror* in 1876:

> The past few weeks have witnessed the fearful and bloody raids on the sheep folds of this county. On Monday night [a] week, Mr. T. C. Paxson, near Clarke's Gap, out of a flock of 104 sheep had 54 killed by dogs, and 40 odd wounded, some of which have since died—making between 70 and 80 head destroyed for him within a fortnight.
> On Sunday night, the 19th., Mr. I. Wilson Bowie, in the same vicinity, lost 24 sheep from the same cause.[42]

---

[40]Ibid., III, 127. A piece of rope four feet in length and five-eighth of an inch in diameter was recommended. The strands on one end of the rope were loosened and bent back and tied securely to an unraveled portion of the rope. A rope thus prepared had an enlarged end that was used as a flexible probe that did not puncture the walls of the animal's throat.

[41]"Minutes of the Lovettsville Farmers' Club," I,59.

[42]*The Democratic Mirror,*November 30, 1876. Both poor and wealthy appear to have been fond of their dogs. Affluent members of the county, who belonged to hunt clubs, considered their hounds as indispensable to them as their horses. Both white and black tenants were also fond of owning numerous curs. All usually refused to get rid of their dogs when confronted with conclusive evidence their canines were responsible for the destruction of others' property.

In the year ending February 1, 1876, dogs had killed 320 sheep in Loudoun. The financial loss was judged to be $1,671.48, or approximately $5.22 per sheep.[43] The following year dogs again killed 320 sheep in the county. In 1874, 460 sheep were killed in the same manner at an assessed loss of $2,583.36. These financial losses were too great for Loudoun farmers to withstand without any compensation.[44] Therefore, a dog tax of seventy-five cents for each animal was levied upon the owners. In 1874 there were over 2,600 dogs upon which the owners were to pay dog taxes. Out of this number, taxes were paid on 2,536 dogs.[45] The money from the yearly dog tax was turned over to the treasurer of the Sheep Fund. From this account farmers who had suffered sheep losses due to dogs were partially reimbursed. From 1875 to 1877, Loudoun farmers received sixty-four, ninety-one, and ninety-eight percent of their assessed losses.[46] The continued threat of dogs to livestock in Loudoun during the twentieth century was also reflected in the legislation enacted by the Virginia legislature in 1914 entitled "An Act to Protect Sheep and Other Stock in the County of Loudoun." Essentially this law demanded the licensing of all dogs in Loudoun and continued the practice of creating a fund from dog taxes for the remuneration of county inhabitants "for any loss they sustain from dogs killing or crippling their sheep, lambs or other stock."[47]

Livestock in Loudoun could legally roam and graze at large from the colonial era until the fence laws of 1866 and 1878. This legislation

---

[43] Ibid., July 6, 1876.

[44] Ibid., July 5, 1877.

[45] Ibid., July 1, 1875. Dogs also posed a threat to both man and animal as carriers of rabies. The November 16, 1865, issue of *The Democratic Mirror* stated that a young Negro girl recently died from hydrophobia after being bitten by a "mad dog." The paper warned all to "Be on the look out for mad dogs."

[46] Ibid., July 1, 1875; July 6, 1876; July 5, 1877. The amount paid to owners who lost sheep naturally depended upon the ratio of dogs assessed and taxes paid as compared to the number of sheep destroyed plus "all incidental expenses" of running the Sheep Fund. The Sheep Fund was $1,700.75 in 1877. After "incidental expenses" were paid, $1,549.69 was divided among the owners who had sheep killed by the fangs of canines.

[47] *Acts of the General Assembly*, 1914, pp. 389-90. Under the 1914 law, the tax rate on all male and spayed dogs was "seventy-five cents per head, and one dollar and fifty cents per head for all unspayed female dogs." All "unlicensed dogs were to be killed" by a constable or deputy sheriff. The state in 1914 also enacted legislation to protect foxes in the counties of Loudoun and Fauquier by making it illegal to shoot, trap, or poison a red or grey fox between April and September of each year (*Acts of the General Assembly*, 1914, pp. 228-29). An additional act was passed in 1916 to protect "certain fur-bearing animals in the county of Loudoun." Anyone "desiring to set traps for mink, muskrat, skunk, opossum, and raccoon in the county of Loudoun shall first procure a license from the commissioner of revenue." The fee for the license was two dollars and fifty cents. Open season for mink, muskrat and skunk was from the first day of November to the first day of March, and for hunting opossum and raccoon from the first day of October to the first of March (*Acts of the General Assembly*, 1916, pp. 26-27).

by the state legislature not only created extensive excitement among county residents but also induced the construction of numerous fences in the county during a period when a similar occurrence was taking place on a salient region of the last great American frontier, the Great Plains.[48] The 1866 law, known as "The Stock Law," emphatically favored the landowner. Owners of animals were held legally and financially liable for any depredation of another's property by their stock. Many humble folk complained that the legislation threatened to deprive them of a way of surviving. They stated they could not afford to rent pasture, which for one cow was $2 a month. Nor did they see the merit of such legislation when extensive unused grazing land existed on another's property.[49] Legislation enacted in 1878 stated that "every freeholder in the county of Loudoun be required to keep a lawful fence along the public highways, and that all partition fences in said county shall be kept in thorough

This attitude of conservation did not extend to hawks in Loudoun. In 1916 the state legislature authorized the county Board of Supervisors of Loudoun to pay a fifty-cent reward for the scalps of "gos-hawk" and "cooper's hawk" killed in the county. No reward was paid for scalps of the "sparrow hawk" (*Acts of the General Assembly*, 1916, p. 9). Other birds had been partially protected by state law since 1870's. For example, in 1878 it was illegal in Loudoun to "kill or capture or offer for sale or buy partridges between the first day of February and the first day of November." Neither was it lawful to kill pheasants between February and August, or robins between April and November. Hunting and killing wild turkeys was prohibited between February and October 15. Violation of any one of these evoked a $10 fine or imprisonment until the fine was paid (*The Democratic Mirror*, April 14, 1878). Crows and sparrows were not protected by law because of their destruction of crops. For this reason the crow was especially disliked by the farmer. A Mr. Carpenter succinctly stated the feeling of local farmers when, while attending the September 14, 1914, meeting of the Lovettsville Farmers' Club, he gave the "crow, hail Columbus," and condemned it as the "worst bird . . . we have, and deserves to be shot."

[48] Walter P. Webb, *The Great Plains* (New York: Ginn and Co., 1959), pp. 238-39. Farmers in the county not only had their crops destroyed by roaming domestic animals, but also had to contend with indomitable weeds. Members of the Lovettsville Farmers' Club in 1912 devoted a meeting to the topic: "The best way to get rid of obnoxious weeds." Most felt the "best way is persistent pulling" of undersized growth. Although this was practical for gardens, it was not feasible for large acreage of crops. Others contended that the cutting of weeds and the grazing of sheep were beneficial. One approach to combat ragweed was the "heavy sowing of orchard grass." Unlike the modern farmer, who has innumerable herbicidal sprays to control weeds, the farmer prior to World War II had to depend upon backbreaking hand weeding, the mower, and hand scythe (see the "Minutes of the Lovettsville Farmers' Club, I, 38-39).

[49] *The Democratic Mirror*, April 11, 1866; Maddex, *The Virginia Conservatives*, 1867-1879, pp.176-78. Both the 1866 and 1878 laws gave each county the right to decide whether the legislation would be in effect in the county. The 1866 law was implemented in some Loudoun districts. The law was applicable for all stock in the second, fourth, and ninth districts in the county, but the first and tenth districts were "exempted entirely" from the legislation, and in districts three, six, seven, and eight the law was "applicable to all stock except milch cows, which as heretofore" were "permitted to roam at large."

repair."⁵⁰ While this law did not remove the liability of owners of roaming stock, it did exempt them from paying damages when "trespasses" were committed by stock in fields along public highways because fences were not in proper and "lawful condition."⁵¹ A number of Loudoun landowners resented this provision. One such gentleman wrote a protest letter to *The Democratic Mirror* and signed it "TRUE FENCER." In an exaggerated claim, he protested the 1878 law:

> . . . *made of Loudoun County a common, free to the happy possessor of any needy mule, ass, horse or horned beast and that he be allowed to pasture the same on any growing grass or grain his more thrifty neighbor may possess, unless such neighbor be fenced in on every side, strong and high to the utmost limits of the law.*⁵²

This farmer also protested against the law because it posed a financial hardship upon the landowner:

> . . . *The cost of fencing is at present a serious evil, and day by day a growing one. The prodigal waste of timber a worm fence requires, must soon reckon that light and airy structure among the has been.*
>
> . . . .
> *Timber and rock are the materials most drawn upon by fencers. The former fast fades from view—the latter, when plenty, can be moved, and when placed in the right way and shape, makes a lasting and strong defense against intruders, but the time and labor required to wrest them from their firm base, and transport them to usefulness, is*

---

⁵⁰*Acts of the General Assembly*, 1878, pp. 61-62. Fences on the boundaries of farms were to be jointly repaired by conterminous landowners. If they could not agree to repair such fences, after ten days either one of them could apply to a justice of the peace in his district, who would appoint "three disinterested freeholders to be known as fence-viewers, any two of whom may " determine the extent and cost of the needed repairs and to "announce their decision in writing to" the landowners. If one of the parties "fail within the specified time to make the required repairs, then it shall be lawful for the other party to make such repairs at the cost of the party so failing." For their services the "fence-viewers," were to receive "one dollar for every day so employed, to be recovered one-half from each party."

⁵¹Ibid., p. 62. The 1878 bill was introduced in the Virginia legislature by a Loudouner in the House of Delegates, Captain John R. Carter.

⁵²*The Democratic Mirror*, April 4, 1878.

> known only to the initiate few. No legislative arm or back was ever framed to stoop and struggle with troubles such as these; and rock, though durable and abiding, when out of place becomes restive in a fence—they tumble down from [storms] and mighty Nimrods, whose stocks in trade embrace both dog and gun.[53]

During the latter 1800's and early 1900's, Loudoun farmers continued old debates as to the best practices in crop and animal husbandry, including such issues as the desirability of raising white or yellow corn, the merits of using commercial fertilizers and lime, and the advantages and disadvantages of new farm equipment.[54] Frequently an "Institute," a county-wide meeting, would be held for the purpose of discussing the techniques and problems of Loudoun agrarians.[55] Also,

---

[53]Ibid. Hunters have continued since 1878 to annoy county farmers by damaging fences while going over or through them, negligently leaving gates open that allow stock to escape, and indiscriminate shooting that occasionally wounds or kills domestic stock. By 1914, the Lovettsville Farmers' Club considered the "best fence for fields to be woven wire with a strand of barb wire on top." For barnyards the club recommended a board fence ("Minutes of the Lovettsville Farmers' Club," I, 42). Since World War II many of the old stone fences in the county have been torn down and used in the construction of homes. The most unusual method of prolonging the life of an old wire fence was advocated by R. N. Legard. He stated "that in dividing his corn field for hogging purposes he had used the stalks of corn to support the fence, tying the fence to the stalks."

[54]"Minutes of the Catoctin Farmers' Club," III, 185, 189; VI, 18; IX, 11. By the 1880's silos were being used to store ensilage, and new equipment was being introduced. However, in 1883 Colonel White of the Catoctin Club "warned" his fellow members to beware of "much useless machinery being introduced for the handling of [the] preparation of ensellage [sic]." One such machine was used to cut fodder. It was first used in the county in 1883 by a local farmer who elatedly claimed he and a boy were able to "cut 60 shocks a day." For some this machine replaced the corn-knife for cutting fodder. The corn fodder cutter was a device with two sharp blades that were pulled by a horse in between the rows of corn. Two seats were mounted on top of the blades for two men to ride and catch the corn stalks as they were cut. White had reason to be chary of this machine: if the blades were not kept sharp, if the stalks were especially thick, and the ground wet, the stalks would not be cleanly cut off several inches above the ground but pulled up by their roots and often remain on and under the blades, requiring frequent stops to clean off the debris. Three years after the corn fodder cutter was introduced into the county, a wheat binder was used. The latter required five horses to pull it. In 1896 when an article about milking machines was read to the members of the Catoctin Club, none of the members were interested in purchasing such a machine. By 1914 "Sharpless" milking machines were being used on Morven Park farm near Leesburg.

[55]Ibid., VII, 145; "Minutes of the Lovettsville Farmers' Club," I, 92. For example during 1905, a "Farmers' Institute" was held at Leesburg under the auspices of the "State Agricultural Experimental Station in Blacksburg." Nothing was done in the county to assist farm women in managing a menage until 1916. During that year the first "Home Demonstration" work was started at Lincoln under the direction of Miss Hallie Hughes.

during this period farmers formed an organization known as "corn clubs" to stimulate the interest of their sons in agriculture and "help train boys in farming."[56] During the same period, county farmers became more interested in obtaining better breeds of livestock. Massive Clydesdale and Percheron horses were by far the most popular work horses in the county.[57] Probably an accurate reflection of the sentiment of many Loudoun farmers in 1914 in regard to breeds of cattle was the rating by a Lovettsville farmer, Clinton Souder, who rated the Durham cow as "the best general purpose breed, for beef the Shorthorn, for butter and cream the Jersey," and for milk the Holstein. A neighbor of Souder's claimed, "Herfords and Holstein stood well in the Cattle World."[58] Farmers' clubs made resolutions to encourage their members and other county residents to breed "all female" domestic herbivorous animals "to pure bred sires."[59] Previously, with the exception of sheep, the only concern that Loudouners had for breeds of livestock was occasionally getting a thoroughbred stallion, usually of some racing fame, to breed one of their mares. A fast-riding horse during the nineteenth century was considered an important source of local status and prestige.[60]

[56]"Minutes of the Lovettsville Farmers' Club," I, 46-47; XI, 15. In 1913 corn clubs were organized in the county. Each boy was to be given the use of an acre of land upon which he was to raise corn. This oganization was the precursor of the "4-H Club" in Loudoun.
[57]Ibid., p. 117; "Minutes of the Catoctin Farmers' Club," III, 145; IX, 108. Many farmers during the late 1800's and early 1900's kept from ten to fifteen horses on their farms as draft and riding animals. A Friend, Isaac Hoge of the Lincoln Farmers' Club and his brother are credited with introducing the "Percheron breed of horse in the county." Isaac also was the first in the county to own a "steam thresher."
[58]"Minutes of the Lovettsville Farmers' Club," I, 44-45. In 1904 a number of Angus beef cattle were purchased from Chicago and brought to Loudoun. By 1914 farmers of Loudoun were supporting a county stock sale.
[59]Ibid., p. 117; "Minutes of the Catoctin Farmers' Club," IX, 180.
[60]*The Democratic Mirror*, March 14, 1866; *The Genius of Liberty*, April 14, 1832; *The Loudoun Times-Mirror*, May 18, 1961; Statement by Edward R. Brown, personal interview, February 4, 1973. During the 1830's, "Tecumseh" and "Industry" were extensively advertised in county newspapers and handbills. After the Civil War a thoroughbred Morgan horse near Winchester, known as "Black Hawk," was much in demand. Antebellum farmers took their mares to the owner of Tecumseh, who lived near Gum Spring in Loudoun. For stud fees and boarding a mare for a season the price was $12. For $20 Tecumseh's owner would guarantee the mare to be "in foal" before the end of the season. Fifty cents extra was charged and given to the groom. Similar provisions and fees were charged by the owner of Black Hawk: $15 "for the season" or $5 for a "Single Leap." Farmers in Loudoun raised draft horses to sell to people in Washington, D. C., to pull wagons and streetcars. Dr. Hugh Grubb, a Purcellville veterinarian, supplemented his income until the advent of the truck by going to Washington and purchasing lame horses for a very low price. He brought the animals to Loudoun, where he treated them. Later, after they were well, he took them back to D. C. and sold them for a handsome profit.

EMERGENCE OF DAIRYING

In terms of Loudoun's twentieth-century agriculture, the most significant development in the county during the nineteenth century was the meager beginning of dairy farming. The stimulus for the development of dairy farming was the large market for milk in Washington, D. C., and the rail line that connected Loudoun with the nation's capital. However, neither of these was eager to accommodate Loudoun farmers. The first dairies in the county emerged during the 1870's within a few miles of the Washington and Ohio Railroad depots in Loudoun. In the early 1870's a "Farmer and Dairyman Association" was organized at Hamilton. But the inability to obtain satisfactory service from the rail line greatly impeded the growth of dairy farming in the county.[61] During the 1880's dairy farming in Loudoun was firmly established, but only on a small scale and around rail depots. Probably the largest dairy herd in the county in the 1880's was that of Dr. Quimby. During the advent of that decade he was "milking 100 cows [and] making about 40 lbs. of butter per diem."[62] Due to continuing problems of rail service and the reluctance of "parties in Washington . . . to contract with Strangers living a distance from the City, fearing" they would not live up to the terms of the contract, many Loudoun dairymen, like Dr. Quimby, concentrated upon making butter.[63] This development, in turn, gave impetus to the formation of a creamery at Hamilton, which had a dairy herd of sixty cows, and in 1887 made "200 lbs. of butter per week put in 1/2lb. prints" that sold for forty cents a pound.[64]

---

[61] *The Democratic Mirror*, March 27, 1872; Herbert H. Harwood, Jr., *Rails to the Blue Ridge* (Falls Church, Va.: Pioneer America Society, 1969), p. 106; "Minutes of the Catoctin Farmers' Club," XI, 17.

[62] "Minutes of the Catoctin Farmers' Club," III, 87. Milking one hundred cows in the early 1800's was quite a feat considering they had to be milked by hand twice a day.

[63] Ibid., IV, March 6, 1886 (the pages of volumes IV, V and VI are not numbered.) C. C. Mercer sent milk to Washington during the 1880's but found he had great difficulty getting his milk cans returned to him so he could ship additional milk. The minutes of the Catoctin Club records that the Washington market required "31/2% butter fat in milk," but unlike many other cities refused to pay more for a higher percentage of butterfat. In 1887 a farmer, Benchler, of Leesburg traveled to Washington to "sell milk and met with great many difficulties." He was "offered 65 cts. per gal. for cream, but did not bargain." Finally "he was forced to sell his milk at 15 cts. per gal." During the latter 1800's and early 1900's, "a cream wagon would visit farms in Loudoun, twice a week and purchase cream even from the small farmer with a few cows."

[64] Ibid., February 5, 1887.

TEMPERANCE AND REVIVALISM

The history of liquor in Loudoun is similar to that which occurred in the rest of Virginia and the nation. Early settlers brought with them from England an attitude that liquor was a part of mankind's natural sustenance. Consequently it was generally maintained that liquor was a "good" and a "normal" aspect of man's existence. This view, which continued to persist into the nineteenth century, was only slowly challenged in spite of the apparent abuses and problems that resulted from the excessive consumption of "ardent spirits." The acceptance of liquor is also illustrated by the limited regulation of liquor by the government of Virginia from the colonial era to the late nineteenth century.[65]

However, state regulation of liquor prior to the twentieth century was not accepted as adequate by all citizens of the "Old Dominion." During the 1820's local temperance societies emerged in the state and throughout the nation in an attempt to address more adequately, and to alleviate, the problems of inebriation.[66] The social ills resulting from "demon rum" were identified as poverty, illness, and vice. These were maladies that not only disrupted the family unit due to drunken husbands, but also brought about instability within the community.[67] To fight against such ills and to work for sobriety, Loudoun residents organized temperance societies, such as the Sons of Temperance. Speeches and parades were extensively used in an attempt to win converts to the cause of temperance. Typical of such a display was a procession of more than 150 Sons of Temperance in Waterford in August 1849. This procession was accompanied by the "Leesburg Band" while, according to *The*

---

[65]C. C. Pearson and J. Edwin Hendricks, *Liquor and Anti-liquor in Virginia 1619-1919* (Durham, N. C.: Duke University Press, 1967), pp. 3-5, 54, 152. Price-fixing and licensing were the basic methods Virginia used in an attempt to regulate the sale of liquor, especially by ordinaries and tippling houses. (Ordinaries were inns or places where a person could sleep, eat, and drink; a tippling house [saloon] was solely a place to purchase and consume alcoholic drinks.) Like the nation, Virginia during the twentieth century turned away from regulation of liquor to the alleged panacea of prohibition. After the failure of the latter and the repeal of the Eighteenth Amendment, the state of Virginia again returned to regulation.

[66]Ibid., pp. 59, 153. Joseph R. Gusfield in *Symbolic Crusade: State Politics and the American Temperance Movement* (Urbana: University of Illinois Press, 1963) suggests that the early temperance movement was an attempt by the Federalist aristocracy, displaced from political power, to reassert control over the growing numbers of middle-class Americans (see pp. 36-57, 59-60).

[67]Pearson and Hendricks, *Liquor and Anti-liquor in Virginia, 1619-1919*, p. 143; June Sochen, *Herstory: A Woman's View of American History* (New York: Alfred Publishing Co., 1974), p. 134. Tyler, *Freedom's Ferment*, pp. 330-32. Antebellum temperance tracts often labeled liquor as the agent of the devil, which among other things brought about "Delirium tremors, Cholera, Murder, Collapse, Epilepsy, and Fever."

Loudoun Chronicle, "ladies looked charming, and put on their sweetest smiles as the band of brothers passed in review before them." This event was followed by an "eloquent and heart-stirring address" by George W. Bradfield of Snickersville." The editor of *The Loudoun Chronicle* added, "We must say that we like these public gatherings, they have a tendency to promote good feeling among the citizens of our county."[68]

However, the efforts and impact of such organizations as the Loudoun Sons of Temperance were severely curtailed and disrupted by the Civil War. The trauma of belligerency exacerbated tippling, and it was not until the 1870's that a resurgence occurred in the temperance movement.[69] During this period Lodges of the Order of Good Templars became common throughout Loudoun and elsewhere.[70] A part of this renascence was a renewed dependence upon parades and speeches. For example, on Monday, September 8, 1875, an all-day "grand Temperance demonstration," free of refractory behavior took place at Leesburg. Forty-seven Lodges of the Order of Good Templars participated in a procession that included 700 "decked out with banners and regalia" and headed by the Leesburg Band. Templars and supporters of temperance came from Washington, D. C., northern Virginia, and Maryland. Between 1,000 and 1,200 members and supporters of the Orders of Good Templars crowded on three "extra trains of the W.&O. Railroad" for the trip from Alexandria to Leesburg. After the morning parade, a crowd of between 3,000 to 4,000 "proceeded to a grove of trees a half a mile" from the town of Leesburg, where "a substantial stand for the speakers" had been previously constructed. There picnic baskets were opened, and abundant provisions spread for all present," followed by speeches until 4:00 P.M. Then the procession "reformed and again marched through the principal streets" of the town. The march was concluded at the railroad depot, where guests and city brethren departed at 6:00 P.M. for their homes outside Loudoun.[71]

After this demonstration the confidence and efforts of Loudoun temperance reformers continued to grow. To coordinate and centralize their efforts, men and women of various Templar orders held a county convention at Waterford on May 18, 1876, and formed the "Loudoun County Lodge, No. 1."[72]

[68] *The Loudoun Chronicle*, August 31, 1849.
[69] Pearson and Hendricks, *Liquor and Anti-liquor in Virginia, 1619-1919*, pp. 152-53, 160-61. Baptist, Methodists, and members of the Society of Friends in Loudoun were especially dedicated to working for temperance.
[70] *The Democratic Mirror*, May 25, 1876. A Rev. Dr. Winfield of Arkansas was one of the main speakers. According to the *Mirror*, he spoke "for nearly two hours" and treated "the large crowd of attentive listeners to one of the strongest, most interesting and effective speeches delivered in these parts for many a day."
[71] Ibid., September 9, 1875.
[72] Ibid., May 25, 1876. The constitution for the county lodge was patterned after the one used in the state of New Jersey. Among those elected to positions in the county lodge

Other examples of a renewed interest and crusade in Loudoun against liquor during the 1870's were the numerous petitions sent to the state legislature, sponsored by residents of the county. For example, the 1872-73 session of the Virginia General Assembly was asked by some Loudouners not only to enact prohibition legislation, but also to make sellers of alcoholic beverages liable for all damages resulting from drinking. During the last part of the decade residents of Loudoun, along with those in other areas of the state, petitioned for legal permission for residents within counties to determine by ballot whether the sale of liquor would be permitted within local jurisdictions.[73]

Since the crusade against strong drink was usually clad in righteousness and moral indignation against an evil that was believed to be the work of the devil, the temperance movement was closely allied with organized religion and revivalism. Of all the religious denominations in Loudoun, the Society of Friends, especially those in the Lincoln community, was the most extensively affiliated with the county's crusade against "strong drink." On May 4, 1878, the first local union of the Woman's Christian Temperance Union in Virginia was organized at Lincoln by Mrs. E. D. Stewart of Ohio, better known as "Mother Stewart."[74] From the nucleus in Lincoln a dozen unions of the W.C.T.U. grew up in other communities in Loudoun. By 1891 these organizations formed a county-wide union with headquarters at Hamilton and periodic county conventions in the hope that the coordination of their efforts would more efficiently further the cause of temperance.

Due primarily to the leadership of Quakers at Lincoln, the W.C.T.U. continued to be an active force in the county until the mid-twentieth century. By that time most of the stalwarts who had traditionally provided the leadership for the W.C.T.U. had died. Leadership provided by Lincoln Quakeresses during the late nineteenth century and first half of the twentieth century went beyond the county to that of the state and even the national organization of the W.C.T.U. Mrs. Sara H. Hoge of Lincoln, a graduate of Swarthmore College in Pennsylvania who later

---

were Thomas E. Taylor as county Templar chairman; Dr. J. W. Taylor, counselor; and Mrs. Clara Janney, vice Templar.

[73]Pearson and Hendricks, *Liquor and Anti-liquor in Virginia, 1619-1919*, p. 68.

[74]The national organization of the W.C.T.U. was formed in 1874. The Declaration of Principles adopted by this organization in 1874 reflected not only an abhorrence to drinking, but the inequality of women and the plight of labor. This document stressed "one standard of purity for both" male and female and equal rights for women and the improvement of wages, working hours of laborers, and fairer treatment of workers by the courts. While Mrs. Stewart visited Loudoun, she also organized unions at Waterford and Hamilton. Soon after Frances E. Willard was elected president of the national W.C.T.U. in 1879, she visited Loudoun to promote temperance work. In 1883 she organized the Virginia W.C.T.U. Membership in the Lincoln union increased from 7 in 1878 to 183 in 1922, 145 in 1925, 155 in 1926 and decreased during the 1930's. For example, in 1936 there were 110 members in this union; in 1940, 83; in 1944, 58; in 1955, 35; and in 1964, 25.

taught school at Lincoln, best illustrates this point. For forty years (1898-1938) Mrs. Hoge was the president of the Virginia W.C.T.U. and also served as recording secretary at national conventions of the W.C.T.U. With the support of her husband, Howard M. Hoge, Sara made their home at Lincoln not only the center of the Virginia W.C.T.U., but also a place where national officers of the organization met for conference.[75] After the death of Mrs. Hoge, Mrs. Mabel A. Taylor, also of Lincoln, became the leader of Loudoun's W.C.T.U. Mrs. Taylor was also active in the state organization, as she was circulation manager of the chief organ of the Virginia W.C.T.U., *The Virginia Call*, for nearly a half a century following World War I.[76]

The work of the W.C.T.U. was deemed by its members to be a religious crusade to uplift the standard of life of all mankind. Members wore white ribbon badges as a symbol of their dedication to a life of purity, total abstinence, and devotion to God.[77] To carry out these goals, women of the W.C.T.U. developed a comprehensive program. Membership consisted of six types: (1) regular (women), (2) White Ribbon Recruits (babies dedicated by their parents to a life of total abstinence), (3) the Loyal Temperance League (grade school age boys and girls), (4) the Youth Temperance League (high school and college age persons, (5) honorary members (sympathetic adult males, often husbands of regular members of the organization), and (6) "Rock of Ages" members (elderly citizens).[78] Numerous committees were

---

[75]Elizabeth H. Ironmonger and Pauline L. Phillips, *History of the Woman's Christian Temperance Union of Virginia and a Glimpse of Seventy-Five Years, 1883-1958* (Richmond, Va.: Cavalier Press, 1958), pp. 34, 64-70; Lincoln W.C.T.U. Minute Book, 1880-87, pp. 1-4. Minutes for 1878 to 1880 have been lost.

[76]Ibid., pp. 44, 145-47. From 1883 to 1886 Mrs. Rebecca D. Wilson of Lincoln was president of the Virginia W.C.T.U.

[77]Lincoln W.C.T.U. Minute Book, 1880-87, p. 4. The bylaws of the Lincoln Club in 1880 states, "Any member who fails to have on the white ribbon at any meeting of [the] Union shall pay to the treasurer a fine of 5¢."

[78]Ironmonger and Phillips, *History of the Woman's Christian Temperance Union of Virginia*, pp. 57, 120-21. A typical pledge taken by women in Loudoun's W.C.T.U. would read:

"That I might help to make the County of Loudoun a better place in which to live, and a safer place for our youth, I hereby wish to join the Woman's Christian Temperance Union. In order to become a member, I agree to pay $1.00 a year dues to the   Union, and hereby sign the pledge taken by all members:

"I hereby solemnly promise, God helping me, to abstain from all distilled, fermented and malt liquors, including wine, beer and cider, as a beverage, and to employ all proper means to discourage the use of and traffic in the same.

"Name

"Address

"Date"

established to work both on state and local levels. The W.C.T.U. exerted considerable effort in an attempt to influence the press and state legislation for local option which would give the voters of each county, city, or town the right to decide by ballot whether the manufacture and sale of "intoxicating liquors" would be permitted within that jurisdiction. Disadvantaged groups—especially blacks, the poor, and prisoners—were deemed to be especially vulnerable to becoming victims to the evils of drink. This attitude was reflected in the activity of the Lincoln W.C.T.U. during the early 1900's at the "county alms house" and in 1911 in the investigation of "the colored church's use of wine" for communion.[79] Also of interest is the fact that the W.C.T.U. singled out railroad employees as in need of uplift due to their alleged propensity for liquor.[80] In 1908, the Lincoln Union wrote to the management of the railroad line that ran through most of Loudoun, the Southern Railroad Company, and complained that employees of the line used "intoxicants." The company responded by stating it would investigate. The same year, in an attempt to promote further their attack on drink and sin, the Lincoln Union placed Bibles and temperance literature in the Purcellville, Round Hill, and Bluemont railroad stations.[81]

Any public gathering was looked upon as an opportunity to spread the creed of W.C.T.U. The Lincoln Union took an active role in the annual Bush Meeting by obtaining guest speakers and was given permission to establish on the meeting grounds a "W.C.T.U. Rest Room," which was "furnished with temperance tracts."[82] State and county fairs were also singled out by the W.C.T.U. as in need of greater regulation because they were centers for the drinking, gambling, and sale of "impure literature."[83]

Women were also chided for frequenting places where intoxicants were sold. A pamphlet published by the national W.C.T.U. entitled *Women and — Women*, an indictment of drinking women, was distributed to Loudoun women. Curiosity was singled out as the basic cause of women drinking. Alarmed at the number of female drinkers, the pamphlet stated that women:

> ... *have gone to the bars in such numbers they are crowding the men. Tap-room babies are a common sight in some cities; the mother is inside drinking and the baby is in its carriage or go-cart on the sidewalk. The cocktail*

---

[79] Lincoln W.C.T.U. Minute Book, 1906-13, pp. 62, 116.
[80] Ibid., pp. 40-42.
[81] Lincoln W.C.T.U. Minutes, 1906-13, pp. 25-32.
[82] Ibid., pp. 137, 142, 151.
[83] Ironmonger and Phillips, *History of the Woman's Christian Temperance Union of Virginia*, p. 57.

> *lounge had attracted many women and now there are "boozing bees." Saloon-keepers are inducing women to meet in the taverns (saloons) to knit, gossip, play bridge, and drink.*
> *We know what the result will be, Drunks! Drugs! Dregs!... Such is the course of the woman drinker....*
> *We appeal to Christian women to join our organization and work with us to make better conditions—for the protection of other women as well as the men and the youth of our country....*[84]

Inspired by such emotional and simplistic appeals, W.C.T.U. members in Loudoun and the nation devoted their greatest efforts on behalf of youth. To mobilize and mold young females on behalf of temperance, an auxiliary organization of the W.C.T.U., Young Woman's Christian Temperance Union, was formed at Lincoln and Hamilton during the late 1800's.[85] The most comprehensive campaign was carried out through the public schools. There the W.C.T.U. devoted extensive amounts of time in an attempt to forward its "Scientific Temperance Instruction."[86] This program included speaking contests, in which medals were awarded to school pupils who delivered the best speeches on temperance, and the distribution of temperance literature that stressed not only the virtue of temperance but also abstinence from other vices or vile habits, like profanity and smoking. In an attempt to obtain commitments to these ideals all students were urged to sign pledges not to drink, curse, or smoke. Those who signed such pledges became members of the Loyal Temperance League or the Youth Temperance League. Induced not so much by a sincere intent to pursue a life of abstinence as by the persistence of the leaders of the W.C.T.U. and the enticement of an

---

[84]Irene B. Taylor, *Women and — Women* (Evanston, Ill.: National W.C.T.U. Publishing House, n.d.). By 1914 the temperance forces in Loudoun, in an attempt to protect the county's youth, obtained the enactment of a state law by the Virginia legislature that prohibited the manufacture of cider in Loudoun within one mile of all public high school buildings.

[85]Their organizations were commonly referred to as "Y's." "Y's" were disbanded during the twentieth century. For example, the Hamilton Y was discontinued in 1911.

[86]Ironmonger and Phillips, *History of the Woman's Christian Temperance Union in Virginia*, p. 224. Public school authorities in Loudoun were sympathetic until the 1950's to the W.C.T.U. This sympathy was due in part that one of its stalwart members, Mrs. Carrie Emerick, was the mother of the Superintendent of Schools, who held that position from the early 1900's to the 1950's. During this period it was a common practice for the W.C.T.U. to have a reception for public school teachers at the start of each school year.

end-of-the-year school party sponsored by this organization, at which time ice cream, cake, and candy were served, many youths signed temperance pledges.[87]

Closely allied with the temperance work of the W.C.T.U. in Loudoun during the late 1800's and early 1900's were annual temperance and gospel meetings and camp meetings. All were dedicated to temperance, piety, and the reading of the Bible as requisites of Christianity and salvation. The month of August was a favorite time for temperance and gospel meetings as well as camp meetings. In 1877 a Prohibition and Evangelical Association of Loudoun County was formed.[88] From that year until the 1930's, this organization sponsored an annual prohibition and gospel meeting, better known from the start as the Bush Meeting at Purcellville.[89] During the early years the week-long affair was held under a big tent. Later the association built a wooden structure for the annual occasion.[90] The first day of this event was usually "W.C.T.U. Day," during which a program was presented for the children, including a speaking competition known as the "Gold Medal Contest." The second and third days were labeled "Prohibition Days," and the fourth, fifth, and sixth days were called "Gospel and Evangelical Days." Devotional exercises launched each day at 9:30 A.M., followed by several preaching services throughout the day conducted by a good evangelist whose eloquence and righteous indignation condemned liquor, Satan, and sin in a manner that evoked fear in the hearts of converts and entertained even nonbelievers.[91]

---

[87]Statement by Betty Brown Poland, personal interview, February 10, 1975. Bronze, silver, gold, and diamond contests were held, depending on the age of the children and the levels of competition. Participants were required to recite verbatim abstracts from temperance literature that the W.C.T.U. liberally supplied to the schools. Prior to giving the speech, copies of the materials being quoted were given to the judges. Small grade school children recited short simplistic passages like "Drinking demon rum will make you dumb. . . ." For each word forgotten or misquoted, points were deducted from the participant's score.

[88]The prohibition and Evangelical Association of Loudoun County, Virginia, *Twenty-Second Annual Temperance and Gospel Meeting* (Washington, D. C.: Norman T. Elliott, 1899), p. 1. By 1912 this association was referred to as the Purcellville Chautauqua Association and by 1917 as the Bush Meeting Association.

[89]Lincoln W.C.T.U. Minute Book, 1906-13, pp. 142, 151; *The Loudoun Times* (Leesburg, Va.), May 23, 1917. For a while the annual meeting was referred to as the Purcellville Chautauqua Convention.

[90]*The Democratic Mirror*, August 8, 1878. This structure was later used for county fairs, and today it is known as the Purcellville Skating Rink.

[91]The Prohibition and Evangelical Association of Loudoun County, Virginia, *Twenty-Second Annual Temperance and Gospel Meeting*, pp. 3-7. Although one minister was the feature speaker, several ministers participated throughout the week in the religious ceremonies.

Similar to the Bush Meetings and popular during the same time span were the annual religious retreats called camp meetings.[92] During August camp meetings were held at sites in the western regions of the county. The most popular during the 1870's were the "Round Hill Camp Meeting, Hillsborough Camp Meeting, and the Loudoun Camp Meeting."[93] The popularity of these occasions is attested to by the fact that they were attended not only by the righteous but also by ruffians and persons looking for excitement. It was not uncommon, in spite of the evangelism of numerous preachers who stressed temperance and a pristine lifestyle, for drinking, gambling, and fighting to take place in such camps. However, these problems were usually controlled by comprehensive rules that regulated camp life and law officials who policed the camps and arrested those guilty of improper conduct. Advertisements in county newspapers admonished the public that these were "religious meetings" and anyone unwilling to comply cheerfully with all rules "should stay away," including all vendors who were excluded from selling items at the camp site unless they had received permission from the organizers of the retreats.[94]

---

[92]*The Democratic Mirror*, August 19, 1875; May 10, 1877. Another organization that attempted to promote Christian ideals among residents of the county was the Young Men's Christian Association of Leesburg. The "YMC Association" had a "hall" in Leesburg, where in addition to business meetings, prayer meetings and Bible classes were held. This organization also distributed religious literature, visited the sick and poor, provided a reading room for public use with 400 volumes on historical, biographical, secular, and religious subjects. During the late spring, the Y.M.C.A. usually held a "Strawberry and Ice Cream Festival" at its "Hall," which was usually well attended. This organization also sponsored Bible classes. These had less appeal than social gatherings and were temporarily abandoned in May 1877 due to "non-attendance and scarcity of funds." To raise money, popular lectures were sponsored by the Leesburg Y.M.C.A. Speakers were brought from Richmond and outside the state. The most popular was Dr. Oscar F. Flippo of Baltimore, Maryland. His humorous and instructive lecture, "Anger or the Folly of Getting Mad," plus his most famous lecture, "Ice on the Pulpit and Who Put It There," earned him the title "Prince of Lecturers." The admission price to such lectures was twenty-five cents. Sixty-three dollars were raised in 1877 from Flippo lectures on behalf of the Leesburg Y.M.C.A. Flippo also delivered lectures in Waterford and Northfork to help raise money for churches. Although not as famous as Dr. Flippo, J. Mort Kilgour of Loudoun, a local politician, often spoke within the county as a "popular lecturer." During the 1870's the Loudoun Bible Society also struggled to promote Christian piety. To achieve this total, the organization attempted to raise money for the purchase and distribution of the "Holy Book" to Loudouners and people of the "destitute portions of the state." Raising money proved to be a difficult task because of the apathy of county residents, who not only gave little financial support but sparely attended annual meetings at the Leesburg "M.E. Church South."

[93]*The Democratic Mirror*, August 9, 1871; August 12, 1875. The Loudoun Camp Meeting was held "in the neighborhood of Bloomfield about one mile and a half from the old Seaton Camp ground." This was a Methodist camp, but non-members of this denomination were welcome.

[94]Ibid., August 9, 1871.

These restraints and the attempt to create a somber religious atmosphere kept few people away. Numerous residents of the county and elsewhere came to live in tents, usually located in a grove of trees, and to attend the nightly revival services for one week. Attendance during the weekend was especially large. Such was the case of the "Round Hill Camp Meeting" during the mid-1870's. Aided by a location only a few hundred yards from a railroad depot, 3,000 to 4,000 "threaded the avenues" of this camp during the Sabbath of August 9, 1875.[95]

The momentum of the anti-liquor movement in Loudoun during the 1870's generated by the Templars, the newly formed W.C.T.U., the popular Bush Meetings, and reinforced at camp meetings culminated in petitions from Loudouners to the state legislature for the enactment of local option. The state legislature responded favorably to this request. Voters of each magisterial district in Loudoun were granted the right to determine by ballot whether the sale of liquor was to be prohibited or permitted in their district.[96] The right to determine the legal status of liquor by local ballot was first exercised in Loudoun during the Presidential election of 1880. Although more county residents cast ballots for Presidential candidates than voted on the issue of liquor, the issue of local option intensely divided local residents. In regard to licensing and selling liquor, 2,089 residents voted for and 2,048 voted against. Local optionists—residents against the licensing and selling of liquor—won three of the six magisterial districts. Voted "dry" were Mt. Gilead, Jefferson, and Lovettsville districts, which comprised the western half of the county. Remaining "wet" were the eastern districts of Leesburg, Mercer, and Broad Run.[97]

The local option issue remained a touchy subject in county politics during the late 1800's and into the twentieth century. During this time no one made a more passionate plea for local option than a lady from Aldie in Mercer District, where local option had been defeated in the 1880 election. In an article in *The Democratic Mirror*, published in 1882 and signed "Myrtle," she stated:

> *I am a woman, and I touch not, taste not, handle not, neither have I husband or brother to fall victims to this terrible monster [liquor]; Yet for the sake of those who*

---

[95]Ibid., August 12, 1875. People came by train from Washington, D. C., Alexandria, and Leesburg.

[96]Pearson and Hendricks, *Liquor and Anti-liquor in Virginia, 1619-1919*, pp. 166-67. Even if a majority of voters within Loudoun County supported the licensing and sale of liquor, the sale of liquor was to be prohibited in each of the magisterial districts where voters were in a majority against licensing. A person who voted against licensing was called a "local optionist" or "dry." The General Assembly did not grant all counties throughout Virginia local option until the enactment of the General Local Option Act in 1886.

[97]*The Democratic Mirror*, November 11, 1880.

have, would I plead that this curse be removed from our land, and each sun that rises, sinks to rest, seeing some poor, deluded soul conquered by King Alcohol. . . .I could tell of the brave little band that joined hands in the old church at Aldie on the 7th of April, 1876, with the determination to fight the enemy to the death. Since that time, many have been our struggles, and our little army, heartsick and sore, have at times almost given up the fight, believing King Alcohol had conquered. But not so. Though the King's forces have been doubled in the past year, we are still to the front, and are fighting on with renewed strength and vigor. We are determined to dethrone this monster King; he shall not destroy the bravest and best of our land, without an effort to put him down - and the only effectual way to do this is for each son of our land, whether he be the King's subject or whether he be fighting to dethrone the King, to come forward and vote for Local Option. If you will cast your vote with us my brother, it will remove from our community this terrible plague, worse by far than the taint of leprosy. O, my brother man, you cannot look upon this matter in the light that I do; if you did, there would be no more liquor license in Virginia. Everytime I see the door of King Alcohol's palace close on a human being, I imagine I can almost hear the terrible fiat, that goes forth in the kingdom above, saying, "another soul is lost!" I know the Recording Angel drops a tear of pity, as he scans the hitherto bright record of that doomed man, and trembles, when he writes murderer by the name of the tempter that lured him in.[98]

By 1916 the forces of anti-liquor in Virginia had shifted the state from local option to statewide prohibition,[99] which added to nationwide prohibition in 1919, made opponents of "ardent spirits" rejoice in victory. Their celebration was premature and short-lived. Like the rest of the nation, Loudouners illegally obtained liquor. For example, James Brent smuggled whiskey into Leesburg until he was caught "as he stepped from" a "train bearing a dress suitcase" filled with twenty-four pints

---

[98] Ibid., February 9, 1882.

[99] Pearson and Hendricks, *Liquor and Anti-liquor in Virginia, 1619-1919*, pp. 262-63, 284, 292. In a referendum in 1914 a majority of the voters supported statewide prohibition. In 1916, the Mapp Law, as the prohibition act was known, was enacted and made Virginia a "dry" state.

of whiskey.[100] Farm sales also afforded opportunities for men to acquire liquor. On May 5, 1924, B. O. Compher of the Lovettsville Farmers' Club wrote J. V. Nichols, demanding something be done about drinking and drunks at farm sales. Compher complained that at one particular sale:

> . . . drinks were there by the dozen. I could not understand where so many were finding something to drink until I got to talking with a young fellow who had just enough on to make him feel that he was smart. I asked him where so many were finding so much to drink? He said they have barrels of it in the cellar, which I found out later, was correct, and selling it out by the glass for 10¢, open and above board. There were three Lawyers there, Connor, Martin, and Gregg, who if they would, could tell the tale. G. E. Thomas, and L. C. James were the auctioneers, they saw how things were going, and dozens of others could testify to same. There will be another sale on the adjoining farm the 17th of the month, at the home of the man who dealt out the drinks. And it is predicted that the same thing will be practiced there. As a member of the Law Enforcement League, I am not satisfied to see such things tolerated. Please act. . . .
> As I am living close to these parties, I would rather be kept in the background.[101]

As prohibition failed to stop the sale and use of liquor, Loudoun women of the W.C.T.U. and men supporters of prohibition watched with great dissatisfaction the demise of what they had worked so hard to obtain and believed to the panacea for the "drinking problem." The culmination of their disappointment took place in 1933 with the termination of prohibition in Virginia and the nation. They found little solace in Virginia's return to regulatory methods to control the sale of liquor through the establishment of the Alcoholic Beverage Control System.[102] The abolition of prohibition was denounced as regressive. As proof, the

---

[100]*The Loudoun Times*, May 23, 1917. James Brant was described in this issue as "an intermittent colored resident of Aldie and Leesburg."
[101]Letter to J. V. Nichols from B. O. Compher in Vol. II of the "Minutes of the Lovettsville Farmers' Club."
[102]Pearson and Hendricks, *Liquor and Anti-liquor in Virginia, 1619-1919*. The membership of the Lovettsville Farmers' Club voted on December 16, 1922, that prohibition was a "success."

Lincoln W.C.T.U. pointed with disdain to the opening of an A.B.C. store in Leesburg in 1935 and the rise in liquor sales at that store from $16,042.07 in 1935 to $48,598.00 in 1946.[103]

Changes in American lifestyles during the twentieth century were significant in the enervation of Victorian standards and the genesis of a moral revolution. The emergence of the United States as a world power and belligerent in World War I, the rise of "organized crime" (spawned and sustained by prohibition), the Great Depression, and the supersedure of a rural-agrarian society by a urban-industrial way of life with a more affluent middle-class weakened or destroyed old values and absolutes upon which the nineteenth-century and early twentieth-century temperance movement was founded. Since 1945, in a modern age of pragmatism and relativism, the temperance crusade for abstinence has been condemned not only as simplistic, but also as naive in an age of affluence and sophistication. Yet in spite of its overly simplistic condemnation of "King Alcohol," the temperance movement's indictment of alcoholism as a major American social problem has proved to be prophetic.

---

[103]Loose newspaper clipping in the Lincoln W.C.T.U. Account and Membership Book, 1920-39. The difference in the annual sales total in 1935 and 1946 was due not only to increased purchases and consumption by area residents, but also to the termination of the Great Depression and inflation.

Chapter 8

THE LAST DAYS OF UNCHALLENGED AGRARIANISM: 1917 TO 1945

By 1917 Loudoun was rapidly approaching the end of an age of evolutionary change and continuity. From 1790 to the First World War the county's history had been a continuum comprised of relative demographic stability and an agrarian lifestyle centered around the bicorporal community. This had been an age in which the horse was the most treasured of the domestic animals. Despite technological innovations in farm implements prior to the Civil War, they were adopted slowly by modern standards. Reform in animal and crop husbandry spanned the whole era, but so did the debates over their merits and validity. Although corn had superseded wheat after the Civil War as the county's main staple, general farming continued to be the primary way of life for most Loudouners, who often lived upon ancestral lands and often in dwellings constructed during the 1700's or early 1800's.[1] This relatively static or continous lifestyle after 1900 was facing forces that would dramatically alter agrarian life in Loudoun from 1917 to 1945.

---

[1]Solange Strong, *Old Stone Houses of Loudoun County, Virginia* ([Leesburg, Va.]: By the Author, 1950), pp. 2-10. Stone houses were constructed by German, Scotch-Irish, and Quaker settlers in Loudoun Valley. They brought with them the desire and technique to build homes like those in Pennsylvania. English settlers favored wooden structures. Log cabins, which were originally built throughout the county, were later replaced in Loudoun Valley by stone buildings. In eastern and southern regions of the county humble folk usually just built additions to original log cabins and eventually covered the logs with clapboard. The more affluent farmers built brick homes in the early 1800's with bricks usually made on their farms by their slaves.

Specialization in farming culminated in dairy farming, raising of beef cattle, and poultry. Extensive changes in lifestyles were induced by technological innovations, such as the tractor, car, truck, and electricity. Although life in Loudoun from 1917 to 1945 remained overwhelmingly rural and agrarian, these developments, coupled with two world wars and a decade of economic depression, accelerated the transformation in the mode of living during the county's last age of agricultural ascendance.

THE INTRUSION OF THE FIRST WORLD WAR AND THE AFFIRMATION OF NATIONALISM

American intervention in World War I temporarily diverted the attention of county residents from the issues of improving roads,[2] education,[3] and the desirability of prohibition.[4] It also brought about an extensive intervention of the federal government in the everyday lives of Loudouners. The war did not disrupt the strong devotion that the majority of Loudouners had for agrariansim or the Democratic party.[5] *The Loudoun Times,* which published its first issue on July 5, 1916, was a devout organ of the Democratic party.[6] Its editor and owner, H.T. Harrison, became an eloquent spokesman for Loudoun's agrarian and Democratic posture. During World War I, he staunchly defended a Loudoun Democrat and Virginia's governor, Westmoreland Davis.[7]

[2] *The Loudoun Times,* July 19, 1916; August 30, 1916; November 8, 1916.
[3] Ibid., September 27, 1916; October 4, 1916.
[4] Ibid., August 9, 1916; May 23, 1917. The Quakers of Lincoln and Purcellville were the leaders in the county's anti-liquor movement. To aid in the fruition of abstinence, they formed the Bush Meeting Association, which sponsored revival meetings linking salvation from sin with the adherence to abstinence.
[5] Statement by Mabel Rice Poland, personal interview, December 31, 1971, and February 9, 1974; *The Democratic Mirror,* October 19, 1893. Devotion to the Democratic party was reflected in the naming of children during the last decades of the nineteenth century. For example, during that period in the vicinity of Pleasant Valley one child was named James Buchanan Poland and another Cleveland B. Rice in honor of two Democratic Presidents.
[6] *The Loudoun Times,* July 5, 1916. Influenced by the intellectual climate of the Progressive era, in which big businesses were indicted as malefic corporate behemoths that dominated America's economic and political institutions, the motto of *The Loudoun Times* was "Uninfluenced by Power, Controlled by None, Devoted Solely to the People and Their Welfare."
[7] Jack T. Kirby, *Westmoreland Davis: Virginia Planter-Politician, 1859-1942* (Charlottesville: University Press of Virginia, 1968), pp. 1, 19-21, 24, 26, 34-37, 40-41. Virginius Dabney, *Virginia: The New Dominion* (4th ed.; Garden City, New York: Doubleday and Co., 1972), p. 441. Davis was well aware of his own importance due to his aristocratic parents and his wealth. He was also ambitious and competitive. As a land speculator and highly successful and sought-after corporation lawyer, he had acquired a

Although Davis could be characterized as an arrogant and recalcitrant gentleman farmer, he, nevertheless, gained the confidence of the farmers of the state because of his espousal of agrarian reform and the leadership he displayed during his eight years as the president of the Virginia State Farmers' Institute.[8] In the gubernatorial contest Davis was depicted as a farmer and his opposition as the voice of urban Richmond. The opposition press called Davis a "Demagog" and ridiculed him because he was a "farmer candidate."[9] *The Loudoun Mirror* responded by vociferously defending Davis, both as a man as a representative of the granger:

> *The Loudoun Times and the people of Loudoun County most strongly resent the fact that, any man or paper should endeavor through impertinent, unwarranted, and unjust ridicule to injure any candidate whom they unitedly endorse, and Loudoun being an agricultural county, in an agricultural state, further resents, as will every farmer in Virginia, that the farmers of the "Old Dominion," upon whose shoulders have rested her material welfare, her material progress, her past, her present and her future, who by the sweat of their brow have made her what she is to-day. . . .*[10]

considerable private fortune. But his marriage to Marguerite Grace Inman, daughter of a wealthy cotton broker, insured his social and economic prominence. In 1903 the Davises purchased Morven Park, a restored colonial plantation with a palatial home and extensive acreage on the outskirts of Leesburg. Upon coming to Virginia, Westmoreland Davis retired from legal practice and became an agrarian reformer and member of Virginia's social elite. The Davises became leaders of the Loudoun Hunt Club, and their new home became the center for the entertainment of local huntsmen. To aid him in his agrarian reform, Davis purchased in 1912, the *Southern Planter*, a farm journal that had been in existence for seventy-two years. Morven Park served as a testing station for raising crops and new methods of husbandry involving horses, poultry, and dairying. In 1907 he helped found the Virginia Dairymen's Association. His work on the Farmers' Institute led to the creation in 1914 of the Legislative Reference Bureau to provide aid to farmer-legislators who lacked legal training in writing legislative proposals. One of Davis' crowning achievements was obtaining the enactment of the Lime Bill over the determined opposition of the National Lime Manufacture Association. Many progressive farmers in Virginia wanted to use lime, but found that $4.85 per ton for kiln-burnt lime was too expensive to use when 1,500 to 2,000 pounds were recommended for each acre. What made the price so frustrating was that usable calcium limestone was found virtually throughout the western portions of the state. To solve this problem, the Lime Act established two state-owned, convict-worked limestone grinding plants that provided burnt lime to Virginia farmers for seventy-five cents a ton.

[8] *The Loudoun Mirror*, March 28, 1917.

[9] Ibid., July 4, 1917. *The Loudoun Times* concluded in an editorial "If Westmoreland Davis is a 'demagog,' then let us have more of them in public office."

[10] Ibid., September 20, 1916. During September 1916, smallpox hit Loudoun; Hughesville was quarantined. Scarlet fever was also contracted by many students who attended Leesburg High School. Misfortune also struck A. G. Adams of Bloomfield, who was killed by a bull.

The paper also defended and applauded national Democratic candidates. In the Presidential election of 1916, it stated:

> That Mr. Wilson and the Democratic Party have saved the American people from the horror, tortures and devastations of an almost world-wide war, is a fact that cannot be controverted by even the Republican Party itself and is a fact that every voter in our land, should, with a thankful prayer in his heart, remember upon election day, and with his ballot partly pay an everlasting debt of gratitude to a leader and a party, whose temperate and judicious course has saved our people and our country from those many devastating and disastrous conditions into which the nations of Europe are now seen plunged.[11]

On November 1, 1916, *The Loudoun Times* called upon county voters to cast their ballots for President Wilson, as he would insure peace and prosperity. A vote for Republican Charles E. Hughes was denounced as a move toward "probable war" and "great uncertainty." In a classic statement of portraying a political candidate in a symbolic mantle of the national interest, *The Loudoun Times* concluded a vote for Wilson was truly a patriotic act:

> Vote for peace—vote for smiles on our women's faces—vote that our boys may live out their allotted lives—vote that our daughters may never face what those of Belgium faced and suffered—vote that crepe be kept from off our doors, sorrow from our hearts and tears of mourning from our eyes — vote for peace at home and abroad — vote as your father voted, FOR MOTHER, HOME AND LOVED ONES.[12]

While claiming the re-election of the incumbent President would insure peace, *The Loudoun Times* unabashedly issued the caveat that America must prepare for war and, if need be, enforce the Monroe Doctrine and America's "rights on the sea."[13] This attitude was indicative of the growing American paranoia that Germany was looking "with longing and envious eyes upon the rapidly increasing wealth of" the United States. The German menace was inaccurately believed to have

---

[11]Ibid., August 16, 1917. This paper conceded that Wilson may have made mistakes when he first took office but that they were "being corrected as experience" taught "both Mr. Wilson and his party what is best for the American people."
[12]Ibid., November 1, 1916.
[13]Ibid., September 27, 1916; February 21, 1917; March 7, 1917.

made imminent an invasion of the United States.[14] Therefore, *The Loudoun Times* pleaded, "We must be prepared to fight for our country, our homes, our honor, and our flag." By the fall of 1916, any pretext of neutrality by most Americans was being displaced by an attitude that vilified and depicted Germany in a most unfavorable light. *The Loudoun Times* was doing its part to bring about such a shift by stressing German atrocities that could reach America:

> *Belgium has disappeared as a nation. In Poland all children under the age of seven have ceased to exist. Women of France have been stripped of their chastity and defiled and carried away to work as slaves under foreign masters. In the "East" thousands of women and children have been brutally murdered that food might be saved for an invading army.*
>
> ....
>
> *The time has come, when we, the American people, must awaken to he fact, that we are living in an atmosphere of false security. We cannot longer afford to disregard danger signals seen on every side nor ignore recent bloody history.*[15]

Loudouners responded to an intellectual diet of jingoistic and bellicose editorials and to America's entry into the war as a belligerent with a degree of unanimity and patriotism heretofore unknown in the county. Boy Scout troops planted an acre of potatoes to help the American cause. "Patriotic Sundays" were observed throughout the county in which patriotism and God became the common subjects of predicants' sermons.[16] Residents eagerly purchased Liberty Bonds and children and more humble folk made financial contributions by buying from the county's War Saving Committee "U. S. Saving Stamps" and "U. S. Thrift Stamps."[17] These purchases were stimulated by ads in

---

[14]Herbert J. Bass (ed.), *America's Entry into World War I: Submarines, Sentiment or Security?* (New York: Holt, Rinehart and Winston, 1964), pp. 1-7; Arthur S. Link, *Woodrow Wilson and the Progressive Era, 1910-1917* (New York: Harper and Row, 1963), pp. 278-81. The United States declared war on Germany April 6, 1917. From the editorial opinion of *The Loudoun Times* from 1916 to 1918, Loudouners believed that American intervention was dictated by American security, neutral rights, and a vague ideal of service to humanity. More recent historians, with a great deal of validity, refer to the above as misguided and sentimental reasons.

[15]*The Loudoun Times*, September 27, 1916.

[16]Ibid., June 16, 1917.

[17]Oscar T. Barck, Jr., and Nelson M. Blake, *Since 1900: A History of the United States in Our Times* (rev. ed.; New York: Macmillan Co., 1952), pp. 222-27. *The Loudoun Times*, January 9, 1918; May 8, 1918. By May 1918 Loudoun's allotment of Liberty Bonds was $294,600. Also by May 1918, 1,123 of Loudoun's citizens had purchased securities, which enabled the county to oversubscribe her allotment by $132,350.

county newspapers and patriotic meetings like the "Big Liberty Loan Meeting" at the Leesburg town hall in May 1918.[18] The best examples of the degree that Loudoun residents were involved in the war effort were the activities of the Local Patriotic Community League, founded in Leesburg in June 1918, and the Committee for United War Work Campaign, chaired by D. C. Sands of Middleburg. In addition to purchasing bonds, the county through the Committee for United War Work Campaign raised an additional $17,764.74 for the war effort. The largest Loudoun contributor was Governor Westmoreland Davis, who donated $1,000 to the Loudoun campaign.[19] A total of $1,236.06 was raised by pupils in the county schools. Of this amount $707.37 was donated by the "Victor Girls" and $528.69 by the "Victor Boys." Nineteen towns, centers of bicorporal communities, were assigned quotas.[20] Conscription also touched many Loudouners. By the middle of September 1918, 2,224 men in the county between eighteen and forty-five had registered in accordance with the draft law.[21] By the end of the war, 591 males from Loudoun had been inducted into military service through the county draft board.[22] The high idealism and belief in service to humanity that accompanied America's entrance into the war was also echoed in the Loudoun press in listing the names of nineteen "Loudoun Soldiers who died in the service of their country fighting for God, Country, and Humanity."[23] Patriotism was depicted not only in terms of military service, but also in the purchasing habits of county civilians. At least one local businessman attempted to combine buying and using county products with patriotism. He ran ads in *The Loudoun Times* stating it was patriotic to purchase and consume local products as it "thereby

---

[18] *The Loudoun Times*, May 1, 1918; June 9, 1918. Over 600 residents attended this meeting.

[19] Governor Davis also gave another $1,000 "through Richmond."

[20] *The Loudoun Times*, June 12, 1918; December 25, 1918. The contributions of "Victor Girls" and "Victor Boys" through their schools were counted toward the fulfillment of the nearest town's quota. The students would have contributed more, but attendance of the 2,700 pupils had been greatly "reduced on account of influenza."

[21] Ibid., September 18, 1918. Of the 2,224 men who had registered by the final months of the war, 1,755 were white, 468 were Negroes, and one was an Oriental.

[22] Ibid., December 4, 1918. On November 11, 1918, fighting terminated in World War I when Germany and the Allies signed an armistice and agreed to discuss a peace settlement based upon Wilson's Fourteen Points.

[23] Ibid., July 31, 1919. These nineteen men were Alexander P. Humphrey, Russell Beatty, Austin Bell, S. Thurbert Conklin, Nathaniel Cooper, Colonel Edward C. Fuller, Grover Cleveland Gray, Lieutenant Frank Hough, Leonard Hardy, John McQuinn, Edward Lester Nalle, Ernest Nichols, Lynnwood Payne, Captain Charles Riticor, Ashton Shoemaker, H. G. Smallwood, John E. Smith, Major B. W. Haxall, Jr.

After World War I, the family cemetery on the farm ceased to be used. Instead Loudouners interred their dead in church and commercial cemeteries.

Table 12. Report of Funds Raised for America's War Effort
in World War I under the Aegis of the
Loudoun County Committee for the
United War Work Campaign.

Town	Quota	Cash	Pledges	Total Subs.
Purcellville	$1,350.00	$1,540.27	$ 679.50	$2,219.77
Middleburg	975.00	1,206.12	347.50	1,553.62
Leesburg	2,625.00	2,415.43	1,722.75	4,138.18
Unison-Bloomfield	1,050.00	1,163.10	312.50	1,475.60
Philomont	675.00	522.85	280.50	803.35
Hamilton	975.00	1,123.90		1,123.90
Waterford	750.00	812.68	72.50	885.18
Aldie	900.00	955.67	57.50	1,013.17
Bluemont	600.00	500.25	29.00	529.25
Lovettsville	1,875.00	1,155.70	163.44	1,319.14
Round Hill	975.00	710.64	13.00	723.64
Hillsboro	900.00	515.77	10.00	525.77
Lucketts	975.00	498.67	51.00	549.67
Arcola, Waxpool, Ryan, Ashburn and Sterling	1,725.00	835.50	69.00	904.50
TOTALS	$16,350.00	$13,956.55	$3,808.19	$17,764.74

Source: The Loudoun Times, December 25, 1918.

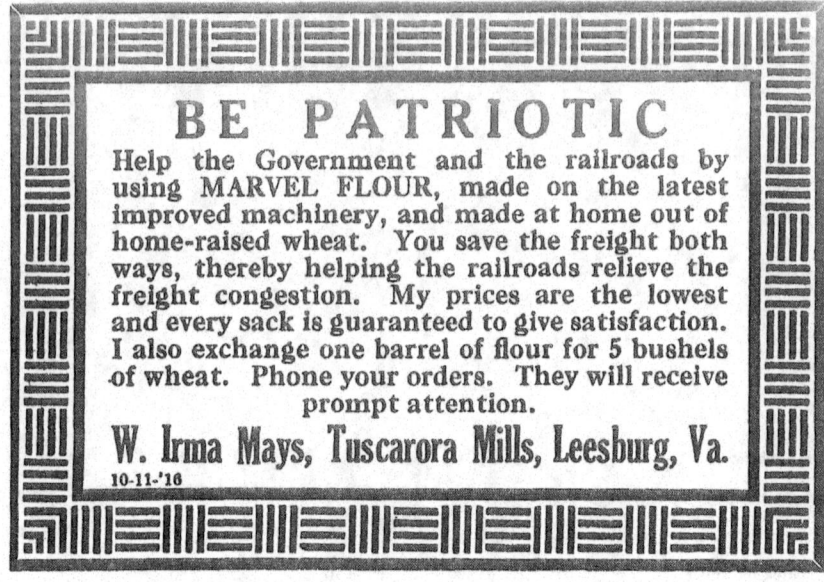

Figure 20. A Patriotic Ad that Ran in The Loudoun Times from October 11, 1916, to December 4, 1918.

relieve[d] freight congestion, and allowed the railroads to be used for the war effort."[24]

The termination of the fighting, the abdication of the Kaiser, and the "cancellation of draft calls" were celebrated by county residents in Leesburg on Monday, November 11, 1918:

> A large parade of flags on bedecked automobiles was formed east of town under the marshalage of Mr. W. Frank Garrett, and passed through town, horns were blown, b e l l s rang, whistles blew and the n o i s e of celebration was heard on every side. The parade extended over several blocks in length and was viewed by a large crowd.[25]

---

[24]Ibid. This ad was originally placed in this paper on October 11, 1916, prior to American intervention in the First World War.

[25]Ibid., November 13, 1918

This celebration of "The Rebirth of Peace" recorded by *The Loudoun Times* was, nevertheless, dwarfed by the Friday, July 25, 1919, celebration at the county seat. Arrangements were planned by "The Boys' Home Coming Celebration," chaired by H. T. Harrison. Over 7,000 people witnessed the parade to the courthouse steps of uniformed Loudoun men who had served in either the army, navy, or the marines.[26] There they heard Governor Davis give an address and present medals, "which were pinned on by the young ladies of the county." Supper, which was served "Loudoun's Fighting Sons by members of the Red Cross," was followed by "Vaudeville" staged on "the courthouse porch" by well-known professionals from New York, who danced, sang, and performed other acts. Celebrations were concluded by a concert by the Minister's Band of Washington, and finally with "Square dancing on the Court House Green and round dancing in the Town Hall until 1 A.M."[27]

The jocosity of the above celebrations was not totally representative of the tenor of the two years following the termination of World War I. Disillusionment with war and Wilsonian idealism, coupled with problems of demobilization, the recession of 1920-1922, labor strikes and violence, and the Red Scare created a milieu in which American fears of communism not only challenged but surpassed their hatred of Germany.[28] Reflecting this tenebrous situation was *The Loudoun Times*. At the end of the war an embittered H. T. Harrison editorialized that Germany was undeserving of mercy. He furthermore believed an attitude of "To Hell with Germany" was "in accordance with the laws of God" and "To Hell with Germany" was "the feeling of the American people."[29] Harrison was only slightly less critical of the League of Nations, which he labeled as a dangerous attempt "'to control the peoples of the world."[30] Disillusionment with Wilson's attempts to establish a magnanimous peace and a world organization to deter future wars, the editor of *The Loudoun Times* also indicted the federal government for its control and management of America's economic life in order to mobilize the nation for war:

> *Government control has been tried and convicted - convicted of being the greatest failure ever known. It has increased taxation both directly and indirectly and*

---

[26]Ibid., July 31, 1919.

[27]Ibid., July 17, 1919. County residents who had served in previous wars were carried in cars as part of the processional. The degree to which the memory of Confederate soldiers was venerated was reflected by the existence of the organization of Sons of Confederate Veterans. Members of this organization also were included in the parade.

[28]Barch and Blake, *Since 1900*, pp. 268-83; Robert K. Murray, *Red Scare: A Study of National Hysteria* (New York: McGraw-Hill Book Co., 1964), pp. 263-64.

[29]*The Loudoun Times*, November 20, 1918.

[30]Ibid., September 11, 1919.

> decreased service in every form. It has catered to a few at the expense of millions. It has created lustful appetites in some and endeavored to satisfy them at the expense of all. It has accomplished nothing constructive but has been proven disruptive. It is wrong in theory, wrong in principle and wrong in operation, and facts prove it.[31]

But some of the most censorious and denunciatory invective was leveled at "bolshevism."[32] In an editorial in 1919, entitled "God Save the Liberties of America," Harrison contended that communism was:

> ... the curse of Europe, a leprosy of the mind that contaminates the body; a scourage that has devastated an old world and now threatens a world of far later birth; a mad desire for what is not and for the breaking of every Commandment given by God to man, from the very first down to the tenth and last; a mad desire to write history with fingers dipped in human blood; a mad lustful yearning to make every man's property the property of all.... Bolshevism is but another name for the desecration of woman, bolshevism is but another name for brutal, cold-blooded murder; bolshevism is but another name for arson ... socialism, anarchism and rebellion, and collectively it represents the mad desire of a lust mad group to take from America her cherished liberties.[33]

On December 10, 1920, the author of the above words and the owner of *The Loudoun Times* died at the age of fifty-nine. With his passing went Loudoun's major voice from 1916 to 1920. The postwar paranoia that he engagingly reflected gradually waned after his death as Loudouners and most Americans returned to less strident rhetoric and to civilian pursuits in the illusion of returning to the "good old days" and "normalcy."[34]

---

[31]Ibid., January 22, 1919.
[32]Ibid., April 2, 1919; April 24, 1919; October 9, 1919; November 13, 1919; January 20, 1920. The violence in the American labor movement during this era caused Harrison to call for "The Death of Labor Unions."
[33]Ibid., April 2, 1919.
[34]Barck and Blake, *Since 1900*, p. 284; *The Loudoun Times*, December 16, 1920. Henry T. Harrison was born at Leesburg on April 29, 1871, to Walter J. and Nannie W. Harrison. After H. T. Harrison's death *The Loudoun Times* was edited and managed for several years by Stilson H. Hall.

THE RESTORATION OF CIVILIAN AND LOCAL PRIORITIES

By the early 1920's Loudouners again turned their primary attention to everyday mundane living and familiar local problems pertaining to taxes, schools, roads, prices of farm products, rising cost of industrial products, labor shortage, and the migration of county youths to Washington, D. C. This decade also witnessed the accelerated use of the tractor, truck, and car in the county.[35]

The general impact of World War I, in addition to the stimulation of emotionalism and activities of mobilization, also elevated the prices of Loudoun farm products to a new high. For example, a bushel of wheat increased from $1 in 1917 to $2.50 in 1919. "Fat cattle" were sold for eight and nine cents a pound in 1917 and twelve cents a pound by 1919.[36] On February 15, 1919, the Lovettsville Farmers' Club devoted their meeting to the topic: "Has the war that has just ended been a benefit to the Farmer from a financial standpoint?" L. W. Hickman declared that "at first glance it would look as though it would have been a benefit to the Farmer, but when you look at the other side" and "consider all the extra expense brought on by the war" and war mobilization, "the Farmer has not been benefited." Some members agreed with this assessment. Others stated the war had "been a benefit" to the farmer "up to the present time," but this trend was being reversed by heavy taxation and rising expenses.[37] These problems emerged due to Wilson's postwar economic policy of balancing the budget, the termination of extensive wartime deficit spending, and the return of American servicemen to the job market, all of which led to a sudden drop in prices and rise in unemployment in 1920, culminating in a severe recession in 1921. Harrison discussed the plight of the farmer in 1920 in one of his last editorials entitled "The Agricultural Crisis."[38] He not only identified

---

[35]"Minutes of the Lovettsville Farmers' Club," I, 100, 127; *The Loudoun Times*, May 1, 1918; December 4, 1918. The increase in the number of cars and trucks was a major factor in the concern in the county for road improvement during the second and third decades of the 1900's. In 1918 some farmers in the area were looking to tractors not only as a solution to labor problems but also as "an inducement to keep the boy on the farm."

[36]"Minutes of the Lovettsville Farmers' Club," I, 126-27, 146, 160-65. In June 1918, "Fat Cattle" were sold for thirteen to fifteen cents a pound.

[37]Ibid., pp. 162-63.

[38]*The Loudoun Times*, December 2, 1920. Harrison stated that the farmers needed to be "assured that they" would "be aided financially so that their crops may be marketed gradually and not en masse as victims of vastly accumulated wealth which will purchase at ruinous prices to the producer and hold for . . . prodigious profit." Apparently the farm loan association in Loudoun under the Federal Loan Act that went in effect in 1916 to provide farmers with long term rates was inadequate.

the farmers' economic maladies arising from a decline in prices of farm products, shortage of money, and inability to obtain credit, but also reminded his readers these conditions were unjust. He reaffirmed the concept of American agrarianism that had its genesis in the colonial era: "Agriculture is the basis of all prosperity and the farmer feeds the world and when crops are curtailed it is necessary that some one shall go without food."[39] By 1922, prices of Loudoun products returned to the prewar level and remained there, or slightly above the 1910 to 1914 average, until 1930.[40]

County farmers during the 1920's demanded frugality in public expenditures, a demand often in conflict with their insistence on improved schools. This conflict made the farmer at that time take an ambivalent position on public education. On the one hand, farmers wanted their sons to go to four years of high school in which "agriculture" would be "a calender subject . . . and other subjects . . . second to it;" but they were opposed to "raising the school tax." Many stated that in a situation in which either the taxes must be increased or the teachers must work for less, the latter was definitely preferable.[41] In 1922, Lovettsville farmers suggested there were too "many teachers for the number of Scholars." They considered "one big leak" of county funds was due to the $930 salary paid to the Superintendent of Schools," which they advocated cutting in half. They also said having a county nurse was an extra and needless expense.[42] The "unnecessary money" that "had been spent in contracts made by the Road Board" and the "excessive Salaries of the officers of the County" were also of concern to them. The communities of Loudoun were canvassed to find candidates for county office who would "work for less pay."[43]

---

[39]Ibid.; Adrienne Kock, *The Philosophy of Thomas Jefferson* (Chicago: Quadrangle Books, 1964), p. 22; Richard Hofstadter, *The Age of Reform: From Bryan to F.D.R.* (New York: Vintage Books, 1955), pp. 23-39, 121-22. Hofstadter referred to the view of agriculture as the basis of American wealth and greatness as the "agrarian myth" that diminished in Vaidity as American approached modernity.

[40]"Minutes of the Lovettsville Farmers' Club," I, 5, 6, 18, 44-45, 86-87, II, 151, 157, 161, 169, 179, 197, 209, 228, 234, 255.

[41]Ibid., I, 108; II, 206. There were 353 fewer pupils in Loudoun schools in 1920 than in 1915.

[42]Ibid., II, 160. In response to a request for financial assistance in 1916 by the president of the county nurse fund to help pay the salary of nurse McCulley, the Lovettsville Club overwhelmingly voted no. However, in 1929, the Lovettsville Club sent a letter to the Board of Supervisors urging them to appropriate money to support "Home Demonstration work in the county."

[43]Ibid., pp. 151, 166, 181. The Lovettsville Club was disturbed to find that the county supervisors could not reduce salaries of county officials because they were set by the state legislature. During the 1920's the highest paid official in Loudoun was the county treasurer. His wages were based upon county and state taxes and could be as much as $6,000. The sheriff's and commonwealth attorney's salaries were $800. The county clerk's salary was $800 plus fees, which amounted to a total annual salary of under $4,000. Probation officers

Despite lamentations about their problems, most Loudoun farmers lived a comparatively good life during the decade of the 1920's. For example, Loudoun in 1922 ranked first in the state in total corn production, with 1,944,000 bushels, and first in average yield of corn per acre during the same year, with forty-two bushels of corn per acre. Loudoun ranked third in Virginia in total wheat production, with 582,000 bushels in 1922, and thirteenth in yield of wheat in bushels per acre, with fourteen.[44] In hog production, Loudoun was sixth in 1922, with 20,500 swine.[45] Loudoun ranked seventeenth in the value of cars, trucks, and motorcycles in 1924, the number of such conveyances having increased from 1,244 in 1920 to 2,134 in 1924.[46] The advent of such vehicles led to a decrease in the number of horses, from 11,157 horses in the county in 1910 to 9,885 in 1920.[47] However, the most drastic decrease was in sheep. In 1910 there were 31,180 sheep in Loudoun as compared to 11,003 in 1920, a decrease of 20,177 head or sixty-six percent in ten years. Rising land prices, use of extensive grazing land for more intensive farming, growth of dairying, and raising beef cattle were responsible for the reduction in the number of sheep.

By the 1920's dairying had emerged as one of the "chief industries in Loudoun County." In 1920 Loudoun ranked fourth in Virginia in total value of dairy products, with $909,253, and eighth in the state in the number of cows, with 10,100.[48] The growth of dairying led to the formation of organizations to assist this industry. Prior to the First World War, "The Loudoun Valley Cow-Testing Association" was formed. Members of this association in 1920 had sixteen herds that totaled 531

received $1,200, the Leesburg jailer $500, and deputy sheriffs from $300 to $400; superintendent of the poor $600, each of the six overseers of the poor $40; and the prohibition inspector $300. Members of the Board of Supervisors received $6 a day, plus a small fee for the expense of traveling to meetings.

[44]Warwick County ranked first in the state in 1922 with an average yield of twenty bushels of wheat per acre.

[45]Deck and Heaton, *An Economic and Social Survey of Loudoun*, pp. 91-93. In 1920 Loudoun was eleventh in the total tons of hay, with 22,750. The county ranked fifteenth in the total number of bushels of orchard fruit harvested in 1920, with 180,895 bushels. Of this number 153,005 bushels were apples; 24,002 bushels, peaches; 2,630 bushels, pears; 632 bushels, plums; and 626 bushels, cherries. During the 1920's the United States Bureau of Agriculture estimated that forty-eight pounds of butter were consumed by each person in Loudoun in a year. However, the county produced only two-thirds of this amount, the rest having to be imported. There also existed what Deck and Heaton called a "deficit" in poultry production in Loudoun. Each person in the county consumed twelve fowls a year. Loudoun produced only three-fourths of the fowl needed for residents.

[46]Ibid., p. 54.

[47]Ibid., p. 87

[48]Ibid., p. 88. Loudoun farmers in the 1920's usually purchased cattle in the fall and winter and sold them the next summer or fall after fattening them on grass and grain raised on the farm. The number of hogs raised in Loudoun also increased considerably from 1910 to 1920.

13. The 1925 Farm Census for Loudoun County by the Department of Commerce.

	Jan. 1, 1925	Jan. 1, 1920
...ed by: White farmers	2,035	1,962
Colored farmers	1,868	1,841
Owners	167	121
Managers	1,498	1,377
Tenants	72	78
	465	507
...d in farms	281,651	305,906
...and, 1924	94,761	...
...vested	86,140	...
...p failure	818	...
...ow or idle	7,803	...
...e, 1924	143,750	...
...vable	109,958	...
...odland	7,734	...
...er	26,058	...
...and not pastured	35,530	...
...her land	7,610	...
...and buildings	$20,984,533	$26,642,195
...d alone	11,941,453	18,128,325
...dings	9,043,080	8,513,870

8,357	9,885
228	223
26,334	28,371
2,751	1,189
10,650	14,600
8,389	8,242
4,544	4,340
15,597	23,084
2,325	3,041

1924			1919		
Acres	Crop		Acres	Crop	
28,743	955,694	bu.	41,601	1,651,903	bu.
793	17,073	bu.	563	9,846	bu.
29,593	387,825	bu.	45,846	573,165	bu.
1,168	12,274	bu.	1,858	17,069	bu.
22,171	26,708	tons	17,597	19,731	tons
	44,736			40,709	
	113,507			91,659	
	172,616			153,005	

months old and over.

cows.[49] By 1920 the leading dairy breeds in Loudoun were the Guernsey, Jersey, and Holstein-Friesian. To promote better breeds of livestock, the Loudoun County Breeders' Association was established prior to 1916. Included in its work was backing the sale of registered stock like the Guernsey sale it sponsored at Purcellville in April 1917.[50] Cooperatives have generally not been successful over the long haul in Loudoun.[51] The most successful exception has been the Maryland-Virginia Milk Producers' Association formed in 1920 for the cooperative marketing of milk produced in the Washington area. This organization eliminated dairymen having to compete with one another over prices and presented a united front, which distributors had to recognize and had to come to terms with.[52] In 1910 the position of agriculture extension agent was established in Loudoun to assist all county farmers in an advisory and service capacity. Thirteen years after this position was established, home demonstration work was organized to offer assistance to Loudoun homemakers.[53]

[49]Ibid., pp. 88-90; 106-107; telephone interview with Edward R. Brown, Purcellville, Virginia, February 16, 1974. The Loudoun Valley Cow-Testing Association helped dairymen to cull out cows that produced milk low in butter-fat. To warrant the top price, milk had to have a certain percentage of butter-fat.

[50]*The Loudoun Times*, November 8, 1916; April 18, 1917. The average price paid for young heifers and bulls at this sale was $298. The top price of $530 was paid "for one of the best young heifers ever seen in Loudoun." In 1916 frequent stock sales were held at Purcellville by the Purcellville Stock Sales Company. This company specialized in selling horses. For any horse sold for $50 or less, the commission to the company was $2.50. If the animal was sold for over $50 the commission was $5. A fee of fifty cents was charged for horses not sold. Halters, sandwiches, and coffee were free.

[51]"Minutes of the Lovettsville Farmers' Club," II, 171. In the 1920's most of Loudoun's farm products were purchased by local buyers, who combined and graded the items and shipped them to market. These buyers usually went from farm to farm buying up eggs, butter, vegetables, livestock, and crops.

[52]Deck and Heaton, *An Economic and Social Survey of Loudoun*, pp. 97, 111-13. The Breeders' Association also sponsored the annual county fair which traditionally had been held at Leesburg, but was moved to Purcellville in 1918.

[53]Ibid., pp. 108-10. In 1910 the first farm extension work in Loudoun was financed by the General Education Board of New York City in cooperation with Westmoreland Davis of Leesburg. Later, Lincoln High School aided in the project by employing the county agent part of the time as an instructor. From 1916 into the 1920's the county Board of Supervisors appropriated funds to enable the continuation of extension work in Loudoun. Later the extension service came under U. S. Department of Agriculture and land grant college, Virginia Polytechnic Institute at Blacksburg, Virginia. The first county agent was H. M. Hoge who was succeeded by E.M. Hunter in 1914. On August 1, 1920, J. Ross Linter, perhaps the most respected of all Loudoun's county agents, replaced Hunter and remained on the job until the 1940's. Home demonstration work was organized in cooperation with the Loudoun County Health Association. Miss Grace Heyl was the first county home demonstration agent in Loudoun. By 1924, there were five home demonstration clubs in the county: Round Hill, Hillsboro, Aldie, Leithton, and Mt. Gilead. Closely allied to this seem to have been the early 4-H clubs in the county which apparently were originally for girls who engaged in cooking, canning, making bread, gardening, and clothing.

In some respects the decade of the 1920's represented a high point in the bicorporal community in Virginia. Throughout the state there existed 1,675 community leagues. In the early 1920's Loudoun had the greatest number of leagues of any county in the state, with sixty-three organizations and combined membership of 1,751. The local community leagues were dedicated to the promotion of "a spirit of cooperation" among the people of each community to work for better schools, health, roads, agriculture, improved "moral and civic conditions," and "better social and recreational conditions." The community around Lincoln had one of the most active leagues in the county. At Lincoln High School, members of the league erected a new shop for wood and iron work "costing $1000, improved the water system, installed" electric power and lights and made other improvements in the school with the $1,109.01 the league had raised. Like the Lincoln league, others in the county also concentrated their efforts on improving school facilities.[54]

The small and modest size farm still remained the dominant economic unit in the county. Industry in the county remained primarily limited to grain, milling, and lime companies.[55] One exception was the Loudoun Light and Power Company organized in 1912, which revolutionized living in the towns of Purcellville, Hamilton, and Round Hill. In addition to providing "electric current for those towns," the Loudoun Light and Power Company produced "artificial ice."[56]

The continuing acendancy of the medium sized farm in Loudoun is evidenced by the fact that of the 1,962 farms in the county in 1920, 1,336 contained fewer than 175 acres.[57] Of the 1,962 farms, 507, or 25.8 percent, were operated by tenants. Of the 507, share tenants operated

[54]Ibid., pp. 79-80. The Lincoln community league also constructed a booth and screen for the "installment of a moving picture machine," bought a set of maps for teaching, a victrola and records, books, equipment for the playground, and refined the fence in front of the school, and improved the school's driveway.

[55]Ibid., pp. 46-49. In 1920's there were two kilns in Loudoun. The Leesburg Lime Company was formed in 1910; its quarry was opened in 1888. It employed twenty people. The Goose Creek Lime Company began by burning lime but by 1920 made pulverized lime. It had between five to fifteen employees. The Round Hill Milling Company started in the late 1800's and with six to eight employees manufactured flour and its by-products, bran and middlings, corn meal, and cracked flour. The Aldie Mills with a smaller labor force provided the same products. W. S. Jenkins Grain Company, though incorporated in 1914, had been in business since 1889; it had its main mill at Leesburg and elevators at Hamilton and Ashburn. C. C. Saffer and Brother was formed in 1910. It ground grain and sold seed, feed, and farm equipment. The Norris Brothers Planing Mill was established in Leesburg prior to the Civil War. During the 1920's it employed six to eight workmen, who made sashes, doors, blinds, and other wood items.

[56]Ibid., pp. 48-49. Until a transmission line was constructed to another plant in 1921, two steam-driven electric plants were located in Loudoun. Leesburg also had electricity during the early 1900's. In 1927 the first electric traffic signals were installed in the county at a crossroads in the town of Leesburg.

[57]Deck and Heaton, *An Economic and Social Survey of Loudoun*, p. 83.

...cal Survey of Industries in Loudoun from 1860 to 1920.

	Amount of Payroll	Annual Value of Product	Value Added by Manufacture	Capital Stock
	$70,889	$750,178	$179,577	$274,786
	38,132	485,054	153,629	264,359
	45,737	433,140	137,440	265,425
	63,674	378,255	132,490	260,967
	52,204	638,136	204,787	351,257
	--	--	--	--
	87,553	633,419	208,417	(No Report)

...aton, *An Economic and Social Survey of Loudoun*, p. 46.
...orts gave no information by counties.

Table 15. Classification of Farms in Loudoun County
According to Size.

	1920	1910
Under 3 acres	18	3
3 to 9 acres	183	347
10 to 19 acres	172	227
20 to 49 acres	265	259
50 to 99 acres	261	274
100 to 174 acres	417	377
175 to 259 acres	292	304
260 to 499 acres	269	266
500 to 999 acres	71	72
1,000 acres and over	14	15

Source: Deck and Heaton, *An Economic and Social Survey of Loudoun*, p. 83.

336.[58] Deck and Heaton held the share tenants in higher regard than the tenant who rented the land "for a cash consideration." The share tenant, they say:

> *. . . will take better care of the land. . . . In most cases, the cash tenant is trying to get all he can out of the soil at the least cost. When he has succeeded in extracting everything from the soil until its natural fertility is used up, he moves to another place and continues the process of wearing out farms.*[59]

Of the farms in Loudoun in 1920 only 4.6 percent were owned by Negroes.[60]

[58] Ibid., pp. 86-87. In 1900 there were 593 farms in Loudoun operated by tenants and in 1910, 538. These figures indicate that tenancy in the county after 1900 was declining. Tenancy, along with sharecropping, evolved during the reconstruction era due to the shortage of cash. The crop was divided in shares of one-fourth to one-third. One share, or one-third of the crop, went to the owner of the land, another share went to those who furnished tools, seed, mules or horses; and the final share, to the laborers. During reconstruction blacks had nothing but their labor so they became sharecroppers working for one-fourth to one-third of the crop. Share tenants, on the other hand, were usually white and rented the land for a percentage of the yield of a crop.
[59] Ibid., p. 86.
[60] Ibid., p. 59.

THE TRAUMA OF THE GREAT DEPRESSION
AND
THE IMPACT OF BIG GOVERNMENT

While the crash of the stock market that began with "Black Thursday" on October 24, 1929, was not pleasant news to Loudouners, it was not deemed calamitous. New York City and Wall Street seemed relatively remote and unrelated to Loudoun's agrarian life. Like the rest of the nation residents were unaware this was the start of a decade of depression and economic malaise. Although Loudoun farmers grumbled about the decline in corn and wheat prices from 1928 to 1930, their major concern and fear were a drought that struck the county and the nation in 1930 with unparalleled severity.[61] Precipitation was unusually light from the summer of 1929 to the spring of 1930. When spring rains failed to materialize during April and May of 1930, Loudoun crops by June were endangered. During July extensive heat waves continued which saw the "thermometer regularly registering from 100 to 105 degrees in the shade" and "as high as 130 in the sun."[62] From the first of May to the middle of November, Loudoun received about one-fifth or less of its average rainfall for that period. According to J. R. Lintner, Loudoun's county agent at that time, the county was reduced to "a barren waste, such as had not been seen since the drought years of 1816 and 1817." The county lost ninety-nine percent of its corn crop and harvested only one-fourth of the traditional amount of hay. The "pasture failures in July and August" and lack of feed "forced many county cattle farmers to sacrifice in Baltimore." Lintner stated that a "conservative estimate of all crop losses, including apples, gardens, and new grass seedings" in Loudoun, "amounted to the impressive sum of $3,250,000.[63]

Economic and administrative theory in 1929 and 1930 dictated that relief from depressions and other disasters must not come from the federal

---

[61]"A Bad Year," *The Agricultural Situation*, XIV (October, 1930), 1. The price of Loudoun corn dropped from $1.55 a bushel in 1928 to $.98 in 1930; wheat prices declined from $1.20 to $.85 a bushel during the same period.

[62]J. R. Lintner, "The Great Drought of 1930," an essay by Loudoun's county agent attached to page 225, volume II of the Lovettsville Farmers' Club Minutes. The thermometer reading would seem to be exaggerated but it is based upon the words of Lintner, a knowledgeable man with integrity, not given to making mendacious statements. Lintner prepared a account of the depression at the request of the Lovettsville Farmers' Club so "that posterity should be forewarned of a possible reoccurrence." Lintner also attended numerous meetings of the Lovettsville Club. In 1945, the farmers clubs of Loudoun collectively presented Lintner with a $500 war bond at a dinner honoring his twenty-five years of service to the farmers of Loudoun.

[63]Ibid. Wells and springs went dry in Loudoun during 1930. Approximately four thousand steers were sold from Loudoun during the month of August. Corn often grew no taller than two feet.

government, but from the states and localities. Therefore, the main relief for Loudoun grangers was provided by the Virginia Department of Agriculture, which commissioned a cooperative known as the Virginia Seed Service to go to Nebraska and "purchase hay in a large way." Railroad companies also responded to the farmers' plight by charging only one-half of their normal rates for carrying water, feed, and hay into drought-stricken areas. Four hundred and fifty railroad cars of "feeds and hay" were shipped to Loudoun in 1930 at a freight saving of approximately $35,000. Drought relief councils were formed on the county level in twenty-three states to advise farmers what they could "do to help themselves."[64] The Loudoun County Drought Relief Council prepared and published a pamphlet entitled *Self-Help: Drought Relief Suggestions for Farmers*. Extensive advice was provided on both crop and animal husbandry, including how to economize on the use of feeds, how to keep the best ears of old corn for seed corn for the following season, and to cull and sell inferior producing cows and pullets. Due to the shortage of hay and other feeds for cows and horses, the pamphlet also urged Loudoun farmers to use molasses as a feed by mixing "one part molasses to three or four parts water and sprinkle the material, or better, mix with cut straw." Farmers were also warned of the "disease menace" following a long drought due to "accumulated filth from farm premises and decaying vegetation" seeping into farm water supply sources when rains finally came. It was recommended that family "drinking water . . . be boiled for some time after heavy rains." The final caveat was that a lesson should be learned from Loudoun's experience with the drought: farmers should "endeavor to carry over at least small surpluses of forage and feed grains until a new crop is assured."[65]

Unfortunately the drought of 1930 coincided with the start of the Great Depression. This development no doubt exacerbated and accelerated the debilitation of Loudoun's economic well-being.[66] One aspect was reflected in the sale of property for delinquent real estate taxes for 1931. Four hundred and fifteen separate pieces of real estate, amounting to thousands of acres of land, were advertised in the December 8, 1932, issue of *The Loudoun Times-Mirror* to be "sold at public auction on the first Monday in January 1933, between the hours of 12 P.M. and 4 P.M., in front of the Court House, unless the amount for which said lands" were "delinquent, together with interest costs, and charges" had been previously paid to the treasurer. Some of the back taxes were on property that had sizeable acreage, such as Catherine E. De Kay's

[64]Ibid. Over 7,500 railroad cars of feeds and hay were shipped to Virginia in 1930.
[65]Loudoun County Drought Relief Council, *Self-Help: Drought Relief Suggestions for Farmers* (n.p.: n.n., n.d.), pp. [1-4].
[66]Walter T. K. Nugent, *Modern America*, (Boston: Houghton Mifflin Co., 1973) p. 201.

605 acres, upon which she owed $225.18 in taxes. Others were for small sums on town lots or a few acres. For example, Amos Jenkins owed $1.56 on one-half a acre of ground.[67] Due to the depression the number of farms operated in Loudoun was reduced from 2,107 in 1930 to 1,645 in 1935.[68]

The policy of the Hoover administration to combat the depression through "voluntary cooperation" and "self-help" was received coolly by Loudoun farmers, who correctly proclaimed it would not help them. The Federal Farm Board was created in 1929 to make loans available to cooperative marketing associations owned and managed by farmers.[69] In the October 26, 1929, meeting of the Lovettsville Farmers' Club the discussion topic was "What can the Federal Farm Board do to best help the Farmer?" The consensus was succinctly stated as "a case of help yourself, if you expect to be helped," because the unorganized farmer would not be assisted by the Federal Farm Board.[70] By March 7, 1931, twenty-six Loudoun farmers had applied to the Federal Farm Board for loans. At that time, seven had been approved for sums averaging just slightly more than $300.[71] The Federal Farm Board request that farmers voluntarily reduce their acreage by thirty percent fell upon deaf ears in Loudoun and elsewhere.[72] By the first of 1932, Loudoun farmers optimistically believed that "times" would "soon improve" and no reduction in livestock and grain was justified.[73] This view occurred at

---

[67] *The Loudoun Times-Mirror* (Leesburg, Virginia), December 8, 1932. *(The Loudoun Times-Mirror* is hereafter referred to as the *Times-Mirror.)* A few of the pieces of property were owned by the same owner. Of the 415 pieces of real estate upon which taxes had not been paid, eighty-three pieces, usually a few acres or town lots, belonged to Negro residents. One black resident, John Ratcliffe, owned two tracts. One was 232 acres and the other, sixty acres. Back taxes on both came to $50.49.

[68] U. S. Bureau of the Census, *United States Census of Agriculture: 1935, Virginia* (Washington, D. C.: Government Printing Office, 1936), pp. 10-11.

[69] "Minutes of the Lovettsville Farmers' Club," II, 241, 248.

[70] Ibid., p. 241; Barck and Blake, *Since 1900*, pp. 439-443. The Federal Farm Board was created by the Agricultural Marketing Act of 1929. The Board was also authorized, if drastic measures were necessary, to establish stabilization corporations to purchase and take surplus farm produce off the market in an attempt to stabilize farm prices. Also in an attempt to help farmers, the Hawley-Smott Tariff of 1930 was enacted that raised tariff rates on farm products from the twenty percent stated in the Fordney-McCumber Tariff of 1922 to thirty-three percent.

[71] "Minutes of the Lovettsville Farmers' Club," II, 118. During the spring of 1931, the average wages for farm laborers in Loudoun were $1 to $2 per day. In the fall of 1934 an average wage of $20 per month "plus house, fire wood, meat, meal, flour, and a cow" was considered "fair for the average hand."

[72] "Minutes of the Catoctin Farmers' Club," XI, 245.

[73] "Minutes of the Lovettsville Farmers' Club," III, February 20, 1932 (pages are not numbered in Volume IV).

the start of 1931, a year that would see Loudoun's farm prices reach their lowest level.[74]

A Democratic county like Loudoun that had cast 1,915 votes for Alfred E. Smith to 1,325 for Herbert Hoover in 1928 found it easy to vote overwhelmingly for Franklin D. Roosevelt in 1932.[75] The new Democratic standard-bearer received 2,439 Loudoun votes compared to Hoover's 685.[76] When F.D.R. assumed the duties of the Presidency in March 1933, many Loudoun farmers agreed they could no longer "hold their own under present conditions."[77] They looked for tax relief and concurred with the county policy of cutting back the salaries of teachers and county officials.[78] They also agreed to "cooperate with the Government in its new plan of farm relief" as set forth in the Agricultural Adjustment Act, which included payments to farmers agreeing to limit and cut back their agricultural production.[79]

Approximately 240, or about one-eighth of Loudoun's farmers, signed contracts under the 1934 Corn-Hog Production Adjustment Program agreeing to cut production in return for payments based on "parity."[80] W. H. Frazier of Lovettsville chaired the three-man county Allotment Committee that supervised the county's participation in this program. Each of the five magisterial districts in Loudoun also had a committee of three to coordinate the program in each district. Acreage cultivated for corn was substantially reduced by Loudoun farmers who participated in the program. In 1933, these same farmers raised 7,289

---

[74]Ibid., II, September 19, 1931 (loose minutes in Volume II with no page number). In June 1832, wheat was sold for forty-five cents a bushel and corn for thirty-three cents a bushel.

[75]*Times-Mirror*, November 8, 1928. The county school tax was eighty cents on "the 100 of assessed" property.

[76]Ibid., November 10, 1932. The Socialist Presidential candidate, Norman Thomas, received ten votes in Loudoun and the Prohibitionist candidate eleven. There were eighty-seven fewer ballots cast in 1932 than in 1928.

[77]"Minutes of the Lovettsville Farmers' Club," III, March 18, 1933.

[78]Ibid., April 16, 1932; April 15, 1933; April 21, 1934.

[79]Ibid., III, July 24, 1933; September 16, 1933; November 18, 1933; William E. Leuchtenburg, *Franklin D. Roosevelt and the New Deal, 1932-1940* (New York: Harper and Row, 1963), pp. 48-52; Dexter Perkins, *The New Age of Franklin Roosevelt, 1932-45* (Chicago: University of Chicago Press, 1957), pp. 18-20. The Agricultural Adjustment Administration obtained funds to pay farmers to restrict production from a processing tax levied on certain farm products. The Supreme Court declared the A.A.A. unconstitutional in 1936 on the grounds the processing tax was an improper use of taxing powers. The A.A.A. had attempted to restore farmers' purchasing power to parity with the period of 1909-1914. This complex formula was to provide farmers with payments for the produce based upon agricultural prices during the pre-World War I era.

[80]Arthur M. Schlesinger, Jr., *The Coming of the New Deal* (Boston: Houghton Mifflin Co., 1959), pp. 62-67; Milton H. Spencer, *Contemporary Economics* (New York: Worth Publishers, 1971), pp. 529-30; *Times-Mirror*, May 24, 1934. Corn and hogs were connected since most corn in the United States was used to feed hogs being raised for market.

acres of corn, compared to only 1,704 acres in 1934.[81] The heart of the "First New Deal" was the A.A.A. and N.R.A.[82] When both were declared unconstitutional by the Supreme Court, formation of a successor to the A.A.A. was needed to continue the approach of the federal government getting money directly in the hands of the farmer and cutting farm production so as hopefully to reduce surplus crops which were depressing farm prices. In 1936 the Soil Conservation and Domestic Allotment Act authorized the federal government to make payments to farmers who used farm techniques that maintained and restored the fertility of the soil and helped curtail erosion. Loudoun farmers received $11 an acre for not raising the soil-depleting crops of corn and wheat and were paid an additional $10 if they planted fewer than ten acres of soil-conserving leguminous crops like alfalfa. An additional dollar per acre was paid to farmers who practiced such crop husbandry exceeding ten acres. Additional funds for Loudoun farmers were obtained under the second A.A.A. created by the Agricultural Adjustment Act of 1938. This agency was similar to the first A.A.A., except in its emphasis upon conservation and in the fact it was not financed by a processing tax.[83]

Despite hard times, Loudoun farmers were unwilling to give up their right to reject federal programs and restrictions upon production. For example, the Lovettsville Club went on record in 1938 as opposing "compulsory wheat control."[84] Farmers scorned New Deal measures, such

---

[81] *Times-Mirror*, May 24, 1934. Loudoun farmers had more acreage in corn in 1932 than in 1933. For example Philip J. Coleman had a 700-acre farm upon which he raised 120 acres of corn in 1932, seventy-five acres in 1933 and, when he joined Corn-Hog Association in 1934, he cultivated only twenty-one acres of corn. Coleman raised 132 hogs for market in both 1932 and 1933. More typical was a 145-acre farm owned by Robert L. Ashby. In 1932, twenty acres of corn were raised on this farm as compared to eighteen the following year. After he joined the Hog-Corn program, only four acres of corn were raised in 1934. In 1932 Ashby raised forty-eight hogs for market, compared to thirty-five in 1933.

[82] The National Industrial Recovery Act (N.I.R.A.) of 1933 established the National Recovery Administration (N.R.A.) to supervise a program of industrial self-regulation by empowering business to draw up fair competition codes. *The Loudoun Times-Mirror* proudly displayed the emblem of the N.R.A. with the slogan "We Do Our Part" on the front page until the Supreme Court declared the N.I.R.A. unconstitutional in 1935. The N.I.R.A. also created the Public Works Administration (P.W.A.) to provide jobs for the unemployed by hiring those out of work to work on projects like the construction of roads and buildings.

[83] Barck and Blake, *Since 1900*, pp. 534-36; *Times-Mirror*, April 30, 1936. The second A.A.A. continued to set quotas for certain crops and established the Commodity Credit Corporation to lend money to farmers for surplus crops and store the crops until prices went up (ever-normal granary concept) in an attempt to establish the farmers' purchasing power at the 1909 to 1919 level (parity-price principle). This act also set up the Federal Crop Insurance Corporation (F.C.I.C.) to insure crops. Farmers who kept within their acreage allotments and followed soil-conserving practices qualified for benefit payments.

[84] "Minutes of the Lovettsville Farmers' Club," IV, June 11, 1938.

as the C.W.A. and N.R.A., because they did not "think the farmer" had "been benefited by the operation of either."[85] Most Loudouners, but not all, continued to support F.D.R. Lovettsville farmers became embittered at the intrusion of "Big Government" into their everyday living. At one of their meetings they attempted to discuss the topic of "How long shall we as good citizens of the United States submit ourselves to dictation of someone who is tearing down the constitution?"[86]

The major concern of the county Board of Supervisors during the 1930's was the care of the indigent, which was the largest "single item of cost to the taxpayers of Loudoun."[87] The care of the needy in a rural county could not be partially met by the soup lines as in more densely populated areas. Local assistance was provided in part by the Tally-ho Theater in Leesburg, which accepted as admission at Friday matinees food, clothing, and toys to be given to Loudoun's indigent.[88] Prior to Christmas in 1932, the nadir of the depression, headlines in the *Times-Mirror* stated, "Food Pressing Need of Poor in Loudoun as Christmas Nears" and "Plight of Destitute Families Is Loudoun's Foremost Thought as Zero Weather Grips Entire County." The *Times-Mirror* praised not only the work during the 1930's of the Tally-ho Theater but also "a benevolent Democratic administration" in Washington,[89] responsible for the Federal Emergency Relief Administration (F.E.R.A.).[90] Mrs. Blanche Melvin, the county F.E.R.A. administrator, supervised the granting of meat, flour, cereal, and blankets to the needy in the county from the F.E.R.A. commissary in Leesburg. For example, during the first of May 1934, the F.E.R.A. succored 368 indigent Loudoun families with the following supplies:

---

[85]Ibid., May 19, 1934. The Civil Works Administration established in 1933 created jobs for millions of unemployed. In 1934 the functions of the C.W.A. were transferred to the Federal Emergency Relief Administration (F.E.R.A.) which in turn became the Works Progress Administration (W.P.A.) in 1935.

[86]The secretary, Roland Legard, recorded in the minutes that this topic "seemed too heavy for the members to handle and most shied off" from debating the subject. Lovettsville was traditionally a Republican area that voted for F.D.R. in 1932. In the 1936 Presidential election F.D.R. received 2,228 votes in Loudoun compared to 867 for Alfred M. Landon.

[87]*Times-Mirror*, July 25, 1934. One of the few cheerful episodes during the tenebrous 1930's was a "baby show" held on October 20, 1934, at the Leesburg school auditorium that was sponsored by the Leesburg Parent-Teacher Association. "Every mother in Loudoun" was invited "to enter her baby and compete for prizes." At least eight classes were "offered for children up to six years" of age. Prizes were offered in each class for the healthiest and prettiest infant. A special class was held for the "most talented baby."

[88]Ibid., December 15, 1932; November 10, 1934.

[89]Ibid., December 15, 1932; December 22, 1932.

[90]Barck and Blake, *Since 1900*, p. 492. The F.E.R.A. was created during the "Hundred Days" at the start of F.D.R.'s administration in 1933.

> ... 1,860 pounds of flour, 2,000 pounds of salt meat, 1,137 pounds of smoked meat; 170 pounds of fresh beef; 792 pounds of canned beef; 600 pounds of cheese; 600 pounds of lard; 1,200 pounds of cereal; 132 blankets.[91]

However, gratuitous relief was too contradictory to the Puritan ethic of hard work so deeply ingrained in the American mind. Doles were, therefore, not the major intent of the New Deal, which considered such relief was to be used only in emergency situations. Both Blanche L. Melvin, the local administrator of the F.E.R.A., and the top New Deal members of the "Brain Trust" agreed that relief and recovery must come from a man's working for his "keep." During the first part of May, Mrs. Melvin told the members of the Board of Supervisors that many "unworthy" persons were being aided by the F.E.R.A.[92] Later in 1934, Mrs. Melvin announced a "no work, no eat" policy of the F.E.R.A. in Loudoun, which set about to provide seeds for needy families to help themselves by raising gardens.[93] If the indigent were negligent "in helping themselves by not planting gardens, then they could not expect handouts from the F.E.R.A." In each county district, a committee was assigned the task "of seeing that the needy" were "forced to make the most out of their gardens."[94]

F.D.R.'s major approach to pull the unemployed out of the depression and "prime America's economic pump" was to get money into the hands of the unemployed by providing them with jobs created by the federal government. This was the purpose of the C.W.A. and the agencies that succeeded it. Administration of the C.W.A. in Loudoun was in the hands of J. T. Hirst. During the winter of 1933-1934, the federal government expended $59,700.78 in Loudoun. Of this sum $40,041.04 was spent for labor and $19,659.44 on materials.[95] The state director of the C.W.A. instructed Hirst to have all employees of the agency to be given physical examinations by county doctors, who were to receive seventy-five cents for each person they examined. Loudoun doctors through their Loudoun Medical Society voted not to participate in the program. The president of this society explained that "the fee of seventy-five cents provided as compensation for each examination was

---

[91] *Times-Mirror*, May 3, 1934.
[92] Ibid., May 10, 1934.
[93] Of the 358 Loudoun families on relief in 1934 the F.E.R.A. only provided seeds for 175 gardens. Due to the generosity of D. C. Sands, Mrs. Melvin was able to provide seeds for all families on relief.
[94] *Times-Mirror*, May 24, 1934.
[95] Ibid., April 26, 1934; May 10, 1934. During the 1933-34 winter, a total of $35,842.90 was spent by C.W.A. in the construction of schools in Loudoun; $725.18 "on the alms house," $172.85 on the jail and $5,031.75 on an addition to the clerk's office building.

too meager to interest doctors" as Loudoun doctors "could not afford the C.W.A. rate of compensation." He also pointed out that Loudoun physicians in 1934 received a $2 "fee for office examination[s] and $5 for examining persons" for life insurance policies.[96] The C.W.A. was discontinued on May 1, 1934, its functions being incorporated with the F.E.R.A., which in turn became the Work Progress Administration (W.P.A.) in 1935. Projects started under the C.W.A., such as school buildings and the addition to the clerk's office buildings in Loudoun, were completed by the F.E.R.A.[97] In spite of benefits to Loudouners from federal-funded projects, county officials and many residents continued to express concern about "excessive" government spending. Subsequently, the county Board of Supervisors urged the state office of the F.E.R.A. to make policy changes so that during the summer months' wages would be reduced and workers on federal work projects would be required to work longer hours.[98]

Roosevelt's New Deal measures were unparalleled in the degree of legislative activity which expanded the power of the federal government, especially that of the Presidency. Never had the federal government intervened so extensively into the daily lives of American businessmen, farmers, and laborers.[99] A majority of Loudouners were hard-working people who strongly supported F.D.R. but, nevertheless, had some ambivalence about New Deal measures, such as the degree of support for the unemployed.[100] Misgivings about the New Deal's intrusion into daily lives were weakened by not only the crisis that spawned government intervention in the first place but also the selection of county residents to administer such agencies as the C.W.A. and F.E.R.A. on the county level.

Of all the legislation of the Roosevelt years none changed more directly the way people lived in Loudoun than the creation of the Rural

---

[96]Ibid., March 1, 1934; March 8, 1934. The state C.W.A. sent "outside doctors to make examinations of county" C.W.A. workers.

[97]Barck and Blake, *Since 1900*, p. 512; *Times-Mirror*, May 10, 1934. Mrs. Blanche L. Melvin was retained as the top administrator of the F.E.R.A., and J. T. Hirst, former administrator of the C.W.A., joined the F.E.R.A. as the supervisor of work projects.

[98] *Times-Mirror*, June 7, 1934. Some residents felt jobs sponsored by the F.E.R.A. should be discontinued during the summer months. The Civilian Conservation Corps (C.C.C.) was established in 1933 to provide work for men between the ages of eighteen and twenty-five, veterans of World War I, and experienced woodsmen. Enrollment was for a six-month period in a camp where work was done in reforestation, soil-erosion control, and road-building. Regulations required that "three-quarters of the base pay," which was $30 a month, be sent home to the C.C.C. members' dependents.

[99]Edwin C. Rozwenc (ed.), *The New Deal: Revolution or Evolution?* (rev. ed.; Boston: D. C. Heath and Co., 1959), pp. v-viii.

[100]*Times-Mirror*, November 9, 1940. F.D.R. received 2,156 votes in the Presidential election of 1940 compared to 1,061 for Wendell L. Willkie.

Electrification Administration (R.E.A.) in the spring of 1935.[101] By sponsoring the creation of nonprofit cooperatives and granting them low-cost government loans, the R.E.A. revolutionized rural life and closed the lacuna between city dwellers who had electricity and modern conveniences and country residents who continued to live in lifestyles of the previous century. Without electricity farm families in Loudoun depended upon kerosene lamps for the home and farm chores done prior to sunrise and after sunset. Farmers had neither the benefit of electric milking machines or electric pumps to provide water for livestock kept in barns. Farm women lived and toiled like their predecessors in the preindustrial age. In 1915 the minutes of the Lovettsville Farmers' Club recorded farmer C. Carpenter's views on the subject of modern conveniences in a pre-electrical age. These consisted:

> ... of water in the house and the wood-pile as convenient as possible to the door, cement walks, a separate building convenient to the house to use for butchering, washing, and all such work to be done without taking it into the kitchen.
> W. H. Frazier followed by saying that Mr. Carpenter struck it right when he spoke of the convenience that water makes in the house, and he added, Heating the house by Furnace in the cellar [was an additional convenience].[102]

The creation of the Tri-County Electric Cooperative in Loudoun by the R.E.A. during the latter half of the 1930's started bringing to Loudoun women and their families conveniences that cities had, such as indoor plumbing, running water, washing machines, refrigerators, electric vacuum cleaners, not to mention electric lights.[103] Until the establishment of Tri-County Electric Cooperative, only the people in the larger towns in Loudoun, like Leesburg, Purcellville, Hamilton, Round Hill, and Middleburg, had electricity.[104]

---

[101] Leuchtenburg, *Franklin D. Roosevelt and the New Deal*, pp. 157-58. Nine out of ten Americans did not have electricity prior to 1935. By 1941 every four out of ten farms in America had electricity, and in 1950 nine out of ten. In 1936 R.E.A. became a loan agency for cooperative power companies.

[102] "Minutes of the Lovettsville Farmers' Club," I, 125. Cisterns were used into the twentieth century in Loudoun to collect water for farm homes that did not have a well or spring that was bountiful.

[103] Leuchtenburg, loc. cit.

[104] *Times-Mirror*, May 3, 1934; June 7, 1934. In 1934 the Virginia Public Service Company bought out the Loudoun Light and Power Company. Residents who lived in towns hoped this shift in management would mean lower rates. The gap between Loudoun town and rural life prior to the New Deal rural electrification program is illustrated by the fact that up until that time only one dairy farm next to Leesburg had electricity.

THE SECOND WORLD WAR AND THE REAFFIRMATION OF NATIONALISM

The termination of the Great Depression was not complete until after war had started in Europe. The stimulus of war mobilization dramatically decreased unemployment and farm surplus while accelerating production.[105] Although the crisis of World War II consumed America's activities and attention, neither the psychological scares left by the Great Depression or New Deal programs were completely terminated. New Deal measures which continued into the 1940's were programs for conservation, farm quota systems, and price supports, and for halting the growing number of tenant farms in the nation. During the early New Deal days, the Roosevelt administration had become concerned about the rising rate of tenancy in America over the last half century. In an attempt to reverse this trend, the Farm Security Administration (F.S.A.), established in 1937 as an agency under the Department of Agriculture, was to make long-term loans to select tenants and laborers to enable them to purchase farms.[106] These loans ran for forty years at three percent interest. The few loans available in Loudoun by 1944 were awarded by a local F.S.A. Committee composed of three local farmers. From 1941 to 1944 F.S.A. loans totaling $34,827 enabled "former tenants, sharecroppers and farmlaborers" in Loudoun to become farm owners.[107]

The second A.A.A. throughout World War II continued to set quotas for Loudoun farmers who signed up under the allotment program and pledged to practice conservation in their husbandry. But unlike the 1930's, the A.A.A. during World War II attempted to escalate farm production to meet war needs. In 1945, each participating farmer in the A.A.A. program received "$1.20 for each acre of cropland, plus 55 cents for each acre of fenced, non-crop, open pasture land."[108] Farmers also

---

[105]"Minutes of the Lovettsville Farmers' Club," IV, October 21, 1939; January 18, 1941; Nugent, *Modern America*, p. 205.

[106]Barck and Blake, *Since 1900*, pp. 536-38. Tenancy had increased from twenty-five percent of all farmers in America in 1880 to forty-two percent in the mid-1930's.

[107]*Times-Mirror*, January 13, 1964. The Loudoun County F.S.A. supervisor in 1944 was T. C. Henderson.

[108]Ibid., January 20, 1944. For example in 1944, the goals set for Loudoun County by the A.A.A. included sixty-five millions pounds of milk as compared to the 1943 goal of seventy-two million pounds; about 125,000 dozen fewer eggs in 1944 than 1943; a reduction of about 600 sows under the 1943 goal; a slight decrease in corn acreage, but a maximum effort to produce hay. At that time, J. V. Nichols was the chairman of the Loudoun Board of Agriculture. Although the goals were less than 1943, Nichols chaired a meeting at Leesburg courthouse on January 13, 1945, to discuss how Loudoun farmers could provide maximum yield for "the war effort."

received lime and fertilizer through this program.[109] Loudoun farmers responded to conservation measures and payments. B. W. McKimmey of Lovettsville stated, "One of the best things that had come from" the A.A.A. "was the payment in fertilizer and lime, thereby improving many farms in the county that would otherwise have failed to get an application of lime and fertilizer."[110] In 1943, "approved soil" conservation practices recommended by the A.A.A. were carried out on "85.3 percent of the county's crop land."[111]

Although Loudoun farmers welcomed this program, they were less than enthusiastic about the "price ceiling" placed upon agriculture products by the Office of Price Administration (O.P.A.) established in 1942.[112] The O.P.A. not only froze prices for agricultural products but also put a ceiling price on all consumer goods, wages, and rents throughout the nation. This agency also rationed scarce commodities, such as gasoline, fuel oil, tires, sugar, coffee, meat, and butter through the issuance of booklets of stamps that had to accompany purchases. Allotments of stamps were issued by the local Loudoun Price and Ration Board. Attempts to circumvent the above restrictions were made by black marketeers, who nefariously operated in Loudoun as well as throughout the nation.[113]

The shortage and cost of labor and the insufficient supply of farm equipment also annoyed the farmer, in some ways more seriously than price controls. As the war demanded additional farm products and the labor shortage became critical, farmers were forced to use more modern farm equipment if it was available.[114] During the later years of the war, attempts were made to alleviate labor shortages in Loudoun by the use of Nazi prisoners of war. Approximately 170 German soldiers, "held under U.S. Army guard in a camp near Leesburg," were taken from there by trucks to work on county farms. In spite of original feelings of hostility toward the German prisoners as malefic people, Loudoun farmers soon came to respect them as efficient laborers.[115]

---

[109] Ibid., March 15, 1945.

[110] "Minutes of the Lovettsville Farmers' Club," IV, June 10, 1944. Also at this time, B. W. McKimmey reflected the view of some Loudouners that "all the payments of relief given out by the government" had "caused lots of people and especially a certain class of people to become shiftless and no account."

[111] *Times-Mirror*, September 14, 1944. In 1943 this program was "21.4 percent greater than" a similar program from 1936 to 1939.

[112] Barck and Blake, *Since 1900*, p. 678. An extensive listng of the O.P.A. ceiling upon food items was printed in the January 13, 1944, issue of *The Loudoun Times-Mirror*.

[113] *Times-Mirror*, November 9, 1944; January 6, 1944; April 20, 1945. During June 1945, the Loudoun War Price and Rationing Board "pleaded for patience on the part of the county residents who" had applied for but "not received canning sugar."

[114] Ibid., January 20, 1944.. J. H. Purcell of Round Hill advertised in the June 29, 1944, issue of *The Loudoun Times-Mirror* for workers to pick cherries. He paid one cent for each pound of cherries picked.

[115] Ibid., June 28, 1945.

Problems of labor and farm equipment notwithstanding, Loudoun's production and income soared during World War II. The United States Census Bureau reported that the value of all Loudoun farm products sold or used by farm households in 1945 approached the $8 million mark. This sum was twice the $4,131,951 value of Loudoun's products in 1940.[116] The number of farms in Loudoun increased from 1,716 in 1940 to 2,015 in 1945. Of the approximate 330,839 acres in the county, "92.2 percent of it" was in farm land in 1945, compared to "84.4 percent of the land devoted to agricultural purposes" in 1940. In 1945 there were 235 dairy farms in Loudoun, 180 poultry farms, 496 livestock farms, fifteen "forest product farms," 218 general farms and 669 subsistent farms.[117]

In World War II, Loudouners once again reaffirmed their nationalism through accelerated farm production, military service, and extensive purchases of war bonds. Unlike the unpopularity of conscription during the 1960's, a number of youths under eighteen in the county during World War II misrepresented their age in their "eagerness to serve with the Armed Forces." A headline in the January 20, 1944, issue of *The Loudoun Times-Mirror* stated, "Jumping of Fight Gun by Loudoun Youths Is Problem." To counteract this trend, the Loudoun Selective Service Board required "all youths registering with it on their eighteenth birthday to have with them either their birth certificate or a satisfactory statement signed and sworn to by their parents."[118]

Loudoun residents purchased several million dollars worth of war bonds. The county was assigned seven war loan quotas by the United States Treasury Department, in each of which Loudoun exceeded her goal. Local responsibility for reaching each quota was vested in the Loudoun War Finance Committee.[119] War bond "saleswomen who made house-to-house canvass[es] in Broad Run and Leesburg districts during the Seventh War Loan Campaign" and the extensive headlines, ads, and illustrations in *The Loudoun Times-Mirror* of American warriors

---

[116]Ibid., September 26, 1946. The actual value set on Loudoun's 1945 produce was $7,817,122. Loudoun dairy products alone increased from $1,173,307 in 1940 to $2,715,062 in 1945; livestock products sold for $2,532,938 in 1945 as compared to $1,617,890 in 1940. The general farms in Loudoun in 1945 produced products valued at $642,453.

[117]Ibid.

[118]Ibid., January 20, 1944. Legislation establishing the first peacetime compulsory military service program was enacted by Congress in 1940. This law established local draft boards and required all men between twenty-one and thirty-five to register with this local board. By October 3, 1940, 3,264 men in Loudoun had registered with the county draft board.

[119]Ibid., January 20, 1944; May 17, 1945. From January 1944 to June 1945 Loudoun met its quota for the fourth through seventh loan drive. The lowest quota for the above was $885,000 in the sixth War Loan drive and the highest was $1,155,000 in the seventh. The quotas for the fourth and fifth loan drives were $900,000 and $920,000, respectively.

struggling against the enemy urged Loudouners to invest in war bonds.[120] The seventh and largest bond drive was aimed at the defeat of Japan.[121] Typical of front page headlines was "Community Puts Zest in Bond Drive Aimed at Beating Japs to Knees."[122] To open the seventh bond drive to assure victory in the Pacific and to celebrate the end of the war in Europe, the Loudoun War Finance Committee held on May 12 a "big Battle Equipment Show" in Leesburg that included:

> ... an amphibious tractor, popularly known as "the duck," which transports men and equipment on land and in water. A T-53 hydraulic bomb carrier . . . with two 1000 pound bombs. A 40 mm. anti-aircraft gun. . . . Three soldiers . . . circulate[d] through the crowds with handitalkie radio sets. . . .[123]

The highlight, however, included "free rides on an Army weasel in Goose Creek for each person who" purchased a bond that day.[124] School children, thrilled by the above celebrations, did their part by purchasing war stamps to put in a booklet. When the proper number of stamps was accumulated, they were exchanged for a war bond. Pupils of county schools also collected scrap metal, such as toothpaste containers, and picked milkweed pods to aid the war effort.[125] Children and adults were rewarded for their support of the war effort by Pitts' Tally-ho Theater in Leesburg. This establishment showed movie matinees for kids who had purchased war stamps. The admission was $1 in stamps for a child under twelve and $2 in stamps for an adolescent. Admission for adults was a war bond.[126] Loudoun churches and their ministers collectively planned days of prayer in the county for victory and the termination of war.[127]

[120]Ibid., December 7, 1944; May 17, 1945; June 21, 1945.

[121]The formal end of the war in Europe was May 8, 1945, and the formal surrender of Japan was August 14, 1945.

[122]*Times-Mirror*, May 17, 1945. During the sixth bond drive, the December 7, 1944, issue of the *Times-Mirror* carried an illustration of an American soldier crawling on a Pacific island with his hand stretched out. Under this was a caption saying, "The Japs are far from being pushovers—there are 73 million of these stubborn, cruel . . . fanatic[s] determined to stop us. Save Loudoun lives by buying that extra Bond today!"

[123]Ibid., May 10, 1945. The 40 mm. anti-aircraft gun was demonstrated before an enthusiastic crowd at three o'clock that Saturday afternoon. The thirty-five piece "Edgewood Arsenal Band" had earlier opened the program at one o'clock.

[124]Ibid.

[125]Milkweed pods were used in making parachutes.

[126]*Times-Mirror*, May 24, 1945.

[127]Ibid., September 7, 1944. The Chesapeake and Potomac Telephone Company ran ads in the *Times-Mirror* that party lines were "Patriotic Lines" because they saved copper that would go into the war effort.

THE LAST DAYS OF UNCHALLENGED AGRARIANISM

These were only some of the ways the war involved civilian life in the county. What the county paper did not reflect was the worry of all residents about members of their families in the armed services and the sorrow of families and friends of the fifty-one Loudouners killed in the war.[128] Loudouners, like other citizens of the nation, were jubilant as World War II came to an end in August 1945.[129] To celebrate, the Loudoun's War Finance Committee organized two "Welcome Home Rallies for the county's" returning service men that were held on Saturday, October 25, 1945.[130] White soldiers were welcomed in the Leesburg High School auditorium and black veterans in the auditorium of "Douglas Colored High School."[131]

[128]Ibid., July 4, 1946. The only domestic development to compete with the apprehension associated with the war during the 1940's was the fear of infantile paralysis that struck the county during the summers. School children and adult members of the county participated in annual fund-raising drives in hope of accelerating the conquest of that dreaded disease. Robert A. Meyers, a county educator, chaired the 1944 drive that raised over $1,200 and R. T. Cordell directed the campaign the following year that netted more than $3,500.

[129]During June 1945, the Leesburg town council pondered what remedial ordinances should be enacted to outlaw the existence of a brothel in the county seat that outraged Loudoun's Ministerial Association and town residents, as well as vexed police officers.

[130]These ceremonies also marked the opening of the "Victory Loan drive."

[131]*Times-Mirror*, October 25, 1945. Plans were discussed in the county during and after the war of "an enduring memorial to the men and women of the county who served their country" in World War II. These did not materialize.

Chapter 9

THE CRISIS OF CHANGE: 1945 TO 1972

Residents of Loudoun County entered the postwar era after 1945 with a reaffirmed identity of their county as a viable agrarian region that would long continue her agricultural heritage. This view was predicated upon an empirical judgment founded in their experiences during the Great Depression and World War II. They had recently witnessed how the demands of World War II not only had brought about a renaissance of Loudoun farming after a debilitating depression but also had accelerated the county's economy to new agricultural heights. As an agricultural county in 1945, Loudoun stood "around the top not only among the 100 counties in Virginia, but in the nation as well." It had recently been ranked "as one of the five best agricultural counties" in the Eastern region of the United States.[1]

In spite of the reaffirmed agrarianism, lifestyles in the county that had been traditionally unaltered were modified during the previous two decades and the forces for change greatly enhanced. The extension of electricity to rural residents was revolutionizing modes of living. Big government had intervened in local life to the point that its programs and agents were a permanent part of county life. The cow unquestionably had replaced the horse as Loudoun's most valuable animal. Although general farming remained important, specialized farming in the form of dairying, poultry, and beef cattle were salient aspects of the county's

[1] *Times-Mirror*, May 15, 1945.

economy. But the most significant force for accelerated change that led to the decline of Loudoun as an agricultural county was the automobile.

THE CAR AS A VEHICLE OF CHANGE

Since 1920 mass-produced and mass-consumed automobiles have revolutionized living in America. Their ultimate social and economic effects upon life in the county as well as in the nation have been prodigious.[2] The magic of the automobile was the mobility it provided people in transcending traditional transportational barriers.

By 1960, 2,395, or 28.6 percent, of the employed Loudoun residents commuted to work outside the county.[3] By 1970, 5,335, or 40.6 percent, of the employed county residents commuted to jobs outside the county.[4] The new-found mobility greatly weakened, and eventually destroyed, the traditional nineteenth-century bicorporal communities. Communities that had been formerly centered around small hamlets which possessed country stores, post offices, mills, and churches lost their cohesiveness. Residents could now conveniently go to larger towns in the county like Leesburg, Middleburg, or Purcellville for socializing and to stores, and with a degree of regularity to much larger urban centers like Winchester, Washington, D. C., and suburban shopping centers in northern Virginia. After 1945, as the result of automobiles, an increasing number of commuters, many of whom were exurbanites, lived in Loudoun with a few acres or a small farm and worked outside the county. By the 1960's, the Loudoun commuter was becoming increasingly a suburbanite who lived in a planned community. These residents were attracted to rural living, but in practice were closely wedded to urban conveniences made possible by the use of the car, which decentralized their places of employment, patronage of stores, and pursuit of recreation. The decline of the bicorporal community also was accompanied by the demise of the nineteenth-century agrarian community consciousness traditionally based upon family ties, common needs, lack of modern facilities, neighbors working together at harvest time, befriending each other in times of grief,

---

[2]Nugent, *Modern America*, pp. 67-69.
[3]Virginia, Division of State Planning and Community Affairs, *Data Summary: Loudoun County* (Richmond, Va.: Office of Research and Information, 1969), p. 8. (Hereafter referred to as *Data Summary* for 1968.) As of 1971, there were 111.42 miles of primary and 670.40 miles of secondary roads in Loudoun. Of the latter only 273.94 miles were hardsurfaced roads.
[4]Virginia Division of State Planning and Community Affairs, *Data Summary: Loudoun County* (Richmond, Va.: Office of Research and Information, 1972), p. 14. (Hereafter referred to as *Data Summary* for 1970.) In 1960, 489 people living outside Loudoun commuted to work inside the county. In 1970 the number had increased to 2,621.

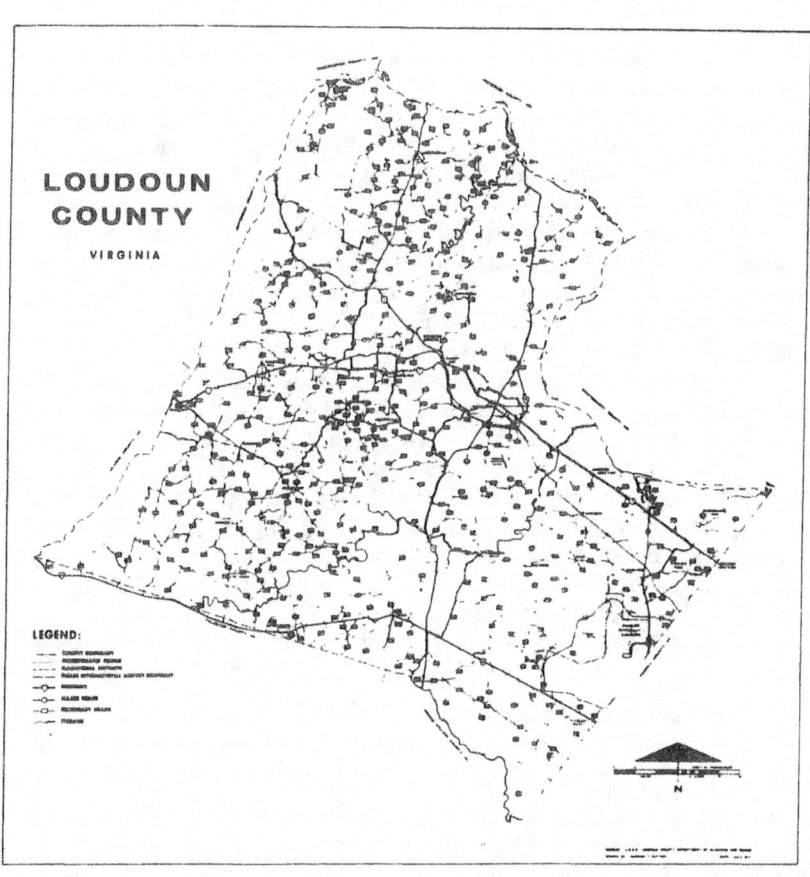

*Figure 21. Loudoun County Roads in 1972.
Source: Loudoun County Data Book*, p. [85].

and frequently associating and communicating as the result of attending the same church, having gone to the same school, and frequenting the same store. In short, the car made possible the transformation of traditional bicorporal communities in Loudoun into bedroom communities, where people slept, but worked and played elsewhere.

The demise of traditional decentralized community life was accompanied by a greater centralization of economic, social, and political institutions.[5] The country store gradually gave way to the chain store, one-room schools were abandoned in favor of larger plants, and churches in smaller hamlets were forsaken in favor of those in the larger towns. A classic example of the decentralized bicorporal community was the existence of fifty-four Methodist churches in Loudoun in 1906, which by 1958 had dwindled as the result of consolidation to nineteen.[6]

Until the car, public education in Loudoun was controlled by District School Boards. Although the District School Board members started meeting occasionally as the Loudoun County School Board in 1898, district board meetings were held until 1922.[7] Since 1922 only a county School Board has been in existence.

Consolidation of public schools was made possible by one of the motorized cousins of the automobile, the school bus. The closing of one, two, and three-room schools was a significant alternation in the traditional composition of the bicorporal community. School consolidation, which started after World War I, culminated in the 1950's in Loudoun with the establishment of one high school. This was, nevertheless, a traumatic development accompanied by as intense a protest movement as had been witnessed in the internal affairs of the county during the twentieth-century.

Between the end of World War I and the mid-1920's thirteen schools

---

[5]Prior to the car and television, farm boys obtained some of their merriment by night-hunting. A small group of boys or men with dogs and kerosene lanterns would often chase a raccoon or possum well into, if not through, the night. By the 1940's this practice was all but abandoned.

[6]Kincaid, "The First Churches in Loudoun," p. 19. In 1916 in Loudoun there were 7,894 church members out of a population of approximately 21,000. Of the one-third of the county residents who were church members 3,360 were Methodists, 2,278 were Baptists, 515 were Episcopalians; 478 were Presbyterians, 139 were members of the Reformed Church, and 120 were Roman Catholics; 1,004 attended other denominations. Loudoun ranked 70th in the state in church membership with only 49.4 percent of her population ten years and over as church members. Deck and Heaton wrote in the 1920's: "It seems deplorable that a county like Loudoun, which stands high among its sister counties in education and other vital items, should be so far behind in the matter of church membership" (*An Economic and Social Survey of Loudoun County*, p. 69). More acceptable to Deck and Heaton was Loudoun's low divorce rate in 1924. Loudoun "ranked 70th" in the state with only "1.75 divorces per 1,000 of the population."

[7]Loudoun County, Virginia, Minutes of the District School Boards, 1904-1922, p. 35; Loudoun County, Virginia, Minutes of the Loudoun County School Board, 1891-1919, pp. 5-8; *Times-Mirror*, March 31, 1949.

had been consolidated. At the latter date there were seventy-nine schools in the county, twenty-four of which were Negro schools; fifty-eight were one-room buildings. All were reported as having "sanitary outhouses." Attending these segregated schools were 3,641 white and 1,022 black students.[8] Despite forces at work that were transforming Loudoun's educational system, Loudoun's school system in the early 1920's was similar to the public education system that was first established in the county during the 1870's. By 1926 twenty white schools had been consolidated; by 1945 the number had reached fifty-five. During this period consolidation had only meagerly touched black schools. There were twenty-four schools for Negroes in Loudoun in 1926 and twenty-one in 1945.[9]

While many county residents favored the abandonment of one- and two-room schools for consolidated schools that offered a more comprehensive and improved curriculum and more specialized instructional staff, others lamented this trend as regressive and not progressive.[10] The issue of consolidation became especially explosive on the question of closing high schools. While closing of elementary schools several miles from each other in favor of a more centralized school still in or near the general vicinity of the community of the closed school was acceptable, the closing of high schools and busing children outside the community ten to fifteen miles was considered by many as a serious threat to their traditional concept of the neighborhood school and local education. An example of such an episode was reflected in the February 15, 1940, headlines of *The Loudoun Times-Mirror*, which read "Masses Debate Revision of High School Sites." More than 250 patrons and taxpayers "aired their views on the proposed plan" to "close the high school departments at Round Hill and Ashburn." H. C. Thompson in a lengthy address strongly opposed the closing of Ashburn High School and transporting pupils approximately ten miles to Leesburg. He further pointed out consolidation of schools was "experimental" and not a guarantee of improved education.[11] The protest against consolidation of

---

[8]Loudoun County, Virginia, Annual School Report for 1925-1926, pp. 1-6. Nine of the seventy-nine schools were white high schools. Two thousand, two hundred and ninety-five white and 618 black students were promoted at the end of the 1925-26 term, while 644 white and 295 black "failed," and 702 white and 109 black pupils "dropped out" during the school year.

[9]Annual School Report of Loudoun County for 1925-1926, p. 6; "Scrapbook on Loudoun County Schools, 1945-1947," n.p. Enrollment in Loudoun's elementary schools increased very little from 1932 to 1952. The major trend in public education during this span, in addition to consolidation, was the increased enrollments in county high schools.

[10]Deck and Heaton, *An Economic and Social Survey of Loudoun County*, pp. 76-77.

[11]*Times-Mirror*, February 15, 1940. Some additional rooms were added to the Leesburg High School to help accommodate the increase due to consolidation with Ashburn. Two rooms were added to Lincoln High School to handle students from Round Hill.

white high schools in Loudoun in 1940 was mild compared to the remonstration from 1947 to 1950. Reluctance to give up the community school, the main cohesive force of the bicorporal community during the late 1800's and the first half of the 1900's, was expressed lucidly in an unsigned editorial from the 1947 issue of the Lincoln High School *Lincolnite*:

> A recent editorial stated that if plans progress according to schedule that soon in Loudoun we shall have one high school and four elementary schools. It is difficult to sort our true thinking and feeling on this subject from the anger and resentment which we feel at such an announcement.
>
> I say anger and resentment, and I realize that this may be a part of my environment, for I come from a farming community which has steadily lost the schooling advantages it once had. First the high school went because it was too little to meet state requirements. Then the elementary school burned and the school board decided not to rebuild it because the children could be hauled on buses to other communities. That left among the permanent residents of my community a feeling of being cheated and thwarted which is not good.
>
> In each instance the argument in favor of consolidation was that children could get more advantages in the larger schools. Might I ask what advantages? For example there are more children in Lincoln, more teachers and a small increase in the subjects from which we might choose. But gone is the friendly intimacy which we felt in the small school. I don't think that this is the fault of Lincoln or the teachers. It is the fault of the school not being nearer my home—near enough for my family to feel that it is their school. It is also the fault of classes being so large. . . . It is the fault of there being little opportunity for the teacher to discover what I do know or, what is more important, what I need to know and have not learned. Of course the bigger the enrollment the more impersonal a school becomes. I do feel that this is a loss which should weigh heavily against further consolidation.
>
> Then too is the toll of time and energy which riding the bus takes. I am a farm boy and in many instances

it has called for real sacrifice and extra labor on the part of my parents in order for me to get to school. I leave too early and get home too late to do much, other than a few chores. In times of emergency, like illness in the family, I have had to get up in the dark hours and help do the farm work and then have someone take me to school. I do think that the extra hours on this bus and the extra miles that the school is from our home is another reason the farm boys and girls fail to make the grades and frequently drop out of school.

Most of the people who make rules and laws about consolidation are town and city people and know very little about rural roads, rural life, and rural weather. Mild days on a bus are a pleasure but the biting aching cold of freezing weather is only a little worse than the hot, crowded, sweaty days of early fall and late spring. This could be corrected partly by putting on more and better buses, but who is going to correct the walk to the bus stop, the wait in the rain or the wind, which must be followed by a lengthy ride in an unheated bus?[12]

From 1947 to 1950 some members of the School Board expressed the view that it would be best for Loudoun to adopt one high school.[13] School Board members who became proponents of such a move did so as the result of the eloquence of Loudoun school superintendent Oscar L. Emerick, who in turn drew on the advice of "state school authorities" that counties in Virginia should build "comprehensive high schools" that provide curricula in college preparatory and vocational courses. The superintendent pointed out that the mere addition to the four existing white high schools after World War II—Aldie, Leesburg, Lincoln, and Lovettsville—would fail to provide suitable shops for industrial arts and agriculture without expensive duplication of facilities. In short, it was impractical and financially inexpedient to provide both the facilities and faculty for four small high schools in an attempt to provide a comprehensive educational program.[14] The existing educational system

[12]A reprint of this article can be found in the "Scrapbook on Loudoun County Schools, 1945-1947."
[13]*Times-Mirror*, January 20, 1949. The official title of the school suprintendent is Division Superintendent of Schools.
[14]Newspaper clipping on school consolidation written in the late 1940's by O. L. Emerick in "Scrapbook on Loudoun County Schools, 1945-1947," n.p. A comprehensive curriculum in 1949 consisted of English, Spanish, Latin, French, mathematics, history, government, social problems, natural sciences, physical and health education, home economics, diversified education, distributive education, vocational, agricultural, industrial arts. Emerick recommended such a school should have between 600 and 1,200 pupils. The

in the county was not as strong as it should have been.[15] By 1947 Loudoun ranked fifth in the state in "ability to pay for support of public education," but was "ninety-first in effort."[16] From World War II to 1960 Loudoun had a problem in filling teaching positions due to low salaries and excessive teaching preparation demanded of high school instructors, which resulted in a high turnover rate as teachers gained employment in better paying jurisdictions like Fairfax County or left the teaching profession for higher paying jobs.[17] Prior to the end of World War II, *The Loudoun Times-Mirror* stated in 1944 that the "stark, somber fact is that" some of Loudoun's schools have reached "the point, on one hand" of "outright lawlessness . . . and on the other hand, children are not receiving the sort of instruction that is likely greatly" to benefit "them when they will be required to shift for themselves."[18]

Though discipline greatly improved after the termination of World War II as male instructors returned to the classroom from military service, the problem of teacher salaries, overcrowded classrooms, and inadequate educational offerings continued.[19] To meet these problems, the school budget was greatly increased by raising Loudoun county taxes on "real estate and tangible personal property" from $1.10 in 1944 to $2 in 1949 per $100 of the assessed value of the realty and personalty.

---

enrollment in the four white high schools in 1949 was approximately 900 pupils: Aldie had 150 pupils; Leesburg, 300; Lincoln, 280; and Lovettsville, 140. In the fall of 1949 an eighth grade was implemented as part of the high schools of the county to promote a smoother transition from elementary to high school work. From 1945 to 1949, the eighth grade had been introduced to a limited extent on the elementary level in the Loudoun school system.

[15] *Times-Mirror*, May 17, 1945. World War II records revealed that more "than one-third of enlisted white Army men from Virginia serving in World War II" had only an elementary education (or less). This was far below "the national average."

[16] Newspaper clipping in the "Scrapbook on Loudoun County Schools, 1945-1947." Ability to pay statistics were based upon the "true value of locally taxable wealth" provided by the State Department of Taxation for 1942 and "divided by the number of pupils in average attendance" during the school year. Effort was calculated by dividing the "true value of local taxable wealth" into "the amount received for education from local sources." In "self help" the county was fifteenth in the state. "Self help" was the amount expended from local funds for the operation of Loudoun schools per child for his average yearly daily attendance. During the middle 1940's it was $46.33 per pupil. In the 1943-1944 term, the total school enrollment in Loudoun of black and white pupils was about 4,000, with 115 white and thirty-five black teachers.

[17] This problem is identified in a newspaper clipping in scrapbooks on Loudoun County schools in the years from 1940 to 1947. It was not uncommon for high school teachers from 1940 to 1954 to teach daily four or five different subjects that might range from history to a foreign language.

[18] *Times-Mirror*, February 24, 1944.

[19] Starting salary for a teacher with a collegiate professional certificate in 1952 was $2,500. Many teachers worked on local permits that paid from $1,800 to $2,160.

The school budget that demanded an increase in tax rate to $2 was deemed drastic and alarmed the taxpayers of the county, especially the farmers who protested to the Board of Supervisors.[20] Angered by "ballooning taxes," county residents, especially in western Loudoun, were increasingly annoyed at the possibility of losing their remaining neighborhood high schools. This fear resulted in over 300 taxpayers from all sections of the county, mainly farmers led by J. V. Nichols, a Purcellville dairyman, crowding on February 7, 1950, into the Leesburg courtroom for a meeting of the Board of Supervisors. Many believed this meeting would decide the fate of the plan for one high school, as recommended by superintendent O. L. Emerick. The result "was one of the most turbulent meetings" in the twentieth-century history of Loudoun. There were "sharp exchanges of repartee and arguments that was caustic" and "thunderous protest against the construction of a single high school."[21] The issue was not resolved at this meeting, and on May 1, 1950, the supervisors "deftly, with noteworthy finesse and scant ceremony" tossed "right back to the School Board the education ball that for months had been bouncing between the two units in the controversy over the number of high schools that" were "to be maintained in Loudoun."[22]

After three years of deliberation by county authorities and oftentimes more vitriolic and emotional than logical discussions by the citizenry, the issue of consolidation of all white high schools remained

[20]Ibid., January 10, 1949; March 31, 1949; May 3, 1949; May 10, 1949. The School Board proposed a $452,000 school budget for the county for the 1949-50 fiscal year. This was an increase of $167,000 over the budget of 1948-49. Much of this budget was to go for the construction of two additional rooms at each of the Leesburg, Lovettsville, and Lincoln high schools; auditorium, clinic, and one classroom at Arcola; four additional rooms at Douglas High School; and a new eight-room elementary school at Douglas. A special committee of the Loudoun Parent-Teacher Association submitted a report that asserted the 1949-50 budget was the "very minimum needed to hold the county's schools at present standards much less raise them." It was pointed out by the *Times-Mirror* that the "proposed tax rate of $2, when applied to low assessment, will result in a tax levy which is lower than any county in this section of Virginia, Maryland, or West Virginia." Neither the position of the P.T.A. or the *Times-Mirror* stilled the residents, who were especially vociferous as they continued to protest to their representatives on the Board of Supervisors and members of the School Board. The pressure on School Board members prompted three to resign during the first of May 1949, and a fourth moved that the entire board should resign. This motion was ruled out of order by the chairman of the board, W. T. Smith.

[21]Ibid., February 9, 1950. Two rulings of parliamentary procedure by chairman I. W. Baker were denounced, the latter by an "uproar" of citizens at the meeting. When J. V. Nichols asked for a show of hands by members of the audience who were opposed to one high school, an overwhelming majority raised their hands.

[22]Ibid., May 4, 1950. The School Board passed the "Hot Potato" to the Supervisors by requesting the two boards meet in a joint meeting to discuss the school issue. The supervisors' rejection of such a joint venture left the resolution of the issue in the hands of the School Board.

unresolved. The *Times-Mirror* in May 1950 stated the School Board had wisely gone on record "as favoring one school." The same issue of the paper explained the tentative proposal by the board that, if a consolidated high school were to be constructed, it would be financed by a state grant-in-aid of $300,000 and the borrowing of an additional $600,000 from the State Literary Fund at two percent interest. The cost of the loan and interest over a thirty-year period would amount to $786,000 or "an average of $2.62 per year for each of "Loudoun's 10,000 taxpayers." The editorial concluded that "for a county so rich as Loudoun the cost would be neither excessive nor burdensome."[23] Nevertheless, opposition to one high school was so strong the School Board remained timorous and irresolute over the implementation of such a plan. Superintendent Emerick became so discouraged he concluded that in spite of the assured $300,000 in state funds, the opposition in the county against consolidation was so strong that the $786,000 loan needed to complete the project could not be approved.[24]

Consequently he proposed at a special meeting of the School Board in the fall of 1950 that the $300,000 available in state funds be expended for the construction of additional rooms for the existing five high schools in the county. The School Board rejected this recommendation of the superintendent and went on to implement the consolidation of all white high schools in the county.[25] Finally in the fall of 1954, white students from all sections of the county entered Loudoun County High School, located on a thirty-acre site near Leesburg.[26] This was the crowning achievement of the four decades of O. L. Emerick's career as superintendent of Loudoun schools. The consolidation of the county's white high schools was a fitting climax of the career of a man who had since 1917 consolidated and reduced the number of schools in the county from approximately one hundred to fifty and had guided Loudoun's school system from the age of the horse and buggy to that of the car and bus.

While the bus enabled consolidation of schools, which improved education in the county for white pupils, Negro students in the county were not sharing in these advancements. The dual school system in the county was the product of the reconstruction era and the caste system

---

[23] Ibid., May 25, 1950. Daniel C. Sands, a member of the Board of Supervisors from Mercer District reported that "two classes of people" came to see him. "One was composed of young married couples who had children to be educated." The other was older people whose children had already been educated. The people with children, according to Sands, were "perfectly willing to pay $200 or more annually in taxes in order to have adequate school facilities." He maintained that the older class made "no mention of improving our school system." All they talked about was cost.

[24] Ibid., November 23, 1950.

[25] Ibid., November 30, 1950.

[26] O. L. Emerick, "Loudoun County Schools," *Virginia and the Virginia County*, VII (January 1953), 31-32.

established after the Civil War, later reinforced by the Supreme Court of the United States, especially in its decision in Plessy v. Ferguson in 1896, which announced the doctrine that segregation of races was legal as long as public facilities were equal. However, the "separate but equal" doctrine usually worked out in practice as "separate and unequal."[27] Essentially this situation was a manifestation of racial attitudes held by many white residents in the county and nation, which took for granted that Negroes were inferior. The segregation of institutions and practices, such as the existence of a dual school system, reinforced and perpetuated racism in the county.

In 1925 the minimum salary for white elementary teachers in the county was $520 as compared to $315 for black. The average salary for white teachers in Loudoun was $836.10 and blacks, $358.12.[28] The average yearly cost to educate a white pupil was $29.27 as compared to $9.81 for blacks. Unlike the facilities for whites with nine high schools, there was not a black high school in 1925 in the county. The average length of the yearly school term was 175 days for white pupils and only 138 for blacks.[29] In 1936-37, the county School Board voted to increase the salaries of all public school teachers; white teachers received a ten percent increase while "colored teachers obtained only a $5.00 per month" increment. [30]

A few one-room white elementary schools still remained in use in the county in 1940, while black students had to attend a number of such structures, the majority of which were generally inferior to those buildings where most white pupils attended.[31]

[27]Robert G. McCloskey, *The American Supreme Court* (Chicago: University of Chicago Press, 1960), pp. 210-11.

[28]Annual School Report for 1925-1926, p. 6. Discrimination was limited not solely to color, but also sex. In 1925 the minimum salary for male high school teachers was $1,530 and female high school teachers $900. Maximum salaries for male and female teachers were $2,700 and $1,485, respectively.

[29]Ibid. In 1936, white schools opened on September 9, but schools for Negro residents of the county were not opened until September 23. Some whites argued the disparity in the money spent to educate white and black pupils was justified because whites paid most of the taxes that supported the county school system.

[30]*Times-Mirror*, May 14, 1936. This increase in wages of black instructors amounted to about $35 a year, but the minimum increment for the lowest paid whites was double that amount. For higher paid white instructors the increase was far more. Salaries of all Loudoun school teachers were reduced during the depression. Even with the ten percent increase white teachers in 1936-37 received ten percent less than in 1929-30. The ten school bus drivers in the county in 1936 received salaries that varied from $90 to $140 a year for transporting county school children. In May 1936, Lincoln High School graduated thirty students, the highest number in the history of that institution, which was "one of the two oldest and accredited high schools in Loudoun."

[31]Thomas E. Sims, Jr., "Inspection and Survey Report." This is an evaluation and description of Loudoun County Schools in 1940 by a special agent of the Garrett Insurance Agency of Leesburg, Virginia. One-room schools varied in dimensions from 17' X 25' to 22' X 34'. They usually had a stone foundation and metal roof. Their insurable value in 1940 varied from $200 to $500.

Blacks protested against the nature of education for their children in Loudoun during 1940. Approximately thirty Loudoun Negro parents, who were members of an organization known as the County-Wide League, appeared before the Loudoun County School Board on March 12, 1940. This group was headed by Charles H. Houston, a black Washington, D. C., attorney, who stated the County Wide League's mission was to obtain "equal educational opportunities for Negro children in the public schools of Loudoun." Houston also stated:

> . . . *research had convinced him that the superintendent and members of the County Board of Education are exposed to personal liability damages for many of the discriminations which they now inflict upon the Negro children.*[32]

Houston "pointed out with ridicule . . . the conditions existing in the Negro high school at Leesburg, particularly with reference to laboratory equipment, building safety and discrimination in class subjects." Although Houston did not ask for integration of schools, this episode, nevertheless, shocked the county as the *Times-Mirror* reported that at "no other time in the history of the Loudoun County school system has quite the same education problems arisen as" in the above meeting.[33]

Integration of some of Loudoun's public facilities did not take place until the spring of 1961. At that time proprietors of "eating establishments" at Middleburg agreed they would serve Negro customers. This decision resulted from an incident that occurred several weeks earlier in which two black students from Howard University in Washington, D.C., had been refused service at one of the drug stores. The students went to William Jackson, a local Negro "builder and representative of the N.A.A.C.P.," who cautioned the youths to pursue "mediation rather than a demonstration," especially when President Kennedy was in Middleburg for weekend respites. The threat of a demonstration stimulated local white civil and religious leaders to negotiate with black

---

[32] *Times-Mirror*, March 14, 1940. In 1933, Houston as a representative of the National Association for the Advancement of Colored People appeared in Leesburg to defend George Crawford, a five-foot two-inch Negro tried in Loudoun for the brutal murders of Mrs. Spencer Ilsely and Mrs. Annie Buckner at the former's home at Middleburg. The January 14, 1932, issue of the *Times-Mirror* ran headlines about the murder, which included "Slayer Uses Hatchet to Crush Skulls of Victims Attacking Them As They Lay in Beds." Citizens offered a $500 reward. Crawford was sentenced to life in prison.

[33] Ibid. Houston also "demanded" accreditation be obtained for the Negro high school and attacked the low salaries for black instructors, lack of "janitor service, electric lights and other conveniences." He also noted "the colored race was deprived of" the benefits of consolidation.

leaders and subsequently decide to "open up" the town's eating establisments to blacks.³⁴

Desegregation of Middleburg's eating establishments encouraged blacks to demand the desegregation of county schools and the firemen's swimming pool at Leesburg.³⁵ Efforts by black residents to desegregate county schools started in 1962 with the request of a dozen Negro students to the State Pupil Placement Board in Richmond to grant them admittance to the two white high schools in the county.³⁶ During the same year, eight Loudoun Negroes brought a suit against the county to desegregate the county schools. As the results of these incidents, Federal District Court Judge Oren R. Lewis ordered that Loudoun comply with "the freedom of choice plan designed to phase out the all-Negro schools as well as to integrate white schools." Progress was made in the integration of the county schools the five years after the above suit, but it was slow. As schools reopened in Loudoun in the late summer of 1967, four Loudoun schools were attended exclusively by blacks; one was a high school and the other three were elementary schools. Ten of Loudoun's twenty-two schools were integrated, with a total of 218 black pupils enrolled in predominantly white schools.³⁷ At the end of August 1965 the Justice Department brought a suit against the Loudoun school officials "for still operating on a dual school system." Judge Lewis decreed that "all Loudoun schools be integrated on both

---

³⁴Ibid., April 13, 1961. John Eisenhard, then the managing editor of *The Fauquier Democrat*, upon learning that a demonstration was being considered, contacted Rev. Albert F. Pereira of Leesburg, who conducted Catholic services at Middleburg often attended by the "first family." Father Pereira called upon Edwin C. Reamer, the mayor of Middleburg, and the various Protestant pastors of Middleburg and civil leaders to discuss the situation. It has also been reported that at one point in the negotiations a member of President Kennedy's staff participated in the discussions.

³⁵Ibid., June 7, 1962; September 16, 1965; May 26, 1966. Lawyers for Mrs. Hazel Berry, her daughter Josephine, and several other local Negro citizens filed a suit in the U. S. Court for the Eastern District of Virginia in September 1965 asking that the court grant a permanent injunction against the pool's policy of segregation on the grounds it violated the Civil Rights Act of 1964. During May 1966, the court issued such an injunction restraining the Leesburg Volnteer Fire Department from operating its pool on its traditional discriminatory basis. The firemen complied with the injunction by permanently closing the pool.

³⁶Ibid., June 7, 1962. Two black students who lived in the Purcellville area asked to be placed in the new Loudoun Valley High School, and ten from the vicinity of Leesburg wanted to attend Loudoun County High School. In 1967 the Loudoun County League of Women Voters made public their three-year study of education in the county, which among other points urged "complete and permanent desegregation of all Loudoun County public schools" and higher salaries for teachers.

³⁷Ibid., September 14, 1967. Despite the request by black students to attend Loudoun County and Loudoun Valley high schools in 1962, those schools were not integrated until the 1965-66 school year. In 1968 there were 1,403 Negro pupils in Loudoun public schools, 519 of whom were enrolled in predominantly white schools.

pupil and staff levels no later than the 1968-69 school year."³⁸ All Negroes were to attend schools nearest to their homes. The manner in which C. M. Bussinger, the successor to O. L. Emerick as superintendent of Loudoun schools, complied with this court order ranks as Bussinger's major achievement during his twelve years tenure.³⁹

By June 1967, black residents within the county generally seemed pleased with the county's school administration and its policies toward blacks, except for the number of black faculty members employed in county schools. At the behest of the Loudoun branch of the N.A.A.C.P., the federal Department of Justice made an inquiry into the county's teacher employment policies. Mrs. Lou Etta Watkins, chairman of "the N.A.A.C.P.'s local education committee," stated that she "was fearful that the Negro teacher" would "disappear from Loudoun County." In 1969 Loudoun had over 400 public school teachers, forty of whom were black. School authorities responded to charges that they were not doing all they should in acquiring and keeping black instructors by stating no Negro instructor had been retired or fired; the school administration had been preoccupied with the other administrative details in order to comply with the desegregation court order; and the obtaining of Negro applicants for teaching positions was difficult.⁴⁰

THE "STEEL HORSE" AND SCIENTIFIC INNOVATIONS IN HUSBANDRY

Agriculture in Loudoun has changed far more in the years since 1945 than in any comparable period in the county's history. Not only have accelerated changes taken place in the techniques of crop and animal husbandry and the use of equipment, but for the first time farming has been declining as the paramount lifestyle in Loudoun.

---

³⁸Ibid., August 31, 1967. Judge Lewis "rapped"Justice Department attorneys for delaying bringing suit against the Loudoun School Board until near the start of a new school year. He stated, "I'm not going to permit the government to interrupt the school system" in August when this could have been done in May. This is the reason why he gave Loudoun school authorities until the 1968-69 school year to desegregate all schools, including "elementary schools to be operated on the basis of non-racial geographic attendance zones." Furthermore, he added that as soon as the new Broad Run High School was completed, that high school was also to come under the court order. All transportation of pupils was to be desegregated by the 1967-68 school term. When school opened in September 1967, the total enrollment was 8,167, an increase of 200 over that of the previous year.

³⁹Ibid., September 1967.

⁴⁰*Times-Mirror*, June 12, 1969. Five hundred and fifty people applied for teaching positions in the county for the 1969-70 school term. Although the county school

The most revolutionary advance of this era has been the extensive use and popularity of the "steel horse" or tractor. Its supersedure of the horse started gradually prior to America's entry into World War I. Debates took place in county farmers' clubs from 1917 to 1940 over the practicality of the tractor. On January 20, 1917, several members of the Lovettsville Farmers' Club stated that it was possible that in the future tractors "could be used very satisfactory" in Loudoun.[41] Members of the same club in 1930, however, reaffirmed that the "tractor is all right in its place . . . but the farm cannot do without the horse."[42] By 1938 most farmers felt that "taken on the whole, the tractor appeared to have it over the horse." As one Lovettsville farmer put it, his twelve-year-old son cultivated thirty acres of corn in one day, doing an excellent job, and he personally had "plowed and put in order for planting" five acres a day. He maintained he could plow as much land with one tractor "as with four good teams" of horses. The farmer went on to say he could cut an average of twenty-two acres of wheat per day, regardless of the heat.[43] Other major advantages were the "saving in man power" and "saving in horse feed" that could be used to raise other livestock profitably. Two Lovettsville farmers, S. C. Legard and R. N. Legard, were less enthusiastic about the tractor. R. N. Legard said he "didn't think much of the tractor, didn't like the noise they made; didn't like the smoke and didn't like the smell of them."[44]

The tractor by 1940 was, nevertheless, the basic source of farm power for crop husbandry, bringing with it an ever-increasing number of expensive implements and machinery that saved labor and

administration attempted to recruit applicants from six black colleges and universities in Virginia, they had only fifteen black candidates for jobs. Of the fifteen black applicants, three were offered teaching positions.

[41]"Minutes of the Lovettsville Farmers' Club," I, 100, 127. Often such debates were related to the use of gasoline engines, trucks, and cars. Members of the Lovettsville Club on November 13, 1916, stated the "motor power" was "an advantage on account of time saved and convenience . . . especially for Doctors and all who were compelled to make quick trips." However, one member, J. L. Bush, stated he didn't "know if the automobile" was "really an advantage to a farming community." It might be "all right if one does not get spoiled in using it." He felt the gasoline engine was of far greater value to the farmer. Gasoline engines were used to power generators for "electric lighting plants," run milking machines, and water pumps.

[42]Ibid., II, 246. At that time the club stated that the truck was a great "money saver," but it was cheaper to hire someone else with a truck to do the work than to own one. In 1918 "motor truck service" from Washington to Bluemont and Hillsboro was available.

[43]If farmers were not careful using their horses in hot weather, they would become overheated and die.

[44]"Minutes of the Lovettsville Farmers' Club," III, April 16, 1938. By 1940 the Southern States Cooperative Association started accommodating the use of the tractor, truck, and car by delivering gasoline and oil to the farmers in the county who desired this service.

revolutionized farming. After 1945 three pieces of equipment pulled by the tractor dramatically altered the techniques of farming in Loudoun: the combine, which made the binder and threshing machine obsolete, the hay baler, and the corn picker which revolutionized the harvesting of corn.[45]

Scientists have invaded farming not only through technology manifested in the form of innovative equipment, but also through chemical fertilizers, chemical sprays, and veterinary medicine.[46] Despite having expressed an ecological concern for the impact of chemical sprays, pesticides and herbicides are deemed by most farmers to be essential to successful husbandry.[47] Since the use of D.D.T. in the 1940's for the control of insects, sprays have been increasingly used for bugs on crops and livestock. Herbicidal sprays have also been increasingly used for weed control. Since 1970 in Loudoun they have been used to kill grass and weeds in a manner that has eliminated for the most part both the traditional procedure of plowing land to prepare a seedbed for corn and the subsequent cultivating of the crop to eliminate weeds.[48]

Science also befriended the farmer with improved varieties of crops, especially the development of hybrid corn, which was satisfactorily introduced in the county during the late 1930's.[49] Scientific advancements by 1940 made possible the use of artificial insemination in dairy husbandry, thereby eliminating the necessity of each dairyman keeping dangerous and temperamental bulls while improving the bloodlines of each dairy herd through the use of artificial insemination.[50] After 1945 most dairymen in the county used this procedure. Advancements in veterinary science brought about improvements in animal surgery and the extensive use of antibiotics, especially penicillin. These have been used

[45]Ibid., January 17, 1942. The Lovettsville Farmers' Club met at Westmoreland Davis' home, Morven Park, and discussed "What New Types of Labor Saving Devices Can Be Profitably Used on the Farm in 1942?" Many members stated they did not believe the combine and corn picker were "generally practical or profitable" for much of Loudoun. The corn picker was extensively used in the county after 1945 but has recently been replaced by the self-propelled combine that harvests not only small grains like wheat and orchard grass seed, but also corn.

[46]Ibid., VI, November 19, 1962; January 19, 1963; September 19, 1964; March 17, 1972; "Worrying About the Wrong Chemicals," *Farm Journal*, LXXXXVIII (March, 1974), 62. By 1972 farmers in the county were using 400 pounds of chemical fertilizers per acre on pasture land, from 400 to 600 pounds of fertilizer per acre when cultivating small grains, and from 200 to 600 pounds of fertilizer per acre for corn. The above is often in addition to lime and manure.

[47]"Minutes of the Lovettsville Farmers' Club," V, April 16, 1955; VI, April 16, 1960.

[48]Herbicidal sprays are used to kill vegetation in a field where corn is to be raised. Later a special corn planter is used to plant corn in the unplowed field. In 1969, 417 farms in Loudoun used "agricultural chemicals" that cost $868,557.

[49]Ibid., III, April 15, 1939; November 16, 1940.

[50]Ibid., June 22, 1940.

effectively to combat infectious diseases and illnesses in livestock that were formerly treated by home remedies and crude veterinary methods.[51]

Since 1960 mechanization has also been applied to raising beef and dairy cattle in Loudoun through the use of elaborate automatic feeding systems. The most drastic changes have occurred in dairying. Milking machines used widely since the late 1930's have been joined by innovations since 1945 that eliminated the heavy and clumsy milk-can and after 1960 the traditional dairy barn. The dairy barn was gadually replaced by the more efficient and more manageable milking-parlor and free-stalls. While in the milking-parlor, cows are fed a high protein feed consisting of a large percentage of soybean meal. The amount of feed is based upon a computer printout formulated on the past production of each cow.[52]

Big government has continued to influence Loudoun's agriculture since World War II. However, the termination of O.P.A. controls in July 1946 had a dramatic and immediate impact upon the prices of Loudoun's farm products. Prices zoomed upward on the Loudoun livestock market at Leesburg. Under the O.P.A. the ceiling for hogs had been $14.75 per hundred pounds. After the ending of all O.P.A. price controls on commodities, hogs sold in Leesburg for $23 per hundred pounds. The ceiling on calves had been $13.60, but, when controls were removed, the top price suddenly increased to $22.75. Poultry prices also increased after June 1946. The top price for "bakers" and "fryers" under the O.P.A. had been thirty cents a pound, hens twenty-six cents a pound, and roosters twenty-two cents a pound. By the first of July after O.P.A. ceilings were removed, bakers and fryers were sold for forty-three cents a pound, hens for thirty-six cents, and roosters for twenty-seven cents a pound.[53]

Despite a dramatic increase in prices after the termination of the O.P.A., prices for farm products did not constantly and uniformly remain high. Problems of overproduction, fluctuation of prices for farm products, and rising expenses still plagued the farmer, although not to the same degree as during the 1920's and 1930's. Through the enactment of additional legislation the federal government continued price support

---

[51]Telephone interview with Edward R. Brown, March 7, 1974. Artificial insemination has not been free from problems. It has been expensive and often cows do not always conceive as rapidly under this system as farmers would like. More recently some farmers have discontinued using the program of artificial insemination and are again keeping their own bulls.

[52]Statement by Edward R. Brown, personal interview, January 27, 1974. Milk from the milking-parlor flows from the milking machines through pyrex pipelines into a refrigerated storage tank, where it is held until picked up by the milk truck. Pyrex glass pipe is used for sanitary reasons,because it can be thoroughly cleaned by running extremely hot water and detergent through it.

[53] *Times-Mirror,* July 4, 1946.

programs, quota systems, loans, and conservation assistance originally set forth during the New Deal.[54]

Raising poultry was a lucrative business for numerous residents of the county during the 1940's. But the competition of larger and wealthier poultry farms and organizations located in the Valley of Virginia that could stand a smaller margin of profit per bird because of the size of their business led to the demise of poultry farming in Loudoun. After 1950 the poultry farms and hatcheries in Loudoun, like the Mountain View Farm's Hatchery, Pleasant Valley Farm Hatchery, and Loudoun County Hatchery, either drastically curtailed their operation or went out of business.[55]

Government programs did not help Loudoun poultrymen or enable small general farmers to compete successfully in an era of inflation.[56] Numerous federal farm programs until 1973 have, nevertheless, attempted to subsidize farming in Loudoun. Under the soil-bank program initiated in 1956, farmers were paid for taking land out of production to help reduce the surplus of certain crops.[57] From 1936 to 1972 over 1,000 ponds were constructed in Loudoun through assistance provided by the United States Conservation Service and the Agricultural Stabilization and Conservation Service. The Agricultural Conservation Program, called the Rural Environmental Assistance Program (R.E.A.P.), provided financial assistance for pond construction and other conservation measures on "a matching basis." Every dollar given by the

---

[54]Barck and Blake, *Since 1900*, pp. 797-98; statement by John M. York, personal interview, December 15, 1972. Mr. York is the executive director of the Agricultural Stabilization and Conservation Service of the U. S. Department of Agriculture for Loudoun County.

[55]Statement by C. Preston Poland, personal interview, March 8, 1974; *Times-Mirror*, June 29, 1944.

[56]Donald V. Gawronski, *Out of the Past: A Topical History of the United States* (Beverly Hills, Calif.: Glencoe Press, 1969), p. 171.

[57]"Minutes of the Lovettsville Farmers' Club," V, May 19, 1956; *Times-Mirror*, July 29, 1972. For example, in 1956 farmers could sign up, prior to October 5, to decrease their wheat production for the next year by as much as fifty acres. For each acre taken out of wheat production, farmers received funds from the federal government computed in accordance with a formula of thirty-two cents per bushel "of the estimated normal yield" of what the land would have produced if wheat had been raised. Payments were "expected to average about $25.00 per acre in the county." Under this act farmers could also sign up for the "conservation reserve." If they agreed to "take crop land out of production for" a period of several years, they would be paid "annually approximately $10.00 per acre." In 1960, $137,712 was given to Loudoun farmers under the soil-bank program, as compared to $135,653 in 1961 and $102,144 in 1962. Under the Agricultural Act of 1970, the federal government made payments to farmers not to exceed $55,000 per farmer who agreed to "set aside part of his land from production in order to meet a national objective of balancing supply and demand . . . in feed grain, wheat and cotton." By the end of July 1972, the 300 Loudoun farmers who participated in this program received approximately $218,000.

federal government had to be matched by the local farmer.[58] Prior to the termination of the R.E.A.P., more than 121 Loudoun farmers filed for assistance under the "emergency conservation measures" of the R.E.A.P. to help them recover from the "more than million dollars worth of damage to farmland" in Loudoun inflicted by the "Agnes Flood" of June 1972.[59]

Most Loudoun farmers did not participate extensively in federal programs after World War II to obtain additional funds from the federal government. The application of funds that were granted to Loudoun farmers was supervised by the Loudoun Agricultural Stabilization Committee, comprised of county farmers elected to that position, and the executive director of the Agricultural Stabilization and Conservation Service for Loudoun County.[60] While grangers did not mind accepting federal funds, many could not tolerate being told they had to comply with quotas and criteria that might fetter their individualism and thus negate one of the more attractive reasons for being a farmer: being one's own boss. This attitude led S. C. Legard to state on April 22, 1961, in a discussion on farm allotments, that he was "opposed to all forms of slobbering in his business." Others felt federal aid helped only the "big western farmer and it was bad because it represented a gradual tightening of control of farm operations" by the government.[61] In regard to the soil-bank program, critics like Campbell Legard stated:

> . . . the principal [sic] is wrong, it is not sound, too much control is bad, and when you fail to recognize [that] principal [sic], you are getting pretty low. Things like this are apt to break the economy of the whole country.[62]

The major trends in Loudoun agriculture since 1945 have been the displacement of the small general farm, the disappearance of farming

---

[58] *Metro Virginia News* (Leesburg, Va.), January 7, 1973; *Times-Mirror*, Januay 17, 1963. The Rural Environmental Assistance Program was abolished on December 23, 1972. The five years prior to the abandonment of the R.E.A.P. program, Loudoun received approximately $325,000 annually in grants. Federal aid for programs like the construction of farm ponds was abolished with the termination of the R.E.A.P.

[59] *Times-Mirror*, June 29, 1972; November 23, 1972. Under this program farmers suffering extensive damage could receive as much as eighty percent of the costs of "certain conservation measures designed to rehabilitate land" damaged as a result of natural disasters. On June 22 and 23, 1972, Loudoun received nearly twelve inches of rain that flooded parts of the county, inflicting damages to homes and other forms of property estimated to be $5,000,000.

[60] Ibid., January 17, 1963; U. S. Department of Agriculture and Bureau of the Census, *1969 Census of Agriculture* (Washington, D. C.: Government Printing Office, 1972), p. 481. (Hereafter referred to as the *1969 Census of Agriculture*.) In 1969, 226 farms out of 761 in the county participated in some form of government farm program.

[61] "Minutes of the Lovettsville Farmers' Club," VI, April 22, 1961.

[62] Ibid., November 22, 1958.

grarian Land Use in Loudoun from 1910 to 1965.

Harvested Acres	Cropland Not Harvest & not pastured-Acres	Land Use in Preceding Year			Woodland	
		Pasture Acres	Other Pasture Acres	Pasture Acres	Other Acres	
—	—	—	—	—	—	
—	—	—	—	—	—	
86,140	8,621	109,958	26,058	7,734	35,530	
91,977	5,896	124,307	6,855	14,819	30,577	
93,675	3,344	135,451	5,494	14,619	37,450	
94,538	3,139	116,412	—	—	—	
108,176	2,030	71,193	61,440	16,389	36,661	
94,316	7,645	84,294	40,348	12,219	40,750	
90,274	3,671	84,245	42,155	17,925	30,123	
79,670	10,829	76,110	31,838	11,888	33,866	
79,886	7,283	53,086	44,407	10,270	29,216	

ure, Statistical Reporting Service, *Farm Statistics, 1910-66: Loudoun County,*

..., and Wool Sold by Loudoun Farmers from 1909 to 1964.

eam sold utterfat Pounds	Chicken eggs sold Dozens	Chickens sold Head	Turkeys raised Head	Wool shorn Pounds
4,400	556,417	—	—	—
35,957	541,294	87,016	—	56,069
248,173	—	—	—	62,032
316,762	607,285	122,896	10,300	75,209
—	—	—	—	84,243
266,737	—	122,917	13,858	66,422
336,188	—	—	14,024	57,609
727,813	560,798	176,762	26,916	40,930
169,483	365,483	111,090	36,308	42,500
78,060	243,656	83,266	51,201	32,690
43,536	306,322	22,956	4,800	20,313

...tatistical Reporting Service, *Farm Statistics, 1910-66: Loudoun County,*

in eastern Loudoun as the urban corridor has grown to include portions of that part of the county, and the emergence of larger and more mechanized dairy farms in western Loudoun. These trends have greatly accelerated since 1960.[63] For example, small general farmers during the late 1950's and 1960's have stopped farming and sought employment elsewhere due to inflation, higher taxes, and the expense of mechanized farming. Often lands formerly used for general farming were rented by dairymen to sustain an increase in their dairy herds.[64] Although fewer, the farms were larger than in the past. The number of acres in corn decreased from 26,000 in 1955 to 4,900 acres in 1966. The number of farms declined from 2,015 in 1950 to 761 in 1969. From 1954 to 1959, the amount of land farmed in the county deceased almost 25,000 acres, an annual decrease of 5,000 acres.[65] In 1950 the population of Loudoun was 21,147, of whom 10,751 lived on farms. By 1960 the total county population was 24,549, with only approximately one-fifth of the residents, 5,784, living on farms.[66]

THE SUBURBAN REVOLUTION

By 1920, urban living had become the way of life for a majority of Americans.[67] However, in Loudoun County significant demographic changes indicative of urbanization did not take place until after 1950. Until that time the population of Loudoun had remained more or less the same since 1800.[68] For example, in 1800 there were 20,523 residents in the county, compared to 21,147 in 1950. By 1960 the population had

---

[63]Ibid., June 17, 1961; *1969 Census of Agriculture*, pp. 417-24; U. S. Department of Agriculture, Statistical Reporting Service, *Farm Statistics, 1910-66: Loudoun County, Virginia* (Washington, D. C.: Government Printing Office, 1967), pp. 1-4. (Hereafter referred to as *Farm Statistics, 1910-66*.)

[64]An example of this change is the career of C. Preston Poland. From the 1940's into the 1950's he was a general farmer and proprietor of Mountain View Farm Hatchery. During the latter 1950's, he abandoned both forms of farming and became a contractor and builder of custom homes. He then rented his farm land to a nearby dairy farmer, Nelson Craun.

[65]*Times-Mirror*, November 17, 1960. This decline was due in large part to the increase in the number of commuters who purchased farms, the disappearance of the small farmer, and the expulsion of residents from 5,000 acres taken for the construction of Dulles Airport.

[66]*1969 Census of Agriculture*, p. 417; *Farm Statistics, 1910-66*, pp. 2-3.

[67]Blake Mckelvey, *American Urbanization: A Comparative History* (Glenview, Ill.: Scott, Foresman and Co., 1973), pp. 110-14; Nugent, *Modern America*, pp. 59-60.

[68]Loudoun County Department of Planning and Zoning, *Loudoun County Data Book*, [1972], p. [33]. (Hereafter referred to as the *Loudoun County Date Book*.)

Table 18. *Acreage and Yield of Corn and Wheat in Loudoun from 1909 to 1966.*

Year	CORN			WHEAT		
	Acreage	Yield Bu.	Production Bu.	Acreage	Yield Bu.	Production Bu.
Census:[a]						
1909	41,904	26.7	1,119,384	33,518	13.8	461,612
1919	41,601	39.7	1,651,903	45,846	12.5	573,165
1924	28,743	33.3	955,774	29,533	13.1	386,929
1929	28,198	35.5	999,982	30,709	15.3	471,118
Estimates:[b]						
1930	35,600	6.1[c]	217,200	27,880	19.0	529,900
1935	35,000	37.0	1,295,000	25,000	17.4	435,000
1940	32,500	42.5	1,381,250	23,000	17.5	402,500
1945	31,400	44.4	1,394,200	23,700	18.0	426,600
1946	27,700	49.0	1,357,300	20,950	21.0	440,000
1947	28,000	46.5	1,302,000	20,300	21.0	426,300
1948	28,200	57.5	1,621,500	19,650	21.5	422,500
1949	25,000	54.0	1,350,000	16,200	19.8	320,800
1950	24,800	55.0	1,364,000	14,500	18.4	266,800
1951	25,600	46.0	1,177,600	13,500	20.9	282,500
1952	25,900	51.3	1,328,700	13,500	23.3	314,600
1953	26,200	34.0	890,800	13,600	21.4	290,700
1954	26,500	45.0	1,192,500	9,700	28.8	279,400
1955	26,000	40.9	1,063,400	8,400	30.5	256,600
1956	23,900	59.0	1,410,100	8,200	28.5	233,700
1957	23,900	29.0[c]	693,100	5,900	20.5	121,000
1958	16,700	64.2	1,072,600	7,200	28.7	207,000
1959	15,800	52.3	826,100	6,600	19.5	128,700
1960	16,900	67.1	1,133,500	6,500	29.0	188,500
1961	16,100	64.2	1,034,400	6,200	27.0	167,400
1962	17,400	63.0	1,096,500	4,900	24.0	117,700
1963	8,500	45.0	382,450	5,200	25.0	129,900
1964	12,200	60.7	740,500	6,100	26.4	161,300
1965	11,700	55.0	643,600	5,800	31.0	179,800
1966	4,900	37.0[c]	181,200	5,500	33.0	181,600

Source: U.S. Department of Agriculture, Statistical Reporting Service, *Farm Statistics, 1910-66: Loudoun County, Virginia,* p. 4.

[a]Corn for grain
[b]All corn (grain, silage, and forage)
[c]Droughts in 1930, 1957, and 1966 greatly reduced corn yield

Table 19. Number of Residents That Lived on Farms in Loudoun from 1910 to 1960.

Year	Population Total	Farm
1910	21,167	—
1920	20,577	—
1925	—	11,631
1930	19,852	10,223
1935	—	12,504
1940	20,291	11,793
1945	—	11,024
1950	21,147	10,751
1955	—	—
1960	24,549	5,784

Source: U.S. Department of Agriculture, Statistical Reporting Service, *Farm Statistics, 1910-1966: Loudoun County, Virginia*, p. 3.

increased significantly to 24,549. Yet even this increase was less than a thousand more than the 23,634 living in the county in 1880.[69] From 1880 to 1930 the population of Loudoun decreased to 19,852 residents. This decline was due to the attraction of jobs and action located in the city, the continued agrarian nature of Loudoun, the lack of industrial growth in the county, and limited job opportunities.[70] The movement of residents from the county, essentially to Washington, D.C., from 1880 to 1930 was reversed after World War II. From 1945 to 1960, exurbanites, residents from the Washington area and other cities moved to Loudoun County, where their way of living was a mixture of urban and rural elements.

Exurbanites were the precursors of the suburbanites that came to the county after 1960 to live in large planned communities. A majority of the latter, who came from the older and impacted suburbs of Washington, continued to work for the federal government and other places of employment in Alexandria, Arlington, and Fairfax counties, the District of Columbia, and even Maryland. They moved in such

---

[69]Ibid.; Deck and Heaton, *An Economic and Social Survey of Loudoun*, pp. 62-64. The population of Loudoun in 1940 was 20,291.

[70]Ibid.; *Loudoun County Data Book*, p. [33]; Virginia, Division of Industrial Development and Planning, *Leesburg . . . People and Economy* (Richmond, Va.: n.p., 1964), p. 3

numbers to eastern Loudoun in search of homes that by 1970 the county's population had increased to the unprecedented number of 37,150, of whom 17,154 lived in Sterling Park and the seven major incorporated towns in the county: Leesburg, Purcellville, Middleburg, Round Hill, Hamilton, Lovettsville, and Hillsboro. Housing units in the county increased 64.7 percent from 1960 to 1970. For example, Loudoun had 7,370 housing units in 1960 as compared to 11,400 in 1970. Of the latter, 10,215 were single units; 954, two or more units; and 231 were mobile homes. New housing units increase annually from 365 in the 1966-1967 fiscal year to 2,293 in 1971-1972. This construction helped increased the population per square mile from 47.5 in 1960 to 71.9 in 1970.[71] Of the 14,339 employed county residents in 1970, 2,712 were professional workers, such as engineers, teachers, and physicians; only 312 were farmers and 765 farm laborers and farm foremen.[72]

The most drastic demographic increases have occurred in the county since 1960. Farming significantly declined in eastern Loudoun during the last half of the 1950's due in large part to the construction of Dulles International Airport on an extensive portion of eastern Loudoun. Five hundred residents of 5,000 acres in Loudoun and 3,000 acres in Fairfax were dislocated and evicted from their homes and property in 1958. This development not surprisingly produced emotional and harsh verbal exchanges between residents of the region and officials of the Civil Aeronautics Administration seeking as rapid a possession of the land as possible in order to begin construction of the airport.[73]

The construction of Chantilly Airport, later officially named Dulles International Airport, not only destroyed the remaining vestiges of many of the bicorporal communities and farming in southeastern Loudoun, but also accelerated the demise of farming in eastern Loudoun to the north of the airport because of extensive purchases of land by corporations for commercial development. Lehman Brothers of New York, one of the nation's largest investment banking houses, operating through the Northern Virginia Development Corporation, quietly led the way by purchasing sizeable acreage north of the airport for $2 million. The impact of the construction of the airport, land speculation for future commercial

---

[71] *Loudoun County Data Book*, pp. [33-34, 72-73]. Of the 37,150 in Loudoun in 1970 only 4,648 were Negroes. Although the number of new housing units dramatically increased from 1960 to 1970, the number did not always surpass that of the previous year. There were 522 new units in 1967-1968 fiscal year, 415 in 1969-1970, and 1,087 in 1970-1971.

[72] Ibid., pp. [35, 49]. There were fifty physicians, dentists, and related practitioners (optometrists and veterinarians) in Loudoun in 1970.

[73] *Times-Mirror*, January 30, 1958; July 13, 1958; August 20, 1958; August 31, 1961. Numerous suits emanated over the assessment and payments for condemned properties and the deadlines for residents to leave as demanded by the government's right-of-eminent-domain.

and industrial development, and the realization that agriculture had ceased as a significant way of life in most of eastern Loudoun led the Planning Commission of Loudoun to zone the vicinity around the airport as suitable for commercial development.[74] This represented a significant shift in the attitude of county planners, because up to 1966 the Planning Commission was opposed to rezoning the northeastern region of the county for industrial use.[75]

County officials and discerning residents were aware during the late 1950's that Loudoun was on the threshold of being transformed. The headline of the December 4, 1958, issue of *The Loudoun Times-Mirror* read: "Growth Begins, Surge Coming in Population." Although many citizens were alarmed, some thoughtful Loudouners felt that Loudoun had "the machinery at hand to handle this transition . . . without too many dislocations."[76] In 1962 another headline in the above county paper, "More Than $101,000,000 in Building Is Under Way," reflected the building boom in Loudoun.[77] Responsible for the direct intervention into Loudoun life were American corporate behemoths and financial giants, including New York banks and "200 millions of U.S. Steel money for a 'planned community' " of 1,700 acres which was predicted to double the county's population in ten years.[78] In 1964 United States Steel Corporation bought out the corporation of M. T. Broyhill & Son, launchers of the planned community known as Sterling Park that had brought urban life to the county on a large scale.

From the fall of 1961 to the fall of 1962 county officials, led by the Board of Supervisors, opposed Broyhills' "Planned City" by refusing to a m e n d the county Zoning Ordinance to accommodate planned communities, such as the one the Broyhills proposed. During the last

[74]Ibid., October 22, 1959. The *Times-Mirror* in this issue had a headline that read: "Industrial City' Seen for Sterling-Ashburn."

[75]Ibid., September 21, 1961. Planners stated industrial development would have an adverse effect upon Goose Creek County Club, Belmont Plantation, and the modest surburban developments known as the Potomac and Broad Run Farms subdivison.

[76]Ibid., December 4, 1958; *The Blue Ridge Herald,* September 2, 1954. This was based on faith in the Planning Commission and Board of Supervisors.

[77]*Times-Mirror,* October 16, 1960. This sum did not include the $90 million cost for the construction of Dulles Airport and $5 million additional being spent by the federal government for the construction of the Federal Aviation Agency's Air Traffic Control Center at Leesburg.

[78]Ibid., April 26, 1963; September 12, 1963. U.S. Steel financed the Broyhill Company prior to buying it out. In 1963 American Telephone and Telegraph built an installation on the Short Hill Mountain costing $4,700,000. In 1969, International Business Machines Corporation purchased the 1,128-acre historic Belmont Plantation east of Leesburg. I.B.M. paid $3 million or approximately $2,600 per acre. Levitt and Sons have attempted since 1970 to build a large "planned community" within Loudoun. This company was the largest residential development firm in America. It was later purchased by I.T.&T. Federal antitrust action has since forced I.T.&T. to divest itself of this firm, and in 1974 Levitt purchased his former company.

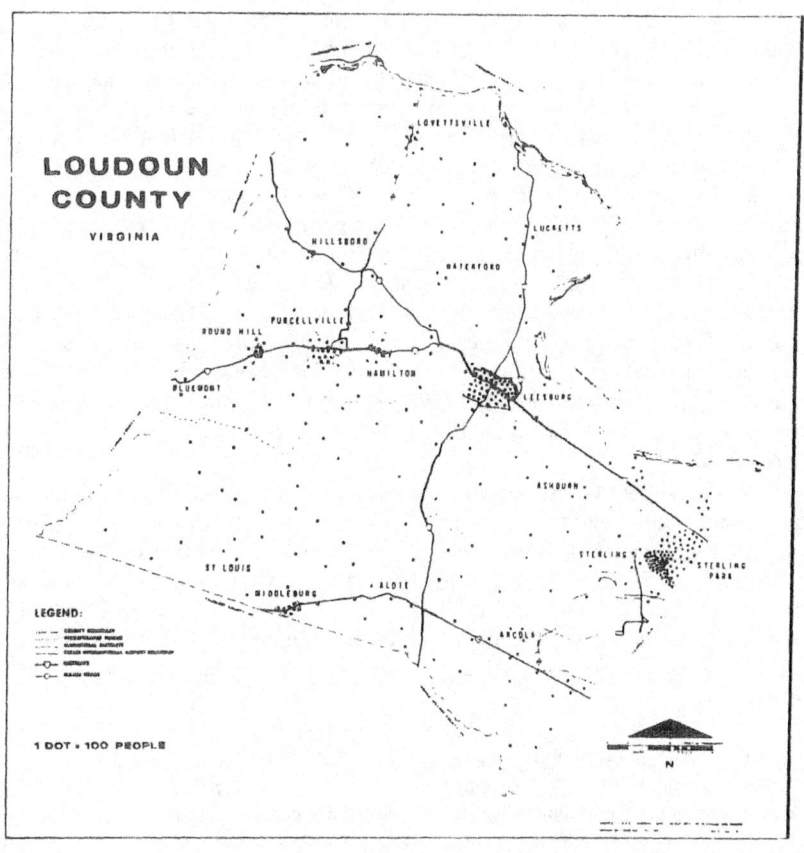

*Figure 22. Distribution of Loudoun's Population in 1970.
Souce: Loudoun County Data Book, p. [36].*

part of February 1962 county supervisors accepted the report of the planning consultant firm of Mott and Hayden, hired by the county to study the Broyhills' proposal for a planned community. This report stated Sterling Park was not needed "to meet the growth" that was anticipated in the county over the next two decades. Supervisor J. T. Hirst expressed the view of many residents when he stated, "I do not think Loudoun can afford this much impact at one time."[79] In the meantime the Broyhill firm started construction of a "1,700-home subdivision" on 500 acres of the 1,700-acre tract that had been zoned residential previously.[80] To counteract the attitude and reasoning of men like J. T. Hirst, the lawyers and public relations men for the Broyhill firm launched a campaign that Sterling Park would house "fewer than one school-age child per house and about one school-age child for each four apartments." Figures submitted as to the anticipated county taxes to be paid by residents of the subdivision maintained that, if "capital investments were not counted" after the first year, the tax returns to the county would exceed "the costs of schooling the children, and providing police and other services." Such logic convinced not only the editors of the *Times-Mirror*, who propagated this view and endorsed the establishment of Sterling Park, but also the Board of Supervisors.[81] By the summer of 1962, the way was paved for the development of Sterling Park by the supervisors, who amended the county Zoning Ordinance to provide for planned communities.[82] By 1973, the development of Sterling Park, although advanced, had not been completed.

In July 1970, the establishment of the second major planned community for Loudoun, Sugarland Run, was approved by the county Planning Commission. Developers of the project, Boise Cascade Building Company, started in the fall of 1970 the construction of a planned community that, when completed, was projected to have "a final population of about 7,800 people" residing in more than 1,000 single family houses, 658 town-houses and over 500 "garden apartment units."[83]

[79]Ibid., September 2, 1961; March 1, 1962.

[80]Ibid., March 1, 1967. On the 500 acres already zoned residential the Broyhill Company needed only to show that their subdivision met county zoning and sanitation standards and provided adequate sewer and water service and satisfactory streets.

[81]Ibid., August 17, 1961; June 21, 1962. During 1962, the Broyhill Company planned to construct 328 homes to sell and 256 apartments to rent. The complex was to include a shopping center, and a seventy-five-acre sports and recreation center. Originally the company planned to complete this project, which would include 3,500 homes, 3,000 apartments, grade schools, a high school, churches, and house 22,000 to 30,000 in ten years.

[82]Ibid., September 20, 1962. During 1965, the Sterling Park Development Corporation, a division of the United States Steel Corporation, updated the original plans for Sterling Park. These included the construction over a period of five to ten years of an additional 5,000 residential units, of which approximately 1,900 units were to be apartments.

[83]Ibid., July 30, 1970; September 24, 1970.

Other significant growth has occurred in the county's most populous towns, Leesburg and Purcellville. Leesburg's population has increased from 1,703 in 1950 to 2,869 in 1960 and 4,821 in 1970 while Purcellville has experienced a demographic growth from 945 in 1950 to 1,419 in 1960 and 1,775 in 1970.[84] Both Leesburg and Purcellville have expanded their territories by annexation and have experienced population increases as the result of the establishment of new subdivisions. Their economies have also been altered as the result of the emergence of new shopping centers that have replaced and transferred many of the major stores and shopping districts from the center to the outskirts of these towns.[85] Much of Leesburg's growth was due to the partial implementation of a planned subdivision to the south of the original town and apartments built to the east of "old" Leesburg.[86]

As of the end of 1973 the development of Sterling Park, Sugarland Run, and subdivisions in Leesburg and elsewhere in the county, while far from being completed, nevertheless have had a salient and revolutionary impact upon the county. They were responsible in large part for doubling the county's population from 21,147 in 1950 to approximately 42,000 residents in 1973. The above subdivisions also have helped to accelerate the demise of agriculture in Loudoun, especially in eastern Loudoun, and have had a profound impact upon county government, education, taxes, and volume of traffic on the major highways in the county.[87]

[84]Virginia Division of State Planning and Community Affairs, *Data Summary: Loudoun County* (Richmond, Va.: Office of Research and Information, 1972), p. 6. (Hereafter referred to as *Data Summary* for 1970.)

[85]*Times-Mirror*, April 4, 1963; August 26, 1965; January 6, 1966. By the first part of 1966, Purcellville had tripled the area of the town. During 1965, twelve acres on the eastern outskirts of Purcellville was purchased by Charles F. Holden, Jr., Dr. William T. Burch, H. M. Ball, Jr., and C. C. Brown for $100,500. They developed a major shopping center that included "a major grocery chain, a drug chain, individual shops and other commercial enterprises" housed in structures "colonial in style" and offering "three acres of blacktop parking."

[86]Ibid., August 17, 1972; December 24, 1972; April 4, 1963; Loudoun County Planning Commission Minutes for September 22, 1970, pp. 4-8. In 1963 there was a plan for $10 million subdivision south of Leesburg on a 336-acre site with 700 homes ranging from $13,000 to $17,000, an eight-acre shopping center, and twenty acres reserved for recreation. The project was proposed by Sidney Z. Mensh and Company of Washington, D.C. Although numerous houses and apartments are currently being constructed on over 100 acres of this site, the development has changed owners and the plans have been substantially altered.

[87]Virginia Department of Highways, *Commonwealth of Virginia: Depatment of Highways* (Richmond, Va.: Traffic and Safety Division, 1971), pp. 5-6. In 1971 traffic on Route 7, from Sterling Park to Leesburg varied in volume from 10,920 to 9,510 vehicles a day, from Leesburg to Purcelllville 10,720 to 7,415, and Purcellville to Round Hill 3,205. The volume has greatly increased since 1971. Although Route 7 is in the process of being made into a four-lane highway, traffic congestion in Loudoun will be exacerbated by new housing and the projected increase of 5,800 vehicles per day to attend the Loudoun Campus of Northern Virginia Community College by 1983. This campus opened on a full-time basis in the fall of 1974.

Demographic growth has had a profound effect upon county institutions, as growth has been the paramount force behind the expansion and modification of the traditional "county Board format" of county government that had gradually evolved from the colonial period.[88] In spite of demographic pressures the Board of Supervisors has remained the most significant branch of the county government. It has continued to determine policies for the county, supervise all fiscal affairs, and appoint most of the members of other county boards.[89] The Board of Supervisors in May 1963 created the position of an executive secretary to assist the board in the administration of county government.[90] Population increases also brought about in 1971 the redistricting of county magisterial districts that increased the number of districts from six to seven. This subsequently increased by one the number of members who served on county agencies like the Board of Supervisors, School Board, and Planning Commission.[91] Between 1960 and 1971 the county sheriff's department increased from approximately a half dozen "field deputies" to twenty.[92] To provide recreation for a growing non-agrarian population, the Board of Supervisors authorized in 1961 the establishment of a Department of Parks and Recreation for Loudoun County.[93] In 1959 the development of eastern Loudoun prompted the supervisors to establish the Loudoun County Sanitation Authority in an attempt to handle the county's

---

[88]George W. Jennings, *Virginia's Government* (rev. ed.; Richmond, Va.; Virginia State Chamber of Commerce, 1971), pp. 115-20; *Loudoun County Data Book*, p. [20]; *Times-Mirror*, July 21, 1949; August 11, 1949; October 27, 1960; November 3, 1966. Attempts to change the existing form of county government in 1949, 1960, and 1966 have not been successful.

[89]School Board members were appointed by a three-man School Electoral Board until 1972. As the result of a county referendum on November 7, 1972, the School Board members were thereafter appointed by the Board of Supervisors.

[90]*Loudoun County Data Book*, p. [20] On July 1, 1972, the title of Executive Secretary of Loudoun County was changed to County Administrator but the duties remained unchanged.

[91]Ibid., p. [33]; *Times-Mirror*, July 1, 1971; October 14, 1971. Not only were the boundaries of these districts greatly altered but former names of districts like Mt. Gilead and Lovettsville were abandoned and new names assigned like Blue Ridge, Catoctin, Dulles and Sterling. The only old names kept were Leesburg, Broad Run, and Mercer.

By 1976, the increase in Loudoun's population (estimated to be 56,612) again brought about the redistricting of the county and the addition of another magisterial district: Guilford.

[92]*Data Summary* for 1970, p. 22. In 1971, the sheriff's department had seventeen support deputies to supplement the regular staff. Four towns had their own police officers plus there were nine troopers of the Virginia state police assigned to the county.

[93]*Times-Mirror*, June 9, 1966. Since its creation, this department has constructed tennis courts, basketball courts, baseball and softball fields, and horseshoe pits on twenty-six school grounds and opened and operated community centers for teen and adult activities.

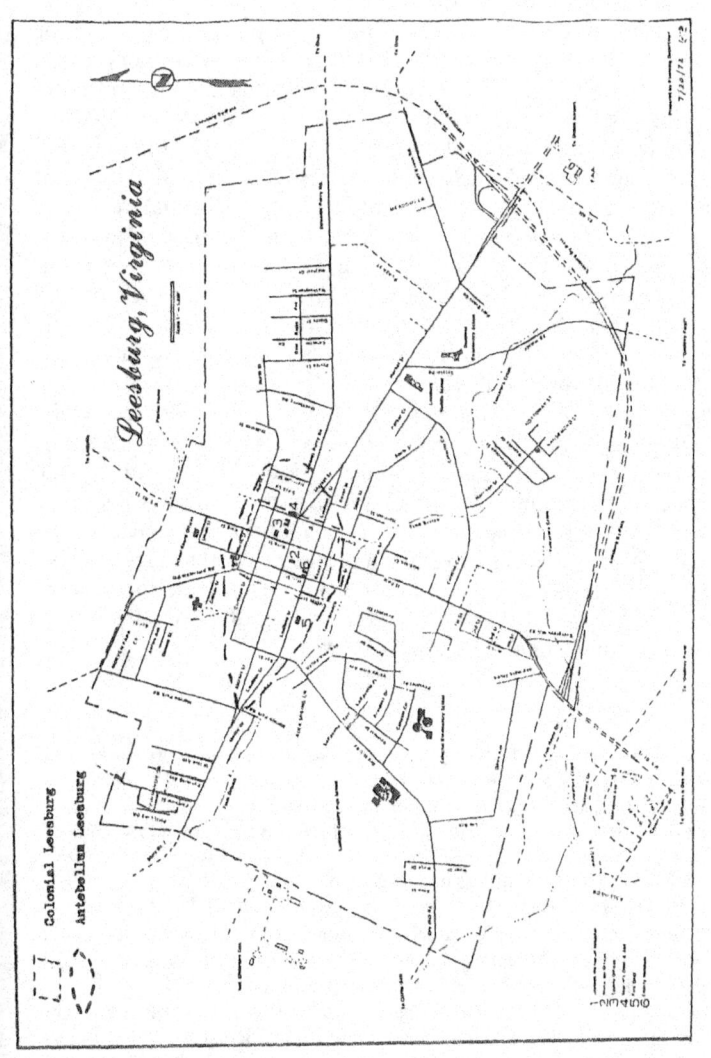

Figure 23. A 1972 Map of Leesburg, Virginia.

sewerage and water problems.[94] Burgeoning construction in the county also caused the Board of Supervisors to establish a building code for Loudoun in 1961 and an electrical code the following year. Building inspectors were subsequently appointed to insure that contractors complied with county construction standards.[95]

Growth has also necessitated the establishment and expansion of the personnel and work of the county Planning Commission.[96] Members of this commission have no legislative power, but serve as an advisory board to the Board of Supervisors. The Planning Commission is assigned the task of studying and making recommendations to the supervisors on "subdivision control, land use and classification." Planning commissioners and the planning staff are also assigned the responsibility of issuing or denying building permits to developers, realtors, or individual residents in such a manner as to insure that a single structure or subdivisions are well-planned, conform to the county's zoning, and subdivison ordinances and comprehensive plan, and contribute to the orderly growth of the county. Further, they allow the development of areas suited to residential, commercial, and industrial building while they attempt to maintain desirable agricultural and rural areas.[97]

The implementation of these guidelines has not been easily achieved. Zoning has increasingly become more complex, and Planning Commission meetings more heated and emotional.[98] Farmers and residents with a lengthy tenure in Loudoun, frightened by development which they deem to be bringing impending economic and social disaster to the communities in which they live, have protested vociferously against rezoning land and the issuance of building permits to developers and realtors in spite of the latter's constant promulgation of the doctrine that "progress" cannot, and should not, be deterred.

[94]Loudoun County Sanitation Authority, *Loudoun County Sanitation Authority: Ten Years of Service and Progress*, 1973, pp. 1-11; *Times-Mirror*, June 25, 1970. Since 1973 the Loudoun County Sanitation Authority has attempted to develop a "major water supply system and a sanitary sewerage system for a greater portion of the eastern section of Loudoun."

[95]*Times-Mirror*, August 17, 1961; January 25, 1962.

[96]Jennings, *Virginia's Government*, p. 120. There existed as of 1972, in addition to the Planning Commission, a full-time Director of Planning, an Assistant Planner, and a Zoning Administrator. In special situations certain zoning cases may be taken to a Board of Zoning Appeals, which is appointed by the Circuit Court judge.

[97]*Data Summary* for 1970, p. 21 *Loudoun County Data Book*, p. [30]; Virginia Citizens Planning Association, *A Planning Commissioner's Handbook* (Richmond, Va.: Virginia Citizens Planning Association, n.d.), pp. 1-8, 20. Statement by C. Preston Poland, personal interview, March 16, 1974.

[98]Loudoun County Planning Commission Minutes, for October 2, 1972, p. 2; October 24, 1972, pp. 2-3; November 2, 1972, p.2; *Times-Mirror*, December 9, 1971. Since 1960 zoning has dominated the headlines of the county newspapers more than any other single topic.

THE CRISIS OF CHANGE: 1945 TO 1972   373

Of all the zoning cases concerning Loudoun, none has been as celebrated or as significant as the county's refusal to rezone 1,270 acres in northeastern Loudoun purchased in 1969 by Levitt and Sons, Inc., at that time the nation's lagest residential development firm. Levitt planned to construct a $125,000,000 planned community designed to house 13,000 people. The Board of Supervisors rejected Levitt's attempt to build such a "planned community on the grounds that it" would adversely affect the county's economy due to the sudden demand for additional schools and services. Levitt appealed the decision to the Loudoun Circuit Court on the grounds that the Loudoun supervisors had acted in an "arbitary and capricious" way and "in a discriminatory manner in light of the county's recent approval of the Sugarland Run subdivison."[99] The court upheld Loudoun's rejection of Levitt and Sons; the corporation then appealed the decision to the State Supreme Court. Subsequently, Loudoun formulated an innovative approach that has become known as Article 12 of the county Zoning Ordinance. Widely applauded by critics of unfettered growth and widely denounced by developers, Article 12 required developers to pay for the establishment of public facilities, such as schools, sewers, and libraries needed to serve residents of a new development. In August 1972 Levitt abandoned its appeal to the Virginia Supreme Court, much to the dismay of developers in northern Virginia, and filed a new application in Loudoun to establish a subdivision in compliance with Article 12. This move also annoyed other developers in northern Virginia.[100]

Demographic growth had its most dramatic impact upon the expansion of the county school system and the subsequent increment in county taxes, the overwhelming proportion of which go to help finance the county's educational system.[101] School enrollment in the county rose

[99]Loudoun County, [Department of Planning and Zoning], *Zoning Ordinance of Loudoun County* (1972), pp. 157-66.

[100]Loudoun County Planning Commission Minutes for August 25, 1970, pp. 2-7; November 14, 1972, pp. 3-7; "Land Use and Abuse," *Central Atlantic Environment News*, II (September, 1972), 2-3; Statement by C. Preston Poland, personal inteview, March 16, 1974; *Times-Mirror*, December 3, 1970; February 4, 1971; December 2, 1971; August 3, 1972. As of March 1974, Levitt's application was before the Loudoun Board of Supervisors, who had up to then delayed ruling upon it. Other counties faced with extensive growth are considering the adoption of an "Article 12" approach. So revolutionary was the concept set forth in Article 12 that it received coverage in an article in *Newsweek* (August 21, 1972, p. 40), entitled "Banning the Boom."

[101] *Times-Mirror*, August 27, 1970. Of the $12,908,758 spent by the county government in the 1971-1972 fiscal year, $10,447,204 was spent on Loudoun's education system. Increase in school enrollment has necessitated not only additional teachers, but also an expansion of the administrative staff to assist the superintendent of schools in planning for the expansion of the educational system, and supervising and providing assistance to the teachers in the existing schools. There were fifty principals, assistant principals, supervisors, and directors in the 1971-1972 school year and sixty the following academic year. The instructional staff was increased from 552 in 1971-1972 to 604 in 1972-1973.

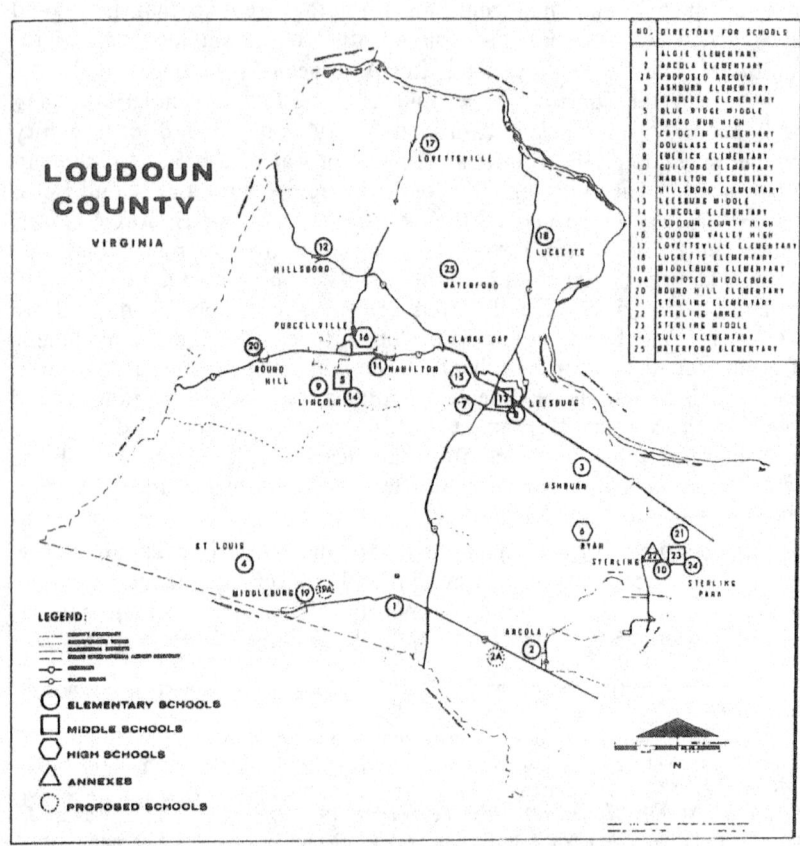

Figure 24. Loudoun County School Sites in 1972.
Source: Loudon County Data Book, p. [36].

New schools that opened from 1972 to 1976 are Rolling Ridge Elementary School in Sterling Park, Sugarland Elementary School in Sugarland Run, J. Lupton Simpson Middle School in Leesburg, and Park View High School in Sterling Park.

from 8,313 in 1967-1968 school year to 11,700 in the fall of 1973.[102] The school budget has risen from $2,544,592 in 1965-1966 to approximately $13,500,000 in 1973-1974. In 1960 the total county budget was only $2,400,000, but by 1967 it had risen to $6,600,000.[103] In spite of dramatic increases in the school budget, overcrowded conditions still existing in eastern Loudoun schools have resulted in the use of trailers, politely referred to as "mobile classrooms," and a twelve-month school program that started in the summer of 1973 for four schools in the Sterling district: Guilford, Sterling, and Sully Elementary schools, and the Sterling Middle School.[104] As school budgets increased during the 1960's, the county became increasingly more dependent on bond referenda and the incrementation of county taxes,[105] especially the local real estate tax, which is the largest single source of county revenue.[106] From 1961 to 1973 the rate of this form of taxation increased from $2.35 to $3.20 per hundred dollars of the assessed value of real estate. The revenue from the county real estate tax increased from $718,651 in 1961 to $4,849,184 in 1971.[107]

During the 1960's the increase in tax rates on real estate and the increase in the appraisal of farm land in Loudoun spiraled to the point some land was appraised 1,000 percent higher than the appraised value at the beginning of the decade. Farmers complained, with considerable justification, of inconsistencies and inequalities in the appraisals of realty.

---

[102] *Loudoun County Data Book*, p. 417; Statement by Don Middleton, personal interview, March 15, 1974.

[103] *Times-Mirror*, March 4, 1965; August 10, 1967; February 12, 1970; *Metro Virginia News*, March 10, 1970. The school budget for 1976-1977 is $2,762,557.

[104] Arcola P.T.A. Executive Committee, Survey of Parents on Twelve-Month School, January 26, 1973; *Times-Mirror*, February 1, 1973. In the Loudoun year-round school program, students went to school for forty-five days, followed by a fifteen-day vacation. This cycle was continued throughout the year. By staggering the vacation periods, a school could accommodate about one-fourth more students than the traditional nine-month school year where all students had a summer vacation.

[105] *Times-Mirror*, February 16, 1961; January 9, 1964; June 20, 1968; October 24, 1968; April 12, 1973; *Metro Virginia News*, April 15, 1973. For example, county voters approved school bond issues in 1964 of $5,500,00, in 1968 for $11,250,000, and in 1973 for $27,900,00.

[106] *Loudoun County Data Book*, p. [79]. Loudoun received during the 1971-1972 fiscal year $6,377,839 in property taxes, $1,309,782 for other local taxes, $3,605,720 from the state government, $824,527 from the federal government, and $934,841 from local licenses pemits, fines, et al.

[107] Ibid., pp. 77-80. The assessed value was only twenty-five percent of the appraised value of realty owned by Loudoun taxpayers. In 1964 the assessed value was increased to forty percent of the appraised value. Other county taxes in 1972 included a personal property tax of $5 per hundred dollars of the fair "market value" of motor vehicles, aircraft, boats, trailers, and business equipment; one percent sales tax; and a ten percent utility tax on telephone, electricity, and gas usage. The county Board of Supervisors discontinued the household personal property tax on January 1, 1967.

Similar property was frequently not appraised in the same manner.[108] For example, in 1964 a large 13,000-acre area between Leesburg and Fairfax County traversed by Route 7 was a region of great disparity in property assessments. Some land in that region was appraised at $2,000 per acre while adjoining land of similar characteristics was appraised from $1,000 to $1,200 an acre.[109]

Rising taxes were the most damaging to residents on fixed incomes, usually the elderly whose finances were already strained by inflation. Such was the case of Mrs. Faye L. Presgrave, who lived at Pleasant Valley on Route 50 in southeastern Loudoun, close to Fairfax County. She had lived on a three-acre plot since 1927. Widowed in 1955 and unable to work, she had to rely upon Social Security payments for her financial needs and commitments. From 1960 to 1970 her property taxes increased from $37.93 to $250.69. In 1970 her property was reappraised, and its assessed value increased from $5,200 to $11,660.[110] This was a significant factor in her selling her property the following year to a speculator.

The county government has not been totally remiss in at least attempting to cope with some of the problems associated with the escalation and inequities of county property taxes. Attempts to slow the escalating tax on realty were made by the implementation of Article 12 of the county Zoning Ordinance and the enactment of new taxes, such as the one percent county sales tax that went into effect in 1966 and the ten percent utility tax established in 1971.[111] To further reduce the burden of property taxes for the farmer in the county, the Board of Supervisors in the fall of 1972 adopted a program enacted by the state legislature earlier that year. This plan, referred to as Land Use Taxation (L.U.T.), was designed to greatly reduce the assessed value of farmland

---

[108] *Times-Mirror*, December 23, 1965; February 18, 1971; February 25, 1971. State law required the county to have a reappraisal of realty for tax purposes within the county at least every six years. Appraisals were made in 1964 and 1969 by a county assessment board. Membership on this body resulted from the appointment of one person from each magisterial district by the judge of the Circuit Court, who usually appointed persons nominated by the county Board of Supervisors. This board's assessment of the value of each piece of property allegedly was based upon "availability and access to highways, schools, sewage, and water." Landowners could seek redress from what they felt were unfair assessments by appealing to a county equalization board, which in a limited number of cases has made adjustments in the assessed value of properties.

[109] Ibid., February 25, 1971; March 4, 1971; March 18, 1971. In 1969 taxes on two farms owned by one farmer were $763.24. After the reappraisal, his property taxes on the same two farms were $1,632.28. Inequities in tax appraisals were not limited solely to eastern Loudoun, because complaints came from all over the county.

[110] Ibid., August 1, 1971. The land upon which Mrs. Presgrave's home was located increased in assessed value 360 percent in the 1970 reappraisal. The assessed value of the three-acre tract in 1969 was $2,000 and in 1970 $7,200.

[111] *Loudoun County Data Book*, pp. [77-78]; *Times-Mirror*, May 26, 1966; March 4, 1971; September 9, 1971; December 9, 1971.

for tax purposes.[112] Much confusion resulted from the lack of precise directives, as only nominal requirements were made of landowners to qualify for assessment on the basis of current use rather than the land's "fair market value."[113] One month after Loudoun adopted the L.U.T. in 1972, 513 landowners picked up forms to apply for tax reductions under this program. Among them was one of the largest land speculation companies in Loudoun, the Northern Virginia Development Company, which sought tax relief on 2,400 acres it had purchased in eastern Loudoun. Speculators were able to qualify on the grounds they were preserving "open spaces."[114] Farmland, which had been appraised at up to $1,000 per acre under the "fair market value system," was reduced under the L.U.T. program to assessments ranging from $50 to $400 per acre.[115] More than half of the $500,000 the county lost in real estate tax revenues during the first year L.U.T. was in operation in the county was "pocketed" by landowners, speculators, and others, who probably could not qualify for tax relief under the 1973 L.U.T. law.[116]

To remedy the fact that land speculators could qualify as easily as farmers for tax relief under the 1972 L.U.T. law, Charles Waddell, a former member of the Loudoun Board of Supervisors who had been recently elected to the Virginia State Legislature as a Senator, introduced a bill in the Virginia Senate in 1973 designed to reduce the ease with which land speculators could qualify for tax relief under L.U.T. The enactment of the Waddell bill into a new land use law set higher standards by making as a requirement for L.U.T. the condition that land must be used in a manner that is "consistent with the land use plan of the county and zoning ordinances." This provision allowed Loudoun to link L.U.T. assessments directly with zoning. Other new qualifications included a certification by landowners that their property was being used in a "planned program for soil management and soil conservation practices" and had been farmed primarily for commercial purposes for at least five years prior to the application for tax relief under L.U.T.[117] However, even the new law does not circumvent all speculators from qualifying for tax relief. By purchasing farms that have produced for the commercial market for the past five years, speculators can rent out

---

[112] *Times-Mirror*, October 5, 1972.

[113] Ibid., January 25, 1973. Under the 1972 law, landowners could qualify for tax relief under four categories: agricultural, horticultural, open space, and forest.

[114] Ibid., October 26, 1972. There were 761 farms in Loudoun, according to the 1969 census.

[115] Ibid., May 3, 1973; June 7, 1973; August 16, 1973. It was estimated the county would lose $518,000 in revenue from property taxes during the 1973-1974 fiscal year as the result of the L.U.T. tax program.

[116] Ibid., August 16, 1973.

[117] Ibid., May 3, 1973; June 7, 1973.

their newly acquired land so that farming is continued. The tax benefits of the L.U.T. program are thereby transferred to the speculators.[118]

Cultivable land in the county not only has been diminished by suburban sprawl, but also has been menaced by plans to inundate significant portions of the county in an attempt to provide additional water for the numerous inhabitants in local jurisdictions to the east of Loudoun.

Demographic growth in northern Virginia and the suburbs of Wasington, D.C., has severely taxed the area's water resources and led to shortages during arid summers. In an attempt to alleviate such problems, plans have been proposed to dam the Potomac River or its tributaries in Loudoun. If these are implemented, numerous Loudoun residents would be evicted from their homes and sizeable acreage of fertile farmland would be inundated. This action would further deplete the county of productive farmland already diminished by the wave of suburbanization. Since 1945 federal and regional agencies, plus county jurisdictions east of Loudoun, have espoused the development of the Potomac basin. Unlike the proposals of the 1960's and 1970's, which were predicated upon the need for water for urbanites, the primary intent during 1945 was to develop the Potomac basin along the lines of the Tennessee Valley Authority to provide hydro-electric power and cheaper electricity. As of 1976, aroused and angry residents of Loudoun, working through local, state, and federal representatives and numerous local protest meetings, have prevented the implementation of plans to develop the Potomac River.[119]

Probably the greatest concern manifested by county residents to a proposal for the construction of a dam on the Potomac River occurred during the ealy 1960's. During that period the Army Corps of Engineers, the advocates of the construction of an eighty-seven-foot-high cement dam, where Seneca Creek flows into the Potomac River, were unanimously viewed by Loudouners as villains.[120] The proposed

---

[118] Statement by C. Preston Poland, personal interview, March 16, 1974.

[119] *Times-Mirror*, April 5, 1945; August 16, 1945. All proposals stressed that the additional and secondary benefits of damming the Potomac River would be the creation of a recreation area and the providing of a degree of flood control. In April 1945, after holding hearings where enraged citizens from Loudoun, Clarke, and Frederick counties vociferously denounced damming the Potomac, the Board of Engineers for Rivers and Harbors rejected a proposed plan whereby the federal government would develop the Potomac River basin to produce electricity. During August of the same year a similar plan, proposed at Hershey, Pennsylvania, by the Interstate Commission on the Potomac River Basin, failed to materialize.

[120] Colonel Warren Johnson of the Army Corps of Engineers was responsible for much of this disdain. Angry citizens at the county courthouse in June 1965 protesting the plan for the construction of Seneca Dam were told by the colonel that their views would in no way affect his recommendation of the dam. However, written comments by citizens were attached as an appendix to his report, which was forwarded to his superiors.

construction of a dam near the northeastern boundary of the county would have flooded 300 homes and removed from the tax rolls 15,000 acres of land, most of it in eastern Loudoun and zoned for industrial development. Led by J. Emory Kirkpatrick, chairman of the Loudoun Board of Supervisors, residents protested that the above threat, coupled with the previous removal by the federal government of 7,500 acres of farmland for Dulles Airport, would drastically alter the county environmentally and cripple it economically. Residents eagerly responded to the request by *The Loudoun Times-Mirror* to "HELP SAVE OUR COUNTY" by sending a form letter, published in the paper to state and federal officials, that protested against the construction of a dam at Seneca Creek.[121]

Demographic growth has also caused municipal and county governments east of Loudoun to advocate and sponsor plans that were not in the best interest of Loudouners. One of the most interesting but vexing to Loudoun residents was the construction of dams and a filtration system by Fairfax City in Loudoun County, which provides water from Goose Creek and Beaverdam Creek for the city of Fairfax. Loudouners have often pondered why a city in another county was allowed to municipalize water from Loudoun's major internal water resources.[122]

Other local jurisdictions have more recently coveted the use of Catoctin Creek that traverses northwestern Loudoun. Officials of the District of Columbia, Fairfax County, and the Washington Suburban Sanitary Commission, which serves Prince George's and Montgomery counties in Maryland, proposed in 1974 the construction of a dam on Catoctin Creek, eleven miles north of Leesburg. They maintain that the construction of such a reservoir would hold a nine-day supply of water for inhabitants of the region most dependent upon the Potomac River

---

[121] *Times-Mirror*, September 28, 1961; June 7, 1962; January 18, 1962; June 27, 1963; May 13, 1965. United States Secretary of Interior Stewart Udal informed Loudoun's Board of Supervisors on May 11, 1965, that they and all areas that would be affected by the construction of the Seneca Dam must continue to "vociferously and dynamically" fight the plan urged by the Army's Corps of Engineers.

[122] Ibid., July 31, 1958; March 24, 1960; August 25, 1966. In April 1956, Fairfax City first asked for permission to build a dam on Goose Creek west of Ashburn (near the intersection of Rt. 659 and 642). A three-year court battle ensued between the two jurisdictions, with Fairfax City arguing the right to construct a dam and use water from Loudoun on the grounds of "public necessity." The matter was settled out of court during the fall of 1959, when Loudoun County supervisors agreed to allow the construction of a water facility (dam and filtration plant) in Loudoun. In 1966, Fairfax City obtained permission from Loudoun authorities to expand their use of county water. They were granted the right to impound an additional 500 acres south of their Goose Creek Reservoir, where a dam was constructed on Beaverdam Creek. Original plans called for the flooding of approximately 160 acres and at a later date the height of the dam increased so a maximum of 500 acres would be inundated. Then the Beaverdam Creek and Goose Creek reservoirs would be capable of providing 25 million gallons of water a day for use by residents of Fairfax City.

for water. Angry residents have exclaimed that the implementation of this plan would flood at least 9,400 acres of productive and usable land and inundate the hamlet of Taylorstown, evicting its seventy-five residents.[123] Furthermore, they claimed it was illogical to take valuable land and disrupt the lives of numerous residents when a reserve-water supply for the people in and around the nation's Capital could be obtained by the construction of reservoirs in the less tillable and less fertile and sparsely settled mountains of West Virginia. Despite the spirited resistance of Loudouners, the possibility of the additional impoundment of water inside the county for non-residents is imminent. Constant pressure for the implementation of such plans emerges from the Army Corps of Engineers in an attempt to meet long-range water needs for Metropolitan Washington, and the demand for more immediate results by utility commissions, such as the Fairfax Water Authority, is ever present. The demands by the latter are especially formidable because Virginia law empowers them to impound water anywhere in the state.[124]

[123] *Metro Virginia News*, June 16, 1974, and November 24, 1974; *Washington Star-News*, June 5, 1974 and June 9, 1974. The residents of northwestern Loudoun formed the Catoctin Valley Defense Alliance (C.V.D.A.) to fight the proposed dam that would flood their homes. An alternate plan to damming Catoctin Creek was also proposed by the Army Corps of Engineers, i.e., to construct another dam on Goose Creek (southwestern Loudoun). The latter proposal prompted citizen protest in the annual meeting of the Goose Creek Association, held on November 20, 1974, at the Middleburg Community Center.

[124] *Metro Virginia News*, November 24, 1974.

Chapter 10

THE URBAN FRONTIER AND THE FUTURE OF LOUDOUN COUNTY

From 1945 to 1972 methods of farming in Loudoun were transformed by technology and scientific innovations. But by far the most significant development was the inception of extensive urban commuter communities dependent upon the car. This phenomenon represented the first major displacement of an agrarian society in Loudoun originally established by European colonists. The 1970's continue to witness the crisis of this transformation.

CURRENT TRENDS AND FUTURITY

The decline in farming, growing urbanization, escalating county budgets, expanding county government, growing school enrollment and increasing local taxes have dichotomized the county into two geographical factions: the eastern-urban areas led by Sterling Park and the western and agrarian regions and older communities in the eastern sectors of the county. This division has manifested itself in numerous emotional and recalcitrant harangues by citizens and citizens' groups who have appeared before the Board of Supervisors, Planning Commission, and School Board. Bitter struggles have ensued over determining county policy, in which citizens of Sterling Park have felt the rest of the county was improperly blocking the establishment of their just county services and educational facilities. Residents of more traditional communities have felt that they were the ones being mistreated as the result of rising taxes, which benefited residents primarily in the new planned communities. People with many domiciliary years in the county were also critical of Sterling Park because they believed residents of more traditional communities were being taxed to establish services for a planned community, which upon reaching maturity and no longer needing the financial support of the rest of the county, would incorporate into a city.[1]

The location of a new high school in eastern Loudoun in 1966, the implementation of a year-round school program in the Sterling Park area in 1973, and the 1973 bond issue are just a few of the recent issues that reflect a bifurcation of residents in new planned communities and older communities.[2] Neither side has totally had its way. Sterling Park wanted what was later known as Broad Run High School located nearer, or in, their community. Despite the efforts of the Sterling Park residents through their civic organizations, the county located the high school away from their community, due in part to the fear of future incorporation by Sterling Park as a city that would thereby take over not only the elementary schools constructed in this planned community with money from county taxes, but also this high school as well.[3] The approval of the $27,900,000 bond issue by the voters of Loudoun was a victory for the urban residents of Sterling and Broad Run districts, whose overwhelming support offset the overwhelming opposition in the other districts.[4] What the farmers of western Loudoun had predicted and feared had been realized, the voting power of eastern Loudoun had demonstrated its nascent political clout in a county-wide election.[5]

However, prior to 1976 the views of the two most populous districts in the county, Sterling and Broad Run, were often ineffectual in determining policies on representative boards, such as the Board of Supervisors, Planning Commission, and the School Board, in which the five other districts could ally or partly form a voting block for determining policy. Although representatives of the five less urban districts rarely voted as a block against the two urban districts, the School Board from 1973 to 1976 was divaricated on the issue of year-round school. The

---

[1] *Metro Virginia News*, April 15, 1973; *Times-Mirror*, April 1, 1971; February 1, 1973; April 12, 1973. Sterling Park wants to abandon the volunteer fire department system in favor of firemen paid by the county. As a bedroom and commuter community, residents find it more difficult to maintain a volunteer system than the more agrarian areas.

[2] *Times-Mirror*, April 28, 1966; May 12, 1966; April 12, 1973; December 6, 1973; January 17, 1974.

[3] Ibid., April 20, 1966.

[4] Ibid., April 12, 1973. The vote was 3,339 for the bond issue and 2,966 against it. Sterling and Broad Run districts cast 2,401 votes for the bond issue and only 221 against it. The remaining five districts cast only 938 votes for and 2,745 against this bond issue.

[5] *Metro Virginia News*, April 15, 1973.

strongest proponents of this system were the School Board representatives from the two populous districts of Sterling and Broad Run. This favoring was representative of the strong support of the residents of those two districts for year-round school. The School Board's decision in January 1974 not to extend year-round school to Broad Run High School further exacerbated the division within the county between urban regions in eastern Loudoun and the rest of the county. Parents in the eastern portion of the county were annoyed at having their children going to Sterling Middle School on a year-round basis and those of high school age going to Broad Run High School on a traditional system.[6] Residents of Sterling and Broad Run districts were resentful of a decision forced upon them contrary to their desires by what they deemed to be recalcitrant board members whose constituency with one exception would not be affected by the implementation of the year-round system at Broad Run High School.[7]

Also accompanying the transition of Loudoun from an agrarian to urban county is the contest between the zoning board and Board of Supervisors attempting to maintain "planned" and "controlled growth" within the county and the demands by developers, realtors, and land speculators promoting unfettered growth which they proclaim as "progress." The county's first line of defense against uncontrolled growth resulting from innumerable plans for accelerating the construction of new homes and planned communities is the Planning Commission and the Department of Planning and Zoning. The outcome of the struggle between the county Planning Commission and Department of Planning and Zoning and Board of Supervisors with developers will determine the

---

[6] *Times-Mirror*, December 6, 1973; January 17, 1974. Students in Sterling Park and Sugarland Run from 1973 to 1975 attended elementary school and a middle school on the year-round system while high school students from those areas remained on the traditional nine-month school year. Children of families in the Arcola and Ashburn areas of the Dulles district attended elementary schools which remained on the traditional system, a middle school on the year-round calendar, and a high school on the traditional system.

[7] Ibid., January 17, 1974; February 15, 1974. Among the reasons given by the four members who voted against extending the year-round system to Broad Run High School was the opposition expressed by students and teachers of that school. Parents in the central and western regions of the county were adamantly opposed to year-round school. The action and statements of some of the School Board members who opposed year-round school implied that it must be stopped or it would spread malevolently throughout the county. The prevention of the implementation of year-round school at Broad Run High School in 1974-75 might prove to be a "pyrrhic victory" for opponents of this system in terms of what is the most realistic alternative to overcrowded schools in eastern Loudoun in a manner that is both financially expedient and academically sound. The asperity and acrimony vented in this struggle could in the near future cause residents in eastern Loudoun to defeat bond referenda needed to construct new schools for the growing population in more western regions of the county like Leesburg and Purcellville. Despite providing a sound educational program and the support of parents with children in the year-round system, the School Board terminated the program in Loudoun during the summer of 1975.

nature of Loudoun County's future. The paramount issue is not whether Loudoun should grow demographically, because the forces of accretion cannot be abrogated, but how the transition to urbanization can be orderly achieved in a manner not financially disruptive of native residents and terminative to agrarianism in the western regions of the county.

The above agencies of the county government have recently shown a degree of administrative acumen by attempting to implement a Land Use Tax program, by developing the innovative concept set forth in Article 12, by approving the establishment of select industrial development in the county, and by updating the county zoning ordinances and comprehensive development plan.[8] Plans are currently being considered by county officials as to the feasibility of restricting the county's "annual residential growth rate to five percent" or of applying a more flexible "phase growth fiscal guide," in which the rate of growth would be determined by anticipated county revenues and thereby hopefully matching "the new costs of additional" residents with "available government revenues."[9] Despite the impressive premise of the concept "phase growth" and the impressive goals of the county's zoning regulations, the pressures that could negate their design for controlled growth and the circumvention of compliance with county goals and regulations are formidable.

Factors that could nullify the intent of county zoning are (1) the financial might of developers in the county that include some of the largest corporate and banking institutions in the nation, which are acutely aware of the expansion of the urban corridor into Loudoun, (2) the promulgation by proponents of development that growth is synonymous with inalterable progress and that the increase in tax base resulting from demographic growth and the establishment of subdivisions more than pay for the expansion of county services, (3 the less-than-sympathetic

---

[8]Ibid., May 24, 1973; August 16, 1973; January 24, 1974; [Loudoun County, Department of Planning and Zoning], *Subdivision Ordinance of Loudoun County, Virginia (1973), p. 1.*

[9]*Metro Virginia News*, August 26, 1973; *Times-Mirror*, August 16, 1973. From 1960 through 1971, Loudoun's population increased approximately 5.5 percent per year. Since 1970 it has increased about 10 percent each year. The crux of the phase growth formula is the Capital Improvements Program (C.I.P.). Under this program the county would determine its plans for capital improvements to provide future services, such as schools, county buildings, and parks, and the projected costs of these projects. Then the county government would examine the rate of county growth and determine on the basis of the local tax base how much growth the county can accommodate. Critics of this plan have called it socialistic and communistic. Developers have acrimoniously damned it. Another approach under consideration to control growth and preserve farmland is land banking, the purchase of land by local governments before it is bought by developers. Such a practice would allow local governments to insure the use of the land in the best interest of the community. The lack of funds plaguing local governments makes it difficult to provide currently needed services, much less to invest in land banking. However, advocates argue, considering the alternatives and current trends, land banking is well worth the effort.

decisions of the county Circuit Court in cases involving county zoning regulations, and (4) the recent role of the town officials of Leesburg and Purcellville that have served as agents of unabated growth.

Investment in Loudoun properties and developments sponsored by such corporate giants as United States Steel, Xerox Corporation, Levitt and Sons, I.T.&T., and I.B.M. brings to bear upon the county sophisticated advertisement and public relations campaigns, talented and experienced legal minds, and unlimited funds for court appeals to obtain reversals of county zoning rulings that attempt to thwart development plans. On a less grandiose scale, numerous local realtors with a dependence on local attorneys are constantly promoting the sale of property and the development of the county.[10]

Public relations campaigns are launched by these developers and realtors to convince the public and local authorities that extensive urban development is benevolent. These are founded on two premises that are not irrefutable because they are based on neither fact nor reality. The first is that extensive urbanization is progressive. This premise in turn connotes that, as developers, they are benefactors promoting the advancement of civilization over a less advanced rural and agrarian lifestyle. The second premise is that the establishment of large planned communities expands the tax base that more than financially compensates for the increase in local government expenditures for additional schools and services involving police, sewage, and water.[11] In reality, suburbs usually cost county jurisdictions far more than the taxes from these new planned communities yield.[12] This fact is testified to by the increasing

---

[10]*Loudoun County Data Book*, pp. [56-58]; *The Sunday Star and Daily News* (Washington, D. C.), January 14, 1973, Sec. R, p. 6. As of 1971 there were forty-one real estate firms in the county and forty attorneys. Xerox has built a large training center in Loudoun. I.B.M. has purchased a large tract of land in the county for development purposes.

Legal transactions, such as the sale and transfer of ownership of realty, can provide a significant portion of a lawyer's income. For example, lawyers in Fairfax County, Virginia, and in many other suburban regions charge a fee of $500 for tracing a title on a $50,000 home in a subdivision. The title search is usually only a fifteen-minute task involving consulting deed books at the county courthouse (see pp. 7-10 in the April 6, 1975, issue of *Parade*, Sunday supplement of *The Washington Post*).

[11]Editors of *Fortune*, *The Exploding Metropolis* (New York: Doubleday Anchor Books, 1958), p. 123; *Times- Mirror*, August 17, 1961; *The Washington Post* (Washington, D. C.), January 2, 1974, Sec. A, pp. 1, 8, col. 1. The cost of extra services needed due to demographic growth is not paid by the new residents; but, due to conventional tax practices of spreading the load, old residents must pay additional taxes without obtaining any additional services.

[12]Richard M. Highsmith, Jr., J. Granville Jensen and Robert D. Rudd, *Conservation in the United States* (3d ed.; Chicago: Rand McNally and Co., 1971), pp. 367-68; *The Washington Post*, January 2, 1974, Sec. A, p. 8, col. 1. The alteration of the landscape by urban development has been referred to by some authorities as "cultural erosion."

dependence of county governments faced with extensive growth upon bond issues and escalating bond debts. In Loudoun's sister county, Fairfax, which has experienced the travail of unfettered growth since World War II, yearly bond payments have leaped from $3,980,000 in 1961 to $27,000,000 for the 1973-74 fiscal year.[13] Prince William County, on Loudoun's southeastern boundary, in the mid-1970's labeled the "fastest growing large county in the nation," was counseled in 1974 by one of Virginia's leading bond experts, Walter Craigie, Sr., that the county faced a "critical debt problem" so severe it should "scrap plans for a $42 million to $53 million school bond issue."[14] Developers maintain that without continued growth local governments will be unable "to collect sufficient tax revenue to pay" increasing expenses without raising local taxes even higher.[15] Most local officials in the Washington area today, unlike a decade ago, refuse to accept the developer's rationale that subdivisions are self-supporting in terms of financing services they require from local governments. Generally such officials now believe, as the result of past experiences, that property taxes are simply insufficient by themselves to finance the costs of residential growth.[16] A study by the Virginia Farm Bureau Federation, an organization less than sympathetic to planned communities, concluded that its study of the Sterling Park subdivision in Loudoun "showed a yearly deficit of nearly $2 million—a deficit 'to be picked up by the other citizens of the county.'"[17]

This deficit resulted in large part from the lack of industrial development in the county to offset Sterling Park's housing of primarily young adults with children. By 1974 Sterling Park, along with the Sugarland Run development, domiciled approximately one-third of the nearly 12,000 children who attend Loudoun's schools. While a high precentage of the families in this area have two or more children in school and an annual income far above the average for the residents of the

[13] *The Washington Post,* January 2, 1974, Sec. A., p. 8, col. 1. During the thirteen years from 1961 to 1974 local support of schools in Fairfax jumped from $10.9 million to $98.4 million; the cost of operating the police department from $1.3 million to $10.3 million; and the fire department budget increased from $655,939 to $8.1 million.

[14] Ibid., March 16, 1974, Sec. A, pp. 1, 4, col. 6. Prince William as of 1974 was $80,000,000 in debt. The proposed school budget for Loudoun County for 1974-75 specified that $2,882,648 must be paid on the 1973 and previous bond issues. This figure represented an increase from the $2,152,315 payment for "debt services" in 1973-74. The Urban Institute stated in 1973, that its study of the Hollymead subdivision near Charlottesville, Virginia, "showed that Albermarle County would have to pay $101,745 more annually over a 30-year period for services to the development than it receives in various taxes and fees." The Hollymead development consists of 800 residential units and thirty acres of commercial development.

[15] Ibid., January 2, 1974, Sec. A, p. 8, col. 1.

[16] Ibid., Sec. A. p.1, col. 2; Robert C. Wood, *Suburbia: Its People and Their Politics* (Boston: Houghton, Mifflin Co., 1958), pp. 72-73.

[17] *The Washington Post,* January 2, 1974, Sec. A, p. 8, col. 2.

rest of the county, because of the present tax system which is the major source of the county government's revenue, residents in developments like Sterling Park and owners of dwellings on small plots throughout the county on the average annually pay (up to 1974) to the county no more than $200 to $500 in real estate taxes.[18]

For the above reasons, urbanization has made the traditional taxation of privately owned land and property obsolete as the basic source of revenue to finance schools and local governmental services. Until the recent Land Use Tax program, this form of taxation was forcing farmers to sell their property. Unless the county is able to regulate growth and attract adequate select industry and commercial development that does not contaminate the environment with pollutants or bring excessive numbers of new people into the county and that at the same time yields sufficient property taxes to support the county's growth rate, the county will be forced to do the following: (1) continue its dependence upon bond referenda, which plunges the county deeper into debt and which people in the western part of the county are becoming more reluctant to support, or (2) increase the current property tax, a measure which will make it increasingly more difficult for the elderly and persons on a fixed income to meet their tax payments or for young families in the county with low or moderate incomes to become homeowners.[19] An escalating county debt could also inadvertently negate the intent of Land Use Taxation by raising the tax rate on farmland out of dire financial necessity to the point that farming would be impractical.

[18]Ibid., April 3, 1974, Sec. C, p. 1; Loudoun County Real Estate Book I, 1974, 2, 4, 22, 48, 61, 77, 80, 86, 197, 279, 470; Book II, 513-18, 521, 527, 530, 541, 604, 666-67, 673, 688, 694, 696, 699, 713, 721, 718, 810, 812, 814; Statement by C. Preston Poland, member of the Loudoun County Planning Commission from Dulles district, personal interview, March 16, 1974. The above real estate tax includes taxes based on assessment of both the land and buildings upon the land. One of the few developments in northern Virginia that pays its way is Reston, located in the northwestern part of Fairfax County. Unlike developments elsewhere in Virginia, such as Sterling Park and Hollymead, Reston apparently has "a significant amount of industrial and commercial areas that yield large tax payments and require few services." For 1973-74 the average family of four in Fairfax county with an income of $10,000 paid $430 in county real estate and $77 in personal property taxes, whereas the same size family in the same county with an income of $20,000 paid $836 in real estate and $167 in personal property taxes.

[19]Times-Mirror, October 26, 1972; Metro Virginia News, January 27, 1974. A 1972 government study released by the Department of Commerce on county business patterns showed that Loudoun supported a greater number of business establishments than many areas of Loudoun's size. By 1972 there were 560 separate businesses in the county that employed one or more persons. Of this number, 277 employed from one to three workers, 126 from four to seven, and 109 from eight to nineteen. Totally, 4,816 persons were employed by businesses within the county, with the combined payrolls reaching $27,092,000. Despite this income the county's revenues are not sufficient to support cost of its current growth rate. However, the Board of Supervisors did establish during the first of 1974 an industrial authority for Loudoun to help attract suitable industry to the county.

Other alternatives that are more promising but difficult to enact include a one-percent land transfer tax, as recommended by Loudoun supervisor from the Leesburg district, Frank Raflo.[20] Another alternative would be to have enacted a school tax based upon the income of Loudoun residents. This tax has not been formally advocated as a revenue panacea by anyone in the county; and, although it is one of the most lucid and equitable alternatives, it currently has no chance of being realized.

When unsuccessful in obtaining the rezoning of properties and approval of their projects by the county with the arguments of progressivism and beneficial financial tax increments to Loudoun, developers have turned to litigation.[21] Underlying all court cases involving Loudoun's zoning restrictions is the conflict between the rights of the community and county government and the property rights of individual developers. The right of the county government to regulate property rights of individuals by demanding compliance to zoning requirements is based upon the amorphous and broad police power that courts have decreed. This power to regulate had its genesis not in a written constitution but in the "indispensable attribute of our society, possessed by the sovereignties before the adoption of the Federal Constitution."[22] The power to zone was subsequently granted by the state legislature to the county Board of Supervisors, who in turn delegated authority to the Planning Commission to approve or disapprove plats of applicants.[23]

Regardless of the theory set forth by court decisions outside Virginia, the Virginia courts have taken a very narrow view of the delegated police powers to a county to regulate through zoning individual property rights for the public welfare. This bent has resulted partially from the dependence upon long-established precedents of property rights in the American judiciary system and the comparative nascent granting of zoning powers to Virginia counties by the state legislature during the 1930's and only extensively applied by county governments since 1950. The judgment of lawyers and judges in Loudoun and elsewhere in the state has usually been fettered by the legal precedent of "vested property rights," therefore imposing past standards to cope with zoning problems resulting from revolutionary changes.

---

[20] *Times-Mirror*, August 16, 1973.
[21] *Metro Virginia News*, January 7, 1973.
[22] *Times-Mirror*, July 27, 1972.
[23] Minutes of the Subdivision Committee of the Loudoun County Planning Commission for July 18, 1972, p. 2; *Zoning Ordinance of the County of Loudoun*, p.1. If a preliminary plat is rejected by the Planning Commission, it cannot go to the Board of Supervisors "since they only consider final plats." The applicant's only alternative, if preliminary requests for rezoning are denied by the Planning Commission, is to appeal to the Circuit Court of Loudoun. This, in turn, leads to "interlocutory decrees" by that court. If the court reverses the ruling by the Planning Commission, the "matter is referred back to" the Planning Commission and the Board of Supervisors for "reconsideration of the preliminary plat."

Problems of growth cannot be resolved by tradition, but demand decisions made upon the criterion of the impact of growth upon the future quality of man's milieu.[24] The Loudoun County Circuit Court has based most of its decisions on a restrictive view of zoning as set forth by the Supreme Court of Virginia in Andrews v. Loudoun County Board of Supervisors. It has continued usually to rule, like the decision of the State Supreme Court in the Andrews case, that the denial of development by the Planning Commission and Board of Supervisors of Loudoun County has been "arbitrary and capricious." This factor was applied by the Loudoun Circuit Court in its interlocutory decree of March 8, 1973, in Rust v. the Loudoun County Board of Supervisors. In turn, recently the Rust case has been cited extensively by the Circuit Court as the precedent for reversing denials by the county Planning Commission and Board of Supervisors of proposed development programs.[25]

Another force counter to the attempts by the county to regulate and control growth has been the policy of Loudoun's two largest incorporated towns, Leesburg and Purcellville. While the county has been intensifying

---

[24]Andrews v. Loudoun County Board of Supervisors, 200 Va. 637, 640 (1959). The Circuit Court has not been favorably impressed by protests by the Loudoun Landowners Association, the Goose Creek Association, and the Lincoln Community League against requests for the establishment of subdivisions in western Loudoun.

[25]Ibid.; Loudoun County Planning Commission Minutes for March 12, 1972, pp. 1-8; July 25, 1972, pp. 1-2; March 12, 1974, pp. 1-19; "Dirt Roads in Exurbia," *Traffic Quarterly* (January, 1971), 104-06, 110-14. Recent cases in which Circuit Court Judge Raymond Snead applied the precedent of the Andrews and Rust cases include Daivi Development Corp. v. Loudoun County Board of Supervisors and the Loudoun County Planning Commission, chancery no. 4359 (1974), and Tyler v. Loudoun County Board of Supervisor and the Loudoun County Planning Commission, chancery no. 4318 (1974). All of these were interlocutory decrees which sent the "matter back to the" Planning Commission. In these and earlier decisions the court has ruled that "the Planning Commission has no power to deny a subdivision plat based on the inadequacy of the State highways." This decision means that, if these developments are established, the public may well have to finance through taxes rebuilding the narrow and serpentine dirt roads in the western region of the county which have great difficulty accommodating two-way traffic. Loudoun's legal leadership and defense in zoning matters such as the above is provided by the commonwealth's attorney, whose time and interest is limited since he must divide his efforts and energies between service to the county government and private practice. This has prompted critics to comment that the commonwealth's attorney often does not appear to display as enthusiastic and vigorous defense of Loudoun's zoning efforts as they would like. Neither does the commonwealth's attorney, critics argue, provide as extensive legal advice to the zoning commission as is needed. The latter appears to be a valid criticism of the March 12, 1974, meeting of the Planning Commission. The commonwealth's attorney was not present. The attorneys and representatives for Daivi, Tyler, and Puelicher forcefully demanded the commission approve their applications, which would allow urban development. The newly appointed assistant commonwealth's attorney, who did attend the meeting, when asked by the commisssion for legal advice, stated he was unfamiliar with the details of the above cases (Loudoun County Planning Commission Minutes for March 12, 1974, pp. 14-19).

its effort to restrain growth, the municipal governments of these two towns, under the influence of businessmen and lawyers, have accelerated the maximum growth of these towns by encouraging subdivisions, shopping centers, and annexation of territory.[26] Land within the corporate limits of an incorporated town is not subject to restrictions set forth in zoning ordinances of the county.[27] The difficulty in this arrangement is that incorporated towns depend upon the county to meet their educational needs. Towns may thereby counteract plans for phased growth by the county government, and exacerbate the financial burdens of the county and significantly contribute to the increase of taxes. In addition to Purcellville and Leesburg spurning cooperation with the county government in regulating expansion, the mayor of Purcellville in 1973 denounced attempts by the county to establish "phased growth." He also voiced strong opposition to "any plan for regulated growth."[28]

The outcome of the contest between regulated and controlled growth espoused by the Board of Supervisors and the Planning Commission on the one hand and the forces for unfettered growth sponsored by municipal governments, large corporate investors, and local realtors, aided by judicial decrees, will determine not only the rate of expansion of county schools and services and the subsequent degree of increases in county taxes, but also the fate of farming in western Loudoun. Increasing cost of mechanistic agriculture, inflation, shortage of labor, farm youths not wishing to be bound to continuous hours and never-ceasing responsibilities of dairying, and the enticing prices for farmland offered by developers and land speculators are unfortunately rapidly displacing farming in the western region of the county.[29] Environmentally this trend is tragic. Loudoun Valley contains some of the most fertile and productive soil in the United States, especially its 105,000 acres of Chester soils which are rated as premium farmland.[30] In light of recent food shortages the nation has faced, it would be a waste of part of our country's natural resources for agriculture to disappear from this area.[31] Eastern Loudoun

---

[26] *Metro Virginia News*, March 4, 1973; *Times-Mirror*, November 30, 1972; August 9, 1973; January 24, 1974.

[27] *Loudoun County Data Book*, p. 28.

[28] *Times-Mirror*, August 8, 1973. According to the *Times-Mirror*, the mayor made a distinction between "phased growth" and "orderly growth." He opposed the former but claimed to support the latter as well as Article 12 of the county ordinance.

[29] *The Washington Post*, March 30, 1973, Sec. D, pp. 1, 5, cols. 1-4.

[30] U. S. Department of Agriculture Soil Conservation Service in Cooperation with [the] Virginia Agricultural Experiment Station, *Soil Survey: Loudoun County, Virginia* (Washington, D. C.: Government Printing Office, 1960), pp. 63-66; Statement by Leslie W. King, District Conservationist, U. S. Department of Agriculture Soil Conservation Service, personal interview, December 14, 1972.

[31] "The New American Land Rush," *Time*, October 1, 1973, p. 85; Eugene P. Odum and others, *The Crisis of Survival* (Glenview, Ill.: Scott, Foresman and Co., 1970), pp.

has inferior soil types compared to those in the western region of the county. Therefore, the demise of farming in eastern Loudoun is not so great a loss agriculturally as would be the total displacement of farming in the western half of the county.

It is questionable whether zoning can save western Loudoun because of the previously discussed pressures. The impending demise of agriculture in the region is supported by the statement of Loudoun's former zoning administrator, Ruth Miller. From her years of experience she has found "no law or ordinance" exists "that can not be gotten around,"[32] a succinct rephrasing of the philosophy of developers, who optimistically believe the impedimenta to growth imposed by zoning can be nullified or negated. If Mrs. Miller's statement proves to be prophetic, then Loudoun's zoning efforts and attempts to regulate growth will offer little protection for agrarianism in western Loudoun.[33]

The threat to the fertile area of Loudoun Valley is in part the result of the attitudinal transformation that accompanied the shift of America from a rural to an urban nation. This shift in attitude resulted in the displacement and obsolescence of the traditional agrarian philosophy embraced by Loudoun grangers and articulated by county newspaper editors throughout the nineteenth century and the first half of the twentieth, that America's past, present and future greatness was derived from the farm. Accompanying industrial-urban growth has been the emergence of a new American credo relegating the agrarian philosophy to the status of a myth while elevating America's faith in technology and education as salutary and progressive conveyances of affluence, abundance of consumer products, and conveniences.[34] Surplus farm products from 1945 until recently, the rising cost of food in chain stores, the federal government's farm-support programs, and the increasing intricacy and abstruseness of American life have bequeathed a new agrarian myth embraced by urban America that ignores the farmer's plight and takes farming for granted. It is predicated upon the illusionary belief that farmers are excessively affluent and that America's

---

74, 123; John Opie (ed.), *Americans and Environment: The Controversy over Ecology* (Lexington, Mass.: D. C. Heath and Co., 1971), pp. xi-xiii, 46-47. The number of U.S. farms has declined from 5.6 million in 1950 to 2.8 million in 1975.

[32]Statement by Ruth Miller, personal interview, December 14, 1972.

[33]*The Washington Post*, June 2, 1973, Sec. E, pp. 1, 17, col. 1. Some students of the problems of urbanization are advocating "land banking," which is "the purchase by any government agency" of "substantial quantities of land and holding these parcels in the public name as a means of influencing development patterns and controlling land prices." The pressure for development in Loudoun has also recently been intensified by the restraint upon construction and development by counties on Loudoun's eastern and southern boundaries.

[34]Hofstadter, *Age of Reform*, pp. 28-30, 121-22; David M. Potter, *People of Plenty: Economic Abundance and the American Character* (Chicago: University of Chicago Press, 1954), pp. 206-08.

agricultural resources will continue to provide adequately and indefinitely for the country's needs for farm products regardless of current urban development.[35] Consequently most Loudoun residents, as those throughout the nation, do not fully comprehend the limits of the nation's agrarian resources and the future consequences of present growth rates and patterns.

The threat to agriculture in Loudoun Valley is disconcerting because (1) it would be a misuse of a natural resource to "plant planned communities" in such a fertile area, and (2) the sprawl of urban areas is not limited to Loudoun but is a national phenomenon that occurs for the most part at the expense of high-quality land permanently lost from actual or potential agricultural production. Between 1942 to 1956, 17 million acres of cultivatable farmlands have been diverted to nonfarm uses. Currently approximately 600,000 acres of rural land are annually being diverted to nonfarm uses, such as residential, industrial, and commercial sites and highways. This trend is especially alarming when most of the loss is in top-quality farmland. Of the 470 million acres of cropland in the United States, only 72 million acres are in the Class I category. By 1958 over half of this highly fertile land was next to urban areas. Since this time considerable acreage has been urbanized. Loudoun County and many other regions within Virginia are a part of this national trend, which has prompted an alarmed Richmond Regional Planning District Commission to ask the Virginia General Assembly to consider state ownership of farmlands to halt the escalating depletion of prime agricultural acreage in Virginia. The report of the commission warned that, if present population and development trends continue, an inadequate amount of land will be available in the year 2000 to accommodate public demands for food.[36]

---

[35] According to Ruth Miller, after most residents move to Loudoun, regardless of whether they live in a subdivision like Sterling Park or not, they do not want the county's population to increase. But these residents with urban backgrounds and even many older residents in the county do not see the impending demise of farming in Loudoun Valley as either a reality or a negative development.

[36] Highsmith, Jr., Jensen, and Rudd, *Conservation in the United States*, pp. 369-71; editors of *Fortune*, *The Exploding Metropolis*, pp. 122-23; "Saving the Farms," *Time*, (April 21, 1975), 48; Miller, *The Urbanization of Modern America*, pp. 208-09; "What To Do: Costly Choices," *Time*, (November 11, 1974), 78; *The Washington Post*, August 13, 1974, Sec. C, pp. 1, 10, col. 2. By the end of 1959 it was estimated by the Department of Agriculture that "27.2 million" acres of land were occupied by urban areas, not counting an additional six to eight million acres that were the sites of towns and nonrural residences. Rural transportation facilities, not counting roads in cities which occupy from twenty to twenty-five percent of the urban area, occupied "25.3 million acres" in highways, railroads, and airports. Taken as a whole, the above occupied only approximately "2.5 percent" of America's total land. This total seems neither significant nor alarming until placed in the context that the above is an accelerating trend reducing America's cultivatable land. Two Virginia counties, Henrico and Chesterfield, located near Richmond, between 1964 and 1969 lost 53.6 percent of their 497 square miles of farmland to urbanization.

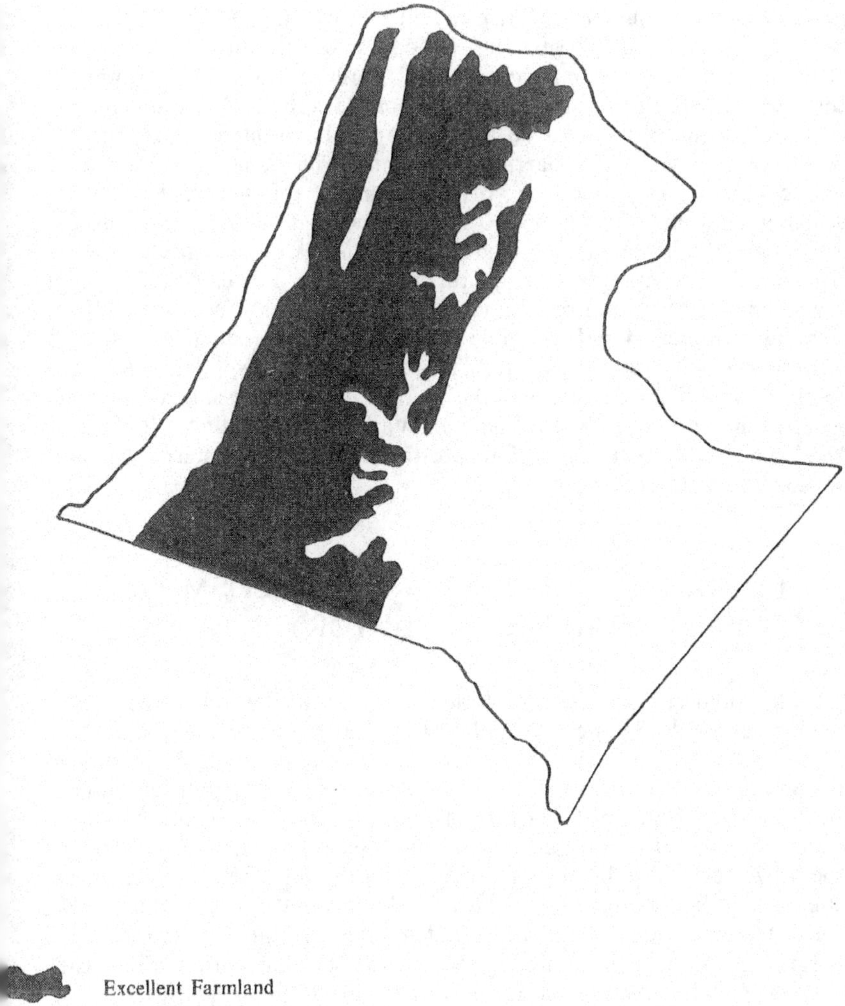

THE URBAN FRONTIER 393

 Excellent Farmland

Figure 25. Premium Farmland in Loudoun County in 1976.
Source: Soil survey: Loudoun County, Virginia, p. [122].

Dwarfed by the statistics of national acreage, the comparatively small area of Loudoun Valley is easily considered insignificant and the fate of agriculture there inconsequential for the agricultural economy of the nation. Continuance of this as a dominant attitude by residents, developers, and judicial officials will assure the utter demise of commercial farming in western Loudoun and will further deplete an already dwindling domain of fertile farmland. Such a posture is comparable with the agrarian philosophy of the eighteenth and nineteenth centuries deeming trees to be an inexhaustible resource that must be zealously removed as a barrier to farming. The answer is not in a renascent agrarian credo or myopic concept of unimpeded urban development, but a synthesis of realistic agricultural and urban development. The challenge facing Loudoun is the implementation of an effective policy that will regulate growth so exurban and urban development are concentrated and restricted to the less suitable soil for farming in eastern Loudoun while maintaining the productive region of western Loudoun for agriculture. The forces of urban sprawl, aided and abetted by judicial decree, and the apathy of many residents, plus the penetration of exurbia into Loudoun Valley and pending subdivision developments for that region, indicate that farming in western Loudoun is near the point of no return.

LOUDOUN'S PAST AS A MICROCOSM OF AMERICAN HISTORY

The domestic history of America is comprised of trends and developments determined by the lifestyles and achievements of innumerable people that have lived in communities traditionally encompassed by political boundaries marking the jurisdiction of county governments. Although the history of any one county or region does not reflect all the salient trends of the developments that brought about modern America, the history of Loudoun, as that of other counties, does reflect a significant cross section of many threads in the nation's historical fabric. These include the settlement and emergence of an agrarian society, its refinement through technological innovations that shifted the focal point of farming techniques from hand-powered implements to those drawn by the horse and subsequently powered by the tractor or by sophisticated self-propelled equipment. Loudoun also serves as a microcosmic example of nineteenth-century American life, such as the sectional confrontation over slavery; fighting, bitterness, and destructiveness of the Civil War; disillusionment of Southerners with reconstruction; and the establishment of public education and the attack upon the evils of drink. Like the rest of the nation, Loudouners during the twentieth century witnessed the emergence of big government and its intervention in their daily lives. This trend was especially evident during the federal government's mobilization of the nation's economic and human resources during World War I and II and through New Deal programs to provide relief and recovery from the Great Depression.

Loudoun is currently experiencing what has been historically the paramount shift in the nation's economy and lifestyle, the transformation from an agrarian to an urban people. Loudoun's agrarianism reigned supreme as a local lifestyle until 1960. Since that time a demographic revolution has taken place, sponsored by a renaissance of land speculators and developers comparable to those of the colonial era. During both eras, these enterprising men, motivated by profit and convinced they were benefactors of "progress," became vital agents for change and ecological revolutions. Those of the colonial era peopled northern Virginia, which displaced not only the aborigine but also larger species of wildlife, and altered the vegetation by clearing land. In contemporary times developers and speculators have ushered in an urban frontier even more revolutionary in its ecological transformation than that of the colonial era. Bulldozers not only have removed many remaining trees as the beginning of a man-made horizon of rooftops and a terrain draped with asphalt roads and cement sidewalks, but also have aided in the supersedure of a topography of rolling fields of farmland and trees. Unlike the first frontier in Loudoun, which was involved essentially in the conquest of nature, the present urban frontier is making further demands upon nature and subordinating not merely the customs of primitive natives but also the lifestyle of modern agrarian American citizens and displacing them from farmlands previously settled by their ancestors.[37] The financial, social, administrative, and legal problems associated with Loudoun's transition from agrarian to urban communities are not unique. They are essentially the same as those of many areas throughout the United States that are going through a similar transition.[38]

---

[37]Based on correspondence between Yardley Taylor and N. F. Cabell, January 11, 1854; Bean, *The Peopling of Virginia*, pp. 147-49; Loudoun County Deed Book B, pp. 282-83; C, pp. 15, 272, 277; D, pt. 2, pp. 638-39, 641-66; Loudoun County Real Estate Book I, 1973, 61, 80 , 86, 197, 279, 470. Statement by Edward R. Brown, personal interview, December 31, 1972. A comparison of current county records with those of the colonial era reveals a continuity of surnames in western Loudoun, while those of families who settled eastern Loudoun have generally been replaced by names of recent suburban residents.

[38]"The New American Land Rush," pp. 80-99; *Times-Mirror*, November 2, 1967; *The Washington Post*, February 20, 1973, Sec. D, p. 1; June 2, 1973, Sec. E, p. 1; October 30, 1973, Sec. D, p. 1. Loudoun is a part of the Virginia urban corridor that is a part of the eastern urban corridor of the United States that runs from Maine to Florida. Similar solutions to growth problems are also proposed throughout the nation by local officials, planners, and conservationists. These consist of regional planning authorities to cope with environmental problems involving water, sewerage, and air; zoning, land use taxes, conservation of open spaces, and cluster planning as controls for " phased growth."

Like that of the nation as a whole, the present challenge facing Loudoun, is not the conquest of the American environment, but the coping with problems emanating from accelerating change, which has been accompanied by the complexities of an increasing interdependency in American life. The solution must be one that will sustain the opportunities for satisfactory human life by using nature's resources judiciously without inflicting irreparable ecological damage. Ironically, the philosophy that maintains growth is synonymous with progress is a product of America's history, especially American capitalism, which was nourished by the conquest of the American environment. This very force that has emerged from America's past must now be regulated and tempered as our well-being can no longer sustain the total subjugation of our environment exclusively to the profit motive. It remains to be seen whether citizens and their institutions are up to this challenge and the continuous crisis inherent in the democratic system, demanding the resolution of confrontations between the conflicting rights and wills of citizens in a manner that will culminate in an ameliorable synthesis approaching the altruistic and elusive goal of progress for all.

EPILOGUE: THE CRISIS OF CHANGE CONTINUES

The dominant theme of the history of Loudoun County is the shift from farm to subdivision. County residents have lived on two frontiers that have brought revolutionary man-made environmental changes. First came the farming frontier, created by European settlers' axes and guns. Much of what was total forest was cleared, Indians were shoved westward, and wildlife was reduced. The second, and even more radical, transformation is being made by the urban frontier. Bulldozers are changing the topography in ways that were impossible with ax and shovel. Since the first publication of *From Frontier to Suburbia* in 1976, urbanization has exploded into an urban revolution that has far exceeded the degree of change discussed in the concluding chapter, "The Crisis of Change: 1945 to 1972." Currently being built upon what was formerly farmland, a sea of houses are moving westward like an unstoppable tidal wave, transforming lifestyles and creating new challenges.

DEMOGRAPHIC REVOLUTION

The population of Loudoun remained constant for one and a half centuries. From 1800 to 1950 Loudoun's population stayed between 21,000 and 23,000. The metro-Washington region's large job base, along with the growth of high-tech companies along the nearby Dulles corridor, Dulles airport, and Dulles Greenway toll road; the shortage of open land; and higher taxes in the more densely populated counties to the east made Loudoun a prime target for growth.[1] By 2002 to 2003 it was the second-fastest-growing county in the nation. The population has recently increased at a spectacular rate. During the year 2000 alone, the population of Loudoun grew by a number equal to

---

[1] *The Washington Post*, June 26, 1999. The Dulles Greenway toll road is fourteen and half miles through the center of eastern Loudoun, the heart of the fastest-growing section of the county. Greenway connects with Dulles Toll Road to Washington, D.C. The daily cost for commuters on Greenway in 1996 was $1.50. Greenway has attracted businesses such as MCI and WorldCom, and especially large subdivisions, such as Ashburn Farms, Belmont Forrest, Broadlands, Carisbrooke, Regency, and Flynn's Crossing.

the total population of the county from the eighteenth century through much of the twentieth century. In the last decade of the twentieth century Loudoun's population nearly doubled (from 86,129 to 169,599). The county's population increased from 169,599 in 2000 to 190,903 in 2001. Most of the growth occurred in the eastern half of the county and in and around Leesburg, Purcellville, and the smaller towns in the west. Leesburg's population increased from 16,202 in 1990 to 30,323 by 2001, while Purcellville grew from 1,744 to 3,965 during the same period.[2]

Families with children make up the largest single group in Loudoun, but the county's senior population nearly doubled from 1990 to 2000. The county's ethnicity during this decade diversified as well. The number of whites dropped from ninety percent to eighty-one percent of Loudoun's population. The percentage of blacks declined nearly ten percent, although the number almost doubled (from 6,169 to 11,683). Hispanics became the county's fasting-growing group, climbing from two and a half a percent in 1990 to six percent of Loudoun's population (10,089), while the number of Asians more than tripled during the decade, to reach 9,067.[3]

Demographic shifts and urban growth have spawned a host of issues that scream for resolution: the need for more schools and county services, rising taxes and crime, decrease in farming, and congested roads.

IMPACT OF THE DEMOGRAPHIC REVOLUTION: REVOLUTIONARY CHANGES

Loudoun has been a magnet for younger families. Nearly half of all homes include children under the age of eighteen.[4] This makes Loudoun one of the fastest-growing school systems in the nation. When the 2002–2003 school year started, more than 37,000 students (nearly 3,000 more than the pervious year) entered fifty-six schools and were greeted by more than 3,000 teachers,

---

[2] Department of Economic Development, 2001 *Annual Growth Summary, Loudoun County, Virginia, USA* (Leesburg, VA, 2002), 5, 11, 18, 48. Hereafter referred to as *Growth Summary*); *Leesburg Today: The Journal of Loudoun County* (Leesburg, VA, January 11, 2002), p. 7. The population growth of the other five incorporated towns from 1990 to 2001 was much less: Hamilton, 562 to 700; Hillsboro, 90 to 96; Lovettsville, 749 to 853; Middleburg, 549 to 637; Round Hill, 500 to 505. Leesburg considered annexing nearly 8,000 acres east and south of the town, but opposition from the county and town residents has, as of 2003, prevented fruition of this plan.

[3] *Loudoun Times-Mirror*, March 14, 2001; *The Washington Post, Loudoun Extra*, May 27, 2001.

[4] According to the 2000 census, the number of children younger than fourteen more than doubled to 44,268 since 1990. Children younger than five increased from 7,613 to 16,461. This is counter to the trend in the rest of the Washington area, which has seen an increase in people living alone. More then forty percent of the households in the nation's capital, Alexandria and Arlington, Virginia, are residences of singles. By contrast, only 18.5 percent of Loudoun homes are occupied by singles.

administrators, and counselors.[5] Some 24,000 pupils arrived on 463 school buses that traveled 11,000 route-miles daily and 6.1 million miles annually to a school system that, despite rapid growth, is a leader in public education. State-of-the-art computer technology can be found in all classrooms and laboratories, and the school system offers a full range of education programs, including programs for gifted and disabled. Its students achieve high scores on the Stanford Achievement Test and the Scholastic Aptitude Test, with a low drop-out rate and 80 percent of the graduated attending college.

But with an anticipated student body increase of 3,000 a year in the foreseeable future, the challenges continue. Staffing is a main concern. About 600 new teachers are needed a year; finding faculty for courses and coping with increasing diversity in the student body, where sixty different dialects are spoken, is challenging. From 2002 to 2005, thirteen new schools will open. In 2000 each new elementary school cost $11,000,000 and each high school cost nearly $42,000,000. In addition to financial cost, the district must address the emotional issues of school location and redrawing school boundaries.[6]

Financing for these schools comes from bonds approved by citizens of Loudoun County in November elections. In November 2000, voters approved $119,865,000 in bonds with a twenty-year construction and a five-year repayment schedule at six percent yearly interest. The annual payment on this debt is $9,768,000. For the homeowner with property assessed at $100,000, the annual cost is $59; for owners of property assessed at $350,000, the cost is $206.

The average cost to educate Loudoun's 37,375 students in forty-four schools for 2002-2003 was $9,366 per student. This was a drastic change

---

[5] *Loudoun County Public Schools Annual Report for 2000-2001*, 4–5, 17, 20. Total full-time staff for 2002–2003 was 5,532.9; 3,052.5 teachers and counselors, 238 administrators and professional staff; and 2,242.4 support staff (cafeteria workers, classroom aids, bus drivers, secretaries, mechanics, maintenance workers, therapists, nurses, and custodians). Of the 56 school facilities, 38 are elementary schools (K–5), eight are middle schools (grades 6–8), one is an intermediate school (grades 8–9), seven are high schools (grades 9–12), and two are instructional centers. The average class size for kindergarten through eighth grade is twenty-two, and for grades 9–12, it's just under twenty-seven. Secondary teachers for grades 6–8 teach six of seven or eight periods per day, and for grades 9–12, they teach five out of seven or eight periods a day. In 2002–2003 teacher's salaries ranged from $34,398 to $77,401, with the average being $51,419. Parents help the county's school system through participating in a Parent Teacher Association (PTA) or Parent/Teacher Organization (PTO) at each school. They coordinate their efforts by sending representatives from each of these organizations to serve on the countywide Loudoun Education Alliance of Parents (LEAP). Elementary schools are constructed to accommodate 800 pupils, middle schools under 1,200, and high schools 1,600 students.

[6] Opening in fall 2002–2003: Heritage High School, Harmony Intermediate School, River Bend Middle School, Forrest Grove Elementary School and Hutchison Elementary School. In 2003–2004, Dominion High School, Belmont Ridge Middle School, Countryside Elementary School, Frances Hazel Reid Elementary, and Mountain View Elementary. In 2004–2005, Mercer Middle School, Stone Ridge Middle School, Smart's Mill Middle School, and Belmont Station Elementary. Future high schools are planned for South Riding and Brambleton.

in the number of students and schools from when Dr. Edgar B. Hatrick III became superintendent, in 1991. Then there were fewer than 15,000 students and 33 schools. Superintendent Hatrick faces a bigger job each year.[7]

The size of county government has also greatly expanded, especially in the largest departments: county administration, sheriff, management services, building and development, fire and rescue, animal care and control, library, health services, parks and recreation, and the division of aging services. Many of these departments exist because of the shift from an agrarian to an urban society, including the shift from volunteer to paid firemen. As people became less self-sufficient and more urban, they looked to more government, even on the county level, to meet their needs. This resulted in not only an expansion in the size of county government but also extensive local regulations. For example, in the year 2000 there were 1,805 county employees, but in 2002 the number increased thirty-eight percent to 2,465. The cost of increased positions, salaries, and fringe benefits escalated sixty-seven percent during this two-year span. The number of county-owned vehicles (not counting school buses) more than doubled from 1999 to 2002.[8] The per-position cost for the county government employees rose to $53,415 in 2002. The same year the county's vehicle fleet was more than 900. Of these, 310 were assigned to the sheriff's department.[9]

Accompanying the expansion in county personnel is the construction of new, large, multimillion-dollar structures to accommodate county workers and the judiciary.[10] In addition to bringing about the emotionally charged, rapidly changing school boundaries, the demographic explosion led to the realignment of the boundaries of the county's eight election districts in 2003. Mercer District was abolished and combined with the Blue Ridge and Dulles Districts. This enabled the creation of a new election district, Sugarland Run,

---

[7] Loudoun County Public Schools, *Loudoun County Public Schools: Annual Report 2001-2002*, (Leesburg, VA, 2002), 5, 8, 14-16; Loudoun Public Schools, *Loudoun's School Bond Referendum Facts*, (Leesburg, VA, 2000); *Leesburg Today*, December 30, 1998 & November 5, 2002. The school budget for 2002-2003 is $347,964,193. From 1983 to 1998 Loudoun voters approved a total of $342.5 million in bonds, with long-term indebtedness. More than $270 million were for schools. A $50 million school bond referendum was defeated in 1986, but since then bond issues have passed.

Loudoun started offering high school classes in 1890, and by 1909, had high schools at Leesburg, Lincoln, and Waterford. By 1916 a dozen high schools were in existence. Many had stables on the school grounds for the horses of students and teachers who rode to school. By 1944 high schools were consolidated into four schools: Aldie, Leesburg, Lincoln, and Lovettsville. In 1954 the four regional schools were consolidated, with the opening of Loudoun County High School at Leesburg. Modern education in Loudoun started with the superintendency of Oscar Leroy Emerick (1917-1957). Mr. Emerick had a staff of one, his sister, the legendary Miss Ruth Emerick. Her brother, Oscar, in a countywide pole was selected as the most influential Loudouner of the twentieth century.

Mr. Emerick was frugal with money but centralized Loudoun's educational system. He brought about the first county school board, replacing the local school boards and commissioners of six local school districts. Emerick purchased the first "motorized" school buses in 1925. Under his watch Frederick Douglass High School was created for African-Americans (1941-1968). Succeeding Emerick as superintendent was Clarence M. Bussinger (1957-1968). When he came aboard the county had 5,156 students, a starting teacher's salary of $3,240, and a total budget of $1,100,000. Robert E. Butt succeeded Bussinger as superintendent (1969-1988).

Potomac, and Broad Run. Leesburg District sits in the center of the county, and in the west are Blue Ridge and Catoctin, making up almost two-thirds of Loudoun.[11]

A RISE IN CRIME

The increased crime rate has put pressure on towns and county law enforcement agencies. The Leesburg police department grappled with a thirty-two percent increase in crime in one year (2000–2001).[12] On the county level, the sheriff's office cites a significant rise in violent crime from 2001 to 2002. Violent crimes rose from 413 in 2001 to 618 in 2002, while total crime in the county rose from 2,131 to 3,357. In 2002, for the first time in the county, what the sheriff's department called a "formal gang involved in criminal activity" made an ominous appearance. The sheriff in 2003 assigned one deputy to the full-time duty of investigating gang activity in the county, and the debate over how to cope with gang activity became an issue in a county election for the first time.[13]

The sheriff's office's full-time employees increased from 321 in 2000 to 444 $33,500,000 in 2003. The decline in the economy and county plans to cut

---

Under his watch, school integration that started in the 1960's was completed. He also dealt with the first significant growth in the county by building fourteen new schools. Dr. David N. Thomas was superintendent from 1988 to 1991.

[8] *Leesburg Today*, February 22, 2002 & July 5, 2002; *Loudoun Times Mirror*, April 4, 2001.

[9] In 2003 there were ten county supported community centers and four senior centers (Arcola, Leesburg, Purcellville, and Sterling). The Area Agency on Aging Senior Centers offered a variety of programs and activities including noon meals for citizens fifty-five or older.

[10] www.loudoun.gov/government. A two-story county office complex in Leesburg opened in 1981 costing $1,670,000, but soon it was too small. It was replaced by a large structure in the mid 1990s. In 1993 county offices were scattered over thirteen locations. All but one of the thirteen sites was leased, costing $2,629,125. County voters in 1993 rejected a bond issue that would have financed the construction of a consolidated government center. After considering numerous proposals, the board of supervisors accepted Gilbane Properties' proposal to build a new office building in Leesburg (158,100 square feet) and to purchase the Shenandoah Building (80,171 square feet) in the town and lease both buildings to the county for twenty-two years, at an annual cost of $2,400,000. This arrangement reduced the cost to the county by the amount of interest savings from debt service (overall cost savings) for the twenty-two years estimated to be $20,000,000. After leasing the two buildings for twenty-two years, the county has the option of purchasing the County Government Center and the Shenandoah Building for one dollar.

[11] See www.loudoun.Gov/Maps/election.

[12] *Loudoun Times Mirror*, April 10, 2002; *Leesburg Today*, April 10, 2003. In 1997 Leesburg had fewer than 1,000 crimes, 1,664 in 2000 and 2,200 in 2001. From 2000 to 2001 the number of rapes tripled (from 4 to 12), burglaries more than doubled (from 33 to 67), and motor vehicle thefts doubled (38 to 58). In a majority of the rape cases the victim knew their attacker. In burglaries, construction sites and unoccupied buildings were the primary targets.

[13] Ibid., July 24, & 31, 2002; April 30, 2003. The sheriff's office believes as many as fifteen members of a Hispanic gang attacked and stabbed (fortunately not fatally) two teenagers at a carnival in Sterling. Less than a week later five Hispanic men arrived with a gun and pepper spray, forced their way into a home in South Riding, terrorizing the family until they left with money, jewelry, a video camera, and a gun they had taken from an upstairs safe.

$8,000,000 from the 2003 fiscal year budget—of which $1,000,000 was from the sheriff's budget—led Sheriff Stephen O. Simpson to re-deploy deputies assigned to DARE (Drug and Alcohol Resistance Education). Simpson announced he was eliminating the drug-education program in middle schools and reducing it in grade schools. Members of the board of supervisors criticized this action.[14]

FINANCING THE DEMOGRAPHIC REVOLUTION

More people means more schools, county services, and more regulations. All of these raise costs. The fiscal year 2002 budget for Loudoun's larger departments rose twenty-eight percent over the previous year.[15] Enrolment in Loudoun schools rose 135 percent between 1992 and 2002, contributing to Loudoun's having the second-highest public debt of Virginia's counties. The per capita debt jumped from $2,000 in 1995 to $3,314 in 2002. The cost of constructing and furnishing a high school rose from about $42,000,000 in 1998 to more than $52,000,000 in 2002. County taxes have been increasing at an alarming rate, with rising assessments and increasing tax rates. Assessments for many, especially those living next to developing subdivisions, increased 300 to 500 percent in 2002. A retired citizen, Austin Grimes, of eastern Loudoun, saw the assessment on his twelve acres leap from $144,800 in 1999 to $553,300 the following year. His tax bill jumped from $1,600 to $6,100 in one year. This was not an isolated incident. Property owners, especially throughout eastern Loudoun, had similar experiences. Retired residents on fixed incomes are especially vulnerable, and some have been forced to sell their land.

Property taxes for fiscal year 2004 were increased $0.06, making the tax rate $1.11 for every $100 of assessed value. But the increase in taxes still fell $12,000,000 short of providing enough money for the original school budget. The county's total debt in 2002 was more than $500,000,000 and by 2004 increased to $700,000,000. What this meant for the average Loudoun

---

[14] *Leesburg Today*, July 5, 2002; *Loudoun Times-Mirror*, July 31, 2002. During the economic downturn, and in wake of WorldCom's scandal in 2002, WorldCom's northern Virginia operation center laid off 525 employees, which was 0.5 percent of Loudoun's more than 98,000 jobs. In 2002 Sheriff Simpson had 338 positions for sworn officers. Ninety-one of these were assigned to jail and court duty, and 142, to field patrol. In 2002 the staff levels of the sheriff's office had 0.76 deputies per 1,000 residents. This rate is higher than the 0.67 officers per 1,000 that the state recommends, but below one officer per 1,000 residents that, Simpson points out, is the national standard. Following the terrorist attacks of September 11, 2001, increased security has been implemented in the Loudoun circuit court complex and county office buildings. Contingency plans have also been made for public schools.

[15] *Loudoun Times-Mirror*, April 4, 2001. The budget for county administration for 2002 was $2,044,868 (36 percent increase); sheriff, $29,306,274 (24 percent increase); management services, $5,127,633 (34 percent increase); general services, $17,351,099 (53 percent increase); building and development, $14,612,342 (43 percent increase); fire and rescue, $19,257,485 (44 percent increase); library, $7,075,968 (33 percent increase); health services, $43,101,318 (58 percent increase); and parks and recreation, $19,233,456 (24 percent increase).

homeowner in 2003 was a forty-two percent increase in real estate taxes. The proposed operating county budget for 2004 increased ninety-three percent since the 2000 budget. Despite Loudoun's being the third richest county in the United States in 2003 and having tax relief programs—especially for elderly and disabled people with low incomes—many on fixed incomes cannot qualify.

Taxes are hitting Loudoun residents hard. Older residents, especially, see the new tax burden as unreasonable, as something that forces them out of their homes and destroys their small communities. Even owners of large estates consisting of more than 1,000 acres are selling because of taxes and the cost of maintaining such properties. Some of the younger residents who inherit land see the rapid growth in the value of the land as an opportunity to make a sizable amount of money. Meanwhile, county tax assessors defend their actions, arguing that they are bound by state law to establish the "market value" of the property without regard to the impact on the community or how long a person has lived on the property.[16]

Funding schools and expanding county government and services have put a financial strain on an out-of-date tax system based on property taxes. Property taxes make up more than three-fourths of the county income. County property tax was formed for the nineteenth-century agrarian society, and it made sense in a society of farmers. But it no longer works in an urban society. The county's urban growth is primarily young families with children, and the yearly educational cost per child in 2003 is nearly $10,000; property taxes of families with children do not pay their children's educational costs. Property taxes on $300,000 to $500,000 of assessed property value in the year 2000 provided $3,000 to $6,000 in revenue for the county. Throw in other needed county services in addition to education, and the costs are staggering, driving property taxes and bond debts skyward.

A shift away from property tax as a key source of county financing is highly unlikely. Voters are not in the mood to approve a local income tax or sales tax, and the Virginia general assembly, from which county powers are derived, blocks attempt to give counties greater regulatory powers, such as requiring developers to provide funding for school construction and more roads. Some see the answer in attracting more businesses, especially high-techcorporations, to the county. Both state and county officials gleefully welcome the world's largest private medical research organization, the Howard Hughes Medical Institute, to Loudoun in 2003.[17]

[16] *Leesburg Today*, July 2, November 15, 2002; January 31, March 14 & 21, 2003; *Loudoun Times-Mirror*, March 19 & 26, 2003; *The Washington Post*, March 7, 2000 & February 6 & May 12, 2003. The proposed operating budget by Loudoun County Administrator Kirby M. Bowles for 2004 is $32,000,000. Spending for capital projects and other items brings the total budget to $802,000,000.
Applicants for tax relief must be sixty-five or older or permanently and totally disabled. For real estate tax relief in 2003 the gross household income cannot exceed $52,000, and the total combined net worth of the applicants must not be more than $240,000.

[17] Loudoun County's revenue sources for the fiscal year 2001 were: 78 percent from local revenues (most from property taxes), 16 percent from the commonwealth of Virginia, 1 percent from the federal government, 4 percent from the Fund balance, and 1 percent from other sources.

Working out the county budget leads to annual differences between the school board and the board of supervisors. This is the result of the contradictory motives of Loudoun voters. They elect school board members who are dedicated to providing the best financial support for education, but for their county supervisors, who have the final say on the county's budget, voters want representatives who will limit spending and not raise taxes.[18]

The Howard Hughes Medical Institute (HHMI) broke ground for a medical research campus along the banks of the Potomac River in eastern Loudoun on May 5, 2003. The half-billion dollar, 760,000 square-foot research facility is scheduled to open in 2006, with a staff of more than 2,000.

GROWTH AND POLITICAL CONFLICT

The bountiful financial gains from developing Loudoun County strongly motivate real estate and development corporations, such as Toll Brothers, Winchester Homes, Pulte, and Trafalgar, to build houses and commercial buildings over as much of the county as possible. They and their supporters call this progress. Any attempt to restrain unfettered development is decried as anti-progressive and a threat to the county's economic well-being. The opposing view condemns escalating development because it is ruining the county's quality of life and causing skyrocketing taxes and debt.

Development in Loudoun during the first decade of the twenty-first century is unstoppable. The fundamental issue is not growth versus no growth, but between development versus retaining some open space. Residents are divided on the development question between controlled growth, or "smart growth," and little or no restriction on the rate of development. The Board of Supervisors and the county Planning Commission late in the 1990s (1996–2000) welcomed extensive and rapid development with open arms. Public reaction, including that of many new residents, and led by Voters to Stop Sprawl, replaced the previous pro-growth board with one that is attempting to slow and control growth. Because of development sites approved by pro-growth supervisors and planning commissions for approximately 30,000 future houses, rapid construction continues after the new supervisors assumed office in 2000.

One major achievement of county supervisors (2000–2004) is a twenty-year planning strategy that includes the revision of the comprehensive plan and 1993 zoning ordinance and zoning map and the creation of the purchase-of-development-rights program (PDR).[19]

---

[18] Interview with superintendent of Loudoun County public schools Dr. Edgar B. Hatrick, Leesburg, VA, January 23, 2003.

[19] *Leesburg Today,* March 23, 2001. The board originally appropriated $4,000,000 to launch the development rights program by buying from select landowners, preferably with fifty or more acres, easements that would permanently restrict development on those properties. The program was started in 2001 and is administered by the purchase development rights board. Originally they received more than 100 applications. The county also established the Loudoun Land Conservation

The revised zoning ordinance and zoning map reflect sensitivity to environmental concerns, especially saving trees. They also attempt to limit development in the western part of the county, to preserve open space, and to slow growth. The revised zoning ordinance is designed to reduce potential residential development by nearly fifty percent. The new zoning map divides the county into three areas: the rural area (of western Loudoun), the transition area (between rural and suburban areas), and the suburban area (in the east). The greatest down zoning—which reduces the number of houses that can be constructed in an area—applies to the rural area. In the northern rural area, the number of houses was reduced from one house per three acres to one house per twenty acres, while in the southern rural area, the number of houses was reduced to one per fifty acres.[20] Before Loudoun's down zoning was adopted in 2003, some landowners, encouraged by developers, tried to rezone their farms into building lots under the 1993 regulations. Public hearings held about down zoning prior to the passage of the revised ordinance were numerous—and were often emotional and loud.

As commendable as the 2003 revisions on zoning are, they have intensified the fight between developers and some citizens who want to sell their land (Citizens for Property Rights), on one side, and the board of supervisors and supporters of slowing development, on the other side. Within a few weeks after the new regulations went into effect, nearly 200 lawsuits had been filed by developers and some pro-growth landowners challenging the legality of the revised regulation. Supporters of down zoning contend the county will successfully defend the revised zoning ordinance in court.

The conflict between the two forces is reaching a climax in the county elections in November 2003. The revised 2003 zoning ordinance and the officials who created it are facing a political assault in this election. The incumbent chairman of the board of supervisors predicts that millions will be spent by pro-development forces to unseat the "smart growth" supervisors and change what cynical critics, including some vocal—and at times vitriolic—members of Citizens for Property Rights (CPR), call "snob zoning," which favors wealthy landowners.

The first stage of the political battle over growth in 2003 elections took place in the county's Republican party. A contentious battle was fought over the method of nominating Republican candidates. When the pro-growth forces, who want to unseat York, were able to shift the nominating process from a direct primary to a nominating convention, the incumbent chairman of the board of supervisors, the commonwealth attorney Robert Anderson, along with several other candidates for county offices, left the Republican Party to run as independents.[21] The election appears likely to be hotly contested. Regardless of the outcome, the issue of growth will contentiously remain.

Fund (LLCF), a special fund created for purchasing conservation easements and preserving open space. It is funded entirely by private contributions (by February 24, 2003, $5000 had been donated). The LLCF complements the work of the PDR.

[20] See www.loudoun.gov, and go to Hot Topics, then Zoning.

[21] *Loudoun Easterner*, March 12, 2003. Another type of criticism of the supervisors and their chairman comes from the Republican county treasurer, Robert Zurn, a former supervisor and

THE END OF TRADITIONAL FARMING: AGRICULTURE'S TRANSITION

The family farm that formed the economic and social nucleus of the county for centuries has all but disappeared. Dairy farming and the production of grain crops that traditionally were the mainstay of Loudoun agriculture have drastically declined. In 2003 only two dairy farms remain. The two remaining farms survive in part by selling breeding stock to South American buyers. The cost of land and equipment has escalated. Farmers have found it difficult to find workers as their sons leave the family farm in favor of jobs that pay better and are less physically demanding. One of the harder jobs to fill has been the task of milking cows twice a day 365 days a year.

Temporary endeavors such as sod farming, hay making, and raising beef cattle have replaced traditional farming on Loudoun's undeveloped land in the early twenty-first century. These are a part of the transition from farming to urban development and often take place on land purchased for development.

In the new type of agriculture in Loudoun, vegetable and herb farms, vineyards, and Christmas trees farms have emerged. Horses and beef cattle have replaced dairy cows as soybeans have replaced corn and wheat. By 2003 most of the county's remaining agriculture is located in the western portion of Loudoun. Even there most of the former family farms have disappeared. These factors, plus the lure of higher prices paid by developers for land, result in the sale of farms. Any reduction in county property taxes the farmer may receive through the Land Use Tax program is not enough to abate the selling of farmland.[22]

The closing of the Southern States store in Leesburg in 2003 is indicative of the western march of urbanization. This store opened in 1934 and served as a supply store for farmers until the late 1900's, when more and more

---

supporter of York. Zurn laments rising government spending and higher taxes and charges York and the supervisors of being overly concerned with land use issues while not paying enough attention to financial matters.

For some, especially within the Republican Party, the litmus test for any political candidate is their stand not on growth, but on abortion. These voters argue that their votes are morally based and that will only support candidates opposed to abortion.

[22] The county adopted the Land Use Assessment Program in 1973. Real estate taxes for owners of land (five acres or more) that qualify for agricultural, horticultural, forestry, or open space uses are deferred by the assessment of these properties under their fair market value. County supervisors in 1999 amended Loudoun's land use ordinance, allowing the option of an additional tax deferment called the sliding-scale option. The taxpayer agreeing to stay in land use for ten to twenty years will receive a 99 percent deferment in taxes during the years of their commitment. Those agreeing to a five- to ten-year commitment would receive a 50 percent reduction. All properties in land use must be revalidated every six years. The deferred, or rollback, tax is due when changes in use occur. Traditional rollback tax is equal to the deferred tax for the current year, tax for the previous five years, plus 10 percent simple interest for each year. Rollback taxes for the sliding-scale option may be more. The minimum number of years for payment of rollback taxes

of the store's patrons were suburbanites.[23]

By the year 2000, hay constituted about four-fifths of Loudoun's land in crops, in large part to feed the county's 36,000 cattle and calves and 15,800 horses. Loudoun at this time has the largest number of horses of any Virginia county. The total value of horses in Loudoun in 2001 was nearly $295,000,000. A key factor in Loudoun's horse industry is the rich soil along the base of the Blue Ridge Mountains; it grows the highest quality of blue grass, which is crucial for raising thoroughbred horses.[24]

The traditional concept of a farm has changed, both in the amount of land used as well as the type of farming. Many residents now consider as little as five to ten acres a farm, instead of the hundreds of acres associated with traditional farming. New residents lacking a rural background but attracted to the idea of farming occasionally contact Loudoun's agricultural extension agent only to discover they do not own enough land for profitable farming and the cost of purchasing enough land and farm equipment is prohibitive.[25]

Farming and urban housing do not often coexist peacefully. Residents of subdivisions find farm smells and the noise of farm equipment used early on weekend mornings intolerable. Farmers find dogs from housing developments chasing their cattle and neighborhood youngsters' playful forays upon private farm land—and occasional trashing part of a crop—not only annoying, but costly.[26]

THE NEW COMMUNITY: THE END OF THE FARM AND THE RISE OF THE SUBDIVISION

The small farm communities centered around a country store or church, where everyone knew each other and their family history, have been replaced by a more impersonal subdivision community. Residents are usually commuters who frequently spend several hours a day traveling to and from work.

Longtime residents disdain the supplanting of original communities with subdivisions. To them, these changes are disturbing, inconvenient, and annoying. They live with the constant noise of large earth-moving equipment,

in the sliding-scale option is the same as the traditional program, but if the number of years in the program is greater than five, then taxes must be paid for each year from the date the sliding-scale option was signed.

[23] *The Washington Post, Loudoun Extra*, March 30, 2003. Two Southern States storesremained in 2003, but both are in western Loudoun, in Middleburg and Purcellville. In 1997 there were 1,032 farms in Loudoun, composed of 184,988 acres on which crops were raised. On 68,216 of these nearly 50,000 acres were in hay. In 2002 there were 36,000 cattle and calves in Loudoun; only 500 were milk cows.

[24] Virginia Agricultural Statistics Service, *2001 Virginia Equine Report* (Richmond, VA, 2002), p. 8. Most of the hay for horses in Loudoun is purchased outside the county.

[25] Interview with Gary Hornbaker, Loudoun County extension agent, Leesburg, VA, January 27, 2003.

[26] *The Washington Post*, July 22, 2000. See "Life on the Edge" in the real estate section for a discussion of conflicting rural and urban lifestyles.

the almost constant beeping of equipment moving backwards, the cracking and crashing of trees being uprooted. Houses and barns are reduced to rubble by the bulldozer's blade and then hauled away. Residents endure the mind-numbing sound, day after day, of drilling through rock. Truck horns wail continuously, warning of impending blasts, which rattle house windows. Residents live with these disturbances while fretting over the fate of their homes and wells. They watch as topsoil is trucked away for sale, and the remaining earth is moved about. Small hills are leveled, changing the topography of land that has existed since its geological formation. Roads formerly constructed for horse and wagon traffic and later adopted for motorized vehicles now give way to potholes and broken pavement under the weight of large, rapidly moving, fume-belching dump trucks. These congest the narrow, crooked roadways, making travel hazardous. Despite the diligent labor of craftsmen who frequently use nail guns and cranes to construct prefabricated sections of new houses, longtime residents lament the loss of pastoral views to a horizon of endless rooftops.[27]

Loudoun's larger subdivisions, such as Country Side, Ashburn Farms, and University Center, have thousands of homes. Smaller subdivisions have hundreds, or less often, a mix of single-family detached houses, single-family attached homes, and condominiums. In 2001 the average price of all types of houses for the more than 9,100 housing units sold was $290,000. The average price for the 3,940 single-family detached house was $396,016.[28]

Wildlife also has to make the adjustment to revolutionary environmental changes. Most animals, including deer, raccoons, geese, hawks, possums, foxes, groundhogs, and skunks, move to the remaining farm, woods, or open space as their traditional habitat disappears. A farmer may enjoy the beauty of a deer grazing in his field, but not the damage it does to his crop, garden, or barbed-wire fence. Nor does he appreciate his malodorous neighbor the skunk's nightly forays digging up his lawn in search of grubs and worms, or the consumption of his garden vegetables by raccoons and groundhogs. The latter dig burrows with open entrances, posing a hazard to livestock's legs. The farmer may not be overjoyed to see the multiplying numbers of Canada geese, one of the most adaptable animals, grazing upon his grass fields. Those in the animal world are trying to survive. They do not recognize legal deeds or the exclusive human ownership of their environment. The new urban homeowner may find that not all animals are ready to forgo their claim to the land.

Life in a subdivision differs greatly from life in a farming community. A subdivision has a high concentration of residents, who have limited contact

---

[27] The author and his family had the following experiences with development around the family farm: Companies employed by developers mistakenly destroyed one-eighth mile of the farm's fence and were only stopped when we saw them. The workers had been told to remove all of the fences on the property and didn't realize that they were no longer on the developer's property. Several weeks later explosives sent rocks hurling on a public road, one striking and nearly going through the hood of our new car. The fence was rebuilt and repairs to the car were for paid by the responsible companies.

[28] Department of Economic Development, County of Loudoun, *2001 Annual Growth Summary* (Leesburg, VA, 2002), pp. 26–29. Loudoun's oldest subdivision, Sterling Park, has 3,080 single detached family homes. The largest development for condominiums is University Center, where

with each other. Residents almost always keep house and car doors locked, and they often install security systems. A farming community, on the other hand, consists of small numbers of people scattered about. Residents know each other and their family histories, and they live in houses that are rarely—if ever—locked. Keys remain in the ignition of unlocked vehicles.

The high concentration of large populations that are found in subdivision-filled areas require recreational facilities such as swimming pools, playing fields, and tennis courts. These are used for organized competition, which has descended even to include preschoolers. Anxious—and at times hyperactive—coaches and parents sometimes react with intensity rivaling a life-or-death struggle.

Farm communities have had fewer amenities and fewer county-provided services. While urban areas need public trash service, in farms, traditionally garbage was fed to hogs, and trash was burned or dumped on remote areas, usually near or in the woods. Vegetable gardening was a standard part of farm life, while urbanites shop for food almost exclusively from stores or farmers. A member of the family would usually mow a farm's fields or yards, while lawn services are caring for more and more urban yards. On farms, chores occupied much of school-age children's free time, leaving them with less free time for organized sports. Sports were often limited to intense high-school competition.

The shift from an agrarian to a densely populated urban society has been accompanied by expanding federal, state, and local regulations. These are designed to protect and benefit the public by restricting individual control and options. Unlike in urban settings, where firearms are restricted or prohibited, on farms guns are used for hunting or eliminating wildlife that's considered a threat or nuisance, without fear of violating a local ordinance or state law. The farm owner was king of his domain. He could cut trees at will and could usually burn brush without a permit. Into the mid 1900s he could construct buildings without having to endure the tedious process of obtaining a building permit or being subjected to zoning and county inspectors. Water for farm dwellings still comes from a spring or well, and sewage is disposed of by a septic tank and drain field constructed next to each house. Neither one is controlled by the county water and sewer authority, and they require no monthly fee.

The modern subdivision has created a new type of regulatory agency: the homeowners' association. By 2003 there were twenty-three such organizations in Loudoun. They are created as part of each planned community to establish regulations that benefit the inhabitants and community. All residents in a community with a homeowners' association are subject to its regulations and must pay monthly fees to the association. Residents also elect the association's board of directors, who are charged with administering or altering regulations, which, in some cases, form a book of 100 or more pages.

more than 2,017 are to be built. The average price among 2,530 units sold in Loudoun in 1991 was $170,246 ($210,048 for single detached family house, $146,303 for a town house, $95,848 for a condominium. The average price of townhouses sold in 2001 is $228,150, and condominiums are $143,159).

Any external changes to a homeowner's property, such as painting a house, building a deck, or cutting down a tree, are subject to the approval of a review board. Some associations require applications to their review board to be accompanied by the approving signatures of four neighbors. Regulations of associations can be meticulous; for example, some require that exterior Christmas decorations must be removed before a specific deadline.[29]

Homeowners' associations for urban dwellers are usually accepted as a necessary, if not benevolent, part of urban life. But to many inhabitants of rural communities steeped in a tradition of independence and self-reliance in agrarian lifestyles, the idea of being told what you can do on or with your property is viewed as repugnant, meddling, and an infringement of rights.

Most urban residents appear to be content with their lifestyle. According to a 2002 survey of county residents living in the densely populated sections of the county, only nine percent were born in Loudoun; one-third had lived in the county for three years or less; and another third, for ten years or less. The reasons for coming to the county, in order of importance, were location of work site, affordable housing, and Loudoun's rural character. Well over ninety percent were satisfied with county services (schools, fire and rescue, libraries, and parks and recreation) and more than half stated that they were willing to pay higher property taxes to maintain or increase select public services (fire and rescue, law enforcement, and public schools).[30]

People in an urban environment have certain economic and cultural advantages, especially in the metropolitan Washington, D.C., area. They would find the traditional county store fascinating but its prices and selection inadequate when compared to large shopping malls and discount stores such as Wal-Mart and Costco. Urban life is more appealing to these people than living on a farm. An urban environment provides higher-paying jobs and a greater selection of job opportunities than are available on the family farm, where hard, sweaty, dirty, and sometimes smelly work is commonplace. Income is lower on the farm, and profit is determined by the uncertainties of the weather and the withering competition of large farm corporations. Caring for farm animals—such as dairy cows, which have to be milked and fed twice a day—limits the daily freedom of farm dwellers. Such activities are a far cry from how urbanites fill their days.

[29] *Loudoun Times-Mirror*, January 15, 2003; *The Washington Post*, March 7, 2003; *The Washington Post, Loudoun Extra*, September 28, 1997; "The Making of Washington; As Far As The Eye Can See," *The Washingtonian*, pp. 56–103, January 2000.

[30] Department of Economic Development, County of Loudoun, *2002 Survey of Loudoun Residents*, pp. 3–4,8. This report is based on the random sampling (one-half in eastern Loudoun, one-fourth in Leesburg, and one-fourth in western Loudoun) of 1,010 households. See Loudoun's website: www.loudoun.gov.

So what is Loudoun County's future? Ironically, the primary and disappearing characteristic of the county, its rural character, attracts the growth that is destroying it.[31] A majority of recent urban residents, as well as old-timers, feel that the county's biggest problem is growth and development. Residents who have recently migrated to the county are also a major force in attempting to slow the county's development. How successful they and their smart-growth county representatives' (the board of supervisors elected in 2000) zoning changes will ultimately be, time will decide. The history of Loudoun since the late 1900's reveals that the only constant for the county is change.

[31] Ibid, p. 3. Thirty-four percent of those surveyed in 2002 "felt that the single best thing about Loudoun was its rural character and countryside." Loudoun's second leading problem after growth, according to this survey, is traffic and transportation. The majority of Loudoun's new residents (forty-one percent), as in years past, came from the county to the east, Fairfax County. Almost as many, thirty-nine percent, came from outside the Washington, D.C., area.

Growth has also increased the need for more hospital services. A new Loudoun Hospital building was constructed in the 1970s next to the old hospital in Leesburg. The closing of the 1970s 120-bed structure and movement in 1997 to a new, only eighty-bed facility at Lansdowne is controversial. It left western Loudoun farther away from a hospital. In 2001 the state health commissioner approved a nineteen-bed addition at Lansdowne costing $5,800,000. Otherwise the commissioner has been a barrier to expanding Loudoun's health-care facilities. Claiming a surplus in excess of 100 hospital beds will exist by 2007 after approved expansion in Loudoun and nearby hospitals in Fairfax County are completed, the commissioner rejected in 2002 a Nashville company's attempt to create a new hospital campus in Loudoun and in 2003 denied the applications of the Loudoun Hospital Center to add thirty-two new beds as well as that of the Hospital Corporation of America to construct a new hospital in Ashburn. The critical need for more beds led to the reopening in 2003 the formerly abandoned Leesburg facility, providing limited services.

APPENDIX

Prices of Agricultural Products Received by Loudoun Farmers from 1911 to 1972.

	Fat Cattle (Priced per pound)	Stockers (Price per pound)	Hogs (Price per pound)	Lambs (Price per pound)	Wool (Price per pound)
	$.05	$	$.05 1/2	$	$
	.06-.07		.07		
bu)	.08-.09		.09-.09 1/2		
	.07 1/2-.08		.08		
	.07-.08		.07		
	.08-.09		.09-.1/2		
bu)	.08-.09		.09-.09 1/2		
	.13-.15		.15-.16	.15-.17	.70
	.12		.17	.16	.58
	.07-.08		10 1/2	.11	.35
	.08 1/2-.09		.06 1/2	.13	.47 1/2
	.08 1/2-.09		.07	.13	.35-.38
	.08 1/2-.09		.11 1/2-.12	.12 1/2	.40
	.08-.09 1/2		.14	.12 1/2	.35
	10-.10 1/2		.09	.12-.13	.35
	.12		.09-.09 3/4	.12-.13	.51-.52
	.13		.10 3/4-.11	.14-.14	.29-.39
	.09 1/2-.10		.10	.10 1/2	.25

APPENDIX (Continued)

orn	Fat Cattle (Price per pound)	Stockers (Price per pound)	Hogs (Price per pound)	Lambs (Price per pound)	Wool (Price per pound)
ou)	$.07 1/2	$	$.07 1/2	$.10	$.15
ou)	.05-.06 1/2		.04-.04 1/2	.05-.06	.08-.09
obl)	.04 1/2-.05 1/2		.05	.05-.07	.15
obl)	.05 1/2-.06 1/2		.04 1/2	.07-.08 1/2	.26
obl)	.07 1/2-.09		.08-.09 3/4	.07-.08 1/2	.28
3.50(bbl)	.06 1/2-.07 1/2		10	.08 1/2-.10	.31c
ou)e	.09-.11	.08-.10	.09-.10 1/2	.10-.12 1/2	.40
obl)	.07-.08 3/4		.08-.08 3/4	.07-.09 1/2	.18-.20
3.00(bbl)	.07-.09		.05-.06 3/4	.07-.11	.25
3.50(bbl)	.08-.09		.04 1/2-.05 1/4	.08-.10	.35-.40
4.25(bbl)	.08 1/2-.10		.08 1/2-.10 1/3	.08-.12	.45f

to the lack of information for the month of June.

not available.

ived for a bushel of shelled corn, which would be substantially greater than that for unshelled
ne barrel; five bushels of shelled corn equal one barrel.

APPENDIX (Continued)

Fat Cattle (Price per pound)	Stockers (Price per pound)	Hogs (Price per pound)	Lambs (Price per pound)	Wool (Price per pound)
$.14-.16	$	$.13-.13 3/4	$.13-.14	$.50-.56
.13-.15		.11-.13 1/2	.11-.15	---
.14-.16		.14 3/4	.15-.17	.48
.15-.17		.14 5/6	.18	.48
.22-.24	.22-.23	.23-.24	.22	.40
.28-.32	.28-.30	.19-.21 1/2	.25-.30	.38
.18-.23 1/2	.20-.25	.15-.20 1/2	.20-.25	.50
.25-.28 1/2	.25-.30	.20	.27	.50
.28-.33	.30-.38	.22	.36	
.27-.31	.28-.33	.20 1/2	.28	.54
.18-.20	.15-.20	.26	.20-.24	
.15-.21	.12-.21	.25	.15-.21	
.15-.23	.15-.22	.21	.16-.25	
.15-.20	.15-.20	.18		
.20-.23	.20-.24	.20 1/2		
.28	.25-.29	.25 1/2		
.26-.29	.28-.33	.17-.17 1/4		
.20-.23	.20-.25	.17 1/2		
.20-.23 1/5	.22-.27	.18		
.23-.25	.25-.35	.19		
.22	.22-.30	.18		
.18-.21	.18-.26	.15-.16		

available information for June 1951.

available information for June 1964.

APPENDIX (Continued)

Corn	Fat Cattle (Price per pound)	Stockers (Price per pound)	Hogs (Price per pound)	Lambs (Price per pound)	Wool (Price per pound)
$7.00(bbl)	$.24-.26	$.29	$.25		
7.00(bbl)	.27-.28	.34	.25 1/2		
	.24-.26	.32	.23 1/2		
6.00(bbl)	.27	.33	.20		
1.20(bu)					
7.50(bbl)	.33	.35	.25		
6.50(bbl)	.28-.29	.30	.26		
8.00-9.00(bbl)	.30	.30-.40	.20		
7.50(bbl)	.34-.36	.35-.52	.27-.27 3/4		

on for June 1967.

the "Minutes of the Lovettsville Farmers' Club" for 1911 to 1972, 7 vols.

BIBLIOGRAPHY

The nature of germane local sources demand some comment about them prior to the extensive listing of all materials consulted in the preparation of this volume. Some of the more illuminating information about Loudoun's past is scattered throughout the myraid of county records, such as the Court Order Books, Minute Books of the County Court, Deed and Will Books, Minute Books of the School Board, and minutes of the County Planning Commission. These should be supplemented with *The Statutes at Large, Being a Collection of All the Laws of Virginia*, edited by William H. Hening and Samuel Shepherd, and the *Acts of the General Assembly of the State of Virginia*. Local newspapers, when available, are the most revealing of source materials. Indispensable for an understanding of antebellum Loudoun are the issues of *The Genius of Liberty*. From the end of the Civil War to the twentieth century a wealth of information can be gleaned from *The Democratic Mirror*.

Just as valuable for the twentieth century are the issues of *The Loudoun Times-Mirror* and its precursors, *The Loudoun Mirror* and *The Loudoun Times*. For those who do not wish to spend the vast number of hours required to examine the aforementioned, several surveys pertaining to Loudoun are available. Among these titles, none of which are based upon an extensive examination of the above sources, are *Legends of Loudoun: An Account of the History and Homes of a Border County of Virginia's Northern Neck* by Harrison Williams, *History and Comprehensive Description of Loudoun County* by James W. Head, *Legends of Loudoun Valley* by Joseph V. Nichols, *The Composition Book* by Asa Moore Janney and Werner Janney. Head's book is more of a geological study than a history, and Nichols and the Janneys' works, while fascinating reading, are for the most part undocumented accounts of folklore and legendry. Two succinct and useful summaries of Loudoun's history up to the 1920's are the *Loudoun County Geography and Supplement* by H. R. Sanders, Eliza Lunceford, and Virginia Fenton and *An Economic and Social Survey of Loudoun* by Patrick A. Deck and Henry Heaton.

The genesis of Loudoun is recounted in the excellent book by Fairfax Harrison, *Landmarks of Old Prince William*. This should be supplemented by articles in *The Bulletin of the Loudoun County History Society*, published during the late 1950's and early 1960's. Witty and opinionated comments of an Englishman's visit to Loudoun during the American Revolution can be found engagingly presented in *The Journal of Nicholas Cresswell*.

Antebellum Loudoun can best be understood from an examination of John A. Binns' work entitled *A Treatise on Practical Farming*; James M. Garnett's *Biographical Sketch of Hon. Charles Fenton Mercer*, Olliver O. Trumbo's unpublished master's thesis "Charles Fenton Mercer, 1778-1858"; Yardley Taylor's *Memoir of Loudo[u]n County, Virginia;* Patricia C. Hickin's doctoral dissertation "Antislavery in Virginia, 1831-1861," and Lewis G. Gray's two-volume *History of Agriculture in the Southern United States to 1860*. Material on antebellum Loudoun and subsequent eras can be found in Samuel M. Janney's *Memoirs of Samuel M. Janney* and Philip diZerega's unpublished master's thesis "History of Secondary Education in Loudoun County Virginia."

The impact of the Civil War upon the county is extensively recorded in *Loudoun County and the Civil War* by John Divine et al.; *History of the Independent Loudoun Virginia Rangers* by Briscoe Goodhart, *The Comanches: A History of White's Battalion* by Frank M. Myers, and the copious volumes entitled *The War of the Rebellion: A Compilation of the Official Records of the Union and Confederate Armies.*

Rail transportation that touched nineteenth and twentieth-century Loudoun is discussed in *Rails to the Blue Ridge* by Herbert H. Harwood, Jr., and *The Washington and Old Dominion Railroad* by Ames W. Williams. Information pertaining to Loudoun and one of her early twentieth-century celebrities is provided by Jack T. Kirby in *Westmoreland Davis: Virginia Planter-Politician, 1859-1942.*

Specific material and insight into farming in Loudoun since the Civil War are in the extensive and enlightening "Minutes of the Catoctin Farmers' Club of Waterford, Virginia, 1868-1943" and the "Minutes of the Lovettsville Farmers' Club of Loudoun County, 1911-1972." Materials indispensable for an understanding of Loudoun politics are contained in the following relevant studies of Virginia: *Sectionalism in Virginia from 1776 to 1861* by Charles H. Ambler, *The Political History of Virginia During the Reconstruction* by Hamilton J. Eckenrode, *The Virginia Conservatives, 1867-1879: A Study in Reconstruction Politics* by Jack P. Maddex, Jr.; *County Government in Virginia, 1607-1904* by Albert O. Porter.

The Bicentennial has increased interest in Loudoun history and spawned several recent titles that provide interesting sketches about the county's past. Among these are *Glimpses of Loudoun* by the Loudoun County Independent Bicentennial Committee, *The Guide to Loudoun: A Survey of the Architecture and History of A Virginia County* by Eugene M. Scheel, *Hillsboro: Memories of a Mill Town* by the Hillsboro Bicentennial History Committee, and *The Town of Leesburg in Virginia: The Middle Century, 1858-1958* by Frank Raflo.

BIBLIOGRAPHY 419

A. PRIMARY SOURCES

1. Unpublished

a. *Official Records*
Fairfax County, Virginia. Court Order Books.
    ————— Deed Books.
    ————— Records of Surveys.
    ————— Records of Roads.
Loudoun County, Virginia. Annual School Reports.
    ————— Court Order Books.
    ————— Decisions of the Circuit Court.
    ————— Deed Books.
    ————— Minute Books of the County Court.
    ————— Minute Books of the County School Board.
    ————— Minute Books of the District School Boards.
    ————— Minute Books of the School Electoral Board.
    ————— Minutes of the County Planning Commission.
    ————— Real Estate Books.
    ————— Reports of Teachers Contracted.
    ————— School, Teacher, Enrollment and Attendance Records.
    ————— Will Books.
United States. National Archives. Population Schedules of the Censuses of Loudoun County, Virginia, for 1790 to 1890.
    ————— National Archives. Slave Schedules of the Census of Loudoun County, Virginia, for 1850.
Virginia. Board of Public Works. *Annual Reports*, 1815-1840.
    ————— House of Delegates. *Journal*, 1838, 1845-1847.
    ————— *Proceedings and Debates of the Virginia State Convention of 1829-30.*

b. *Manuscript Materials*

Bray Collection. Private Collection of Mrs. Virginia Ballard Bray, 910 Seneca Road, Herndon, Va. The Collection consists of letters, clippings, and account books of the New Baltimore Academy.

Gott Collection. Private collection of John K. Gott, librarian, Langley High School, Va. Extensive material on Northern Virginia, including the minutes of the Ketocton Baptist Association, 1792-1815.

Hammond, Frank. Collection. Private collection of Frank B. Hammond, 7500 Nancemond, Springfield, Va. Unpublished diaries of Kathryn Carper and William G. Hammond, plus letters and photographs.

Hammond, Richard. Collection. Private collection of Richard M. Hammond, 128 Elden Street, Herndon, Va. An extensive and fascinating collection of letters, deeds, photographs and collector items.

Janney, Asa M. Collection. Private collection of Asa M. Janney, Lincoln, Va. Extensive collection of materials on Janney family and Society of the Friends in Loudoun.

Janney, John. Collection. Thomas B. Library, Leesburg, Va. An extensive collection of private and business letters, scrapbooks, and ledgers of perhaps Loudoun's most distinguished nineteenth-century citizen.

Leigh Collection. Private collection of Lewis Leigh, Sr., 3989 Chain Bridge Road, Fairfax, Va. Materials on the Day family.

Loudoun County Historical Society Collection. Purcellville Library, Purcellville, Va. Much informative material can be found in the numerous items, including mill books, account books, and minute books of Loudoun temperance organizations.

Loudoun Museum Collection. Leesburg, Va. Miscellaneous collection of deeds, photographs, account books, and museum items dealing with Loudoun County and vicinity.

Manuscript Collection of the Maryland Historical Society. Baltimore, Md. Account Book of Joseph Janney, 1773-1776.

Manuscript Collection of the Historical Society of Pennsylvania, Philadelphia, Pennsylvania. Pemberton Papers.

Plaskett Collection. Private collection of Paul C. Plaskett, 2516 North Stevens Street, Alexandria, Va. An interesting collection of deeds, clippings, photographs, letters, and genealogical information on the Coleman family.

Taggart Collection. Library of Congress. MSS. Division. Account books of the Fall Bridge Co. and the Georgetown-Leesburg Turnpike Co., 1816-1853.

Taylor Collection. Private collection of L. L. Taylor, Lincoln, Va. Collection of materials relating to the Taylor family and Society of the Friends including Yardley Taylor's "Surveying Notebook, 1832."

Thomas Balch Library Loudoun Collection. Leesburg Va. Miscellaneous collection of letters and other papers pertaining to some of Loudoun's more influential citizens, including the historical papers of the late Wilbur C. Hall. Also in this collection are the Minutes of the Board of Trustees of the Leesburg Academy from 1833-1860.

Manuscript Collection of the Virginia Historical Society Library. Richmond, Va. Letters and petitions of Loudoun Valley citizens to the federal government for remuneration for property destroyed by Union soldiers during the Civil War.

Manuscript Department of William R. Perkins Library. Duke University, Durham, N. C. Minutes of the Female Mite Society of the Episcopal Church of Leesburg, Va., 1823-1846.

Virginian Collection. Fairfax County Library, Fairfax, Va. Newspaper clippings on northern Virginia.

Virginia State Library. Archives. Vestry-Books for Shelburne Parish, Loudoun County, 1771-1805, N. F. Cabell Papers, Petitions of Loudoun Citizens to the Virginia General Assembly and numerous other materials related to Loudoun.

Society of the Friends Collection. Sandy Spring, Maryland. Minutes and records of the Fairfax and Goose Creek monthly and quarterly meetings.

c. Unpublished Studies

Arcola P.T.A. Executive Committee Survey of Parents on Twelve-month School, January 26, 1973. This survey is kept by the secretary of the Arcola P.T.A.

"Loudoun County." 5 vols. Thomas Balch Library, Leesburg, Va. Scrapbooks of newspaper clippings of the early 1900's pertaining to Loudoun County.

"Minutes of the Catoctin Farmers' Club of Waterford, Virginia, 1868-1943." 12 vols. Volumes I, II, IV and IX are missing; the rest are kept in a vault at the First and Merchants National Bank, Leesburg, Va.

"Minutes of the Lovettsville Farmers' Club of Loudoun County, 1911-1972." 7 vols. All records of this organization are kept by club's secretary.

"Scrapbooks on Loudoun County Schools, 1940-1947." 2 vols. Loudoun County School Board Office, Leesburg, Va. Newspaper clippings and other items.

Rowberg, A. A., compiler. "Loudoun County." 4 vols. Purcellville Library, Purcellville, Va. Collection of newspaper articles published in the *Blue Ridge Herald* and *Loudoun Times-Mirror* from 1957 to 1966.

Sims, Thomas E., Jr. "Inspection and Survey Report." Evaluation and description of Loudoun County Schools by a special agent of the Garrett Insurance Agency of Leesburg, Va., 1940.

d. Oral History

Atwell, George. Director of the Business Department of Loudoun County Schools. Personal interview. December 28, 1972.

Brown, Edward R. Dairy Farmer. Personal interview. December 3, 1972; December 31, 1972; February 4, 1973; January 27, 1974. Telephone interview, February 16, 1974; March 7, 1974.

Brown, W. Jack. County Extension Agent. Personal interview. December 15, 1972.

Douglas, James E. Owner, Aldie Mill. Telephone interview. August 18, 1973.

Fletcher, Gordon W., Jr. Planning Specialist for Loudoun County Schools. Personal interview. March 15, 1973.

Haston, Robert C., Jr. County Assistant Extension Agent. Personal interview. December 14, 1972.

Homes, Oliver Wendell. "Stage Lines, Inns and Taverns of Fairfax County." Lecture given at Marshall High School, Tysons Corner, Va. October 3, 1972. Tape available at the Central Fairfax County Library, Fairfax, Va.

King, Leslie W. District Conservationist, United States Department of Agriculture Soil Conservation Service. Personal interview. December 14, 1972.

Middleton, Don M. Planning Specialist for Loudoun County Schools. Personal interview.

March 15, 1974

Miller, Ruth. Zoning Administrator. Personal interview, Department of Planning and Zoning. December 14, 1972.

Poland, Betty B. Personal interview. February 10, 1975.

Poland C. Preston. Member of the Loudoun County Planning Commission. Personal interview. October 22, 1972; November 26, 1972; February 9, 1974; March 8, 1974; and March 16, 1974.

Poland, Mabel Rice. Personal interview. December 31, 1971.

Raflo, Frances. Director of the Loudoun Museum. Personal interview. December 13, 1972.

Reid, Frances H. Associate Publisher of the *Loudoun Times-Mirror*. Personal interview. December 8, 1972.

Stanley, Fred A. Employee of the Department of Highways for the Loudoun District. Personal interview. December 15, 1972.

Welch, Arthur A. Director of Planning for Loudoun County Schools. Personal interview. March 15, 1974.

York, John M. Executive Director of the County Agricultural Stabilization and Conservation Service of the U. S. Department of Agriculture. Personal interview. December 15, 1972.

e. Maps

A Plan and Profile of an unfinished Survey and Level for a proposed Canal from Goose Creek in Loudoun County to Hunter Creek near Alexandria. Made in obedience to the orders of the President and Directors of the Board of Public Works of Virginia, 1818. Virginia State Library, Richmond, Va.

2. Published

a. Official Records

Fairfax County, Virginia. Planning Division. *The Vanishing Land: Proposals for Open Space Preservation, Fairfax, Virginia*. Annadale, Va.: Turnpike Press, 1962.

Leesburg, Virginia. *Charter and Ordinances of the Town of Leesburg in Virginia*. 1902.

―――― Restoration and Redevelopment Commission. *Report of the Leesburg Restoration and Redevelopment Commission*. 1962.

Loudoun County, Virginia. Department of Planning and Zoning. *Loudoun County Data Book*. (1972).

BIBLIOGRAPHY

_____ (Department of Planning and Zoning). *Zoning Ordinance of Loudoun County.* 1972.

_____ Loudoun County Sanitation Authority. *Loudoun County Sanitation Authority: Ten Years of Service and Progress.* [1973].

U. S. Bureau of the Census. *United States Census of Agriculture: 1935, Virginia.* Washington, D. C.: Government Printing Office, 1936.

U. S. Congress. House. *Certain Loyal Citizens of Loudoun County, Virginia.* H.R. Rept. 806 to accompany H.R. 2451. 53rd Cong., 2d Sess., 1894.

U. S. Congress. Senate. *A Bill for the Relief of Loyal Citizens of Loudoun County, Virginia.* S. Rept. 99 to accompany S. 48. 43d Cong., 1st Sess., 1874.

U. S. *Congressional Record.* Vols. CVI, CVII.

U. S. Department of Agriculture and Bureau of the Census. *1969 Census of Agriculture.* Washington, D. C.: Government Printing Office, 1972.

U. S. Department of Agriculture, Statistical Reporting Service. *Farm Statistics 1910-66: Loudoun County, Virginia.* Washington, D. C.: Government Printing Office, 1967.

U. S. Department of Agriculture Soil Conservation Service in Cooperation with (the) Virginia Agricultural Experiment Station. *Soil Survey: Loudoun County, Virginia.* Washington, D. C.: Government Printing Office, 1960.

U. S. Department of Commerce and Bureau of the Census. *Statistical Abstract of the United States.* Washington, D. C.: Government Printing Office, 1971.

U. S. Department of War. *The War of the Rebellion: A Compilation of the Official Records of the Union and Confederate Armies.* 128 vols. Washington, D. C.: Government Printing Office, 1880-1910.

Virginia. *Acts of the General Assembly of the State of Virginia.* Richmond, Va.: 1809-1972.

_____ Auditor of Public Accounts of Virginia. *1921 Roster of Confederate Pensioners of Virginia.*

_____ Administrative Division of State Planning and Community Affairs. *Virginia Planning Legislation, 1970.* Richmond, Va.: Office of the Governor, 1970.

_____ Department of Highways. *Commonwealth of Virginia: Department of Highways.* Richmond, Va.: Traffic and Safety Division, 1971.

_____ Division of Industrial Development and Planning. *Leesburg. . .People and Economy.* Richmond, Va.: [n.p.]. 1964.

_____ Division of State Planning and Community Affairs. *Data Summary: Loudoun County.* Richmond, Va.: Office of Research and Information, 1969.

———— Division of State Planning and Community Affairs. *Data Summary: Loudoun County.* Office of Research and Information, 1972.

———— *Proceedings and Debates of the Virginia State Convention of 1829-30.* Richmond, Va.: Samuel Shepherd & Co., 1830.

———— Report of the Governor's Ad Hoc Committee to Review the Virginia Area Development Act. 1972.

———— Report of the Secretary of the Commonwealth to the Governor and General Assembly. Richmond, Va.: 1905.

———— *The Statutes at Large, Being a Collection of All the Laws of Virginia,* ed. William H. Hening and Samuel Shepherd. 16 vols. Richmond, Va.: 1808, 1823-1836.

———— Virginia Metropolitan Areas Study Commission. *Governing the Virginia Metropolitan Areas: An Assessment.* Richmond, Va.: Printed by the Division of Planning, 1967.

b. *Diaries, Memoirs, and Other Pertinent Data*

Alexander, John H. *Mosby's Men.* New York: Neale Publishing Co., 1907.

Announcement of the Twelfth Session of (the) Leesburg Academy. Leesburg, Va.: Mirror Office, 1898.

Berkhofer, Robert F., Jr. (ed.). *The American Revolution: The Critical Issues.* Boston: Little, Brown, and Co., 1971.

Binns, John A. *A Treatise on Practical Farming.* Frederick-town, Md.: Printed by John B. Colvin, 1803.

Blackford, William Willis. *War Years with Jeb Stuart.* Charles Scribner's Sons, 1945.

Boogher, William Fletcher (ed.). *Gleanings of Virginia History.* Baltimore: Genealogical Publishing Co., 1965.

Burnham, W. Dean. *Presidential Ballots, 1836-1892.* Baltimore: The Johns Hopkins Press, 1955.

Business Directory of Leesburg. Leesburg Va.: William L. Stork, Publisher, 1860.

Caldwell, S.B.T. *To the Voters of Loudoun.* [n.p.]: August 5, 1831.

Catalogue of Loudoun Valley Academy for Young Ladies and Gentlemen: Session 1869-1870. Alexandria, Va.: Printed at the Commercial Advertiser, 1870.

Circular for 1873-74 of the Loudoun Valley Academy for Young Ladies and Gentlemen. [n.p.: n.n., n.d.].

Crawford, J. Marshall. *Mosby and His Men.* New York: G. W. Carleton and Co., 1867.

Cresswell, Nicholas. *The Journal of Nicholas Cresswell, 1774-1777.* New York: The Dial Press, 1924.

Daughters of the American Revolution, National Society. *DAR Patriot Index.* Washington, D. C.: 1966.

Eckenrode, H. J. *List of the Colonial Soldiers of Virginia.* Baltimore: Genealogical Publishing Co., 1965.

Fairfax, Thomas. *Journey from Virginia to Salem.* London: Printed for private circulation, 1936.

Glazier, Willard. *Battles for the Union.* Hartford, Conn.: Filman and Co., 1878.

———— *Three Years in the Federal Cavalry.* New York: R. H. Ferguson and Co., 1871.

Goodhart, Briscoe. *History of the Independent Loudoun Rangers.* Washington, D. C.: Press of McGill and Wallace, 1896.

[Goose Creek and Little River Navigation Company.] *A Plan of Inland Navigation for the County of Loudoun.* [n.p.]: November 14, 1831.

Gwathmey, John H. (ed.). *Historical Register of Virginians in the Revolution.* Richmond, Va.: The Dietz Press, 1938.

Halkett, Peter. *Halkett's Orderly Book and Braddock's Defeat.* Norman: University of Oklahoma Press, 1959.

Henderson, Fenton M. *Loudoun County: Its Social, Agricultural and Manufacturing Advantages.* Leesburg, Va.: By the Author, 1868.

Hunton, Eppa. *Autobiography of Eppa Hunton.* Richmond, Va.: The William Byrd Press, 1933.

James, Charles F. *Documentary History of the Struggle for Religious Liberty in Virginia.* Lynchburg, Va.: J. P. Bell Co., 1900.

Janney, Samuel M. *Memoirs of Samuel M. Janney.* Philadelphia: Friends' Book Association, 1881.

———— *The Yankees in Fairfax County.* Baltimore: Snodgrass and Wehrley, 1845.

Jefferson, Thomas. *Notes on the State of Virginia,* ed. William Peden. Chapel Hill: University of North Carolina Press, 1955.

Jewell, Aurelia M. (comp.). *Loudoun County, Virginia, Marriage Bonds, 1762-1850,* 2d ed. Berryville, Va.: Chesapeake Book Co., 1962.

Johnson, Robert U. and Clarence C. Buel (eds.). *Battles and Leaders of the Civil War.* 4 vols. New York: The Century Co., 1897.

Loudoun County Drought Relief Council. *Self-Help: Drought Relief Suggestions for Farmers.* [n.p.: n.n., n.d.].

Marshall, John A. *American Bastile.* Philadelphia: Evans, Stoddart, and Co., 1870.

Martin, Joseph (ed.). *A New Comprehensive Gazetteer of Virginia.* Charlottesville, Va.: Mosely and Tompkins, Printers, 1835.

Matthews, William. *Report on a Survey and Estimate for the Improvement of Navigation on Goose Creek, Little River and Beaver's Dam.* N.p.: November 1832.

McCaskey, Thomas G. *Destination Loudoun: A Study of Tourism in Loudoun County.* [n.p.: n.n., n.d.].

Moore, Frank (ed.). *Rebellion Record.* 11 vols. New York: Putnam, 1861-1863; Van Nostrand, 1864-1868.

Mosby, John S. *The Memoirs of Colonel John S. Mosby,* ed. Charles Wells Russell. Bloomington: Indiana University Press, 1959.

Munson, John W. *Reminiscences of a Mosby Guerrilla.* New York: Moffat, Yard, and Co., 1906.

Myers, Frank M. *The Comanches: A History of White's Battalion.* Baltimore: Kelly, Piet and Co., 1871.

Prize List Horse and Colt Show, Association of Loudoun County, Virginia, June 7-8, 1922. [n.p.: n.n., n.d.].

The Prohibition and Evangelical Association of Loudoun County, Virginia. *Twenty-Second Annual Temperance and Gospel Meeting.* Washington, D. C.: Norman T. Elliott, 1899.

1923-24 Report of the Financial Condition of the Loudoun Hospital, Inc., Leesburg, Virginia. [n.p.: n.n., n.d.].

Semple, Robert B. *A History of the Rise and Progress of the Baptists in Virginia.* Richmond, Va.: By the Author, 1810.

Springwood Select Home School for Young Ladies, Near Leesburg, Virginia; Session 1866-7. [n.p.: n.n., n.d.].

Scott, John. *Partisan Life with Col. John S. Mosby.* New York: Harper and Brothers, Publishers, 1867.

Taylor, Yardley. *Memoir of Loudo[u]n County, Virginia.* Leesburg, Va.: Thomas Reynolds, Publisher, 1853.

To Yardley Taylor Esq. [n.p.: n.n.]. July 28, 1857.

Torrence, Clayton (ed.). *Virginia Wills and Administrations, 1632-1800*. Richmond, Va: William Byrd Press, 1930.

Tucker, Henry St. George. *Commentaries of the Laws of Virginia*. 2 vols. Winchester, Va.: By the Author, 1837.

Virginia Citizens Planning Association. *A Planning Commissioner's Handbook*. Richmond, Va.: Virginia Citizens Planning Association, [n.d.].

Ward, Robert D. (comp.). *An Account of General Lafayette's Visit to Virginia*. Richmond, Va.: West, Johnson, and Co., 1881.

Warinner, N. E. (comp.). *A Register of Military Events in Virginia 1861-1865*. (Richmond, Va.): Virginia Civil War Commission, 1959.

Washington, George. *The Diaries of George Washington*, ed. John C. Fitzpatrick. 39 vols. Boston: Houghton Mifflin Co., 1933-1944.

_____. *Journal of My Journey over the Mountains*, ed. J. M. Toner. Albany, N. Y.: Joel Munsell's Sons, Publishers, 1892.

White, E. V. *History of the Battle of Ball's Bluff*. Leesburg Va.: The Washington Print Co., 1900.

Wilson, Samuel M. (ed.). *Catalogue of Revolutionary Soldiers and Sailors of the Commonwealth of Virginia to Whom Land Bounty Warranty Were Granted by Virginia for Military Services in the War for Independence*. Baltimore: Southern Book Co., 1953.

Wise, George. *History of the Seventeenth Virginia Infantry*. Baltimore: Kelly, Piet and Co., 1870.

c. *Periodicals*

"Ashburn and Round Hill Volunteer Fire Depts.," *Virginia and the Virginia County*, VII (January, 1953), 28.

"A Bad Year," *The Agricultural Situation*, XIV (October, 1930), 1.

Baker, Irvey W. "Lovettsville District," *Virginia and the Virginia County*, VII (January, 1953), 27, 50.

"Banning the Boom," *Newsweek*, LXXX (August 21, 1972), 40.

Birchfield, James. "Rural-Urban Broad Run," *Virginia and the Virginia County*, VII (January, 1953), 23.

Blume, George T., and D. Upton Livermore. "Virginia's Population Shifts," *The Southern Planter*, August 1, 1960, [n.p.].

Campbell, William. "Autobiographical Sketch," *William and Mary Quarterly*, 2d ser., XXIX (January, 1929), 88-109.

Carter, Councillor. "From the Letter-Books of Councillor Carter," *Virginia Magazine of History and Biography*, VI (July, 1908), 88-90.

Chamberlin, Arthur, and A. Aubrey Bodine. "Town with a Past," *Sunday Sun Magazine*, June 5, 1967, 13-17.

Davis, John. "Diary of Capt. John Davis of the Pennsylvania Line," *Virginia Magazine of History and Biography*, I (July, 1893), 1-16.

"Diary of William Beverly," *Virginia Magazine of History and Biography*, XXXVI (January, 1928), 27-35.

Dodd, William E. (ed.). "Correspondence of Leven Powell: Letters on Jefferson's Election and Some Monroe Letters," *The John P. Branch Historical Papers of Randolph-Macon College*, III (June, 1903), 217-55.

———(ed.). "Correspondence of Leven Powell, 1775-1787," *The John P. Branch Historical Papers of Randolph-Macon College*, II (June, 1902), 111-38.

Dudley, John R. "The Heart of the Hunt Country Is Middleburg," *Virginia and the Virginia County*, VII (January, 1953), 14, 41-46.

"Execution of Deserters," *Harper's Weekly*, (August 8, 1863), 509, 510.

Emerick, O. L. "Loudoun County Schools," *Virginia and the Virginia County*, VII (January, 1953), 31-32.

"Hamilton, Center of Rich Farming Area," *Virginia and the Virginia County*, VII (January, 1953), 29.

Harrison, Fairfax (ed.). "With Braddock's Army: Mrs. Browne's Diary in Virginia and Maryland," *Virginia Magazine of History and Biography*, XXXII (October, 1924), 305-13.

Henry, William Wirt (ed.). "House of Burgesses, 1766 to 1775," *Virginia Magazine of History and Biography*, IV (April, 1897), 380-86.

"Historical and Genealogical Notes and Queries: Memoranda from the Fredericksburg, Virginia, Gazette, 1787-1803," *Virginia Magazine of History and Biography*, XII (April, 1906), 433.

Jefferson, Thomas. "Unpublished Letters of Jefferson," *Virginia Magazine of History and Biography*, VIII (October 1900), 114-18.

"Land Use and Abuse," *Central Atlantic Environment News*, II (September, 1972), 1-4.

"Letter Published in the 'Genius of Liberty,' Leesburg, Va., from John M. McCarty, in Answer to Gen. Armistead T. Mason," *Virginia Magazine of History and Biography*, XXXV (January, 1927), 74-76.

"Letters Bearing on the Election of 1800," *The John P. Branch Historical Papers of Randolph-Macon College*, I (June, 1901), 54-63.

"Letters of Rev. David Griffith, to Leven Powell, 1776-1778," *The John P. Branch Historical Papers of Randolph-Macon College*, I (June, 1901), 39-53.

"Letters of the Byrd Family," *Virginia Magazine of History and Biography*, XXXVIII (October, 1930), 347-60.

"Leven Powell," *The John P. Branch Historical Papers of Randolph-Macon College*, I (June 1901), 22-23.

"A List of Parishes and the Ministers in Them," *William and Mary Quarterly*, 1st ser., IV (April, 1897), 200-02.

"List of Tithables in Virginia, Taken 1773," *Virginia Magazine of History and Biography*, XXVIII (June, 1920), 81-82.

"Loudoun's Board of Supervisors," *Virginia and the Virginia County*, VII (January, 1953), 15.

"Loudoun County Community College," *Virginia and the Virginia County*, VII (January, 1953), 25.

"Miscellaneous Colonial Documents," *Virginia Magazine of History and Biography*, XVIII (January, 1910), 159-69.

"Miscellaneous Colonial Documents," *Virginia Magazine of History and Biography*, XIX (January, 1911), 156-66.

"Miscellaneous Colonial Documents," *Virginia Magazine of History and Biography*, XIX (December, 1911), 156-65.

"Muster Roll--The Loudoun Guards: Company C, 17th Virginia Infantry, C.S.A.," *The Bulletin of the Loudoun County Historical Society*, III (1962), 49-54.

"The New American Land Rush," *Time*, (October 1, 1973), 80-99.

Nichols, Joseph V. "Loudoun County: One of America's Wealthiest and Most Attractive Rural Sections," *Virginia and the Virginia County*, VII (January, 1953), 7-8, 38-40.

"The Number of Men of Military Age in Virginia in 1776," *Virginia Magazine of History and Biography*, XVIII (December, 1910), 34-35.

"Proceedings of the Virginia Committee of Correspondence, 1759-70," *Virginia Magazine of History and Biography*, XII (June, 1905), 157-69.

"Proceedings of the Virginia Historical Society," *Virginia Magazine of History and Biography*, IX (October, 1922), i-xii.

"Purcellville Progress: One of Northern Virginia's Newest and Fastest Growing Communities," *Virginia and the Virginia County*, VII (January, 1953), 21-22.

"Resolutions of Loudoun County," *William and Mary Quarterly*, 1st ser., XII (October, 1903), 230-36.

"Saving the Farms," *Time*, (April 21, 1975), 48.

Stowe, Jonathan P. "Life with the 15th Mass," *Civil War Times Illustrated*, XI (August, 1972), 4-11.

Thomas, R. S. (ed.). "Members of His Majesty's Council of Virginia for 1768," *Virginia Magazine of History and Biography*, III (June, 1896), 426-29.

Van Sickler, Lake. "Round Hill," *Virginia and the Virginia County*, VII (January, 1953), 33-34.

"Virginia Council Journals, 1726-1753," *Virginia Magazine of History and Biography*, XXXVII (April, 1929), 229-41.

"Virginia Militia in the Revolution," *Virginia Magazine of History and Biography*, XV (July, 1907), 87-92; XVI (December, 1908), 419-21.

"Virginia State Troops in the Revolution," *Virginia Magazine of History and Biography*, XXX (December, 1922), 56-59.

"Virginia Troops in the Continental Line," *Virginia Magazine of History and Biography*, II (January, 1895), 241-58.

Wanner, Harry C. "Fore," *Virginia and the Virginia County*, VII (January, 1953), 20.

West, George. "Papers Relating to the College William and Mary," *William and Mary Quarterly*, 1st ser., XVI (January, 1908), 162-73.

"What To Do: Costly Choices," *Time*, (November 11, 1974), 76-83.

d. Newspapers

The Advance Guard (Leesburg, Va.), March 12, 1862.

The Blue Ridge Herald (Purcellville, Va.), 1924-1957.

The Democratic Mirror (Leesburg, Va.), 1858-1861, 1865-1906.

The Denver Post (Denver, Col.), 1974

The Genius of Liberty (Leesburg, Va.), 1817-1823, 1829, 1832, 1840-1841.

Genius of Universal Emacipation (Baltimore, Md.), 1825, 1828.

The Globe (Fairfax, Va.), 1972.

The Loudoun Chronicle (Leesburg, Va.), 1849-1850.

The Loudoun Mirror (Leesburg, Va.), 1914-1916.

The Loudoun News (Leesburg, Va.), 1935-1952.

The Loudoun Times (Leesburg, Va.), 1916-1927.

The Loudoun Times-Mirror (Leesburg, Va.), 1929-1976.

The Loudoun Whig (Leesburg, Va.), 1840.

The National Era (Washington, D. C.), 1849-1850.

Metro Virginia News (Leesburg, Va.), 1972-1974.

Piedmont Virginian (The Plains, Va.), 1972.

The Record (Leesburg, Va.), 1903-1905.

The Richmond Whig (Richmond, Va.), 1829.

The Washingtonian (Leesburg, Va.), 1854, 1869-1901.

The Washingtonian Times (Leesburg, Va.), 1905-1906.

The Waterford News (Waterford, Va.), 1864.

The True American (Leesburg, Va.), 1800.

The Washington Post (Washington, D. C.), 1966, 1968, 1972-1976.

The Washington Star (Washington, D. C.), 1940, 1949, 1973-76.

e. Maps

Atlas to Accompany the Official Records of the Union and Confederate Armies. Calvin D. Cowles. Washington, D. C.: Government Printing Office, 1891-1895.

The George Washington Atlas. Lawrence Martin. Washington, D. C.: United States George Washington Bicentennial Commission, 1932.

An Historic Map, Loudoun County, Va. Arthur W. Arundel, Frances H. Reid, and Roy F. Clancy. Loudoun Times-Mirror, Leesburg, Virginia, 1969.

Loudoun County, Commonwealth of Virginia. Eugene M. Scheel. Washington, D. C.: William and Heintz, 1972.

Loudoun County Primary and Secondary Highway Systems. Richmond, Va.: Department of Highways, 1971.

Loudoun County Virginia from Actual Surveys. Yardley Taylor. Philadelphia: Thomas Reynolds and Robert Pearsall Smith, Publishers, 1853.

Map of Loudoun County Virginia. H. H. Hardesty, Publisher, 1883.

North-Eastern Virginia and Vicinity of Washington. Comp. by the Topographical Engineers' Office, Division Headquarters of General Irving McDowell. Washington, D. C.: Government Printing Office, 1962.

Purcellville, Loudoun County, Virginia. Sanborn Map Co. 1933.

Site Analysis: A Planned Community, Loudoun County, Virginia. Levitt and Sons, 1970.

Virginia-Maryland-Mt. Vernon Sheet. Department of Interior, U. S. Geological Survey, 1912.

Virginia-Warren Sheet. Department of Interior, U. S. Geological Survey, 1928.

Zoning Map of Loudoun County, Virginia. Approved and adopted by the Board of Supervisors, Loudoun County, 1972.

B. SECONDARY WORKS

1. Unpublished

Diehl, George West. "A True Confederate Soldier: Col. Elizah Viers White." [n.d.]. Thomas Balch Library, Leesburg, Va. (Xeroxed.)

diZerega, Philip V. "History of Secondary Education in Loudoun County, Virginia." Unpublished Master's thesis, University of Virginia, 1948. (Typewritten.)

[Goodhart, Briscoe (comp.).] "Loudoun County." 5 vols. Thomas Balch Library, Leesburg, Virginia.

Hickin, Patricia C. "Antislavery in Virginia, 1831-1861." Doctor's dissertation, University of Virginia, 1968. (Typewritten.)

Janney, Asa Moore. "A Short History of the Society of Friends in Loudoun County." Unpublished, typewritten manuscript, Goose Creek Meeting Library, Lincoln, Va. Has material not included in the published article.

"L.C.H., 1919-1942: Short Sketch of the Loudoun County Hospital and Nurses Training School." Unpublished program commemorating the above on June 20, 1942. Purcellville Library, Purcellville, Va. (Typewritten.)

"Loudoun County." The Loudoun Museum, Leesburg, Va. (Xeroxed.)

Marsh, Helen Hirst. "Purcellville, Virginia, 1852-1952." Purcellville Library, Purcellville, Va. A history of the town of Purcellville based primarily upon county newspapers. (Typewritten.)

Nichols, William D. "The Hoge, Nichols and Related Families; Biographical-Historical: A Sequential Arrangement of Genealogical Data." Fairview Park, Ohio, 1969. Thomas Balch Library, Leesburg, Va. (Typewritten.)

Ray, L. V., Jr. "Remarks on History of the Little River Baptist Church." Paper presented at the ground-breaking ceremony, Aldie, Va., July 8, 1972. (Mimeographed.)

Trumbo, Olliver O. "Charles Fenton Mercer, 1778-1858." Unpublished Master's thesis, Madison College, 1966. Thomas Balch Library, Leesburg, Va. (Typewritten.)

Writers' Program of the Work Projects Administration in the State of Virginia. "Historical Inventory of Loudoun County." Loudoun County School Board Office, Leesburg, Va. 216 reports by Elizabeth Morgan and Robert L. Preston on personalities, homes and other aspects of Loudoun history. (Typewritten.)

2. Published

a. Books

Abernethy, Thomas Perkins. *Three Virginia Frontiers.* Gloucester, Mass.: Peter Smith, 1962.

Adams, Evelyn T. *The Courthouse in Virginia Counties, 1634-1776.* Warrenton, Va.: The Fauquier Democrat, 1966.

Ambler, Charles H. *Sectionalism in Virginia from 1776 to 1861.* Chicago: University of Chicago Press, 1910.

Ammon, Harry. *James Monroe: The Quest for National Identity.* New York: McGraw-Hill Co., 1971.

Banfield, Edward C. *The Unheavenly City Revisited.* Rev. ed. Boston: Little, Brown and Co., 1974.

_____ and James Q. Wilson. *City Politics.* New York: Vintage Books, 1966.

Barck, Oscar T., Jr., and Nelson M. Blake. *Since 1900: A History of the United States in Our Times.* Rev. ed. New York Macmillan Co., 1952.

Barck, Oscar T. Jr., and Hugh T. Lefler. *Colonial America.* New York: Macmillan Co., 1958.

Bass, Herbert J. (ed.). *America's Entry into World War I: Submarines, Sentiment or Security?* New York: Holt, Rinehart and Winston, 1964.

Bean, R. Bennett. *The Peopling of Virginia.* Boston: Crescendo Publishing Co., 1938.

Beard, Charles A., and Mary R. Beard. *The Rise of American Civilization.* 2 vols. in 1. Rev. ed. New York: Macmillan Co., 1962.

Benedict, Michael L. *The Impeachment and Trial of Andrew Jackson.* New York: W. W. Norton and Co., 1973.

Bennett, Lerone, Jr. *Before the Mayflower: A History of the Negro in America, 1619-1964.* Rev. ed. Baltimore: Penguin Books, 1970.

Beverley, Robert. *The History and Present State of Virginia.* Chapel Hill. University of North Carolina Press, 1947.

"Binns, John Alexander," *Dictionary of American Biography*, I, 283.

Board of Supervisors of Loudoun County. *A Group of Historical Murals Painted by Members of the Loudoun Sketch Club in Honor of the Two Hundredth Anniversary of the Founding of the County.* Leesburg, Va.: Board of Supervisors of Loudoun County, 1957.

Brant, Irving. *James Madison.* 6 vols. New York: Bobbs-Merrill Co., 1961.

Brenaman, J. N. *A History of Virginia Conventions.* Richmond, Va.: J. L. Hill Printing Co., 1902.

Bridenbaugh, Carl. *Cities in the Wilderness.* New York: Capricorn Books, 1964.

———. *The Colonial Craftsman.* Chicago: University of Chicago Press, 1971.

Brown, Richard (ed.). *Slavery in American Society.* Lexington, Mass.: D. C. Heath and Co., 1969.

Brown, Robert E., and B. Katherine Brown. *Virginia 1705-1786: Democracy or Aristocracy?* East Lansing, Mich.: Michigan State University Press, 1964.

Bruce, Philip Alexander. *Social Life of Virginia: In the Seventeenth Century.* New York: Frederich Ungar Publishing Co., 1964.

Buck, J. L. Blair. *The Development of Public Schools in Virginia.* Richmond: State Board of Education, 1952.

Buck, Paul H. *The Road to Reunion, 1865-1900.* Boston: Little, Brown and Co., 1937.

Bugg, James L., Jr. (ed.). *Jacksonian Democracy: Myth or Reality?* New York: Holt, Rinehart and Winston, 1965.

Burchard, John, and Albert Bush-Brown. *The Architecture of America.* Boston: Little, Brown and Co., 1966.

Burgess, John W. *Reconstruction and the Constitution.* New York: Charles Scribner's Sons, 1902.

Cappon, Lester J. *Virginia Newspapers, 1821-1935.* New York: Appleton-Century-Crofts, 1936.

Cash, W. J. *The Mind of the South.* New York: Vintage Books, 1941.

Cochran, Thomas C., and Thomas B. Brewer (eds.). *Views of American Economic Growth: The Agricultural Era.* Vol. I. New York: McGraw-Hill Co., 1966.

Conrad, Alfred H., and John R. Meyer. "The Economics of Slavery in the Antebellum South," *Did Slavery Pay?* Edited by Hugh G. J. Aitken. Boston: Houghton Mifflin Co., 1971.

Coulter, E. Merton. *The South During Reconstruction, 1865-1877.* Baton Rouge: Louisiana State University Press, 1947.

Cox, Lawanda, and John H. Cox. *Politics, Principle and Prejudice, 1865-1866.* New York: Free Press of Glencoe, 1963.

Craven, Avery O. *Reconstruction.* New York: Holt, Rinehart and Winston, 1969.

──── *Soil Exhaustion as a Factor in the Agricultural History of Virginia and Maryland, 1606-1860.* Reprint. Gloucester, Mass.: Peter Smith, 1965.

Craven, Wesley F. *The Southern Colonies in the Seventeenth Century, 1607-1689.* Baton Rouge: Louisiana State University Press, 1949.

Curry, Richard O. (ed.). *The Abolitionists.* New York: Holt, Rinehart and Winston, 1975.

──── and Joanna D. Cowden. (eds.). *Slavery in America: Theodore Weld's American Slavery As It Is.* Itasca, Ill.: F. E. Peacock Publishers, 1970.

Curti, Merle. *The Growth of American Thought.* 2nd ed. New York: Harper and Row, 1965.

Dabney, Virginius. *Virginia: The New Dominion.* 4th ed. Garden City, N. Y.: Doubleday and Company, 1972.

Dangerfield, George. *The Awakening of American Nationalism. 1815-1828.* New York: Doubleday and Co., 1965.

Davis, David B. (ed.). *Ante-Bellum Reform.* New York: Harper and Row, 1967.

Davis, Richard Beale. *Intellectual Life in Jefferson's Virginia, 1790-1830.* Chapel Hill: University of North Carolina Press, 1964.

Deck, Patrick A., and Henry Heaton. *An Economic and Social Survey of Loudoun.* Charlottesville, Va.: University of Virginia, 1926.

Detweiler, Robert, Jon N. Sutherland, and Michael S. Werthman (eds.). *Environmental Decay in Its Historical Context.* Glenview, Ill.: Scott, Foresman and Co., 1973.

Dickinson, Josiah Look. *The Fairfax Proprietary.* Front Royal, Va.: Warren Press, 1959.

Dowdey, Clifford. *The Golden Age: A Climate for Greatness, Virginia 1732-1775.* Boston: Little, Brown and Co., 1970.

———. *The Virginia Dynasties: The Emergence of "King" Carter and the Golden Age.* Boston: Little, Brown and Co., 1969.

Dunning, William A. *Reconstruction, Political and Economic, 1865-1877.* New York: Harper and Row, 1962.

Earle, Alice Morse. *Stage-Coach and Tavern Days.* New York: Dover Publications, 1969.

Eaton, Clement. *The Freedom-of-Thought Struggle in the Old South.* New York: Harper and Row, 1964.

Eberlein, Harold D., and Cortlandt Van Dyke. *Colonial Interiors: Federal and Greek Revival.* New York: Bonanza Books, 1938.

Eckenrode, Hamilton J. *The Political History of Virginia During the Reconstruction.* Gloucester, Mass.: Peter Smith, 1966.

———. *The Revolution in Virginia.* Hamden, Conn.: Archon Books, 1964.

Editors of Fortune, *The Exploding Metropolis.* New York: Doubleday Anchor Books, 1958.

Eisenberg, William Edward. *The Lutheran Church in Virginia, 1717-1962.* Roanoke, Va.: The Trustees of the Virginia Synod, Lutheran Church in America, 1967.

Ekirch, Arthur A., Jr. *Man and Nature in America.* New York: Columbia University Press, 1963.

Elkins, Stanley M. *Slavery.* New York: Grosset and Dunlap, 1963.

Engerman, Stanley L. "The Effect of Slavery upon the Southern Economy: A Review of the Recent Debate." *Did Slavery Pay?* Edited by Hugh G. J. Aitken. Boston: Houghton Mifflin Co., 1971.

Forbush, Bliss. *A History of Baltimore Yearly Meeting of Friends.* Sandy Spring, Md.: Baltimore Yearly Meeting of Friends, 1972.

Ford, Alice. *Edward Hicks, Painter of the Peaceable Kingdom.* Philadelphia: University of Pennsylvania Press, 1952.

Franklin, John H. *From Slavery to Freedom.* 3d ed. New York: Alfred A. Knopf, 1967.

Freehling, William W. *Prelude to Civil War.* New York: Harper and Row, 1968.

Freeman, Douglas S. *George Washington: A Biography.* 6 vols. New York: Charles Scribner's Sons, 1951.

French, Leigh, Jr. *Colonial Interiors.* New York: William Helburn, 1923.

Gage, Charles E. *Tobacco, Tobacco Hogsheads and Rolling Roads in Northern Virginia.* Falls Church, Va.: Falls Church Historical Commission, 1959.

BIBLIOGRAPHY

Garnett, James Mercer. *Biographical Sketch of Hon. Charles Fenton Mercer.* Richmond, Va.: Whittet and Shepperson, 1911.

Gatell, Frank O. (ed.). *Essays on Jacksonian America, 1815-1840.* Englewood Cliffs, N. J.: Prentice-Hall, 1970.

―――― and John M. McFail (eds.). *Jacksonian America, 1815-1840.* Englewood Cliffs, N. J.: Prentice-Hall, 1970.

Gawronski, Donald V. *Out of the Past: A Topical History of the United States.* Beverly Hills, Calif.: Glencoe Press, 1969.

Genovese, Eugene D. *The Political Economy of Slavery.* New York: Random House, 1967.

Gewehr, Wesley M. *The Great Awakening in Virginia, 1740-1790.* Durham, N. C.: Duke University Press, 1930.

Glassie, Henry. *Pattern in the Material Folk Culture of the Eastern United States.* Philadelphia: University of Pennsylvania Press, 1968.

Graham, James R. *The Planting of the Presbyterian Church in Northern Virginia.* Winchester, Va.: George F. Norton Publishing Co., 1904.

Gray, Lewis C. *History of Agriculture in the Southern United States to 1860.* 2 vols. Reprint. Gloucester, Mass.: Peter Smith, 1958.

―――― "Economic Efficiency and Competing Advantages of Negro Slavery under the Plantation System," *Did Slavery Pay?* Edited by Hugh G. J. Aitken. Boston: Houghton Mifflin Co., 1971.

Grigsby, Hugh Blair. *The Virginia Convention of 1829-30: A Discourse Delivered Before the Virginia Historical Society at the Annual Meeting.* Richmond, Va.: MacFarlane & Ferguson, 1854.

Guild, June Purcell. *Black Laws of Virginia: A Summary of the Legislative Acts of Virginia Concerning Negroes from Earliest Times to the Present.* New York: Negro University Press, 1969.

Gusfield, Joseph R. *Symbolic Crusade: Status Politics and the American Temperance Movement.* Urbana: University of Illinois Press, 1963.

Gutheim, Frederick. *The Potomac.* New York: Rinehart and Co., 1949.

Harrison, Fairfax. *Landmarks of Old Prince William: A Study of Origins in Northern Virginia.* 2d ed. Berryville, Va.: Chesapeake Book Co., 1964.

Hartz, Louis. *The Liberal Tradition in America.* New York: Harcourt, Brace and World, 1955.

Harwood, Herbert H., Jr. *Rails to the Blue Ridge.* Falls Church, Va.: Pioneer America Society, 1969.

Hawkins, Hugh (ed.). *The Abolitionists.* 2d ed. Lexington, Mass.: D. C. Heath and Co., 1972.

Head, James W. *History and Comprehensive Description of Loudoun County, Virginia.* [Leesburg, Va.]: Park View Press, 1908.

Heatwole, Cornelius J. *A History of Education in Virginia.* New York: Macmillan Co., 1916.

Hendrick, Burton J. *The Lees of Virginia.* Boston: Little, Brown and Co., 1935.

Hening, William W. *The Virginia Justice.* Richmond, Va.: Shepherd and Pollard, 1825.

Herndon, Melvin. *Tobacco in Colonial Virginia: "The Sovereign Remedy."* Williamsburg, Va.: Virginia 350th Anniversary Celebration Corporation, 1957.

Highsmith, Richard M., Jr., J. Granville Jensen, and Robert O. Rudd. *Conservation in the United States.* 3d ed. Chicago: Rand McNally and Co., 1971.

Hinshaw, William Wade. "Fairfax Monthly Meeting," *Encyclopedia of American Quaker Genealogy*, 1950, VI, 463-66.

―――― "Goose Creek Monthly Meeting," *Encyclopedia of American Quaker Genealogy*, 1950, VI, 609-14.

Historical Society of Fairfax County, Virginia, Yearbook, 1955. Vol. IV. Vienna, Va.: Historical Society of Fairfax, 1955.

Hobbs, Horace P., Jr. *Pioneers of the Potowmak.* 2d ed. Ann Arbor, Mich.: University Microfilms, 1964.

Hofstadter, Richard. *The Age of Reform.* New York: Vintage Books, 1955.

Howe, Henry. *Historical Collections of Virginia.* Charleston, S. C.: W. R. Babcock, 1847.

Ironmonger, Elizabeth Hogg, and Pauline Landrum Phillips. *History of the Woman's Christian Temperance Union of Virginia and a Glimpse of Seventy-Five Years, 1883-1958.* Richmond, Va.: Cavalier Press, 1958.

Jacob, John J. *Biographical Sketch of the Life of the Late Capt. Michael Cresap.* Cumberland, Md.: J. W. Buchanan, 1826.

Janney, Asa M., and Werner Janney. *The Composition Book: Stories from the Old Days in Lincoln, Virginia.* Bethesda, Md.: By the Authors, 1972.

Janney, E. Edward. *Quakerism and Its Application to Some Modern Problems.* Philadelphia: Walter H. Jenkins, Publisher, [n.d.].

Janney, Eli Hamilton, *Dictionary of American Biography*, V, 609-10.

Janney, Samuel McPherson. *History of the Religious Society of Friends from Its Rise to the Year 1828*. 4 vols. Philadelphia: Hayes and Zell, 1860.

"Janney, Samuel McPherson," *Dictionary of American Biography*. V, 611.

Jennings, George W. *Virginia's Government*. Rev. ed. Richmond, Va.: Virginia State Chamber of Commerce, 1971.

Jernegan, Marcus Wilson. *The American Colonies, 1492-1750*. New York: Frederick Ungar Publishing Co., 1963.

Johnson, Laurence A. *Over the Counter and on the Shelf: Country Storekeeping in America*. New York: Bonanza Books, 1961.

Johnston, Angus James II. *Virginia Railroads in the Civil War*. Chapel Hill: University of North Carolina Press, 1961.

Jones, Rufus M. *The Quakers in The American Colonies*. New York: N. W. Norton Co., 1966.

Jordan, Winthrop D. *White over Black: American Attitudes Toward the Negro, 1550-1812*. Chapel Hill: University of North Carolina Press, 1968.

Judson, L. Carroll. *The Sages and Heroes of the American Revolution*. Philadelphia: By the Author, 1852.

Judy, Ida M. *John Champe: The Soldier and the Man*. Strasburg, Va.: Shenandoah Printing House, 1940.

Kegley, F. B. *Kegley's Virginia Frontier*. Roanoke, Va.: The Southwest Virginia Historical Society, 1938.

Kercheval, Samuel. *A History of the Valley of Virginia*. 3d ed. Woodstock, Va.: W. N. Grabill, 1902.

Kerr, K. Austin (ed.). *The Politics of Moral Behavior: Prohibition and Drug Abuse*. Reading, Mass.: Addison-Wesley Publishing Co., 1973.

Kirby, Jack Temple. *Westmoreland Davis: Virginia Planter-Politician, 1859-1942*. Charlottesville: University Press of Virginia, 1968.

Klein, Herbert S. *Slavery in the Americas: A Comparative Study of Cuba and Virginia*. Chicago: University of Chicago Press, 1969.

Kock, Adrienne. *The Philosophy of Thomas Jefferson*. Chicago: Quadrangle Books, 1964.

Kohn, Hans. *American Nationalism*. New York: Collier Books, 1961.

Lathrop, Elise. *Early American Inns and Taverns.* New York: Tudor Publishing Co., 1956.

The League of Women Voters of Loudoun County, Virginia. *Know Your County.* Leesburg, Va.: Westinghouse Electric Corporation, DECO Communication Department, 1968.

Leesburg, Virginia, and Vicinity. Washington, D. C.: Inter-State and Engraving Company, [n.d.].

Leuchtenburg, William E. *The Perils of Prosperity, 1914-1932.* Chicago: University of Chicago Press, 1958.

Lewis, John G., and Elisabeth D. Lewis. *The Minor Bartlow House.* Hamilton, Va.: By the Authors, 1970.

Link, Arthur S. *Woodrow Wilson and the Progressive Era, 1910-1917.* New York: Harper and Row, 1963.

Long, Charles M. *Virginia County Names.* New York: The Neale Publishing Co., 1908.

Loudoun County Bicentennial Program Committee. *Official Program and Historical Booklet.* Leesburg, Va.: Loudoun County Bicentennial Program Committee, 1957.

Loudoun: Virginia's Garden County. [n.p.]: Loudoun County Chamber of Commerce, 1961.

Lynd, Staughton (ed.). *Reconstruction.* New York: Harper and Row, 1967.

Maddex, Jack P., Jr. *The Virginia Conservatives, 1867-1879: A Study in Reconstruction Politics.* Chapel Hill: University of North Carolina Press, 1970.

Mason, F. E., L. R. Edwards, and M. F. Harrison (eds.). *Glimpses of Leesburg: A Colorful Sketch.* [n.p.: n.n., n.d.].

McCloskey, Robert G. *The American Supreme Court.* Chicago: University of Chicago Press, 1960.

McColley, Robert. *Slavery and Jeffersonian Virginia.* Urbana: University of Illinois Press, 1964.

McKelvey, Blake. *American Urbanization: A Comparative History.* Glenview, Ill.: Scott, Foresman and Co., 1973.

Mercer, Henry C. *The Dating of Old Houses.* Doylestown, Pa.: The Bucks County Historical Society, 1923.

Methodist Historical Society of Northern Virginia. *Methodist Historyland: A Tour Guide to Methodist Sites in Northern Virginia.* Alexandria, Va.: [n.n.], 1966.

Meyers, Marvin. *The Jacksonian Persuasion: Politics and Belief.* Stanford, Cal.: Stanford University Press, 1966.

Miller, Zane L. *The Urbanization of Modern America: A Brief History.* New York: Harcourt, Brace, and Jovanovich, 1973.

Moore, C. Lee (comp.). *Virginia.* Richmond, Va.: Auditor of Public Accounts, 1920.

Morrison, Alfred J. *The Beginning of Public Education in Virginia, 1776-1860.* Richmond, Va.: Davis Bottom, Superintendent of Public Printing, 1917.

Morton, Louis. *Robert Carter of Nomini Hall: A Virginia Tobacco Planter of the Eighteenth Century.* Charlottesville: University Press of Virginia, 1964.

Murray, Robert K. *Red Scare: A Study of National Hysteria.* New York: McGraw-Hill Co., 1964.

Munford, Beverley B. *Virginia's Attitude Toward Slavery and Secession.* New York: Negro University Press, 1969.

Nichols, Joseph V. *Legends of Loudoun Valley.* Leesburg, Va.: Potomac Press, 1961.

Nichols, Roy F. *The Disruption of American Democracy.* New York: Macmillan and Co., 1948.

Northern Virginia Regional Planning Commission. *Historic Northern Virginia Buildings and Places.* [n.p.: n.n.], 1961.

Nugent, Walter T. K. *Modern America.* Boston: Houghton Mifflin Co., 1973.

———. *The Money Question During Reconstruction.* New York: W. W. Norton and Co., 1969.

Odum, Eugene P., and others. *The Crisis of Survival.* Glenview, Ill.: Scott, Foresman and Co., 1970.

Olmsted, Frederick Law. *The Slave States.* Rev. ed. New York: Capricorn Books, 1959.

O'Neal, William B. *Architecture in Virginia: An Official Guide to Four Centuries of Building in the Old Dominion.* New York: Walker and Co., 1968.

Opie, John (ed.). *Americans and Environment: The Controversy over Ecology.* Lexington, Mass.: D. C. Heath and Co., 1971.

Osterweis, Rollin G. *The Myth of the Lost Cause, 1865-1900.* Hamdem, Conn.: Archon Books, 1973.

Parker, Horatio N., and others. *The Potomac River Basin.* Washington, D. C.: Government Printing Office, 1907.

Patch, Joseph Dorst. *When the British Captured Washington.* [n.p.: n.n., n.d.].

Pearson, C. C., and Edwin Hendricks. *Liquor and Anti-Liquor in Virginia, 1619-1919.* Durham: University of North Carolina Press, 1967.

Pearson, C. C. *The Readjuster Movement in Virginia*. Reprint. Gloucester, Mass.: Peter Smith, 1967.

A People of God, 1765-1965: New Jerusalem Lutheran Church. 200th Anniversary Celebration Program, 1965.

Perkins, Dexter. *The New Age of Franklin Roosevelt, 1932-45*. Chicago: University of Chicago Press, 1957.

Perman, Michael. *Reunion Without Compromise: The South and Reconstruction, 1865-1868*. Cambridge: Cambridge University Press, 1973.

Phillips, Ulrich B. *American Negro Slavery*. Baton Rouge: Louisiana State University Press, 1966.

───── *Life and Labor in the Old South*. Boston: Little, Brown and Co., 1951.

Poland, Charles Preston, Jr. *Dunbarton, Dranesville, Virginia*. Fairfax, Va.: Fairfax Office of Comprehensive Planning, 1974.

Porter, Albert O. *County Government in Virginia, 1607-1904*. New York: Columbia University Press, 1947.

Potter, David M. *People of Plenty: Economic Abundance and the American Character*. Chicago: University of Chicago Press, 1954.

Randall, J. G., and David Donald. *The Civil War and Reconstruction*. 2d ed. Boston: D. C. Heath and Co., 1961.

Randall, J. G. *Constitutional Problems Under Lincoln*. Rev. ed. Urbana: University of Illinois Press, 1964.

Ratner, Lorman. *Pre-Civil War Reform*. Englewood Cliffs, N. J.: Prentice-Hall, 1967.

Rice, Otis K. *The Allegheny Frontier: West Virginia Beginnings, 1730-1830*. Lexington: University Press of Kentucky, 1970.

Richards, Leonard L. *Gentleman of Property and Standing*. New York: Oxford University Press, 1970.

Rose, C. B., Jr. *The Indians of Arlington*. Arlington, Va.: Arlington Historical Society, 1966.

Rozwenc, Edwin C. (ed.). *The New Deal: Revolution or Evolution?* Rev. ed. Boston: D. C. Heath and Co., 1959.

───── (ed.). *Reconstruction in the South*. 2nd ed. Lexington, Mass.: D. C. Heath and Co,. 1972.

Ryland, Garnett. *The Baptists of Virginia, 1699-1926*. Richmond, Va.: The Virginia Baptist Board of Missions and Education, 1955.

Sale, Edith T. *Colonial Interiors: Southern Colonial and Early Federal.* New York: Bonanza Books, 1930.

Samuels, Harriet Brockman (ed.). *Loudoun County: Past and Present.* Princeton, N. J.: The Graphic Arts Press, 1940.

Sanderlin, Walter S. *The Potomac Valley: A Student's Guide to Localized History.* New York: Teachers College Press, 1969.

Sanders, H. R., Eliza D. Lunceford, and Virginia Fenton. *Loudoun County Geography Supplement.* Charlottesville, Va.: Loudoun County School Board, 1925.

Scheiner, Seth M. (ed.). *Reconstruction: A Tragic Era?* New York: Holt, Rinehart and Winston, 1968.

Schlesinger, Arthur M., Jr. *The Age of Jackson.* New York: The New America Library, 1945.

_____. *The Coming of the New Deal.* Boston: Houghton Mifflin Co., 1959.

Shanks, Henry T. *The Secession Movement in Virginia, 1847-1861.* New York: AMS Press, 1971.

Sheldon, William D. *Populism in the Old Dominion: Virginia Farm Politics, 1885-1900.* Reprint. Gloucester, Mass.: Peter Smith, 1967.

Shurtleff, Harold R. *The Log Cabin Myth.* Reprint. Gloucester, Mass.: Peter Smith, 1967.

Simkins, Francis Butler. *A History of the South.* New York: Alfred A. Knopf, 1958.

Simms, Henry H. *The Rise of the Whigs in Virginia, 1824-1840.* Richmond, Va.: The William Byrd Press, 1929.

Sochen, June. *Herstory: A Woman's View of American History.* New York: Alfred Publishing Co., 1974.

Slaughter, Phillip. *The History of Truro Parish in Virginia.* Philadelphia: George W. Jacobs and Co., 1908.

Smith, Jean H. *Snickersville: The Biography of a Village.* Miamisburg, Ohio: Printed by The Miamisburg News, 1970.

Spencer, Milton H. *Contemporary Economics.* New York: Worth Publishers, 1971.

Sprouse, Edith Moore. *Mount Air, Fairfax County, Virginia.* [n.p.]: Fairfax County Division of Planning, 1970.

Stampp, Kenneth M. *The Era of Reconstruction, 1865-1877.* New York: Alfred A Knopf, 1965.

Steadman, Melvin Lee, Jr. *A Walking Tour of Leesburg, Virginia.* Leesburg, Va.: Potomac Press, 1968.

———. *By Fence and Fireside*. Annandale, Va.: The Turnpike Press, 1964.

———. *Leesburg's Old Stone Church, 1766*. Manassas, Va.: Virginia-Crafts Printing Co., 1964.

Strong, Solange. *Let's Look at Loudoun County, Virginia*. [n.p.: n.n.], 1949.

———. *Old Stone Houses of Loudoun County, Virginia*. [Leesburg, Va.]: By the Author, 1950.

Sweet, William Warren. *Virginia Methodism: A History*. Richmond, Va.: Whittet and Shepperson, 1955.

Swem, Earl G. *Virginia Historical Index*. Roanoke, Va.: Stone Printing and Manufacturing Co., 1936.

Sydner, Charles S. *The Development of Southern Sectionalism, 1819-1848*. Baton Rouge: Louisiana State University Press, 1962.

Talpalar, Morris. *The Sociology of Colonial Virginia*. 2d ed. New York: The Philosophical Library, 1968.

Taylor, Alrutheus A. *The Negro in the Reconstruction of Virginia*. New York: Russell and Russell, 1919.

Taylor, George R. *The Transportation Revolution, 1815-1860*. New York: Harper and Row, 1951.

——— (ed.). *The Turner Thesis*. Boston: D. C. Heath and Co., 1956.

Taylor, Irene B. *Women and — Women*. Evanston, Ill.: National W.C.T.U. Publishing House, [n.d.].

Thomas Balch Library. Leesburg, Va.: [n.n.], 1923.

Thomason, John W., Jr. *JEB Stuart*. New York: Charles Scribner's Sons, 1929.

Trelease, Allen W. *White Terror: The Ku Klux Klan Conspiracy and Southern Reconstruction*. New York: Harper Torchbooks, 1972.

Tyler, Alice F. *Freedom's Ferment*. 2d ed. New York: Harper and Row, 1962.

Underhill, Ruth M. *Red Man's America*. 2d ed. Chicago: University of Chicago Press, 1971.

Unger, Irwin, and David Reimers (eds.). *The Slavery Experience in the United States*. New York: Holt, Rinehart and Winston, 1970.

Van Deusen, Glyndon G. *The Jacksonian Era, 1828-1848*. New York: Harper and Row, 1959.

Virginia Book Company. *Virginia Books and Pamphlets Presently Available*. Berryville, Va.: Virginia Book Co., 1972.

Virginia Highway Historical Markers. *The Tourist Guide Book of Virginia.* Strasburg, Va.: Shenandoah Publication House, 1931.

Virginia Historic Landmarks Commission. *Virginia Landmarks Register.* [n.p.: n.n.], 1970.

Virginia State Dairymen's Association. *A History of Seven Decades of Service to Virginia's Dairy Industry.* [n.p.: n.n.], 1971.

Virginia State Library. *Virginia Local History: A Bibliography.* Richmond, Va.: Virginia State Library, 1971.

Wade, Richard C. *Slavery in the Cities.* New York: Oxford University Press, 1970.

Warner, Sam B., Jr. *The Urban Wilderness: A History of the American City.* New York: Harper and Row, 1972.

Wagstaff, R. E. *Sully Plantation.* [n.p.: n.n.], 1967.

Ward, John W. *Andrew Jackson—Symbol for an Age.* New York: Oxford University Press, 1962.

The Waterford Foundation. *Twenty-Ninth Annual Homes Tour and Crafts Exhibit.* Waterford, Va.: [n.n.], 1972.

Waterford Home Tour. *The James Moore House.* [n.p.: n.n.], 1972.

Waterman, Thomas T. *The Mansions of Virginia, 1706-1776.* Chapel Hill: University of North Carolina Press, 1945.

Webb, Walter P. *The Great Plains.* New York: Ginn and Co., 1859.

Weinberg, Albert K. *Manifest Destiny.* Chicago: Quadrangle Books, 1963.

Weisberger, Bernard A. *They Gathered at the River.* Chicago: Quadrangle Books, 1966.

Whiffen, Marcus. *American Architecture Since 1780: A Guide to the Styles.* Cambridge, Mass.: Massachusetts Institute of Technology Press, 1969.

Whitfield, Theodore M. *Slavery Agitation in Virginia, 1829-1832.* Reprint. New York: Negro University Press, 1969.

Wilkinson, J. Harvie III. *Harry Byrd and the Changing Face of Virginia Politics, 1945-1966.* Charlottesville: University Press of Virginia, 1968.

Williams, Ames W. *The Washington and Old Dominion Railroad.* Springfield, Va.: Capital Traction Quarterly, 1970.

Williams, Harrison. *Legends of Loudoun: An Account of the History and Homes of a Border County of Virginia's Northern Neck.* Richmond, Va.: Garrett and Massie, 1938.

Williams, Henry L., and Ottalie K. Williams. *Old American Homes.* New York: Bonanza Books, 1967.

Wingo, Alfred L. *Virginia's Soils and Land Use.* Richmond, Va.: Baughman Co., 1949.

Wood, Robert C. *Suburbia: Its People and Their Politics.* Boston: Houghton Mifflin Co., 1958.

Worsley, Lizze (comp.). *Old St. James Episcopal Church, Leesburg, Virginia, 1710-1877.* Leesburg, Va.: [n.n., n.d.].

Wright, Louis B. *The Atlantic Frontier.* Ithaca, N. Y.: Great Seal Books, 1963.

───── *The First Gentlemen of Virginia.* Charlottesville: University Press of Virginia, 1964.

Writers' Program of the Work Projects Administration in the State of Virginia. *Virginia: A Guide to the Old Dominion.* New York: Oxford University Press, 1940.

Wust, Klaus. *The Virginia Germans.* Charlottesville: University Press of Virginia, 1969.

───── (comp.). *Virginia German Bibliography.* Edinburg, Va.: Shenandoah History, 1970.

───── *Virginia Fraktur: Penmanship as Folk Art.* Edinburg, Va.: Shenandoah History, 1972.

Wynes, Charles E. *Race Relations in Virginia, 1870-1902.* Charlottesville: University of Virginia Press, 1961.

Vandiver, Frank E. *Jubal's Raid.* New York: McGraw-Hill Co., 1960.

b. *Periodicals*

Brown, Stuart E., Jr. "Manors on the Frontier," *Virginia Cavalcade,* XVI (Winter, 1967), 42-47.

Bushnell, David I., Jr. "The Virginia Frontier in History—1778," *Virginia Magazine of History and Biography,* XXIII (June, 1915), 256-68.

Cabell, N. F. "Some Fragments of an Intended Report on the Post Revolutionary History of Agriculture in Virginia," ed. E. G. Swem, *William and Mary Quarterly,* 1st ser., XXVI (January, 1918), 145-68.

Cady, Edwin H. "A Bequest from James Monroe," *The Bulletin of the Loudoun County Historical Society,* II (1960), 7-16.

"Centennial Ceremony for the Battle of Ball's Bluff," *The Bulletin of the Loudoun County Historical Society,* III (1962), 7-30.

Coleman, Charles Washington. "The County Committees of 1774-75 in Virginia," *William and Mary Quarterly*, 1st ser., V (October, 1896), 94-106; and (April, 1897), 245-55.

"Confederate Monument in Leesburg," *The Bulletin of the Loudoun County Historical Society*, IV (1965), 25-26.

Divine, John. "The Comanches," *The Bulletin of the Loudoun County Historical Society*, IV (1965), 21-23.

────── "The Passage of the Armies Through Loudoun: 1861-65," *The Bulletin of the Loudoun County Historical Society*, II (1960), 33-35.

Garnett, James Mercer. "James Mercer," *William and Mary Quarterly*, 1st ser., XVII (October, 1908) 85-99 and (January, 1909), 204-23.

"Genealogical Queries," *William and Mary Quarterly*, 2d ser., I (October, 1921), 297-99.

Gibbens, Paul H. "The Co-Operation of the Southern Colonies in the Forbes Expedition Against Fort Duquesne," *Virginia Magazine of History and Biography*, XXXVI (January, 1928), 1-16; (April, 1928), 145-60; and (October, 1928), 305-37.

Hall, Wilbur C. "Commander of the Morman Battalion," *The Bulletin of the Loudoun County Historical Society*, I (1958), 44-50.

────── "The Future of Education in Virginia," Richmond, Va.: Reprint from February, 1931, issue of the *Virginia Journal of Education*.

"Historical Notes and Queries: Virginia Vestry-Books and Parish Registers," *Virginia Magazine of History and Biography*, III (July, 1895), 85-86.

"Homes of the Past," *Rural Living*, February, 1972, 6-7, 20.

Hord, A. H. "Genealogy of the Triplett Family," *William and Mary Quarterly*, 1st ser., XXI (July, 1912), 33-34 and (October, 1912), 115-34; XXII (October, 1913), 175-91.

Janney, Asa Moore. "A Short History of the Society of Friends in Loudoun County," *The Bulletin of the Loudoun County Historical Society*, IV (1965), 29-42.

"Jefferson and the Ketoctin Baptist Association," *The Bulletin of the Loudoun County Historical Society*, I (1958), 56-60.

Kelly, John Bailey. "Quaint Village Preserved by Waterford Foundation," *Virginia and the Virginia County*, VII (January, 1953), 24-50.

Kincaid, Nan Lin. "The First Churches in Loudoun," *The Bulletin of the Loudoun County Historical Society*, I (1958), 9-20.

Marsh, Helen Hirst. "Early Loudoun Water Mills," *The Bulletin of the Loudoun County Historical Society*, I (1958), 21-26.

———. "The Loudoun Company," *The Bulletin of the Loudoun County Historical Society*, III (1962), 43-48.

Morrison, A. J. "Virginia Patents," *William and Mary Quarterly*, 2d ser., II (July, 1922), 149-56.

Nichols, Joseph V. "Tales of Old Virginia," *The Bulletin of the Loudoun County Historical Society*, I (1958), 40-43.

"Notes and Queries: A Map of Fairfax County in 1748," *Virginia Magazine of History and Biography*, XXXVI (April, 1928), 180-82.

Osburn, Penelope M. "Exeter: Its History and Architecture," *The Bulletin of the Loudoun County Historical Society*, II (1960), 17-32.

———. "Historic Leesburg Often Took Part in Great Events," *Virginia and the Virginia County*, VII (January, 1953), 16-17, 46.

———. "The Oldest Town Established in Loudoun," *The Bulletin of the Loudoun County Historical Society*, I (1958), 51-55.

———. "The True American," *The Bulletin of the Loudoun County Historical Society*, I (1958), 27-39.

Putnam, Eben. "Queries," *Virginia Magazine of History and Biography*, V (December, 1897), 337.

Rowberg, Andrew A., and Marie C. Rowberg. "Post Offices of Loudoun County," *Virginia and the Virginia County*, VII (January, 1953), 57-72.

Scheel, Eugene M. "Dirt Roads in Exurbia," *Traffic Quarterly*, January, 1971, 103-15.

Trout, W. E. III. "The Goose Creek and Little River Navigation," *Virginia Cavalcade*, XVI (Winter, 1967), 30-34.

True, Rodney H. "John Binns of Loudoun," *William and Mary Quarterly*, 2d ser., II (January, 1922), 20-39.

Vandevanter, C. O. "The Chapel, Loudoun County," *Virginia Magazine of History and Biography*, XXXVIII (April, 1930), 169-72.

"Virginia War History Commission Supplement No. 1," *Virginia Magazine of History and Biography*, XXIX (January, 1921), 65-66.

"Virginia War History Commission Supplement No. 4," *Virginia Magazine of History and Biography*, XXIX (October, 1921), 449-96.

Wade, William A. "Lovettsville's New Jerusalem Lutheran Church," *Virginia and the Virginia County*, VII (January, 1953), 26.

White, E. V. "History of the Battle of Ball's Bluff," *The Bulletin of the Loudoun County Historical Society*, IV (1965), 7-18.

ADDITIONAL BIBLIOGRAPHICAL MATERIAL ABOUT LOUDOUN COUNTY

Since the late 1970s numerous additional titles have been added to the list of historical works about Loudoun County. An important contributor and now the most valuable depository of Loudoun materials is the Thomas Balch Library, in Leesburg, Virginia. It was a private library without a copying machine when I was originally researching *From Frontier to Suburbia*, and many months were spent reading hardbound volumes of original county newspapers. On Saturdays my wife and two daughters, one in preschool and the other in early elementary school, would spend the day with me at Balch. The girls' only reward was a fast-food lunch and the "privilege" of feeding paper into and pushing the start button on my portable and crude copying machine. The machine frequently overheated and smoked, producing unreadable blackened pages. Since then the Balch Library has gone from a private institution to a county library to being under the auspice of the town of Leesburg. It has flourished. Guided by the Friends of the Thomas Balch Library and the library staff, the building has been renovated and expanded, holdings increased, and an extensive and impressive mural by the renowned artist William Woodward has been placed on the upper walls of one of the rooms that traces the history of the county (see Charles P. Poland Jr. and Rachel Yarnell Thompson, *The Thomas Balch Library Mural: A Loudoun County Story* (Leesburg, VA, The Friends of the Thomas Balch Library, 2002). Balch also houses numerous genealogical and historical reference materials (such as indexes to wills and deeds, death registers, tithables, and marriages). The most intriguing of the titles is Louise Skinner Hutchison's *Apprentices, Poor Children and Bastards Loudoun County Virginia 1757–1850* (Westminister, MD: Willow Bend Books, 2002). The Friends of the Thomas Balch Library also publish books on Loudoun history, especially about her communities and African-American residents. The most ambitious and valuable of their publications is Eugene M. Scheel's *Loudoun Discovered: Communities, Corners, and Crossroads*, in five volumes (Leesburg, VA: The Friends of the Thomas Balch Library, 2002–2003). Each volume is devoted to a geographical section of the county; *Eastern Loudoun: 'Goin' down the Country*, vol. I; *Leesburg and the Old Carolina Road*, vol. II; *The Hunt Country and Middleburg*, vol. III; *Quaker Country and the Loudoun Valley*, vol. IV; *Waterford, The German Settlement and Between the Hills*, vol. V. These volumes are a collection and updating of more than 120 articles written for the *Loudoun Times-Mirror* and include maps, illustrations, and an annotated bibliography. Scheel continues his almost three decades of study of Loudoun's past in his bimonthly articles in the *Washington Post*.

Information on the county's formative years and before can be found in William F. Rust III's *Loudoun County Prehistory* (Leesburg, VA: Loudoun's Archeological Center, 1986); Margaret Lail Hopkins' *Cameron Parish* in

Colonial Virginia (N.P.: Privately printed, 1988); John Phillips II's *The Historians Guide to Loudoun County: Colonial Laws of Virginia and County Court Orders, 1757–1766*. (Leesburg, VA: Goose Creek Publications, 1996). Useful source material in addition to that found in Phillips' book can also be found in *The Ledger of Israel Janney, 1784–1793*; three volumes, compiled by Werner Janney (Lincoln, VA: At the Sign of the Pied Typer, 1989). The Quakers are important in the settlement and the history of Loudoun. A fine starting point is Werner and Asa Moore Janney's *Ye Meeting House Smal: A Short Account of Friends In Loudoun County, Virginia, 1732–1980* (Lincoln, VA: privately printed, 1980). Both authors are Friends and descendants of Quakers who settled in the county. Asa Moore, who for years ran a country store and post office in Lincoln, became a county legend, interspersing humor and a vast command of Loudoun's past in entertaining stories and conversation.

Books and booklets on Loudoun's towns and homes are numerous (see the bibliography of *Loudoun Discovered* for a more extensive listing that includes tours and maps). The history of Middleburg and the vicinity is discussed in Audrey Windor Bergner's *Old Plantations and Historical Homes Around Middleburg, Virginia, and the Families Who Lived and Loved Within their Walls* (New York: Cornwell Books, 2001), and in Eugene Scheel's *The History of Middleburg* (Middleburg, VA: Middleburg Bicentennial Committee, 1987). Scheel's *Story of Purcellville* (Purcellville, VA: First Virginia Bank, rev. ed. 1977) provides an overview. Asa Moore and Werner Janney deal with the town's history during the early 1900s in *A Medieval Virginia Town, 1914–1919* (Lincoln, VA: At the Sign of the Pied Typer, 1986). Residents of Waterford, Virginia, one of the few national landmark towns in the United States, are deeply committed to historical preservation through their Waterford Foundation. They sponsor a large annual craft fair to fund the foundation's activities, which include publications about their unique town. Some of their publications are *Waterford Perspectives* (1983), edited by the foundation's education committee, and two books by John Divine, Bronwen C. Souders, and John M. Souders, *To Talk Is Treason: Quakers of Waterford on Life, Love, Death and War in the Southern Confederacy* (1996) and *When Waterford and I Were Young* (1997). John Divine's encyclopedic knowledge of the Civil War and cheerful benevolence in helping other students and Civil War authors earned him the unofficial title of "Mr. Civil." The Souderses have continued and expanded Divine's work on Waterford. See *The Burning Cow Question and Other Tales from the Waterford Town Council, 1891–1909* (2000), edited and annotated by John Souders.

Information about the county seat, Leesburg, during the 1900s can be found in Frank Raflo's tome, *Within the Iron Gates: Stories Remembered* (Dulles, VA: Printed by TechniGraphix, 1998). In 1976 The Hillsboro Bicentennial History Committee authored and published *Hillsboro: Memories of a Mill Town*. Information about another town in northwestern Loudoun, Lovettsville, can be obtained from the Lovettsville History Society Museum.

The publication of Civil War material continues to escalate. For the county's most famous battle, see the fine work of Kim B. Holien in the *Battle of Ball's Bluff* (Orange, VA: Moss Publications, 1985); Byron Farwell, *Ball's Bluff: A Small Battle and Its Long Shadow* (McLean, VA: EPM Publications, 1990), and William F. Howard, *The Battle of Ball's Bluff: "The Leesburg Affair"* (Lynchburg, VA: H.E. Howard, 1994). The origin, combat, and consequences of the battle of Ball's Bluff are traced in the soon-to-be-published *Glories of War: Small Battles and Early Heroes of 1861* by Charles P. Poland Jr. The best study of the cavalry battles in Loudoun during the Gettysburg campaign is Robert F. O'Neill's *The Cavalry Battles of Aldie, Middleburg, and Upperville* (Lynchburg, VA: H.E. Howard, 1993). For the 8th Virginia's history throughout the war, consult John Divine's *8th Virginia Infantry* (Lynchburg, VA: H.E. Howard, 1984). Divine also authored another history of a cavalry unit composed of many Loudouners, *35th Battalion Virginia Cavalry* (Lynchburg, VA: H.E. Howard, 1982). The life and activities of Confederate partisan leader John Singleton Mosby continue to fascinate Civil War readers, leading to the formation of a John Mosby society. The society is responsible for naming much of Route 50 in northern Virginia the John S. Mosby Highway, with roadside markers denoting any area in the region where the Gray Ghost set foot or rode through as a Mosby Heritage area. The society continues to publish material about his life and guerrilla activities, much of which occurred in Loudoun. See Kivin H. Siepel's *Rebel: The Life and Times of John Singleton Mosby* (New York: St. Martin's, 1983); Jeffrey Wert's, *Mosby Ranger* (New York: Simon and Schuster, 1990); Thomas Evans and James M. Mayer's *Mosby's Confederacy: A Guide to the Roads and Sites of Colonel John Singleton Mosby* (Shippensburg, PA: White Maine, 1991); Hugh C. Keen and Horace Mewborn's *43rd Battalion Virginia Cavalry: Mosby's Command* (Lynchburg, VA: H.E. Howard, 1993) and James A. Ramage's, *Gray Ghost: The Life of Col. John Singleton Mosby* (Lexington, KY: University Press of Kentucky, 1999). One of Mosby's most successful confrontations with the Union is presented by Wynne C. Saffer in "Colonel Mosby's Action at Mount Zion Church," *The Bulletin of the Historical Society of Loudoun County, Virginia*, 1997, 2nd. ser., vol. I. Less significant or restrained were the activities of John W. Mobberly. The guerrilla antics of this little-known member of White's Comanches are presented in Richard E. Crouch's *"Rough-Riding Scout": The Story of John W. Mobberly* (Arlington, VA: Elden Editions, 1994). Dealing with civilian problems during the war is Taylor M. Chamblin's *Crossing the Line: Civilian Trade & Travel Between Loudoun County, Virginia and Maryland During the Civil War* (Waterford, VA: Waterford Foundation, 2003).

Bibliographies of prominent figures who lived in Loudoun include Mary S. Skutt and Rachel Y. Thompson's *American Hero to the World: George C. Marshall* (Leesburg, VA: George C. Marshall International Center, 1999); Carolyn Green's, *Morley: The Intimate Story of Virginia's Governor and Mrs. Westmoreland Davis* (Leesburg, VA: Goose Creek Productions, 1998); Douglas R. Egerton's, *Charles Fenton Mercer and the Trial of National Conservatism* (Jackson, MI: University Press of Mississippi, 1989); Russell

Baker's, *Growing Up* (New York: Congdon and Weed, 1982). *Charlotte Haxall Noland 1883-1969*, edited by Mary Curtis, Lee deButts, and Rosalie Noland Woodland (Middleburg, VA: Foxcroft School, 1971), is a collection of reminiscences of people who knew the venerable headmistress of Foxcroft School. Information on another Loudoun female educator, Margaret Mercer, a crusader against slavery and supporter of women's rights, can be found in Byron A. Lee's *The Mercers and Parkhurst* (Harwood, MD: published by the author, 1999). For the autobiography of one of Loudoun's wealthiest residents, see Paul Mellon's *Reflection in a Silver Spoon: A Memoir* (New York, NY: Morrow, 1992).

Recent years have seen the appearance of a number of books dealing with African-American life in Loudoun: Brenda E. Stevenson, *Life in Black and White: Family and Community in the Slave South* (New York, NY: Oxford University Press, 1996); the Black History Committee of the Friends of the Thomas Balch Library, *The Essence of A People: Portrait of African-Americans Who Made a Difference*, vol. I and II (Leesburg, VA: Friends of the Thomas Balch Library, 2001-2002); and Bronwen and John Souders, *A Rock in a Weary Land, a Shelter in a Time of Storm* (Waterford, VA: Waterford Foundation, 2003). Additional information on African-Americans and many other aspects of Loudoun's past can be found in the Loudoun Museum, in Leesburg, Virginia.

An important recent addition to the understanding of the county's history is the Loudoun Heritage Farm Museum, at Claude Moore Park in Sterling, Virginia. It now ranks with the Thomas Balch Library, county court records in the judiciary center, and the Loudoun Museum as important depositories of historical information about Loudoun. The Farm Museum provides exhibits about agriculture in Loudoun, stressing the lives of select farmers and farm technology, and a book on the subject, *It's Just A Way of Life: Reminiscing About the Family Farm* (Winchester, VA: Winchester Printer, 2002), compiled and edited by Allison Weiss. The sage of Lincoln, Asa Moore Janney and his brother Werner add to our knowledge by editing *John Jay Janney's Virginia* (McLean, VA: EPM Publications, 1978). This is a readable and informative account of farm life of the ordinary farmer (1812-1831) written by a ninety-year old man. Relevant for an understanding of agriculture in the county at the turn of the twenty-first century are the *2001 Virginia Equine Report* and *Census Data* compiled by the Virginia Agricultural Statistics Service (www.nass.usda.gov/va).

Photographic histories of the county have appeared, starting with Nan Donnelly-Shay and Griffith Shay's *The County of Loudoun: An Illustrated History* (Norfolk, VA: The Downing Co., 1988) and followed by five books by Mary Fishback, published by Arcadia Publishing, Charleston, South Carolina: *Loudoun County: Two Hundred and Fifty Years of Towns and Villages* (1999); *Loudoun County, People and Places* (2000); *Loudoun County: The Family Album* (2002); *Northern Virginia's Equestrian Heritage* (2002); and *Leesburg* (2003).

Inside Loudoun: The Way It Was (Leesburg, VA: *Loudoun Times-Mirror*,

1986), by Frances Reid, traces the history of county newspapers, with emphasis on events and developments during her more than half-century's employment at the *Loudoun Times-Mirror*. Miss Fanny, as Miss Reid was known, along with Asa Moore Janney and John Divine, were three of the most respected, well-liked, and well-known Loudouners during the last half of the 1900s.

A valuable sourcebook on the county's political history was written by Wynne C. Saffer: *Loudoun Votes, 1867–1966: A Civil War Legacy* (Westminster, MD: Willow Bend Books, 2002). Saffer has also authored *Mount Zion Cemetery, Aldie, Virginia* (Westminster, MD: Willow Bend Books, 1997).

For recent political developments and other issues, important sources include the *Washington Post*, especially their *Loudoun Extra* section, and county newspapers: the *Loudoun Times-Mirror* and two papers that came into existence more recently, *Leesburg Today* and *Loudoun Easterner*. Technology had revolutionized the availability of materials about Loudoun, especially the county government. A vast array of information about the county government and regulations, including the revised zoning ordinance of 2003, can be found at www.loudoun.gov. An informative presentation about growth can be found under Burton on this website entitled "Loudoun County: A Case Study in Unbridled Growth." Jim Burton, an Independent two-term incumbent of the Board of Supervisors and a major force in slowing growth, is a sought-after speaker by many counties to the west of Loudoun that are concerned about growth. Published materials are also available about Loudoun's growth. The most useful is the *2002 Annual Growth Summary, Loudoun County, Virginia, USA* (Leesburg, VA: Department of Economic Development, 2003). Also see the website www.Loudoun.gov/business.

Information about Loudoun public schools is available through a website (loudoun.k12.va.us) and materials published by the Loudoun County public school public information office at Leesburg, Virginia: *2002–2003 Guide/Directory*; *Annual Report 2001–2002*; *Program of Studies: Academic Year 2002–2003*; and *Employee Handbook: 2002–2003*.

The Loudoun Convention and Visitors Association (LCVA) has published an official visitor's guide for 2003–2004 entitled *Birds of Every Feather Visit Loudoun County, Virginia*. Although it was issued to attract tourists, it is a useful research tool. It provides information about towns, organizations, and museums; presents maps; and lists many websites. *Loudoun Magazine*, a recently established monthly magazine, deals with current developments but includes historical essays as well.

INDEX

Abel, R. B., 83
Abolitionists, 130
Aborigine, 395 (*see also* Indians)
Adams, A. G., 309*n*
Adams, John Quincy, 102,109,111
Admiralty Courts, 50
Agrarianism, 95
  myths, 318*n*
  philosophy, 85-86,391
"Agricola," 243-44
Agricultural Adjustment Act (A.A.A.)
  first, 330
  second, 330,335-36
Agricultural Society of Loudoun, 92-93
Agricultural Stabilization and Conservation Service, 358
Agriculture (*see also*, Agrarianism, Farmers)
  during antebellum era, 80-81
  during colonial era, 79,80
  dairy farming, 294,319,322,356
  decline, 359-62,391-92,395
  during the Great Depression, 326-30, 335-36
  effects of Civil War, 185,213-14,218-20, 223-27
  equipment, 80-81,279-80
  extension agent, 322
  future, 391
  golden age, 279-94
  and labor, 81-84
  livestock, 74-77
  methods of farming, 74-94, 279-88, 292, 294,307-08
  from 1917 to 1945, 307,317-30,334-36
  during 1920's, 317-25
  since 1945, 354-64,381
  prices of farm products, 397-400
  during reconstruction, 223-30
  reform, 74-94,354-57
  and slave labor, 131,138
  during World War II, 335-38
Alcoholic Beverage Control System, 305-06
Aldie, 2,68,69*n*,72,75,76,98,126,238,347
  origin of name, 98
  mill, 98*n*, 323*n*
  skirmishes at, 207,210-11
Aldie Farmers' Club 281
Aldie Mill, 98*n*,323*n*
Alexander, J. H., 124*n*
Alexandria Canal Company, 122
Alexandria Gazette, 147
Alexandria and Harper's Ferry Railroad, 127
Alexandria, Loudoun, and Hampshire Railroad Company, 127,237
Alexandria, Loudoun, and Hampshire Turnpike Company, 118*n*
Alexandria Road, 10,30,34 (*see also* Roads)
Allen, Thomas E., 260
Ambrister, Robert, 106*n*
American Antislavery Society, 148
American Colonization Society, 142-43,145

American Revolution
  causes of, 50-51
  Champe, John, 56-57
  Griffith, David, 56-57
  Hessian prisoners, 32*n*
  impact upon Loudouners, 52-54,59-61
  militiamen, 53-54
  and Quakers, 52
  revolutionary committees, 51-52
  Tories, 52
American System, 102
Andrews, John, 36*n*
Andrews vs. Loudoun County Board of Supervisors, 389
Anglican Church, 13,38-40,42,48,59
Animal husbandry, 286-88,292-94
Antietam, 205
Antifunders (*see* Readjusters)
Antislavery movements, 141-50, 158-67
  (*see also* Abolitionists)
  meetings, 145-46
  petitions, 145-46
  and religion, 141-42
Apprentice system,
  purpose, 81
  runaways, 81-82
Arbitrary arrests, 215-18
Arbuthnot, Alexander, 106*n*
Arcola, 72,75 (*see also* Gum Spring)
Army Corps of Engineers, 378-379*n*
Army of Northern Virginia, 184,204
Army of the Potomac, 184,207
Arnold, Benedict, 56
Ashbury, Francis, 44*n*
Ashburn, 71*n*, 75 (*see also* Farmwell)
Ashby's Gap, 29,206*n*
Ashby's Gap Turnpike Company, 115, 118,119,125
Ashby, Robert L., 330*n*
Automobile, 308,381
  as vehicle of change, 342-45
Avis, John, 139
Awbrey, Francis, 8,39*n*

Baby show, 331*n*
Baker, Edward D.
  at Ball's Bluff, 196,198,202
  death, 198,202
Baker, I. W., 349*n*
Balch, L. P. W., 142*n*
Ball, Charles B., 142*n*
Ball, George W., 264*n*
Ball, G. Washington, 246*n*
Ball, Harvey M., Jr., 369*n*
Ball, Henry, 216
Ball, Langtree, 145*n*
Ball's Bluff, battle of, 188*n*,191,193-202
Baltimore and Ohio Railroad, 34,126
Balthrop, John, 89
Bank of the United States, 103,105,130
Bank of the Valley, 113-14

456 INDEX

Banks, 105,113-14,130,236
Battles, Civil War, 189-213 (*see also* specific listings as Ball's Bluff)
Baptists, 42,44,46,47,48
Baseball, 254
Bayley, Sydner, 142*n*
Beagle Club of America, 94*n*
Beanton, William, Jr., 230*n*
Beard, Lewis, 104*n*
Beatty, Russell, 312*n*
Beaver Dam, 122-23
Beeson, Edward, 145*n*
Bell, Austin, 312*n*
Bell, John, 176
Belmont, 71*n*, 75,163
Belt, Campbell, 186,216
Belt's Ferry, 32*n*
Benedict, W. B., 153*n*
Benevolent Society of Alexandria, Virginia, 147
Benton, Benjamin H., 93
Berkeley, William, 48*n*
Berry, Hazel, 353*n*
Berry, Josephine, 353*n*
Biays, Ned, 134,135
Bicorporal communities, 307,312
  boundaries of, 69*n*
  characteristics, 67-69,71,72,75
  decline, 342-48,365-69
  importance of 66-69
Big government, 394-95
"Big Spring," 8
Binns, Charles, 19*n*,85
Binns, Charles, Jr., 19*n*
Binns, Dewanner, 85*n*
Binns, John A.
  agrarian philosophy, 85-86
  agrarian reformer, 85-91
  on causes of illness, 87-88
  critics, 90-91
  on deep plowing, 88
  experiments with gypsum, 86-90
  influence, 85,88-89,91
  and the Loudoun system, 85
  on red clover, 88
Binns, Thomas Neilson, 85*n*
Birkley, Samuel S., 109*n*
Blacks, 64-65,272,350-54
  colonization, 161
  education, 132,345,352
  free blacks prior to Civil War, 137,139
  owners of farms, 325
  and reconstruction, 238-44,272,274
  as slaves, 6-7,131-41
  and World War II, 339
Blacksmiths, 81
Bloomfield, 72,75,121 (*see also* Frog Town)
Bluemont, 42*n*,71*n*,75 (*see also* Snickersville)
Blue Ridge Mountain, 15,19,184
Board of Public Works, 118-20,124
Board of Supervisors, 63*n*,331,

333,349,366,368,370,372,376-77,379,381, 382-83,388*n*,390
Bogue, William L., 166
Bohannan, A., 54*n*
Boise Cascade Building Company, 368
Bond, Asa, 216
Bond issues, 382,386
Boston Tea Party, 50
Bounan, Robert C., 230*n*
Bowie, I. Wilson, 288
Braddock's expedition, 36
Braden, Noble S., 104*n*
Braden, Robert, 113*n*
Bradfield, Benjamin, 80
Bradfield, George W., 296
Brawner, Frank, 249*n*
Breckinridge, John C., 176
Brent, James, 304-05
Brislan, John, 255
Broad Run (stream), 2,6,211
Broad Run High School, 354*n*,382-83
Brown, C. C., 369*n*
Brown, Isaac, 142*n*
Brown, John, 170-73
Brown, Robert E., 26
Browne, Mrs., 36-37
Broyhill and Son, 366
Bruin, Joseph, 139*n*
Buckner, Annie, 352*n*
Bull Run, battle of, 193
Bull Run Mountain, 29
Bull, William 190*n*
Buoy, Major, 135
Burch, William T., 369*n*
Burt, E. R., 198
Bush, J. L., 355*n*
Bush Meeting, 299,301-02
Bush Meeting Association, 308*n*
Businesses, 72,230-38,323-34
Bussinger, C. M., 354

Cabell, N. F., 90,91*n*
Caldwell, S.B.T., 106-07, 145-46
Calhoun, John C., 168*n*
Campbell, Aeneas, 10*n*,19,24,28*n*
Campbell, B. M., 139
Campbell, John, 15
Campbell, W. L., 139
Camp meetings, 301-03
Canals, 114-15,122-25,128
Capital Improvements Program, 384*n*
Carlyle, John, 33
Carolina Road, 10,29-30,32-34
Carpenter, Charles, 284*n*,334
Carter, Elizabeth A., 228*n*
Carter, George, 142*n*
Carter, John A., 82,145*n*,161*n*,174*n*,178
Carter, John R., 178,230*n*,277,291*n*
Carter, Landon, 79*n*
Carter, Robert (of Nomini Hall), 8,27-28, 48*n*
Carter, Robert "King," 8
Carter, William, 241

Carter's Gap, 126
Cass, Lewis, 103
Catoctin Creek, 125,379-80
Catoctin Farmers' Club 83,252-53, 283-88,294n
Catoctin Mountain, 127
Catoctin Presbyterian Church, 42
Catoctin Valley Defense Alliance, 380n
Cattle, 74,218,223-25,286-87,319-22, 397-400
Caven, John 42n
Centennial of American independence, lack of celebration in Loudoun, 276n
Chamberlain, A. W., 226
Chamblin, Charles T., 234
Champe, John, 56-57
Chantilly Airport (see Dulles International Airport)
Charles II, King, 7
Chesapeake and Ohio Canal, 74,106,122-23
Chesapeake and Potomac Telephone Company, 338n
Chichister, George M., 145n
Children, illegitimate, 22,24
Chilton, Elizabeth, 24
Chilton, George, 22
Chinn, Charles, 24
Chinn, R. S., 230n
Churches, 12,39-49
 and bicorporal communities 344
 church wardens, 24
 discipline of members, 48-49
 political duties, 23-24
 and slavery, 142-43
Circleville, 75,121
Circuit Court, 389
Circus, 254
Cisterns, 334n
Civilian Conservation Corps, (C.C.C.), 333n
Civil Rights Act (1964), 353n
Civil Rights Bill, 266-67
Civil War, 183-221,394
 battles, 189-213
 Brothers' War, 189-90
 causes of, 167-68
 impact, 183-87,214-27
 political meetings, 168
 troop movement, 202-09
Civil Works Administration (C.W.A.), 331-33
Clagett, Henry, 145n
Clapham, Josias, 10n18n,19n,32n., 51n,53,61n
Clapham, Samuel, 113n
Clapham's Ferry, 32n,35
Clark, Gidney, 8n
Clark's Gap, 127
Clay, Henry, 103
Clemons, James, 50n
Clerk of Court, 16,19n,63n
Cleveland, Johnson, 142n
Cocke, Catesby, 8

Cockran, W. B., 230n
Coe, Spencer A., 262
Cogswell, Milton, 196,199
Cokongoloto, 3 (see also Goose Creek)
Colchester Road, 30
Colclough, Charity, 22
Colclough, Robert, 22
Coleman, James, 24
Coleman, Jermima, 53
Coleman, Joel, 53
Coleman, Philip J., 330n
Coleman, Richard, 6n,19n
Comanches, 185n,188-90,216
Combs, Joseph, 39n
Command of the Army Act, 265
Commercial development of Loudoun County, 365-69
Committee for Loudoun's Public Safety, 51-52
Committee for United War Work Campaign, 312
Commission of revenue, 19n
Community leagues, 323
Compher, B. O., 305
Compromise of 1850, 167,170
Compromise of 1877, 277
Conestoga wagons, 28-29
Confederate soldiers, reverence for, 261-62
Confiscation Act, 229
Congressional reconstruction policy, 256,265-72,278
Conklin, S. Thurbert, 312n
Connolly, Thomas C., 149-50
Conoy Island, 4
Conrad, Alfred H., 138
Conrad's Ferry, 194
Conrad, Robert Y., 264
Constables, 16
Constitutional Convention of 1829-30, 108
Continental army, 53-54,57
Colonial era, 23,26n,27-29,395
Colonization of blacks, 161
Colored Man's Aid Society, 244
Conscription, 337
Conservation, 1,330,335-36,358-59, 395-96
Conservatism, 255-56
Conservative clubs, 272-76
Conservation party, 270-77
Cooper, Appolis, 39n
Cooper, Nathaniel, 312n
Cordell, Presley, 118n,142n,145-46
Cordell, R. T. 339n
Corn, 6,79,307,321,329-30,356,397-400
Corn clubs, 293
Coroner, 16,63n
Corum, Euroch, 242n
County agent (see Agriculture)
County court, 18-25 (see also Loudoun County)
 judicial functions, 20,72
 legislative functions, 20,21

County government (see Loudoun County)
County justices, 16,18,19,22 (see also
    County court)
County lieutenant, 12
County-wide League, 352
Courthouse, 10,19-20
Craigie, Walter, Sr., 386
Crane, Philo, 230n
Craun, Nelson, 362n
Crawford, George, 352n
Crawford, Willam H., 102
Cresswell, Nicholas, 42-43, 52,54-55
Crime, 22-25,48-49,55n,240-42,357
Crooked Valley Factory, 76n
Cross, James H., 240n
Culpeper, John, 7
Culpeper, Thomas 7

Dabney, Virginius, 246n
Dairy breeds, 321
Dairy farming, 294,319,322,356
Daivi Development Corporation v. Loudoun
    County Board of Supervisors, 389n
Dams, 378-80
Dana, Charles A., 217
Dangerfield case, 164-67
Dangerfield, Daniel, 164-67
Darish, John, 137n
Davis, Gideon, 80
Davis, John, 12n
Davis, Sith, 24
Davis, Westmoreland, 308-09
  agrarian reformer, 309,322n
  Governor of Virginia, 308-09
  owner of Morven Park, 309n
  owner of the *Southern Planter*, 309n
  and World War I, 312,315
Davis, William, 54n
Daysville, 75
DeBow, James D. B., 170
DeBow's Review, 170
Declaration of Independence, 51
DeKay, Catherine E., 327-28
Democratic Mirror, The 82,138
    139,166,167,170-76,178n,180n,
    187,193,201,229,246,251
  and blacks, 242-3
  impact of Civil War upon, 231,235,236,239
  on farming, 280n,281,288,291-92
  on the Freedmen's Bureau, 244
  on reconstruction, 258-60,262,266-68,
    271-72,276
Democratic party, 100,168,174-76,
    271-78,308-10,329
Demographic growth, 384,395
  impact upon county institutions and
    services, 370,372
  impact upon magisterial districts, 370
  impact upon schools, 373,375
  impact upon water resources, 378-80
Department of Parks and Recreation, 370
Department of Planning and Zoning, 383
Desegregation, 350-54

Developers, 365-69, 373,383-91,395
Devens, Charles, 194-95,199
Difficult Run, 15-16
Diseases, 24-25,36n
Dixon, Henry, 190n
diZerega, Philip, 245n
Dogs, menace to sheep, 288-89
Dog tax, 288
Douglas, Charles, 104n
Douglas, James E., 98n
Douglas, Stephen A., 176
Douglas, William, 43n,53
Dover, 75,126
Downey, J. Madison, 258
Downey, William B., 234,260n
Draft, 312
Dranesville, 117,127
Drought of 1930, 326-28
Drovers, 34
Duff, W. L., 195
Dulaney, Richard, 230n
Dulles International Airport, 365-66,379
Duncan, John, 82
Dungan, David, 89n

Eaches, Daniel, 113n
*Early History of Agriculture in
    Virginia* (Cabell), 90-91
Early, Jubal A., 209,218
Eastern Ridge Road, 30 (see also Roads)
Eaton, John H., 105n
Ecology, 1,63,395n,396 (see also
    Environment)
Education (see also Schools)
  in antebellum Loudoun, 151-56
  of blacks, 350-51
  costs, 251-53,348,375,382
  night school, 248
  private, 151-56,245-50
  public, 250-52,344-54
  during reconstruction, 245-52
Edwards, Benjamin, 12
Edwards, Thomas W., 244-45,264n
Edwards' Ferry 32n,35,193,194,200,207
Eisenhard, John, 353n
Elections, 98-107,260,273-78
  1824, 102,106
  1828, 102,106
  1832, 103,106
  1836, 103,106
  1840, 103,106
  1844, 103,106
  1848, 103,106
  1852, 103,106
  1860, 175-76
  1876, 274-77
  1928, 329
  1932, 329
  1936, 331n
  1940, 333n
Electricity, 308,323,333-34
Ellzey, William, 61n,142n
Ellzey, Thomas S., 161n

INDEX 459

Embrey, George, 53
Emerick, Carrie, 300*n*
Emerick, Oscar L., 347,350,354
Emerson, Ralph Waldo, 1
Emorie, Stephen 50*n*
Emory, W. H., 209
English, Mary, 22
English Toleration Act, 40
Enoch, Fenton, 227
Environment
 alteration in, 3-4,25-26,396
 exploitation of, 1
Episcopal Church, 13,39-40 (*see also* Anglican Church)
Era of Good Feelings, 101
Eskridge, Charles G., 19*n*
Established church, 13,39-40
Evans, Nathan G. ("Shanks"), 193,195, 198,201,202
Evans, Thomas, 32-33
Evergreen Mills, 71,75,124
Execution of Union deserters, 207*n*,208
Exurbanites, 364-65 (*see also* Urbanization)

Fairfax, Ferdinando, 128*n*
Fairfax and Loudoun Turnpike Company, 116*n*
Fairfax County, 13,16,379,386
Fairfax Meeting, 41
Fairs, 92-93,254-55,280
Farmer and Dairyman Association, 294
Farmers (*see also* Agriculture, Agrarianism)
 from Civil War to World War I, 279-94
 clubs, 280-88
 communication inadequacies, 285
 displacement of, 359-62,365,381,392-94
 expenses, 359-62
 farm sizes, 323-25
 labor problems, 323-25
 from 1917 to 1945, 307,317-30,334-36
 subsidized by federal government, 358-59
 techniques of husbandry, 26-29,74-94, 354-57,394
 transportation inadequacies, 285
Farmers' Alliance, 282
Farmers' Assembly, 282
Farmers' Institute, 292
Farming frontier, 395
Farm Security Administration (F.S.A.), 335
Farmwell, 71*n*, (*see also* Ashburn)
Fauquier County, 15,16*n*
Fawcett, Elisha, 145*n*
Featherston, Winfield S., 198
Federal Emergency Relief Administration (F.E.R.A.), 331-33
Federal Farm Board, 328
Federalist party, 61*n*,96-99
Fences, 289-92
Ferree, James J., 244-45
Ferry, 8,25,32-33
Fertilizers, 336
Festivals, 254

Flax, 28
Flippo, Oscar F., 302*n*
Flour, 74
Fort Bacon, 10*n*
Fort Beauregard, 186*n*
Fort Evans, 186
Fort Johnson, 186
Fort Sumter, 179,186
Foster, J. William, 83
4-H Clubs, 93*n*,293*n*,322*n*
Fox, George K., Jr., 260
Franklin, Benjamin, 15*n*
Frankville, 75
Frazier, W. H., 329,334
Free blacks prior to Civil War, 137, 139 (*see also* Blacks)
Freedmen's Bureau, 229-30,239,244-45,264*n*, 265,266 264*n*,265,266
Free schools, 151*n*, (*see also* Education, Schools)
Free Soil party, 103*n*
French, Daniel, 19
French and Indian War, 15,16*n*,28*n*,36,50
Friends, Society of, 49,239 (*see also* Quakers)
Frog Town (*see* Bloomfield)
Frontier, 3,25,63
Frye, Christopher, 44*n*
Fugitive slaves, 164-67 (*see also* Slavery)
Fugitive Slave Act (1850), 164-65,169-70
Fuller, Edward C., 312*n*

Gag rules, 130
Gant, Thomas, 22*n*
Gap Meeting, 41 (*see also* Potts' Meeting)
Garrett, W. Frank, 314
Garrison, William Lloyd, 147
Geary, John W., 203
Genius of Liberty, The, 92,99,100,101, 104,107,114,120,121,132,140,144,152*n*
Genius of Universal Emancipation, 140,149*n*
George, John, 181
George III, King, 51
"George Town," 10,12*n* (*see also* Leesburg)
Georgetown Turnpike Company, 117-18,119
"German Settlement," 6
German settlers, 6,41,131
Gettysburg, 184,218
Gibson, Rebecca, 49
Giles, William B., 99*n*
Gilmore, William, 53
Giver, E. R., 258
Glebe, 39-40,60
Glendening, Andrew, 89*n*
Goal (*see* Jail)
Gohongarestaw, 3 (*see also* Goose Creek)
Goodhart, Briscoe, 189*n*
Goose Creek, 2-3,6,8,15,32,122-25,211,379, 380*n*
Goose Creek and Little River Navigation Company, 122-25
 construction of, 122-24
 cost of, 123,124

failure of, 124
Goose Creek Association, 380n
Goose Creek Baptist Church, 46,47,48
Goose Creek Chapel, 14,39
Goose Creek Lime Company, 323n
Goose Creek Meeting, 41,49,144-45,147
Gordon, Charles, 82
Gore, Thomas, 50n
Goresville, 75,186 (see also Lucketts)
Gorman, Willis A., 195
Gover, Jesse, 145n
Grange, 254,282-83
Grant, Ulysses S., 212-13
 visits Loudoun, 254-55
Gray, Grover Cleveland, 312n
Great Awakening, 41-42
Great Depression, 326-34,335,395
Greeley and Brown clubs, 273
Greeley, Horace, 273
Gregg, George, 226
Gregg, Gibson, 230n
Gregg, William, 170
Griffith, David, 40,56-58
Griggsville, 71,72
Grimes, John T., 267
Growth
 impact, 387-96
 issue of, 383-96
Grubb, Adam, 81
Grubb, Hugh, 293n
Guilford Station, 71n,75
Gulick, George, 135
Gulick, J. H., 165n,166
Gum Spring, 13n,42,72,75 (see also Arcola)
Gypsum, 85-91

Hague, Francis, 10n
Hall, James, 135n
Hall, Stilson H., 316n
Hamilton, 66,69n,71n,75,122,213n, 261,323,334,237,365
Hamilton, James, 10n,18n,19n, 20n,122n
Hamilton, John, 113n
Hamilton, Robert, 43
Hammerly, John W., 232-33
Hammett, Edward, 137
Harding, William H., 86n
Hardy, Leonard, 312n
Harmony Church, 261
Harper's Ferry, 170-71
Harris, Sophia, 53
Harrison, Henry, 204
Harrison, Henry T.,
 on agrarianism, 308-09,317-18
 on communism, 316
 death, 316
 on government, 315-16
 and *The Loudoun Times*, 308
 and World War I, 314-15
Harrison, H. T., 104n,249
Harrison, Nannie W., 316n

Harrison, Nathaniel 180,181
Harrison, Sally, 57n
Harrison, Walter J., 316n
Harrison, William H., 103
Harrison's Island, 194-97,199-200
Hatcher, T. C. L., 180n
Hayes, Rutherford, P., 277
Hays, Ann, 24
Hay soldiering, 219
Head, George R., 274
Head, James M., 179n
Head, John W., 267
Head v. Hough, 44n
Heater's Ferry, 32n,
Heaton, Albert, 129n
Heaton, James, 142n
Hemp, 28
Hempston, C. F., 228
Hempstone, W. D., 120n
Henderson, Fenton M., 83
Henderson, Richard H., 108,118,125n,128
 142n
Henshaw, J. J., 181,258
Herndon, John G., 283
Heronimous, Francis, 22
Heronimous, Paldos, 23
Heryford, John, 38
Hessians, 32n,55
Heyl, Grace, 322n
Hibbs, Benjamin, 242n
Hibbs, William, 219n
Hickin, Patricia C., 146n
Hickman, L. W., 317
High schools, 345-50 (see also Education, Schools)
Hill, Daniel H., 186,202-03
Hillsboro, 66,68,72,75,121,171,209,251,365
Hillsboro Border Guard, 172
Hillsboro Camp Meeting, 302
Hillsborough and Harper's Ferry Turnpike Company, 118,119
Hirst, J. T., 332,333n,368
History and Comprehensive Description of Loudoun County, Virginia (Head), 179n
Hoe, James Hall, 135n
Hoge, D. J., 283n
Hoge, Eli, 227
Hoge, H. M., 322n
Hoge, Isaac, 293n
Hoge, James M., 274n
Hoge, Sarah H., 297-98
Hogs, 76,213,223-25,287,319,321,329-30n,397-400
Holden, Charles F., Jr., 369n
Hollingsworth, Robert, 216
Holmes, Oliver W., 200
Holmes, William, 226
Holmes, William, Sr., 145n
Hooker, Joseph, 206
Hoover, Herbert, 328,329
Horse racing, 253-54,293n
Horses, 74,223-25,288,293,319-22

INDEX 461

Home demonstration agent, 322
Home Demonstration clubs, 322n
Hough, Frank, 312n
Hough, John 8,10,28n33,122n,142
Hough, William H., 76n
Hough, W. S., 150,169,170
Housing, 235-36,365,368
Houston, Charles H., 352
Howard, Oliver O., 230,234,245
Hoysville, 72
Hughes, Charles E., 310
Hughes, Hallie, 292n
Hughesville, 40,75,121
Humanitarian reforms, 96
Humphrey, Alexander P., 312n
Hunter, E. M., 322n
Hunting regulations, 289n
Hunton, Eppa, 195,198,200,275,283n
Hurley, Rueban, 139
Hurricane Agnes, 359
Hutchinson, Benjamin, 48n,
Hutchinson, James, 45n
Hydrophobia, 289n

I.B.M., 366n,385
Illnesses, 23,87-88
Ilsely, Mrs. Spencer, 352n
Immigrants, 6,8,82-83
Indentured servants, 24,81
Indians, 3-6,29
  Algonquin, 3-4
  contributions, 6
  culture, 3-4
  Piscataway, 4
  Seneca, 4n
Indigent, 331-32
Infantile paralysis, 339n
Inman, Marguerite Grace, 309n
Integration, 352-54
Internal improvements, 96
Intolerable Acts, 50
Invincible Club, 274
I.T.&T., 366n,385

Jackson, Andrew, 102,105
Jackson, William, 352
Jacksonian era, 95-130
Jail, 19-21,112-13,240
James, John, 82
Jamison, Robert, 51n
Janney, Amos, 8
Janney, Asa M., 257
Janney, Charles P., 227-249n,260n
Janney, Daniel, 90-91,145n
Janney, George, 113n
Janney, Hannah, 41n
Janney, Israel, 76n,90,91n,142n
Janney, Jacob, 41n
Janney, John, 104n,109,145n,168,175n,203,
  chairman of state convention, 178
  views on secession, 178-79

Janney, Pheneas, 76n,115

Janney, Samuel M., 103n
  author, 147,149n,150n,159
  and the Civil War, 214n,216-19,225
  crusade for Indians, 257
  crusade for public education, 150-52,157-58
  crusade against slavery, 135,137,147-50
  on the death of Lincoln, 257
  early life, 147
  founder of Springdale school, 148
  interest in newspapers, 149-50
  trial in Loudoun, 158-61
Jefferson, Thomas, 60n,61n,86n,248n
Jenifer, W. H., 195,198
Jenison, Ozro P., 152n
Jenkins, Amos, 328
Jenners, Abiel, 113n
Jockey Club of Leesburg, 254n
Johns, A. Deane, 250n
Johnson, Andrew, 230
  conflict with Congress, 265-68
  impeachment, 268
  reconstruction policy, 262-66,272
Johnson, Bill, 135
Johnston, Joseph E., 203
Johnson, Thomas, 128n
Johnson, Warren, 378n
Johnston, George, 51n
Joint Committee on the Conduct of the
  War, 202
Jones, Alexander, 60n
Julian, George W., 230

Kansas-Nebraska Act, 170
Keenan, John F., 153n
Kelly, Oliver H., 282n
Kemper v. Hawkins, 160
Kemp's Stagecoach Company, 237
Kennedy, J. F., 352
Kephart, Virginia, 163n
Ketoctin Baptist Church, 45,46,47,48
Ketocton Baptist Association, 44,45n,
  46,48,60n
Key's Gap, 19
Kilgour, James, 104n
Kilgour, J. Mortimer, 179n,263n,302n
Kilpatrick, Hugh J., 205
King, William, 82
Kirkpatrick, J. Emory, 379
Ku Klux Klan, 238-39

Labor, 82-85,131-41,317
Lacey, Israel, 86n
Lacey, Joseph, 34n
Ladies Central Memorial Association,
  The, 262
Lafayette, Marquis de, 54n,109-11
Land banking, 384n,391n
Landholding
  colonial period, 26-27
  during the Civil War, 228-30
Landon, Alfred M., 331n
Land speculators, 41,376-78,390-91,395
Land Use Tax (L.U.T.), 376-78,387,395n

Lane, Hardage, 51n
Lane, James, 51n
Law Enforcement League, 305
Lawyers, 234-35,385n,388
Lee, Francis "Lightfoot," 10n,12,18n
Lee, "Light Horse" Harry, 56
Lee, Ludwell, 111,142n
Lee, Philip Ludwell, 10n
Lee, Richard B., 116n
Lee, Richard H., 274
Lee, R. H., 142n
Lee, Robert E., 171,204
Lee, Thomas, 8
Leesburg, 11,66,68-69,70,71n,72,75,108, 112-13,121-22,127,233,235-37,314-15, 334,339,342,347,
 claim as capital of the United States, 97n
 colonial era, 10-12,38-39
 description of, 111-13
 economic life, 72,230-31,236
 formation of, 10-12
 Lafayette's visit, 109-11
 population, 66,369
 skirmishes at, 204n,209
 town government, 110
Leesburg Academy, 152-54
Leesburg and Aldie Turnpike Company, 118
Leesburg and Snickers' Gap Company, 118,119
Leesburg Building Association, 236
Leesburg Civil Guard, 172
Leesburg Female Academy, 110
Leesburg Institute, 110
Leesburg Lime Company, 323n
Leesburg Railroad Company, 125-26
Leesburg Star Fire Company, 112
Leesburg Turnpike Company, 74,117-18, 119,120-21
Leesburg Volunteer Fire Department, 353n
Legard, R. N., 292n,331n,355
Legard, S. C., 355,359
Legends of Loudoun Valley (Nichols), 179n
Leithton, 71n
Lemon, Jacob, 214n
Lewis, E. K., 250n
Lewis, John, 6,51n,53
Lewis, John H., 231
Lewis, Oren R., 353
Lewis, Thomas, 51n,116n
Levitt and Sons, 366n,373,385
Lexington and Concord, 51
Liberty Bonds, 311-13
Liberty party, 148
Lincoln, 297-99,323,347
Lincoln, Abraham, 176,179,180n,216,257
Lincoln Community League, 389n
Lincoln High School, 323
Lincolnite, 346-47
Lincoln-Johnson reconstruction policy, 256
Linter, J. Ross, 124n,322,326
Liquor, regulation of sale, 295,303-06
Literary Fund, 151n,251
Littleton, Thomas, 232-33

Little River, 122-23
Little River Church, 46,47,48
Little River Turnpike Company, 74, 115-21
 regulations as precursors of modern traffic laws, 117
 success, 175,120
 toll rates, 116
 weight limitations, 117
Livestock, 74-76,77,293
 breeds, 293
 diseases and maladies, 286-88
 impact of Civil War upon, 213,222,225
 menaced by dogs, 288-89
 remedies, 286-88
Lloyd, Emily E., 240n
Local option, 303-04
Local Patriotic Community League, 312
Lord Shelburne, 15n
Loudoun Agricultural Society, 254,280
Loudoun Bible Society, 302n
Loudoun Board of Agriculture, 335n
Loudoun Camp Meeting, 302
Loudoun Campus of Northern Virginia Community College, 369n
Loudoun Chronicle, The 104,149-51, 169,295-96
Loudoun Colonization Society, 142-43, (*see also* American Colonization Society)
Loudoun Commonwealth's attorney, 389n
Loudoun Company The, 113
Loudoun County
 agriculture, 25-39,74-94,279-94,307, 317-30,334-36,341-42,354-64,359-62, 391-94
 and the American Revolution, 50-61
 during the antebellum era, 63-181
 banks, 113-14,236
 boundaries, 15-16,69n
 businesses, 33-38,71-72,323-24
 and the Civil War, 183-221
 battles, 118-214
 border area, 183-84
 Confederate "bread basket," 184,219
 determinates of military activity, 183-84
 division of loyalties, 183,187-90
 forts in, 185-86 .
 impact upon civilian life, 184-86, 212-20,221-42,245,255-78
 mobilization, 184-87
 and colonial era, 3-48
 crime, 22-23,240-42,352n
 current trends, 381-94
 division within, 6-7,161-90,214-20,318
 drought, 326-27
 education, 151-58,245-53,344-54,373-75
 formation of, 13-16,
 from 1877 to 1917, 279-306
 geography, 2-3
 government, 16-25,63n,214-15,238-60, 366-68,370,372-80,381-94
 and the Great Depression, 326-34

INDEX 463

as microcosm of American history, 394-96
name, 15
nationalism, 107,310-16,335-39
newspapers, 99,100,101,104,107,114,120,
  132,138,139,140,144,149-51,150,
  152n,158,159,166-67,168,170-
  76,178n,180n,187,193,201,212,
  215,229,231,233,235,236,239,242-
  44,246,251,253-54,256,258-60,262,
  266-68,271-72,276,280n,281,
  288,291-92,295-96,303-04,308-16,
  327,331,337-39,345,348,349n,
  350,352,366,368,379
from 1917 to 1945, 307-40
from 1945 to 1972, 341-80
petitions to Congress, 225-27
politics, 16-18,61,96-109,167-81
  255-78,308-11,329,344-50,378-86,
  389-91
population, 64-66,137,362-65
and reconstruction, 221-78
reform movements in, 141-56
religion, 39-49,59,141-42
and sectionalism, 168-81
settlement of, 6-13
and slavery, 131-50
and taxes, 16n,52,54,251-52,262,
  289,318,327-28,348,49,
  375-78,381-82,387-88
towns, 66-69,71,72,75,365
transormation from agrarian to
  urban society, 362-95
transportation, 29-30,114-28,237-38,
  342-44
and World War I, 308-11
and World War II, 335-39
zoning, 372,384-91
Loudoun County Agricultural Academy
  and Chemical Institute (The Institute),
  93-94
Loudoun County Breeders' Association, 322
Loudoun County Builders Association, 236
Loudoun County Drought Relief Countil,
  327
Loudoun County Hatchery, 358
Loudoun County Health Association, 322n
Loudoun County High School, 350,353n
Loudoun County League of Women Voters,
  353n
Loudoun County Livestock Exhibition
  Association, 93
Loudoun County Ministerial Association,
  339n
Loudoun County Sanitation Authority,
  370,372
*Loudoun County Virginia: It's Social,
  Agricultural and Manufacturing
  Advantages* (Henderson), 83
Loudoun County War Finance Committee,
  339
Loudoun, Fourth Earl of (*see* John
  Campbell)
Loudoun Guard, 172,185

Loudoun Hunt Club, 309n
Loudoun Landowners Association, 389n
Loudoun Light and Power Company,
  323,334n
Loudoun Manumission and Emigration
  Society, 143-45,162
Loudoun Medical Society, 332-33
Loudoun Price and Ration Board, 336
Loudoun Rangers, 187-90,206n,218
Loudoun Savings Bank, 236n
Loudoun Selective Service Board, 337
Loudoun Times, The
  on agrarianism, 308-09
  on the 1916 election, 310
  on Westmoreland Davis, 308-09
  on World War I, 311-16
Loudoun Times-Mirror, The
  and dams, 379
  and education, 345,348,349n,350,352
  and the Great Depression, 327-31
  and urbanization, 366,368
  and World War II, 337-39
Loudoun Valley, 2
  burning of, 213-14
  future of farming, 390-94
  quality of land, 391
Loudoun Valley Cow-Testing Association,
  319-22
Loudoun Valley High School, 353n
Loudoun villages, 66-69,71,72,75 (*see
  also* Towns)
Loudoun War Finance Committee, 337
Loudoun Whig, 150
Love, Samuel, 116n
Lovett, Landon T., 241
Lovettsville, 66,72,75,171,180,193,347,
  365
Lovettsville Farmers' Club, 83,283-86,
  288,305,317,318n,319n,328,334,
  355
Lowell, J. J., 200
Loyalists, 52n, (*see also* Tories)
Loyal Temperance League, 298,300
Lucas, Jesse, 129n,130n
Lucas, Mars, 129n,130n
Luckett, Cooke D., 277
Luckett, Robert T., 104n
Luckett, Samuel, 260n,272
Lucketts, 75 (*see also* Goresville)
Lucketts, Francis, 166
Lundy, Benjamin, 144n
Lutheran Church, 41
Lynch, William B., 150n

Macaulet, John T., 261n
Madison, James, 108
Magisterial districts, 71n,370,382
Manassas Gap Railroad, Loudoun
  branch of, 126-27
Manifest Destiny, 95-96
Major, Richard, 48
Mann, Joseph B., 255
Markets for Loudoun's farm products,

74,76
Marks, John, 45-46
Marshall, John, 108
Maryland-Virginia Milk Producers' Association, 322
Mason, Armestead T., 98-99,134
  death, 99n
  duel with John M. McCarty, 99n
  feud with Charles Mercer, 98-99
Mason, George, 61n,98n
Mason, Francis, 229
Mason, Mary, 137n
Mason, Stephen Thomas, 61n
Mason, Thomas, 10n,18n,28n
Mason, W. T. T., 111n
Matildaville, 69n
Matthew, William, 277
McCabe, Charles P., 138,232,277
McCabe, J. B., 254n
McCabe, John H., 110
McCarty, Daniel, 7n
McCarty, John M., 99n,100n,104n
McCarty, William M., 110
McClellan, George B., 194,202
McColley, Robert, 146n
McCormick, Stephen, 89
McFarlan, Alexander, 60n
McGinnis, Sally, 24
McGuffey, William H., 156
McIntire, C. C., 150n,158
McIntire, Patrick, 150n
McKimmey, B. W., 336
McNeil, Gibbs, 124n
McQuinn, John, 312n
Mead, John, 8n
Means, Samuel C., 193,206n
  and the Loudoun Rangers, 187-90
  property confiscated by Confederates, 187
  Unionists, 187-88
Mechanicsville, 75
Medicine, 233-34
Melvin, Blanche, 331-32,333n
Memoir of Loudoun County, Virginia (Taylor), 92
Memoirs of Samuel M. Janney, 135,147
Mendenhall, Jacob, 113n,142n
Mercer, C. C., 294n
Mercer, Charles F.
  for colonization of free Negroes, 97, 143
  critic of Jackson, 105-06
  death of, 97n
  feud with Armistead T. Mason, 98-100
  founder of Aldie, 98
  for internal improvements, 97,116,122
  and nationalism, 127
  party affiliations, 58,97-99
  political career, 97-102,105-06,108,109
  president of the C. & O Canal Company, 97
  for public education, 97,157-58
Mercer, Eleanor, 97n
Mercer, Hugh, 98n

Mercer, James, 97n
Mercer, John, 8,97n
Mercer, John Francis, 163n
Mercer, Margaret, 163
Mercer, W. F., 181
Merritt, Wesley, 213
Methodists, 42-44,173,261,344
Mexican Cession, 95
Mexican War, 103n,109n,129,168
Meyer, John R., 138
Meyers, Robert A., 339n
Middleburg, 16n,66,68,69n,72,73, 75,121,126,207,237,334,342,352-53, 365
Middleburg Academy, 152
Middleburg Community Center, 380n
Milhaney, James, 145-46
Militia, 16,50,53,171-73,185-86
Millennialists, 96
Miller, John, 12
Miller, Ruth, 391
Mills, 28,69n,74,98n
Millsville, 75
Mines, John, 142n
Minor, John W., 181
Minor, Nicholas, 10-13,19n,20n,34,43
Minor's ordinary, 34
Mirror, The, 150n
Miskel Farm, skirmish at, 211-12
Missouri Compromise, 129
Mobberly, John, 219n
Monkhouse, Jonathan, 24n
Monocacy River, 32
Monroe Doctrine, 310
Monroe, James, 98n,108,111
Moore, Asa, 113n,142n
Moore, James, 113n,142n
Moore, John, 98n
Moran, Dick, 211
Morgan, John, 113n
Morlan, Richard, 51-52
Morticians, 232-33
Mosby, John S., 184,207,209-14,221
  battle tactics, 210
  and conscription, 218
  skirmishes:
    Aldie, 210-11
    Miskel's Farm, 211-12
    Mount Zion, 212
Mosby's Confederacy, 209-14,221 (*see also* Mosby)
Mosby's Rangers, 209-14
Moss, John, 19n
Mother Stewart (*see* E. D. Stewart)
Mott, Alexander, R., 233,234
Mott, Lucretia, 165
Mountains,
  Appalachian, 2-3
  Blue Ridge, 2
  Bull Run, 2,6,17
  Catoctin, 2,6
  Short Hills, 2,6
Mountain View Farm's Hatchery, 358,362n

Mount Gilead, 72,75
Mountsville, 72,75
Mount Zion Church, skirmish, 212
Mucklehany, John, 19n
Murray, Samuel, 142n

N.A.A.C.P., 352,354
Naale, Edward Lester, 312n
Nationalism, 95-96,107,127-28,255,335-39
National Recovery Administration (N.R.A.), 330
Neersville, 41n,71n,75,121
Nergin, Margaret, 245
New Church Road, 30 (see also Roads)
New Deal, 329-36,395
New Lisbon, 75
Newton, Charles A., 242n
Newton, Enos W., 152n
Newton, Sarah, 49
New Valley Baptist Church, 45,49
Nichols, Joseph, 226
Nichols, Joseph V., 179n,305,335n,349
Nichols, Samuel, 142n
Nighthunting, 344n
Night school, 248
Nixon, Joel L., 104n
Noland, B. P., 180,181,187n,230n
Noland, Philip, 6,20n,32,35
Noland, Thomas, 32n,35,122
Noland, William B., 138,142
Noland's Ferry, 29-30,32,54n,121
Norris Brothers Planning Mill, 323n
Norris, John, 104n,186n
Northern Neck, 3,7,12
Northern Turnpike Company, 118
Northern Virginia Development Corporation, 365,377
North Fork, 71n
Norwood, v. Gaver, 44n
Nourse, Charles H., 153n
Nullification, doctrine of, 106-07

Oak Hill, 8,98n,109,110n
Oatlands, 8
Oatland Mills, 71,75
Office of Price Administration (O.P.A.), 336,357-58
Old Carolina Road, 19
Old Leesburg Road, 30 (see also Roads)
Old Stone Church, 43, (see also Methodists)
O'Neal, Margaret (Peggy), 105n
Order of Good Templars, 296
Ordinaries, 10,33-38,295n
  centers of community life, 34
  decline, 33-34
  origin, 33
  regulation of, 37-38
  services, 34,36-37
  significance, 33
Oregon issue, 95
Orr, John M., 234
Osburn, Joel, 135

Osburn, John, 52n
Osburn, Joshua, 113n
Osburn, Penelope M., 228n
Osburn, Tarleton, 52n
Overseer of the poor, 60
Owens, John, 135
Owings, Richard, 44n
Owsley, Thomas, 23
Owsley, William, 23,53
Ox, 74

Paeonian Springs, 71n
Parent-Teacher Association, 349n
Patowmack Company, 122
Patriotism, 311-15,337-39
Patton, John W., 166
Patrons of Husbandry (see Grange)
Paxson, T. C., 288
Peers, Henry, 111
Pelham, John, 206
Pemberton, James, 142
Pereira, Albert F., 353n
Perfectionists, 96
Peyton, Francis, 18n,19n,50,51n
Philips, Thomas, 125
Philomont, 72,75,121,206
Phoenix Factory, 76,78
Physicians, 57-58,233-34,332-33
Picnics, 254
Pierce, Franklin, 103
Pie rooting, 219
Pierpoint, Francis H., 258n
Planning Commission, 366,368,370,372, 381,388-90
  (see also Zoning)
Planned communities, 9,366-69,382,385,386
Planters' Club, 283n
Plaster (see Gypsum)
Plaster, George Emory, 234
Pleasant Valley, 75,376
Pleasant Valley Farm Hatchery, 358
Pleasonton, Alford, 205,206-07
Plessy v. Ferguson, 351
Point of Rocks, 128n
Poland C. Preson, 362n
Poland, James Buchanan, 308n
Political parties, 96-108,148 (see also Democrats, Federalists, Republicans, Whigs)
Polk, James K., 103
Pollard, Burr, 241
Poorhouse, 60n
Population, 64-66,364,369-72
Populist party, 282-83
Postal service, 121-22,214,236-37
Potomac Baseball Club, 254n
Potomac Company, 32
Potomac Rangers, 4
Potomac River, 2-6,7,15,25,29,32,122, 184,378-80
Potts' meeting, 41
Poultney, John, 12
Poverty, 331-32

Powell, Burr, 142
Powell, Cuthbert, 110n
Powell, E. B., 241
Powell, George C., 104n
Powell, Humphrey, B., 124
Powell, Leven, 51n,56-58,61,116n
Presbyterian churches, 42
Presgrave, Faye L., 376
Pressing, 218-20
Prince William County, 13,15,386
Prisoners of war, 215-17,336
Progress, idea of, 95-96,372,386,391, 395-96
Prohibition, 304-06
Prohibition and Evangelical Association of Loudoun County, 301
Property rights, 388
Prostitution, 339n
Providence Baptist Church, 241
Public schools, 344-54 (see also Education)
 advent of in Loudoun, 248,250-53
 cost, 251-53,348-50
 criticism of, 252-53
 segregation, 350-54
Punishment, colonial, 22-24
Purcell's Store, 122 (see also Purcellville)
Purcellville, 66,71n,75,122,126,209,322, 323,334,342,365,369,385,389
Purcellville Stock Sales Company, 322n
Putman, J. C., 200

Quakers, 8,37,59,90,183 (see also Society of Friends)
 and the Civil War, 215-19,227-28
 meetings, 41
 opposition to slavery, 135,141-50,156-65
 setters, 6-7,131
 and temperance, 297-98
Quarantine, 25

Raflo, Frank, 388
Railroad towns, 71n,126-28,237-38,285
Ramsey, Sanford I, 140
Randolph, Peyton, 51
Raney, Sanford J., 104n
Rape, 22,241,242n
Raspberry Plain, 20
Ratcliffe, John, 328n
Rattle-band, 255
Readjusters, 277
Realty appraisals, 375-76
Reamer, Edwin C., 353n
Reamer's Stagecoach Company, 237
Reconnaissance, 183-84,194-95
Reconstruction, 221-78,394
 and blacks, 238-45
 housing shortage, 235-36
 mail service, 236-37
 military rule, 261,265-69
 plans, 222
 taxes, 351-52,362
 transportation, 236-38

whites' disillusionment with, 264-70
Reconstruction acts, 265,269
Recreation, 253-55
Red Scare, 315
Reed, Jacob, 51n
Reform movements, 141-56
Reith, Howard, 230n
Religion, 39-49,59,173-74,261 (see also Churches)
 colonial era, 23-24
 church membership, 344n
 denominations, 344
 diversity, 41-49
 and slavery, 141-42
Republican party, 230,273-77
Reston, 387n
Revolutionary War (see American Revolution)
Rhodes, Jacob, 53
Rhodes, Mary, 53
Rice, Cleveland B., 308n
Rice, Hannah, 53
Rice, James, 53
Richards, George, 107n
Richmond Regional Planning District Commission, 392
Ritocor, Joshua, 124n
Roach, James, 124
Roads, 14,17,29-32,115-21,285,343 (see also Turnpikes)
Robinson, Robert, 89n
Rodeffer, H. L., 286
Rogers, A. H., 140
Rogers, A. L., 173
Rogers, Asa, 161n,178,217n
Rogers, Hamilton, 161
Rogers, Sandford P., 165n,166
"Rogues Road," (see Carolina Road)
Rokeby, 97n
Roosevelt, Franklin D., 329,331-33,335
Rose, John, 142n
Roszel, Sarah, 40n
Roszel, Stephen A., 40n,44n
Roszel, Stephen C., 134,142n
Roszel Chapel, 43n
Round Hill, 66,71n,75,323,365
Round Hill Camp Meeting, 302-03
Round Hill Milling Company, 323n
Ruffin, Edmund, 170
Rural Electrification Administration, 333-34
Rural Environmental Assistance Program (R.E.A.P.), 358-59
Russell, Anthony, 19n,51n
Russell, Robert, 89
Rust, Peter, 6n
Rust v. Loudoun County Board of Supervisors, 389
Ryan, 71n
Ryan, John F., 283n

Sanborn, J. J., 153n
Sands, Daniel C., 312,332n,350n
Schofield, John M., 256

School Board, 347-54,370-75,382-83
School commissioners, 151n
School districts, 151n
Schools, (see also Education)
and the bicorporal community, 345-50
private, 152-53
  Bashaw's English school, 152n
  Belmont school, 246
  Ben Bridges' school, 152
  Blue Ridge Academy, 246
  Dover school, 246
  Edward Hazen's school, 154
  Franklin Taylor's school, 152
  Gibson's Female school, 152n
  Hillsboro school, 152
  John Woods' English school, 152n
  Leesburg Academy, 152-54,246,249-50
  Leesburg Female Academy, 152n
  Leesburg Female Seminary, 246
  Leesburg Female Institute, 246
  Leesburg Male School, 246
  Loudoun School, 246
  Loudoun Valley Academy, 246-48,250
  Middleburg Academy, 152
  Middleburg Seminary, 246
  Mountsville Academy, 246
  P. Saunder's school, 152n
  Rehoboth Academy, 152
  Samuel A. Jackson's English School, 152n
  Springdale Boarding school, 152
  Springwood Select Home school for young ladies, 246
  Upperville Academy, 152
  Waterford school, 152
  William Williamson's Middleburg school, 152
public
  consolidation, 344-54
  origins, 150-51,250-52
  poor schools, 156-57
Scott, Winfield, 103
Secession, 176-81
Sectionalism, 63-64,95-96,167-80,394
Segregation, 339,350-54
Seldon v. the Overseers of Loudoun, 60
Seldon, W. C., 132
Seldon, Wilson Cary, 60n
Seldon, Wilson C., Jr., 145n
Self-Help: Drought Relief Suggestions For Farmers, 327
Seneca Creek, 378-79
Settlers, 6-7,27,41,131,183
Sharp, George, 145n
Shawen, Cornelius, 113n
Sheep, 76,286,288-93,319,397-400
Sheep Fund, 289
Sheetz, Benjamin F., 180n,229
  on the Civil War, 258-59
  and the Conservative party, 272-73
  editor of *The Democratic Mirror*, 258
  on presidential election of 1876, 275-77
  on reconstruction, 258,263-64,266-69,271-77

Shelburne parish, 15,16n,17,39n,40,57,60
Shenandoah Valley, 30,115
Sheridan, Philip H., 217,221
Sheriff, 16,19,63n,370n
Shippy, John, 48n
Shore, Thomas, 51n
Short Hill Mountain, 6,127
Shreve, D. T., 173n
Shumate, L. M., 248n
Sidney, Algernon, 100
Silcott Springs, 71n,75
Simpson, Elizabeth, 165n166
Simpson, French, 164-166
Simpson, John S., 249n,250
Sims, Thomas 61n
Skinner, Christian, 24
Slaves, 27,29-30,81,101,113,129-50
  crimes, 22,139-40
  as divisive issue, 129-31
  literacy of, 135
  movement to free, 142-50
  numbers in Loudoun, 131-33,137
  runaways, 133-37
  shift in attitude of white Loudouners 161-62
  symbol of sectional differences, 131
  traders, 138-39
  treatment of, 132-41
Slocum, Henry W., 206n
Smarr, John, 48n
Smith, Alfred E., 329
Smith, Balaain, 81
Smith, David, 145n
Smith, Rufus, 242n
Smith, William, 24,51n
Smith, William A., 158
Smith, W. T., 349n
Smith's Ferry, 32n
Smoot, Charles, 190
Smoot, William, 190
Snickers' Gap, 30
Snickers' Gap Turnpike Company, 115, 118,119
Snickersville, 71n,72,75,237-38
  (see also Bluemont)
Society of Friends, 256,297-98 (see also Quakers)
Soil-bank program, 358
Soil Conservation and Domestic Allotment Act, 330
Some Considerations on the Keeping of Negroes (Woolman), 142
Sons of Confederate Veterans, 315n
Sons of Temperance, 295-96
Souder, Clinton, 293
Souder, J. C., 286
Southern Railroad Company, 299
Southern Rights Convention, 168,180
Southern States Cooperative Association, 355n
Sower, B. W., 101
Spirit of Democracy, The 104
Spotswood, Alexander, 4,6

468 INDEX

Stafford County, 13
Stagecoach service, 121-22, 237-38
Stanton, Edwin M., 187-202,216
States' rights, 101-02,127,238,270
Steer, Isaac E., 145n
Sterling, 71n
Sterling Middle School, 383
Sterling Park, 365,368-69.381-82,386-87
Sterling Park Development
    Corporation, 368n
Stevens, Thaddeus, 230
Stewart, E. D:, 297
Stock Law, 290
Stone, Charles P., 193-95,202
Strawbridge, Robert, 43
Stuart, J. E. B., 205,206-07,209
Subdivisions (see Planned communities;
    Urbanization)
Suburbanities, 364-65 (see also
    Urbanization)
Suburban revolution, 362-80 (see also
    Urbanization)
Suffrage, 104-05 (see also Voting)
Sugarland Path, 30 (see also Roads)
Sugarland Run (creek), 16
Sugarland Run (subdivision), 368,369,386
Summers, George, 53
Superintendent of schools, 252
Surveyors, 16
Sycoline Creek, 6

Talbot, Elisha, 145n
Talbott, Joseph, 113
Tariffs, 96,106-07, 129
Taxes, 16n,251-52,262,288-89,318,
    327-28,348-49,375-78,381-82,387-88
Tavenner, Lot, 227
Tayloe, John, 8,10
Taylor, Benjamin F., 145n
Taylor, Henry S., 145n
Taylor, Jonathan, Jr., 144n
Taylor, Jonathan K., 246-48
Taylor, Mabel A., 298
Taylor, Mahlon, 142n
Taylor, Richard Henry, 279-80
Taylor, Thomas E., 297n
Taylor, Timothy, Jr., 104n
Taylor, Yardley, 74n,76n,80,90-92,
    111-12,143n,145n,156-57,162-64
Taylor, Zachary, 103
Taylorstown, 71n,75,380
Tea Act, 50
Teachers, 348n,351 (see also Education)
Tebbs, Charles B., 104n,234
Telephone 285
Temperance, 295-306
Temperance societies, 295-306
Tenantry, 82,325,335
Tenure of Office Act, 265
Texas, 95,97n
Thacher, George A., 234
Thomas, John, 51n
Thomas, Mahlon, 227

Thomas, Norman, 329n
Thompson, Amos, 42
Thompson, H. C., 345
Thompson, S. G., 250n
Thompson's ordinary, 37
Thoreau, Henry David, 1
Thrift, Sanderson, 264n
Tilden and Hendricks clubs, 273-75
Tilden, Samuel J., 276
Tillett, Samuel, 86n
Tithables, 13,23
Tobacco, 27-28,30
Tomson, Tommy, 134n
Tories, 51,52,61
Tournaments, 253
Towns, 66,68-73,75,368-69,
    colonial, 38-39
    formation of, 67-69,72
    government, 69
    incorporation of, 69n,365
Township, 63n,71n
Tracey, Jacob, 53
Tractor, 308,354-57 (see also Agriculture)
Trade, 28-29,74
    flour, 27-29
    regulation of, 29n
    tobacco, 27-29
Transcendentialists, 1
Transportation (see also Roads)
    railroads, 126-28
    during reconstruction, 236-38
    revolution in, 114-28
    stagecoaches, 121-22
    turnpikes, 114-21
Trappe, 71n
Treatise on Practical Farming, A.
    (Binns), 85
Treaty of Albany, 4-6
Treaty of Lancaster, 4n
Tri-County Electric Cooperative, 334
Triplett, Simon, 53
Truro parish, 13
Tucker, Henry St. George, 60n
Turner, Fielding, V
Turner, Frederick Jackson, 6
Turner, Nat, 145-46
Turnpikes, 114-21,238 (see also Roads)
    degree of success, 120-21
    demise, 120-21
    origin of, 115-16
    regulations, 117
    toll rates, 116
Tuscarora Creek, 6,186n
Tutt, Charles P., 254n
Tyler, Charles, 19n
Tyler v. Loudoun County Board of
    Supervisors, 389
Tyler, William B., 145n

Udall, Stewart, 379n
Underwood Constitution, 271
Union (Unison), 68,72,75,121,206
Union Cemetery, 200,232,261-62

United States Conservation Service, 358-59
United States Steel Corporation, 368n,385
Upperville, 121,125,207
Urban frontier, 362-96
Urbanization, 362-96
   cost, 385-86
   impact upon farming, 378,392
   and progress, 385

Valley Forge, 58
Van Buren, Martin, 103
Van Deusen, Glyndon, 95
Van Devanter, C. H., 287
Verts, Conrad, 86n
Vestal Gap Road, 30(see also Roads)
Vestal's Gap, 14
Vestrymen, 23
Veterinary medicine, 356-57
Villages, 71n
Virginia Call, The 298
Virginia Colonization Society, 143
Virginia Dairymen's Association, 309n
Virginia Farm Bureau Federation, 386
Virginia General Assembly, 13,15,16n,18, 69,392
Virginia Public Service Company, 334n
Virginia State Farmers' Institute, 309
Virtz, Henry, 287
Voting, 102-04,104-05,106,107n,108n, 176-78,180-81,257,264,275-77,329,331n, 333n (see also Elections)

Waddell, Charles, 377
Walker, J. E., 286
Wallman, John, 81
Ward, Samuel, 86n
Warner, John, 8
War of 1812, 97n
War of the Rebellion, 184
Washington, Bushrod, 144n
Washington, George, 8,33n,55,56-57,58n,168
Washington, W. H., 86n
Washington and Leesburg Turnpike Company, 120-21
Washington and Ohio Railroad, 237n,285, 294,296
Washingtonian, The, 99,100,104,150n, 158,159,167,175,231
Washingtonian-Mirror, The, 150n
Waterford, 42n,66,68,69n,72,75, 121,180,188-90,191,206n,295
Waterford and Point of Rocks Turnpike Company, 118
Waters, 180
Watkins, Lou Etta, 354
Watkins, S. V., 250n
Waxpool, 71n
W.C.T.U., 297-301,303,305-06
Webster, Charles A., 188n,189
Welch, Elizabeth, 53
West, Charles, 34n
West, George, 19n
West, William, 10n,19n,34,48n,69n,

West's ordinary, 34
Whaley, James, Jr., 24
Wheat, 27-29,30,74,77,79-80,307,321,397-400
Wheatland, 71n,75
Wheatland convention, 185
Whig party, 97-104,108-09,168,174-75, 271,278
White, Benjamin V., 44n
White, E. B., 286
White, Elijah (Lige) Viers, 188-90,193, 199n,205,207,218,272
White, R. J. T., 287
White's Battalion (see Commanches)
Whitfield, Theodore M., 146n
Wilcox, Eleanor, 53
Wildlife, 3-4
Wildman, Charles B., 199
Wildman, John W., 251
Willard, Frances E., 297n
Williams, John, 113n
Williams, Syddah, 228n
Williams, Thomas, 112
Williams, William, 216
Williamsburg, 51
Williams' Gap, 14,30, (see also Snickers' Gap)
Willkie, Wendell L., 333n
Wilmot Proviso, 168
Wilson, J. B., 153n
Wilson, Rebecca D., 298n
Wilson, Woodrow, 310,315,317
Windon, Sarah Hamrick, 22
Wise, C. W., 250n
Witherow, W. P., 233
Women and _____ Women (Taylor) 299-300
Wood, John W., 249n
Woodgrove, 75,209
Woodly, William, 121n
Woolen factories, 76,78 (see also Woolen Mills)
Woolen mills, 76,78
Woolman, John, 142-43
Work Progress Administration, 333
World War I, 308-16,395
   celebration of termination, 314-15
   concripts from Loudoun, 312
   impact upon Loudouners, 317
   readjustment after war, 317-18
   reasons for American intervention, 312
World War II, 395
   casualties, 339
   celebration of termination, 339
   children's war effort, 338
   draft, 337
   and farming, 335-37,341
   labor shortages, 337
   prisoners of war, 336
   war bonds, 337-38
Wright, George, 240n
Wright, H. G., 209
Wright, Thomas, 145n

W. S. Jenkins Grain Company, 323*n*
Wyckoff, A. C., 233*n*

Xerox Corporation, 385

Year-round school, 383
Yinger, Nicholas, 4*n*
Young, Francis A., 198
Young, Thomas, 226-27
Young Men's Christian Association, 302*n*
Young Woman's Christian Temperance Union, 300

Youth Temperance League, 298,300-01

Zacharias, J. F., 234
Zerega, Alfred L. B., 281
Zoning, 383-91,395*n*
  Article 12,376,384
  and the courts, 388-89
  legal basis, 388
  opposition to, 384-91
  ordinances, 366,368,372-73,376-78, 384
  and property rights, 388-89

Photograph by Betty B. Poland

ABOUT THE AUTHOR

Charles P. Poland, Jr. is a native of Loudoun County, Virginia, where his ancestors settled over two hundred years ago. As a resident of the county, he has witnessed the westward movement of urbanization from the nation's capital into Loudoun. After teaching throughout northern Virginia, he is currently Professor of History and Director of the Civil War Museum on the Annandale Campus of Northern Virginia Community College. He received his Ph.D. from Western Colorado University and has authored *The Glories of War: Small Battles and Early Heroes of 1861; An Introductory Outline of American History; Dunbarton: Dranesville, Virginia* and numerous articles and reviews for magazines and journals.

www.ingramcontent.com/pod-product-compliance
Lightning Source LLC
Chambersburg PA
CBHW071136300426
44113CB00009B/986